Provinces

second edition

Provinces

Canadian Provincial Politics

second edition

edited by
Christopher Dunn

Originally published by Broadview Press 2006

Library and Archives Canada Cataloguing in Publication

Provinces : Canadian provincial politics / edited by Christopher Dunn. — 2nd ed.

Includes bibliographical references.
ISBN-13: 978-1-44260-068-3
Previous ISBN 978-1-55111-754-6

1. Provincial governments—Canada—Textbooks. I. Dunn, Christopher J. C., 1948–

JL198.P73 2006   320.971   C2006-902773-0

We welcome comments and suggestions regarding any aspect of our publications–please feel free to contact us at the addresses below or at news@utphighereducation.com

North America   5201 Dufferin Street North York
                         Ontario, Canada, M3H 5T8
                         2250 Military Road
                         Tonawanda, New York, USA, 14150
                         Tel: (416) 978-2239 Fax: (416) 978-4738
                         email: customerservice@utphighereducation.com

UK, Ireland, and   NBN International
continental Europe   Estover Road, Plymouth PL6 7PY
                         Tel: + 44 (0) 1752 202300; Fax: + 44 (0) 1752 202330
                         email: enquiries@nbninternational.com

www.utphighereducation.com

Higher Education University of Toronto Press gratefully acknowledges the financial support of the Government of Canada through the Book Publishing Industry Development Program for our publishing activities.

Copy-edited by Betsy Struthers.

PRINTED IN CANADA

This book is printed on paper containing 100% post-consumer fibre.

For Christopher and James

Contents

Introduction

This is the second edition of a very successful work on Canada's provinces. When it was first published, it was long overdue: a generation of students had come and gone in Canada without the benefit of comparative, subject-specific studies of provincial societies. There were, and there continue to be, a number of province-specific reviews of provincial affairs—and well done they are indeed. Yet the time had come to re-emphasize the comparative tradition in Canada.

Now it is time to integrate into the provincial studies some of the vital concerns of the new decade and millennium: a disquiet about the quality of democracy, concern about women's place in provincial societies, interest in the nature and potential of governance in the north, unease on the question of the fiscal imbalance between all orders of government, a sensitivity to the needs of cities and communities, assessment of the retrenchment of the state, and consideration of the policy futures influenced by the changing demography of the provinces, among other things.

There is a certain paradox of course in this country regarding its provinces and territories. Unquestionably important to the well-being and prosperity of citizens, they are at the same time largely ignored by political scientists and other social scientists. This is unfortunate. Let us explain.

Provinces is at once a study of provincial government and a review of comparative politics. The benefits of comparative studies are well-known: they allow governments to recognize their relative position on the policy networks of the polity and innovators to search for new ideas to use in their own arena. On the other hand, they provide a useful backdrop for policy conservatism, as the more adventuresome jurisdictions experiment and pass their lessons on to others. For the political scientist, perpetually fascinated with, as Richard Simeon called it, "the problem of the dependent variable," they provide social laboratories for the study of policy determinants. For the publicly minded citizen, they offer a rough set of policy indicators to situate the progress of his or her province in matters institutional, administrative, or policy-related.

The essays in this collection are arranged so as to approximate major concerns of the political science discipline. There are five major sections: political landscapes, the state of democracy in the provinces, political structures and processes, provincial political economy, and provincial public policy.

The contributors mean the essays to be accessible to introductory students, yet do not indulge in over-simplification. They agreed that their work would focus on explaining entry-level material in provincial government and politics:

gone would be any preoccupation with esoteric and ingrown academic debates. In this we feel we have succeeded.

In that spirit, the accompanying chart—a simplified form of systems analysis—is included as a method of clarifying both the decision-making system operative at the level of provincial politics and the sections of the book. "Surveying Provincial Political Landscapes" investigates the cultural norms of the system, with an emphasis on regionalism, and plumbs the feedback that citizens give to their provincial governments, in the capsule provincial political history sense. "Democracy, Provincial Style" reviews the dynamics surrounding the primordial political ritual of citizens electing their legislatures, the meaningfulness of the ritual, and the relative status of the parties that mediate the process. "Provincial Political Economies" stresses systemic inputs of an economic nature. The "Provincial Structures and Processes"—the executive, legislative and judicial powers, and the local governments—are of course the "institutions" that characterize provincial government. We also review the distinctive constitutional aspects generic to the territories and how they differ from provinces. "Provincial Public Policy" examines the executive and joint outputs that governments and legislatures produce. Needless to say, the categories overlap to a great extent. Yet, the mind needs a somewhat simplified road map before the detours and detail are outlined.

Part I: Surveying Provincial Political Landscapes

The landscapes involved in this section are historical in nature. One is expansive in its history, one is recent. Together they provide an excellent place to start for readers who are either new to the study of provincial politics or who want to review the history they have already lived.

Nelson Wiseman's essay on provincial political cultures, reprinted from the original edition of this book, has been widely acknowledged as a classic in the literature. He offers one of the few comprehensive overviews available on provincial political cultures in Canada. He elaborates on this early ground-breaking work by applying the fragment theory to some provincial societies, but this time expands it to a pan-Canadian context. Wiseman stresses the complementary nature of those political culture approaches that Canadian academics have previously considered in splendid isolation from one another: political economy, formative events, and the fragment theory.

Rand Dyck discusses major political developments in each province, beginning with what experiences they had in common over the last decade. Starting about 1985, most of the provinces were influenced by the nearly universal global spread of the ideology of neoconservatism or neoliberalism, which called for a reduction in the role of the state and the annual balancing of government budgets. To ideology was added economic stresses: a recession in the early 1990s and federal transfer reductions later in that decade. The need to engineer a smaller

Decision-Making in a Parliamentary System

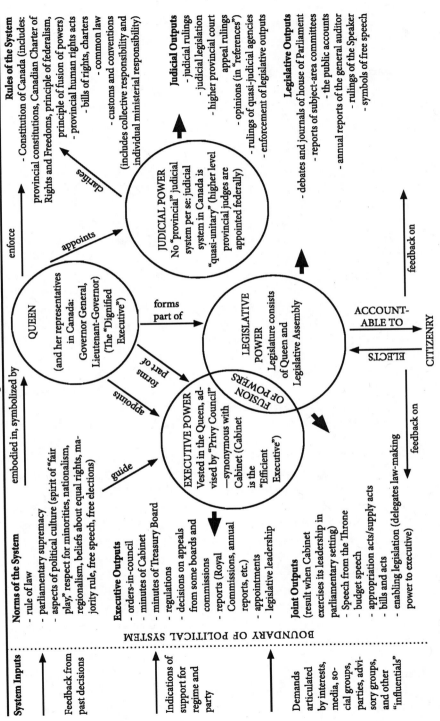

Rules of the System (includes:
- Constitution of Canada (includes: provincial constitutions, Canadian Charter of Rights and Freedoms, principle of federalism, principle of fusion of powers)
- provincial human rights acts
- bills of rights, charters
- common law
- customs and conventions
(includes collective responsibility and individual ministerial responsibility)

Judicial Outputs
- judicial rulings
- judicial legislation
- higher provincial court appeal rulings
- opinions (in "references")
- rulings of quasi-judicial agencies
- enforcement of legislative outputs

Legislative Outputs
- debates and journals of house of Parliament
- reports of subject-area committees
- the public accounts
- annual reports of the general auditor
- rulings of the Speaker
- symbols of free speech

JUDICIAL POWER
No "provincial" judicial system per se: judicial system in Canada is "quasi-unitary" (higher level provincial judges are appointed federally)

clarifies

enforce

embodied in, symbolized by

appoints

QUEEN
(and her representatives in Canada: Governor General, Lieutenant-Governor) (The "Dignified Executive")

forms part of

forms part of

appoints

guide

EXECUTIVE POWER
Vested in the Queen, advised by "Privy Council" —synonymous with Cabinet (Cabinet is the "Efficient Executive")

LEGISLATIVE POWER
Legislature consists of Queen and Legislative Assembly

FUSION OF POWERS

ACCOUNT-ABLE TO

CITIZENRY

ELECTS

feedback on

feedback on

Norms of the System
- rule of law
- parliamentary supremacy
- aspects of political culture (spirit of "fair play," respect for minorities, nationalism, regionalism, beliefs about equal rights, majority rule, free speech, free elections)

Executive Outputs
- orders-in-council
- minutes of Cabinet
- minutes of Treasury Board
- regulations
- decisions on appeals from some boards and commissions
- reports (Royal Commissions, annual reports, etc.)
- appointments
- legislative leadership

Joint Outputs
(result when Cabinet exercises its leadership in parliamentary setting)
- Speech from the Throne
- budget speech
- appropriation acts/supply acts
- bills and acts
- enabling legislation (delegates law-making power to executive)

System Inputs

Feedback from past decisions

Indications of support for regime and party

Demands articulated by interests, media, social groups, parties, advisory groups, and other "influentials"

BOUNDARY OF POLITICAL SYSTEM

state resulted in all provinces to some degree or other reducing public services, programs, and public sector remuneration, as well as moving to more user fees, deregulation, privatization, and downloading. However, Dyck sees that the neo-conservative consensus of the last 20 years is bound to break down under the demands for protection and better services from government. The province-by-province summaries review the political tensions engendered by these demands.

Part II: Democracy, Provincial Style

The new millennium in Canada has been marked by a rebirth of interest in the vitality of democratic institutions and processes. Six provinces introduced special commissions or task forces to investigate the health of their democracy. As these chapters reveal, much remains to be done to strengthen it.

David K. Stewart and **R.K. Carty** are two of the most respected experts of political parties in Canada. In this volume, they examine the various parties that have organized and contested the provincial political systems in Canada during the decade after the great national political earthquake of 1993. This permits them to present an analysis of the party systems of the provinces and compare them to the structure of national party competition. They then look at differences in provincial party organization, membership, and the methods of leadership selection, one of the most important party activities. They conclude by noting the increasing difficulty of re-election, the drop-off in voter participation, and the increased interest in electoral system reform. The latter, of course, has the potential to transform party politics in the provinces.

Donald E. Blake is generally acknowledged as the country's foremost authority on provincial and territorial electoral system procedures and outcomes. He examines these here as an indicator of the quality of democracy that each jurisdiction exhibits. To be sure, he says, the quality of democracy has been examined in the literature with reference to political development, political culture, economic preconditions for democracy, and institutional development. He maintains nonetheless that elections are the principal mechanism for calling our representatives to account; they are "defining institutions" in the quest for modern democracy. There are four dimensions used to explore interjurisdictional differences in electoral democracy: the fairness of the electoral map, laws governing who can vote and be a candidate, rules governing party and election expenses, and election outcomes. Comparisons to rules and regulations at the federal level are made as well. The chapter concludes with an overall assessment of the state of electoral democracy in the provinces and territories and the extent to which regional divisions, especially between Atlantic Canada and the rest of the country, persist.

Gregory Tardi presents a legal portrait of the 2003 Ontario General Election. Although it focuses on Ontario, the chapter's concerns and themes can be generalized to the other provinces as well since it covers matters of universal interest to those concerned with the vitality of election mechanics: the constitutionality of timing of the election, the federalism factor in the representation of Ontario electors, the mechanics of dissolution, the legal framework of election administration, campaigning according to the law, ensuring a democratic standard in campaign speech and political rhetoric, interactions between campaign promises and legality, legally sanctioned broadcasting and the leaders' debate, the decision about whether and how to vote, and the effects of shifting to a permanent register of electors. Tardi analyzes these through the optic of "political law," the interaction between law, public administration, and political principles.

Alan Siaroff has assembled statistical data on provincial politics since 1900. Covered in this collection is such information as provincial electoral systems; provincial election results; measures of electoral concentration, competition, and bias; and Canadian provincial premiers since 1900. We believe that this is the most complete collection of political statistics in one place.

Part III: Provincial Structures and Processes

The concern with the democratic ethos has also affected the standard institutions of government—the powers (branches) of government, local government, and territorial government. Although centralization of power in provincial government is still a fact of life, the degree of centralization has been mitigated somewhat. This is a theme that draws all of the following contributions in this section together.

Christopher Dunn provides an introduction to the role of premiers and cabinets and to the basic machinery of cabinet governance. He investigates the constitutional position of the provincial executive, compares federal and provincial premiers and cabinets, reviews the design of various provincial cabinets, and describes the three models of cabinet governance, namely, the unaided or departmental cabinet, the institutionalized cabinet, and the prime minister- (premier-)centred cabinet. Such literature as exists is split about whether cabinets have remained in the institutionalized mode or whether they have moved towards a post-institutionalized or premier-centred government. In fact, Paul Martin's current federal government may mark the return of institutionalization.

It is not clear any more what it means to be in cabinet, as the line between cabinet and other actors in the governing caucus has been obscured to some extent. The policy process is increasingly, if not exclusively, driven by caucus in British Columbia (BC), Alberta, and Manitoba. Junior cabinet ministers have the ability to check the ministerial prerogative in Quebec. Cabinet secrecy has lost some of its potency with the holding of open cabinet meetings in BC and the expansion of cabinet committee membership in Ontario. This may be a miniature revolution in the making, a change in the centuries-old Westminster model, which, along with the change in legislatures, means that institutional change of a fundamental nature is in train.

The principal focus of **Graham White**, one of the country's leading institutionalists, is on the relative role of legislatures in policy-making, along with issues of representation and accountability. Along the way, he reviews the fundamental similarities among provincial and territorial legislatures, which he briefly compares to the House of Commons. Subsequent sections examine the representativeness, size, and party composition of Canadian legislatures. He finds uneven development but an overall trend towards more effective provincial and territorial legislatures. Members are better paid and have more extensive resources. Procedural and administrative advances have enhanced provincial legislatures' independence from government and their overall capacity to influence public policy, to hold the government accountable, and to represent the people. These advances have not, however, reversed the underlying cabinet domination of provincial legislatures in any fundamental way. The provincial and territorial legislatures are indeed our central democratic institutions, but their effectiveness along many dimensions—not least in safeguarding and strengthening democracy—leaves much to be desired.

Carl Baar has a distinctive approach that makes his chapter required reading for students of the courts: he looks at provincial court systems from a political perspective. He adopts two contrasting approaches. First, he argues that Canadian provincial court systems are disengaged from the central processes of provincial politics to a greater extent than the courts in other federal systems, due to the distinctive organization of Canadian provincial courts and the broad authority of the Supreme Court of Canada. His second argument is that this system's disengagement requires that its political dimensions be examined separately. Politics enters in areas where courts are normally asked to exercise their authority. Accordingly, the second half of his chapter examines the authoritative role of provincial trial and appellate courts in criminal, civil, and family matters (the three major types of court work) and the advocacy role of the judiciary as an interest group in provincial politics.

Richard Tindal and Susan Nobes Tindal observe local government through the lens of intergovernmental relations, a suitable one in light of the federal government's new deal for cities and communities. Theirs is a comprehensive review, which examines, province by province, the recent history of provincial-local relations, changing provincial-local fiscal and legal relationships, the new federal-local relationship, and the impact of globalization and international organizations. Their chapter is sensitive to the needs of modern local governments, whom they say should not let themselves be defined by, and limited to, formal, hierarchical relationships such as those established by international, national, and provincial actors. Local governments especially need to stop seeing their roles and potentials through the constitutional perspective, as merely creatures of the provinces.

Gregory Tardi reviews the evolution of Canada's three northern territories. Nunavut, the Northwest Territories (NWT), and the Yukon are the modern successor jurisdictions to the lands of the Hudson's Bay Company, known as Rupert's Land, and to those of the original North West Company. Without these lands, Tardi reminds us, Canada would have remained a small country wedged between the Great Lakes and the northern Atlantic seaboard. Territories, in contrast to provinces in the 1867 Constitution, had only a limited form of local autonomy, with the remaining powers and the financing of government exercised from the federal level in Ottawa. Since Confederation, there have been developments: some territorial lands were granted provincial status, and there was separation of parts of the 1870 version of the NWT into separate territories. Potential provincehood is a perennial theme, but there is still an insufficient population base and an inadequate level of economic activity to render government and politics self-sustaining to the point of autonomy. The financial assistance of the federal government is still required in order to enable territorial public authorities to function. With the funding comes a certain degree of political control. Despite this, each of the three northern territories is a microcosmic Canadian-style democracy.

Part IV: Provincial Political Economies

Political economy examines the interaction between state and economy. One author here stresses a similarity between provincial political economies; the other stresses differences.

Michael Howlett notes that a common flaw of comparative provincial studies is their tendency to emphasize differences and to downplay either similarities or tendencies toward convergence. He outlines the changing nature of provincial political economies, concluding that provincial "myths" or stereotypes that emphasize differences need correcting. Most of these myths originated in an earlier era of primary sector production, but the reality is that all provinces have highly developed service sector (tertiary) political economies wherein well over two-thirds of the gainfully employed are found. Such a development has important implications, notes this leading Canadian political economist and internationally known public policy authority.

Few people are closer to the provincial fiscal scene than **Geoffrey E. Hale**. In this collection he has done a path-breaking review of provincial fiscal and tax policies. To begin with, he reviews the structures of provincial public finance and the changing face of fiscal federalism. This is followed by an analysis of the various approaches to fiscal sustainability that provinces have used since the 1990s: balancing budgets, 1992-96; stabilizing provincial finances, 1996-2000;

and managing fiscal dividends, 2000 to present. One important innovation in the 1990s, Hale notices, was the introduction of "budget rules," which featured governments committing themselves to self-imposed disciplines on budgetary processes in reaction to chronic deficits and international economic shocks. Long a characteristic of American state budgeting but not Canadian, such "rules" have included contingency funds, fiscal stabilization or reserve funds, balanced budget legislation, standardized accounting procedures, consolidated budgets, debt restrictions, tax or expenditure controls, and referendums for new taxes. He explains one significant development that took place in the late 1990s: the "provincialization" of provincial fiscal regimes, especially the initiation of the new "Tax on Income" system. He follows this already significant contribution with a province-by-province review of the different paths to tax reform and an assessment of the so-called "fiscal imbalance." This is a must-read for those interested in the fiscal and economic forces that affect provincial futures.

Part V: Provincial Public Policy

The area of comparative public policy is not an easy one at the best of times, and the difficulty is exacerbated when the subject involves subnational governments like Canada's provinces. This section of the book pushes the envelope by expanding the level of knowledge about public policy in the areas of governance, demographics, the status of women, social policy, environmental policy, and collective bargaining.

Karen Bridget Murray assesses "The Realignment of Government in the Provinces." This is a job whose difficulty is hard to convey, since, by and large, it has never been done before in a comprehensive fashion. She succeeds wonderfully. Murray describes the ebb and flow of welfare governance, the changing public-private mix in social and economic policy, and the refocusing of responsibilities between local and provincial authorities. These sound prosaic in summary, but the reader is invited to contemplate the richness of the per-province summaries with regard to each of these categories and the depth of the literature base which informs this essay. Murray comes to the conclusion that all these transformations have altered the relationships between citizens and their government, in terms of democratic processes and citizenship.

David K. Foot has a striking contention: the future roles of provincial governments will, in large part, be determined by demographic trends, but demographic information, although readily available, is insufficiently used. This chapter, by one of the country's preeminent demographers, is a call for proactive strategic planning based on demographic and life-cycle analysis at the provincial level to aid in the formulation of appropriate provincial government policies. It provides an introduction to the use of demographic analysis in the context of Canada's provinces and territories, beginning with a review of the size and growth of the total population of each province and territory. The next section examines the associated age structure and introduces the concept of demographic dependency as a convenient summary measure of demographic influences on government. This concept and the associated data are then extended to incorporate relevant economic information. These measures in place, the chapter introduces population projections to develop an overall vision for the future for each province and territory. Finally, this overview is broken down, and selected individual program expenditures are briefly reviewed to illustrate the role that demographics play in influencing specific government policies and programs. With this information the student of government is equipped to better understand provincial and territorial governments in Canada, both in the past and into the future, and provinces are equipped to be able to shift resources gradually from programs in diminishing need to those programs with growing needs.

Brenda O'Neill attempts to explain the question of provincial variation in the status of Canadian women, an important one given the decentralized Canadian federalism, various signs that the provinces' power relative to the federal government is increasing, and the fact that the provinces have jurisdiction over key areas of social policy. Substantial variation is found on a range of policy issues and in women's status. "Place" matters for Canadian women in the degree of economic independence and reproductive freedom they enjoy, the level of child care services available to them, and the level of political representation afforded to them. Her investigation suggests that provincial variation in policy and status is shaped in part by a mix of factors and that this mix varies, depending on the policy or status indicator in question. Horizontal fiscal imbalance provides only limited mileage in explaining this result. She therefore suggests a next step: developing a more sophisticated set of indicators for assessing the various factors that might be brought to bear on policy-making at the provincial level.

Debora L. VanNijnatten and Gerard W. Boychuk compare state and provincial public policy. They argue that two important patterns in North America—regional cross-border economic integration and decentralization—require that policy comparisons focus on the Canadian provinces (and relevant American states) rather than simply on national-level comparisons. Using selected subnational comparisons of social and environmental policy, they show that there are differences among provinces and among states that call into question the methodological appropriateness of generalizing about national policy attributes. This conclusion is supported by a closer look at neighbouring states and provinces where, in some cases, social and environmental policy differences are less marked than differences between neighbouring states or neighbouring provinces. Whether cross-border examinations of policy at the provincial and state level reveal convergence or divergence, they constitute a more appropriate test of the impacts of increasing cross-border economic integration on policy distinctiveness than comparisons of national statistical aggregations or a more singular focus on federal-level policy.

Gene Swimmer and Tim Bartkiw simplify the Byzantine world of collective bargaining in the provinces. With the bulk of constitutional jurisdiction over labour relations resting with provincial governments, what these governments do in the private sector or public sector can be vitally important. The chapter, with its authoritative summaries of provincial regimes, reviews the provincial state's private sector interactions, its public sector interactions, the effect of provincial deficit on collective bargaining, and prospects for the future. Impelled to bolster provincial competitiveness, governments are likely to follow incremental change, but with public finances so volatile, more radical moves to control the largest controllable budget item, public sector compensation, are possible. The authors devote considerable attention to reviewing the various methods used by the provinces in restraining public sector compensation. One approach involves using legislation to impose restraint by suspending collective bargaining and/or overriding existing collective agreements—or just threatening to do so. The second strategy is to obtain concessions through a combination of hard bargaining and reductions in transfer payments, a technique identical to concession bargaining in the private sector. The third strategy involves the "social contract": the provincial government attempts to develop a cooperative arrangement with the public sector unions where the unions voluntarily agree to increase productivity and/or restrain compensation in return for other policies. The most likely prospect for the future, Swimmer and Bartkiw predict, is a return to the "adversary" (concession) system of collective bargaining in both the public and private sectors.

Most of the participants in the *Provinces* project gathered at a "mini-conference" in Toronto in 2002. Unlike the participants in other joint collections, ours had the opportunity to meet each other and to share insights about the various papers, topics, and approaches.

Others deserve appreciation. Broadview's President, Michael Harrison; Barbara Conolly, Managing Editor; Greg Yantz, Assistant Politics Editor; and Tara Lowes, Production Editor, were supportive of the project. The copy-editor, Betsy Struthers, has done an admirable job of a difficult text. Thanks also to my MUCEP (Memorial University Undergraduate Career Experience Program) students, Johnny McLevey and Mandy Leriche, and to the MUCEP Program itself.

Provinces offers the student of Canadian affairs fascinating opportunities to investigate the human drama inherent in provincial politics. For the student of comparative politics, it offers ten socio-political laboratories. In many ways, provincial politics are more interesting than the federal, which in comparison seem more hidebound by convention and constraint. But read on and discover for yourself....

PART I

Surveying Provincial Political Landscapes

CHAPTER 1

Provincial Political Cultures

NELSON WISEMAN

Political culture refers to deeply rooted, popularly held beliefs, values, and attitudes about politics. Culture is pervasive, patterned, cross-generational, enduring, and relatively stable. It is more like climate than like the weather of transitory political events. It is an abstraction, an idea, and as such it is more elusive, more open to interpretive dispute, and harder to fix than a society's composition or economic status. By the 1960s there were over 250 available definitions and uses of the concept of culture.[1] Cross-national comparative studies of political cultures and cultural change are as old as the study of politics; indeed, there is a rich established literature comparing and contrasting Canadian and American political cultures,[2] while in recent decades some comparative cross-provincial studies of political culture have emerged.[3]

This study juxtaposes three complementary rather than competing approaches to studying provincial political cultures. Culture is a holistic concept, one informed by many variables which are not mutually exclusive; however, I focus here on one specifically: Louis Hartz's *fragment theory*. This theory has never been applied consistently at the provincial level but is the richest of the three as an explanatory theory. While it does not claim to explain everything about a society's culture, it is a powerful analytical lens through which to view it. Hartz and his collaborators focused on the ideologies of new societies spun off from Europe: Canada, the United States, South Africa, Australia, and Latin America.[4] So what are the fragment theory's suggestive possibilities when pursued at the provincial level? Like Hartz, we must strive for historical breadth and imagination, comparative analysis, and the identification of cultural-ideological origins. To a limited extent, however, other approaches do this as well. On which one should we then rely?

The departures taken in this chapter are to apply fragment methodology consistently across regions and provinces, as well as to stress the complementary nature of what some consider to be competing views of political culture in Canada. Hartz himself recognized that economic factors—the availability of capital, the formation of new classes, and urbanization—were interconnected with ideological fragmentation. Accordingly, I examine how external control of the markets for raw materials and resources throughout Canada's history, as described in the *staples tradition*, can explain the variegated aspects of regional cultures as well as power relations. Similarly, Seymour Martin Lipset's *formative events* or founding moments approach to Canadian and American political culture has a certain resonance with Hartz because both stress the transplantation of cultural traits. Ultimately, however, I stress the fragment theory because the staples approach historically has not devoted much attention to the interplay between different ideologies or to the processes by which cultural ideas endure, and the formative event described by Lipset in Canada—our "counterrevolution" to the American "revolution"—does not explain all regional cultures across Canada, only some.

Staples and Society

In the Canadian context, the staples theory of economic growth spotlights the exploitation of a successive series of raw or natural resources.[5] The backward and forward economic linkages required for staples extraction and export may be used to explain culture as well as economic development. From this perspective, society's collective psyche is conditioned by Canada's lack of control of staples markets. Just as Britain's colonies/provinces were settled in response to external demand for staples *and* external social upheavals and dislocations, much of Canada's economic, social, ideological, and institutional development has been driven from abroad. From a political economy perspective, culture may be said to reflect the forces of production surrounding a staples economy. From this vantage point, the inputs of production—capital and labour—and the staples to which they are applied, shape power relations and political consciousness or culture.

Table 1.1 lists five staples, chronological periods of their formative exploitation, and the provinces or regions most affected. *The fishery* fed the early settlement of the Atlantic colonies and the Gaspé. Before Confederation, the Maritimes' Golden Age was characterized by a water-based trading system that exchanged Maritime fish (and then lumber) for finished British goods, New England wheat, and West Indian rum and sugar. *The fur trade* overlapped the fishery's growth and entailed British and, especially, French-Canadian penetration of North America, south through the Great Lakes and the Mississippi to Louisiana, and west and north across Rupert's Land and beyond. The surplus generated by the fur trade provided the capital for the Bank of Montreal's establishment in 1817 and that city's financial and economic hegemony until the mid-twentieth century. Europe's craving for wooden ships led to the harvesting of New Brunswick, and Lower and Upper Canadian *forests* in the first half of the nineteenth century. Subsequently, an appetite for newsprint had the same effect, and BC's timber became an economic factor in the twentieth century with the opening of the Panama Canal in 1914. Along with the transcontinental railway, this ensured BC's dynamic growth and Vancouver's entrepôt status. Completed in 1885, the Canadian Pacific Railway (CPR) served as the Prairies' transmission belt, turning the region into the British Empire's breadbasket in the first quarter of the twentieth century. *The wheat economy* fuelled Central Canada's protected manufacturing engine. Mining in northern Ontario before and after the turn of the century helped shift the centre of economic gravity westward. Western *fuel and mineral development*, presaged by BC's 1850s gold rush and based on coal, was complemented after the Second World War by the discovery of oil, natural gas, and the extraction of potash, uranium, nickel, gold, and other metals. Manitoba and Quebec harnessed the Arctic watershed for hydro-electric power.

Table 1.1. Staple Development by Approximate Period and Region

Staple	Period	Province/Region
1. Fish	18th–19th centuries	Atlantic Canada
2. Fur	18th–19th centuries	Quebec
3. Forests	19th century	Central and Atlantic Canada
	20th century	BC
4. Farms	early 20th century	Prairies
5. Fuels/Minerals	late 19th and 20th centuries	northern Ontario and Quebec
	late 20th century	Alberta and BC

From a political economy perspective, provincial political cultures reflect the interplay of economic forces that envelop them. Thus, Atlantic fishermen may carry an individualistic ideology based on their individual ownership of boat and gear or a historical memory of such, even though many of them may be employees or deeply in debt and not effective or real entrepreneurs. Comparatively, Maritime farmers have been more likely subsistence farmers whereas those in the Western grain trade have been commercial farmers. The former have been less dependent on dealing with bankers, transport firms, merchants, and others who could be identified as common exploiters. Where Western farmers embraced cooperatives as alternative economic structures, Maritime farmers had less need for cooperatives, tended to spurn them, and were less affected by the volatile cycles in commodity markets.[6] Such differences in provincial economic cultures may be said to drive differences in provincial political cultures.

Formative Events and Quakes

Table 1.2 identifies formative events or founding moments in provincial histories. This notion, used by Lipset, is compatible with and complementary to the fragment theory's focus on the transplantation of cultural genes. Lipset defined and contrasted Canadian and American political cultures as products of a single formative event: the American Revolution.[7] This hinge in the two national histories, however, is more critical for some provinces (Ontario, the Maritimes) than for others (the West, Newfoundland, Quebec).

If formative events cast cultures, let us remember that casts are subject to stress, to periodic assault, to possible modification and cracking. In the US, the

Revolution's northern liberalism—and it is from the northern states that most of the Loyalists came—was confronted in the Civil War by the lingering quasi-feudal conservatism of the South. The war between the states was not the US's formative event, but it was certainly a monumental tremor or "quake": a landmark that cast a shadow on future political development. In emancipating blacks and undermining the plantation culture, it confirmed and extended the Revolution's liberal egalitarian predilections.

One can also search for and fix formative events and lesser quakes in provincial histories. In Newfoundland, the formative events of *responsible government* and *Confederation* were retarded. Local reformers agitated for responsible government as they did elsewhere, but it came about only after it was achieved in other places. Britain could grant responsible government to Newfoundland but could not impose Confederation on it; rejecting Confederation in the 1860s was pivotal to Newfoundland's evolution just as embracing it was in 1949. Aloofness from Canada was the product of physical separation and cultural differences with the Maritimes and Ontario. The Loyalists ignored and avoided the island, as did most of the third British wave of immigration who saw in Confederation entrepreneurial possibilities for national and Western economic development. Remote and isolated, Newfoundland was a world unto itself. While the promise of the Inter-Colonial Railway—capturing a Canadian market for Maritime industry—helped induce Maritime entry into Confederation, it was not relevant to the island's prospects. Moreover, financial scandals in the twentieth century rattled confidence in Newfoundland's parties and government. The political system collapsed in a way that it did not elsewhere, and Newfoundland had no Ottawa to turn to in the Dirty Thirties to alleviate its impossible financial predicament. It reverted to direct British rule, *Commission Government*, which was overtaken by the Second World War. As an American military outpost, Newfoundland became exposed to the culturally integrating influence of the Allied war effort. Britain was keen to dispose of a financial millstone, and, after the war, it did all it could to set the stage for union with Canada.[8] Commission Government therefore qualifies as a "quake" in Newfoundland history.

In the Maritimes we might arguably see the *Acadian expulsion* in 1755 as the region's formative event. It assured a future British, rather than dualistic French-English, mould for Nova Scotia and Prince Edward Island (PEI). New Brunswick proved something of an exception: a number of Acadian "fugitives"[9] escaped to it and settled its northeast, a region to which future generations of expelled Acadians would eventually return. Here too, in the meantime, government was established and controlled by Loyalists. The result was a broadly similar and pervasive political culture throughout the Atlantic region: elite-oriented, conservative, and traditional. The Conservative and Liberal parties that emerged were not divided by ideological differences. The American Revolution helped populate the Maritimes with settlers, and the region was more liberal than Newfoundland but, like it, had no liberal or nationalist rebellion, no equivalent to those in Upper and Lower Canada. Like them, however, it had its Family Compacts and Reformers, a tension between the established and the aspiring classes. The Maritimes were not as liberal as Upper Canada because fewer early nineteenth-century liberals, in what I will later call the "third immigrant wave," settled there. Nevertheless, many did, and they struggled for responsible government. One battle they fought which had no Ontario parallel was for "better terms" in Confederation's early years. Whereas Ontario's relative wealth fuelled that province's determination to lessen federal power in the late nineteenth century, the relative poverty of the Maritimes contributed to the region's eventual embrace of strong central government. The theme of improving local conditions through federal power, through equalization grants and regionally designated programs, has thus characterized the Maritimes' constitutional position in recent decades.[10]

Table 1.2. Formative Provincial Events

Province	Formative Events Founding Moments	Quakes
Newfoundland	Responsible Government and Confederation 1855, 1860s, 1949	Commission Government 1934-49
Maritimes	Acadians expelled 1755 Responsible Government 1848	American Revolution 1780s
Quebec	Conquest 1760 Quiet Revolution 1960	1837 Rebellion
Ontario	American Revolution 1780s 1837 Rebellion and Responsible Government 1848	War of 1812
Manitoba	Riel and CPR 1870s	Winnipeg General Strike 1919
Saskatchewan	Riel and CPR 1880s	Great Depression 1930s
Alberta	"Last Best West" 1896	Oil 1947
BC	CPR and Panama Canal 1885 and 1914	Social Credit 1952

The *Conquest* was Quebec's formative event. Symbolically, Quebec's "sovereignty" referendums may be seen as attempts to undo at the ballot box—a twentieth-century battleground—what Wolfe's muskets accomplished on the Plains of Abraham in 1759. The evacuation of New France's economic and political elite shifted societal leadership to the Catholic clergy and economic leadership to a new class of English-speaking merchants. The recognition and protection of French language and religious expression in the *Quebec Act* of

1774 fed a festering contradiction in the polity: a French society governed by an anglophone executive. Hence, Papineau's *patriotes* and the *Rebellion of 1837*. The Rebellion, an ethnic struggle with a claim for responsible government, was thus unlike the political battle in Upper Canada at the same time. Although the fight for self-governance was won, a new liberal society in French Quebec was not forthcoming. The clergy supported the British Crown, condemning the Enlightenment and assaulting change. Confederation offered Quebec not a new beginning but a consolidation of its traditions, entrenched in Sections 92, 93, and 133 of the British North America (BNA) Act. Thus, Quebec kept political modernization at bay,[11] but, inevitably, the contradiction between what Quebec became in the twentieth century—socially and economically urban—and its nineteenth-century rural-based ideology was too stark to continue. It exploded in the *Quiet Revolution*, as sharp and as precise as the Conquest itself had been. Overnight, the authoritarian, traditional, rural, conservative, corrupt, patronage-driven government of Maurice Duplessis's Union Nationale gave way to the democratic, rationalist, urban, liberal, merit-based public service of Jean Lesage's Liberals. Where Duplessis's regime had been essentially passive, with the Church providing services which in English Canada were governmental, Lesage's regime was aggressive and active. Secularization and a modernized provincial state combined to yield a nationalism that was, and is, both linguistic and governmental. Linking past, present, and future, language became the new religious icon. Thus, Quebec's ethnically rooted *pure laine* tribalism runs back over three centuries.

The *American Revolution* was English Canada's founding moment, but it was especially so for Ontario. Its political institutions were based explicitly on the belief in the superiority of Britain's more conservative institutions. The British determined that the pre-revolutionary American governments had been overly democratic and too subject to popular measures. More of a frontier and less established than Atlantic Canada, Upper Canada attracted many energetic, liberal, and entrepreneurial American farmers in the decades following the Revolution and the Loyalist influx. Reinforcing Upper Canada's innate conservatism, however, was the *War of 1812*. Its main effect in the Maritimes was commercial enhancement; in Ontario—where it was mainly fought—it buttressed a fierce and aggressive Tory ideology.[12] American immigrants who refused to fight for the Crown were expelled, others decamped. The war stimulated patriotic passion and cemented the control of the conservative elite, the Family Compact. Within this broad conservative cultural disposition, liberal ideology was reflected by the Baldwins, Irish Protestant immigrants in the third wave, Mackenzie, and the *1837 Rebellion*. This outlook, however, was a secondary and minoritarian one. When *responsible government* came in 1848, it had a strong conservative stamp on it. The High Tory right was destroyed, but the newly emergent Liberals and Conservatives—led by George Brown and John Sandfield Macdonald—were in agreement on the evils of American democracy and the virtues of British constitutionalism. Partisans on both sides contrasted favourably their society's stability to the US's civil discord. But an ideological and economic difference between the two parties, despite their agreement to the project, was their view of Confederation: Conservatives preferred to project a new national economic empire guided by the state; Liberals saw the potential for expanded private economic opportunities. Ontario's centrality and power could facilitate both outlooks.

The *coming of the railway* was a formative event common to all four Western provinces. As in the Maritimes, it was a condition for BC's entry into Confederation; on the Prairies, it was a precondition for settlement. In light of the West's provincially differentiated political traditions, however, it is necessary to look beyond the CPR. As with the expulsion of the Acadians, the *defeat of Louis Riel's Métis* in 1870 ensured that Manitoba would be English. The *tide of Ontarian immigrants* in the 1870s and 1880s shunted aside the French Catholic Métis and the language and religious educational guarantees they had negotiated in the Manitoba Act, the province's constitution. The *Official Language Act* of 1890, confirming English and denying French, was no administrative *coup d'état*: it simply mirrored the new demography. In the 1871 census, only nine souls in Winnipeg claimed to be Indian or Métis. French Canadians appeared as merely one of the many new and smaller ethnic groups of the fourth immigrant wave. The CPR meant Winnipeg's growth and hegemony in the West as gateway, grain market, and wholesale/retail distribution centre for communities stretching over the Rockies into BC. The *Winnipeg General Strike* crystallized the differences between the dominant tory-touched Ontario liberals and the British labour-socialists of the fourth wave. Moreover, the Strike begat the Independent Labour Party (ILP), and exactly a half-century after the Strike's collapse, the ILP's direct genealogical and ideological grandchild, the New Democratic Party (NDP), won power in the province.

The Manitoba pattern was reprised in the North-West. The *defeat of the displaced Métis* and the *execution of Riel* in Regina in 1885 cleared the path of the Ontarians and the CPR. The most rural province, Saskatchewan had no comparably dominant urban centre as did Manitoba and BC, but the burgeoning wheat economy quickly made it the third most populous province. In less time, however, the *Great Depression* devastated it. Whatever economic glory it was to recover awaited the 1970s and its new staples: oil, gas, and potash. Saskatchewan is now the least populous province outside Atlantic Canada. Harsh climate, one-crop dependency, boom and bust economic cycles, and immigrant Britons experienced in cooperativism all contributed to the formation of more cooperatives in Saskatchewan than in any other province in the first half of the twentieth century. The Great Depression did not directly produce a Cooperative Commonwealth Federation (CCF) government as it did a Social Credit one in Alberta, but it graphically exposed Saskatchewan as a dependent and unstable province. This and the efficaciousness of war-time planning were supportive backdrops to the

CCF's cooperative-socialist message and its preference for strong central government. The leadership of immigrant British socialists, in combination with the voting support of continental Europeans in this fourth immigrant wave, swept the CCF into office in 1944. It confirmed, consolidated, and reflected a left-right dynamic common to Western Canadian politics.

Tentatively and imaginatively, one may offer up the *evaporation of the US's "Last Best West"* in 1896 as Alberta's formative event. To be sure, the CPR had opened the province, but the 1890s was when the American frontier was spent: good, free farm land was no longer available to willing homesteaders. The last North American agricultural frontier, therefore, was the unstaked Prairies: western Saskatchewan and especially southern Alberta. Large numbers of transplanted Nebraskans, Dakotans, and others moved up into the western Prairies and became the backbone of Alberta's formative farmers' movement, the United Farmers of Alberta (UFA). Indeed, a contemporary Alberta journalist encountered such a Dakotan, who came to the province by wagon in 1910, at a 1982 convention of the separatist, populist Western Canada Concept.[13] The UFA grew out of branches of the American Society of Equity to which many of its members had belonged, and its Board of Directors in 1918 contained more American-born than either Canadian- or British-born members.[14] Inflationary monetary reform ideas and direct democracy proposals—which swept the American plains in the late nineteenth century—were popularized by American UFAers such as credit expert George Bevington and former Kansas Governor J.W. Leedy. These ideas were then co-opted by Social Credit as the UFA was saddled with the Great Depression, a sex scandal involving the premier, and a popular sense that it was time for a change in government if not in ideological outlook. The *postwar discovery of oil* and the reorientation of the provincial economy eased Social Credit's transformation from enemy of big business to Cold Warrior. Social Credit Premier Ernest Manning went from leading a government that had attacked the "Fifty Big Shots of Canada" and the banks to serving as a director of the Canadian Imperial Bank of Commerce. Like the American government, Alberta's government became an implacable foe of socialism. This was, and is, sound strategy, because socialism has always been weaker in Alberta than in the other western provinces.

BC's isolation and distance from the rest of Canada and Europe may suggest that linkage to them—through the completion of the *CPR* (1885) and the *Panama Canal* (1914)—were formative events. As on the Prairies, population growth exploded. BC's frontier economy, however, was corporate rather than agrarian. Conditions in the remote mining and forestry towns helped to generate class consciousness, and the radical ideological make-up of the fourth wave of immigration to those towns and to Vancouver also fed class struggle: labour versus capital, workers versus management, blue collar versus white collar, left versus right. BC's dynamic growth—it went from second smallest to third largest province in less than a half-century—made it a magnet for entrepreneurs and wage labourers, many of whom came from an industrial, urban, and distressed Britain. Furthermore, the left-right dynamic in BC provincial politics was more engrained than elsewhere, even producing a unique right-wing coalition government of Liberals and Conservatives. (In Manitoba, in contrast, the coalition leaders presented themselves as populist "non-partisans" rather than as primarily anti-CCF.) In 1952, the BC CCF lost despite its victory in the popular vote. The overnight *emergence of Social Credit*—it had been sudden in Alberta as well—soon consolidated and clarified the left-right dialectic in provincial politics. In both provinces, Social Credit moved to the right after gaining power. In BC, however, unlike Alberta, a symbiotic ideological tension between left and right continues into the new millennium.

The Fragment Theory

Hartz's idea that the politics of new societies are shaped by the older societies from which they come is neither novel nor radical. It appears obvious: immigrants and their ideas come from elsewhere. Less evident and counter-intuitive is Hartz's claim that socialism's emergence in a new society required a pre-existing conservatism; the two ideologies share some common assumptions and views of society. According to Hartz, the rejection of conservatism in the US explained its antagonism toward and inability to comprehend the future appeal of socialism.[15] Hartz's theory, applied to Canada by Gad Horowitz, suggested that Canada's relative flirtation with socialism and the US's fanatical rejection of it was connected to Canada's relative ideological diversity, tolerance, and toryism.[16] Horowitz offered the Canadian corollary to Hartz's analysis of American absolute liberalism and intolerance of classical conservatism or tory philosophy. From a Hartzian perspective, Canada had dual founding cultural fragments: the older society is rooted in pre-revolutionary, pre-liberal France. It was imbued with an organic-collectivist-corporatist, quasi-feudal ideology that revolved around the conservative principles of tradition, hierarchy, and authority or social order. The second, and newer, English-Canadian fragment rejected and fled the American Revolution but was infected with a rationalist-egalitarian ideology. It revolved—unlike a Tory world view—around the liberal principles of freedom and competition, giving priority to the individual rather than the community. The Loyalist outlook was fundamentally liberal but unmistakably streaked with a tory or conservative touch. Let us call it conservative liberalism: more liberal and less conservative than New France, but more conservative and less liberal than the revolutionary, republican US where the people, rather than monarchs, are sovereign. Lord Durham's image of two cultures living and quarrelling within the bosom of a single state is older than the Dominion of Canada and as current as Quebec's referendums on sovereignty.

As 1995 began, Ontario, BC, Saskatchewan, and Quebec had something oddly in common: governing parties calling themselves social democratic. How un-American! Place this against the backdrop of the Hartz-Horowitz fragment theory, whose essence is this: "the relative strength of socialism in Canada is related to the relative strength of toryism."[17] It holds that conservatism—English toryism and French quasi-feudalism—contained the seeds for Canada's future receptivity to socialism. When one looks at the provincial level, the pattern is perplexing, simultaneously supportive and contradictory of the Hartzian principle. It works better for French Canada—Quebec—than for English Canada. In Quebec, the connection between traditional conservatism and modern social democracy is reflected in the ideological evolution of the union movement; in the corporatist impulses before and since the Quiet Revolution; in the "Je me souviens" motto, reminiscent of pre-liberalism; and in the familial linkage between Daniel Johnson's conservative Union Nationale and son Pierre-Marc Johnson's social democratic Parti Québécois (PQ). In that province, socialism arose as Hartz noted that it had in Europe, through the interaction of, and a reaction to, feudal and liberal ideas. Socialism appeared later in Quebec than in English Canada or Europe because Quebec's liberalism—a concomitant condition for socialism's appearance—was retarded until its explosion in the 1960s. Socialism's emergence, according to the fragment theory, required not only conservatism but liberalism too, however brief its rush.

Yet in English Canada, the Hartzian application confounds. Socialism has been strongest where toryism has been weakest: in the West. Conversely, socialism has been weakest where toryism has been strongest: in Atlantic Canada and eastern Ontario. In confirmation of the Hartz-Horowitz thesis, however, socialism in the West has been weakest in Alberta, the province where toryism has been weakest and which appears most like the American case: pure, unalloyed liberalism.

Fragments, nationally, were cut off from the ideological evolution of their mother societies in Europe. The US embraced Locke but, thrown off from Europe, did not experience the successors and reaction to Locke: the Chartists, the Fabians, the Labour Party. French Canada embraced the *ancien régime* but, it too thrown off from Europe, did not experience the Jacobins or (until the 1960s) the Enlightenment. Australia was formed out of the crucible of Britain's Industrial Revolution and embraced the Labour Party but, cut off from Europe, did not experience Labour's successors: scientific socialism and revolutionary communism. Hartz described the fragment as congealing, living an interior life,[18] frozen and limited by its point of departure from an evolving European ideological constellation where competing philosophies interacted as parents and children. He foresaw the collapse of fragment ideologies in a new era of unavoidable world impact, globalization, cultural diversity, cosmopolitanism, and ideological bombardment.

Immigrants and ideas

The ideological evolution of *provincial* fragments is similarly bounded by the point of departure and cultural baggage of specific waves of immigration. Five distinct immigrant waves and broad periods are discernible, the identification of which is critical to pursuing the fragment theory at the provincial level. Immigrants from quite different societies, carrying differing ideological baggage, settled in dramatically differing proportions in the various provinces. Cross-national comparative analyses fudge such differences, for their primary interest is to characterize a dominant ethos or charter national outlook. Provincial-level analysis requires subnational detail and refinement. For example, Loyalism's hierarchical, elitist, and ascriptive preferences for social order, stability, and continuity have been used to describe Canada's political culture in contrast to that of the US. These conservative hallmarks once rang true in Ontario and still resonate in Atlantic Canada, but they never have in the West. Moreover, the new polyglot, polyethnic, and multiracial social order of metropolitan Ontario now seems far from exhibiting the characteristics of tory orderliness and deference to authority associated with the Loyalists. A diverse, non-immigrant ethnic group has been Aboriginal peoples. Their ideas counted for naught in politics until recently, however, due to their disenfranchisement from the political system until the 1950s and 1960s. Similarly, the Chinese in Western Canada who were imported to build the CPR had, like the Aboriginal peoples, low status, no votes, and no political clout.

Canadian provincial politics have been shaped by five successive immigrant waves, as Table 1.3 demonstrates. The first and oldest, from pre-revolutionary France, was transplanted to New France and Acadia. This fragment represented, as we have suggested, quasi-feudal conservatism. The Conquest reinforced it: a pre-Enlightenment Catholic clergy filled the vacuum of a decapitated

Table 1.3. Immigrant Waves by Period, Region, Orientation

Immigrant Waves	Period	Primary Region	Dominant Orientations
1. France	to 1760	Quebec/Acadia	quasi-feudal conservative
2. Loyalist	1780s	Maritimes/ Ontario	tory-touched liberal
3. Britain	1815–51	Ontario/ Maritimes	Reform liberal
4. Britain/US/ Eastern Europe	1890s–1920s	West/ Ontario	a) labour-socialist b) populist-liberal c) deferential
5. Asia/South Europe/ Caribbean/ Latin America	1945–	Metro Canada	individual/equality rights/liberal

middle-class lay leadership. Fewer than 10,000 French immigrants multiplied—in a context of minimal French migration after 1759—to over 7 million by the late twentieth century. Duplessis's death, exactly 200 years after the Conquest, symbolically represented the expiration of the old conservative ideology of mere *survivance*. The Quiet Revolution gave birth to the liberal ideology of *rattrapage* and *épanouissement*.

The second immigrant wave, the Loyalists, were expelled by the liberal American Revolution.[19] They swelled Nova Scotia with nearly 30,000 new settlers and established New Brunswick. About 10,000 of them anchored what became Ontario. In English Canada, Loyalists became the elite. They were politically Tory but relatively liberal compared to Quebec's ideological leadership.

A half-century after the Loyalist influx, coinciding with the growth of British reform liberalism, an even larger third immigrant wave appeared. Between the end of the Napoleonic wars and 1851, the population of what became Ontario exploded tenfold, from fewer than 100,000 residents to nearly 1 million.[20] Largely composed of labourers and artisans—few of them were middle class—this wave was more liberal than the Loyalists and reflected Whig and Reform ascendancy in Britain. They demanded and secured responsible government in the Maritimes and the Province of Canada in 1848. They modified the more authoritarian political order of the Family Compact. This wave had a greater impact in Ontario than in the Maritimes because embryonic Ontario was, relatively, a frontier society. Thus, Upper Canada's liberal reform Rebellion of 1837 was led by a Scottish immigrant who arrived in 1820 to seek his fortune in the new world: William Lyon Mackenzie.

The fourth immigrant wave at the turn of the twentieth century was more diverse because it was composed of three overlapping ripples. The largest, from the mother country, contained Britain's emerging labour-socialist politics. Many of these immigrants were British liberals, some more tory than others. Most were city-bred labouring folk; many of them were sympathetic and open to the new egalitarian and distributional promises of socialism. Their greatest impact was in the sparsely settled West. Some settled in urban Ontario, fewer still in the Maritimes. Jimmie Simpson, for example, became Toronto's labour-socialist mayor in the 1930s. Some British miners went directly into Cape Breton's mines, established a labour party, and launched labour wars there in the 1920s. By far, however, the new British impact was greatest on the new, shifting frontier: the West. The radical British outlook was reflected in the leadership and personnel of numerous nascent Labour parties and the CCF. These parties proved strongest and most resilient where institutions were rudimentary. The Prairie population exploded from about 100,000 in 1881 to 2 million in 1921, and that of BC tripled in half that time.

A second, relatively small but regionally influential ripple in this fourth wave was a populist-liberal American one, flowing northwest from the American great plains. In 1911, Americans comprised nearly one-quarter of all Albertans, and their dominance in rural areas dictated the shape of provincial politics. Their American plebiscitarian-democratic instincts were devoid of toryism, and while this outlook attracted some socialists, it rejected socialism itself. This populist strain, moving steadily to the right over the years, came to be expressed in a long string of unorthodox (by Eastern Canadian standards) parties: the Non-Partisan League, the UFA, Social Credit, and the Reform Party.

The third and last ripple in this fourth wave was a diverse lot of continental Europeans: Ukrainians, Germans, Poles, Jews, Scandinavians, and others. They were not influential ideologically because their origins and outlooks were mixed and their languages foreign. In social status, Scandinavians were somewhat below those of British ethnic origins, but above the others. In order to avoid suspicion and to gain acceptance, the Europeans deferred ideologically, and by the time the first generation learned English, they had bred a second generation that assimilated some of the prevailing values. As they acculturated, they came to the fore politically. In the early 1990s, for example, for the first time, none of the three Prairie premiers was of British ethnic origin.

The fifth immigrant wave—coming from southern Europe, Asia, the Caribbean, and Latin America, as well as from the older, more traditional sources—is the most socially and ideologically variegated. Coming since the Second World War, it has been overwhelmingly urban and metropolitan, drawn especially to the largest centres. Many of the visible minorities in the fifth wave spoke English or French, unlike the continental Europeans of the fourth and fifth waves. Those from the British Crown colony of Hong Kong and most of the Caribbean (the former British West Indies) tended to settle in metropolitan English Canada while many from Haiti, the former French Middle East, and Vietnam gravitated to Montreal. We may differentiate between two broad ripples within this broadest of waves. The southern Europeans—Italians, Greeks, Portuguese—are somewhat older in origin and now relatively well established compared to the Asians and those from the Caribbean and Latin America. More visible, multicultural, and multiracial, this wave is loosely tied together in its stake in a recent ideological emblem: the *Canadian Charter of Rights and Freedoms*. This wave's absolute numbers are large, but its relative numerical, ideological, and political impact is weak, for provincial political cultures are now too established to be overwhelmed. It has not created new political parties, preferring to attain status within the established ones; right-wing and left-wing, liberal, socialist, and conservative, this wave is the most motley.

Cultural imagery

The Hartzian approach to political culture is creatively bold: comparative, historical, dialectical, and holistic. In such a creative vein, Table 1.4 presents metaphorical images of the provinces. They are limited and imperfect but serve as heuristic devices. In considering them, think of provincial societies and cultures as reflecting the political discourse of other societies and cultures, and strive to appreciate provincial cultural differences rather than similarities. Exaggeration via caricature and stereotype is intended as an imaginative, rather than literal, technique whose purpose is to illuminate the exceptionality of each provincial political culture.

Table 1.4. Provincial Metaphorical Images

Province	Metaphorical Images
Newfoundland	Canada's Ireland and West Country England
Maritimes	Canada's New England
Quebec	New (Old) France
Ontario	The US's Counter-Revolution
Manitoba	The Prairies' Ontario
Saskatchewan	The Prairies' Britain
Alberta	The Prairies' US
BC	Canada's Australia

Newfoundland: Canada's Ireland and west country England

Newfoundland as *Canada's Ireland and west country England* is a simultaneously false and insightful metaphor. The contention is merely that Newfoundland politics have appeared—relatively more so than the politics of any other province—like old Irish and west English politics. This is the primary comparative point and all that is hinted. The collapse of Newfoundland's fishery in the 1990s may be seen as the New World equivalent of the Irish potato famine. After the Napoleonic wars, the fishery encouraged Newfoundland's settlement. Organized around a semi-feudal relationship between outport fishermen and St. John's fish merchants, money was virtually absent in the "truck" system. For his catch, the fisherman received credit and goods in exchange. Settlers "came predominantly, and in about equal number, from Ireland and the west of England, and it is from them that the present population of the island is largely descended." Newfoundland society "was largely determined by the cultural norms and patterns of social organization and behaviour of the two founding groups, the Irish and the English," writes S.J.R. Noel. His description is consistent with that of the fragment theory:

> For the Irish brought with them a national heritage of poverty, Roman Catholicism, and hatred of their English oppressors; while the English brought with them from the west country a heritage of puritanical Protestantism, social deference, and semi-feudal

economic relationships. Thus the constituent elements of the new community from the very beginning contained in their respective traditions and memories from the old world the seeds of social conflict in the new.[21]

Newfoundland's cultural duality, like Quebec's, was reinforced by residential segregation, unwritten law, and custom. The Irish Catholics gravitated to St. John's and the Avalon Peninsula, the English to the outports. In the Protestant north of the island, the Orange Lodge was particularly strong. Not one constituency beyond the Peninsula had a Catholic majority.[22]

Political divisions mirrored the economy and society: the urban centre of St. John's versus the isolated outposts was Newfoundland's version of the metropolis-hinterland paradigm. Neither Catholic in leadership nor policy, the early Liberal party was sustained by Irish Catholic voters, while the early Conservatives represented the English merchant class and adopted "Protestant Unity" as their rallying cry. Old World politics drove the colony's first constitution of 1832, suggesting an uncongealed and still evolving political culture. This constitution was the product of British Whiggism's ascendancy: manhood suffrage and eligibility for office unfettered by property, rent, income, or literacy requirements.[23] Still, Newfoundland was partly of Ireland but also unlike it. It "was not to become simply a colonial microcosm of Ireland, for, unlike Ireland, political oppression was not in the economic interest of the Protestant ruling elite." The English Tory Protestant oligarchy opposed Confederation in the 1860s, but the heart of the opposition was among the Liberal Irish Catholics. Their "bitter folk memories were stirred by such effective propaganda as the comparison of confederation to the 1801 *Act of Union* between Britain and Ireland." Nearly a century later, Newfoundland in the 1940s was still "poorer than its North American neighbours but also different from them, holding to more conservative values, and preserving a culture historically rooted in the pre-industrial societies of Ireland and the west of England."[24]

In the 1860s, the Conservatives were "converted" into "liberal democrats," partly because Protestants now made up a slight majority but, more critically, because sectarianism became safely institutionalized. As in the Maritimes, elections, public appointments, and patronage reflected religious considerations. Newfoundland adopted a religious denominational basis of electoral representation[25] which disappeared only in the 1970s. In Newfoundland, "the denominational compromise of the 1860s had crystallized into an established principle of government and denominational segregation had become an unwritten law of social organization."[26] David Bellamy described the province in the 1970s as dominated by a "rural fundamentalism" and as "only a partially secularized society."[27] This is quite a contrast to BC, where Catholics are outnumbered by non-believers and non-Christians.[28] As in conservative Quebec but somewhat less than in the Maritimes, in conservative Newfoundland beyond St. John's the virtues of rural society were idealized and the impact of civilization derided.

More than any other province, Newfoundland has been like Ireland *and* closer to Britain, known as "Britain's Oldest Colony." St. John's is geographically nearer London than it is Vancouver, and, until 1980, the Union Jack served as the provincial flag. Like Canada in the First World War, Newfoundland was automatically in Britain's war. Unlike Canada in the Second World War, however, it was again automatically at Britain's side. In 1934 it asked for direct British rule in the midst of financial distress. It surrendered its self-governing dominion status which it had just recently gained in the Statute of Westminster. Intimately and institutionally connected to Britain, Newfoundland was to be generationally isolated from it in a way that Canada was not. The fourth immigrant wave passed it by, even more so than it did the Maritimes. Thus, Newfoundland's flirtation with labour-socialism was abstract and stunted whereas in the West it was real and potent. In Newfoundland, "the activities of the British Labour party were avidly reported" in the 1910s;[29] in the West they were avidly lived and replicated. Newfoundland's fishermen's union of 1913, organized by native farmer William Coaker, drew on a self-reliant, archetypally individualistic, and largely self-employed class "more closely akin to an agrarian peasantry than to an industrial proletariat."[30]

Newfoundlanders' self-image was congruent with the colony's settlement: prohibited by British law until the nineteenth century, the outports emerged as isolated outlaw communities tucked away in remote coves entered neither by the Royal Navy nor by outside fishing boats. This fostered a self-image quite unlike the class solidarity of the British-born unionists who voted for a general strike in Calgary in 1918, imposed one on Winnipeg a year later, dabbled in the syndicalism of the One Big Union, and initially applauded the Russian Revolution. The socialist phase of Joey Smallwood, who led Newfoundland into confederation with Canada, is noteworthy for its brevity, one of intellectual conversion quite different from the rooted, transplanted, and sustained socialism of, for example, John Queen and M.J. Coldwell, the Manitoba and Saskatchewan ILP leaders. There was never much popular ideological support for socialism in Newfoundland.

Voting in the two 1948 referendums that led to Confederation cut across religious and ethnic lines, forcefully exhibiting the cleavage between St. John's and the outports. Nevertheless, Catholics and Protestants were identified with the anti- and pro-confederate forces respectively: the Catholic Archbishop of St. John's was one of union's most vociferous critics. In the aftermath, the Confederate Association was converted into the Liberal Party and the anti-confederate Responsible Government League became the core of the new Progressive Conservatives (PCs).[31] Newfoundland's relative preference for oligarchic, hierarchical, personal, and deferential politics survived through the Smallwood era.

As in the nineteenth century, in the 1960s virtually all members of the Assembly lived in St. John's, and many had tenuous links with the ridings they represented. Smallwood treated many constituencies as if they were the rotten boroughs of pre-Reform Britain, parachuting into them candidates who were the sons of cabinet ministers and prominent personal supporters.

The Maritimes: Canada's New England

As in Newfoundland, Britain ruled the Maritimes in the eighteenth century. It was *New England*, however, that helped shape Maritime political culture more so than elsewhere in Canada. Even before 1712, New Englanders were a power on the scene, "a strong formative influence in the making of the Atlantic Provinces," providing it with its "surplus population."[32] Today, many Maritimers continue the connection through relatives in the "Boston States." British pre-Loyalist and Loyalist fragments shared common New England origins; the former laid the foundations of permanence for the region, the latter reorganized it. In fact, in many respects the Maritimes were the northern social extension and economic partner of New England. Even after its firm implantation in the new British Empire, the region remained a theatre for international rivalry. A political colony of Britain, it was an economic and cultural satellite of pre- and post-revolutionary America. Massachusetts settlers and their system of courts took root in the Maritimes in the 1750s and 1760s under justices striving to enforce New England precedents. Britain actively encouraged migration to the Maritimes from New England and discouraged it from the British Isles. Nova Scotia offered New Englanders in the mid-eighteenth century what Alberta offered mid-western Americans in the early twentieth century: free land. An early fragment of 7,000 settlers "imparted to the province the character of a northern segment of New England and appeared as the logical completion of the process by which New Englanders had, for generations, come to regard Nova Scotia as their own."[33] Many immigrants came directly from Britain—Irish Ulstermen, some Yorkshire farmers, and a mass movement of Highland Scots—but the region was culturally more akin to New England than old Scotland. In terms of political style too, the Maritimes were in a New England sphere of influence: "The political patricians of the Atlantic Provinces bore little resemblance to those of the mother country and appeared to be in the grip of the demeaning influences of the pork-barrel that flowed in from the United States."[34]

Despite the formative presence of New Englanders, nascent democratic liberal impulses were subdued in the Maritimes. Toryism was stronger in the region before as well as after the American Revolution, while the Loyalist influx overwhelmed but also fused with the pre-Loyalist order. In Upper Canada, in contrast, Loyalism by itself was formative. Liberalism took root in both regions, but its Maritime variant was more tory-tinged. Loyalists were relatively more important in the struggle for responsible government in the Maritimes than in Upper

Canada because Maritime society was relatively less influenced by the third immigrant wave—British nineteenth-century liberals—the wave that brought John A. Macdonald and his family to Kingston in 1820. Contrast Joseph Howe's liberalism with George Brown's: the former looked eastward to Britain, the latter westward to the backwoods of Canada. The son of a Loyalist, a group with an identity of collective persecution, "Howe's loyalty for his native province may have approached fanaticism, but it in no wise exceeded his loyalty for the mother country." He was "the loyalist *par excellence*" whose "highest ambition"[35] was to secure Nova Scotian representation in the British House of Commons, an idea not common to Upper Canadians, not the aspiration of a Mackenzie nor a Baldwin. Howe's political evolution from "Mild Tory to Reforming Assemblyman"[36] reflected the Maritimes' cautious ideological evolution.

Nova Scotia's rugged frontier, out of which New Brunswick was carved, imposed a measure of equality on those settling in its isolated rural areas. The governmental institutions that arose, however, were more aristocratic and exclusive than liberal and egalitarian. As Hugh Thorburn notes, "the Loyalists were inclined to fear liberal reforms involving popular control of government after their experiences in the former colonies."[37] Government evolved, however, and after 1837 it "came to resemble the American rather than the British pattern"[38] in extending the powers of the elected Assembly. Nevertheless, all three Maritime colonies operated with unelected upper houses; Nova Scotia's survived until 1928. Parochialism and social immobilism prevailed rather than liberal acquisitiveness, enterprise, and materialism. The American Civil War simultaneously frightened Maritimers and stimulated their economy. The termination of free trade in 1866 and the Fenian menace from the US made Confederation appealing for conservative reasons in the Maritimes, whereas the expansionary possibilities excited Upper Canada's economic and political elites. The American Revolution represented a political upheaval; Confederation was more of an economic rearrangement.

In many respects, therefore, Maritime politics did not change significantly between the late eighteenth and mid-twentieth centuries. The touchstones of conservatism—localism, tradition, caution, stability, social order, hierarchical religions, and elitism in the economic and political realms—took root, survived, indeed thrived. Cementing them were a pervasive system of patronage, a climate of deference to authority, and cross-generational, familial, cradle-to-grave partisan loyalties which were more pronounced in the region than anywhere else in English Canada. As in Newfoundland, partisan sectarianism in the Maritimes proved more symbolic than substantive. Parties differed by virtue of the personalities and puffery of their leaders, not their principles or policies; religion and patronage reinforced partisanship, structuring political inputs and outputs. Frank MacKinnon noted that PEI "has four political parties: Liberal, Conservative, Catholic, and Protestant."[39] For decades, one could not foretell the winning party in PEI elections, but one could be certain that 21 Protestants and nine Catholics would be elected. Multi-member ridings arose in all three provinces to accommodate and dampen the religious cleavage which, in much of the Maritimes, appeared superficially like the future class cleavage in the urban West, the hub around which politics revolved. Yet Maritime religious and Western class divisions were profoundly dissimilar in that the former were non-ideological and the latter intensely so. To be a non-partisan in the Maritimes was akin to being a heathen; to switch partisan affiliation was akin to renouncing one's religion and converting. What was remarkable was not the early sway of conservative liberalism or liberal conservatism, but rather its lasting power; New Brunswick's Quiet Revolution came no sooner and arguably later than Quebec's, after the election of Louis Robichaud in 1960. "Provincial politics in New Brunswick," begins one account in the 1970s, "might best be described as parochial, stagnant, and anachronistic—reminiscent, in some ways, of politics in nineteenth century Britain before the reform movement."[40]

The Acadians who returned and re-emerged were culturally distinct but ideologically compatible with Maritime Loyalism and conservatism. Despite their solidarity and growth—they constituted about two-fifths of New Brunswick by the 1950s—the Acadians were geographically clustered as a secondary and less privileged fragment. They barely held one-sixth of the legislature's seats in nearly a century of elections.[41] Franco-Manitobans, in contrast, came to be overrepresented in their legislature despite their alleged linguistic and cultural oppression.[42] Yet still, Acadians attained in the *Charter of Rights* an entrenched status for themselves and their language exceeding that for Franco-Manitobans or anglophone Quebecers. That these were achieved under PC Richard Hatfield, whose power base was the Loyalist southwest rather than the Acadian northeast, reflected only a partial eclipse of the politics of ethnicity. The appearance of the Confederation of Regions party as Official Opposition in 1991—a rump of disenchanted, anti-bilingualism former PCs—was evidence of the continuing social fissures of ethnicity and language.

The simultaneous weakness of agrarian radicalism and the isolated, concentrated presence of socialism in the Maritimes is indicative of the region's relative conservatism. Socialism languished in Atlantic Canada in comparison to Ontario and especially the West because the carriers of labour-socialism in the fourth wave of immigration bypassed the region. The sole and revealing exception to this pattern, the one that confirms the rule, is Cape Breton, where the Maritime coal and steel industries are located. They attracted working-class Britons who formed a Cape Breton ILP in 1917, and this became the heart of Nova Scotia's ILP three years later.[43] While agricultural and rural interests could drive politics in the Maritimes as they did on the Prairies, they did so in quite different ways. Subsistence rather than commercial farming was the Maritime order: a way of life rather than a business. It was diverse (fruit, dairy, potatoes, poultry) rather than specialized and mechanized. Having no wheat, Maritime agriculture had no King. Maritime agriculture did not foster and could not sustain large numbers of cooperatives as on the Prairies. Thus, the agrarian revolt in the Maritimes was inaudible compared to its roar on the Prairies and in Ontario, where farmers' parties formed governments.

The relative conservatism of Maritime farmers and the relative radicalism of more westerly farmers were reinforced by their respective relationships to the land. The Maritime farmer inherited or divided long-held family farms, often on marginal land. In the West, pioneers cleared prime, virgin lands. Many of western Ontario's nineteenth-century farmers were of the third wave of immigration, bringing liberal ideas and an expansionary outlook driven by notions of progress. As in the Maritimes, mixed agriculture prevailed in Ontario but it was prosperous rather than subsistent. Further west, on the Prairies, the fourth immigrant wave brought American physiocratic, Jeffersonian notions as well as British socialist schemes for land nationalization. Such influences, evident and powerful in the West, were feeble when they were present in the East.

Quebec: New (Old) France

The image of Quebec as *Canada's New France* is neither historically contentious nor problematic. Spun off from the monarchical, aristocratic, clerical, and quasi-feudal *ancien régime* before the 1760s, this fragment escaped the liberal French Revolution but not the Seven Years' War. It was thus cut off, as well as thrown off, from Europe in a way that the British North American colonies were not. New France was in tune ideologically with Old France rather than with the new European France of the Age of Reason. Whereas British developments—the rise of Whig liberalism and the repeal of the Corn Laws and colonial trade preference—materially affected the Canadian colonies, French developments were too worldly and hence irrelevant to Quebec. To its societal leaders, the Catholic clergy, Mother France had been monstrously violated and ideologically disfigured. It was logical that the Church serve as guardian and agent of French-Canadian identity and nationalism, for although the British took political command, they guaranteed New France's religious and linguistic continuity. The new hierarchical and authoritarian British political order was more consistent with French Canada's heritage than with the rival American model of 1776. But the *habitants* were less keen to see the emergence of representative government than were their British masters. Where the American colonists had insisted on no taxation without representation, many French Canadians resisted representative government precisely because to them it implied inevitable taxation.[44] Indeed, into the 1950s, Quebec's French political class purposefully and repeatedly professed loyalty to the British Crown and a hereditary monarchy.

Until the Quiet Revolution, conservatism or pre-liberalism prevailed. But liberalism was weaker in the province than in any other region. Why? Where conservatism and liberalism collided in Europe's more homogeneous national societies, cultural separation in Quebec facilitated the collusion of liberal English and conservative French elites. Quebec's nineteenth-century liberalism or *rougisme*—first Louis Papineau and then the Institut Canadien—was never too lively. As Hartz noted, the illiterate *habitants* identified with Papineau's nationalism but could not fathom his liberalism.[45] Life and work within separate but complementary solitudes meant that social policy for the French was decreed by the Church while economic policy beyond agriculture was dictated by English Montreal and a few American corporations. The respective strength and weakness of liberal thinking in English and French Quebec was mirrored institutionally: in 1911, over 1,300 of the province's 200,000 English were at universities, compared with just over 700 of some 1,300,000 French.[46] And anglophone students were ten times as numerous in the sciences as were francophones. Laurier's liberalism, just as Trudeau's would be later, was self-taught, not derived from his own culture. At the elite level there were some consociational linkages that transcended Quebec's borders. Duplessis, for example, endorsed Drew and Diefenbaker and spurned St. Laurent because of their ideologies. But at the mass level it does not matter much: in every federal election where a Quebecer has been a party leader (Laurier, St. Laurent, Trudeau, Mulroney, Bouchard), Quebecers have voted for him. In lamenting Quebec's antipathy to democratic liberalism before the Quiet Revolution, Trudeau cited the unlikely intermeshing of the Church and the Canadian Broadcasting Corporation (CBC). On the morning of Duplessis's last electoral hurrah in 1956, the following conservative prayer was broadcast:

> Sovereign authority, by whatever government it is exercised, is derived solely from God, the supreme and eternal principle of all power.... It is therefore an absolute error to believe that authority comes from the multitudes, from the masses, from the people, to pretend that authority does not properly belong to those who exercise it, but that they have only a simple mandate revocable at any time by the people. This error, which dates from the Reformation, rests on the false principle that man has no other master than his own reason.... All this explanation about the origin, the basis, and the composition of this alleged sovereignty of the people is purely arbitrary. Moreover, if it is admitted, it will have as a consequence the weakening of authority, making it a myth, giving it an unstable and changeable basis, stimulating popular passions and encouraging sedition.[47]

The triumphant breakthrough of liberalism in the 1960s had dual political expressions. Those exerting their energy at the provincial level (Lesage, Lévesque, Laporte) turned to the provincial state to modernize society. Those who entered the federal arena (Lamontagne, Trudeau, Marchand) sought modernization and *rattrapage* via equal access with liberal English Canada at the centre. These alternative visions were reflected in the conflicting language laws of 1977 and 1982: Quebec's Charter of the French Language versus Ottawa's *Charter of Rights*. And within the Quebec state, divisions arose between business liberals (à la Bourassa) and welfare liberals (à la Lévesque). This paralleled divisions within English Canadian liberalism (notably between Gordon and Sharp).

The clash of Quebec's receding conservatism and its ascending liberalism in the 1960s helped to produce, as Hartz's dialectic suggested, the rise of a self-conscious socialist outlook. It merged with and reacted to the communitarian, *organiciste*, and authoritarian traditions of historical Quebec as well as the democratic, capitalistic, and egalitarian innovations of the Quiet Revolution's liberalism. Nascent leftist parties in the 1960s, such as the Ralliement indépendistes nationale (RIN) and the Parti socialiste du Québec (PSQ), contextualized Quebec's quest for national self-determination as part of a worldwide movement for decolonization and national liberation. Let us recall that 1960 was no less a revolutionary year in West Africa where the French colonial empire was formally dismantled. The PQ of Lévesque and Parizeau, as well as Bouchard's Bloc Québécois (BQ), proclaimed itself "social democratic," a term no other governing party in Canada, besides the CCF-NDP, had ever used to describe itself. Indeed, the PQ applied to join the Socialist International. The transformation has continued to the present day: in spurning native son Jean Chrétien in 1993, French Quebec revealed how modernized its politics had become.

The interaction and development of ideologies in Quebec may appear more muddled than in English Canada because Quebec's ideological movements have been relatively more fluid and unstable. They have been overshadowed, mediated, and shaped by a relatively coherent ethnic nationalism in contrast to its diluted English-Canadian counterpart. Thus one nationalist family, the Johnsons, has produced premiers for three ideologically competitive parties: the conservative Union Nationale, the social democratic PQ, and the liberal Liberals. The relative strength of Quebec nationalism was confirmed in a cross-cultural survey of university students in the 1980s in Britain, Australia, New Zealand, the US, and Canada. A left-right divide, determined by respondents' self-location, overshadowed nationality as a predictor of predispositions to notions of equality, the role of government, women, and minorities among all the national groupings, but it was significantly and especially weakest among French Quebecers.[48]

The story of conservative, quasi-feudal Quebec demonstrates that fragments may escape their pasts as well as be trapped by them. Ideological evolution in English Canada was fed by successive immigrant waves. In Quebec, as in the US, ideological development was internal, feeding on itself. Liberalism's appearance was a case of spontaneous combustion, a product of and reaction to lengthy immobilism. An expression of Quebec's conversion from conservatism to radicalism was that before the Quiet Revolution its separate Catholic union movement attacked the American Federation of Labour (AF of L) for discussing the public ownership of railways; after the Quiet Revolution it attacked the AF of L for its allegiance to private enterprise. At the same time, radicalism has been mediated by caution, by Quebec's lingering conservatism: in the 1970s, the PQ promised to adopt a congressional-presidential system and proportional representation; once in office it did nothing on either account. Symbolically, Quebec replaced the Speech from the Throne with a Premier's Inaugural Address. Concretely, it embraced the British Westminster model rather than rejecting it. So too in substantial constitutional negotiations: with the possible exception of the Meech Lake Accord, Quebecers have repeatedly opted for the status quo over proposals for change. Through five rounds—from the Fulton-Favreau formula and the Victoria Charter to the Constitution of 1982 and the Meech Lake and Charlottetown Accords—Quebec's radical and nationalist elites said "no." Lévesque went to London to plead his case for constitutional continuity with British Prime Minister Margaret Thatcher. In the plebiscitarian rounds of 1980, 1992, and 1995 weighing in on constitutional rearrangements, the cautious masses also said "no." Quebec has given simultaneous mandates to unabashed federalists and sovereigntists.

Quebec conservatism, liberalism, and socialism have been so moulded by the province's unique nationalist context that their links to their English-Canadian equivalents have always been temporary and tenuous. Thus PC Brian Mulroney captures Alberta and Quebec, but their alliance and discourse is so improbable that it dies with his departure; thus, Liberal Lester B. Pearson promotes the equality and universality of two languages while Quebec's provincial Liberals insist on linguistic particularism, on the sanctity of Montreal's French *visage*; thus, the NDP builds a coherent and genuinely national party in English Canada, while its Quebec connection is so flimsy that it is captured by Paul Rose, the murderer of Laporte; thus, Social Credit wins easy money adherents in Quebec and Alberta but fragments into ideologically similar but nationally exclusive parties. In short, then, because it is culturally descended from New France, Quebec has unfolded ideologically differently from the other provinces because they are culturally of British North America.

Ontario: The US's counter-revolution

Ontario has been both of the US and against the US. An immediate byproduct of the American Revolution, it has also been inextricably connected to the US's development as a nation. Terms identifying Ontarian values are often used to distinguish Canada from the US: "elitism, ascription, hierarchy, continuity, stability, and social order."[49] Of course, Canada is neither Ontario writ large, nor is Ontario a microcosm of Canada—despite what Ontarians may think. Nevertheless, it is Ontario's relative dominance and centrality that make it easy and tempting to extrapolate from it onto English Canada. Ontario's national population share is much larger than the combined California and New York shares. Ideologically, Ontario is different from the US in both its genesis and more recent politics. In the late eighteenth century, western Quebec—the future Upper Canada, then Canada West, and then finally Ontario—was settled by Loyalists espousing a relative conservatism, rejecting the US's more extreme liberalism. In the late twentieth century, it elected a social democratic government which contrasted with the US's preference for right-wing business liberalism. Under both Liberal and NDP regimes, Ontario opposed continental economic integration via free trade. Moreover, English-Canadian nationalism—largely defined by what it is not: American—has always been centred in Ontario, in its historically shielded manufacturing and cultural industries.

And Ontario's founding conservatives, or to some more precisely, conservative liberals, were American *counter-revolutionaries*. Loyalism began with loyalty to the British Crown and entailed rejecting weak executive government. It also refused to sever the bond between religion and the state as both the European French and Americans had done. Along with their sons and some British Tories such as William Allan and D'Arcy Boulton who came to the province in the 1790s, Loyalists became the backbone of the ruling Family Compact. Like British Tories, they denounced early reformers as "Jacobins." While supportive of developing their new province, many in the Compact—quite unlike Quebec's Château Clique—"may even have held a quasi-aristocratic contempt for business and mere money-making.... The Compact came out of the war [of 1812] with a finely-developed sense of loyalty and an awareness that they had led in the battle to keep out the Americans, their institutions, and their ideas." The French Revolution and the War of 1812 were pivotal in shaping the elite's world view: "The first imparted to them a 'tory' attitude towards change and reform, the second gave them an acute sense of leadership, loyalty to Britain and a strong anti-Americanism."[50] The Loyalists were more than frustrated Whigs,[51] although their toryism was certainly infused with whiggism. It had to be: the purer British toryism of Elizabeth I, Hooker, and the Stuarts had been swept away more than a century earlier in the Glorious Revolution of 1688. Conservative liberalism thus prevailed initially, but reform challenges to it were not long in coming.

There is a schizophrenic, contradictory element in Ontario's anti-Americanism, for it has been deeply touched by American reform liberalism, arguably as much as by its British counterpart. Upper Canadian liberalism, as expressed by the Reformers, drew heavily on the voting support of post-revolutionary, non-Loyalist American farmers who came to the western reaches of the province. It also drew on American examples. Whether the subject was education, primogeniture, canal building, the ballot, the structure of government, or its cost, William Lyon Mackenzie and his allies pointed to American, more often than British, practice. In 1826, Mackenzie noted that the province's liberalism was "owing chiefly to our neighbourhood to the United States, and the independent principles brought into the colony with them by settlers from thence...."[52] Certainly, the heavy British tide in the third wave of immigration in the 1830s "carried radical and democratic ideas with them to the colonies," but "most of the contemporary evidence points in the other direction, however, and suggests that the British immigration contributed a distinctly conservative influence to Upper Canada."[53] English radicals often became Upper Canadian Tories once they became land owners. The conservatism of the nineteenth-century British wave, suggests Gerald Craig, "appears to have been much stronger than that of the old Loyalist Population, who were accused by some contemporaries of being strongly tinged with 'republican principles.'"[54] Just as the Loyalists' conservatism was moderated by American liberal influences, Upper Canadian liberalism was in turn tempered by the Loyalist legacy. Thus, as Wise notes, "Upper Canadian conservatism was a major formative influence upon the nature of the reform tradition in the province."[55] The mainstream of reform came to be represented by moderates such as Baldwin and Brown rather than the "across-the-board democratic radicalism" of Gourlay and Mackenzie. John A. Macdonald's first dominion government was aptly titled Liberal-Conservative; that is what it was ideologically.

As immigration receded in the second half of the nineteenth century, and as more native Ontarians appeared, the province developed an identity and outlook separate from Ottawa as well as from Britain and the US. "Grit" is a distinctly Ontarian term which arose at mid-century. Noteworthy are the farm organizations that surfaced after the 1870s, the Grange and the Patrons of Industry, which were branches of American organizations. As agrarianism waned, however, and as urbanization waxed, rural liberalism came under stress. Its fading bellow, if not last gasp, was the United Farmers Organization (UFO) victory of 1919, a lashing out at apparently irreversible, inexorable industrialization. E.C. Drury's reform liberalism was reflected in the common cause he sought with the newly arriving British labour-socialists of the fourth wave of immigration. They were also wary of the new factory society. His democratic-liberal attitude to government legislation was that it "should be the responsibility of all members of the legislature instead of emerging full-blown from the cabinet and being passed by a submissive majority"; forthwith, the 1920 legislative session saw a record number of private members' bills enacted with greater freedom for backbenchers "under his regime than at any other time in the province's history."[56]

A farmer-labour, liberal-socialist alliance was doomed to fail, and it did so in quick order in the 1920s. The backgrounds and interests of its members were too dissimilar. The same happened on the Prairies: the rise of the ILP, and then the CCF, came with the growth of the city, not its arrest, as the UFO's rural liberalism preferred. A union class subculture emerged whose outlook and personnel were as heavily British as was the ILP name. Some of Ontario's early craft unions had

American affiliations, but the dynamic industrial unions—those that breathed life into the CCF—were spiritually if indirectly British creations. As Charles Millard, a CCF member of the Provincial Parliament (MPP) and the first national director of the Steelworkers' Union put it: "It's a mistake to believe that we adopted our industrial unions from the States, because they in turn got it ready-made from Britain."[57] Massive wartime planning and controls in the 1940s confirmed the CCF's prescriptive analysis favouring a planned, centralized economy over a collapsed and exploitative capitalist one. After the war, Keynesianism won over both welfare liberals and social democrats. Although the CCF-NDP, Liberals, and PCs appeared to be converging ideologically, the NDP was unmistakably on the left (the other two alternated as centre and centre-right parties) and still is. The Cold War and capitalism's success retarded the CCF's advance, but it survived because it had struck solid roots.

The Ontario NDP's unlikely 1990 election victory was facilitated by its dampened radicalism in changing times, by the fumbling of its opponents, and by voting support from many in the diverse fifth wave of immigration after the Second World War. The NDP appeared to many immigrants and others as part of the Canadian ideological establishment, rather than as a radical party: former NDP leader Stephen Lewis represented a PC government at the United Nations, and the NDP joined the Liberals and PCs to embrace the Meech Lake and Charlottetown Accords. It won office by scoring in metropolitan Ontario, where the fourth and especially fifth immigrant waves had their greatest impact. The media and the party referred to the government as socialist, but what unfolded was the NDP behaving much like its predecessors. It broke some long-standing campaign pledges and came to boast of shrinking, rather than expanding, the public sector.[58] An ideological gulf developed between the Bob Rae cabinet and many in the party mass and unions. In the 1990s, the NDP demonstrated that its socialism was not as radical as it or its opponents had contended; in the 1950s, the CCF had also been considered a becalmed protest party.[59] In electing a social democratic government—indeed, in electing *any* social democrats—Ontario confirmed again, reminiscent of its origins, how unlike the US it is. Ideologically influenced by its neighbour to the south, it has also repelled and been repulsed by it.

Manitoba: The Prairies' Ontario

Manitoba is the *Prairies' Ontario*, a fragment of another fragment society. Unlike Ontario, however, Manitoba and the West did not share the Upper Canadian loyalist fragment's proximity and sensitivity to Quebec nor its common affinity for the "Laurentian myth." Manitoba entered Confederation as a bilingual, bicultural province of 12,000 of whom more than 10,000 were Métis. Ontarians soon flooded in, however, and manned its skeletal institutions. The 1880s, in fact, represented "The Triumph of Ontario Democracy."[60] Ontarians transplanted their municipal system, provoked a Schools Question as they did in Ontario, and re-produced large sections of Ontario statutes into Manitoba law. It seemed fitting and telling that the premier at the turn of the century, Hugh John Macdonald, was the son of John A. All but two of Manitoba's premiers (Ed Schreyer, Gary Filmon) in this century were born in Ontario or have been of Ontarian herit-age. On the new frontier, agrarian liberalism and urban socialism were stronger while toryism was weaker than in Ontario or the Maritimes. Nevertheless, owing to early Ontarian settlers, what there was of toryism was stronger in Manitoba than it was further west. In the 1910s, for example, all Prairie parties but one—Sir Rodmond Roblin's Manitoba Conservatives—favoured direct legislation via referendums. Sir Rodmond dismissed it as "A Socialistic and Un-British Plan" and "degenerate republicanism."[61] Manitoba is the only Western province where the Conservative party has never collapsed and is the only Prairie province to have voted against free trade in both 1911 and 1988. Transplanted Ontarian T.A. Crerar was a good reflector of the dominant rural liberal outlook: between 1919 and 1922 he was offered the premierships of both his old and new provinces.[62] Crerar's Manitoba Progressives, like Ontario's Progressives, made their peace with their former party—Mackenzie King's Liberals—and re-entered its fold by the late 1920s.

The fourth immigrant wave of working-class Britons and land-hungry Eastern Europeans was weightier than in Ontario because the Prairies were relatively emp-ty. British labour-socialism sank roots which now run back more than a century: in 1895 an ILP was established (its constitution required that at least three-quar-ters of its members be wage earners), and in 1900 a Labour MP was elected for Winnipeg. Britain's future Labour prime minister (Ramsay MacDonald) and the party's founding leader (Keir Hardie) spoke at political rallies in the city in 1906 and 1907. Between 1901 and 1916 Winnipeg's population quadrupled. More than half the city's population was born abroad; there were as many British-born as there were native-born Manitobans. All the leaders of the Winnipeg General Strike, except J.S. Woodsworth, emigrated from Britain between 1896 and 1912. The Strike's legacy was a left-right fissure that defined subsequent elections. In the 1920s, 85 per cent of the ILP's aldermen were British-born; in the 1930s, 70 per cent.[63] Concentrated in Winnipeg and systematically underrepresented in the legislature, British labour-socialism was relegated to a secondary position to the dominant, rural, Anglo-Saxon Ontarian, liberal influence.

A smaller left grouping, the Communist Party (CP), drew its inspiration from the Russian Revolution and scientific, rather than evolutionary, socialism. It was backed almost exclusively by Ukrainians and Jews. Between 1919 and 1945, not one Labour alderman in polyglot Winnipeg was of German, Polish, or Ukrainian descent. Decimated by the Cold War, the CP's base of support either died off or was eventually absorbed by the CCF-NDP. A good example was Roland Penner, the NDP attorney-general in the 1980s, the son of a long-serving Communist first elected in the 1920s. When Manitoba adopted an electoral map in 1969 that came reasonably close to equalizing the value of rural and urban voters, the NDP came to power, winning the support of large numbers of first- and especially second- and third-generation Eastern Europeans who no longer deferred to the established Ontario-origin parties and leaders.

Saskatchewan: The Prairies' Britain

Depicting Saskatchewan as the *Prairies' modern Britain* at the turn of the century appears at first incongruous. The most rural of the Western provinces and not founded until 1905, it escaped the Industrial Revolution but not its residue. The city-bred British who inundated the West headed generally for the cities: Winnipeg, Vancouver, Calgary. Saskatchewan's geography produced an odd equation: although it had relatively fewer British-born than either Manitoba or Alberta, it had almost as many of them as farmers as the other two provinces combined.[64] Saskatchewan also had the largest number of continental and Catholic Europeans. As in Manitoba, these rural non-English-speaking European immigrants initially deferred to the Ontarian-led farm organizations and parties, the Grain Growers' Association and the Liberals. Unlike Manitoba and Alberta, however, Saskatchewan's rural Britons were sufficiently numerous and mobilized to sustain the only viable socialist farm organization in the land. Contrast the Saskatchewan's Farmers' Union—whose motto was "Farmers and workers of the world, unite"[65] and which was founded by a former British railway worker—with the conservatively liberal United Farmers of Manitoba (UFM) and the radically populist UFA. The UFMers opposed the Winnipeg General Strike and ridiculed the eight-hour day; they were branded anti-labour and were ineligible for membership in the ILP until 1927. The UFA's motto was "Equity"—drawn from the American Society of Equity—and it was driven primarily by inflationary monetary theories rather than socialist ones. Where the Saskatchewanians wanted a compulsory wheat pool and saw it as a socialist vehicle, the Albertans insisted on a voluntary one, defining the grain problem as one of uncompetitive trade relations. The United Farmers of Canada (Saskatchewan Section)'s labour-socialist British and agrarian heritages could be summed up in two planks of its 1930 platform: "Abolition of the competitive system and substitution of a cooperative system of manufacturing, transportation, and distribution" and "Free trade with the mother country."[66]

Agrarian socialism is something of a misnomer for the Saskatchewan experience. The CCF-NDP has always fared better in the cities than on the farms. When the UFC(SS) and the Saskatchewan ILP merged in the 1930s to form the Farmer-Labour Party, and soon after the CCF, the vanguard that emerged was British-born urbanites, not farmers. The Saskatchewan and then national CCF leader, M.J. Coldwell, was a schoolteacher and member of the Fabian Society in England. Tommy Douglas was born in Scotland and socialized in working-class, socialist Winnipeg. There were, of course, some non-socialist Britons and Liberals. Ideologically, they blended easily with the early Ontarian liberal influence. Consider British-born Charles Dunning who, after serving in the liberal Grain Growers' Association, became premier. Later he was elected in PEI, which he represented as finance minister in Mackenzie King's cabinet. Where in Atlantic Canada could a Coldwell or Douglas have been elected in the 1930s or 1940s? Only in Cape Breton, which had other British labour-socialists like themselves. Dunning and other Liberals governed Saskatchewan owing to their hold on the rural, deferential, continental Europeans, but Dunning had contempt for them, thinking "that they deteriorate in this country particularly if they are educated. He says they can be educated all right but that they cannot be civilized, at least not in one generation; and that the educated Ruthenian [Ukrainian] is a menace to his own countrymen and to the community."[67]

By the 1940s, enough Europeans felt sufficiently secure to desert the Liberals, to combine with the British socialists, and to catapult the CCF to office. The Great Depression confirmed that the headiest days of agricultural expansion were in the past, its future would be even more mechanized and capital-, rather than labour-intensive. At the same time, the socialist base came to be even more firmly dependent on the cities and larger towns. It was the NDP's weakness in the countryside and electoral maldistribution that kept it from office; in 1986 it swept the two major cities, capturing a plurality of voters but a minority of seats, three of which were rural. Liberals and PCs became ideologically indistinguishable, expediently polarizing under one banner or the other as the anti-socialist standard-bearer. Saskatchewan, like BC, imitated the British pattern of a left-right dynamic. In Saskatchewan, in recent decades, a conservative party and a social democratic one affiliated with the Socialist International have been the major competitors for office in a Westminster parliamentary system.

Alberta: The Prairies' US

Alberta politics have come closest to imitating the politics of an *American midwestern or Great Plains state*. "Alberta," declared an MP in 1907, "from the border northward to Edmonton, might be regarded as a typical American state."[68] It represented North America's last agricultural frontier; after the US's own had been staked and settled in the 1890s, Americans poured over the border into Alberta and western Saskatchewan. The Albertan who served as Laurier's immigration minister confirmed the Americans' high status, describing them as "desirable in every way. They are people of intelligence, of energy, of enterprise, of the highest aspirations." In contrast, "we resent the idea of having the millstone of this Slav population hung around our necks."[69] In 1911, American-born Albertans outnumbered the British-born; Canadian-born Albertans were in a minority. The early sway of Ontarian liberalism was soon overshadowed and fused with the more dynamic liberal populism of the Americans. Americans and their ideas shaped provincial politics because they settled in the rural areas. In contrast, the immigrant British working-class wave gravitated toward the politically underrepresented cities. The Americans espoused a populist rural liberalism, one uninfected by toryism, one more radical and plebiscitarian than Crerar's Progressives who made quick peace with parliament's strong, centralizing executive. Some Albertan members of the Legislative Assembly (MLAs), in contrast, described parliamentary responsible government as "limited state dictatorship" and their government refused to appear in front of the Royal Commission on Dominion-Provincial Relations, addressing its comments instead to "the Sovereign People of Canada." By the late 1920s, the federal Progressives were decimated in every province west of Quebec; only in Alberta did the federal UFA Progressives gain seats and votes because they and their constituency were cut from a different ideological cloth. It seemed fitting and telling that the UFA president, "the uncrowned King of Alberta," was Henry Wise Wood, a veteran Missouri populist who rejected both the premiership and a knighthood on account of his American background.

Whereas monetary reform was rarely debated at UFO or UFM conventions, it was all the rage in the UFA. As newly minted Albertans, Americans spread the gospel of inflationary monetary theories and plebiscitarian populism. These outlooks dovetailed with Alberta's American-inspired evangelical, fundamentalist predilections, the faith of a "quite exceptional" 20 per cent of the province's Protestants, including Wood.[70] William Aberhart effectively merged the prophetic Christian gospel with Social Credit—the British name for a theory whose Albertan parentage was essentially American (the Greenback movement)—and rode them to power. Where Woodsworth and the British Social Gospel offered to help man, Aberhart's fundamentalist, messianic gospel promised to save man; where Canadian socialists lauded the welfarism of Britain's Beveridge Report, Social Credit dismissed it as planning for the redistribution of poverty. S.D. Clark noted that "the religious-political experiment in Alberta resembled very closely that tried much earlier in Utah."[71] Social Credit's national leader in the 1950s, Albertan Solon Low, was the son of Mormon Utah; the Reform Party leader in the 1990s, Preston Manning, is Aberhart's godson. Relatively few Americans came to Alberta in the fifth wave of immigration, but they counted in the vital oil industry as managers and executives: "From 1995 to 1970, nine of the fifteen presidents of Calgary's exclusive Petroleum club were Americans."[72] Manning's contemporary proposals for parliamentary reform—free votes for members of Parliament (MPs), plebiscites, a Triple-E Senate—continue to be patterned on American models.

Saskatchewan and Alberta were divided by an artificial border but their differing settlement patterns led to starkly differing dominant ideological traditions. The former produced a powerful cooperative movement and the country's most successful socialist party. The latter regarded the CCF as "a repudiation of the rugged individualism which had always characterized the farmers of Alberta," making it "inevitable that a Social Credit rather than a socialist movement would prevail."[73] Certainly Social Credit at first was radical and appealed to some socialists, but by the 1940s Social Credit's new enemy became socialism rather than the banks and corporations. The anti-socialist baton was passed on to the PCs in the 1970s in the same way as the UFA's penchant for monetary reform had been passed on to Social Credit in the 1930s.

BC: Canada's Australia

More than any other province, BC and its politics have resembled *Australia* and its politics. Both were first settled in the nineteenth century on the edges of the Empire: both represented Greater Britain on the Pacific. Both had gold rushes in the 1850s. Both have resource-based economies with staples located and extracted in the far-flung nooks and crannies of their hinterlands. Both came out of and are largely urban societies. Both were aided by the opening of canals on other continents (Suez, Panama), linking them to the metropolitan economies and cultures of Europe and North America. Both developed distinguishing myths—the Australian Bush Myth and British Columbians' self-image of their splendid isolation in paradise. Settlers in both thought of their new Eden as the location for utopian ends. Both were radical offshoots of Europe: Australian settlement came earlier in the nineteenth century and inherited the then radical liberal ideology of Bentham's utilitarianism; BC's settlement came later, inheriting the ideology of labour-socialism. Both developed left-right, urban-rural, and class-driven political cleavages with parties offering the rhetoric of class conflict. Both represent upstart parvenu societies offering rags-to-riches success, liberation, and class mobility. Radicals in both societies saw them as a potential "workingman's paradise."[74] Both require referendums for constitutional change.

Gordon Galbraith has insightfully used the Hartzian thesis to depict BC as a fragment of Edwardian Britain of the turn of the twentieth century.[75] Transplanted Britons were the single largest component of the population, larger than that born in the province or the rest of Canada. In the 1990s, BC continued as a magnet for migrants, the only province where those born within it are outnumbered by outsiders. In the critical first two decades of the twentieth century, the cast of BC's politics for the rest of the century was set. Like Australia, BC offered indolence, opportunity, and a new beginning. Some "strange and exotic remnants of the British upper classes"[76] took up residence in the Okanagan and on Vancouver Island, but what was especially marked was the British working-class influence on labour organization and residential segregation. As on the Prairies, Britain's labour leaders and their causes had strong followings in this very British society, *British Columbia*. Late Victorian and Edwardian Britain was dominantly liberal but in a time of anxiety and flux: increasing class consciousness, stagnating real wages, the emergence of trade unions, and the establishment of the Labour Party. Upper-, middle-, and working-class Britons were united in BC in their imperial link and their imperialist consciousness. Consider the titles of Kingston's *Whig Standard*, the *Winnipeg Free Press*, and the *Victoria Colonist* for a flavour of contrasting ideological dispositions, eras, and locales.

BC's linkage with Canada via the CPR meant that the Canadian parties, Liberals and Conservatives, appeared not much sooner than in Alberta or Saskatchewan. Much of their impetus, however, came from the strength of provincial labour rather than from the Canadian metropolis: unions "had become so influential by 1903 that fear lest the voters might align as labour and anti-labour was one of the factors in the move to introduce party lines."[77] Farmers' parties were less viable than on the Prairies because agriculture was more diverse (fruit, cattle, vegetables, dairy, as well as grains). Farmers were fewer, relatively fragmented, and isolated in distant valleys, plateaus, and the island. In 1921, only 16 per cent of the workforce was engaged in agriculture; in 1931, less than 6 per cent. The United Farmers of BC (UFBC) proved to be a political joke compared to the UFO, UFM, UFC (SS), and the UFA. The dynamic political force was organized labour in the mining, lumbering, and fishing industries of the remote, one-industry towns of the interior and the coast. It also transformed Vancouver into the premier city of the West. Long before the CCF appeared in the 1930s, labour and socialist parties had been active. Only in BC have there been socialist MLAs in every decade of this century. The 1933 election confirmed a bipolar, discordant, and divided political culture: in its first outing, the CCF attained major party status with about one-third of the vote. Coalition governments in the 1940s were driven by the ideological cleavage of left and right, of working class versus the entrepreneurial and privileged classes. When Social Credit appeared in the 1950s, it simply served as the new anti-socialist, coalitionist standard-bearer. BC Social Credit had nothing to do with "funny money" as in Alberta; this confirmed that its label was convenient rather than principled. In the 1970s and 1980s, the Social Credit cabinets regularly included former Liberals and PCs as well as *bona fide* Socreds. To British Columbians, the ideological space between these improbable allies appeared narrower than that between Social Credit and the NDP. Such an alliance was foretold in the 1930s by a student of BC party politics: "if the C.C.F. lives and grows, the two old parties will have to unite to save the social and economic institutions with which they are so intimately related."[78]

Conclusion

As time passes, the provinces move farther away from the points of departure from their older founding societies. Is the fragment theory less relevant to future developments or have provincial political cultures congealed so that the legacy of the past will weigh on the future? Are toryism and socialism relevant in the new, contemporary world order and, beyond that, in postmodern ideological discourse? New parties—Reform and the BQ—are reflective of older ideological traditions. A now old party, the NDP, is in decline as the century draws to a close. Even if it disappears, its principles and policies are deeply embedded in the national and provincial political cultures—from pensions and labour law to health care and Crown corporations. This is no less true in provinces it has never governed. The older Liberals and PCs exhibited the capacity to reverse ideological directions: toryism is arguably stronger now in Liberal circles than it is in Conservative ones. Conversely, American ideas and models are now more cited by the formerly anti-American Conservatives than by the Liberals.

The irreversible exposure of the provinces to global markets, finance, and media penetration suggests some potential for a new ersatz politics. Evolving provincial economies and the fiscal crisis of the provincial state in the context of federal cutbacks suggest the possibility of shifts in political orientation: witness Ontario's embrace of fiscal conservatism in 1995. Similarly, cultures do undergo revolutions: witness Quebec. Provincial societies, even those that appear relatively stagnant, are also in steady flux. Consider Saskatchewan where soon, at the turn of the twenty-first century, one of every two children entering the school system will be of Aboriginal origin. Does this qualify as a quake, if not formative event, in political culture? Revolution, however, cultural or otherwise, has not been English Canada's *raison d'être*, style, or tradition. A historical overview of provincial political cultures suggests evolutionary change and the persistence of continuities rather than otherworldly breaks with the past. That is why the ideological fragment approach to provincial political cultures continues to offer insight and revelation. When synthesized with the complementary approaches of political economy and formative events, its explanatory power is further enhanced.

Notes

1. Heinz Eulau, *The Behavioral Persuasion in Politics* (New York: Random House, 1963) 62-63.
2. For example, Seymour Martin Lipset, *Continental Divide: The Values and Institutions of the United States and Canada* (New York: Routledge, 1990).
3. For example, Richard Simeon and David Elkins, "Regional Political Cultures in Canada," in David Elkins and Richard Simeon, eds., *Small Worlds: Provinces and Parties in Canadian Political Life* (Toronto: Methuen, 1980); and John Wilson, "The Canadian Political Cultures: Towards a Redefinition of the Nature of the Canadian Political System," *Canadian Journal of Political Science* 7,3 (September 1974): 438-83.
4. Louis Hartz, *The Founding of New Societies* (New York: Harcourt, Brace and World, 1964).
5. Harold A. Innis, *Essays in Canadian Economic History* (Toronto: University of Toronto Press, 1956).

6. Robert J. Brym, "Political Conservatism in Atlantic Canada," in Robert J. Brym and R. James Sacouman, eds., *Underdevelopment and Social Movements in Atlantic Canada* (Toronto: New Hogtown Press, 1979) 65-66.
7. Seymour Martin Lipset, *Revolution and Counterrevolution* (New York: Anchor, 1970).
8. S.J.R. Noel, *Politics in Newfoundland* (Toronto: University of Toronto Press, 1971) 254-55.
9. W.S. McNutt, *The Atlantic Provinces: The Emergence of Colonial Society, 1712-1857* (Toronto: McClelland and Stewart, 1965) 46.
10. Robert Finbow, "Dependents or Dissidents? The Atlantic Provinces in Canada's Constitutional Reform Process, 1967-1992," *Canadian Journal of Political Science* 27,3 (September 1994): 465-91.
11. Kenneth McRoberts, *Quebec: Social Change and Political Crisis* (Toronto: McClelland and Stewart, 1988) Ch. 4.
12. S.F. Wise, "The Ontario Political Culture: A Study in Complexities," in Graham White, ed., *The Government and Politics of Ontario* (Scarborough: Nelson, 1990).
13. Mark Lisac, *The Klein Revolution* (Edmonton: NeWest, 1995) 234-35.
14. W.L. Morton, *The Progressive Party in Canada* (Toronto: University of Toronto Press, 1950) 39.
15. Louis Hartz, *The Liberal Tradition in America* (New York: Harcourt, Brace, 1955).
16. Gad Horowitz, *Canadian Labour in Politics* (Toronto: University of Toronto Press, 1968) Ch. 1.
17. Horowitz 3.
18. Hartz, *The Founding of New Societies* 64.
19. Margaret Ells, "Loyalist Attitudes," in G.A. Rawlyk, ed., *Historical Essays on the Atlantic Provinces* (Toronto: McClelland and Stewart, 1967).
20. Kenneth D. McRae, "The Structure of Canadian History," in Hartz, *The Founding of New Societies* 245.
21. Noel 4-5.
22. Gertrude E. Gunn, *The Political History of Newfoundland, 1832-1864* (Toronto: University of Toronto Press, 1966) 207, Appendix E, Table III.
23. Gunn 11.
24. Noel 24-25, 263.
25. Gordon O. Rothney, "The Denominational Basis of Representation in the Newfoundland Assembly, 1919-1962," *Canadian Journal of Economics and Political Science* 28, 4 (November 1962): 557-70.
26. Noel 25.
27. David Bellamy, "The Atlantic Provinces," in David Bellamy, J.H. Pammett, and D.C. Rowat, eds., *The Provincial Political Systems* (Toronto: Methuen, 1976) 8.
28. Rand Dyck, *Provincial Politics in Canada* (Scarborough: Prentice-Hall, 1991) 20, Table c.8.
29. Noel 87.
30. Noel 77.
31. Susan McCorquodale, "Newfoundland: Plus ça Change, Plus C'est La Même Chose," in Martin Robin, ed., *Canadian Provincial Politics* (Scarborough: Prentice-Hall, 1978) 145-46.
32. McNutt 4, 29.
33. McNutt 61.
34. McNutt 269.

35. J. Murray Beck, "Joseph Howe: Opportunist or Empire-builder?", in Rawlyk 143, 146.
36. J. Murray Beck, *Joseph Howe: Voice of Nova Scotia* (Toronto: McClelland and Stewart, 1964) Part One.
37. Hugh Thorburn, *Politics in New Brunswick* (Toronto: University of Toronto Press, 1961) 5.
38. Thorburn 8.
39. Frank MacKinnon, "Prince Edward Island: Big Engine, Little Body," in Robin 237.
40. P.J. Fitzpatrick, "New Brunswick: The Politics of Pragmatism," in Robin 120.
41. Thorburn 201, Table XXV1.
42. James A. McAllister, *The Government of Edward Schreyer* (Montreal and Kingston: McGill-Queen's University Press, 1984) 148.
43. J. Murray Beck, "Nova Scotia: Tradition and Conservatism," in Robin 181.
44. Louis Massicote, "Quebec: The Successful Combination of French Culture and British Institutions," in Gary Levy and Graham White, eds., *Provincial and Territorial Legislatures in Canada* (Toronto: University of Toronto Press, 1989) 71-72.
45. Hartz, *The Founding of New Societies* 30.
46. Marcel Rioux, "The Development of Ideologies in Quebec," in Hugh G. Thorburn, ed., *Party Politics in Canada*, 6th ed. (Scarborough: Prentice-Hall, 1991) 371.
47. Quoted in Pierre Elliott Trudeau, *Federalism and the French Canadians* (Toronto: Macmillan, 1968) 110-11.
48. Neil Nevitte and Roger Gibbins, *New Elites in Old States: Ideologies in the Anglo-American Democracies* (Toronto: Oxford University Press, 1990) 127-29.
49. Dyck 299.
50. Robert E. Saunders, "What Was the Family Compact?", in J.K. Johnson, ed., *Historical Essays on Upper Canada* (Toronto: McClelland and Stewart, 1975) 130, 131, 134, 136.
51. David Bell, "The Loyalist Tradition in Canada," *Journal of Canadian Studies* 5,2 (May 1970): 22-33.
52. Quoted in G.M. Craig, "The American Impact on the Upper Canadian Reform Movement Before 1837," in Johnson 334.
53. Craig 330.
54. Craig 336.
55. S.F. Wise, "Upper Canada and the Conservative Tradition," in Ontario Historical Society, *Profiles of a Province: Studies in the History of Ontario* (Toronto: OHS, 1967) 36.
56. F.F. Schindeler, *Responsible Government in Ontario* (Toronto: University of Toronto Press, 1969) 179.
57. Quoted In J.T. Morley, *Secular Socialists: The CCF/NDP in Ontario, A Biography* (Montreal and Kingston: McGill-Queen's University Press, 1984) 26.
58. *1994 Ontario Budget* 14.
59. Leo Zakuta, *A Protest Movement Becalmed: A Study of Change in the CCF* (Toronto: University of Toronto Press, 1964).
60. W.L. Morton, *Manitoba: A History*, 2nd ed. (Toronto: University of Toronto Press, 1967) Ch. 9.
61. "Initiative and Referendum," pamphlet, January 27, 1913 in *R.A.C. Manning Papers—Provincial Archives of Manitoba*.
62. Foster J.K. Griezic, "The Honourable Thomas Alexander Crerar: The Political Career of a Western Liberal Progressive in the 1920s," in S.M. Trofimenkoff, ed., *The Twenties*

in Western Canada (Ottawa: Papers of the Western Canadian Studies Conference at Calgary, 1972) 118.

63. J.E. Rea, "The Politics of Class: Winnipeg City Council, 1919-1945," in Carl Berger and Ramsay Cook, eds., *The West and the Nation* (Toronto: McClelland and Stewart, 1976) 235.

64. Robert England, *The Colonization of Western Canada* (London: F.S. King and Son, 1936) 280-81. See also *Census of Canada, 1921*, Vol. 5, 80, Table 58.

65. Morton, *The Progressive Party in Canada* 276.

66. Quoted in S.M. Lipset, *Agrarian Socialism: The Cooperative Commonwealth Federation in Saskatchewan*, rev. ed. (Garden City, NY: Anchor, 1968) 106.

67. J.W. Dafoe to Clifford Sifton, January 13, 1923, in Ramsay Cook, ed., *The Dafoe-Sifton Correspondence 1919-1927* (Winnipeg: Manitoba Record Society, 1966) 137.

68. Quoted in Karel Denis Bicha, *The American Farmer and the Canadian West, 1896-1914* (Lawrence, KS: Coronado Press, 1968) 130.

69. Frank Oliver in *House of Commons Debates*, April 12, 1901 and July 14, 1903. Quoted in Harold Troper, *Only Farmers Need Apply* (Toronto: Griffin House, 1972) 22.

70. W.E. Mann, *Sect, Cult, and Church in Alberta* (Toronto: University of Toronto Press, 1955) 4.

71. S.D. Clark, *The Developing Canadian Community*, 2nd ed. (Toronto: University of Toronto Press, 1968) 134-35.

72. Howard Palmer and Tamara Palmer, *Alberta: a New History* (Edmonton: Hurtig, 1990) 306.

73. John A. Irving, *The Social Credit Movement in Alberta* (Toronto: University of Toronto Press, 1959) 230, 344-46.

74. Diana Brydon, "Regions and Centres: The Literary Images of the Two Countries," in Bruce W. Hodgins, *et al.*, eds., *Federalism in Canada and Australia* (Peterborough, ON: Frost Centre for Canadian Heritage and Development Studies, 1989) 491-92.

75. Gordon Galbraith, "British Columbia," in Bellamy, Pammett, and Rowat.

76. Martin Robin, "British Columbia: The Company Province," in Robin 34.

77. Edith Dobie, "Party History in British Columbia, 1903-1933" [orig. pub. 1936], in J. Friesen and H.K. Ralston, eds., *Historical Essays on British Columbia* (Toronto: McClelland and Stewart, 1976) 72.

78. Dobie 79.

CHAPTER 2

Provincial Politics in the Modern Era

RAND DYCK

This chapter looks at a few of the prominent features of the politics of each of the ten Canadian provinces over the past 15 or 20 years. Before discussing some of the highlights in each province, however, it is worth noting what they had in common. In fact, despite their many differences, the provinces were very similar over this period, primarily in terms of public finance. They were all subject to a general consensus that the role of the provincial state should be reduced and that their budgets should be balanced on an annual basis. The distinctiveness of this set of priorities provides the context for this overview of developments in provincial politics in what might be called the modern era.

Over the first 85 years or so of the twentieth century, government operations expanded enormously at both the provincial and federal levels. This was especially true from 1945 to 1985, when a kind of consensus pervaded political and economic life in the provinces. That consensus, derived in part from the writing of British economist John Maynard Keynes, called for increased government intervention to provide for economic stability as well as to promote human welfare against the ravages of unemployment, poverty, illness, disability, and old age. Since the latter problems fall largely within provincial jurisdiction, the provinces set up extensive social programs over this period, although they were often cost-shared with the federal government. Universal health care and greatly expanded public education operations, including post-secondary colleges and universities, began to consume huge amounts of provincial funds. And until about 1985, virtually everyone agreed that this was good.

Starting about 1985, however, most of the provinces were influenced by the nearly universal spread of the ideology of neoconservatism or neoliberalism, which called for more self-reliance, a reduction in the role of the state, and the annual balancing of government budgets. It was widely felt that governments were spending, taxing, regulating, employing, owning, and owing too much. This profound ideological shift was then reinforced by a worldwide recession from about 1990 to 1995 which significantly reduced provincial government revenues but increased demands in certain policy areas. The provinces' problems were exacerbated by the federal government's determination to balance its own budget, which meant significant cuts in federal-provincial transfers, especially in the Paul Martin budget of 1995.

Together, these developments had the overall effects of reducing provincial government's revenues at the precise moment that governments were trying to balance their budgets; they therefore sought to reduce their costs by cutting their services. Sometimes they would increase provincial taxes or other revenues, but such a move was now totally out of favour, so that, whatever they tried to do, all of the provinces were in economic difficulty in the mid-1990s. They all accumulated deficits during the first half of that decade, but by 1995 they were all constrained by the orthodox view that they should not only balance their budgets but also reduce their taxes, usually in that sequence. The following years have generally been more prosperous, and by the turn of the new century, most provinces had balanced their budgets. Nevertheless, given the resistance to tax increases, they were all concerned to run a lean operation.

There exist a plethora of instruments at the disposal of provincial governments which are faced with the prospect of engineering a smaller state. They include the following:

- reducing public services (e.g., eliminating kindergartens)
- reducing the size of the public service (e.g., layoffs)
- freezing or reducing public service remuneration
- demanding more money from Ottawa
- restructuring government (e.g., fewer departments or fewer municipalities)
- imposing user fees or generating revenues from gambling
- deregulation, that is, removing provincial regulations (e.g., environmental)
- privatization of services or Crown corporations
- downloading responsibilities to municipalities

Depending on the seriousness of the provincial finances and the ideology of the party in power, the government could select a few or many of these instruments, but all of the provinces moved in this direction in the modern era. Let us examine them in turn, traveling from east to west.

Newfoundland and Labrador

Given that Newfoundland and Labrador was Canada's poorest province by many measures, its crisis in public finance dominated everything else in provincial politics in the early 1990s. After the May 1993 election, in which Liberal Premier Clyde Wells was re-elected, teachers and nurses agreed to cuts to pension plan contributions in return for job protection, but the province's finances did not improve. The 1994 budget required another $50 million reduction in total public sector compensation costs, along with $30 million in program spending cuts and $20 million in additional taxes. The government changed student grants to loans and closed 50 acute care hospital beds. Such retrenchment provided for the loss of 800 teaching jobs over the following few years and culminated in a month-long strike. At the same time, the government continued to decrease corporate taxes and remove regulations that bothered business. "Promote Business Investment" became the government's dominant theme, and the budget provided a ten-year tax holiday and minimal regulation for new and expanding businesses.

Given the difficulties, Wells decided to retire, preferring the position of a judge, and was succeeded as Liberal leader and premier by Brian Tobin in January 1996. Tobin had been a popular federal MP and Minister of Fisheries, with his greatest claim to fame being his command of the Canadian naval fleet that took on a Spanish vessel that was overfishing for turbot the previous year. Tobin called a quick election and won a massive majority in February 1996.

One of the issues Tobin inherited from Wells was the implementation of the new non-denominational school system. Newfoundland had joined Confederation in 1949 with up to six separate denominational school systems. Wells's decision to discontinue these was supported by a majority of the public in a referendum in 1995, but the process had been delayed by Catholic and Pentecostal groups. Tobin felt it necessary to call a second referendum on this issue in September 1997 and received overwhelming popular support to cut the churches completely out of the administration of education. This required a constitutional amendment that was eventually passed by the federal Parliament. Soon afterwards, Tobin announced that he would seek another constitutional amendment to change the name of the province to Newfoundland and Labrador, as it was already referred to in many government documents, rather than just "Newfoundland."

The fishing industry had always been a mainstay of the Newfoundland economy, but when the supply of groundfish almost disappeared in the late 1980s, the federal government had virtually prohibited the catching of cod. Since fishing is constitutionally a federal responsibility, although one the province would like to share, the provincial government was not the primary target of the pressure to deal with the problem. The federal Atlantic Groundfish Strategy (TAGs) program, which sought to provide financial assistance to those dependent on groundfish until they found another livelihood, ended in May 1999, but even with licence buy-backs, early retirement incentives, coverage of educational and moving expenses, and job training, the fishing labour force had not been reduced as much as was anticipated. Luckily, the shellfish industry—crab and shrimp—suddenly showed promising prospects and soon brought in greater revenue than had ever been achieved by cod. There has never been any concrete sign of improvement in the supply of groundfish, however, and new worries have begun to surface about whether shellfish will meet the same fate.

The offshore oil development at Hibernia pumped its first petroleum in November 1997 and, especially in the wake of the crisis in the fisheries, has become the province's main symbol of hope. Premier Tobin insisted that Hibernia oil be brought to shore in Newfoundland for transshipment to American refineries, and the storage terminal constructed at Whiffen Head opened in 1998. Moreover, progress continued on the two other principal offshore oil fields, Terra Nova and White Rose.

The other main source of hope was the International Nickel Company (INCO) mine at Voisey's Bay, Labrador. Tobin was insistent that the company build a smelter within the province, and Argentia, 120 kilometres from St. John's, was the mutual choice for its location. The development was then delayed by Aboriginal land claims and environmental assessments, but once these were settled, INCO changed its mind about the proposed Newfoundland smelter. It was largely Hibernia revenues that enabled Tobin to take a hard line on the issue, in contrast to so many predecessors who sold out other provincial resources at rock-bottom prices, and as long as he was premier the two sides remained in a stalemate. The Inuit land claim in Labrador was more quickly approved than others in the country and included giving the Inuit a share of eventual Voisey's Bay profits.

Another long-festering issue in the province was the hydro-electric project at Churchill Falls, also in Labrador. The 1969 contract on which the development was based had greatly favoured Quebec at Newfoundland's expense, and Tobin made a number of plaintive public speeches leading to marginal changes in the original contract. All the while, he pushed for the development of the Lower Churchill River on Newfoundland's own terms. The two provinces came to a tentative deal in 1998 which involved re-routing rivers and laying an underwater transmission line to Newfoundland. To obtain a mandate to take a strong stand with Quebec on Churchill Falls, as well as with INCO on Voisey's Bay, Tobin called an election in February 1999, exactly three years after the last. He was returned with a reduced majority, the hydro deal later unravelled, and Newfoundland began a scaled-down project of its own.

Hibernia revenues also allowed Tobin to follow up on the massive budget cuts made by Wells and in his own early budgets with more generous spending and even tax cuts. Some of this revenue came from Ottawa, of course, including Jean Chrétien's pre-2000 election package to win back Atlantic Canada. Ottawa also reversed the changes it had made to Employment Insurance which were of major benefit to Newfoundlanders. In 2000, the province entered the call-centre era, enticing a major American company to Newfoundland, and then Tobin resigned as premier to run in the 2000 federal election. His departure angered many people, partly because he left unresolved the two major issues on which he had campaigned, Voisey's Bay and Churchill Falls.

Former Health Minister Roger Grimes was elected to head the Liberal party in February 2001. He inherited a (worldwide) economic slowdown, a delayed and over-budget Terra Nova, and a scaled back and Quebec-less Lower Churchill Falls. One of Grimes's first initiatives was to promote the export of fresh water from the province, an activity frowned upon by virtually every other Canadian including the federal government. Meanwhile, the provincial Progressive Conservatives (PCs) chose a wealthy, dynamic, new leader, Danny Williams.

In 2002, production began from the Terra Nova offshore petroleum field, a project led by Petro-Canada, and the Husky Oil White Rose project was given the green light to begin production in 2006. Both were expected to have a 15-year life. Meanwhile, a federal arbitration panel gave Newfoundland about 75 per cent of a major offshore petroleum deposit called the Laurentian Sub Basin in disputed ocean territory between that province and Nova Scotia. The latter got about 16 per cent, and the rest went to France.

On the Voisey's Bay front, Grimes resumed talks with INCO. His new policy involved allowing the company to process some of the ore outside the province in the early years, in return for a promise to import an equivalent amount of ore for processing in Newfoundland later on. The agreement in principle was signed in 2002, with production to start in 2006. INCO will build an experimental hydrometallurgical processing plant at Argentia. If successful, it will be expanded to smelt all the Voisey's Bay nickel ore; if not, INCO will build a conventional smelter there. Opposition politicians claimed that the agreement lacked iron-clad guarantees, but Aboriginal groups enthusiastically endorsed it. This was largely because the latter saw the project as a way out of the depressing state of Aboriginal life in Labrador, characterized by high unemployment and a level of suicides and substance abuse that alarmed the whole country.

As the anticipated 2003 provincial election approached, Grimes appointed a royal commission on Newfoundland's relations with Ottawa—the Royal Commission On Renewing and Strengthening Our Place in Canada. Unfortunately, it did not come up with many new solutions to Newfoundland and Labrador's problems. Then, when Ottawa closed three small areas where a much reduced cod fishery had been allowed to reopen in 1997, Grimes renewed the call for a constitutional amendment to give the province joint jurisdiction over fisheries with Ottawa. But even more election-oriented was his statement that his government would not help enforce the new fishing ban, virtually inviting fishers to defy it. As fishers and fish plant workers blockaded the road, Ottawa promised $44 million for economic development in the communities affected.

Despite Grimes's many election-oriented initiatives, he lost to the PCs in October 2003. Danny Williams's party took 34 seats with 59 per cent of the vote, compared to Grimes's 12 seats and 33 per cent. The NDP gained 2 seats with 7 per cent of the vote. Williams brought in a 2004 budget intended to cut the $840-million deficit by eliminating 4,000 public sector jobs over four years. This precipitated an angry month-long strike in April of 20,000 government, health care, and school board workers. The strike ended with tough back-to-work legislation which imposed a two-year wage freeze and limited wage increases over the following two years.

On the offshore front, speculation surfaced in 2004 that the three operating oil fields might eventually be joined by a fourth, Hebron, as well as by a fifth, the South Whale Basin. Other possible future developments included construction of an underwater tunnel between Newfoundland and mainland Labrador, yet another study of which was begun, while the Labrador Inuit supported a land claims agreement that could create a new Aboriginal territory, Nunatsiavut.

In 2005, Premier Williams aggressively attacked Ottawa on the issue of equalization payments, claiming that the federal government clawed back some 70 per cent of the tax revenue received by the province from the offshore petroleum industry so that it could never get ahead. After revising the equalization payments formula generally, Prime Minister Martin was persuaded to make a side-deal with Newfoundland and Nova Scotia in which they would be able to retain all offshore revenues without a reduction in equalization payments for at least eight years. With increased oil revenues and other federal transfers, Williams brought in a more optimistic 2005 budget, just as production began at both Voisey's Bay and White Rose.

Prince Edward Island

Throughout its history, transportation between PEI and the mainland has been a leading issue in the province's politics. In the 1990s, therefore, the most distinctive feature of PEI political life was that it finally became linked in a fixed way to New Brunswick. After prolonged controversy and environmental objections, the 13-kilometre bridge across Northumberland Strait was given the green light in 1993, and four years later the Confederation Bridge was completed. Its private developer, Strait Crossing, was a consortium of French, American, and Canadian companies, which would operate the bridge for 35 years and then turn it over to the federal government. In the meantime it would receive an annual federal subsidy of $42 million, the previous cost of the ferry service, and charge tolls of about $18 million per year. For the 600 displaced ferry workers, a workforce adjustment package was provided, and in case the dredging for piers disturbed the scallop and lobster grounds, a $10 million compensation fund was established for the fishermen affected. A constitutional amendment was required to the effect that the bridge would replace the 1873 obligation on Ottawa to provide a steamship service from the mainland to the Island.

As in other provinces in the early 1990s, the PEI government was seriously stretched financially. After the retirement of Premier Joe Ghiz, Catherine Callbeck was crowned as the new Liberal leader and premier in January 1993, only the second woman to serve in that position anywhere in the country. Callbeck immediately showed she meant business by bringing in a tough 1993 budget with a promise to balance the budget by 1996. She then called an election, so far the only one in Canadian history to see the two major parties both led by women.

The results were virtually unchanged: the Liberals won 31 seats, while the PCs elected only their leader.

Since the 1993-94 deficit had ballooned to $69 million, the government devoted even more attention to its finances in 1994-95. The budget imposed a wage rollback for provincial public servants; provincial judges successfully challenged their inclusion in the rollback, unlike those affected by the reduction in welfare benefits. Such retrenchment measures, including health care cutbacks, were not particularly popular, so rather than face the electorate again, Callbeck resigned and was replaced as Liberal premier by Keith Milligan. He led the party in the 1996 election, by which time the PCs had chosen Patrick Binns as their new leader. That election was fought on a new 27-single-member electoral map, replacing the former two-member constituencies. Binns gained 18 seats to the Liberals' eight, while the NDP won its first seat in the province. Bean farmer Binns had been a provincial minister from 1978 to 1983 and had then served for four years as a federal MP. As a demonstration that political patronage was still alive and well in PEI, he promptly fired 800 government employees with Liberal connections.

The Binns government continued to be primarily concerned to balance the budget. This was accomplished by 1999, partly as a result of increased federal funds. In the following year, the "good news" budget even included tax cuts, so that Binns called an April 2000 election and was returned with 26 seats to one Liberal. Rising revenues allowed the province to provide publicly funded kindergartens for the first time, as well as to buy an MRI machine. On the downside, the discovery of a potato wart problem in one corner of one field provided the US with an excuse to ban imports of PEI potatoes, the province's leading product. Canada saw this as a means of protecting the American market for its own producers, not a genuine health issue, and the US continued to hassle the province on the question until July 2001. Meanwhile, both provincial and federal governments came to the rescue of impoverished potato farmers. Lobster is normally the second most important primary product in PEI, but in 2004, the province's largest lobster processor went bankrupt because of overcapacity in the industry.

The province's population continued to be divided over further tourism developments, now more likely with the advent of the fixed link, which environmentalists claimed would threaten its fragile ecology, and traditionalists said would change the province's tranquil way of life. Otherwise, few demographic issues arose during this period, except for the question of French-language schools. The Supreme Court of Canada ruled that a small group of francophone parents in Summerside should be provided with French elementary education in their own community, rather than have their children travel to the French school 30 kilometres away.

The next Liberal leadership convention chose the 29-year-old son of former Liberal Premier Joe Ghiz, Robert, as the new party leader. In the September 2003 election that followed, Premier Binns was easily returned, gaining 23 seats with

54 per cent of the vote. The Liberals won 4 seats with 42 per cent of the vote, while the NDP gained only 3 per cent of the vote, not enough to elect any members.

Perhaps the most distinctive feature of PEI's current political and economic life is the prospect of becoming a Kyoto-friendly model of generating electricity from wind-power. With virtually no energy sources of its own, PEI imports most of its electricity from New Brunswick via an underwater cable. But a wind farm located on the northern tip of the island already produces 5 per cent of the province's electricity by harnessing the nearly constant gale-force winds, and many proponents are working to increase that proportion significantly through the establishment of several wind farms across the province. A proposal to add an element of proportionality to the PEI electoral system was made in 2005, but was turned down in a plebiscite, perhaps ending the most promising case of electoral reform at the provincial level.

Nova Scotia

The government of Nova Scotia, led by Liberal John Savage, was also in financial trouble in the 1990s. The 1994 budget would have reached a deficit of $400 million, so once again the government curbed public sector wages with a 3 per cent wage rollback and a three-year salary freeze in order to bring the deficit down to $300 million. As in Newfoundland and Labrador, teachers and nurses were particularly affected, and as in several other provinces, the government undertook a radical reform of the health care system. Legislation created four regional health boards, which would determine the number and type of hospitals needed in each region and the method of paying doctors. They would supervise community health boards, which would emphasize prevention and community health centres in place of expensive acute-care hospitals. The government planned to increase its revenues from the establishment of two new casinos, one in Halifax and one in Sydney, while each of these two large urban areas was forced into a new one-tier metropolitan structure.

After serving as premier for four unhappy years in difficult circumstances, the unpopular Savage threw in the towel in 1997, and the Liberal party chose a long-standing Nova Scotia MP, Russell MacLellan as leader. When he called an election in March 1998, MacLellan gained the same number of seats as the NDP, but carried on in a minority position. This gave the PCs, now led by Dr. John Hamm, the balance of power.

Although MacLellan was not a strong premier, most of his problems were inherited, including the collapse of the Sydney Steel plant and Cape Breton Island coal mines. These two operations were the most important industrial projects on Cape Breton, but they had both relied on government subsidies and ownership since the 1960s in an attempt to strengthen the flagging regional economy. The good economic news throughout this period related to the development of petroleum off the shore of Nova Scotia's Sable Island. After the completion of the $3 billion Sable Island Offshore Energy Project, attached to the $1 billion Maritimes and Northeast Pipeline, the natural gas began to flow to the US at the start of 2000 (even before pipeline extensions were finished to Halifax and Saint John).

MacLellan governed with minimal legislative activity, since he was continually at risk of losing a vote. After 18 months, the NDP and PCs did defeat the Liberal government, leading to a July 1999 election, in which the PCs were victorious, and the NDP and Liberals were tied for second. Once outnumbering the Liberals in the Assembly as a result of by-elections, the NDP became the Official Opposition in 2001.

John Hamm inherited one of the few provinces that was still running an annual deficit by 1999, and he was obsessed with balancing the budget. Apart from hiring more nurses, he slashed everything in sight, restructuring and dismantling government departments, promoting privatization (including NS Resources, the government's agent in the development of offshore petroleum), introducing user fees (such as for seniors' prescription drugs), and eliminating over 1,000 government jobs in the process. Such actions precipitated many protest demonstrations, especially in the education field, and some budgetary adjustments had to be made. In 2001 he increased health expenditures and created a new Crown corporation, NS Business Inc., to try to attract new industry to the province, but was unable to cut taxes, as other provinces had done.

The turn of the new century witnessed the near collapse of the Cape Breton economy. The coal mines had continued to lose money due to poor sales until the federal government decided to close one mine in 1999 and sell the other. A potential American buyer fell through in March 2001, so that Ottawa closed both mines, with a total loss of some 1,600 jobs. The limited pension and severance packages for laid-off workers generated great anguish and controversy, including a two-week wildcat strike.

Meanwhile, the proposed sale of SYSCO, the provincially owned Sydney Steel Corporation, reached ludicrous proportions. Attempted sales to Chinese, Mexican, Dutch, American, and Swiss companies all fell through in turn. Thus, having invested some $3 billion over 34 years, the province decided to liquidate the assets of the plant, with a loss of about 800 jobs, necessitating another controversial pension deal. Ottawa stepped in to provide funds for a Cape Breton call centre, which might eventually employ 900 people.

Unfortunately, even the final closure of the plant was not the end of the story. It left behind an environmental mess called the Sydney tar ponds, which contain 700,000 tonnes of stinking toxic sludge and raw sewage, including 40,000 tonnes of carcinogenic PCBs. The sludge, including the contaminant arsenic, had been seeping into adjacent residential properties, and the area had a high incidence of birth defects, premature births, and high cancer rates. Nevertheless, it took a 17-day hunger strike on Parliament Hill by Elizabeth May of the Sierra Club to persuade the federal government to test the residents for toxic poisoning. Public meetings on the issues were also marked by violence. When the federal study showed that nothing was wrong, the Sierra Club did a study of its own which came to opposite conclusions. In 2004, the federal and Nova Scotia governments unveiled a $400-million cleanup plan that would remove more than 45,000 tonnes of contaminated sediment from the area, but many doubted that it would ever happen.

In 2000, Premier Hamm began a public debate on the unfairness of the 1986 offshore petroleum deal with the federal government, as well as the equalization payment formula. He claimed that 70 per cent of offshore revenues flowed to Ottawa and that the federal government reduced equalization payments in proportion to the province's resource revenues. He was supported by Premier Grimes in Newfoundland, and even by Ralph Klein of Alberta, in his argument that more of the profit should remain with the province. But Mike Harris in Ontario likened the situation to a welfare recipient who wanted to stay on social assistance after winning the lottery! Hamm later left Newfoundland's Premier Williams to lead this fight, and, as noted, they were successful in their joint negotiations with Prime Minister Martin.

The year 2003 was quiet on the drilling front, as EnCana Corp. announced that it was putting on hold the Deep Panuke natural gas field located not far from Sable Island. Some observers feared that there might not be as much natural gas in the area as originally estimated, and most other energy companies allowed offshore exploration licences to expire. As mentioned, a federal arbitration panel gave Nova Scotia only 16 per cent of a major offshore petroleum deposit in disputed ocean territory between that province and Newfoundland. EnCana was more optimistic about the Deep Panuke field in 2004 and revived a smaller version of the project.

As for demographic problems, the province had some small outbreaks of racial tension relating to Black high school students and had to address certain Aboriginal questions. The latter primarily involved fishing rights and the cutting and selling of trees on Crown property. The courts gave varying interpretations to eighteenth-century treaties with the Mi'kmaq on these points. On the question of establishing French-language schools in the province, the Supreme Court of Canada ruled that judges may have to become involved in ensuring that governments actually carry out their orders.

Premier Hamm called a provincial election for August 2003, perhaps in the hope that nobody would notice. In the campaign, the governing PCs emphasized previous tax cuts, which saw each taxpayer receive a rebate cheque of $155, and proposed a further 10 per cent tax reduction to stimulate the economy. At the same time, Hamm promised increased spending on schools, health care, and roads, the three areas subject to greatest opposition criticism. The Liberals opposed a new tax cut, saying that the province could not afford the loss of over $600 million from the public purse. The NDP supported reducing the sales tax on essential items, but pushed for a publicly run car insurance program, since soaring car insurance premiums were a big issue, as they had been in New Brunswick a few months before. When the votes were counted, the PCs were reduced to a minority government (25 seats with 36 per cent of the vote); the NDP took 15 seats with 31.5 per cent of the vote, to form the Official Opposition; and the Liberals had 12 seats, with 31.0 per cent.

In April 2004, Premier Hamm rescinded a major part of the tax cut on which he had been re-elected. He explained that this was necessary in order for the province to run a surplus budget rather than a deficit, and the move won the support of both opposition parties. After the 2004 federal election, Hamm suggested that Prime Minister Paul Martin could learn how to operate a minority government by observing the one in Nova Scotia.

Many observers were surprised in 2005 when a plan emerged to revive the coal industry on Cape Breton, given that the decline in supply had raised the price to a level that might make it economically viable. The province also welcomed the construction of a liquefied natural gas (LNG) terminal on the island.

In February 2006, Hamm was replaced as leader by Rodney MacDonald, at 34 the youngest premier in the land. A general election in June of that year returned the third minority government in four elections. The NDP was happy with 20 seats (from 15), the PC 23 seats (from 25), and the Liberals 9 seats (from 12). Even the popular vote was close—PC 40 per cent, NDP 35 per cent, Liberals 24 per cent, and Greens 2 per cent.

New Brunswick

Frank McKenna took over as the Liberal premier of New Brunswick in 1987 and was a dominant premier for ten years. As in other provinces, his first main concern was the government deficit, against which he battled aggressively. Within the public service, he emphasized rationalization, restructuring, privatization, and voluntary unpaid time off. The budgets of the early 1990s severed over 2,500 public service positions; made cuts to programs, such as the seniors' drug plan; eliminated or amalgamated government agencies; closed hospital beds; levied a surtax on high incomes; and broke collective agreements by imposing a freeze on public service salaries (provoking an illegal public service strike). In 1993 McKenna also passed a law requiring the government to produce a balanced budget with respect to operating expenses over a four-year period. As a result of these concerted efforts on both the revenue and expenditure sides, he balanced the 1994 operating budget, one of the first provinces to do so.

If budgetary restraint was McKenna's first priority, his second was to attract new business to the province. He succeeded in getting well over a dozen firms to set up "back office" or other communications branches in New Brunswick—telemarketing, billing, data processing, telephone orders, and market research. Most settled in Moncton to take advantage of its bilingualism, but some also went to Fredericton and Saint John.

The third main thrust of the McKenna strategy was reform of social policy. In this respect, too, it had a somewhat conservative dimension. The Royal
Commission on Education recommended that the education system needed
more money, more basics (math, science, and language skills), more testing, and
more teaching days per year. McKenna immediately began to implement these
ideas, but he saw the situation in a broader light. Education, social assistance, and
unemployment insurance (UI) were all linked, and he wanted to use education
and training to reduce the reliance on UI and welfare. He established over 100
literacy centres for upgrading purposes, the NB Works training programs, and
the NB Jobs Corps. Federal-provincial pilot projects were also set up under which
those on income assistance programs would get supplements for such things as
transportation and child care that would make it easier to find employment. In
this mild version of workfare, McKenna was insistent that through the discipline
of work or training, people would increase their sense of dignity and self-esteem.

With 5,000 call centre and 1,000 other information technology jobs behind
him, McKenna resigned in 1997, and Camille Thériault was chosen to succeed
him as Liberal leader. But in the June 1999 election, the Liberals were greatly
surprised to lose office to the new young PC leader, Bernard Lord, who had been
elected to the legislature only eight months before.

One of the main issues in the campaign was the toll highway between
Fredericton and Moncton. Lord promised to remove the tolls, and did so, but
at the cost of adding almost $1 billion to the provincial debt. Another issue was
health care, where he promised to hire 300 nurses, and did so. He engaged in
the same full review of government operations as the newly elected PC premier
in Nova Scotia, although his actions were less draconian: restructuring government departments, eliminating and amalgamating agencies, an early retirement
package for civil servants, and restoring school boards in place of parent advisory groups. The province's finances were not strong, but partly because of larger
federal contributions, Lord balanced the budget, reduced taxes, and increased
spending on health care while curtailing services in other areas. He also held a
provincial referendum on video lottery terminals (VLTs), which 53 per cent of
the electorate favoured.

Over the 2001-02 period, the three most prominent issues were natural gas,
official bilingualism, and Aboriginal rights. On the natural gas front, Lord went
before the National Energy Board in July 2002 to make the case for a guaranteed
Canadian share of Sable Island gas reserves. Lateral pipelines had not been built
to northern parts of the province, and plants and mills were being constructed in
the New England states using Sable Island gas, developments that might otherwise have been built in New Brunswick.

Responding to a judicial decision, Lord strengthened the *Official Languages
Act* by requiring all cities and other municipalities having at least 20 per cent
francophones to operate on a bilingual basis: bylaws, documents, and services.

Moncton in particular went happily and fully bilingual. Health care facilities also had to serve patients in the language of their choice, and a Commissioner of Official Languages would see that the *Act* was effectively implemented.

The immediate Aboriginal problems began with Mi'kmaq Donald Marshall, newly released from having served over ten years in jail for a crime he did not commit in Nova Scotia. Marshall then claimed a treaty right to fish for eels and was partially supported by the Supreme Court of Canada, which said that Aboriginal peoples had a treaty right to gain a moderate livelihood from fishing and hunting. The issue got transformed into one of lobster fishing, especially in the Burnt Church region of northeastern New Brunswick, and led to violent clashes among the federal Department of Fisheries and Oceans, non-Aboriginal fishers, and Aboriginal fishers. Peace had been restored by the summer of 2002, but violence in the crab fishing industry the following summer was also partly related to Aboriginal participation. Fishing being under federal jurisdiction, this was primarily Ottawa's problem, but Premier Lord signed a deal on Aboriginal logging operations in the province.

Although these problems were not central to the June 2003 election call, they were among the many issues that did not show Lord in a particularly good light. While some regarded his smooth, steady, cautious approach to be an advantage, others accused his government of not doing very much. Lord was caught off-guard when the dominant election issue became car insurance rates—New Brunswick residents paid the highest premiums in the country, and they had increased dramatically over the past few years. The Liberals, under an even younger and less experienced Shawn Graham, latched onto this issue, promising to roll back rates by 25 per cent and to put a public system in place if the insurance companies did not like it. The NDP considered car insurance to be its particular issue, with the solution being a public plan, but the party did not benefit much in the circumstances.

After a suspenseful night, the results could not have been closer: Lord's PCs won 28 seats, to Graham's Liberals 26, with the NDP re-electing only its leader. The PCs also edged the Liberals in popular vote, 45 per cent to 44 per cent, while the NDP got its typical 10 per cent. It was the barest majority government imaginable. In the aftermath of the election, Lord was courted to lead the old national Progressive Conservative Party and then the new national Conservative Party of Canada, but in the end he demurred. He had his hands full with the auto insurance problem. However, when a legislative committee recommended the adoption of a public plan, as supported by the two opposition parties, Lord opted instead for changes in the privately owned system.

Meanwhile, the two family economic empires in New Brunswick were also in the news. The McCain family, the world's largest producer of frozen French fries, as well as a leader in frozen pizza, vegetables, and dessert, announced that it had begun construction of a French fry plant in China, after ensuring that enough of the right kind of potatoes could be grown in that country. Construction of plants in Russia and India were expected to follow. The Irving family, owners of almost everything else in the province, including firms in the petroleum, transportation, forestry, and newspaper industries, came into controversy in national politics. It was revealed both that five federal cabinet ministers had accepted Irving hospitality and that the Irving empire was offered a $55-million grant to reduce the economic impact of the shutdown of the Saint John shipyard, without having to specify how the money would be used. The Irvings were also involved in a proposed liquefied natural gas (LNG) terminal in Saint John, where they typically extracted tax concessions.

Quebec

Robert Bourassa's federalist Liberal party was in power in Quebec as the 1990s began. Bourassa had been premier between 1970 and 1976, and then staged a miraculous resurrection to get re-elected in 1985. Although the Quebec budgetary deficit was not the focus of as much attention as in other provinces, public sector workers were handed successive wage freezes over the 1991-95 period, and hundreds of jobs were eliminated. All departments suffered from repeated budgetary cuts, and municipalities were particularly hard hit. The government cut back on welfare recipients; hired 150 new welfare inspectors, whom social assistance recipients found to be extremely invasive; and penalized able-bodied recipients if they would not take part in make-work projects. In a commentary that could be extended to other provinces, a Quebec report said that the poor and unemployed were more likely to experience mental health problems than other citizens and it was therefore often inappropriate to coerce them into finding work, into training programs, or into menial jobs. Despite these measures, the government ran up a series of large deficits.

On the revenue side, Bourassa harmonized the provincial sales tax with the federal GST and approved the establishment of casinos. On the economy more generally, the government adopted an industrial strategy called "Québec Inc.," which emphasized the development of five industrial clusters: aerospace, pharmaceuticals, information technology, electric power generation, and metals and minerals processing.

Bourassa was most noted for his obsession with electricity, especially his promotion of the James Bay Hydroelectric project in the 1970s. When he proposed a similarly massive diversion of northern rivers in the Great Whale project in the early 1990s, however, the Aboriginal peoples affected, environmentalists, and American consumers combined to force him to abandon his dream. He developed malignant melanoma, the most serious kind of skin cancer, and resigned at the end of 1993. The Liberals unanimously chose Daniel Johnson as his successor, and he formed a new government in January 1994.

Johnson was less autonomy-minded than Bourassa and took the position that true independence came through jobs, jobs that would be threatened by talk of separation.

Meanwhile, Jacques Parizeau's stern leadership turned the separatist Parti Québécois (PQ) into a strong party once again, and Mario Dumont took over the Action Démocratique du Québec (ADQ) party. Johnson called an election for September 1994, emphasizing that a PQ government would have a serious effect on the Quebec economy. Parizeau, on the other hand, promised a separate referendum on sovereignty within a year of the election. The Liberals almost tied the PQ in terms of popular vote, but the PQ won a clear majority of seats.

Premier Parizeau blamed the Liberals for a residual deficit of $5.7 billion and immediately began to implement his carefully prepared referendum strategy. In December 1994, he tabled a bill that would declare Quebec a sovereign country if approved in the referendum. The bill anticipated a new Quebec constitution with its own Supreme Court, but many observers were surprised at the number of links which the PQ expected to retain with Canada: an economic association, joint citizenship, and use of the Canadian dollar. Many opponents retorted that the rest of Canada might not be agreeable to such sharing; moreover, they rejected the claim that Quebec would retain its existing boundaries. They were also not impressed that Parizeau talked vaguely of "sovereignty" rather than "separation." With Jean Chrétien's federal government asleep at the switch, 50.6 per cent of Quebecers voted against the Parizeau proposal in October 1995 compared with 49.4 per cent in favour. The premier promptly resigned, to be replaced in early 1996 by federal Bloc Québécois (BQ) leader, Lucien Bouchard.

Bouchard's first priority was to get the provincial government's finances under control. This entailed slashing public expenditures in every direction, especially in the health care field, as well as adopting many other policies that were at odds with the PQ's traditional social democratic approach. This priority naturally led to serious confrontations with the provincial public service. Among the few progressive measures adopted were a clampdown on smoking, including the sale of tobacco in drugstores, and $5 per day childcare. This program, along with free daycare for welfare recipients—light years ahead of the rest of North America—had the beneficial side-effect of significantly reducing the number of single mothers on welfare.

Daniel Johnson resigned, and after a national outpouring of support, federal PC leader Jean Charest was persuaded to change parties and levels of operation in April 1998 to become provincial Liberal leader in Quebec. Then, in August, the Supreme Court of Canada rendered its decision on the question Prime Minister Chrétien had submitted to it a year earlier as to whether Quebec had a right to a unilateral declaration of independence. The Court answered in the negative, except for saying that if a clear question in a Quebec referendum was supported by a clear majority in the province, Ottawa and the other provinces would be obliged to negotiate. This set the stage for the November 1998 provincial election: a showdown between Bouchard and Charest. The Liberals received more votes than the PQ, but Bouchard won more seats. Such results were an encouragement to Bouchard to continue governing well but not to call another referendum.

On the federal-provincial front, Ottawa and nine provinces agreed to the Social Union Framework Agreement to guide future federal-provincial relations, but Bouchard refused to sign it. On the other hand, when Ottawa transferred responsibility for labour market training to Quebec, the province did not exercise its new responsibility in an impressive manner. In 1999, Chrétien unveiled his *Clarity Act*, which translated the Supreme Court decision into legislation. It enunciated the conditions Quebec would have to meet before the federal government would engage in negotiations over separation. Negative reaction in Quebec was not as vocal as anticipated, although the PQ government passed *Bill 99* which rejected Ottawa's claim that it could rule on the referendum question.

On the financial front, the province's coffers improved, partly as a result of increased federal equalization payments, and Quebec was able to balance its budget by 1999. This did not mean that all was well, however, especially in the health field, and Bouchard faced a four-week nurses' strike. The 2000 budget provided increased funding for health and education and even included tax cuts, while the 2001 budget helped the poor on the one hand and gave a tax holiday to small manufacturers on the other.

Other decisions over this period related to the substitution of linguistic for religious school boards and a controversial merging of municipalities, especially in the major metropolitan centres. This was particularly contentious on the island of Montreal. Besides the anticipated loss of jobs, local identities, and the high level of services, the amalgamations had linguistic implications for anglophone enclaves like Westmount. Opposition to these mergers was one factor that contributed to the decline of the BQ in the November 2000 federal election, in which the Liberals outpolled the separatists. Bouchard established Quebec's own blood system, hired more minorities in the public service, broadened its same-sex law, and continued the fight against criminal biker gangs.

The province had little choice in allowing English trademark names to be used in signs, such as Burger King, Second Cup, and Canadian Tire, but a new wrinkle emerged in the language wars when French-speaking parents went to court to demand that their children be allowed to attend English-language schools. Their case was rejected by the Supreme Court of Canada in 2005. A variety of Aboriginal problems also erupted, especially with respect to logging rights, although the PQ was ready to discuss Aboriginal self-government, and the federal government purchased land to settle the Oka Crisis ten years after it erupted.

Having concluded that he could take Quebec no further on the road to sovereignty, Bouchard resigned as premier in March 2001. He was succeeded by

Deputy Premier and Finance Minister Bernard Landry. Landry announced his intention of pursuing sovereignty much more vigorously than Bouchard, but his two years in office were not particularly happy ones. Even though the economy was relatively strong and the government adopted several popular measures, it seems that the premier's fixation on sovereignty turned people against him. His government both strengthened and weakened the language laws. First, it prevented immigrant and francophone students from entering the English school system by closing a loophole that many had exploited, but at the same time, it increased the number of English classes in French schools to prepare students for work in a world where English was the dominant language. It also refused to put further restrictions on signs or on access to English-language community colleges and passed a law dictating where and when doctors must work. On a different ethnic front, the government signed an agreement with the James Bay Cree to extend the James Bay hydro-electric complex.

When Landry called the April 2003 election, Jean Charest's Liberals made significant inroads into francophone support and ended up with 76 seats (46 per cent of the vote) to the PQ's 45 seats (33 per cent of the vote), while Mario Dumont's ADQ won only four seats (18 per cent of the vote). Health care waiting lists and municipal mergers were two leading issues, but for many voters it was just time for a change.

The first unambiguous federalist premier in decades, Charest had close ties to federal politicians and many fellow premiers. One of his priorities was to establish a Council of the Federation which would give the provinces a strong, united voice in dealing with Ottawa, and at their 2003 meeting, the other premiers happily agreed to the creation of such a body. Charest put aside constitutional changes, at least for now, and wanted more tax points and money, citing a "fiscal imbalance" between the federal and provincial governments.

Charest claimed he had a mandate to "re-engineer the state" of Quebec to catch up with the other provinces that had been reducing the size of government for over ten years. By most standards, Quebec was the most highly taxed province in Canada, with the most adequate public services, but neoconservatism had never been totally embraced in the province before. In the new government's first budget, it reneged on immediate tax cuts because of the $4.3 billion deficit it inherited from the PQ, but the budget was balanced, with no tax increases, and with increased funding for health care and education. Other areas of government spending were cut, the government began dismantling aspects of state intervention, and laws were passed to reduce the power of trade unions. Symbolically, $5 a day child care was increased to $7 a day.

More than residents in other provinces, Quebecers protested the reduction of public services and privatization of government agencies, such that Charest decided in his second year of office to slow the process down. The government still intended to cut 16,000 government jobs (20 per cent of the civil service), but only

over a decade and mostly by attrition; it also planned additional cutbacks in program spending and to sell off $880 million in assets. Arguing that public-private
partnership agreements did not constitute privatization, Charest continued to
involve the private sector in the provision of services and construction of infrastructure projects. Charest's unpopularity had a negative effect on Paul Martin's
Liberal efforts in Quebec in the 2004 federal election.

On the other hand, the government brought in tax cuts, but the middle class
was angry that the cuts went mostly to lower income families with children.
Moreover, in contrast to many other provinces, especially Ontario, Quebec abolished coercive measures to get welfare recipients to find employment, offering
cash incentives instead. As in Ontario and BC, the Quebec Court of Appeal
declared same-sex marriages legal, but in a 2004 referendum across Quebec, a
majority in many communities voted to divorce themselves from the PQ municipal mergers.

Electricity never being far down the political agenda in Quebec, controversy
surrounded the plan to divert water from the Rupert River to generating sta-
tions on other rivers. Given the freeze in construction of massive hydro-electric
installations since the abandonment of the Great Whale project in 1992, Quebec
surprised many observers by opting to build a plant at Bécancour to produce
electricity by burning natural gas. Quebec was also a national leader in developing windpower. But because the province no longer had a great excess of
electricity to offer to aluminum companies at a discount, Alcoa announced that
it would cancel a $1 billion expansion of its Baie-Comeau smelter.

The Supreme Court of Canada made a controversial decision in 2005 when
it ruled that the prohibition on private insurance for core medical services was a
violation of the Quebec Charter of Rights. In the first instance, the ruling applied
only to Quebec, which already had more private health services than most other
provinces, but many observers expected it to lead to the legitimizing of two-tier
health care in Canada. At the end of 2005, the opposition PQ elected a dynamic
young André Boisclair to lead the separatist cause.

Ontario

There was no sign of either economic difficulty or neoliberalism in Ontario before 1990. The David Peterson Liberals had constructed a minority government
pact with the NDP between 1985 and 1987, and then governed with a massive
majority for the next three years. Meanwhile, the PCs, which had held Ontario
for 42 straight years up to 1985, were a dismal third. Suddenly, in 1990, however,
the bottom fell out of the Ontario economy, just as the provincial electorate decided to replace the Liberals with Bob Rae's NDP. Then, in 1995, Ontario opted
for extreme neoliberalism under the decidedly *unprogressive* Conservatives led
by Mike Harris.

An electorate that merely wanted to teach David Peterson a lesson in 1990 woke up to find it had put a majority NDP government in power, and new premier Bob Rae was as surprised as anyone. His regime has often been faulted for not keeping its promises, raising taxes, running deficits, and freezing public sector wages, but all of these actions can be linked to, if not necessarily excused by, the five years of savage recession starting in 1990 and the resulting shortage of government revenues.

The NDP government did not keep its foremost promise—to establish a public car insurance system, as its counterparts had done in Saskatchewan, Manitoba, and BC. Rae explained that the province did not have the revenues to provide fair compensation to the private insurance companies it would have had to purchase and that would have resulted in a significant layoff of employees. Given the party's spending priorities and the reduced amount of money flowing in, it was probably less surprising that the NDP *did* raise taxes. Although the party in office did not emphasize corporate tax increases as much as it had earlier promised, many people resented the tax hikes because they had less income during this period and because the new "tax cut" orthodoxy was beginning to get established across the land.

The Rae government will always be remembered for adding approximately $10 billion to the provincial debt during each of its five years in office. This was not, however, because its spending was out of control. In fact, the party would have liked to spend much more than it did on social programs. The more objective explanation is that its revenues were severely curtailed in the recession, and the bad economy in turn automatically added to certain program costs.

In an effort to keep the deficit within bounds, the Rae government introduced its "social contract" in 1993. This terminology gave the misleading impression of more consultation between government and employees than was actually involved, but the result was to freeze public sector salaries (over $30,000) for three years and marginally reduce them through unpaid days off. Many public sector workers and all public sector union leaders were irate, and Rae was not successful in trying to persuade them that the alternative would have been massive layoffs.

Despite the economic difficulties, the Rae government was able to pursue several of its own priorities. Apart from the social contract, it passed union- and worker-friendly labour legislation, and the premier was proud of the partnerships he established with industries in the private sector in the saving of jobs. The government promoted non-profit and cooperative housing, and enacted the most comprehensive employment equity legislation in the country.

Given the generally negative public image of the NDP government, no one expected it to be re-elected in 1995, but the surprise was that the election was won by the PCs rather than the Liberals. Mike Harris had rebuilt the PC party over the five-year period and had unveiled a neoliberal election platform, the "Common Sense Revolution," in 1994. Abandoning the longstanding "progressive" policies of the PC party in Ontario, Harris promised tax cuts, eliminating the deficit, getting rid of NDP labour legislation and employment equity, and making those on social assistance go to work.

Harris promised not only to balance the provincial budget over four years, but also to reduce taxes. The only way this could be done was by massively cutting public expenditures, both at the provincial level and in its transfers to municipalities, school boards, hospitals, and institutions of higher education. While cuts were made across the board, the most immediate and draconian was the 21.6 per cent reduction in social assistance rates. Harris promised that the province would be unrecognizable after he was finished, and, in fact, virtually nothing the NDP had done was left intact. Confirming what Rae said about the social contract, Harris eventually cut some 20,000 public service jobs.

One of the Harris government's most significant moves was to create a Hospital Restructuring Commission with the authority to close hospitals. It ordered some 40 hospitals to close, sometimes to be replaced with new ones, but creating great controversy in almost every case. Harris also thought that costs could be reduced by amalgamating the lower tier municipalities within Metropolitan Toronto into one great "megacity" and later extended the same amalgamation logic to Ottawa, Hamilton, and Sudbury. Perhaps even more significant was the downloading of provincial responsibilities to municipalities. Harris claimed that if the province absorbed more of local school board budgets in return for such downloading, the whole exercise would be "revenue neutral," but municipalities did not find this to be the case.

The Harris government also took many other initiatives in the education field. First, by absorbing a larger portion of the education budget at the provincial level, the government aimed to increase its control over school board policies and expenditures. In a similar pursuit, it halved the number of school boards in the province and downgraded the status of school trustees. Second, it established provide-wide standards with respect to class size, student testing, and a rigorous new curriculum. In fact, throughout its term, the Harris government was at war with the teaching profession on a variety of issues such as teacher testing, teachers' preparation time, and supervision of extra-curricular activities. Third, it abolished Grade 13, bringing Ontario into line with most other provinces.

On the welfare front, besides reducing benefits, Harris brought in workfare, based on the general principle that all able-bodied social assistance recipients should go to work. By 2000, the government claimed that 500,000 people had been removed from the welfare rolls, although only a small proportion of these were absorbed by workfare, and many were simply transferred to other assistance programs. It also decreed that anyone who abused the welfare system would lose social assistance benefits for life and repealed all the NDP labour and employment equity laws.

Protecting the environment was not a priority of the Harris government, and it made severe program cuts in this field. After seven people died of E.Coli contamination of the water supply at Walkerton, a judicial inquiry held the reduction in environmental funding and standards and the downloading of water and sewer responsibilities to be largely responsible.

The government sent juvenile offenders to strict discipline boot-camp and built two superjails, one of which was later privatized to an American profit-oriented firm. When an Ontario Provincial Police officer shot and killed Aboriginal protester Dudley George at an unarmed protest outside Ipperwash Provincial Park, there was evidence that the force was under pressure from the Premier's Office, but Harris refused to set up a judicial inquiry into the incident.

Electricity is a major concern in Ontario, and various aspects of the operation of the Crown corporation, Ontario Hydro, have long been questioned. Harris took many of its nuclear reactors out of service because of safety concerns; broke the company into separate producing and distributing organizations, Ontario Power Generation and Hydro One respectively; welcomed private competition into the industry; and deregulated rates. The government leased the operations of the Bruce nuclear plant to a private firm and in 2001 announced the privatization of Hydro One. As for the privatization of other government assets, the record was surprisingly sparse—mainly the toll highway 407. But Harris deregulated wherever he could.

The North American economy started to improve about the time the PCs came to power, so that even though the budgets of Finance Minister Ernie Eves contained many tax cuts, the government began to take in increased revenues. The government passed a balanced budget law, but was soon spending more than Bob Rae had done, and did indeed balance the Ontario budget by the turn of the century.

Harris was re-elected in 1999, partly because he had changed the rules regarding election finance to the benefit of his own party. But coming under increasing criticism after the election, he resigned in early 2002, to be replaced by Eves. The new premier began by repudiating much of the Harris right-wing record and abrasive style. The first major reversal was with respect to electricity: Hydro One would not be privatized after all, and rates would be capped rather than deregulated. The second came in the 2002 budget, which delayed promised tax cuts for a year, including the private school tax credit introduced in 2001, and even increased cigarette taxes. The third reversal was to restore the money that had been removed from the education budget by Eves in his previous capacity as finance minister. The new premier was also active in settling rather than fomenting public service strikes.

In 2003, however, Eves seemed to turn to the right, and the March "balanced budget" resurrected many of the tax cuts and tax credits deferred a year earlier. Even more controversial than its contents, the budget was delivered in the auditorium of a Magna International auto parts plant in Brampton because the legislature was not in session and to avoid opposition criticism. Thwarting his plan to call a spring election, Eves faced a number of unanticipated problems. In March, a SARS outbreak in Toronto hospitals created havoc for the regional economy, especially in terms of a major decline in tourism. In August, a province-wide electricity blackout occurred, and a meat packing plant was charged with illegally processing dead animals and delivering tainted meat.

It was possible to link some of these problems and others to the Harris/Eves record of dismantling the provincial state, but in the campaign leading up to the September 2003 election, Eves continued on this right-wing tangent. The core of the PC platform was tax cuts rather than the restoration of public services. The Liberals, under Dalton McGuinty, promised that they would neither increase nor decrease taxes, but would be able to rebuild the provincial social infrastructure and still maintain a balanced budget. The results were a repudiation of the Harris/Eves regime: 72 Liberal seats with 46 per cent of the vote, compared to 24 PC seats (35 per cent of the vote) and seven NDP seats (15 per cent of the vote).

McGuinty formed a government in October 2003. One of its first acts was to ask recently retired Provincial Auditor Erik Peters to do a quick audit of the provincial books. Peters reported that the Liberals had inherited a $5.6 billion deficit rather than the balanced budget that the PCs had claimed. Moreover, since only about one-third of this discrepancy could be attributed to SARS or other unforeseen problems, it was widely agreed that the PCs had deliberately falsified their numbers to mislead the public just before the vote. The Liberals then played up the deficit for all it was worth and used it as an excuse to ease themselves out of many of their election promises.

The Liberals immediately backtracked on several issues. Instead of balancing the budget for the fiscal year, they might have to run a deficit. Instead of halting urban development in the Oak Ridges Moraine, 5,700 out of the intended 6,600 houses would be built. Instead of canceling the 3P (public-private partnership) hospitals planned by the PCs, they would go forward with a minor adjustment. And instead of leaving electricity rates fixed at 4.3 cents per kilowatt, they would increase on April 1, 2004.

Nevertheless, most of the McGuinty government's early decisions were consistent with its election platform. These included the appointment of a judicial inquiry into the killing of Dudley George at Ipperwash, banning partisan advertising paid for at public expense, and passing a bill declaring two-tier health care illegal. McGuinty also repealed the lifetime ban for those accused of welfare fraud, did away with the 60-hour work week, changed the definition of "Northern Ontario" to exclude the Muskoka region, and vetoed the long-standing proposal to transport Toronto garbage to the Adams Mine in Kirkland Lake. In addition, he suspended the automatic annual 2 per cent increase under rent control and provided new funds for school maintenance and repair.

The long-awaited 2004 budget did indeed run a deficit *and* raise taxes, especially those related to tobacco and alcohol. Most controversial was the reintroduction of provincial health care premiums, graduated by income, of between $60 and $900 per year to help pay for increasing health expenditures. At the same time, certain health care services were delisted from free medicare coverage: chiropractic treatments, physiotherapy, and most eye examinations. But the government also found money to fund and finish partially completed hospitals and raised nursing home standards.

On the education front, McGuinty legislated a two-year freeze on post-secondary tuition fees, cancelled the PCs' teacher testing program, and appointed former NDP premier Bob Rae to head a task force on post-secondary education. The new government was also more committed to the environment than its predecessor, changing the *Planning Act* to make the Ontario Municipal Board less developer friendly and removing its chair, appointing more water quality inspectors, imposing a one-year ban on urban sprawl in the Golden Horseshoe greenbelt, and proposing a plan to target future urban development in southern Ontario more efficiently.

As in so many other provinces, car insurance rates became an election issue, with the Liberals promising an average 10 per cent cut in premiums. After imposing an initial 90-day freeze in such rates, the government persuaded insurance companies to reduce premiums to some extent, but few car owners experienced the full reduction promised. The car manufacturing industry being at the core of the Ontario economy, many of the large auto makers took advantage of federal and provincial government assistance at this time to build new assembly plants, revamp existing ones, or at least keep open plants that were scheduled for closure. These grants were not enough, however, to avoid significant layoffs for 2006 and 2008 at General Motors.

Within the legislature, the election had left the NDP with seven seats, one shy of official party status, but after fighting for semi-official status, the party won a by-election to bring their number up to eight. As a consequence of the austerity budget, McGuinty decided that MPPs would forego their expected 2.7 per cent pay increase. The government gave the provincial auditor powers to examine the books of outside agencies—hospitals, schools, colleges, and universities—and Ontario then joined BC in establishing fixed election dates (October 4, 2007).

Apart from problems in public finance, the McGuinty government's most challenging issue was electricity. Its first move was to dump three key executives at Ontario Power Generation. Then, relying on the advice of former federal cabinet ministers Jake Epp and John Manley, the government decided that the quickest response to the looming electricity crisis was to rely even further on nuclear power. The party had already promised to phase out the province's five coal-fired plants by the end of 2007, and advisers saw little scope for new production based on water or natural gas. The immediate decision was to complete the refurbishment of one of the idle nuclear reactors at Pickering A, with similar decisions on other out-of-commission reactors likely to follow. Many observers were hostile to an even greater dependence on nuclear power, partly because of the problem of what to do with the radioactive waste produced, and argued that the government should put greater emphasis on conservation and renewable sources instead. McGuinty also created a new agency, Ontario Power Authority, to be responsible for projecting future needs and signing contracts to buy electricity from suppliers other than Ontario Power Generation.

The 2005 budget forecast a deficit of $2.8 billion, while containing increased funding for education, health, and infrastructure. Responding to the side-deals Prime Minister Martin was making with other provinces, however, McGuinty asked for, and eventually received, a $5 billion down payment on the $23 billion difference between what Ontario sent to Ottawa and what it got back.

Manitoba

Following an NDP regime under Howard Pawley from 1981 onwards, PC Gary Filmon took over the reins of power in Manitoba in 1988. He ran a successful, moderate government which eschewed the more determined right-wing ideology of counterparts like Mike Harris in Ontario and Ralph Klein in Alberta. The Meech Lake Accord dominated Manitoba politics in the 1988-90 period, with Filmon in a minority government position. In the end, an Aboriginal MLA, Elijah Harper (NDP) refused unanimous consent to rush the Accord through the Manitoba legislature, and combined with Clyde Wells' opposition in Newfoundland, Meech Lake died.

Then, having been returned to office in 1990 with a majority, the Filmon government had to cope with the recession, although Manitoba was not as seriously affected as most other provinces. No longer dependent on Opposition support, Filmon turned to the right, repealing or amending what he considered to be pro-labour legislation left by the NDP. He also provided business with a wide range of tax breaks and tax credits.

Fiscal conservatism was most apparent in the series of Filmon budgets. In 1990, the government imposed a 3 per cent ceiling on public sector wage increases, except for nurses, but in 1991, it froze the wages of 48,000 public service employees and eliminated about 1,000 jobs, only half of them by attrition. In 1992, it cut another 300 government positions and, in the following two years, about 900 more. The 1993 budget was particularly harsh: it included a wage rollback and work week reduction plan (10 days off without pay called "Filmon Fridays") for 100,000 public sector workers, including teachers; elimination of the children's dental plan; and reduction of tax credits for pensioners, renters, and property taxpayers, and for those receiving social assistance and workers' compensation benefits.

The 1994 budget contained ten more Filmon Fridays, which were protested by provincial judges who challenged their inclusion in the legislation. Victims of government retrenchment in 1994 included foster parents, home care, student bursaries, and schools and universities. The government also carried on with its privatization initiatives and provided a wide variety of corporate tax breaks. Despite adopting such measures and exhausting the provincial fiscal stabilization fund, the government continued to run large annual deficits which added some $2 billion to the accumulated provincial debt. In 1993, however, the government declared its intention to balance its books over the following four years. Not surprisingly, many of these actions resulted in protest rallies. Due to the recession, Ontario cancelled an earlier deal that would have seen Manitoba construct a new Conawapa dam on the Nelson River.

On the demographic front, the report of the Aboriginal Justice Inquiry was published in 1991, detailing systemic discrimination against Aboriginal peoples by the legal system and police forces in the province. Filmon also had to contend with various aspects of Supreme Court-enforced official bilingualism, including independent French-language school boards.

Filmon was narrowly re-elected in 1995, partly because of his own personal popularity. The Liberals collapsed, with most of their vote going to the NDP. Manitoba experienced another horrendous flood in the spring of 1997, which necessitated calling in the armed forces. The Red River floodway, the huge ditch previously dug around Winnipeg for this purpose, did its job, but much of the province south of the capital was covered with water. By the budget of 1997, Filmon was able to lower taxes to some extent, as well as devote increased funding to health care, but cutbacks in this field had gained Manitoba the label of "hallway medicine." He cracked down on welfare recipients and was frequently engaged with Aboriginal issues.

By 1998, Filmon faced serious allegations that people close to him had engaged in a vote-rigging scheme in three northern constituencies in the 1995 provincial election. They had surreptitiously funded Independent Aboriginal candidates to split the NDP vote. Although Filmon denied any personal knowledge of the scheme, an assistant was found to have lied about the improprieties, and the affair developed into a full-scale scandal. The judge investigating the scheme wrote as follows: "In all my years on the bench I never encountered as many liars in one proceeding as I did during this inquiry.... A vote-rigging plot constitutes an unconscionable debasement of the citizen's right to vote."[1] Such charges did the PCs no good in the election they called for September 1999, after another serious flood that spring. Thus, after 11 years in office, the Filmon government was defeated by the NDP.

NDP Premier Gary Doer formed a government which included two Aboriginal MLAs in his cabinet. Although he was considered fairly conservative by NDP standards, and was concerned about balanced budgeting, several of his government's early actions revealed its social democratic character. It banned water exports from the province, brought in tax cuts for low-income residents, and reduced tuition fees. Drawing on the Quebec model, it banned political contributions from corporations and unions, leaving parties to be financed only by individuals. Doer approved Aboriginal casinos and resurrected the Aboriginal Justice Inquiry which had examined cases of Aboriginal injustice in the late1980s. He enacted new labour legislation (vehemently opposed by business) that he claimed brought more balance into the collective bargaining process and planned to use the Crown corporation, Manitoba Hydro, as a catalyst for economic development. In view of the province's recent experiences with flooding, he doubled the size of the Red River floodway.

Over the 1999-2003 period, Doer governed in a cautious, practical, fiscally responsible way. He balanced four budgets, while at the same time managing modest tax reductions along with increased investment in health care and education. The economy was generally strong, and the government was scandal-free. Taking advantage of the party's popularity as well as his own, Doer called an election for June 2003. The new PC leader, Stuart Murray, tried to inject an ideological tone into the campaign with the promise of massive tax cuts, but this idea was not particularly appealing, and Doer's NDP was returned with an increased majority. Doer won 35 seats with 49 per cent of the vote; Murray picked up 20 seats with 36 per cent; and the Liberals won two seats (13 per cent of the vote). Murray's stay was comparatively short, however. In April 2006 he was replaced by Hugh McFadyen, who won two-thirds of a leadership vote, the first contested one since 1983, when Gary Filmon became leader.

As noted above, water is a multi-faceted issue in Manitoba. Abundant rain in 2004 probably guaranteed better crops than usual, for example, and would also make it possible to increase the production and sale of hydro-electricity. In the future, Manitoba might benefit from revisiting the Conawapa dam project to supply Ontario with electricity, given that province's serious shortages. Besides serious flooding in 2005, the province faced the problem that the state of North Dakota would open the taps on the Devils Lake water diversion project. Many observers maintained that this would send mercury, salts, sulphates, and fish parasites into the Red River system, polluting Manitoba waters, but the Americans refused to recognize the authority of the Boundary Waters Treaty.

Saskatchewan

After a decade of PC rule under Grant Devine, the NDP was returned to power in Saskatchewan in 1991 under Roy Romanow. Over the years, the NDP in Saskatchewan had developed a reputation for fiscal responsibility, in contrast both to its counterparts in certain other provinces, and to its PC predecessors. Beyond this party tradition and his own personal predilections, Romanow was pushed in a conservative direction by the $5.2 billion debt accumulated by the Devine government and by the recession of the early 1990s.

Predictably, Romanow raised taxes rather sharply, but many observers were surprised to see an NDP government cut transfers to hospitals, schools, municipalities, and universities in such a dramatic fashion. In fact, given that so much of the Canadian health care system had been pioneered by his party in Saskatchewan, Romanow stunned the province with his reduction in spending in the health sector. He even eliminated funding to 52 small-town hospitals, arguing that Saskatchewan had the highest per capita number of hospital beds in the country. In fact, many former hospitals were converted to primary health centres providing basic medical services but not overnight or acute care.

Romanow was easily re-elected in 1995, as the Liberals took hold of second place and the PCs dropped to third. By that time, the government had balanced the budget and afterwards reduced taxes on an annual basis, increased social spending, and still ran a surplus. This was despite a continuation of poor annual grain harvests and was certainly helped by rising petroleum revenues. The premier made repeated pilgrimages to Ottawa to plead for increased federal aid to the farming community. As a rather conservative New Democrat, Romanow did little over the next five years of a pioneering nature, and rural areas perceived that he did nothing for them at all.

In 1997, the Liberal caucus split apart, and four members joined with four remaining PCs to form a new party, the Saskatchewan Party (SP), which became the Official Opposition in the legislature. By this time, many members of the former PC government and party were in jail or had at least been discredited for siphoning personal benefit from the public purse between 1982 and 1991. Remaining PC MLAs were thus happy to find a new party name; indeed, the PC Party rendered itself inactive for the next two provincial elections. The SP adopted a platform similar to that of the Reform-Canadian Alliance Party and elected ex-Reformer Elwin Hermanson as its leader.

Everyone including the pollsters expected Romanow to win the 1999 election easily. But when the NDP was returned with 29 seats to 25 for the SP and four Liberals, Romanow was forced to form an NDP-Liberal coalition government, including two Liberal ministers and a Liberal Speaker. It was the most geographically polarized electoral outcome in Saskatchewan's history, as urban areas went NDP while rural constituencies voted for the SP.

The coalition worked reasonably well, but its position was always a bit shaky. Farmer protests continued, but Romanow held Ottawa responsible for such problems and did little to try to regain NDP support in rural areas. Tensions with teachers and doctors arose periodically, but more money seemed to solve them. Saskatchewan's unique family of Crown corporations brought in millions of dollars a year in profits, which helped the government to balance the budget, increase spending, and cut taxes simultaneously.

Not enjoying the anxieties of a coalition government, Romanow announced in September 2000 that he had taken the NDP as far as he could. The party chose Lorne Calvert as his successor in January 2001. Calvert announced his intention to reconnect the party with rural communities and had to sign a new coalition agreement with the Liberals. When the dust settled by mid-2001, the NDP had 29 members and the Liberals two, both of whom were in the cabinet, while the SP held 26 seats.

Romanow was appointed to head a national royal commission on health care. In that capacity he was able to draw upon Saskatchewan's own Fyke Commission on Medicare whose report was issued in April 2001. Beyond the hospitals that Romanow had already closed, Fyke recommended closing 50 more. He suggested that the province retain six urban and 14 regional hospitals—fewer, stronger hospitals. Fyke also recommended grouping various health care professionals into integrated teams that shared work and avoided duplication, more telephone health advice lines, and more money for research and education. Premier Calvert welcomed many of the recommendations, but emphatically refused to close any more hospitals.

The main story in Saskatchewan over the 1998-2002 period was the weather, mostly drought: there was virtually no rain in the central grain-growing region of the province during those four years. Where grain did grow, as it did with some moisture in 2003, grasshoppers significantly reduced the amount harvested. Not only was this lack of grain production disastrous for the farmers themselves, but it had severe reverberations for other aspects of the economy. Moreover, Canadian grain farmers do not receive much financial support from government. According to an Organization for Economic Cooperation and Development (OECD) study of agricultural subsidies in 2001, a Canadian farmer receives $31 subsidy per tonne of wheat compared to $108 for American farmers and $130 for those in the European Union. And it is not just grain farmers who suffered: cattle farmers ran out of hay to feed their livestock, with the result that they had to sell much of their herds which had been scientifically developed over generations.

In the 2003 election, Calvert brought the NDP back to a bare majority of 30 seats (45 per cent of the vote) compared to 28 seats (39 per cent of the vote) for the SP. The Liberals attracted 14 per cent of the vote, but no seats. The Calvert government's performance obviously did nothing positive for the NDP in the federal election of 2004, where the party lost all of its seats.

Two of the main issues that faced the premier in 2003-04 were the equalization payments formula and the racism rampant in some of the province's police forces. While Newfoundland and Nova Scotia complain that their offshore petroleum revenues serve to reduce their equalization payments, Saskatchewan actually has a stronger case that the equalization payments formula is unfair. The province loses more than a dollar in equalization payments for every dollar it takes in from energy revenues, as Premier Calvert has made clear in pleading with Ottawa that this should be changed. Perhaps Ottawa did not consider the issue to be urgent because Saskatchewan had just moved from the ranks of the "have-not" to the "have" provinces. This was due to soaring revenues from the petroleum industry as well as from uranium sales.

As for anti-Aboriginal racism among police officers in the province, Saskatchewan appointed a Commission on First Nations and Métis Peoples and Justice Reform in 2001. Its final report confirmed that racism exists in the provincial police system. Several cases came to light of police officers abandoning inebriated Aboriginal men on the outskirts of Saskatoon in deadly cold.

Alberta

The government of Alberta has been securely in PC hands since 1971, although leadership changed from Peter Lougheed to Don Getty in 1985 and to Ralph Klein in 1992. Alberta was largely cushioned from the recession of the early 1990s by the health of the petroleum industry, which is its main source of prosperity at any time. Even so, during the years that he was premier, Getty accumulated a provincial debt of some $15 billion. This was a striking figure for a province that had experienced such prosperity for the preceding 40 years. In the 1990-92 period, the government continued to cut public service jobs, raised medicare premiums, limited transfer payments, and promised to balance the budget without success. Not surprisingly, Getty's government fell low in the polls and opposition to his uninspiring leadership precipitated his resignation in 1992.

The PC party decided on a leadership selection process based on the principle of one member-one vote. Memberships cost $5 and were often bought in blocks and given away by leadership candidates. On the first ballot, Health Minister Nancy Betkowski led Environment Minister Ralph Klein by one vote, but a final frenetic week of campaigning put Klein on top with 60 per cent support. In many similar cases where an unpopular party switched leaders just before an election, the new leader did not manage to save the day, but Klein went on to secure another PC victory in 1993. Adopted under closure in the legislature, the controversial new election map continued to underrepresent Calgary and Edmonton, the main sources of opposition support.

On the economy, Klein delivered an economic strategy paper in early 1993 that promised to balance the budget by 1997 and to do so without raising taxes. The first priority was to reduce the government payroll. Well over 4,000 public service jobs disappeared by means of the amalgamation or elimination of government agencies. Another 1,800 government jobs were eliminated by privatizing 200 liquor stores, as well as motor vehicle and property registration services. The sale of the last block of Alberta Energy Co. shares along with other privatizations would also help the financial situation, and the government brought in 80 new or increased fees. In 1994, all government departments had to cut 20 per cent from their operating budgets, all public servants had to absorb a 5 per cent pay cut (partly in the form of seven unpaid days of leave) and had their salaries frozen for the next two years. *Bill 57* permitted the cabinet to delegate the operation of almost any government program to the private sector by means of a contract, such that it could be provided on a fee-for-service basis without much legislative scrutiny.

As in other provinces, the second main objective was a leaner health delivery system. The government amalgamated 204 hospital boards into 17 regional authorities and gave them the power to decide which hospitals would be closed. It was mainly urban hospitals in Alberta that were affected—two in Calgary and one in Edmonton, with others reduced to the status of community clinics. The number of acute care beds was halved over three years, and many other medical services were reduced or eliminated. Nevertheless, the government raised medicare premiums yet again, and Alberta fought with Ottawa over the funding of private clinics.

A third priority was to reduce the welfare budget by getting social assistance recipients into jobs or training programs or out of the province. In the hope of reducing the welfare caseload by 10,000 people a year for three years, the government introduced a variety of programs involving make-work projects and/or training, as well as drastically cutting welfare allowances and related services. The government's ultimate objective was to provide welfare only for the unemployable, not the unemployed. Fifteen support programs for seniors were either eliminated or reduced, while Klein increased nursing home fees.

In the fourth place, the education sector, the government reduced the number of school boards from 142 to 60 and rendered them virtually impotent. Klein reduced grants to kindergartens by 50 per cent, which normally resulted in user fees being charged. Class sizes increased, as the government cut education budgets by 12 per cent and post-secondary grants by 14 per cent, while raising tuition fees. Cuts in operating grants to municipalities forced them to make up the difference with increased property taxes.

Critics such as Kenneth Taft in his book, *Shredding the Public Interest*, argued that Klein misled the public about the magnitude of the deficit problem and pointed out that Alberta had a revenue problem, not a spending problem.[2] To the extent that it *was* a spending problem, the expenditures had largely gone to corporations, not to social programs. As luck would have it, however, government resource revenues for 1994-95 rose to $800 million more than expected, leaving the budget balanced by 1995—two years early!

Within four years or so, Klein had redefined the role of government in Alberta society. The 1997 election, therefore, was focused on the issue: "what do we do with the *surplus*?" After a lavishly financed campaign, the PCs were re-elected with 63 seats and 51 per cent of the vote, the Liberals gained 18 seats, and the NDP picked up two.

Petroleum revenues have continued to gush into the province's coffers ever since. On the one hand, this allowed the government to increase health care funding, as well as education and social services, and to raise public servants' wages; on the other hand, it was also able to reduce taxes. Indeed, Treasurer Stockwell Day announced that Alberta would de-link its income tax system from that in Ottawa, providing for a "flat tax" of 10 per cent to come into effect in 2001. Day went on to succeed Preston Manning as the national leader of the Canadian Alliance. Alberta held a second unofficial "senatorial election" in 1998, and although two Reformers were "elected," neither expected imminent appointment to the upper chamber by the Liberal Prime Minister.

If governing Alberta has not been difficult in recent years, a number of issues aroused some controversy. Many individuals and municipalities were alarmed at the rampant growth of VLTs across the province, although the government saw these as an excellent source of provincial and municipal revenue. Klein had to reverse himself on at least two issues: his limited compensation to those who had been sterilized by order of a government in an earlier era and his refusal to protect homosexuals under Alberta's *Individual Rights Protection Act*. Before the reversals, however, the premier was very tempted to go his own way by using the notwithstanding clause in the *Charter of Rights and Freedoms*, and he did pass a law prohibiting same-sex couples from "marrying," although he was probably trespassing on federal jurisdiction.

Klein continued to fight with Ottawa over legislation to allow profit-making clinics and hospitals in the province. Several bills on this subject were withdrawn under public pressure, but Klein saw one through in 2000—*Bill 11*, which was enacted despite nightly protest rallies at the legislature. The bill allowed private for-profit clinics to perform minor surgeries previously performed only in hospitals and to keep patients overnight. Federal Health Minister Allan Rock expressed grave reservations, but the federal government did not deem it to violate the *Canada Health Act*, although many other observers believed that it did.

The main issue in the winter of 2001 was the deregulation of the provincial electricity industry. Instead of going down, as promised by neoconservative theorists, prices skyrocketed, the whole operation being carried out rather incompetently. Moreover, it was abnormally cold weather and the price of natural gas (some of which was used to produce the electricity) also rose sharply. Klein responded with provincial rebate cheques for residential, non-residential, and business consumers, the total cost of which was $4 billion. Only Alberta would be able to afford an unexpected expenditure of such a magnitude, and the cheques were particularly important because Klein called an election for March 2001.

By this time, Klein's rival for the PC leadership had crossed the floor (and changed her name), and as Nancy MacBeth had become provincial Liberal leader. It was a relatively smooth campaign for the premier, and he actually increased the PC share of the vote and number of seats. When MacBeth lost her own seat, she resigned as Liberal leader.

Klein's first move after the election was to go to Washington, DC to tell the new George W. Bush administration that he shared its rejection of the Kyoto Accord on greenhouse gas emissions and that Alberta was prepared to sell the US as much petroleum as it wanted. Seemingly oblivious to the environmental damage caused by the province's coal, oil, and natural gas emissions, Klein continued to spar with the federal government in 2002 over whether Canada should ratify the Accord. Alberta estimated that it would cost the economy some $30-40 billion, including the loss of 450,000 jobs, but defenders of Kyoto claimed that those figures were wildly pessimistic. Klein proposed a "made-in-Canada" plan and reminded other premiers that if the Alberta economy suffered, Ottawa would have less money to redistribute to them in equalization payments. Surprisingly enough, many petroleum company executives pledged to work to reduce their emissions even in the absence of a concrete Canadian implementation plan.

On the health care front, the Mazankowski Report recommended more choice, more private involvement, more competition and accountability, less comprehensiveness (de-listing certain services), and requiring patients to pay part of their own medical bills. Although this report supported Alberta's moves in a privatizing direction, it was not as radical as some observers feared. In the 2002 budget, the government promptly raised medicare premiums and tobacco and liquor taxes, eliminated dental and optical subsidies for senior citizens, but cut corporate taxes. Like Quebec, Alberta balked at joining the new Canadian Health Council, a proposal stemming from the Romanow report on the future of medicare, which was designed to provide more accountability in the field of health care spending.

As mentioned above, the drought in the prairie provinces got progressively worse over the 1999-2002 period. Although the lack of moisture also affected grain growers, it was primarily the cattle industry that suffered in Alberta. Farmers could not grow enough hay to begin to feed their herds and began to sell their cattle before they were ready for market. On top of that, a single case of mad cow disease in 2003 prompted the US and Japan to ban imports of Canadian beef. Cattle farming being the leading source of agricultural income in Alberta and Alberta leading the country in cattle production, these actions devastated the industry, until the American ban was rescinded.

As in so many other provinces, car insurance became a leading political issue in Alberta in 2003-04, but with an election on the horizon, the government delayed decisive action. Similarly, while Klein was still inclined to make major changes to the health care system, and even threatened to do so in the midst of the 2004 federal election campaign, he backed down again until he could discern the results of federal-provincial negotiations on the issue. What he did do, with typical fanfare, was to announce at his annual Calgary Stampede Breakfast that the province had accumulated enough money to make itself debt-free.

Combining his massive 1990s neoconservative budgetary cuts and the soaring petroleum revenues flowing into the province's coffers, this unique accomplishment was virtually inescapable. Many areas of public life that had been starved for 15 or 20 years, such as education, health, and municipal infrastructure, might now be given the attention they deserved.

In the 2004 election, Klein's PCs dropped to 47 per cent of the vote and 61 seats, compared to the Liberals' 29 per cent and 17 seats, and the NDP's 10 per cent and four seats. Klein welcomed the Supreme Court of Canada decision on private health care insurance, but not the one on same-sex marriage. Meanwhile, the high price of oil and the dwindling conventional supplies put a premium on the exploitation of the tar sands. In 2005, new projects were announced almost daily, and new pipeline proposals were also made, with China showing considerable interest in both. The expansion of the tar sands in particular and the increase in the province's wealth in general did not come without drawbacks, however: labour shortages, the difficulty of coping with dramatic population growth, and the annoyance of other provinces which lost top-notch professionals to higher remuneration in Alberta. In 2006, Klein resigned after a leadership vote gave him lackluster support, ending his anything-but-lackluster fourteen years in power.

British Columbia

After 15 years of right-wing government under the Social Credit party, the NDP under Mike Harcourt took power in BC in 1991. Touting himself as a peacemaker rather than an ideologue, Harcourt's term as premier was generally seen in a positive light. In particular, he brought all sides together—forestry companies, loggers, environmentalists, and Aboriginal peoples—in a variety of difficult forestry disputes. The most controversial concerned the old growth rain forest in Clayoquot Sound on Vancouver Island, but this was followed up by a general new forestry policy for the province which emphasized reforestation, a ban on massive clear-cuts, and increased Aboriginal participation. Given that forestry is one of the two leading primary industries in BC (along with mining), this was a welcome development. Unfortunately, the US continued to take action against Canadian softwood lumber exports, despite the Canada-US Free Trade Agreement, an action that affected BC more than any other province.

The second area in which Harcourt represented significant progress in BC was in terms of Aboriginal issues. Previous provincial governments had tried to avoid such problems, pretending that they were Ottawa's responsibility, but Harcourt enthusiastically joined in the tripartite negotiations on land claims, creating the BC Treaty Commission to oversee the process.

Harcourt also took many typical NDP-type initiatives, such as focusing on child poverty, making it easier to form a new union in a workplace, and promoting environmental protection. While he had inherited a deficit from the preceding government, the provincial economy remained relatively strong in the early 1990s and the deficit gradually declined.

In spite of his generally favourable performance, Harcourt suddenly resigned in 1996 over the "Bingogate" scandal. This involved an ostensible charitable fund-raising organization whose proceeds found their way into the coffers of the NDP. While the whole affair happened before Harcourt was even leader and did not touch him personally, he "fell upon his sword" as the leader responsible. He was succeeded by Glen Clark, whose style was very different from the moderate, consensus-seeking Harcourt. On the Opposition side of the legislature, the long-time government party, Social Credit, gradually withered away, while the chronically weak Liberal party awaited a more successful fate. Despite doing well in the 1991 election, Liberal leader Gordon Wilson was dumped in favour of Gordon Campbell, the mayor of Vancouver.

Clark led the party into the 1996 election campaign, in which the NDP eked out a majority government, even though the Liberals received a larger share of the popular vote. During that campaign, the NDP promised that it had balanced the budget, but when the final figures emerged some years later, this turned out not to be the case. Although BC was not the only province to experience this problem, a group of disgruntled citizens went to court, accusing Clark of making fraudulent promises about the balanced budget in the 1996 campaign, and the phrase "fudge-it budget" emerged.

Clark was premier for three controversial years. The economy remained dismal throughout this period, especially the crucial forestry industry, making it difficult for the government to *ever* balance the budget. Part of the problem related to the Asian economic crisis, that part of the world being such a large market for BC goods. Clark experimented with tax cuts to stimulate the economy, a timber accord with major forestry companies, and increased funding for health and education, but financial recovery remained elusive.

Various aspects of the salmon industry, another leading BC product, were always on the agenda, and Clark was particularly aggressive in fighting the US on this issue. Finding Ottawa unsupportive, he sometimes took matters into his own hands and applauded a fishermen's blockage of an Alaskan state ferry in Prince Rupert harbour. Ottawa finally signed a salmon-sharing accord with the US in 1999, but it did not please BC.

If he had mixed reviews on that issue, Clark ran into nothing but trouble on the "fast ferry" project, a proposal to introduce three faster moving ferries on the Vancouver to Vancouver Island run. These proved to be way over budget in the construction phase and then repeatedly broke down when finally delivered. On other issues, Clark was seen to move away from the pro-environmental stance of his predecessor, but more positively, from an NDP point of view, he froze tuition fees, expanded same-sex rights, and was in the forefront of taking on the tobacco companies with a major legal suit.

One accomplishment, on which BC opinion was predictably divided, was the Nisga'a Treaty. Clark ensured that this initiative received provincial, federal, and Aboriginal approval before he was driven from office. The Nisga'a Treaty is often called the first modern-day treaty and was particularly important in BC because few of its Aboriginal residents are covered by historic treaties. The Nisga'a First Nation involved gained title to land, cash, and self-government powers, which went beyond those of municipal governments, in return for giving up the right to make future land claims and tax-exempt status. Among other things, the complex document had sections on forestry, mining, wildlife and the environment, public access, the administration of justice, finance, and taxation. The provincial Liberals (unlike the federal Liberals) opposed the treaty with all their might and called for a provincial referendum on the issue.

It was the problem of casinos that ultimately did Clark in. A controversy erupted with respect to the casino licence application of a friend and neighbour, who also did renovations on Clark's home and helped to build a deck at his cottage. Clark was forced to resign in mid-1999 and was later charged with fraud and breach of trust. He was acquitted of the criminal charges when the judge said that he was guilty of nothing more than poor judgement in the circumstances in hiring his neighbour to do the renovations. However, the conflict of interest commissioner found that Clark broke the rules because the discharge of his duties as premier appeared to be compromised by his personal dealings.

Clark was replaced as NDP leader and premier by Ujjal Dosanjh, his attorney general and the first Canadian premier of East Indian descent. Meanwhile, figures showed that the 1999-2000 budget had finally been balanced, while the government passed a balanced budget law to ensure that this would always be the case in the future. Dosanjh also ensured better control over the whole gaming industry, while his most innovative action related to an expansion of subsidized child care in the province. As in other provinces, the health care budget was repeatedly increased. Dosanjh raised the minimum wage to the highest in the country, created new parks and protected areas, and paid out modest electricity bill rebates compared to Alberta's.

Much of the action in BC in 2000-01 was on the Aboriginal front. Some new treaties were signed, based on the Nisga'a model, but not all of the negotiations were fruitful. First Nations were successful in demanding environmental assessments of certain new tourism and mining proposals and won a legal fight with commercial fishermen, but lost a case over the rent charged on land leased to the affluent homeowners in a Vancouver suburb.

Dosanjh was personally popular and tried to repair the damage caused by Clark, but he was unable to raise public support for the NDP as a party and government. He waited until the very last minute to call an election for May 2001. Liberal leader Gordon Campbell unveiled an election platform with over 200 promises that included massive tax cuts, a provincial referendum on the principles of Aboriginal treaties, restructuring labour laws, fixed election dates, and scrapping photo radar. On the other hand, whenever a typical voter thought of the NDP, it was in terms of fast ferries, the "fudge-it budget," and casino scandals. Dosanjh didn't stand a chance, and the Liberals garnered 77 seats with 58 per cent of the vote compared to two seats and 22 per cent for the NDP. Dosanjh was personally defeated but later resurfaced in federal politics as a Paul Martin Liberal.

Gordon Campbell immediately cut personal income taxes by 25 per cent. A mini-budget later cut corporate taxes proportionately, while also reducing the money available for such purposes as environmental protection, children, and welfare. Campbell conscientiously implemented many of the 200 promises mentioned above, such as fixed election dates, and his first real challenge was the threat of a mass resignation of the province's nurses. In what was a sign of things to come, he promptly legislated them back to work, a fate also met by BC's teachers after education was declared an essential service. A year later, a study showed that except for the wealthy, the income tax cuts had almost been wiped out by higher user fees such as increased medicare premiums and day care costs.

At the same time, however, the income tax cuts created a deficit of over $4 billion which then necessitated an increase in the retail sales tax. The February 2002 budget announced that one-third of civil service positions—12,000 jobs—would be cut over three years, reduced the spending of all departments except education and health by 25 per cent, and froze the salaries of those government employees left, ripping up more collective agreements. The government also deregulated all university fees, reduced welfare benefits, and imposed tighter eligibility criteria for social assistance, including a two-year time limit. Even though education was supposedly spared the cutbacks, its annual budget was frozen for three years and the government only picked up half of the salary increase it legislated for teachers. This resulted in school boards reducing programs, closing schools, or laying off teachers.

Another dramatic move was a massive redesign of the health care system. The government closed three rural hospitals; converted others to "assisted living centres" for seniors (with fewer services than in nursing homes); closed hundreds of long-term hospital beds, preferring day treatment and home care; charged user fees for a wide range of formerly free medical services; contracted out all non-medical hospital functions; and in the process laid off thousands of health care workers. Campbell later announced plans to contract out many types of surgeries to for-profit suppliers—privatized doctors in privatized clinics. Ottawa did not lift a finger in support of the *Canada Health Act*.

Not surprisingly, Campbell's labour reforms were also somewhat reminiscent of Mike Harris's Ontario. The new legislation reduced benefits for injured workers under the *Workers Compensation Act*, made it easier for employers to thwart efforts to form a union, and severely curtailed overtime pay by allowing employers to average work time over two, three, or four weeks. In a province wracked by discriminatory offences, the government also fired the head of the BC Human Rights Commission as a first step in abolishing the commission entirely.

As promised, the Campbell government held a referendum on Aboriginal issues. It included eight anti-Aboriginal questions and received an approval rate of 85 per cent and higher. But the reality of the referendum was that only 36 per cent of eligible voters cast their ballots and that many of those opposed to the questions destroyed their ballots instead of voting NO. To some extent, the referendum results flew in the face of Aboriginal rights already recognized by the courts and certainly did nothing to encourage Aboriginal groups to return to the negotiating table. As one Aboriginal spokesperson said: "You cannot take away our rights by referendum simply because you are the majority and you can outvote us."[3]

Campbell was charged with impaired driving on a vacation in Hawaii, but he refused to resign, and the controversy largely evaporated. Not so with his radical neoconservative (or neoliberal) reforms. The first opportunity to vote against the so-called Liberal government was in the 2002 municipal elections. Those elections re-energized the moribund NDP, and anti-government candidates were elected in large numbers, including the new mayor of Vancouver. More happily, the province as a whole rejoiced over being awarded the 2010 Winter Olympic games.

The BC economy remained sluggish in 2004 and 2005 despite the tax cuts and as a result of the continuing softwood lumber dispute with the US, the mad cow crisis, the decline of tourism on account of SARS, horrendous forest fires, and other factors. One bright spot for some observers was the possibility of drilling for offshore oil and gas all along the BC coast. Rumours persisted that a moratorium imposed on such drilling that had been imposed in 1972 would be lifted. Environmentalists and Aboriginal peoples were generally opposed.

Among other recent lively issues were Campbell's privatization of the provincial Crown corporation, BC Rail, and the decision of the BC Court of Appeal to allow same-sex marriages. Then, at the same time as the public service strike in Newfoundland and Labrador, over 40,000 hospital workers went on strike in BC, many of them destined to lose their jobs due to contracting out. The week-long strike was ended with harsh back-to-work legislation which might have fomented a general province-wide protest except for last-minute concessions. Even so, the employees saw their wages rolled back by 10 per cent and their work week extended by 90 minutes, the equivalent of another 4 per cent cut. Over the following two years, the government was not allowed to contract out more than 600 additional jobs. Another blow to the Campbell regime was the police raid on the legislative offices of government aides which led to speculation about a variety of criminal activities. All of these government difficulties and controversial decisions breathed new life into the opposition NDP under its new leader, Carole James.

The year 2005 was kinder to Gordon Campbell. First, the economy picked up due to soaring prices for BC resources and the insatiable demand for them from China. Such demand, together with Chinese exports to Canada, led to a congestion of BC ports and plans to expand them. Second, the fixed election date of May 17 saw Campbell's Liberals returned to power, but against a much reinvigorated NDP. Campbell won 46 seats to James's 33, with a 4 per cent difference in popular vote. The election coincided with a referendum on electoral reform. Although 57 per cent voted in favour of reform, this did not meet the earlier established threshold of 60 per cent.

Conclusion

Each of the ten provinces is delightfully distinctive in many ways, such as in stock and array of natural resources, geography, economy, diversity of ethnic groups, cultures, and languages, mix of basic political values, and political leadership. Yet, in the modern era—since about 1985—the provinces have become increasingly similar in their policies and priorities. While ideology and size of government revenues still count, they have all have been determined to balance their budgets, trim expenditures wherever possible, not raise taxes unless absolutely unavoidable, and generally engineer a smaller provincial state. At the same time, however, provincial governments cannot ignore demands for secure supplies of electricity, affordable car insurance, educational systems that produce graduates capable of global competition, and, most of all, an adequate health care system. Such common problems have in fact required the provinces to move beyond the neoconservative consensus of the previous 20 years: the provinces are taking in more revenues, spending more money to compensate for earlier cutbacks, and not necessarily balancing their budgets on an annual basis.

Notes

1. Alfred M. Monnin, *Report of the Commission of Inquiry into Allegations of Infractions of the Elections Act and the Elections Finances Act during the 1995 Manitoba General Election* (Winnipeg: Government of Manitoba, 1999) 16.
2. Kevin Taft, *Shredding the Public Interest: Ralph Klein and 25 Years of One-Party Government* (Edmonton: University of Alberta Press, 1997) 1-3.
3. Robert Matas and Brent Jang, "B.C. and Natives Square Off," *Globe and Mail*, 4 July 2002, quoting Herb George.

PART II

Democracy, Provincial Style

CHAPTER 3

Many Political Worlds? Provincial Parties and Party Systems

DAVID K. STEWART AND R. KENNETH CARTY

In 1993, Canada's national party system was hit by an electoral earthquake that fundamentally reshaped the country's politics. The changes that flowed helped to usher in what Carty *et al.* have described as the fourth party system.[1] In this new party system, the Liberal Party has been able to dominate its opponents and form governments despite winning little more than 40 per cent of the popular vote in an era of declining turnout. Opposition support has been divided among several parties, each with some regional strength, but none with a realistic chance of winning office. Indeed, the Liberal Party's vote was greater than the sum of its two largest opponents in each of the first three elections of this new era.

This political earthquake, which so shook federal electoral competition, has had virtually no significant impact at the provincial level. That continues a process that has, for some decades, seen federal and provincial party politics in Canada becoming increasingly disentangled. Parties, even with the same name, that contest elections in the political system's two different arenas are no longer necessarily linked organizationally nor are their fortunes obviously intertwined. It is a striking reality that a description of the new federal party system does not apply to a single province. Unlike the national system, the parties that dominated provincial life in 1993 generally continue to do so today. This is especially evident of the Progressive Conservatives. Nationally, the party was reduced to a dismal fifth place in the House of Commons and then merged with the Canadian Alliance. Provincially it prospered, winning more provincial elections (43 per cent) than any other party over the decade and outstripping the federally hegemonic Liberals who managed to win only a third (32 per cent) of the provincial elections in the same period.

This marked absence of a relationship between federal success and provincial success is a long-standing characteristic of Canadian party politics. In the Trudeau Liberal era, provincial Liberal parties were extremely weak, winning only 16 per cent of elections. During the subsequent Progressive Conservative (PC) years, from 1984 through 1992, the provincial Liberals were revitalized, capturing 12 of the 25 provincial elections, to the PCs eight. Apparently, having a federal party of the same name in national office provides little electoral benefit to a provincial party.

In this chapter we examine the various parties that have organized and contested the provincial political systems in Canada in the period following the great national political earthquake of 1993.[2] That allows us to present an analysis of the party systems of the provinces and compare them to the structure of national party competition. We then look at differences in provincial party organization, membership, and methods of leadership selection, one of the most important party activities. We conclude our examination of provincial parties by noting the increasing difficulty of re-election, the drop-off in voter participation, and the increased interest in electoral system reform. The latter, of course, has the potential to transform party politics in the provinces.

Parties in the Provinces

Although the fragmentation of the national party system was significantly increased by the entry of new parties in 1993, the same has not been true at the provincial level. For the most part, the provincial party systems continue to be shaped by parties long familiar to their voters. Rather than providing a province-by-province descriptive tour of several party systems, we explore the comparative success of the major national parties at the provincial level. The Alliance (formerly Reform) Party did not contest provincial elections and, reorganized as a new Conservative Party of Canada, has yet to establish formal links with any provincial Progressive Conservative Party. In Quebec, the Bloc Québécois (BQ) remains a very junior partner to the provincial Parti Québécois (PQ) in the nationalist cause. This leaves us with the three parties that dominated national politics before 1993 and a few remaining provincially distinctive minor parties.

The Liberals

Since 1993, the Liberal Party has easily dominated federal politics, regularly receiving support in each area of the country. Perhaps not surprisingly then, it is the only party to contest provincial elections in every province. Figure 3.1 illustrates the strength of its support in the provinces in the period immediately following the national realignment.

Dominant federally for a decade, Liberals have enjoyed rather more modest success at the provincial level, winning just ten of the 31 elections held since 1993. It is clear that the party does significantly better in the five eastern provinces than it does in the western ones. The great majority of Liberal provincial successes took place in Atlantic Canada, although the party also managed to capture office in Ontario, Quebec, and British Columbia. (In the latter two provinces Liberal parties won the largest vote share but lost the elections of 1998 and 1996 respectively.) The BC story may be somewhat misleading, for the 1990s saw the reconstruction of the long-governing Social Credit Party's electoral coalition under the Liberal banner. Thus the BC Liberal Party is really quite a distinct organization with few connections to Liberal organizations in other provinces or to the national party—if anything, it has more in common with PC parties in Alberta or Ontario.[3]

If the Atlantic region is the area of greatest provincial Liberal presence and strength (it won seven of 13 elections there), it is clear that it is not a competitive force on the prairies (where it won none of the 12 elections). The party did manage to provide a coalition partner for the New Democratic Party in Saskatchewan after 1999, but that proved to be a mixed blessing. The party's caucus was small and soon fell to quarrelling over the arrangement, a conflict that left it divided and weaker than before. Two of the Liberal members who entered the coalition government ended up running in the 2003 election as NDP candidates and were promptly defeated. Indeed, in that election the Liberals received their lowest vote share in 17 years and, for the first time since 1982, elected no one to the Saskatchewan legislature. In neither neighbouring Alberta, where it plays second fiddle to a long dominant PC government, nor Manitoba, where it is a weak third force, has the party been a significant contender for office.

Provincial parties in Quebec divide over the issue of independence for the province with the Liberals representing the federalist, pro-Canadian side of the cleavage. While the provincial party shares this basic orientation with its federal namesake, their organizations are quite distinct. Pursuing an opportunistic strategy, the provincial Liberals chose Jean Charest, a national PC party leader (and former minister) to lead it. He went on to take it to power in the 2003 provincial election.

One important dimension on which the Liberal Party's national dominance is reflected at the provincial level is in its capacity to compete across the country. At the beginning of 2003, the Liberals were the only Canadian party represented in each of the provincial legislatures, and following the eight elections that

Figure 3.1. Provincial Liberal Parties: Mean Vote 1993–2005

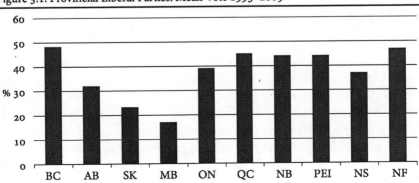

year they retained a legislative presence in every one but Saskatchewan. As 2003 closed, it governed in three provinces (Ontario, BC, and Quebec) and formed the official opposition in four others (New Brunswick, PEI, Newfoundland, and Alberta). In Nova Scotia it holds the balance of power in a divided legislature, and as we noted above, it was recently in government (if as a very junior partner) in Saskatchewan. Only in Manitoba does it play a completely minor role in the parliamentary life of the province.[4]

This unique capacity of the Liberals to compete in every province has come at a cost, for to survive the party has had to adapt itself to the provinces' distinct and different party systems. This means that it stands for quite diverse positions and policies across the country depending upon the local structure of competition it faces. In provinces like Newfoundland or New Brunswick the party is generally seen as at the progressive end of the political spectrum. The opposite is true in BC where the party defines the conservative position by feeding off voters opposed to the NDP. In still other provinces, such as Ontario, Saskatchewan, or Manitoba, the Liberals assume a middle position between parties of both the left and the right. While occupying the centre has proved a winning strategy for the Liberal Party in national politics, more often than not it has been a losing one in the provinces.

The Progressive Conservatives

In the years after the 1993 electoral realignment virtually wiped them off the national electoral map, the PCs were the country's most successful provincial political party, winning more elections than any other party. Figure 3.2 illustrates the pattern of PC provincial strength and reveals that this large number of PC victories came despite the fact that the party had no presence at all in Quebec or BC, and it has now disappeared into the Saskatchewan Party in that province. Those three provinces have long had the most polarized provincial party systems, and for different historical reasons the provincial PC Party was the loser in the polarizations that recast their respective party systems.

In Quebec the PCs disappeared during the 1930s into the Union Nationale, which governed the province for long periods before the provincial system was again transformed by the rise of the PQ in the 1970s. Given that the Conservative label had been blackened in the province by the conscription crisis of the First World War, the party's inability to compete provincially is hardly surprising. In BC, the Conservatives spent the 1940s in a coalition government with the Liberals but then disappeared into an anti-CCF Social Credit party in the early 1950s. When the Social Credit Party dissolved in the early 1990s, the right side of the party system was reorganized under the Liberal label. The PCs lasted longer in Saskatchewan and governed during the 1980s in opposition to the NDP. The party's government ended badly in a scandal that ultimately saw several of its prominent former ministers going to jail.[5] Unable to present the party as a credible alternative to the electorate, the right-wing of the provincial system re-organized itself as the Saskatchewan Party.[6]

Figure 3.2. Provincial Progressive Conservative Parties: Mean Vote 1993–2005

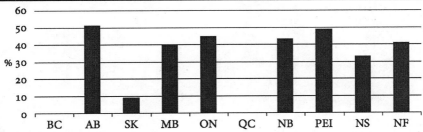

Although they have disappeared in three provinces, the PCs easily dominate in another—Alberta. Since deposing a long-time Social Credit government in 1971, the PCs have won every successive election. In two of the last three elections the PCs won a majority of the vote, capturing more than 60 per cent in 2001. In no other province does the party do so well—in no other province does *any* party do so well. This is despite the fact that since the national party system was overturned in 1993 the national PC Party has been blanked in federal electoral contests in the province. In the three national general elections from 1993 the party managed to elect only one member, and he only once.

In the other six provinces the PC Party has been one of the major competitors for office, generally finding itself in government or as the official opposition after each election. Its opponents differ from province to province: in Manitoba it has faced the NDP, in Ontario and Nova Scotia both Liberals and NDP, and in the rest of Atlantic Canada mainly Liberals. In all cases the party has defined the conservative, right-wing alternative of the local political spectrum, although given the distinctive traditions of each province this has meant that they do not necessarily agree on policy questions. For example, in the last decade the Ontario party has adopted far more right-wing economic policies than would be acceptable to most of the parties in Atlantic Canada, while the New Brunswick party, facing a bilingual electorate, has been more open to constitutional and linguistic issues than have many of its sister parties.

The New Democratic Party

Nationally the NDP, like its predecessor the Cooperative Commonwealth Federation, has never managed to establish a real competitive presence in every province. In part, this reflects its uneven provincial success, for the national party organization has rested on its provincial machines. Figure 3.3 provides a portrait of the party's provincial electoral record in the years following the restructuring of Canadian national politics.

Figure 3.3. Provincial New Democratic Parties: Mean Vote 1993–2005

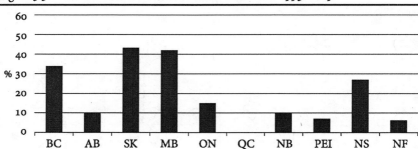

The prairies gave birth to the Canadian socialist movement in the 1930s, and Saskatchewan and Manitoba continue to give the party its greatest support. The NDP currently governs both provinces and has won most of the elections of the past decade over distinctly conservative opponents. The only two other provinces where the party has ever won elections are Ontario and BC, and indeed for a proud moment in the early 1990s the party was able to boast of being the government of over half the Canadian population. However, in both Ontario and BC the experience of governing ended badly. The government in Ontario fell on hard economic times and unprepared, or unable, to make politically acceptable choices was massively defeated. Its vote share fell to just 17 per cent in 1995, and in the two subsequent elections the party did not manage to improve on this weak third place status. Following the 2003 election it did not even have enough elected members to receive official party status in the legislature. Much the same story occurred in BC where an NDP government, re-elected with fewer votes than the Liberals in 1996, was not able to manage the economy successfully. Mired in difficulty and leadership scandal, the party unsuccessfully reorganized behind a hastily chosen new leader—the first person of Indo-Canadian origins to lead a major government in Canada—but saw its vote share plummet to 22 per cent of the electorate producing just two seats in a legislature of 79. The polarized nature of politics in that province could be seen, however, in the NDP recovery in the 2005 election in which they secured 41 per cent of the popular vote. Nonetheless, in both of these large provinces the NDP has experienced a reduction in its role.

The NDP has never won an election in any of the other six provinces and, as Figure 3.3 indicates, is hardly a competitive presence in most of them—the party simply does not exist in Quebec where the federal organization is without even a nominal partner. The one exception to this generalization is in Nova Scotia. Indeed one of the most striking changes in provincial electoral politics in the post-1993 era is the rise of the NDP in that province.[7] For over a century Nova Scotia possessed a traditional two-party system in which only Liberals and Conservatives had a realistic chance at forming the government. Though the

NDP was somewhat stronger in the province than across the rest of the Atlantic region, it was never able to win more than 20 per cent of the provincial vote. Then, in a stunning reversal of fortune in 1998, the party won as many votes as the governing Liberals and came within one seat of matching them in the provincial House of Assembly. The party subsequently slipped when the PCs replaced the Liberals' minority government a year later, but with 30 per cent of the vote it has established itself as major player in a newly fashioned three-party system.

Other provincial parties

The history of Canadian provincial politics has often been coloured by the rise and fall of a series of locally distinctive political movements, some of which transformed themselves into successful governing parties. Over the last half-century there were three important parties that governed for substantial periods. Rather different looking Social Credit parties governed in British Columbia for four decades from 1952 (with a three-year hiatus in the early 1970s) and in Alberta from the Great Depression until 1971. The Union Nationale dominated Quebec's politics from 1944 to 1960, winning again in 1966. The province's party system was then restructured around the independence question in the 1970s, allowing the PQ to form two governments based on four electoral victories. Taken together, these three other parties enjoyed almost as many electoral victories as the NDP.

In the last decade however, "other" parties have been much less successful: only the PQ has won an election. In Quebec, challenges to the polarized character of the party system have given growth to the Action Démocratique (ADQ).[8] This new party provides an option for voters between the stark choice of the separatist PQ and the federalist Liberals, and it does best in the polls when seen in this light. The party has won as much as one-fifth of the popular vote (in 2003), but the first-past-the-post electoral system has given it many fewer seats. New Brunswick's Confederation of Regions Party reversed the ADQ's centrist strategy and sought to exploit their province's linguistic cleavage. For some years after 1991 this proved a successful tactic,[9] but the party then evaporated in the face of internal leadership conflict and a moderation in the tensions over French-English language issues.[10]

BC's politics saw a host of other parties contesting its elections in the aftermath of the collapse of the long dominant Social Credit Party. A local Reform Party (unconnected to the federal party of the same name) emerged on the right, while the Progressive Democratic Alliance broke off from the Liberals. Neither survived the reshaping of the provincial system, and by the turn of the century their supporters had been absorbed into one of the two major parties.[11] The province's politics remain volatile and its party system fragile. That allowed a Green Party to emerge in 2001 with 12 per cent of the provincial vote (but no seats)—the highest vote share ever won by a Green Party in any Canadian election. The party's future is uncertain, but it exists as a major threat to the NDP's monopoly of the left end of the provincial political spectrum, securing almost 10 per cent of the popular vote in the 2005 election.

In 2004 the Alberta Alliance managed to elect a member of the legislature and garnered over 9 per cent of the vote. Founded in 2002 this avowedly "conservative" party, which traces its root to the federal Reform Party, claimed that the Klein PC government had lost touch with "conservative" values. The Alliance attracted almost 15 per cent of the votes in rural Alberta, and, arguably, its split of the right wing vote with the PCs in some ridings in Edmonton and Calgary allowed the Liberal Party to increase its legislative representation substantially.[12] It remains to be seen whether the Alliance Party will remain a part of the Alberta party system, but its "success" again demonstrates the unique nature of Alberta's party system.

Finally, Saskatchewan provides the home for one of the most successful contemporary alternate provincial parties. As we have already noted, the locally discredited PC Party disappeared, only to have most of its former supporters come together with disgruntled Liberals under the banner of the Saskatchewan Party. This new party has made its greatest inroads in rural areas of the province and in the 1999 election actually outpolled the NDP, only to have the electoral system reward the NDP with more seats. The party was led in 1999 and 2003 by a former federal Reform MP and appears to have drawn its strongest ideological inspiration from the former national Reform and Alliance parties.

The Provincial Party Systems

Any account of party politics in the provinces must move beyond an account of the place of individual parties to map the distinctive elements of the individual party systems they constitute. The most striking feature of the ten provincial party systems is the degree to which they, unlike the federal party system, are dominated by two parties. The largest parties typically command almost 48 per cent of the vote, and the two largest parties take about 84 per cent, leaving other parties in distinctly minor positions. By comparison, the largest party in national elections commanded only 40 per cent of the vote, the two largest only 61 per cent of the vote over the same period (Table 3.1). Rae's Index of Fragmentation[13] demonstrates how far less fragmented provincial party politics is compared to those at the national level. Each province has a fragmentation score that is at least .10 lower than the federal score, and the average vote share of the largest party in every province is higher than the comparable federal figure. This is but another indication of how little changed provincial party systems were by the national realignment of 1993 and just how far the dynamics of the two systems have been driven apart.

The two-party character of provincial party systems is enhanced by electoral systems that continue to generate major advantages for the largest parties. In eight provinces, governing parties occupy more than three-fifths of the seats, a share well beyond their popular vote. As a consequence, minority governments rarely occur: after only two of the 31 elections held since 1992 has a government failed to occupy at least half of the legislative seats.[14]

Table 3.1. Party System Measures: 1993–2005

	Vote Share of Largest Party	Vote Share of 2 Largest Parties	Party System Fragmentation[1]
NF	53.0	92.0	.56
NS	40.3	72.3	.65
PEI	53.5	93.5	.54
NB	49.7	87.0	.60
QC	45.0	85.0	.62
ON	45.7	81.0	.64
MB	45.7	82.3	.62
SK	44.0	81.7	.63
AB	51.3	83.5	.61
BC	48.3	82.3	.63
CANADA (federal)	40.2	61.4	.75

1. Rae's Index of Fragmentation

Our general characterization of provincial politics as being structured by two-party dominant party systems provides a sharp contrast to the patterns of national political competition, but it also hides important differences among the provinces. To begin, Alberta stands out as in a class by itself as a genuinely one-party dominant system.[15] It has been that way for most of its history, and its federal politics have often followed suit. The majority of the province's MPs have been on the opposition side of the House of Commons more frequently than those of any other province. It is Canada's really distinct polity!

Rae's Index of Fragmentation provides an important clue to the workings of the other provincial systems. It helps us shake out several distinct variations of the provincial party systems. Three provinces—Newfoundland, PEI, and New Brunswick—all have comparatively lower levels of fragmentation. All these provinces are in the Atlantic region of the country and possess the oldest, most traditional form of Canadian party competition in which Liberals and PCs monopolize electoral debate and alternate in power. New Brunswick has always been threatened by linguistic (and religious) polarization, but the two old parties have generally managed to incorporate the divisions between and within them. In the absence of other divisions, party politics in these provinces is often driven by traditional appeals to leadership, patronage, and the old appeals for change and a call to throw the rascals out.

Two provinces with relatively high levels of fragmentation—Ontario and Nova Scotia—have less stable party systems and come the closest to having genuine multi-party politics of any of the provinces. Ontario has been governed by all three major parties in recent memory; Nova Scotia's new three-way competition has suddenly made its politics (with two minority governments) the most volatile of any in the country. In the absence of a simple choice between two well-defined alternatives, the voters and politicians in both provinces must now struggle with the uncertainties created by the logic of competing sets of political possibilities.

Sitting between these two groups of provinces are the other four, characterized by more intermediate levels of party system fragmentation. Their party systems can best be described as polarized. Like the traditional party systems of the eastern provinces, they offer a clear two-party choice. They differ in that their parties are aligned along a basic line of social or political division that structures much of the province's political life. In Manitoba, Saskatchewan, and BC the division is often articulated in left-right ideological terms, although in the two prairie provinces it tracks equally fundamental regional and rural-urban dimensions. Not surprisingly, given its social democratic orientation, the NDP provides one end of each of these three-party systems. And it is these three more polarized provinces in which the NDP has been strongest (recall Figure 3.3). The other provincial party system that is polarized is Quebec's. There the basic division turns on questions of national identity and orientations to the appropriate political status for Quebec. Despite the efforts of the ADQ, the major parties in that system define themselves in those terms and so do not correspond to those in any of the other provinces.

As we suggested above, the considerable stability of most of the provincial party systems has been reinforced by the workings of the single-member plurality system. However that system carries its own problems, two of which have become more obvious, and so more troubling, over the last decade. The system is well known for the lack of any direct correspondence between vote shares earned and seats won in an election. In its most perverse form this can result in so-called "wrong winners," that is, situations where the party with the most votes does not capture the largest number of seats and so may actually lose the election. This has happened three times in recent years resulting in governments of Quebec (1998), Saskatchewan (1999), and BC (1996) being elected with a smaller vote than their opponents. Inevitably the legitimacy of such governments comes into question.

The second dysfunctional effect of the electoral system is its propensity to greatly over reward the largest party. In the small legislatures of the provinces, this can result in oppositions that simply do not have the human resources to act as effective checks on the government. Several times in recent years the opposition has been so reduced in New Brunswick, PEI, and BC that it has all but disappeared. The result is legislatures that are not able to operate as meaningful parts of a parliamentary system of responsible government. Both these electoral system effects have led to increasing demands for reform of the provincial electoral systems, a question we will return to in our conclusion.

Despite their differences, party competition in all of these provincial systems is simpler than that in national general elections. The federal party system is far more fragmented, riven by crosscutting divisions of region, economy, and identity. This disjuncture is at the heart of the organizational fragmentation of political life across the two levels. It is most apparent in the patterns of party organization and membership.

Party Organization and Membership

All Canadian political parties, at whatever level they operate, have fluctuating memberships organized in constituency associations and primarily concerned with electoral organization and mobilization.[16] The formal structures of the parties vary widely as does the degree to which parties of the same name and orientation are integrated across the federal-provincial divide. The Canadian Alliance, the country's major opposition party in 2003, had no provincial counterparts, and when its members sought to be active in provincial politics, they were forced to do so through some other political party. The reverse is true for members of provincially specific parties such as the ADQ or the Saskatchewan Party. In Quebec, the provincial PQ and the federal BQ have a close working partnership rooted in their commitment to promoting Quebec sovereignty, but there are no formal linkages between these two nationalist parties.

At the other end of the organizational spectrum is the NDP.[17] The provincial and federal wings of that party are tightly integrated, and, indeed, membership at one level carries with it membership at the other as well. The national party organization, and ultimately its political success, rests heavily on the provincial party organizations. It is the real variation in provincial NDP party strength that we observed in Figure 3.3 that lays at the heart of the national party's fortunes over the past decade. Provincial-federal organizational integration has meant that declines in the vitality of the provincial party in the two largest English-speaking provinces (Ontario and BC) has spilled directly into national political competition. The only province in which the party is not formally linked across levels is Quebec, but the NDP is so weak in that province at both levels that this structural dislocation has no significant impact on political competition in either arena.

The Liberal Party has a more complex structure and so varies in its level of cross-level integration. In five provinces—the four in Atlantic Canada and Saskatchewan—those who join their local provincial Liberal Party automatically also become members of the federal party, and vice versa. However, in the five largest provinces, the two Liberal parties are organizationally distinct and membership in one does not carry with it membership in the other. Along with this basic structural difference are huge fluctuations in Liberal membership levels. Some flow from the electoral cycle, with local associations being mobilized in election years,[18] but other differences reflect significant diversity in the individual parties' rules and ethos. For instance, the Liberal Party in New Brunswick claims more than 148,000 members, while in neighbouring Nova Scotia it has only about 26,000.[19] This difference reflects the New Brunswick party's decision to turn its very open memberships into a "life sentence," while in Nova Scotia—as in most provinces—the party requires annual renewals with the payment of a modest membership fee. The relatively meaningless nature of the New Brunswick membership figures were demonstrated in the 2003 federal Liberal leadership election in which the number of participants in its local constituency selection meetings was roughly comparable to those in Nova Scotia.

When still an autonomous party, the PC federal and provincial organizations were formally separated in all the provinces. In practice the degree of real integration of its partisans across levels was not dissimilar to the Liberals. There was a relatively high degree of integration in federal and provincial party activity in the Atlantic region, much less so in the other provinces where there was a provincial organization. In three—Ontario, Manitoba, and Alberta—many supporters, members, and even elected politicians in the provincial PC parties were publicly committed to the federal Alliance Party. It seems likely that this formal organizational separation will remain now that the PCs have been folded in with the Alliance in a new national Conservative Party.

These structural divisions reinforce the distinctiveness of the many political worlds that shape Canadians' electoral politics. They also work to minimize any cooperation between parties of the same name. Sometimes this simply takes the form of politicians scrupulously avoiding comment about politics at the other level, even in their own province. But sometimes it can facilitate political leaders crossing partisan boundaries. The Alliance Party chose a provincial PC cabinet minister as its first leader, and the Quebec Liberal Party is led by a former national PC party leader. In the 1988 national general election, the Liberal Party leader and premier of Quebec quietly supported the federal PCs; in 2000, Alberta's PC premier was an outspoken supporter of the Alliance Party, and in 2004 a former BC NDP premier was elected to the House of Commons as a Liberal. In Canada, such apparent partisan promiscuity is now accepted as an integral part of the realities of federal-provincial party life.

Party leadership selection

One of the most significant powers held by members of Canadian parties is the right to select (and remove) the leader of the party. It is through that prerogative that members have engaged in internal contests to shape party policy and direction. The degree of participation in leadership selection reveals wide variations among provincial parties and provides some indication of the active nature of a party's membership. For several decades, leaders were almost universally chosen in delegate conventions, but provincial parties have pioneered a shift away from leadership conventions to newer, more inclusive processes. The result is that a wide variety of methods are now being used and experimented with.[20] Table 3.2 summarizes the leadership selection processes utilized by provincial parties since 1993. If traditional conventions seem still to be the preferred leadership selection process of the largest single group of provincial parties, that is because no consensus has yet emerged on an alternative. It is immediately obvious that there is no longer any consistency, either within parties of the same name or within individual provinces.

Table 3.2. Provincial Leadership Selection Method by Party[1] (1993–2005)

	Liberal	Conservative	NDP[2]	Other
Traditional Convention	NF QC SK	NF MB	NS ON AB BC	
Modified Convention[3]	NB ON			
All-Member Vote - Single Site	PEI	PEI	NS	
All-Member Vote - Multiple Sites	NS AB	NB ON AB		
All-Member Mail Vote	MB		SK	SK Party
All-Member Tele-Vote	BC NS AB	NS		

1. Some parties appear in more than one category having used more than one method in recent leadership selections.
2. In Manitoba the party has not a chosen a new leader since 1988.
3. Modified conventions generally have delegates bound by constituency preferences on the first ballot.

There is a good deal of variation among provincial Liberal parties. Three of the ten have retained traditional conventions, but others have experimented with a full range of alternatives. In Ontario and New Brunswick the party has opted to combine a convention with a universal membership vote in the local associations, a format also utilized by the federal Liberal Party in 2003. By contrast, other provincial parties have all used some variation of an all-members vote—in PEI, members gathered at one central location, while in Nova Scotia and Alberta they had the option of voting at a polling station closer to home. In Manitoba, party members could mail in their vote while in BC, Nova Scotia, and Alberta Liberals have used electronic technology to cast their leadership ballot by telephone.

All-members votes have been very popular with provincial PC parties and used in five provincial parties (six if we were to count the now vanished Saskatchewan wing). The elections in governing PC parties in Ontario and Alberta have been among the most participatory direct elections in Canada, involving a large number of members: more than 78,000 voted in the 1993 Alberta contest and almost 50,000 in Ontario in 2002. In both cases the total numbers of partisans involved was significantly higher than in the national party's leadership race in 2000.[21] Only in Newfoundland and Manitoba have the provincial PCs resisted this trend and stayed with conventions, although in both the most recent leadership vacancies were filled by acclamation.

The NDP, in part to satisfy the demands of its affiliated labour members, has been slow to abandon using delegated conventions. However, the party has recognized that Canadian party members are now increasingly expecting to have a direct vote for their leader, and in two of their strongest provinces—Nova Scotia and Saskatchewan—has moved to variations on an all-members vote. Building on this provincial experience, the national party has now followed suit, the last federal party to do so.

The Many Worlds of Provincial Party Politics

Perhaps the most striking feature of this review of provincial party politics is just how distinctive and varied it is. The range and presence of the parties, the structure of the respective party systems, the pattern of organizational congruence, and the critical tasks of leadership selection differ from province to province and between federal and provincial politics within the provinces. Canadians live in a system of many (party) political worlds.

These worlds are changing. Over the past half-century, governing parties have won about 75 per cent of all provincial elections, but increasing electoral volatility is making life harder for them. In the elections since 1990, governing parties' electoral success rates slipped to just over 60 per cent. As the re-election rate of governments continued to fall, even seemingly popular one-term governments in Nova Scotia and New Brunswick barely managed to survive in recent elections. The result has been a large number of changes in governing parties since the previous edition of this book in 1995: only in Alberta and Saskatchewan has the same party remained in office for this relatively short period.

Falling voter turnout rates have characterized the national party system over the past decade, and provincial politics has been characterized by much the same trend. In the most recent provincial elections, only PEI reported a provincial turnout in excess of 75 per cent (see Table 3.3) while three provinces (Ontario,

Manitoba, and Alberta) had a turnout below 60 per cent. In all ten provinces the participation rate in the last election was below that of the 1980s: on average the over-all decline is more than 8 percentage points.

Table 3.3. Recent Voter Turnout Compared with Average for 1980s

	BC	AB	SK	MB	ON	QC	NB	PEI	NS	NF
Last Election	58%	45%	70%	54%	57%	70%	65%	83%	64%	72%
1980s Average[1]	77%	57%	83%	71%	64%	79%	82%	84%	72%	79%

1. Data from Lawrence Leduc and Jon H. Pammett, "Elections and Participation: The Meanings of the Turnout Decline," paper presented at the Annual Meeting of the Canadian Political Science Association, Dalhousie University (2003).

This decline in turnout, in conjunction with one-sided legislatures, "wrong winners," and the continued underrepresentation of women in provincial legislatures,[22] has led to an increasing interest in the issue of electoral reform. As this chapter is written, at least half the provinces are actively considering major changes to the single-member plurality system that has been the staple of most provincial politics for decades. In PEI, a one-man commission recommended a system of proportional representation designed to strengthen the hand of opposition parties in the legislature. Islanders themselves however, were less enthusiastic about the prospect of changing their traditional system. In a referendum in November 2005 almost two-thirds of those voting rejected a proposal calling for a mixed-member proportional system.[23] In New Brunswick, a major reform commission is underway with a mandate to recommend a more proportional electoral system. Quebec's new Liberal government, perhaps reflecting on its 1999 loss despite winning the largest share of votes, has appointed a minister for electoral reform, and plans are in hand to introduce a German-style form of a mixed-member proportional electoral system. A newly elected Ontario Liberal government has designated a minister responsible for democratic renewal as part of its pledge to review the electoral system. And in BC, the legislature created a Citizens' Assembly on Electoral Reform. The Assembly, made up of 160 voters drawn at random from the voters list (and excluding active politicians) was charged with reviewing the electoral system. They recommended the province adopt a single transferable vote form of proportional representation, a recommendation that the electorate narrowly failed to approve in a referendum on 17 May 2005.[24] It is difficult to foresee the consequence of all this activity, but it seems possible that before the next edition of this book appears some provinces may have changed their electoral systems. Changes of that sort will almost certainly generate a new set of party systems and a new set of provincial political worlds.

Notes

1. R. Kenneth Carty, William Cross, and Lisa Young, *Rebuilding Canadian Party Politics* (Vancouver: University of British Columbia Press, 2000).
2. For a more historical review of provincial party fortunes, see R.K. Carty and David K Stewart, "Parties and Party Systems" in Christopher Dunn, ed., *Provinces* (Peterborough, ON: Broadview Press, 1996). The data in this chapter report election results from 1993 until 2005.
3. Donald E. Blake, "The Politics of Polarization: Parties and Elections in British Columbia," in R.K. Carty, ed., *Politics, Policy and Government in British Columbia* (Vancouver: University of British Columbia Press, 1996); Donald E. Blake and R.K. Carty, "Partisan Realignment in BC," *BC Studies* 108 (1995-96).
4. In the two most recent elections in Manitoba, the Liberals garnered less than 15 per cent of the popular vote and elected only one or two members to the legislature. With a vote share regularly in this range it becomes essentially a "marginal" party. For a discussion of marginal parties, see Peter McCormick, "Provincial Party Systems, 1945-1993," in A. Brian Tanguay and Alain-G. Gagnon, eds., *Canadian Parties in Transition*, 2nd ed. (Toronto: Nelson, 1996).
5. Gerry Jones, *SaskScandal* (Calgary: Fifth House, 2000).
6. Linda Haverstock, "The Saskatchewan Liberal Party," in Howard Leeson, ed., *Saskatchewan Politics* (Regina: Canadian Plains Research Centre, 2001); Howard Leeson, "Introduction," in Howard Leeson, ed., *Saskatchewan Politics* (Regina: Canadian Plains Research Centre, 2001).
7. David K. Stewart, "Political Realignment in Atlantic Canada?," in Lisa Young and Keith Archer, eds., *Regionalism and Party Politics in Canada* (Toronto: Oxford University Press, 2002).
8. Maurice Pinard, *A Great Realignment of Political Parties in Quebec* (Ottawa: Centre for Research and Information on Canada, 2003).
9. Geoff Martin, "We've Seen It All Before: The Rise and Fall of the COR Party of New Brunswick," *Journal of Canadian Studies* (1998); R. Kenneth Carty and Munroe Eagles, "Party Activity across Electoral Cycles: The New Brunswick Party System, 1979-1994," *Canadian Journal of Political Science* 36:2 (2003).
10. Jacques Poitras, *The Right Fight: Bernard Lord and the Conservative Dilemma* (Fredericton: Goose Lane Editions, 2004).
11. Blake, "The Politics of Polarization."
12. In six ridings in Edmonton and Calgary (and Lethbridge), the combined PC-Alliance vote exceeded that of the Liberal who won the riding. The combined PC-Alliance vote was also greater than that of one of the victorious NDPs.
13. The Index measures the extent to which a party system is fragmented and ranges from a low of 0 (when everyone supports the same party) to a high of 1 (a situation where every voter supports a different party). For details, see Douglas Rae, *The Political Consequences of Electoral Laws* (New Haven, CT: Yale University Press, 1971).
14. Both cases were in Nova Scotia: 1998 and 2003. In the 1999 Saskatchewan election, the NDP won exactly half the seats.
15. David Stewart and Keith Archer, *Quasi-Democracy? Parties and Leadership Selection in Alberta* (Vancouver: University of British Columbia Press, 2000).
16. R. Kenneth Carty, "The Politics of Tecumseh Corners: Canadian Political Parties as Franchise Organizations," *Canadian Journal of Political Science* 35,4 (2002).

17. Rand Dyck, "Relations between Federal and Provincial Parties," in Alain-G. Gagnon and Brian Tanquay, eds., *Canadian Parties in Transition* (Toronto: Nelson Canada, 1996).

18. R.K. Carty, *Canadian Political Parties in the Constituencies* (Toronto: Dundurn Press, 1991).

19. Liberal Party of Canada Web site, <http://www.liberal.ca>, 24 July 2003.

20. John C. Courtney, *Do Conventions Matter?* (Montreal and Kingston: McGill-Queen's University Press, 1995).

21. David K. Stewart and R.K. Carty, "Leadership Politics as Party Building," in William Cross, ed., *Political Parties, Representation and Electoral Democracy in Canada* (Toronto: Oxford University Press, 2002).

22. Linda Trimble and Jane Arscott, *Still Counting: Women and Politics Across Canada* (Peterborough, ON: Broadview Press, 2003).

23. Although no new electoral registration was conducted for the referendum, using the 2003 voter registrations as a base indicates that less than 40 per cent of the electorate participated.

24. Fifty-seven per cent of those who voted in the referendum supported changing the electoral system. However, the support of 60 per cent of those voting was required in order for the changes to be approved.

CHAPTER 4

Electoral Democracy in the Provinces and Territories[1]

DONALD E. BLAKE

Canadians live in two political worlds. They are simultaneously members of the national polity and of the provincial or territorial polity in which they reside. Although part of the same federation, within the limits set out by constitutional provisions such as the parliamentary system and the *Charter of Rights and Freedoms*, provinces are free to vary their constitutions, including their electoral systems, arrangements for redrawing constituency boundaries, and the rules governing election campaigns. Although lacking the constitutional status of provinces, the territories of Yukon, NWT, and Nunavut have considerable authority over electoral procedures as well.

For much of the twentieth century, the provinces figured prominently in litigation alleging provincial infringement of democratic rights such as freedom of speech, freedom of the press, freedom of assembly, and freedom of association. The province of Quebec was particularly notorious in this regard. During the 1950s alone, seven civil liberties cases involving Quebec were considered by the Supreme Court of Canada. In a stinging indictment of Quebecers and their governments before 1960, Pierre Trudeau went so far as to question whether they considered democracy a legitimate form of government.[2]

Although the four western provinces and Ontario extended the right to vote to women before they became eligible in federal elections, other provinces lagged behind, and women were not enfranchised provincially in Quebec until 1940. BC prohibited most Asian Canadians from voting until 1947. As discussed in more detail below, since entrenchment of the *Charter* three provinces and NWT have had their electoral boundaries challenged in court. On the other hand, the first independent boundary commission at any level was established by Manitoba in 1957. The pioneer in elections expenses legislation was Quebec in 1963.

This chapter focuses on electoral procedures and outcomes in the provinces and territories as an indicator of the quality of democracy these jurisdictions exhibit. Elections are the principal mechanism for calling our representatives to account. Richard Katz calls them "the defining institutions of modern democracy."[3] Elections help to determine how power is exercised, by whom, and for what policy objectives.[4] It is also difficult to see how we could do without them. One can envision a future in which technology permits direct and instantaneous voting by citizens on all sorts of issues, bypassing the need for electing representatives in elections. But, for now, and probably for a long time to come, we appear to be stuck with periodic elections, organized by officially recognized parties, who compete for single seats in a system of territorial representation.

We already know that the first-past-the-post system of electing members of the national, provincial, and Yukon legislatures is biased towards the largest party.[5] Governments elected by a majority of citizens are rare, and, occasionally, the party forming the government will have fewer votes (but more seats) than one of its opponents. Some of these distortions can be created or exacerbated by malapportionment, or inequalities in the populations of electoral districts. All jurisdictions have made significant changes to boundary drawing procedures, but as shown below significant differences among them remain.

The role of money in politics is now extensively regulated, in an effort to level the playing field and prevent elections from being "bought." Some critics argue that these changes represent attempts by the established parties to protect their own position and thwart challenges by new parties or pressure groups.[6] Whatever the motivation for their adoption, these changes have not produced a uniform regulatory regime across the provinces and territories.

Even the right to vote and be a candidate, the only individual democratic rights defined in the *Charter*, varies across jurisdictions. Studies of the provinces point to differences in history, wealth, demography, and political culture,[7] all factors that have been associated in the comparative politics literature with the development of democracy.[8] Does the quality of electoral democracy vary across provinces as well?

Table 4.1 offers us some idea of what to expect in this regard. It summarizes four major attempts to classify provinces in ways relevant to the quality of democracy: political development,[9] political culture,[10] economic preconditions for democracy,[11] and institutional development.[12] All four studies imply that electoral democracy is less developed in all or part of Atlantic Canada, an expectation supported by Nelson Wiseman's account of provincial political culture in this volume. However, there is no consensus on which provinces are most developed. Three of the four studies put BC and Ontario in the top group based on an assessment of public opinion, political cleavage patterns, wealth, or institutional development. Four provinces (Saskatchewan, Manitoba, Quebec, and PEI) appear in the top grouping in only one each of the four classifications.

In short, while there is reasonable consensus, based on studies of mass political attitudes and institutions, about the level of political development in Atlantic Canada (low) and in BC and Ontario (high), the placement of the other provinces is more problematic. Perhaps Dyck's ranking is the most persuasive. While based mainly on qualitative assessments, it is relatively recent and incorporates differences on a wide range of indicators, including history, political culture, political institutions, the party system, the electoral system, leadership, and policy.

Table 4.1. Provincial Groupings on Indicators of Development

Political Development (Jenson)	Political Culture (Simeon and Elkins)	Economic Preconditions (Kornberg, et al.)	Institutional Development (Dyck)
Modern	*Citizen Societies*	*Affluent*	*Developed*
SK	BC	BC	ON
BC	ON	AB	QC
PEI	MB	ON	
Transitional	*Intermediate*	*Moderate*	*Intermediate*
AB	SK	SK	BC
NF	ON	MB	AB
MB	QC	QC	SK
QC	NS		MB
ON			
Traditional	*Disaffected*	*Hard-pressed*	*Traditional*
NB	NB	NB	NB
NS	PEI	NS	NS
	NF	PEI	PEI
		NF	NF

The territories, sparsely populated and having more limited experience with representative institutions, have not been subject to the same attempts at classification. In fact, elections and legislatures in NWT and Nunavut are not organized along party lines, and political parties were not introduced into Yukon politics until 1978. The territories also face more significant challenges in implementing the one person-one vote standard than any other jurisdiction in the country. Nevertheless, they are included, where possible, in the comparisons made in this chapter.

The remainder of this chapter explores interjurisdictional differences on four important dimensions of electoral democracy: the fairness of the electoral map, laws governing who can vote and be a candidate, rules governing party and election expenses, and election outcomes. While the provinces and territories are the primary focus, comparisons to rules and regulations at the federal level are made as well. The chapter concludes with an overall assessment of the state of electoral democracy in the provinces and territories and the extent to which regional divisions, especially between Atlantic Canada and the rest of the country, persist.

Equality of Representation

Despite the importance of the equality principle in democratic theory, until entrenchment of the *Charter of Rights and Freedoms* in 1982, equality of the vote was not a major focus of representation concerns. For most of Canada's history, regular readjustment of constituency boundaries (after every decennial census) occurred only at the federal level, dictated by constitutional requirements for balanced representation across the provinces and mandated guarantees to small provinces and provinces with declining populations,[13] rather than concern for strict equality of the vote.[14] Gerrymandering, or the drawing of constituency boundaries to maximize partisan benefit, has been more of an issue, accounting, in part, for the decision in most jurisdictions to establish independent boundary commissions.

A member of the judiciary or a non-partisan official such as the Chief Electoral Officer (CEO) chairs the typical independent commission. Other commission members will have no partisan affiliation, although, in some cases, the government party and the opposition may recommend an equal number of commission members. Since 1982, virtually all commissions have been directed to respect the principle of voter equality, but are permitted to deviate from that principle to respect community of interest, municipal boundaries, minority representation, and related considerations and to ensure that ridings do not become too large in geographical area. A commission generally will hold public hearings to receive suggestions on boundary adjustments and present its recommendations in a report to the legislature. In some cases, the commission may prepare a preliminary report that is the basis for further public hearings before a final report is completed. In all but two jurisdictions (Canada and Quebec), the legislature has the final say on boundaries and may make adjustments before finalizing changes.

Assuming that legislatures do not tamper too much with commission recommendations, these procedures should prevent gerrymandering. However, considerable latitude remains with respect to malapportionment, the problem of unequal electoral district populations. As noted above, the most important court cases involving equality of the vote have been generated at the provincial level. The *Saskatchewan Reference* case[15] and the BC Civil Liberties Association challenge to electoral boundaries in that province, [16] have effectively established the limits to departures from the principle of one person-one vote. While the Supreme Court of Canada has argued that the *Charter* guarantee of the right to vote is a right to "effective representation" rather than strict equality, it has implicitly accepted a maximum 25 per cent deviation as a reasonable standard.[17]

Twenty years have elapsed since the appearance of the first systematic interprovincial comparison of redistribution procedures by R.K. Carty.[18] Since then, the rules governing the timing of redistributions and the makeup of electoral boundary commissions have changed in several respects. As we shall see, the quality of democracy on this dimension has improved considerably.

Redistributions in the 1970s and 1980s analyzed by Carty in PEI, Nova Scotia, New Brunswick, and Ontario were generated *ad hoc*, rather than dictated by a timetable given by statute. Ontario has since committed itself to a fixed schedule for redistribution by tying itself to Canada's *Electoral Boundary Readjustment Act*. The most recent redistribution in New Brunswick was still established at the discretion of the governing party, but it was conducted by the first independent boundary commission used in this province. The first Nova Scotia redistribution triggered automatically by statute (and the second by an independent boundary commission) filed its final report in the fall of 2002.

Yukon is the only one of the three territories where redistribution occurs according to a specific timetable. In NWT and Nunavut, redistributions are authorized by order-in-council at a time chosen by the government of the day.

In all provinces and territories, except Quebec, the legislature continues to have the final say in implementing boundary revision recommendations. In most cases, changes made by the legislature are minor. However, this is not always the case. The most recent (1994) boundary commission in PEI recommended a new electoral map based on 30 electoral districts. However, the legislature subsequently reduced this to 27 electoral districts, producing a significant increase in departures from the one person-one vote standard. Four of the districts created by the legislature had deviations exceeding 25 per cent compared to none in the boundary commission plan. The NWT legislature rejected the recommendation for additional seats for Yellowknife made by its electoral boundary commission in 1998 only to have its action declared invalid by the NWT Supreme Court. The legislature subsequently approved an increase from 14 to 19 seats (two more than originally proposed by the boundary commission) to address the malapportionment issue. On the other hand, the Nunavut legislature added two seats to the 17 recommended by its boundary commission to increase representation for Iqaluit (from two seats to three) and Rankin Inlet (from one seat to two), which otherwise would have had electoral districts 46.6 per cent and 43.0 per cent, respectively, above the electoral quota used by the commission.[19]

Table 4.2[20] summarizes procedures for the provincial, territorial, and federal redistributions for boundary revisions as of 2002. For jurisdictions with fixed timetables, redistributions normally occur every eight to ten years either because the number of years is specified by statute or because eight years would typically cover two election cycles. The 1993 redistribution in New Brunswick was the first in nearly 20 years. The 2002 redistribution in Nova Scotia was the second one by an independent boundary commission.

Again, PEI stands out. Its most recent boundary commission was established after PEI's Supreme Court ruled that the province's *Elections Act* violated the *Charter*.[21] The province was directed to fix an electoral map established in 1962. That map, together with provisions of the *Elections Act*, had established electoral districts where the *minimum* deviation from equality exceeded 30 per cent and the maximum reached 115 per cent.

PEI is the only jurisdiction whose current boundaries were established by a commission containing members of the legislature.[22] In fact, all of the commissioners were MLAs, albeit from both sides of the House of Assembly. Quebec is the only province with a permanent electoral boundary commission, consisting of the CEO and two eligible electors elected for five-year terms by a two-thirds vote of the National Assembly. However, BC, Manitoba, and Yukon also include

Table 4.2. Redistribution Rules

	Year	Timetable	Composition	Deviation
NF	1995	every 10 years	judicial[1]	10% except for 25% in one district and four required districts in Labrador
PEI	1994	ad hoc	bipartisan	no specified limit[2]
NS	2002	every 10 years	independent	25% except in "extra-ordinary circumstances"
NB	1993	ad hoc	independent with judicial involvement	25% except for one district
QC	1992	every second election	independent with CEO	25% except for one district
ON	1997	every 10 years	independent with judicial involvement	25% except in "extra-ordinary circumstances"
MB	1998	every 10 years	independent with CEO and judicial involvement	10% south 25% north
SK	1993	every ten years	independent with judicial involvement	5% except for two districts
AB	1996	every second election	independent with judicial involvement	25% 50% for up to four districts
BC	1999	every second election	independent with CEO and judicial involvement	25% except in "very special circumstances"
YT	2001	every second election	independent with CEO and judicial involvement	no specified limit
NWT	1999	ad hoc	independent with judicial involvement	no specified limit
NU	1997	ad hoc	independent with judicial involvement	no specified limit
Canada	1996	every 10 years	independent with judicial involvement	25% except in "extra-ordinary circumstances"

1. The 1995 Commission consisted of a single judge. However, evidence obtained by the 1994 Commission consisting of a judge and four commissioners, the commission established by statute, was made available to him.
2. The commission decided itself to work with a 15 per cent deviation limit.

their CEO as a member of boundary commissions. These three jurisdictions also include members of the judiciary in redistribution exercises, as do Alberta,[23] New Brunswick, Newfoundland, Ontario, Saskatchewan, NWT, Nunavut, and Canada. The Quebec and Nova Scotia commissions were the only independent commissions without any members from the bench.

Of course, one question to ask about any redistribution exercise is: how fair is the result? That has been perhaps the most important question since the entrenchment of the *Charter* in 1982. On the basis of a review of jurisprudence since then, Kent Roach has already concluded that "'One person, one vote' will not be the constitutional standard for distribution and districting in Canada."[24]

Roach bases his assertion on the comparatively large departures from the one person-one vote standard sanctioned by the courts—25 per cent and more. Australia, a country with similar geography and demography sets a maximum deviation limit of 10 per cent.[25] In the US, deviations are typically much less than 5 per cent.[26]

The 25 per cent limit was first endorsed in litigation respecting provincial electoral boundaries. In deciding the *Dixon Case* (1989), Justice Beverly McLachlin, then of the BC Court of Appeal, ruled that the province's electoral map was unconstitutional on the grounds that so many electoral districts violated an equality of the vote standard. Rather than nullify the results of the most recent election based on those districts, she determined that a standard of 25 per cent within which all districts would fall, as proposed by the Royal Commission on Electoral Boundaries (the Fisher Commission) that was currently examining provincial boundaries[27] and which was then in effect at the national level, would satisfy the constitutional requirement.

However, the *Saskatchewan Reference* (1991) is the only case involving deviation limits to be decided by the Supreme Court of Canada, making it the definitive case on redistribution. In reviewing boundary proposals for Saskatchewan, the Supreme Court let stand legislative limits of plus or minus 25 per cent deviation for the southern part of the province but as high as plus or minus 50 per cent for the north. In doing so, a majority of the court (that now included Justice McLachlin, the judge in *Dixon*), argued that s. 3 of the *Charter*, guaranteeing the right to vote, does not require absolute equality of voting power but rather the right to "effective representation." The court noted that geographical factors, such as population density, difficulty of communication, or community interests, might justify deviations from voter parity. The decision implicitly endorsed the 25 per cent deviation as acceptable in most cases but set no limit on the number of districts that could exceed this standard given the right circumstances.

As Table 4.2 shows, the recent boundary commissions in all jurisdictions except PEI and the territories were given specific limits for deviations from voter parity. The commission in PEI decided, after reviewing the relevant jurisprudence, to work within a 15 per cent deviation limit.

Commissions in six provinces in addition to Saskatchewan (Newfoundland, Nova Scotia, New Brunswick, Quebec, Ontario, and Alberta) were given legislative authority to exceed the 25 per cent limit in specific ways. Newfoundland legislation requires that four districts containing certain specified communities be established in Labrador. Two of them had deviations that exceeded minus 25 per cent. New Brunswick legislation specified that Fundy Isles be a separate electoral district. Accordingly, the 1993 New Brunswick commission "recommended" a district whose population was 64 per cent below the one person-one vote standard. Quebec requires a separate electoral district for Isles-de-la-Madeleine. After the redistribution of 2001, that district had an electorate 76 per cent below voter parity. Alberta allows for up to four districts with deviations as high as 50 per cent. Its boundary commission produced two such constituencies.

BC specifies a 25 per cent limit but allows greater deviations where "very special circumstances exist." A similar provision, "extraordinary circumstances," governs redistributions in Ontario, where the ridings produced by the federal Boundary Commission are also used in provincial elections. Nova Scotia legislation allows exceptions to the 25 per cent limit in "extraordinary circumstances" but specifically defines them as: "the desire to promote the representation of Nova Scotia's Acadian and Black communities." Following this provision the Nova Scotia Boundary Commission recommended four districts whose populations fall below the -25 per cent limit, from -39.5 per cent to -49.6 per cent.

This escape clause was used even more enthusiastically by the BC Electoral Boundaries Commission. Six out of the 79 districts it recommended in 1999 have populations more than 25 per cent below parity, although the smallest is "only" 34.3 percent below. No other jurisdiction in Canada, federal or provincial, has as many districts departing by more than 25 per cent from parity. Only two federal districts proposed in 2002 (one in Newfoundland and one in Quebec) exceed a 25 per cent limit calculated using a within-province electoral quotient. None of the Ontario districts exceeds the limit.

Legislation in the territories appears to be silent on the question of deviation limits. Boundary commission reports in all three territories contain reference to the 25 per cent standard but acknowledge the difficulty of achieving it given demographic and geographical circumstances. The 1997 Nunavut Boundaries Commission report recommended six (out of 17) districts with deviations greater that 25 per cent, three on the plus side and three on the minus side (ranging from -35 percent to +47 percent). As noted above, underrepresentation of Iqaluit and communities on Rankin Inlet was substantially reduced by the legislature when it acted on the commission report. The NWT Boundary Commission Report (1999) came up with only four districts (out of 16) within plus or minus 25 per cent of an equal population standard. The range went from -66 per cent to +46 per cent. However, equality was diluted even further when the territorial legislature rejected additional seats for the Yellowknife area, a move subsequently challenged, successfully, in court.

The 2001 Yukon Boundary Commission came up with four of 18 districts outside the 25 per cent guideline. However, only one of them (Vuntut Gwitchin at -81 per cent) was on the low side. The range for the three underrepresented areas went from +25.5 per cent to +38.1 per cent.

Federal redistributions are governed by rules that require boundary commissions to aim for a maximum deviation of 25 per cent using a quotient obtained by dividing the provincial population by the number of seats to which the province is entitled. If electoral district populations are compared across provinces, the federal jurisdiction does not look so egalitarian. If one divides the combined population of the provinces by the total number of seats they have been allocated to obtain a "national quotient," the August 2002 redistribution proposals produced 28 districts with deviations greater than 25 per cent ranging from minus 71.6 per cent (Labrador with a population of 27,864) to plus 25.4 per cent (Scarborough Centre at 123,089). However, federal redistributions are governed by an initial allocation of seats between provinces that is governed by the Constitution. As noted by Roach,[28] the rules that no province can have fewer MPs than senators and that no province can lose seats as the result of redistribution have constitutional status, making them immune to *Charter* challenge. Moreover, it would require unanimous consent of the provincial legislatures and federal Parliament to change them.

Table 4.3 provides information on several different ways of measuring equality of the vote.[29] The second column shows that provincial and territorial boundaries commissions have produced maps with considerable range of deviations from an equal population standard. The large deviations in the territories can be expected, given the vast distances between scattered communities and, in the case of Yukon, a concern to guarantee representation for the Vuntut Gwitchin First Nation. Among the provinces, Nova Scotia stands out with an average deviation of 14.2 per cent. The average district in Saskatchewan, which has the strictest limits on deviations outside the north, differs by only 1.8 per cent from perfect equality, even with northern districts included in the calculation.

The theoretical minimum percentage of the population required to elect a majority of the legislature is relatively small in the territories, but also in some provinces. It ranges from 44.2 per cent in Quebec to 51.0 per cent in Saskatchewan.

Another measure of equality, the ratio of the largest district to the smallest in each province—the "voting power ratio" in the table—also varies substantially across jurisdictions, with highs of 7.3 in Yukon, 5.3 and 4.4 in Quebec and Newfoundland, respectively, and a low of 1.3 in both PEI and Manitoba. However, by this measure, inequality has also declined in every province. The most dramatic decline occurred in BC, from 14.9 in the 1980s to 1.8 after the 1999 redistribution.

The gini index[30] is one of the most commonly used measures of inequality because its calculation is based on all district populations, not just a few extreme

Table 4.3: Equality of the Vote[1]

	Most Recent Redistribution	Average Absolute Deviation[2]	Minimum for Majority[3]	1980s Voting Power Ratio	Current Voting Power Ratio[4]	1980s Provincial/ Territorial Gini Index	Current Provincial/ Territorial Gini Index[5]	Rank on Provincial/ Territorial Gini Index	1980s Federal Gini Index	2002 Federal Gini Index[6]
NF	1993	6.8	49.0	8.7	4.4	0.131	0.051	5	0.074	0.163
PEI	1994	8.4	49.2	5.6	1.3	0.295	0.054	6	0.010	0.024
NS	2002	14.2	45.4	2.7	2.4	0.155	0.096	10	0.085	0.045
NB	1993	10.6	45.7	4.1	3.4	0.195	0.040	3	0.114	0.037
QC	2001	12.7	44.2	5.1	5.3	0.075	0.088	9	0.097	0.019
ON	2002	6.4	48.7	5.1	1.5	0.150	0.046	4	0.114	0.046
MB	1998	3.2	49.3	2.8	1.3	0.093	0.023	2	0.111	0.016
SK	1993	1.8	51.0	2.3	1.6	0.077	0.013	1	0.100	0.025
AB	1996	9.1	46.2	5.2	2.1	0.219	0.062	7	0.077	0.042
BC	1999	10.3	45.8	14.9	1.8	0.201	0.071	8	0.105	0.054
YT	2001	19.9	45.7	7.0	7.3	0.131	0.151	12	n/a	n/a
NWT[7]	1999	31.1	41.0	n/a	4.3	n/a	0.218	13	n/a	n/a
NU[7]	1997	20.6	42.8	n/a	2.3	n/a	0.148	11	n/a	n/a
Canada[8]	2002	12.3	44.4	5.2	3.8				0.121	0.084

1. Figures for previous voting power ratio and 1980s federal and 1980s provincial Gini indexes are from R.K Carty, "The Electoral Boundary Revolution in Canada," American Review of Canadian Studies, XV (1985): 284. His figures are based on the most recent election through June 1984. The comparison may be affected by the fact that Carty's figures are based on election results, not redistribution reports. All other calculations were made by the author using data from the most recent redistribution in each jurisdiction. The figure in the "1980s Gini Index" column for Yukon were calculated by the author using data in the 1991 Electoral District Boundaries Commission Report.

2. Average deviation (positive or negative) of electoral district populations from the provincial quotient.

3. Percentage of the population contained within the smallest 50 per cent plus 1 electoral districts.

4. Ratio of largest to smallest electoral district.

5. Gini index of inequality ranges from 0 (complete inequality) to 1 (complete equality).

6. The federal Gini index measures inequality across federal electoral districts within the province. The figure in the Canada row measures inequality across all federal electoral districts in the country excluding the territories.

7. The results in these rows are based on the first boundary commissions report prepared after the NWT was divided into Northwest Territories and Nunavut, hence, no over time comparisons are possible. With only one federal constituency per territory, no federal Gini index can be calculated.

8. The figures in this row compare all federal electoral districts, excluding the territories, using data from the 2002 preliminary recommendations of the federal boundary commissions.

cases. It also has intuitively appealing mathematical limits. A jurisdiction in which electoral districts had equal populations would score 0, indicating perfect equality. As populations diverge, the index approaches 1, indicating complete inequality. All provinces have scores toward the low (equal) end, but there is still substantial interprovincial variation. Nova Scotia and Saskatchewan bracket the distribution across provinces with scores of 0.096 (comparatively unequal) and 0.013 (comparatively equal), respectively. Inequality in the territories is more marked than in the provinces and is comparable to 1980s levels in several provinces.

Still, voter equality in all provinces except Quebec is substantially greater than it was before the Supreme Court's ruling in the *Saskatchewan Reference*. This conclusion is evident by comparing the gini coefficient of inequality after the most recent redistribution in each province to the coefficient in the early 1980s. The largest changes are found in Alberta, BC, New Brunswick, and PEI where the coefficient dropped from approximately 0.20 or more to less than 0.10. The coefficients for Quebec for the two periods are quite similar, but the current map is slightly more inegalitarian than the one it replaced. The gini coefficient for federal districts based on a national population quota also declined, from 0.121 to 0.084 across the ten provinces.

Moreover, with the exception of Newfoundland, compared to the early 1980s the gap between gini indexes for provincial and federal districts within the same province is also somewhat less. In the 1980s, federal districts in Newfoundland were substantially more egalitarian than provincial ones. The situation has now reversed. Populations of provincial electoral districts are now more equal than those in federal districts. This suggests that, on the whole, provincial commissions are being stricter than their federal counterparts.

However, regression can also occur. The current Quebec map has a gini index of 0.088, more unequal than in the 1980s (0.075) and more unequal than the 1992 map (0.082). While Nova Scotia has made huge strides towards greater equality, the final map proposed by the 2002 Nova Scotia boundaries commission is also more unequal (gini index = 0.096) than that produced by the previous boundary commission (gini = 0.089).

As far as the provinces are concerned, there is no obvious cultural, economic, or institutionalization pattern to interprovincial differences. Using the gini index rank as the criterion, two western provinces, Manitoba and Saskatchewan, have the most egalitarian electoral maps; however, Alberta, despite comparable topography, is in the most inegalitarian half of provinces. BC, Ontario, and Quebec are the largest provinces with significant populations in remote or sparsely populated areas, but Ontario is relatively egalitarian compared to the other two. The Atlantic province of Nova Scotia is the most inegalitarian in the country, but New Brunswick is among the most egalitarian. PEI, the last jurisdiction to involve incumbent politicians in redistribution, is more egalitarian than Quebec, the province with the most bureaucratized boundary revision procedure.

In the early 1980s the principal differences were between those provinces whose redistributions had been triggered by statutory provisions (Newfoundland, Quebec, Manitoba, Saskatchewan, and Alberta) and those without such legislative provisions. All five had substantially more egalitarian electoral maps than PEI, New Brunswick, Nova Scotia, Ontario, and BC. With the exception of Alberta, they also had become more egalitarian over time.[31] In the 1990s, redistributions in two of those provinces (PEI and New Brunswick) continued to be governed by *ad hoc* procedures, but neither province's map was noticeably more inegalitarian than that in provinces with statutory timetables.

The Right to Vote and Be a Candidate

S. 3 of the *Charter* states that "every citizen of Canada has the right to vote in an election of members of the House of Commons or of a legislative assembly and to be qualified for membership therein." However, like all *Charter* provisions, this one is subject to s.1: "reasonable limits prescribed by law as can be demonstrably justified in a free and democratic society." Arguably, the right to vote is the most important democratic right; however, as Richard Katz points out, "no country allows all adults to vote."[32]

In his cross-national analysis, Katz identifies three categories of qualifications for voting: community membership, competence, and autonomy.[33] The first category covers citizenship and residence requirements. The second typically includes age and mental health, although in the past "competence" requirements have been used to exclude certain racial groups and women. The autonomy requirement is mainly of historical interest and includes financial independence (used to justify restriction of the right to vote to property owners) and other markers of dependency. In Canada it might be expanded to include restrictions on the right to vote of election officials and judges on the grounds that those with legal responsibility for ensuring fairness should themselves have no part in elections. Most jurisdictions in Canada exclude at least two other groups, those incarcerated for criminal offences and those convicted of corrupt or illegal electoral practices. In a sense, these groups have been excluded from the political community, at least temporarily.

All jurisdictions have established 18 as the minimum age for voting and, except for Nova Scotia and Saskatchewan, restrict the franchise to Canadian citizens. Nova Scotia enfranchises British subjects, and Saskatchewan allows British subjects to vote if they were eligible on 23 June 1971. Table 4.4 summarizes the other qualifications (and disqualifications) for voting in the provincial and national elections.

Canada and all the provinces except Newfoundland and Ontario establish a six-month residency requirement. In fact, Newfoundland stipulates that to be eligible a citizen must be resident in Newfoundland only on the day before

Table 4.4. Qualifications for Voting

Jurisdiction	Minimum Residency	Disqualified from Voting					Absentee Provisions
		CEO	Returning Officer	Inmates	Conviction for Election Offences	Other	
NF	no minimum, district resident						proxy voting unrestricted
PEI	6 months, district resident	yes	yes				mail ballot unrestricted
NS	6 months, district resident	yes	yes	yes		federal judges, legally restricted mentally ill or physically infirm	proxy voting, some restrictions
NB	6 months, district resident	yes	yes, except to break a tie	yes	five-year disqualification	legally restricted mentally ill or physically infirm	mail ballot, some restrictions
QC	6 months				five-year disqualification		mail ballot, some restrictions
ON	no minimum, district resident						proxy voting unrestricted
MB	6 months	yes	yes, except to break a tie	yes, if sentence five years or more[1]			mail ballot unrestricted
SK	6 months, district resident	yes	yes, except to break a tie	yes	five-year disqualification	Assistant CEO	mail ballot, some restrictions
AB	6 months, district resident		yes, except to break a tie	yes[2]	eight-year disqualification		mail ballot unrestricted
BC	6 months, registered in district	yes		yes, if sentence two years or more	seven-year disqualification	Deputy CEO	mail ballot unrestricted
YT	12 months	yes		yes		Assistant CEO	proxy voting unrestricted; mail ballot, some restrictions
NWT	12 months	yes	yes	yes, if sentence two years or more	seven-year disqualification		proxy voting, some restrictions; mail ballot unrestricted
NU	12 months	yes	yes	yes, if sentence two years or more	seven-year disqualification		proxy voting, some restrictions; mail ballot unrestricted
Canada	no minimum, district resident	yes		yes, if sentence two years or more	five- to seven-year disqualification	Assistant CEO	mail ballot, minimal restrictions

1. Restriction ruled illegal of Manitoba Court of Queen's Bench, 1999.
2. Except for inmates sentenced for ten days or less or for non-payment of fines.

polling day. The territories have strictest residency requirements—12 months. All jurisdictions require that citizens be registered in order to vote, but all but Ontario,[34] Quebec, and Yukon make it relatively simple to register on the day of the election itself. All jurisdictions permit some form of absentee voting, but in three provinces (Newfoundland, Nova Scotia, and Ontario) this must be done by proxy (i.e., by a delegate), making it impossible for an absentee voter to ensure that her or his true preference has been registered.

Given *Charter* provisions, we would expect to find few exclusions from the franchise. Two Atlantic provinces, New Brunswick and Nova Scotia, are the most restrictive, disenfranchising key election officials; all inmates, no matter how insignificant their offences might be; and those legally deprived of liberty or the right to manage their own property by reason of mental or physical infirmity. Nova Scotia is the only jurisdiction in the country that continues to disenfranchise federal judges, a restriction eliminated at the federal level in 1993. On the other hand, Newfoundland has no exclusions, and PEI has fewer restrictions than any other jurisdiction except Quebec.[35] Two of the three territories (NWT and Nunavut), Alberta, BC, New Brunswick, Quebec, Saskatchewan, and Canada treat election offences as grounds for denial of the franchise, for up to eight years in the case of Alberta. While most jurisdictions specifically prohibit inmates from voting, in October 2002 the Supreme Court of Canada struck down the provision of the Canada *Elections Act* depriving inmates of the right to vote. This presumably means that similar restrictions in other jurisdictions are unconstitutional as well.

Again, there is no obvious pattern to differences among provinces in qualifications for voting. In numerical terms, the most restrictive jurisdiction in so far as voting is concerned is probably Nova Scotia, which disenfranchises CEOs and returning officers, federal judges, and all inmates, as well as those legally restricted by reason of mental or physical disability. Next is New Brunswick whose exclusions from the franchise are nearly identical except for federal judges. New Brunswick but not Nova Scotia disqualifies those convicted of election offences. However, one presumes (hopes) that there are more federal judges than there are people convicted of corrupt or illegal electoral practices in Nova Scotia.

The least restrictive is Newfoundland, which enfranchises all citizens and has no real residency requirement.[36] Ontario is next. That province disqualifies no one who meets basic citizenship and residency requirements. Ontario is followed closely by Quebec and PEI. Quebec disqualifies only for election offences, although these include failure to comply with financial reporting requirements by candidates or official agents. PEI does not penalize election offenders, but it does disenfranchise its CEO and returning officers, a total of 28 people.

Of the remaining four provinces (Alberta, BC, Manitoba, and Saskatchewan), Manitoba appears to be the least restrictive. Its disqualifications are similar to those in BC, but Manitoba is more forgiving of convicted felons, allowing those serving sentences of less than five years to vote compared to less than two years in BC. Moreover, the Manitoba restriction on inmates was ruled unconstitutional by its courts in 1999. Alberta and Saskatchewan are more restrictive—no inmates are allowed to vote in provincial elections, but otherwise they are basically tied. Assuming no real difference in the frequency of convictions for election offences, Saskatchewan disenfranchises only two more people than Alberta, the CEO and Assistant CEO.

The provinces fall roughly into three groups from the perspective of qualifications for voting. Newfoundland and Ontario, polar opposites on most indicators of development, tie for most democratic. The other three Atlantic provinces are found at both ends of the spectrum—Nova Scotia and New Brunswick at the low end and PEI on the more democratic side. The other provinces fall between these two groups. If ranked together with the provinces, Canada would appear toward the less democratic end. Canada has low residency requirements, but, as of the 2000 election, more exclusions from voting than six out of ten provinces.

The territories are even more restrictive. Nunavut and NWT have restrictions similar to those for Canada, but much more stringent residency requirements (12 months). Yukon, except for having no explicit disqualification for election offences, resembles the other territories in most other respects.

As noted above, the *Charter* guarantees to Canadian citizens the right to "to be qualified for membership" in the House of Commons or a legislative assembly. However, Canada, the provinces, and territories, like most countries, regulate candidacy as well. According to Katz,

> [r]egulation of candidacy is forced by the conflict of democratic ideals and reality. The ideal is free and unfettered competition among all comers ... [but] without some way of identifying candidates, the vote might be meaninglessly fragmented. Unfettered competition, far from being fair, may perpetuate (and magnify) the advantages (like private wealth) that some candidates enjoy, to say nothing of the possibilities of deceit and intimidation.[37]

There are at least two ways to determine eligibility to run for office. All provincial and territorial elections acts outline the necessary qualifications and procedures. However, some jurisdictions also specify separately, in legislative assembly acts or the equivalent, who may sit in the legislature. In some cases these restrictions are more extensive. Typically these exclude individuals such as civil servants or government contractors who present potential conflict of interest problems. Direct restrictions on candidacy specified in elections acts as well as indirect ones contained in legislative assembly acts are both considered in this section.

Qualifications for candidacy generally parallel those for voting. In fact, several elections acts simply state that eligibility to vote is the basic requirement for being nominated aside from fulfillment of procedural requirements.[38] Interjurisdictional differences in eligibility are summarized in Table 4.5.

All jurisdictions require the signatures of eligible voters to secure a nomination, although the range in the number required is considerable, from five in Nova Scotia to 100 in Quebec and for national elections. Deposit requirements are relatively low, from nothing (in Manitoba and Quebec) to $100 or $200 almost everywhere else except for Canada, which demands $1,000. In keeping with the increased regulation of election expenses and public funding of political parties, discussed in the next section, all but Ontario require some official endorsement by a registered political party. Even in Ontario, party approval of nominations is implied by the requirement that candidates register with the CEO under the *Election Finances Act*. Since deposit requirements are relatively low or non-existent, except for national nominations, the fact that substantial support is required (at least 10 per cent of the vote) before the deposit is returnable cannot be considered much of a barrier to candidacy. Even for national nominations, where the deposit is higher, half the deposit is returned upon receipt of the required election expense statement, making the effective deposit only $500.

All jurisdictions except Yukon, New Brunswick, and PEI specifically forbid those convicted of corrupt or illegal electoral practices from standing for office or sitting in the legislature. However, the restriction is implied in New Brunswick because eligibility to vote is a requirement for candidacy and those convicted of election offences are not eligible to vote. By extension, certain election officials who are disenfranchised in most jurisdictions would also not be allowed to stand as candidates even if not explicitly disqualified in candidacy requirements. Ontario, one of the few jurisdictions that allow all election officials to vote, still prohibits some from standing as candidates.

Nova Scotia and Ontario prohibit most provincial *and* federal employees from sitting in the legislature. Canada, Newfoundland, Manitoba, NWT, and Nunavut restrict only their own employees, although they provide for leave of absence for those wishing to contest elections. Relatively few provinces specifically exclude MPs, but, since the *Parliament of Canada Act* prohibits members of any provincial or territorial assembly from sitting in Parliament, the restriction is redundant. Moreover, since all provinces require members of their assemblies to be residents of their province, no one would be eligible to sit in more than one provincial assembly.

Exclusion of government employees from legislatures and Parliament is often justified on conflict of interest grounds. Similar reasoning applies to government contractors or suppliers, but only Newfoundland and Canada explicitly exclude them in their elections act or acts covering legislative membership. Another category of government employee, judges, is specifically excluded in BC, New Brunswick, Quebec, Saskatchewan, and Canada.

Table 4.5. Qualifications for Candidacy

	Nomination	Deposit	Return of Deposit	Disqualified from Candidacy or Legislature			
				Government Employees	Election Officials	Conviction for Election Offences	Other
NF	10 signatures, party endorsement	$100	15% of vote	except if employed when House is not sitting or member of armed forces			government contractors
PEI	10 signatures, endorsement by party	$200	half the votes of winner				
NS	five signatures, signature of party leader	$100	15% of vote	federal or provincial employee		five-year disqualification	MPs or candidate for Parliament
NB	25 signatures, signature of party leader	$100	half the votes of winner				mayor, councillor, judges, MP, or senator
QC	100 signatures, signature of party leader	none	N/A			yes, duration of disqualification not specified in Act	MPs, judges, official agent of party, or candidate
ON	25 signatures	$200	10% of vote	federal or provincial except members of armed forces and certain public officials	returning officer, election clerk, enumerator, revision assistant		
MB	100 signatures, party endorsement	none	N/A	except if granted leave of absence	election officer, revising officer, or enumerator	convicted of provincial or federal offense	
SK	four signatures, endorsement by party	$100	at least half the votes of winner			up to five years	federal or provincial judges
AB	25 signatures, party endorsement	$200	half the votes of winner			five- to eight-year disqualification	MP or senator
BC	25 signatures, party endorsement	$100	15% of vote			seven-year disqualification	MP, federal judge
YT	25 signatures	$200	at least 25% of votes of winner	territorial or federal with some exceptions	yes		inmates
NWT	25 signatures	$200	at least 50% of votes of winner	any paid holder of office, commission or employment	yes	five- to seven-year disqualification	inmates
NU	15 signatures	$200	at least 50% of votes of winner	any paid holder of office, commission or employment	yes	five- to seven-year disqualification	inmates
Canada	100 signatures (50 in large, sparsely populated districts), signature of party leader	$1000	50% of deposit for 15% of vote, 50% for election expense statement	yes (except members of armed forces or reserves on active duty because of war)	yes	five- to seven-year disqualification	federal judges (except citizenship judges), members of provincial or territorial legislatures, government contractors, inmates, other public officials

A comparison similar to that used for voter qualifications is more difficult in the case of candidates. Differences in formal nomination requirements, number of signatures and amount of deposit, are trivial. On the other hand, restrictions on candidacy by government employees, potentially the numerically largest group, are hard to assess because of the number of statutes that would have to be consulted in order to ensure completeness and because of difficulties in determining the number of government employees prohibited from sitting in provincial legislatures where the exclusion is specified as well as the ease with which they may obtain leave. Nova Scotia, for example, the most restrictive of the right to vote, requires federal and provincial government employees to request a leave of absence before nomination. Manitoba, on the other hand, allows a 90-day leave of absence (longer than an election campaign) and provides that every application for leave "shall be granted."

That said, the provinces and territories appear to fall roughly into three groups if we use exclusions listed only in elections acts and legislative assembly acts. The least restrictive are Alberta, BC, PEI, Quebec, and Saskatchewan. Manitoba, New Brunswick, and Newfoundland are slightly more restrictive. The most restrictive, then, are Nova Scotia, Ontario, and the territories. Three of the four western provinces rank on the more democratic end on this measure, but so do two of the four Atlantic provinces. The two most "institutionally developed" provinces according to Dyck's scheme (Quebec and Ontario) appear at opposite ends. If we were to apply the same rules governing candidacy at national level, Canada would appear in the most restrictive group with higher deposit requirements and extensive disqualifications, including government employees, all election officials, and most federal judges.

Party and Election Finance

Regulation of party and election finance in Canada began in 1963 with passage by the Quebec National Assembly of legislation governing candidate and party election spending. This was followed by the national *Election Expenses Act* (1974) and Ontario's *Election Finances Act* (1975). By 1990, all provinces except Alberta, BC, and Newfoundland had passed legislation establishing spending limits.[39] All provinces and territories now have regulations covering one or more of the following topics: the amount and sources of campaign funds, spending, and third party advertising. However, BC, Newfoundland, and Yukon still have no spending limits.

The arguments for regulation essentially rely on notions of equity and fairness. While competition is integral to electoral democracy, some measures may be necessary to protect voters from undue pressure and fraud. More recently, arguments have expanded to include a justification for public subsidies to parties and candidates. As summarized by Katz,[40] these include the need to ensure that reasonable resources are available to all serious candidates, desirability of wide dissemination of information and competing ideas, relief from dependence on major contributors, and the desirability of freeing politicians from dependence on members of their own parties. In Canada and most provinces, a *quid pro quo* has resulted. Parties have agreed to submit to regulation in return for campaign subsidies or other benefits.

These regulations are not immune to criticism. By accident or design, they may restrict competition from new parties or non-party groups.[41] Rules that allow only individuals to contribute to candidates or parties may disadvantage parties such as the NDP that depend heavily on contributions from trade unions or parties that rely on corporate donations. Spending restrictions can benefit incumbents over challengers who may have to spend more to compensate for an incumbent's advantage of name recognition and record of constituency service.[42] Incumbency effects in Canada are weaker than in the US,[43] making restrictions on candidate spending less of an issue. However, restrictions on spending by parties or formulae that base campaign subsidies on electoral strength may give an advantage to larger, established parties over weaker or insurgent parties. Finally, restrictions on spending and advertising by non-party groups raise serious free speech issues. As discussed below, such restrictions have been declared unconstitutional by the courts in challenges to federal spending laws and to legislation in BC.

Table 4.6 summarizes the essential features of provincial and territorial regulation as well as legislation at the national level for comparative purposes. Four provinces (Newfoundland, PEI, Nova Scotia, and BC) and Yukon have absolutely no rules governing the size or source of contributions. Saskatchewan and Canada are only slightly more restrictive. They have no limits on contributions but prohibit donations from non-residents.

Detailed reporting requirements (not covered in the table) vary. Some jurisdictions require formal disclosure by candidates and parties to a public official such as the CEO. Others require the information to be included in annual reports by parties. However, all require reports of some sort, including the name of the donor. In Nova Scotia, this applies to all donations over $50, whereas in Alberta names are required only for donations over $375. The other jurisdictions fall in between.

Of the provinces limiting donations, Alberta and New Brunswick are the most permissive followed by Ontario. Quebec is strictest with maximum donations of $3,000 to parties and candidates.

As far as the source of donations is concerned, Quebec and Manitoba are clearly the strictest, permitting donations from voters only. The remaining provinces that restrict the size of donations also claim to restrict sources. However, it is difficult to determine who would *not* be eligible to donate in Alberta (individuals, corporations, unions, and employee organizations can donate) or in Ontario and New Brunswick where the lists are identical to Alberta's except for "employee organizations."

Table 4.6. Party and Election Finance

	Amount	Source	Anonymous Contributions	Spending Limits[1]	Annual Allowance to Parties	Party Reimbursement	Candidate Reimbursement	Third-party Advertising
NF	no limit	no restriction	up to $100	party $3.125 per voter (min $12,000); candidate $3.125 per voter (max $12,000)	none		1/3 of actual expenses to candidate receiving 15% of vote	
PEI	no limit	no restriction	no	party $6.00 per voter; candidate $1.75 per voter	rate based on valid vote for parties with at least one seat		$0.75 per voter to candidate receiving 15% of vote, min $1,500, max $3,000	name of sponsor
NS	no limit	no restriction	no	party $0.40 per voter; candidate sliding scale $1.00 and up based on number of voters	none		$1.12 per voter to candidate receiving 15% of vote	prohibited
NB	$6,000 to each party or association and to one independent candidate	individuals, corporations, and trade unions	up to $100	party $1.00 per voter; candidate $1.75 per voter (min $11,000-max $22,000)	rate based on valid vote for each party in legislature or fielding ten candidates		lesser of actual expenses or $0.35 per voter plus one mail out to candidate receiving 15% of vote	name of sponsor
QC	$3,000 total to each party, independent member, and independent candidate	voters only	up to $200	party $0.60 per voter; candidate $1.00 per voter	rate based on valid vote for all authorized parties	50% if party obtains 1% of vote to maximum of $0.60 per voter	50% of expenses to max $1.00 per voter to candidate winning 15%	prohibited
ON	$4,000 to each party; $750 to each association; additional to parties ($4,000) and candidates ($750) during campaign[2]	individuals, corporations, or unions	no	party $0.60 per voter; candidate $0.96 per voter	none	$0.05 per voter in each district where party obtains 15% of vote	20% of expenses to candidate receiving 15% of vote	advertising over $100 approved by candidate treated as campaign contribution
MB	$3,000 to each party, candidate, or constituency association	voters only	up to $10	party $1.40 per voter; candidate limit sliding scale $2.20 per voter and up based on population density	none	50% of expenses if party obtains 10% of vote	50% of expenses to candidate receiving 10% of vote	included as reimbursable election expense if purchased with approval of party or candidate; no other restrictions

	Amount	Source	Anonymous Contributions	Spending Limits[1]	Annual Allowance to Parties	Party Reimbursement	Candidate Reimbursement	Third-party Advertising
SK	no limit	no contributions from non-citizens outside Canada	up to $250	party $651,355; candidate $52,108 in north and $39,082 in south	none	lesser of $195,407 or 1/3 of actual expenses if party wins 15% of vote	50% of expenses to candidate receiving 15% of vote	advertising approved by candidate or party treated as election expense; otherwise prohibited
AB	$15,000 to each party; $750 to association; additional to parties ($15,000) and candidates ($1,500) during campaign[3]	individuals, corporations, unions, employee organizations	up to $50	no limits	none			name and address of sponsor
BC	no limit	no restriction	up to $50	party $1.25 per voter; candidate $50,000 and up	none			$5,000 per campaign[4]
YT	no limit		up to $50	no limit	none			
NWT	$1,500 to candidate		up to $100	no parties; candidate $30,000	none	no parties		
NU	$1,500 to candidate		up to $100	no parties; candidate $30,000	none	no parties		
Canada	no limit	Canadian citizens or residents	up to $200	party $1.40 per voter; candidate $2.07 per voter and up based on sliding scale of number of voters	none	22.5% of expenses if party wins 2% of votes overall or 5% of votes in districts where it fielded a candidate	15% reimbursement for candidate receiving 15% of valid vote; 50% (less amount above) if candidate spending exceeds 30% of limit	$3,000 per district to maximum of $150,000 nationally during election campaign[5]

1. Per voter limits based on constituencies where party runs candidates; limits adjusted by CPI except in Alberta and the territories.
2. Annual contributions to constituency associations must not exceed $3000. Total contributions to candidates during campaigns are limited to $3000.
3. Annual total contribution to constituency associations must not exceed $3750. There is a total party limit ($30,000) and candidate limit ($7500) during campaigns.
4. Limit ruled unconstitutional by BC Supreme Court, February 2000.
5. Ruled unconstitutional by Alberta Court of Queen's Bench, 2000.

Campaign spending has attracted stricter regulation. Only two jurisdictions, Alberta and Yukon, have no prescribed limit. While the amounts vary slightly, every other province uses a formula based on the number of voters to cap spending by parties and/or candidates. Candidate spending is limited to $30,000 in NWT and Nunavut, but is not tied to the size of the electorate.

All but three jurisdictions where elections are held along partisan lines (Alberta, BC, and Yukon) reimburse candidates and/or parties for some part of their election expenses. However, reimbursements are made available only once a minimum vote threshold has been achieved, ranging from 10 per cent in Manitoba to 15 per cent in the other provinces. New Brunswick, PEI, and Quebec also provide annual allowances to registered parties based on their performance in previous elections.

The most controversial regulation, and the only one challenged in court to date, is restriction on so-called "third party advertising," typically defined as advertising aimed at endorsing or opposing particular candidates that is not purchased by a candidate or registered party. Three jurisdictions (Nova Scotia, Quebec, and Saskatchewan) effectively ban third party advertising. BC established a limit of $5,000 but that was ruled unconstitutional by the BC Supreme Court (February 2000), a decision that has not yet been appealed. In the remaining provinces, restrictions are non-existent or minimal, requiring only the disclosure of the identity of the advertiser. The federal restriction was ruled unconstitutional by the Alberta courts in 2000, a decision that was overturned by the Supreme Court of Canada in May 2004.

Ranking jurisdictions in terms of party and election finance is more problematic than for the other dimensions of electoral democracy. On one hand, regulations exist to make elections fairer. On the other, litigants have successfully argued in court that restrictions on third party advertising violate freedom of speech guarantees in the *Charter*. Regulations at the federal level have been successfully challenged in the Alberta Court of Queen's Bench as have provincial regulations in BC, although the Supreme Court has yet to rule definitively on the issue. An injunction against enforcement of the advertising restrictions was obtained at the beginning of the 2000 election campaign but suspended by the Supreme Court of Canada before the campaign was over.

If we accept the arguments justifying restrictions on contributions on democratic fairness grounds, provinces and territories fall into three groups— those with no contribution limits (Yukon, Newfoundland, PEI, Nova Scotia, Saskatchewan, and BC), those limiting contributions but not sources (NWT, Nunavut, New Brunswick, Ontario, and Alberta), and two provinces (Quebec and Manitoba) that limit contributions and allow only voters to contribute to candidates or parties. The groupings would change if restrictions on third party advertising are included, because three provinces at the lower end of the ranking

(BC, Nova Scotia, and Saskatchewan), as well as Canada, either prohibit such advertising or attempt to limit spending on it.

Grouping jurisdictions on spending limits or reimbursement schemes would also alter the order of provinces except for Quebec and Manitoba. For example, Yukon and Alberta regulate contributions, but they have no spending limits and no reimbursement scheme. On the other hand, PEI's (and Canada's) rank would rise because it limits spending and subsidizes candidates and parties even though it has no contribution limits.

Election Outcomes

Election outcome is the final dimension on which electoral democracy in the provinces is assessed. There is a different quality to this dimension because it includes components that are related weakly or not at all to the legal framework governing elections: redistribution rules, voting and candidacy requirements, and party and election finance. The biggest debate about electoral systems, whether single-member plurality systems are more or less democratic than proportional systems, is irrelevant in Canada at present since all jurisdictions now have identical systems. The last remaining interprovincial variation disappeared with double member ridings in PEI before the 1996 election.

Nevertheless, there is general agreement that election outcomes exhibiting genuine competition are probably healthier for democracy than one-sided contests. Moreover, one-sided outcomes could be a sign that redistribution rules are less fair, overrepresenting rural areas, for example, or that elections have been manipulated by fraudulent means or influenced by disparities in financial resources possessed by the competitors. Indeed, these are reasons for introducing many of the rules and regulations discussed in previous sections.

Table 4.7 offers five measures of election outcomes. Three of these could, in principle, be directly affected by election rules—turnover, the effective number of parties, and proportionality.[44] Turnout could be indirectly related if rules are perceived as so unfair that some eligible voters decide not to participate in the electoral game. There might even be an indirect link to the success rate of female candidates to the extent that candidate subsidy programs make a difference or turnover creates openings in the legislature. In fact, none of these dimensions is correlated with the provincial gini index, perhaps the best measure of electoral fairness. Statistical comparisons with the other dimensions (especially party and election finance) make little sense given the small number of cases and crudity of rankings. However, comparison among measures of election outcomes themselves offers another picture of life in subnational democracies.

Turnout rates differ substantially, ranging from below 50 per cent in Alberta and Ontario to over 80 per cent in PEI and Nunavut. The Islanders have consistently had high turnout rates, but most provinces are experiencing lower rates,

Table 4.7. Election Outcomes

	Year	Turnout	Turnover, Last Election[1]	Average Turnover, Last 5 Elections	Effective Number of Legislative Parties[2]	Female Legislators	Proportionality[3]	Rank on Proportionality
NF	2003	72.0	41.7	18.4	1.8	20.8	87.9	4
PEI	2003	83.3	11.1	27.8	1.3	22.2	68.8	10
NS	2003	65.6	9.6	29.6	2.7	9.6	88.2	2
NB	2003	73.6	29.1	33.2	2.1	13.0	90.8	1
QC	2003	70.4	24.5	18.1	2.0	30.4	82.4	7
ON	2003	57.0	35.9	35.0	1.8	21.3	76.6	8
MB	2003	54.2	8.8	13.2	2.0	22.8	88.0	3
SK	2003	70.5	5.2	25.8	2.0	19.0	84.0	6
AB	2004	44.7	15.1	18.5	1.7	14.5	73.5	9
BC	2005	63.8	39.2	43.9	1.9	13.9	87.3	5
YT	2002	78.1	66.3	46.4	1.7	16.7	67.1	11
NWT[4]	2003	68.5	n/a	n/a	n/a	10.5	n/a	
NU[4]	2004	81.2	n/a	n/a	n/a	10.5	n/a	

1. Turnover is calculated by finding the absolute difference between a party's percentage seat share in the most recent election and the preceding one, summing across parties and dividing by 2 to eliminate double counting. Average turnover is the average of similar calculations for the most recent election and the four preceding elections, effectively going back to the late 1970s and early 1980s.

2. The effective number of parties is calculated by squaring each party's vote share, summing across parties, and taking the reciprocal of that sum. Essentially, it adjusts the absolute number of parties in a legislature by taking each party's strength into account.

3. Proportionality is calculated by finding the absolute difference between percentage vote share and percentage seat share for each party, summing the differences, and dividing by two. That sum is then subtracted from 100. If all parties won the same percentage of votes as seats, the index value would be 100, signifying perfect proportionality.

4. This was the first election after the NWT was divided into Northwest Territories and Nunavut; hence, no over time comparisons are possible.

although only three (Ontario, Nova Scotia, and Alberta) have lower rates than in national elections.

At the national level, Canada has had some of the highest turnover rates among democratic countries.[45] Newfoundland, Quebec, Manitoba, and Alberta excepted, this also appears to be true at the provincial level over the five most recent elections in each province as well as in Yukon. Even provinces with relatively low turnover rates in the most recent election (Nova Scotia and Saskatchewan, for example) have average turnover rates of roughly 25 per cent or higher.

Higher turnover rates are not unequivocal signs of healthier democracy. Very high rates may produce a legislature populated excessively by amateurs. On the other hand, as documented in the US, very low turnover limits opportunities for women and other marginalized groups.[46] However, as Lisa Young notes, "systemic barriers exist: they are only masked by low turnover rates."[47] Her own study shows that even in Canada, a country with high turnover, under a best-case scenario it would take five general elections for the percentage of women in the House of Commons to reach 50 per cent from the 13.2 per cent level in 1988.[48] Still, turnover is obviously a necessary if not a sufficient condition for improving the representation of women.

However, turnover does not appear to be related to another measure of competitiveness—the effective number of parties. Alberta has low turnover and a relatively uncompetitive system. Manitoba has a comparable turnover rate, but close to perfect two-party competition in the legislature (effective number of parties equals 2.0). The chance of women being elected to the legislature is also presumed to be greater with higher turnover. However, that is not the case in the provinces and Yukon.

Newfoundland, PEI, Quebec, Ontario, Manitoba, and Saskatchewan have percentages of legislators who are female comparable to or rather higher than that at the national level, 21.1 per cent after the 2004 federal election.[49] Again, there is no obvious pattern to interprovincial differences. Alberta, the province with the lowest average turnover rate, one party dominance, and low proportionality has a below average percentage of female legislators. But the lowest percentage is found in Nova Scotia, a province with a much more competitive party system, higher turnover rate, and substantially higher percentage of NDP members (the party with the strongest commitment to gender equity) in the legislature, 15 of 52 compared to two of 83 in Alberta.

The proportionality index is perhaps the best intuitive measure of the fairness of election outcomes. This is certainly the position taken by advocates of proportional representation. It measures the relationship between vote shares and seat shares across parties in a given election—the higher the index number, the closer the relationship. A score of 100 represents a situation where the seat share of each party is equal to its vote share. While all jurisdictions use the first-past-the-post method of election, proportionality differs substantially across the provinces, ranging from a low of 67.1 per cent in Yukon to a high of 90.8 per cent in Quebec. Ranks on proportionality for the provinces and Yukon are given in the last column of Table 4.7. The ranking provides no support for a view that the fairness of election outcomes varies by region. PEI has among the least proportional election results, but Newfoundland has one of the most proportional (it ranks fourth out of 11). While proportionality is high in three of four western provinces, Alberta ranks very low (ninth of 11). Of course, alternative measures of election outcomes might yield different jurisdictional rankings. These alternatives are discussed in the next section.

Conclusion

Interprovincial differences on each of the dimensions examined in this study were summarized at the end of each section. As noted there, provincial rankings differ to some extent depending on what dimension is considered and in the case of qualifications for voting and candidacy are relatively minor. Manitoba and Saskatchewan have the fairest electoral maps and election outcomes on the egalitarian side but diverge on voter qualifications: Saskatchewan is slightly more restrictive than Manitoba as far as qualifications for voting are concerned.

Ranking the provinces on the other dimensions is more problematic. The interprovincial differences summarized above on qualifications for voting and candidacy and election finance are qualitative, and depend on how much emphasis is given to particular components—contribution limits versus disclosure requirements, for example, in the case of party and election finance. The main story is one of convergence, although five provinces—Newfoundland, PEI, Nova Scotia, Saskatchewan, and BC—still have no limits on contributions to parties and candidates. On the other hand, neither does Canada, and all six jurisdictions limit spending and require disclosure of contributions as well.

One might have expected differences on the basis of the ideological position of the governing party. However, none are apparent here and have been discounted in previous studies of redistribution rules[50] and party and election finance.[51]

While substantial interprovincial differences still exist, on the whole, the quality of democracy in the provinces has clearly improved. Huge improvements have been made to the electoral map. All but one province used non-partisan redistricting procedures to create the electoral map that governed their most recent election. The one exception, PEI, has since committed itself to a statutory timetable and an independent boundary commission. Almost all provinces have significant regulation governing contributions to and spending by political parties.

What about the provinces compared to the nation as a whole? Using a national quotient, that is, one person-one vote regardless of province, Canada's federal electoral map is more unequal than that for all but one province, Nova Scotia.[52] It places more restrictions on the right to vote than Newfoundland, Ontario, and

Quebec. Alberta, New Brunswick, Ontario, and Quebec all have stricter party and election finance legislation. Seven out of ten provinces have higher turnout rates. The proportion of legislators who are women is higher in four out of ten. In short, federal election procedures and outcomes are not more democratic than provincial ones, and the national level is no longer unequivocally the leader in setting standards of fairness.

Notes

1. This chapter draws extensively from my "Electoral Democracy in the Provinces," *Choices: Strengthening Canadian Democracy* 7 (March 2001), published by the Institute for Research on Public Policy. I am grateful to the IRPP for permission to use that work here. Neither the IRPP nor the editors of the *Strengthening Canadian Democracy* are responsible for the views expressed herein.
2. Pierre Elliott Trudeau, "Some Obstacles to Democracy in Quebec," in P.E. Trudeau, ed., *Federalism and the French Canadians* (Toronto: Macmillan, 1968) 103–23.
3. Richard S. Katz, *Democracy and Elections* (New York: Oxford University Press, 1997) 3. Katz looks at over 800 elections in 70 countries.
4. Lawrence LeDuc, "Elections and Democratic Governance," in Lawrence LeDuc, Richard G. Niemi, and Pippa Norris, eds., *Comparing Democracies: Election and Voting in Global Perspective* (Thousand Oak, CA: Sage Publications) 344.
5. Richard Johnston and Janet Ballantyne, "Geography and the Electoral System," *Canadian Journal of Political Science* 10 (1997): 857–66.
6. See Filip Palda, *Election Finance Regulation in Canada: A Critical Review* (Vancouver: The Fraser Institute, 1991).
7. A good summary is provided by Rand Dyck, *Provincial Politics in Canada*, 2nd ed. (Scarborough: Prentice-Hall, 1991).
8. See for example, Seymour Martin Lipset, "Some Social Requisites of Democracy," *American Political Science Review* 53 (1959): 69–105; and Deane Neubauer, "Some Conditions of Democracy," *American Political Science Review* 61 (1967) 1002–09.
9. Jane Jenson, "Party Systems," in David J. Bellamy, John H. Pammett, and Donald C. Rowat, eds., *The Provincial Political Systems* (Toronto: Methuen, 1976) 121.
10. Richard Simeon and David J. Elkins, "Provincial Political Cultures in Canada," in David J. Elkins and Richard Simeon, eds., *Small Worlds: Provinces and Parties in Canadian Political Life* (Toronto: Methuen, 1980) 68.
11. Allan Kornberg, William Mishler, and Harold D. Clarke, *Representative Democracy in the Canadian Provinces* (Scarborough: Prentice-Hall, 1982) 261.
12. Dyck 632–33.
13. Constitutional rules guarantee that a province can have no fewer members of the House of Commons than the number of senators from that province and that no province can lose seats as a result of periodic redistributions.
14. R.K. Carty, "The Electoral Boundary Revolution in Canada," *Canadian Review of American Studies* 15 (1985): 274.
15. *Reference re Provincial Electoral Boundaries* [1991], 5 W.W.R. 1 (S.C.C.), 81, D.L.R. (4th) 16.
16. *Dixon vs. Attorney General of British Columbia* [1989], W.W.R. 393, 413.
17. Royal Commission on Electoral Reform and Party Financing, *Final Report, Volume 1: Reforming Electoral Democracy* (Ottawa: Government of Canada, 1991) 148. Also

see the discussion in Keith Archer, "Conflict and Confusion in Drawing Constituency Boundaries: The Case of Alberta," *Canadian Public Policy* 19 (1993): 179–82.

18. Carty 273–87. For a longer times series on electoral inequality in provincial legislatures, see Harvey E. Pasis, "Electoral Distribution in the Canadian Provincial Legislatures," in J. Paul Johnston and Harvey E. Pasis, eds., *Representation and Electoral Systems: Canadian Perspectives* (Scarborough: Prentice-Hall, 1990) 251–54.

19. The mandate given to the commission by the legislature was to consider options for 10 or 11 dual member districts and 20 to 22 single members districts. It is clear from reading its report that the commission recommended only 17 single member districts because of strong sentiment at public hearings that a 20- to 22-seat legislature would be too expensive. In fact, the report contains this statement "If in the final analysis, the Governor-in-Council determines (notwithstanding our recommendations) that there should be more than 17 electoral districts, we recommend that the next one, two or three seats be assigned to Iqaluit, Rankin Inlet and/or High Arctic (in no particular order)."

20. Information about legal provisions in this and subsequent tables is drawn from an examination of provincial and territorial elections acts and legislative assembly acts supplemented by *Compendium of Election Administration in Canada: A Comparative Overview* (Canada: Elections Canada, 2002). I am indebted to Carrie Hill for her assistance.

21. *Mackinnon v. Prince Edward Island* [1993], 101 D.L.R. (4th) 362 (P.E.I.S.C.).

22. Recent changes to the PEI *Electoral Boundaries Act* provide that the next redistribution will be by an independent commission consisting of a judge and two individuals who are not members of the legislature or Parliament and not provincial government employees. One will be nominated by the premier and the other by the Leader of the Opposition after consultation with other opposition party leaders. The province has also committed itself by statute to redistribution after every three elections.

23. The participation of the judiciary in Alberta is optional. The Alberta *Electoral Boundaries Commission Act* provides for a chair who must be the Ethics Commissioner, the Auditor-General, a university president, a judge or retired judge, or someone whose "stature and qualifications" are similar. The chair of the 1996 commission was, in fact, a judge.

24. Kent Roach, "One Person, One Vote? Canadian Constitutional Standards for Electoral Distribution and Districting," in David Small, ed., *Drawing the Map: Equality and Efficacy of the Vote in Canadian Electoral Boundary Reform* (Toronto: Dundurn Press, 1991) 65.

25. "Equality and Efficacy of the Vote," in Royal Commission on Electoral Reform and Party Financing, *Final Report: Reforming Electoral Democracy*, Vol. 1 (Canada: Department of Supply and Services, 1991) 140.

26. "Equality and Efficacy of the Vote" 200, Appendix C.

27. *British Columbia, Royal Commission on Electoral Boundaries for British Columbia, Report* (Victoria: Queen's Printer, 1988).

28. Roach.

29. Calculations in this table were made by the author using data from the most recent electoral boundaries commission report in each jurisdiction. I am grateful to Graham White for providing population figures for the electoral districts proposed for Nunavut which are missing from the version available on the Government of Nunavut web site.

30. The Gini index was originally developed to measure the degree of inequality in the distribution of family income. The smaller the proportion of families who possess the largest share of total family income, the larger the magnitude of the index.

31. Carty 284–85. Carty attributes Alberta's exceptionalism to its use of different apportionment criteria for rural and urban districts.

32. Katz 216.

33. Katz 216. For a more recent comparative examination of the right to vote in 63 democracies, see André Blais, Louis Massicotte, and Antoine Yoshinaka, "Deciding Who has the Right to Vote: A Comparative Analysis of Election Laws," *Electoral Studies* 20 (2001): 41–62.

34. Urban residents in Ontario can obtain a certificate of entitlement to vote up to the day before polling day. Rural residents can become registered on polling day itself if vouched for by a registered voter.

35. The disqualifications in Table 4.4 are based on a reading of the relevant elections act. Other statutes may specify disqualifications that have been missed.

36. Citizens must be "ordinarily resident" in the province prior to an election, but no minimum period of residence is stipulated.

37. Katz 246.

38. Nova Scotia is the only jurisdiction to stipulate a different minimum age for candidacy, age 19, than for voting. It is also the only province that allows British subjects who are not citizens to stand for election.

39. See F. Leslie Seidle, ed., *Provincial Party and Election Finance in Canada* (Toronto: Dundurn Press, 1991).

40. Katz 263–64.

41. Some have argued that public funding of political parties leads to (or is produced by) a cartel joining dominant parties in the system, in effect constraining voter options. See Heather MacIvor, "Do Canadian Parties Form a Cartel?" *Canadian Journal of Political Science* 29 (1996): 317–34. For a rebuttal of MacIvor's argument see Lisa Young, "Party State and Political Competition in Canada: The Cartel Model Reconsidered," *Canadian Journal of Political Science* 31 (1998): 339–58.

42. See Gary Jacobson, "Public Funds for Congressional Campaigns: Who Would Benefit?" in Herbert Alexander, ed., *Political Finance* (London: Sage Publications, 1979) 99–127.

43. John Ferejohn and Brian Gaines, "The Personal Vote in Canada," in Herman Bakvis, ed., *Representation, Integration and Political Parties in Canada* (Toronto: Dundurn Press, 1991) 275–302.

44. For a study of electoral volatility at the national level in Canada using the turnover index, see Donald E. Blake, "Party Competition and Electoral Volatility: Canada in Comparative Perspective," in Herman Bakvis, ed., *Representation, Integration and Political Parties in Canada* (Toronto: Dundurn Press, 1991) 253–73. For a national level study on Canada using the proportionality index, see R. Kent Weaver, "Improving Representation in the Canadian House of Commons," *Canadian Journal of Political Science* 30 (1997): 473–513.

45. Peter Mair, *Party System Change: Approaches and Interpretations* (New York: Oxford University Press, 1997) 218–19.

46. See Susan J. Carroll, *Women as Candidates in American Politics* (Bloomington, IN: Indiana University Press, 1985); and Carol Nechemias, "Changes in the Election of Women to US. State Legislative Seats," *Legislative Studies Quarterly* 12 (1987): 125–42.

144 DONALD E. BLAKE

47. Lisa Young, "Legislative Turnover and the Election of Women to the Canadian House of Commons," in Kathy Megyery, ed., *Women in Canadian Politics: Toward Equity in Representation* (Toronto: Dundurn Press, 1991) 95.
48. Young 91–95. Her "best case" assumes the percentage of women who are candidates increases by five percentage points in each election and that women are given a six-point advantage in being nominated in winnable ridings.
49. I am grateful to Lynda Erickson for this calculation. Female representation in most provinces reached or exceeded the federal level in the early 1990s. See Donley T. Studlar and Richard E. Matland, "The Dynamics of Women's Representation in the Canadian Provinces," *Canadian Journal of Political Science* 29 (1996): 273.
50. See Carty.
51. See F. Leslie Seidle, "Preface," in F. Leslie Seidle, ed., *Party and Election Finance in Canada* (Toronto: Dundurn Press, 1991) xix–xxii.
52. If districts in the territories are included in the calculation, Canada and Nova Scotia have identical gini indexes.

CHAPTER 5

Legal Portrait of the 2003 Ontario General Election[1]

GREGORY TARDI

On Tuesday, 2 September 2003, the PC premier of Ontario, Ernie Eves, announced that the province's thirty-eighth general elections were to be held on Thursday, 2 October 2003. This call gives us an opportunity to look at elections as one of the vital components of democracy, focusing on the applicability of the rule of law and, more particularly on the role of law in matters electoral.

The Necessarily Interdisciplinary Approach

The perception generally held of electoral events is that they are not only exclusively political in nature, but also that they are the highlights of the political life of a jurisdiction, recurring at regular, but relatively distant, intervals. Voters focus their attention on the identity and the symbolism of those who may head the next government. The media engage in limited discussion of public issues, often with a perspective predetermined according to the orientation of their respective owners and, possibly, readers or viewers. Electoral opinions are formed and options are chosen on the basis of politically oriented information. Most citizens and electors tend to direct their attention exclusively to the readily apparent elements of the election, the partisan conflict among political parties and candidates.

The analysis which political law[2] can offer on elections as an exercise in democracy is more comprehensive, coherent, and certainly more democratically informative.

The first component necessary to the inclusive political law method of analysis of an election is comprised of the *political principles* which underlie it. These are the temporary nature of the public trust in government, the opportunity for alternance of parties in public office, the right of all citizens to participate and to organize in public life, and citizens' freedom of choice among divergent political options.

Working in conjunction with these political principles are the *institutional arrangements, policies, and practices of public administration* that support them. The most important among these are an electoral administration that is independent of the government of the day and neutral *vis-à-vis* all political parties and candidates, the measures ensuring transparency of the electoral process, and

145

certainty and timeliness in publishing the results. These latter factors dealing with process and results are the ones commonly indicated by the expression "free and fair" elections.

Building on the political principles and the public institutional framework are the *legal aspects* of elections. The primary elements of legality ensuring electoral democracy are that there be a normative statement of democratic and/or electoral rights in the form of a law; equality among voters to the extent possible; equal opportunity for all parties and candidates (which is colloquially known as the level playing field); and clarity, certainty, and predictability in the legal process.

There is a criterion in respect of the law relating to elections that is even more significant in ensuring democracy. If it is important that the electoral administration be independent and non-partisan, it is even more determinative that the law and its administrators and guardians be independent of both the current holders of public office and even of the electoral administration itself. The singular loyalty of the legal advisors of the body overseeing elections is to the Constitution and the legal system. Independence, in the present sense, should not be equated with the idea of being divorced or isolated from the proper and practical functioning of the state. Law functions best when it infuses public administration and politics with legally based norms such as fairness, equity, and equality among citizens. Law also functions best in tandem with public administration and politics when, in turn, it reflects the values it adopts from these disciplines. The independence of law consequently means that it provides rules that are inherently applicable, but which are nevertheless subject to enforcement by litigation and compliance by prosecution. In a democratic election, this is the sense of both the rule of law and the role of law.

What is the *proper balance among law, public administration, and politics* which provides a political regime, and more specifically an electoral system, with its democratic characteristic? In fact, law, public administration, and politics are mutually interdependent. If any of these elements is missing, the resulting electoral system is defective.

This, however, is only half the answer. Democracy implies the rule of law, not the rule of public administration and certainly not the rule of politics. It is law that provides the normative framework for public administration and politics. We must therefore conclude that the legal component of elections is the most fundamental and indispensable. The contribution of law is both to translate the public administration and politics of the event into perceptible rules and to instruct public administration and politics with inherently legal—that is, rules-based—concepts such as structure, organization, and procedure, without which elections would remain mere *pane et circenses*.[3]

This is the conceptual basis from which we now propose to analyze the 2003 Ontario election from a lawyer's perspective.

Constitutionality of Timing the Election

The five-year maximum duration of the thirty-seventh Legislative Assembly of Ontario began on the date fixed for the return of the writs after the thirty-seventh general election.[4] The last general election was held on 3 June 1999. The writs were returned on or after 11 June 1999,[5] and this legislature could therefore have lasted into June 2004. This constitutional norm is supplemented by Ontario's own legislative provision which clarifies that every legislature may last no longer than five years from the fifty-fifth day after the date of the writs for an election.[6] On the basis of the supremacy of the Constitution,[7] we must conclude that if the dates derived from the application of these constitutional and legal provisions differ, the calculation based on subsection 4(1) of the *Constitution Act, 1982* takes precedence.

The doctrine of the supremacy of the Constitution also leads us to note an historical anomaly in the texts. Section 85 of the *Constitution Act, 1867*,[8] a provision never repealed, states that the life of an Ontario legislature is four years. The *Legislative Assembly Act*[9] allows legislatures to remain in place for five years, and this has become the norm, notwithstanding the apparent contradiction between s. 85 of the *Constitution Act, 1867* and the *Legislative Assembly Act*. This practice is not a customary derogation. In fact, it may be explained by the capacity of the legislature to amend the Constitution of the Province, which was granted originally by s. 92 (1) of the *Constitution Act, 1867* and which is now continued by s. 45 of the *Constitution Act, 1982*. In other words, s. 85 of the *Constitution Act, 1867* makes provision for matters which were, under the former subsection 92 (1) of the same *Act*, subject to amendment as being in relation to the internal constitution of the province.

This helps to resolve the apparent textual inconsistency between the four-year limitation period of s. 85 of the *Constitution Act, 1867* and subsection 4 (1) of the *Constitution Act, 1982*, which limits the life of a legislature to five years. The key to this difference may be that the drafters of the 1982 constitutional text believed that s. 85 was not worth deliberately repealing, as it had in any event been rendered spent by Ontario's *Legislative Assembly Act*.[10]

Within these constitutional and statutory parameters, the timing of a dissolution of the legislative body is, firmly, a matter of convention.[11] The Ontario political system is entrenched in the Westminster mould. The convention therefore recognizes that the decision is at the discretion of the head of government. Some Canadian commentators, and, in particular, some political figures have, in recent years, expressed a preference for elections at fixed terms, as exist in the US. The jurisdictions in which such a system has traditionally been instituted are the ones in which political parties do not exist and where, consequently, the government is not, strictly speaking, responsible to the legislature. At present, only the Northwest Territories and Nunavut fall into this category.

Notwithstanding the apparent incompatibility between responsible government and fixed term elections, an experiment is presently being carried on, ostensibly to integrate these two elements of parliamentary life, in BC (a populated province, as opposed to a sparsely inhabited and far-flung territory), which clearly has political parties in its system of governance. Here, the royal prerogative of dissolution was set out in legislation. Subsection 23 (1) of BC's own *Constitution Act*[12] spelled out that the lieutenant-governor could prorogue or dissolve the Legislative Assembly when he or she saw fit, by means of a proclamation in the name of the sovereign. Subsections 23 (2) and (3) incorporated into provincial law the intent of the *Charter* five-year limitation on the life of a legislature.

Following up on a campaign promise, the Liberal government elected into office on 16 May 2001 left subsection 23 (1) in place but substituted new provisions for subsections 23 (2) and (3).[13] The key change brought about by the amendment is that a mandatory voting day was set, in 2001, for 17 May 2005. Thereafter, according to the new text, a general election must be held in the fourth calendar year following each previous general election.

In fact, despite the partisan rhetoric, this reform is more superficial than institutional. As the power of the lieutenant-governor to dissolve the legislature does not seem to have been amended, the government remains responsible to the Legislative Assembly. The consequence of the amendment is thus only that the provincial legislation tightens the limit set out in the *Charter*; the maximum life of a legislature is reduced from five years to four. If the government remains responsible in the Westminster constitutional sense despite this amendment, we may be allowed to wonder why, if not for partisan political reasons, the BC government had the Legislative Assembly set a term on its own duration. To date, the constitutional validity of BC's scheme has not been litigated. If such a challenge ever arises, it would likely focus on whether the amendment to the *Constitution Act* affects the prerogatives of the lieutenant governor.

In Ontario, the fact that the convention on dissolution recognizes the premier's discretion means that as long as the constitutional bounds are observed, the decision on when to call an election is, essentially, a political one. Premier Eves may have given serious consideration to factors such as the time elapsed since the last general election and to the effect of the change of leadership in government. Since 1999, when the people of Ontario re-elected Mike Harris, his predecessor, the premiership changed hands as a result of Harris's resignation as leader of the PCs and Eves's assumption of the office, effective 15 April 2002. Other considerations which may have influenced the premier's decision are of an equally political nature: the electorate's desire for change after two consecutive terms of PC government; the fluctuations of public opinion polling; the impact on voters of political controversies such as the deregulation of the hydro system and the recent black-out; the tainted water scandal of Walkerton and the tainted meat controversy in Aylmer, as well as other alleged impacts of deregulation; public health issues relating to the delivery of medical care and the establishment of private sector hospitals; the handling of the SARS epidemic and whether it was compromised by cutbacks in the health sector; the debate surrounding the 2003 extra-parliamentary budget;[14] and the possible outcome of litigation involving political matters, such as the *George v. Harris* case.[15] Ultimately, the choice of when to dissolve the legislature and to go to the polls is a matter for the political sense and judgement of the premier, as advised by party officials and supporters. Beyond the constitutional limitations of the five-year cycle, this aspect of electioneering is relatively untouched by legal norms. At present, the legality and practice on this point are the same in Quebec as in Ontario.[16]

Ontario's traditional adherence to this Westminster-based convention changed after the Liberal Party win in the 2003 elections. Chapter 5 of the Liberal platform, entitled "The Ontario Liberal Plan for a More Democratic Ontario" contained a part designated "Strengthening our Democracy."[17] Among other promises, this indicates that if the Liberals take office, they will provide for elections to occur normally every four years, at fixed dates, while still retaining the possibility of government defeats on motions of non-confidence. This proposal is remarkably similar to the scheme enacted in BC. Pursuant to the most recent version of section 9 of the Election Act, a general election is to be held on Thursday, 4 October 2007. Subsequent general elections are to be held on the first Thursday in October every four years.[18] Apart from the fact that democracy is a constantly evolving system of governance, how this change would strengthen democracy or make elections more fair is not elucidated.

The question of the timing of the election reflects, in a broader sense, on the issue of the electoral regime used in Ontario. Among the parties contesting the election of 2003, the PCs addressed this matter most specifically. In their campaign booklet entitled "The Road Ahead," one of the chapters outlines "A Stronger Democracy for Ontario." The section designated "Your Vote—The Cornerstone of Democracy" attributes to both the Liberals and the NDP a desire to bring in proportional representation. The PCs completely reject this idea, because in their view MPPs elected through proportional representation would be accountable only to their party's leadership, not to their constituents. No substantiation of this position is offered.[19]

Federalism Factor in Representation of Ontario Electors

In 1991, the Supreme Court of Canada established the constitutional norm that while electoral districts need not conform to the "one person-one vote" standard, the concept of "effective representation" must guide the design of electoral districts.[20] The system of representation in Ontario at the time of the 1995 general election, which brought the PCs back to office after an absence of some ten years, complied with this standard. The legislature then comprised 130 electoral districts, each represented by one member.

For ideological reasons emanating from the overall program of the administration elected in 1995, the "Common Sense Revolution," the government decided to reduce the membership in the Legislative Assembly. The easiest way to accomplish this was to align representation in the legislature on Ontario's deputation in the federal House of Commons, which then consisted of 101 seats. This was done by means of enacting the statute bearing the blatantly partisan title of *The Fewer Politicians Act*.[21] This Act repealed several earlier versions of the *Representation Act*[22] and substituted for them the *Representation Act, 1996*.[23] This *Act* was worded not only so as to link the composition of the Ontario legislature to Ontario's federal deputation, but also to maintain this link in lockstep with future decennial federal redistributions.

Had a provincial general election been held immediately following the royal assent of the *Fewer Politicians Act* on 9 December 1996, the legislature would thus have been made up of 101 members. However, on 8 January 1997, the federal *Representation Order, 1996*[24] came into effect. Consequently, by the time of the next provincial general election on 3 June 1999, Ontario became represented by 103 MPPs at Queen's Park, a number equal to the MPs representing Ontario at the federal level in Ottawa.

The next subsequent federal redistribution began in the spring of 2002 and resulted in the *Representation Order, 2003*,[25] which, by virtue of the federal *Electoral Boundaries Redistribution Act*,[26] was to come into effect on 25 August 2004. This *Representation Order* raised the deputation of Ontario in the House of Commons from 103 to 106 members. In light of the apparent desire of some politicians to enable a federal general election to be held in the spring of 2004 rather than later, the one-year delay for the coming into effect of the *Representation Order* was amended by Parliament so as to bring the new, enlarged electoral map into effect by 1 April 2004.[27]

Ontario legislation does not provide a mechanism for shortening the delay for bringing the new federal electoral map into effect. Consequently, in order for the province to remain linked to the new electoral map, Ontario would have had to wait until 25 August 2004 to hold its election. The province's only other option would have been to enact legislation to provide for shortening of the representation schedule, similar to the federal scheme.

Whether the deadline was to be April or August 2004, the impact of the 2 September 2003 election call for Ontario was to defeat the purpose of the *Fewer Politicians Act, 1996* by de-linking the level of representation in the legislature from Ontario's representation in the House of Commons. For at least one round of elections, Ontario voters will be represented by 103 MPPs in Toronto and 106 MPs in Ottawa, each acting on behalf of differently constituted electoral districts. It is perhaps ironic, however, that after 3 October 2003, there were indeed fewer Ontario politicians in Toronto than in Ottawa. In this respect as well, the decision to go to the polls at this time was an eminently political one, although entirely within the boundaries of the constitutional and legal framework.

The effort to reinstate the link between the electoral districts of Ontario and the province's representation in the House of Commons has, during the tenure of office of Premier McGuinty, taken a slight turn. In legislation adopted by the Legislative Assembly in December 2005, the province was divided into two notional areas. In the south, comprising 96 of Ontario's 106 federal electoral districts and coterminous with these, the provincial electoral districts are now once again the same as Ontario's federal ridings. In the remainder of the province, comprising the 10 northerly federal electoral districts, the legislation establishes 11 provincial electoral districts. Thus, while Ontario is represented by 106 federal MPs at Queen's Park, as of the entry into force of the new law, there will be 107 MPPs.[28]

Dissolution: The Legal Mechanics for Democratic Choice

It is not the premier's mere statement to that effect which initiates an electoral process. Once he has determined the date preferred for dissolution of the legislature and the holding of elections, the legal actors in the system must observe the required formalities, each of which is recorded in an instrument of a legal nature.

Upon the premier's advice, the lieutenant-governor of the province issues a proclamation dissolving the previously elected legislature, which instrument is signed by the president of the Management Board of Cabinet. This is an expression of the royal prerogative of dissolution.[29] Pursuant to the statutory power arising from the *Election Act*,[30] the lieutenant-governor also includes in that proclamation the dates for the close of nominations and for the conduct of the vote.[31] The entire election period can vary from 28 to 56 days. In the present case, it was 30 days, not counting polling day itself. According to federal practice, the representative of the sovereign issues three separate proclamations: one to dissolve Parliament, one to command the issue of writs for the elections, and a further one to call together the newly elected Parliament on a specific date. Ontario's practice is limited to a single proclamation. Immediately following that proclamation, the Ontario Gazette carries a Parliamentary Notice of Election, signed by the Chief Election Officer (CEO).[32]

On the basis of the proclamation, the province's CEO actually issues writs of election, a form inherited from immemorial British practice, addressed to the returning officers in each of the electoral districts.[33] In turn, the returning officers prepare their own Notices of Election, which set out the particulars of the revision of the lists of electors, those of the close of nominations, as well as those for the holding of advance polls and general voting.[34] It is the combination of these instruments which are legally required to trigger the election process.

Legal Framework of Election Administration

The important consideration in managing the electoral process is that the administrative machinery required by the province be geared toward the legal principles which are the prerequisites of democracy. In Ontario, responsibility for the administration of the *Election Act* is vested with the CEO, appointed as an officer of the Legislative Assembly by the Lieutenant-Governor in Council.[35] The CEO is supported in the fulfilment of this mandate by an Office,[36] comprising the Assistant Chief Election Officer and others, as necessary. At the constituency level, the administrative process of an election is managed by a returning officer, also appointed by the Lieutenant-Governor in Council.[37] The political neutrality of all functionaries involved with elections is not only customary, it has become a constitutional convention, the existence of which has been recognized by the courts.

From a lawyer's perspective, the principal task of the CEO is to ensure that citizens' democratic rights are secured and that the entire electoral process unfolds according to the dictates of constitutional norms and legal requirements. Toward this end, the CEO must be supportive not only of the advice of his legal officers over technical administrative issues, but also of their accountability to law above any other consideration. Although the fulfilment of these requirements is usually a given in a jurisdiction as democratic as Ontario, administrative anomalies entailing risks for democracy and legality can occur.

In the 1999 general elections, for example, there was a particular problem with the late opening of the polls in some parts of Metropolitan Toronto. The *Election Act*[38] requires that on voting day the polls open at 9 a.m. and close at 8 p.m. (except in those northwesterly areas which fall into the Central Time Zone). The late opening of some polls occurred for entirely frivolous reasons not in keeping with either the text or the spirit of the legislation. This not only created a media fury, but also necessitated the extension of opening hours at some polls. It is likely, although difficult to prove, that this occurrence deprived some citizens of their ability to cast their ballot. In April 2000, as a consequence, the CEO issued a report[39] on this and other problems encountered in the thirty-seventh general elections, which acknowledged that electoral administration needed to return to a strict observance of legal norms. The recommendations included not only better training and more adequate compensation for electoral staff, but also greater use of technology and a realignment of responsibilities among election officials responsible for the conduct of elections. A new CEO was appointed and instituted measures to avoid a repetition of the problems so recognized.

In modern reality, money drives the electoral machines of political parties, party candidates, and even independent candidates. The regulation of political party and election financing is thus one of the most significant aspects of election legislation. Many jurisdictions, including Canada, combine the regulation of financial issues in the electoral field into the statute which deals with other aspects of the electoral process. In Ontario, there is a separate *Election Finances Act*.[40] In addition to his other functions, the CEO also administers this statute and oversees the election financing process.

Campaigning Under the Umbrella of Law

The *Election Act* does not establish legal parameters for the conduct of actual political activity in general or campaigning in particular. Parties and candidates must therefore seek, accept, and rely on legal advice in respect of their search for public office and power. In the context of campaigning within the bounds of legality, an allegation surfaced on September 11 that a PC organizer in the electoral district of Nipissing, held by former Premier Harris, had offered funding to a candidate of the Green Party so as to draw votes away from the Liberals. When the PC sympathizer stepped forward publicly and the PC Party distanced itself from him the very next day, the matter seemed to be closed.[41] Even if the statute organizing the electoral process is silent on the legal norms to be applied in campaigning, the influence of law on electoral conduct must be taken seriously. Allegations similar to the one mentioned here were made in relation to events in Manitoba and caused years of disruption.[42]

An analysis of the interaction among the law, public administration, and politics relating to elections would be incomplete if it did not mention the legal provisions aimed at separating the politically neutral public service from the partisan activity of campaigning. The *Public Service Act*[43] sets out a comprehensive regime of rules defining political activity and indicating who, among public servants, may, and in which circumstances, engage in this type of activity. It is worth noting that being a government lawyer is not, *per se*, a bar to participation in public life. Within this general category, those who hold positions at the Crown Counsel 5 level belong to the category for which political rights are legally restricted.[44] Such legislation on the avoidance and/or limitation of political activity by some public servants and this use of the law in separating prosecutorial functions from partisanship has been deemed entirely justified by the courts[45] and is not expected to cause controversy. It is worth mentioning primarily in comparative terms, to show how the topic is still subject to legal development. At the federal level, Bill C-25 of 2003, the *Public Service Modernization Act*, which deals with this issue among various others, was presented for first reading by the president of the Treasury Board on 6 February 2003.[46] This bill was amended in some respects and then passed by the Commons on 3 June 2003; it was passed by the Senate on 4 November 2003. The *Public Services Modernization Act* has received Royal Assent and its various parts are being brought into force as circumstances dictate.

A Democratic Standard in Campaign Speech and Political Rhetoric

The fundamental rule applicable to the publications and pronouncements emanating from political parties and candidates in the course of an election campaign is that embodied in paragraph 2 (b) of the *Charter*, namely freedom of expression. In the spirit of constitutional norms guaranteed by s. 52 of the *Constitution Act, 1982*, this freedom is close to being unassailable. Nevertheless, the wise practice of the rule of law in a democratic setting might be cited as an inducement to use this freedom to advance the public interest purpose for which it was designed, rather than as a justification for anything and everything.

Two examples from this campaign need to be mentioned. Much of the PC campaign rhetoric directed at the principal opposition party, the Liberals, was said to be negative, particularly in the initial stages of the election period.[47] This may be expected in the circumstances of a hotly disputed election in which public opinion polls show the opposition as being likely to win more seats than the outgoing government. More to the point here, it is certainly not contrary to legal norms. However, on 12 September 2003, PC headquarters sent a press release to a number of news organizations in which the following words appeared: "Dalton McGuinty: He's an evil reptilian kitten-eater from another planet."[48] Much later in the campaign, it was reported that the quote could be attributed to a well-established PC adviser.[49] Another instance of an unscripted *ad hominem* rhetorical flourish occurred on September 30, when, in the course of commenting on "uncosted campaign promises," Premier Eves stated that the Liberal leader "just says whatever pops into his little sharp pointy head because he thinks that's what you want to hear."[50] Recognizing the inappropriateness of the comment, or more likely the fact that it was unnecessary in order to get his point of view across, Eves later reportedly apologized.

What is the proper legal view of such a statement of political speech? Subject to any determination by a court if this matter is litigated, the cited words probably do not amount to defamation. More importantly, though, the statement would seem to amount to misuse of the freedom of expression. It is not pertinent to the electoral process, to the issues at stake in the election, nor to the *Peace, Order and Good Government* of the province during the time of the thirty-eighth Legislature. As such, this kind of characterization of one's opponent reflects more on those who uttered it than on the person to whom it is directed, and it seriously demeans campaign rhetoric and the interlocutor's wise use of the constitutionally recognized norm. A similar analysis may be valid about the PC's insistent claim that Dalton McGuinty "needs professional help" because of his political views.[51]

One may accord the benefit of doubt in respect of statements expressing political passions, however derogatory and misplaced, which are made in the heat of electoral battle. The same cannot necessarily be true of television advertisements, which are far more deliberately planned, scripted, and timed, and which involve the caution that goes with great expenditure. In this campaign, extensive use was made of so-called attack ads, which Canadian commentators readily ascribe to the influence of American political operatives and advertising techniques. Such ads are also subject to *Charter* protection. Despite that, while they may in some cases be useful in wooing voters in the direction of the party which airs them, it can be argued that such ads ought also to be considered in the light of judicial pronouncements favouring an informed electorate. Democracy, the rule of law, and the integrity of the electoral system indeed require the unfettered transmission of information. In this context, however, the democratic public interest is not necessarily the same as the unrestricted search for partisan advantage through bombardment of the airwaves with advertising that provides material to voters that does not "inform" them in the sense in which the Supreme Court of Canada used the verb "to inform."[52]

This avenue of discussion opens the prospect for comparison of the objective standards of legality and the subjective views of interested parties. It is extremely difficult to distinguish constitutionally and legally between political speech that is intrinsically protected by s. 2 (b) of the *Charter* and that which enjoys protection perhaps unintended by the drafters of the *Charter* because it distorts or abuses the benefit of such protection. The democratic standard for the conduct of elections requires, however, that Canadian society engage in this discussion. The question of relevance in this article is what the law can contribute to that public discussion.

It must be noted that Ontario political figures hold no monopoly on the use of inappropriate and needlessly offensive political speech. No sooner had the campaign in that province ended with the voting on 2 October 2003, than electoral attention shifted to Saskatchewan, where dissolution was expected to occur. On 7 October, the Toronto-based *Globe and Mail* reported that the two major political parties in the election then upcoming in Saskatchewan were proposing to avoid mudslinging, claiming specifically that they had no intention of running a campaign similar to that of Ontario.[53] The writs were eventually issued on 8 October 2003, for the election to take place on 5 November 2003.

The intention to avoid verbal partisan excess that would be contrary to the spirit of the *Charter*'s protection of freedom of speech could, however, not be maintained in the face of electoral zeal. On 13 October 2003, the news broke that sometime earlier, a consultant engaged by the NDP in the capacity of a communications manager had drawn and circulated a cartoon, portraying the leader of the Saskatchewan Party in the role of an SS guard. By the following day, the cartoon was reproduced on the front page of the *Saskatoon Star Phoenix* as well as inside the *National Post*.[54] The incident led to the communications officer's resignation and to the firing of an NDP ministerial assistant.[55] It forced the premier, whose position in the campaign and whose prospects of forming the next government were already precarious, to apologize publicly.[56]

The cartoon's most serious consequence was that its publication, being an acknowledged abuse of legally protected political speech in a campaign, could be said to have pointed out the NDP's organizational weakness and inadequate attention to legality.[57] It can also be said to have contributed to the NDP's near defeat. While it is difficult to generalize, in instances such as this where an electoral campaign is closely contested, an incident of blatant disregard for constitutionally protected rights or for legality can help to tip the balance against the offender. Constitutionalism and legality are very much part of the political culture throughout Canada. Political parties may not necessarily draw electors merely by professing allegiance to legality. Conversely, they are prone to losing votes by reason of electoral tactics which seem to fly in the face of legal norms and sensitivities, whether the faults are committed wilfully or by misplaced zeal.

Interactions Between Campaign Promises and Legality

The focal point of an election campaign may, at a popular and strictly political level, be the competition among the visions which competing political formations hold of society and public life and the images they project to the electorate in order to achieve power and to hold public office. Vision and imagery, as well as the symbolism of leadership, are indeed important in a democratic context. With an expression of respect for each individual voter who has reasons to arrive at an electoral decision, however, these political factors do not give a complete, nor even a sufficient, view of the stakes in electoral reality.

In a democracy, political ideas, ideals, and visions cannot be built without reference to constitutionalism and legality. Moreover, the execution of all political promises and platforms entail legal consequences. Most also require legal instruments, or at least instruments which must conform to legal norms, to be realized. As such, while all voters may wish to take account of parties' and candidates' visions, images, and leadership symbolism, informed voters need to be aware of the central place of legality in making campaign promises. This is even truer for specialized analysts of the interaction among law, policy, and politics for whom certain key questions arise. Let us dissect the 2003 Ontario campaign from this point of view.

There are issues of campaign discussion that produce promises with constitutional implications. Where, for example, a political party advocates that Ontario exercise closer control over the immigration process and come to a federal-provincial agreement similar to that in effect for Quebec, provincial involvement in an s. 91 federal area of jurisdiction comes into play, and federal-provincial negotiations become inevitable to realize the promise. The same is true for labour market agreements, which were mentioned during the leaders' debate on 23 September 2003.

Similarly, where a party leader expresses preference for a return to the death penalty, the subject matter not only delves into the exclusively federal jurisdiction over substantive criminal law, but also opens up a debate which pertains to the Parliament of Canada and which, despite occasional political pronouncements to the contrary, has been a matter of settled law for decades. Such promises may be better understood by the electorate when those making them indicate that their realization is not just a matter of political will but of constitutional jurisdiction, intergovernmental negotiation, in some cases parliamentary consent, and always ongoing popular discussion.

There are other issues of campaign discussion resulting in promises with implications on existing law. In this campaign, the topics of health care delivery; deregulation, including the reform of power generation and delivery, as well as food inspection services; the deductibility of mortgage payments; tax reductions for senior citizens; and the banning of teachers' strikes, all fit into this category. This is an area where the linkage between politics and law is extremely close and interdependent. The carrying to fruition of every one of the cited campaign promises requires change to existing legislative schemes. In these scenarios of reform, we must address the question of cause and effect. Is the law, whether in its pre-election state, or after its election-induced reform, a mere instrument, an expression of the political will? Or, is the law a motivating factor in society and aimed at the resolution of societal problems, independent of politics, but of course working together with politics? The best answer is that it seems to be both. The law is the written record of the decision of the legislature, based on public and political debate. Simultaneously, legal norms such as justice, equity, fairness, and the public welfare have informed and influenced that very political debate which produces the reformed statute. Voters will only be able to interpret and assess such campaigns properly if they are informed in the electoral sense, that is, if they are led to see the legal parts of democracy required for their eventual realization. In short, there can be no political promise without legal foundation.

Other issues of campaign discussion entail promises that carry implications for proposed legislation. Without a doubt, the overriding matter of this nature during the 2003 Ontario campaign was that of the recognition of same-sex marriages. The legislative definition of marriage had been uncontroversial ever since Confederation. By contrast to the foregoing category where attention was paid to existing law and its gradual reform in the direction of campaign promises, here the focus is on what is, essentially, a completely new legislative scheme.

In this scenario of fundamental change to be effected by a legal/legislative process, we must address the question of means and ends. Is the legal solution proffered by each of the competing political parties a mere means to achieving a social goal, or is it an end in itself? The best answer, again, is that it is both. Voters interested in this matter want to achieve both a specific social goal and the instrumental certainty, stability, and relative guarantee that a legal norm expressed in statute provides to sustain that goal. Here, as in the category of promises with implications for existing legislation, the debate is infused not only with what politicians or members of the electorate believe in their "political heart of hearts" to be true and correct, but equally with constitutionally grounded notions of justice, human rights, and equality. Taken as a self-standing instrument, the statute eventually resulting from this debate may, ironically, be a goal of politically visible result. In reality, the means of reaching that goal—that is, the debate—as well as the end itself, are an inseparable mixture of constitutional, legal, and political norms. The mere campaign assertion of the need for a permissive or restrictive solution is insufficient without reference to the legalities involved.

In respect of this issue, there is a sidebar story from the campaign. Throughout the election and even in the leaders' debate, an allegation was made that the Liberal leader had contacted the prime minister of Canada to obtain postponement in dealing with the matter at the federal level. The benefit of this would presumably have been that the solution envisaged in Ottawa not impede the Ontario Liberals' electoral opportunities. McGuinty avowed that he did have such contact but, it seems, to no avail. The politics and the legality of legislative change can indeed be exceedingly controversial.

Issues of campaign discussion engendering political promises that have implications on political life arise from litigation. It is necessary to sound a note of democratic caution here. In a jurisdiction such as Ontario, with a judiciary independent of politics and by extension independent of electioneering, there can be no accusation that a campaign could affect the conduct or the outcome of a litigious process. No such allegation is made here. Rather, what we must envisage is the possibility of influence in the opposite direction, where a trial contemporaneous with an election campaign has an impact on political discussion and decision. In this campaign, the case of *George v. Harris*[58] was clearly perceived as being so relevant to the images of the competing parties as to exert a potential influence on voters' decisions. Long before the election was called, this trial had been scheduled to start on 22 September 2003. Specifically in order to avoid having the trial influence the campaign or impact on its outcome, the incumbent minister of Public Safety and Security, Bob Runciman, one of the defendants, filed a motion on 17 September 2003 to have the start of the trial delayed beyond voting day.

The Ontario Superior Court rendered its decision on the Runciman motion on September 18 in the form of an Endorsement. The judge recounted that Runciman, as one of the defendants, argued for a brief adjournment of the trial on the ground that he would otherwise not be able to participate in the trial as needed, given the necessary time committed to his campaign. In support of the motion, the minister's chief of staff filed an affidavit indicating that the candidate was committed to attending to events and canvassing in his own and in neighbouring ridings each day until 2 October 2003. The plaintiffs, respondents on the motion, objected to the adjournment, arguing that it was simply a politically motivated request to prevent damaging evidence coming out during the campaign, that would prove embarrassing and harmful to Runciman and the PCs.

The court granted the motion, based primarily on the proposition that every person has an inherent right to be present at a trial or at any other proceeding to which he is a party. The judge also felt that a four-day delay in a trial scheduled to last for six months, in an action which had been ongoing for over eight years, was not significant.

Going beyond the parameters of the election period, the court left a noticeable gap in its reasoning. The Runciman motion also pleaded that this defendant would not be able to attend court because of his ongoing duties as minister of Public Safety and Security. By not dealing with this part of the motion, the court avoided setting the precedent that would have been made if it had decided that the applicant's quality of being a minister of the Crown was also sufficient to warrant the requested delay.

The *George v. Harris* trial would inevitably have focused on the legality of the Harris government's attitudes and actions in general. The deliberation, in the context of a campaign, of whether the past actions of an incumbent government were legal or not, are indeed pertinent to the party's image and to voters' opinions and choices. Only the courts, however, not the voters, can determine legal responsibility and liability. Nevertheless, the desire of the defendant minister in this situation can only underline the obvious and inherent electoral benefit of appearing to have acted legally in the past. In politics, there is a perceptible, perhaps even measurable, benefit to be derived from adherence to legal norms. In a democratic environment, the public perception of upholding the constitutional and legal rights of those whom one governs is vital. In this sense, the lesson of *George v. Harris* is that one must not only come to court with clean hands, but one must also face the electorate with hands that are legally clean and that appear to be legally clean. Again, democracy and legality reinforce each other. Interestingly, it was on 2 October 2003, the day of the election itself, that the parties reached a comprehensive settlement, altogether forestalling the need for a trial. Incoming Liberal Premier McGuinty promised that the settlement would also lead to a public judicial inquiry. The formation of such an inquiry was eventually announced on 12 November 2003; it began its hearings on 20 April 2004, and its report was released on 1 November 2005.

Campaign discussion leading to political promises with legal implications may also arise where a legal instrument, such as a contract, is itself the source of the discussion. This scenario arose in the 2003 campaign in respect of the so-called P3 (public-private partnership) hospitals. During its lifetime, the outgoing government had made policy decisions to arrange for the construction of new hospitals using this semi-private method for the delivery of public services. There is some room for doubt as to whether this mechanism of public administration readily fits into the scope of the *Canada Health Act*[59] or the *Ontario Public Hospitals*

Act.[60] Whether it does or not, such use of public funds is highly controversial. In the midst of the campaign, the government indicated its intention to close a P3 agreement for the construction of a new wing for a hospital in Ottawa. By extrapolation from the idea of the P3 method for providing capital projects in the domain of social services, this move concentrated the attention of voters on the actual legal instrument used for the carrying out of the plan. The contract itself became the issue: should the government enter into it or not? *Prima facie*, the campaign promise with legal connotations was to sign or not to sign.

On a more fundamental constitutional level, the matter of the contract called into question both the constitutionality and the political wisdom of what the government had seemingly decided to do during election time. There is a constitutional convention to the effect that between the dissolution of the legislature and either the entry into office of a new government or the renewal of the incumbent one's mandate by means of the election, the government should only act as a caretaker, without engaging in major new initiatives. In this case, the way each of the political parties addressed the issue indicated that they were well aware of the convention. This convention formed the basis of their argumentation relating to the contract. The PC view was that the major policy decisions required to establish the P3 mechanism had been taken during the life of the government and so the signing of the contract was mere public service execution of policy. By contrast, the Liberal's position on the constitutionality of the P3 mechanism was not clear; they opposed signing the contract during the election campaign, but indicated that rather than litigate to cancel it, a Liberal administration would fold the P3 hospitals into the public hospital system. The NDP was most strenuously opposed to both the P3 concept and the contract itself, promising to litigate to end it "at any cost" and "to the ends of the earth."[61]

While the three major political parties expressed their respective positions and made campaign promises which reflected those positions, in the final days of the election period, an *ad hoc* coalition of outside parties started an application against the implementation of the P3 scheme, particularly in respect to hospitals in Ottawa and Brampton. This motion for stay was reported in the media to be that P3 privatization would violate the *Public Hospitals Act*, but they were also said to rely on the constitutional convention against major new initiatives in an *interregnum*.[62]

The applicants included the Ontario Council of Hospital Unions, the Ontario Health Coalition, and the Ontario Public Service Employees Union. The respondents were listed as Tony Clement, Minister of Health, and Her Majesty the Queen.[63] Specifically, the action was for judicial review of the ministerial authorizations for P3 contracts. Specifically, the applicants' motion sought, *inter alia*: (1) an order staying any approval by the minister of any plans by a number of specified hospitals to permit for-profit corporations to design, build, finance, lease/own, maintain, operate, manage, and use any hospital facility, pending the outcome of the application for judicial review; and (2) an order requiring the minister or his delegate to revoke any approvals he may have granted with respect to any such plans.[64] In light of the fact that constitutional conventions are not justiciable, the applicants relied on a variety of pleadings to the effect that the P3 scheme was contrary to the *Public Hospitals Act*. They argued, principally, that P3 would interfere with the ability of the minister to effectively direct the subject hospitals, that it would frustrate the purposes and objectives of the statute, that it would subjugate certain hospital functions to the control and governance of for-profit corporations, and that it would constitute a fundamental change in the manner in which hospitals are governed in the Province of Ontario.

Even though the applicants could not explicitly rely on conventional rules in their action, they could not refrain from mentioning the political context. In doing so, they came as close as possible to pleading that the harm the convention intended to avoid in fact should be avoided:

> A provincial election campaign is currently underway and two of the three major political parties have signified their opposition to the P3 schemes. In light of the fact that the contracts the Minister intends to approve include provisions imposing significant financial penalties if the contracts are revoked, approval now may make the P3 scheme irreversible by a future government for a significant period of time, notwithstanding its opposition to the scheme. Further, the proponents of the P3 schemes have said that the cancellation of the schemes will expose public hospitals in Ontario to significant financial penalties. Such financial penalties would inevitably be borne by the taxpayers of Ontario.[65]

The hearing of the motion for interim order to stop the minister or his delegates from approving the P3 schemes pending the outcome of the application for judicial review took place in the Divisional Court of the Ontario Superior Court of Justice on 30 September 2003. The hospitals showed up in court and complained that they should have been made respondents in the case, along with the minister and the Crown. They said they needed time to prepare their own evidence and arguments, and they therefore asked the court to adjourn the motion. The judge agreed to grant an adjournment. The issue then arose whether the court should stop the minister from approving the schemes, pending the rescheduling of the motion. Effectively, the only thing the judge decided was whether the adjournment was to be granted, with or without conditions. The court applied the same test to that question as it would have applied if it had gone ahead and heard the motion.

In the decision dated 2 October 2003, election day, Justice Patrick Gravely specifically indicated the he was applying to the motion the same rules as those for the granting of injunctive relief. He was not convinced by the applicants' arguments and deferred the motion until the merits of the case could be heard. He reasoned that "I am not satisfied on the evidence presented by the applicants that the P3 projects will likely be in breach of the *Public Hospitals Act* or the *Regulations*. The Minister retains control under the *Act* and in the public interest may revoke approvals under s. 4 (5). Absent any contravention of the statute, this court has no right to become involved in these government decisions."[66] In effect, the judge adjourned the motion without imposing any conditions and referred the matter to the registrar to set a new date for the motion to be heard. It could come on again at any time, depending on what the parties decided to do. If this motion is ever heard, such a hearing will occur long before the merits of the case are determined on the application for judicial review. From the perspective of this article, the important consideration is that, despite the P3 contracts, the litigation prevented breach of the constitutional convention involved.

Finally, platform promises relating to the attorney general portfolio—that is, promises about law and legality itself—are also issues of campaign discussion that carry legal implications. The manner in which the question of legality is best addressed here is to ask whether law, and in particular law enforcement, is the handmaiden of politics or a democratic virtue in and of itself. In more practical terms, are campaign issues in this field raised, and are solutions in this field proposed, so that the party making them may assume office and wield power, or so that it may serve justice and legality? In a sense, campaign promises of political parties in the field of justice are all somewhat predictable. In this campaign as in earlier ones, these promises all arose from the overall vision each party has of society. Most parties, however, tend to make justice-related campaign promises strictly within democratic bounds, respecting at least the fundamental rules of legality. The best conclusion, therefore, must be that in designing campaign promises in relation to the administration of justice, parties combine legal and political considerations in the hope that these will help them achieve a capacity to govern.

While most serious political parties engage their trust in carrying out the campaign promises they undertake, in this campaign none seemed to venture so far as to propose that political or campaign promises become legally enforceable. The doctrine of legitimate expectations has not, or perhaps not yet, extended into this area.

Legally Sanctioned Broadcasting and the Leaders' Debate

The socio-cultural trend of mass communications in North America has for several decades been in favour of television to the detriment of newspapers. In the McLuhanesque world, television can deliver messages more rapidly, more to the viewer's than to the reader's ease, and apparently more effectively than print.

These are all reasons for the prominence of television as the medium of choice in elections.

The legal plain on which broadcasting is situated is exclusively comprised of federal law.[67] The *Radio Regulations, 1986* and the *Television Broadcasting Regulations, 1987*, both made pursuant to the *Broadcasting Act*, define political broadcasts for purposes of an election period. The guiding principle in the statutory and regulatory framework is that broadcasting of programs, advertisements, and announcements of a political character be conducted on a basis equitable toward all accredited political parties and rival candidates in the election. The practical applications of this principle are that no party or candidate may be excluded from access to the airwaves and no party or candidate may disproportionately dominate the airwaves.

In furtherance of the broadcasters' and the public's awareness of the applicable rules at each election, the Canadian Radio-television and Telecommunications Commission (CRTC) issues a broadcasting circular specifically relating to that electoral event. In the present circumstance, on 5 September 2003, the Commission issued *Broadcasting Circular CRTC 2003-456*,[68] which applied the rules to Ontario's electoral circumstances and schedule.

While the legal and regulatory rules on political broadcasting were used and observed in a routine fashion in respect to party advertisements, the same is not true of the party leaders' debate, scheduled for 23 September 2003. The fact that a televised leaders' debate has become the focal point of every general election is now acknowledged. This event underscores not only the visions of the competing political parties, it also reveals the leaders' knowledge of the law which lies at the root of their political platforms. In turn, the debate itself raises contentious issues of legality.

As early as September 6, a consortium of broadcasters comprising the CBC, CTV, CanWest Global, CHUM Television, TV Ontario, CPAC, and OMNI-TV announced that they would organize and diffuse a debate, but one limited to the leaders of the PCs, the Liberals, and the NDP, the only parties within a much larger field which the broadcasters believed capable of electing candidates. The legality of this decision needs to be examined in the context of the serious controversy which the exclusion of the leaders of the other political parties from the debate caused.

On 9 September 2003, the Green Party of Ontario launched a campaign to have its leader included among the debaters.[69] On 14 September, counsel for the Greens lodged a formal complaint with the CRTC. The complaint, made against the seven broadcasters, was that they were "contravening the requirements of equitable coverage during the election period," and it requested that the Commission "act very expeditiously in dealing with this complaint."[70] The complaint letter proposed that the Commission inform the consortium that the leader of the Greens be included in the debate. In the absence of a CRTC power to force the consortium to include the Greens' leader, the Commission's assumption of this role would have been a form of public pressure. In the alternative, the complaint requested that the CRTC inform the broadcasters to give the Green Party of Ontario what it called "extraordinarily wide coverage in other public affairs broadcasts if the balance requirement is to be met."[71] While this argument is clever, it seems to have been crafted with the understanding that it is unlikely the CRTC has the power to issue such remedial instructions, even in the name of the principle of equity. We may thus ponder the nature of the argument: is it legal or political?

The Greens' complaint did raise serious legal issues. The CRTC's discussion of "Equity in Public Affairs Programming" in *Broadcasting Circular 2003-456* included party leaders' debates. The relevant portions of that instrument indicated that, pursuant to s. 3 of the *Broadcasting Act*, broadcasters would have to apply the ground-rule of equity in debates. However, it went on to state that the Commission had, since 1995, no longer required that so-called debates programs feature all rival parties or candidates. The complaint contrasted this position to the principle of "electoral fairness" adopted by the Supreme Court of Canada in the *Libman*[72] and *Figueroa*[73] decisions. It relied in particular on the Court's holding in *Libman* that "Elections are fair and equitable only if all citizens are reasonably informed of all the possible choices and if parties and candidates are given a reasonable opportunity to present their positions."[74] On this basis, the Letter of Complaint went on to conclude that "However, it is at least clear that the concept of electoral fairness developed in *Libman* and *Figueroa* must inform all constitutional considerations of equitable allocation of broadcast time during election periods. I would submit that these cases imply that there is a constitutional requirement of equitable allocation of broadcast time, independent of any statute."[75]

The CRTC dealt with the complaint through a staff response letter dated September 19, which was approved in a letter from the Commission's secretary general on 22 September 2003. In conformity with its apolitical public service mandate, the Commission's response was solely based on norms of law. It decided to take no action at this time, relying principally on the decision of the Ontario Court of Appeal in the case of *R. v. CBC*.[76] That case, also dealing with the participation of leaders of political parties in debates, held that debates were not programs of a partisan political character within the meaning of the *Regulations*, thus rendering the *Regulations* not applicable to the debates. That court's key finding was the distinction between partisan political broadcasts and broadcasts about political matters. The Commission noted that in their response to the Greens' complaint, the broadcasters had relied on the same jurisprudence. For added measure, the consortium members had also added that forcing them to include certain leaders in the debate would be a door to interference with their free expression.

The Green Party's complaint called attention to a recurring issue in democratic political life. Despite the attempts of the legal system to achieve a level of fairness and equity in the conduct of political life and in electioneering in particular, there are irreparable imbalances inherent in politics. One of these is the persistence of smaller parties' relegation to secondary rank status until they reach mass appeal. No legal mechanism has yet been devised to adjust or correct this situation. The CRTC's handling of this complaint follows in a long line of not only Canadian jurisprudence on similar demands for inclusion,[77] it also reflects the manner in which this issue has been dealt with in several like-minded democracies.[78] The lesson is that there are limits to the reach of law into political life, short of a dictatorship of legalism.

The Democratic Decision Whether and How to Vote

Discussion of the vote itself reflects the intimacy between law and politics in the bosom of democracy. The first consideration here is whether it is worthwhile for a citizen to vote. Democracy is the political system which offers the individual citizen the right to participate in political life through the freely expressed choice of a ballot. In its Canadian and Ontario versions, the legal instruments securing the democratic nature of the political system do not require citizens to vote. The declining trend in voter participation is now so pronounced that it was noted publicly by the CEO of Canada in the period following the thirty-seventh federal general election, held on 27 November 2000. His conclusion was against making the vote legally binding. We may contemplate whether such a solution could be contrary to the *Charter* s. 3 right to vote. Nevertheless, in the absence of a legally binding norm, Elections Ontario has engaged in a number of policy initiatives to induce as many voters as possible to participate.

The legal basis of electoral democracy is not just participation, but participation that is politically meaningful. The election administration's advertising campaign has itself thus become contentious. One of the groups criticizing it is Fair Vote Canada, an association aimed at changing the "first-past-the-post" system to one at least partially based on proportional representation.[79] In the view of Fair Vote Canada, the Elections Ontario ads were misleading in that they implied that everyone's vote counts. Whether the goal is that more citizens avail themselves of an existing right protected by law, or a reform such as that sought by Fair Vote Canada, the path toward a useful and effective electoral system must necessarily run through the law.

For those citizens who do use the right to vote, and for many of whom this is their only link to democracy, the highest decision is the choice among competing political options. Having envisaged the matter from the point of view of parties and candidates' political speech and platform promises, we must ask whether citizens choose the way they mark their ballot for legal considerations, political ones, or a combination of factors involving other motivations as well. It is unlikely that the question of voter motivation has been studied from this specific vantage point. If this hypothesis is true, this gap in our knowledge of public affairs is worth noting.

In the absence of clear empirical evidence for now, let us surmise that, subjectively, voters make choices based on a combination of their respective world views, their reaction to the political images projected at them, the impact on them of the political leadership role played by each party head, and their notion of enlightened self-interest. On a more objective, analytical level, the vote would seem to be a comprehensively civil decision, involving the totality of perceptible factors. The vote is not a business decision with voters susceptible only to being convinced by the use of their own tax resources to what they see as beneficial to themselves, although for some it can be principally that. Nor is the vote a religious or exclusively morality-based decision, although for some it has become that. While personal religious or philosophical convictions can, and perhaps inevitably do, colour electoral decisions, the Canadian constitutional tradition of the separation of Church and State implies that belief is only one of a number of factors which voters may wish to take into account. Otherwise, single-issue politics distort the more global, civic perspective of the political system. Moreover, in Ontario society with its rush toward the centre, the vote is not an ideological decision where votes are uniquely susceptible to being enticed by a radical or another form of single-issue choice toward a particular model of society, although for a few, it could be primarily that. Similarly, the vote is unlikely to be a primarily legal decision, with voters solely desirous of achieving a particular legal system or scheme, although for a number, it could be that. Most likely, subject to social science evidence, the decision on how to vote combines partisan, political, and legal considerations together with other policy factors among which economic ones can be mentioned as important.

Democratic Participation and the State of the Law

On 2 October 2003, with whatever combination of motives, the voters spoke democratically. Many others rejected the opportunity offered to them through their constitutionally guaranteed rights and the legal framework of elections implementing those rights. This is a significant issue from the perspective of democracy. In a political legal system which affords rights and liberties such as that of participation in public life through voting, it is inherent that use of the right by the greatest number is beneficial. Moreover, in modern terminology, the participation of the citizenry in public life is in the public interest. The official statistics of elections Ontario indicate that only 56.8 per cent of eligible Ontarians voted. There is a need to question whether the 43.2 per cent electoral abstinence, and more significantly whether the progressive decline in electoral participation, can be attributed to the *Election Act* and to the method of registration of electors that it mandates.

The traditional method of assembling voters' lists in Canada was, for a long time, by enumeration of electors, conducted during each campaign and separately in each jurisdiction. There was a hypothesis that the visits of enumerators to each household contributed to the voters' awareness of the campaign and that it sustained a relatively high level of voter participation, as compared to that in like-minded democracies. This hypothesis itself contributed to the perpetuation of enumeration as the method of compiling voters' lists, enshrined in the electoral statutes of various Canadian jurisdictions, including that of Ontario, even though it could never be conclusively verified.

During the 1990s, ostensibly both as a cost-cutting and an efficiency-promoting measure, Elections Canada decided to abandon the practice of enumeration specific to each election in favour of the establishment of a permanent register of electors. This decision found expression in several sets of amendments to the *Canada Elections Act*. One feature required to make the federal register system succeed according to the wishes of its designers was its adoption by provinces and other subnational jurisdictions. The ideal was a single, multi-use, Canada-wide register. Ontario signed on to this system by amending its legislation so as to grant authority to the CEO to establish and maintain a permanent register of electors for Ontario.[80]

The effect of these changes in the law dealing with the manner of constituting the voters' list on the rate of participation in elections has become a subject of great public controversy. Generally, we may surmise that the legal framework of an electoral regime and the public administration systems which underlie it exert an influence on voter participation, just as they contribute to the outcome of elections.[81] However, we must face the inability of the social sciences to develop precise methods of measurement and the scarcity of precise information available. Consequently, in fairness, attributing the decline in voter participation to the permanent register of electors is just as hypothetical today as attributing higher voter turnouts to event-specific enumeration used to be. The only serious assumption allowing us to believe this new hypothesis is that of *res ipsa loquitur*. Applying this maxim, if it is true that the decline in voter participation is approximately contemporaneous with the shift from enumeration to the register, that decline must be due to the change in the law. Despite the well-established status of the maxim, we may question whether its conclusion can be supported by hard evidence.

One attempt, mandated by the CEO of Canada, has recently been made by academics to analyze the reasons for the decline in voter turnout over the decade of the 1990s.[82] While this is a serious work investigating a variety of possible factors, it devotes minimal attention to the change from the enumeration system to the permanent register and in effect fails to analyze this change as one of the possible factors causing, or contributing to, the decline in voter participation. Quite to the contrary, this study takes a "forge ahead" attitude in its concluding paragraph: "Finally, with regard to *election administration*, there is considerable evidence from this study that more needs to be done to ensure the registration of the maximum number of citizens, particularly young people becoming eligible by virtue of age, in the National Register of Electors."[83]

This incomplete analysis has done nothing to dispel among parliamentarians the attitude that it is the register of electors, as presently enshrined not only in federal but also in Ontario legislation, which diminishes voter participation in elections. "Some provincial and federal politicians say the permanent voters' list is driving down voter turnout provincially and federally, and point to the historic low turnout of only 57 per cent which swept Dalton McGuinty and his Liberals into power on Oct. 2 in Ontario."[84]

Another academic analysis was prepared independently of any electoral authority by a McGill University political scientist, under a mandate from the Institute for Research on Public Policy.[85] According to this study, the register came to replace enumeration primarily on the basis of the expenditure reduction argument put forward by Elections Canada. This impetus combined with political support from the government of the day in the mid-1990s, as well as with the benefit it was thought likely to provide in the field of federal-provincial relations based on the register's multiple use. Consequently, planning for the register included inadequate or no consideration of its potential negative impacts. Notwithstanding this lack of planning, the study regards the negative effects of the register on voter participation in elections to be well grounded in the specialized literature. The real issue then becomes the magnitude of the impact. The change from enumeration to the register seems to have particularly disadvantaged the young and the poor among potential voters. The study concludes by advocating that the issue of how best to enrol voters be revisited and "to ensure that the discussion and the policy choices reflect the ideal that registration regimes should primarily operate to uphold the key democratic principle of facilitating the participation of all citizens."[86]

While cross-jurisdictional comparisons cannot definitely settle an inquiry into the effect of legislation on political activity, they can at least offer some collateral evidence. While the 2003 general election was going on in Ontario, PEI was also conducting one. That province's *Election Act*, like Ontario's, provides for a register of electors.[87] However, unlike the Ontario legislation, the PEI *Election Act* also mandates at each election, in addition to the register, that there shall be a confirmation of all electors on the register.[88] This is, in effect, full enumeration under a different label. PEI's *Election Act* thus contains a mandatory combination of both the enumeration and the register systems. It may be indicative of the value of the *res ipsa loquitur* maxim that in PEI's general election of 29 September 2003, the electoral system based on this legislation produced a voter turnout officially gauged at 83 per cent. This was so despite the intemperate conditions then being caused by Hurricane Juan.

Even discounting the differences between Ontario and PEI in terms of political culture, and those based on differences of geography and proportions of population, the divergence between turnouts of 57 per cent and 83 per cent are too significant to ignore the impact of legislative regimes.

Whether in the field of elections, as here, or in democratic governance which follows electoral events, the combination of political, legal, and public administration—in particular, the influence of legality on the other two elements of public life—is worth studying in greater depth.

Notes

1. The views expressed here are exclusively those of the author and are entirely non-partisan. This article was prepared as an academic paper, not on behalf of the House of Commons, its members or its administration.

2. "Political law" is the interdisciplinary study of (1) the *interaction* among law, public policy, and administration, and politics; and (2) the *influence* of law on the other types of instruments of democratic governance. The approach taken in the study of political law incorporates the elements of constitutional and administrative law with public administration and political science. It goes beyond earlier treatments of "law and politics" by considering jointly all the disciplines relating to governance along a single continuum and by exploring how they interact in complement to, or in conflict with, each other. Political law deals specifically with topics such as: the factors motivating the choice of instruments for governing; the balance of law and politics in the legislative process; the precedence of law and its accommodation with other types of instruments in government management; the legal value to be ascribed to political and campaign promises; and the relative weight of legal, administrative, and political influences in the adjudication of political disputes on issues of public governance. This analysis of the influences on, and forces in, the conduct of public affairs means that political law is more concerned with the role of law than are traditional studies of the rule of law. The study of political law is a reflection of the increasing legalization of politics and public administration, especially in an era dominated by the *Charter*. The use of political law is to demonstrate that in democratic regimes, good governance involves not only respect for civil and political human rights, but also for their natural counterpart, the accountability of public institutions and officials to law. This interdisciplinary focus is deliberately distinct from either a purely legal analysis of the relevant case law or an analysis exclusively grounded in political science or public administration.

3. The Latin expression for "bread and circuses" refers to popular entertainment designed to distract the public from serious participation in civic duties.

4. *Constitution Act, 1982*, s. 4 (1).

5. Parliamentary Notice—Return of Members; *The Ontario Gazette* Vol. 132-26 (Saturday, 26 June 1999): 1.

6. *Legislative Assembly Act*, R.S.O. 1990, c. L. 10, s. 3.

7. *Constitution Act, 1982*, s. 52 (1).

8. R.S.C. 1985, App. No. 5.

9. R.S.O. 1996, c. L.10.

10. The footnotes appearing in *A Consolidation of The Constitution Acts 1867 to 1982*, prepared by the Department of Justice of Canada, are particularly helpful in understanding the relationships among the constitutional statutes, as well as between the relevant federal and provincial statutes. The latest version of this book is updated to 1 January 2001.

11. Andrew Heard, *Canadian Constitutional Conventions: The Marriage of Law and Politics* (Toronto: University of Toronto Press, 1991) 31–34.

12. R.S.B.C. 1996, c. 66.

13. *Constitution (Fixed Election Dates) Amendment Act, 2001*, S.B.C. 2001, c. 36; in force B.C. Reg. 330/2002, s. 1, effective 9 December 2002.

14. Many constitutionalists are of the view that a convention exists, according to which a government is bound to present its budget in the legislature. Nevertheless, on 27 March 2003, the government of Ontario made public its last budget before the election outside the Legislative Assembly, in a car parts factory. This gave rise to a lively public debate as well as a battle of legal opinions regarding the constitutional validity of the tabling.

15. *George v. Harris*, Ontario Superior Court of Justice, File 96-CU-99569. In this action, the family of Dudley George, an Aboriginal protester killed at Ipperwash Provincial Park on 5 September 1995 by the Ontario Provincial Police, initiated a claim for compensation from Mike Harris while he was premier and from other political figures. The political elements of this case relate first to the litigation against a head of government in office and secondly to the allegations against the defendants of motives politically inimical to the deceased.

16. Henri Brun, et Guy Tremblay, *Droit Constitutionnel*, 4e éd. (Montréal : Yvon Blais, 2002) 601–04.

17. 2003 Platform of the Ontario Liberal Party, <http://www.ontarioliberal.on.ca/en/platform/5/index.cfm>; accessed 12 September 2003.

18. *An Act to Amend the Election Act, the Election Finances Act, the Legislative Assembly Act, to repeal the Representation Act, 1996 and to enact the Representation Act, 2005*; Bill 214 of 2005, s. 1(3), enacted 13 December 2005, awaiting Royal assent as this book is going to print.

19. "The Road Ahead: Premier Ernie Eves' plan for Ontario's future," <http://www.ontariopc.com/TheRoadAhead/section_a_stronger_democracy.htm>; accessed 23 September 2003.

20. *Reference Re Prov. Electoral Boundaries (Sask.)* (1991) 2 S.C.R. 158.

21. S.O. 1996, c. 28.

22. *Representation Act*, R.S.O. 1990, c. R.26; *Representation Act, 1991*, S.O. 1991, c. 2; *Representation Act, 1993* (No. 1), S.O. 1993, c.2; *Representation Act, 1993* (No. 2), S.O. 1993, c.30.

23. S.O. 1996, c. 28, Schedule.

24. *Proclamation Declaring the Representation Order to be in Force Effective on the First Dissolution of Parliament that Occurs After January 8, 1997*; SI/96-9, 7 February 1996 and Representation Order 1996, *Canada Gazette*, Part II Extra, 130, 1 (12 January 1996).

25. *Proclamation Declaring the Representation Order to be in Force Effective on the First Dissolution of Parliament that Occurs After August 25, 2004*; SI/2003-154, 29 August 2003 and Representation Order 2003, *Canada Gazette*, Part II Extra, 137, 6 (29 August 2003).

26. R.S.C. 1985, c. E-3.

27. *An Act Respecting the Effective Date of the Representation Order of 2003*, Bill C-49 of 2003, introduced 15 September 2003. At the time of writing, this bill was at the stage of having been adopted by the Standing Committee on Procedure and House Affairs, on 23 September 2003.

28. *An Act to amend the Election Act, the Election Finances Act, the Legislative Assembly Act, to repeal the Representation Act, 1996 and to enact the Representation Act, 2005*; Bill 214 of 2005, s. 4 and Schedule 1, enacted 13 December 2005, awaiting Royal Assent as this book is going to print.

29. Peter Hogg, *Constitutional Law of Canada*, Vol 1 (Toronto: Carswell, 1999) 9–25.

30. R.S.O. 1990, c. E.6, s. 9.

31. *Proclamation of Dissolution and for the Issue of the Writs*, 2 September 2003. *The Ontario Gazette*, Vol. 136-37 (Saturday, 12 September 2003) 1.

32. *Election Act*, R.S.O. 1990, c. E.6, s. 11 (3).

33. *Election Act*, R.S.O. 1990, c. E.6, s. 10 (1).

34. *Election Act*, R.S.O. 1990, c. E.6, s. 11 (1).

35. *Election Act*, R.S.O. 1990, c. E.6, s. 4 (1).

36. *Election Act*, R.S.O. 1990, c. E.6, s. 114 (1).

37. *Election Act*, R.S.O. 1990, c. E.6, s. 7 (1).

38. *Election Act*, R.S.O. 1990, c. E.6, s. 40 (1).

39. *Meeting the Needs of a Modern Electorate*, prepared by the Office of the Chief Election Officer (Ontario, April 2000).

40. R.S.O. 1990, c. E.7.

41. Green Candidate, "PC backer offered me cash," *The Toronto Star* (11 September 2003), <http://www.thestar.com/NASApp/cs/ContentServer?pagename=thestar/Layout/Article_T>; accessed 12 September 2003; and "Business owner says he offered contribution," *The Toronto Star* (12 September 2003), <http://www.thestar.com/NASApp/cs/ContentServer?pagename+thestar/Layout/Article_T>; accessed 12 September 2003.

42. *Report of the (Monnin) Commission of Inquiry into Allegations of Infractions During the 1995 Manitoba General Election*, 29 March 1999.

43. R.S.O. 1990, c. P. 47.

44. *Public Service Act*, R.S.O. 1990, c. P.47, s. 28.3 (3) item 5.

45. *Tremblay c. Commission de la Fonction publique* (1990) R.J.Q. 1386.

46. Gregory Tardi, "Modernization of the Rules on Political Neutrality in the Public Service," *Newsletter of the Constitutional, Civil Liberties and Human Rights Section of the Ontario Bar Association* 3, 3 (April 2003): 17.

47. "Negative campaign a gamble," *The Toronto Star* (4 September 2003), <http://www.thestar.com/NASApp/cs/ContentServer?pagename=thestar/Layout/Article_T>; accessed 12 September 2003; and "Ontario election campaign gets nastier," *The Globe and Mail* (8 September 2003), <http://www.theglobeandmail.com/servlet/story/RTGAM.20030908.wontelect0908/BNSto>; accessed 8 September 2003; and "Tories pull McGuinty attack ads," *The Ottawa Citizen* (20 September 2003), <http://www.canada.com/ottawa/ottawacitizen/story.asp?id=3E06CCBE-!FD-4278_B01>; accessed 23 September 2003.

48. "Eves HQ: McGuinty a 'kitten-eater,'" *The Toronto Star* (12 September 2003), <http://www.thestar.com/NASApp/cs/ContentServer?pagename=thestar/Layout/Article_T>; accessed 12 September 2003; and "Eves acknowledges insult to McGuinty 'over-the-top,'" *The Globe and Mail* (12 September 2003), <http://www.theglobeandmail.com/servlet/story/RTGAM.20030912.wonta0912/BNStory/>; accessed 12 September 2003.

49. "Memo blamed on key Harris adviser," *The Toronto Star* (30 September 2003), <http://www.thestar.com/NASApp/cs/ContentServer?pagename=thestar/Layout/Article_T>; accessed 30 September 2003.

50. "McGuinty makes light of Eves jab," *The Toronto Star* (1 October 2003), <http://www.thestar.com/NASApp/cs/ContentServer?pagename=thestar/Layout/Article_T>; accessed 1 October 2003.

51. "Families angered by Tory memo," *The Toronto Star* (16 September 2003), <http://www.thestar.com/NASApp/cs/ContentServer?pagename=thestar/Layout/Article_T>; accessed 19 September 2003.

52. The Supreme Court of Canada has extended the meaning of the right to vote set out in s. 3 of the *Charter* to encompass the right to an informed vote, through several of its recent decisions, notably *Thomson Newspapers Co. v. Canada* (1998) 1 S.C.R. 877. The concept of "informing" voters should be understood in this context as providing them material on the basis of which they are better able to make choices among political options, than without them.

53. "Saskatchewan parties promise to curb mudslinging," *The Globe and Mail* (7 October 2003), <http://www.theglobeandmail.com/servlet/story/RTGAM.20031007.wsasko8/BNStory/Nat>; accessed October 8, 2003.

54. "NDP cartoon spurs outrage," *The Saskatoon Star Phoenix* (14 October 2003), <http://www.canada.com/saskatoon/starphoenix/archives/story.asp?id=11D086FA-A1C8-4>; accessed 15 October 2003; and "Sask. NDP cartoon has Nazi overtones," *The National Post* (14 October 2003): A-1, A-7.

55. "NDP fires official for role in cartoon," *The Regina Leader-Post* (15 October 2003), <http://canada.com/national/story.asp?id=FAA476B6-E5BB-4E4A-A955-2A818CD523DA>; accessed 15 October 2003.

56. "NDP apologizes for cartoon," *The Saskatoon Star Phoenix* (15 October 2003), <http://www.canada.com/saskatoon/starphoenix/story.asp?id=DDF38735-99F0-4AAA-B5>; accessed 15 October 2003.

57. "Odious cartoon damages NDP," *The Saskatoon Star Phoenix* (15 October 2003), <http://www.canada.com/saskatoon/starphoenix/editorials/story.asp?id=C9169699-0BAE->; accessed 15 October 2003.

58. See note 13.

59. R.S.C. 1985, c. C-6.

60. R.S.O. 1990, c. P.40.

61. "Liberals won't stop P3 hospitals at taxpayers' expense," CBC: Ontario Votes 2003, <http://toronto.cbc.ca/regional/servlet/View?filename=onel_p3mcguinty2003 0925>; accessed 26 September 2003; and "McGuinty slams hospital contract," *The Toronto Star* (26 September 2003), <http://www.thestar.com/NASApp/cs/ContentServer?pagename=thestar/Layout/Article_T>; accessed 29 September 2003.

62. "Unions to seek injunction on sale of hospitals," Canada Newswire #CNNW000020 030930dz9u000jx (30 September 2003).

63. Ontario Superior Court of Justice—Divisional Court; Court File No. 586/03.

64. *Ontario Council of Hospital Unions et al. v. Tony Clement, Minister of Health, et al.*; Factum of the Moving Parties, 29 September 2003; Amended Notice of Motion, 29 September 2003.

65. *Ontario Council of Hospital Unions et al. v. Tony Clement, Minister of Health, et al.*; Amended Notice of Motion, 29 September 2003, para. 16.

66. *Ontario Council of Hospital Unions et al. v. Tony Clement, Minister of Health, et al.*; Endorsement, 2 October 2003.

67. *Broadcasting Act*, S.C. 1991, c. 11, with amendments.

68. See <http://www.crct.gc.ca/archive/ENG/Circulars/2003/c2003-456.htm>.

69. "Green Party to challenge TV networks' debate snub," *The Canadian Press* (13 September 2003), <http://www.canada.com/toronto/features/ontariovotes/story.html?idF195B65B-CA3C-4>; accessed 13 September 2003; and "Green Party launches campaign to be included in televised leaders' debate," <http://greenparty.on.ca/news/press_release/fulltext.shtml?x=97>; accessed 13 September 2003.

70. Green Party Letter of Complaint, dated 14 September 2003 by Roach, Schwartz & Associates, per Peter M. Rosenthal, Solicitors for the Green Party of Ontario, to the CRTC.

71. Green Party Letter of Complaint.

72. *Libman v. Quebec (Attorney General)* [1997] 3 S.C.R. 569.

73. *Figueroa v. Canada*, 2003 SCC 37.

74. *Libman v. Quebec*, para. 47, quoted on Green Party Letter of Complaint 2.

75. Green Party Letter of Complaint 5.

76. (1993) 51 C.P.R. (3d) 192.

77. *National Party of Canada v. Canadian Broadcasting Corporation* (1993) 106 D.L.R. (4th) 575; *Natural Law Party of Canada v. Canadian Broadcasting Corporation* (1994) 1 F.C. 580; *Dumont v. Johnson et Côté* (1994) R.D.J. 460.

78. *Perot v. Federal Election Commission* 97 F. 3d 553 (D.C. Cir. 1996); *Scottish National Party v. Scottish Television and Grampian Television*, 1998 S.L.T. 1395; *Becker v. Federal Election Commission* 230 F. 3d 381 (1st Cir. 2000).

79. "Elections Ontario ads aimed at getting people to vote under fire," <http://www.canada.com/toronto/features/ontariovotes/story.html?id=67E0C86D-B560-46>; accessed 24 September 2003.

80. S.O. 1998, c.9, enacting into the *Election Act* various provisions dealing with the permanent register of electors, enumeration (to supplement the register), as well as the addition of electors to the register on polling day.

81. The notion that an electoral system has an impact on the outcome of an election may seem controversial. Nevertheless, it is genuine. In Ontario, for example, had the 2003 general election been conducted on the basis of proportional representation rather than through a first-past-the-post system, the results would have been significantly different. This reality is not an aspersion on the legitimacy of either system.

82. Jon H. Pammett, and Lawrence LeDuc, *Explaining the Turnout Decline in Canadian Federal Elections: A New Survey of Non-voters* (Ottawa: Elections Canada, March 2003).

83. Pammett and LeDuc 74.

84. F. Abbas Rana, "MPs worried permanent voters' list drives down voter turnout," *The Hill Times* (13 October 2003) 1.

85. Jerome H. Black, "From Enumeration to the National Register of Electors: An Account and an Evaluation," *IRPP Choices* 9, 7 (August 2003).

86. Black 36.

87. R.S.P.E.I., c. E-1.1, s. 24.1.

88. R.S.P.E.I., c. E-1.1, s. 31.

CHAPTER 6

Provincial Political Data Since 1900

ALAN SIAROFF

The following tables provide for the period since 1900: (i) a summary of all election results; (ii) statistics on electoral concentration, competition, and bias; (iii) information on electoral systems; and (iv) a list of all premiers with related information.

Note that vote percentages are based on total valid votes. In certain provinces individual voters did cast multiple votes in dual-member or multi-member districts, but it is the total votes (not voters) that matter here.

Note also that the term Conservative is used continuously for simplicity, rather than switching to "Progressive Conservative".

The material has been drawn from various sources, in particular:

J. Murray Beck, *The Government of Nova Scotia* (Toronto: University of Toronto Press, 1957), Appendix F.

Canadian Parliamentary Guide, various years.

Robert H. Cuff et al. (eds.), *Dictionary of Newfoundland and Labrador Biography* (St. John's: Harry Cuff Publications Ltd., 1990).

Rand Dyck, *Provincial Politics in Canada: Towards the Turn of the Century*, third edition (Scarborough, Ontario: Prentice-Hall Canada, 1996).

Elections Prince Edward Island, *Prince Edward Island Historical Review of Provincial Election Results 1900 to 26 February 2001*, researched, compiled, and edited by Lowell Croken and Norma E. Palmer (July 2001).

Mark W. Graesser, "Religion and Voting in Newfoundland: Party Alignment and Realignment, 1889-1949", paper presented at the annual meeting of the Canadian Political Science Association, Carleton University, June 1993.

Harold Jansen, "The Single Transferable Vote in Alberta and Manitoba", Ph.D. thesis, University of Alberta, 1998.

Ontario, Office of the Chief Election Officer, *Electoral History of Ontario: Candidates and Results With Statistics From the Records, 1867-1982* (1985).

Terence H. Qualter, *The Election Process in Canada* (Toronto: McGraw-Hill, 1970).

Loren M. Simerl, "A Selection of Canadian Provincial Election Results, 1905-1976", pp. 599-637 in Paul W. Fox, ed., *Politics: Canada*, fourth edition (Toronto: McGraw-Hill Ryerson, 1977).

Other relevant provincial reports and websites.

Table 6.1. Provincial Election Results Since 1900

Newfoundland and Labrador	total seats	Conservatives vote %	seats	Liberals vote %	seats	Fisherman's Protective Union vote %	seats	vote %	seats	others and independents vote %	seats
pre-Federation											
1900	36	35.3	4	62.9	32					1.8	0
1904	36	39.5	6	60.1	30					0.4	0
1908	36	49.4	18	50.2	18					0.4	0
1909	36	52.5	26	47.5	10						
1913	36	45.5	21	34.7	7	19.6	8			0.1	0
1919	36	37.7	13	38.7	12	20.5	11			3.0	0
1923	36	48.0	13	27.0	12	24.5	11			0.5	0
1924	36	57.9	25	28.0	4	12.9	6			1.2	1
1928	40	43.3	12	42.3	19	12.9	6			2.2	0
1932	26	70.8	24	28.3	2	12.2	9			0.9	0

Responsible government ended in 1934.

since Federation	total seats	Conservatives vote %	seats	Liberals vote %	seats	CCF / NDP vote %	seats	vote %	seats	others and independents vote %	seats
1949	28	32.9	5	65.5	22					1.6	1
1951	28	35.6	4	63.6	24					0.9	0
1956	36	32.0	4	66.3	32					1.7	0
1959	36	25.3	3	58.0	31	7.2	0	*United Nfld. Party* 8.2	2	1.3	0
1962	42	36.6	7	58.7	34	3.6	0			1.1	1
1966	42	34.0	3	61.8	39	1.8	0			2.4	0
1971	42	51.3	21	44.4	20	1.8	0			2.5	1
1972	42	60.5	33	37.2	9	0.2	0			2.1	0
1975	51	45.5	30	37.1	16	4.4	0	*Liberal Reform Party* 11.9	4	1.1	1
1979	52	50.4	33	40.6	19	7.8	0			1.2	0

	total seats	Conservatives vote %	seats	Liberals vote %	seats	Progressives / CCF vote %	seats	Labrador Party	others and independents vote %	seats
1982	52	61.2	44	34.9	8	3.7	0		0.2	0
1985	52	48.6	36	36.7	15	14.4	1		0.3	0
1989	52	47.6	21	47.2	31	4.4	0		0.7	0
1993	52	42.1	16	49.1	35	7.4	1		1.3	0
1996	48	38.7	9	55.1	37	4.5	1		1.8	1
1999	48	40.8	14	49.6	32	8.2	2		1.4	0
2003	48	58.7	34	33.2	12	6.9	2	0.9 0	0.4	0
Prince Edward Island										
1900	30	46.5	9	53.5	21					
1904	30	45.9	8	54.1	22					
1908	30	48.4	13	51.6	17					
1912	30	60.2	28	39.8	2					
1915	30	50.1	17	49.9	13					
1919	30	45.7	5	54.3	25					
1923	30	52.3	25	44.0	5	2.4 *(Progressives)*	0		1.3	0
1927	30	46.9	6	53.1	24					
1931	30	51.7	18	48.3	12					
1935	30	42.1	0	57.9	30					
1939	30	47.0	3	53.0	27					
1943	30	46.1	10	51.3	20	2.1 *(CCF)*	0		0.5	0
1947	30	45.3	6	50.3	24	4.3	0		0.1	0
1951	30	46.7	6	51.6	24	1.7	0			
1955	30	45.0	3	55.0	27					
1959	30	50.9	22	49.1	8					
1962	30	50.6	19	49.4	11					

PEI (cont.)

	total seats	vote %	seats	vote %	seats	vote % NDP	seats NDP	vote %	seats	vote % others and independents	seats
1966	32	49.5	15	50.5	17						
1970	32	41.6	5	58.4	27						
1974	32	40.2	6	53.9	26	5.9	0				
1978	32	48.1	15	50.7	17	0.9	0			0.2	0
1979	32	53.3	21	45.3	11	1.3	0			0.2	0
1982	32	53.7	21	45.8	11	0.5	0				
1986	32	45.5	11	50.3	21	4.0	0			0.2	0
1989	32	35.8	2	60.7	30	3.5	0				
1993	32	39.5	1	55.1	31	5.4	0				
1996	27	47.4	18	44.8	8	7.9	1				
2000	27	57.9	26	33.7	1	8.4	0				
2003	27	54.3	23	42.7	4	3.1	0				

Nova Scotia

	total seats	Conservatives vote %	seats	Liberals vote %	seats	CCF/NDP vote %	seats	Farmer—Labour vote %	seats	others and independents vote %	seats
1901	38	41.7	2	56.7	36					1.6	0
1906	38	42.1	5	53.2	32					4.7	1
1911	38	45.4	11	51.1	27					3.5	0
1916	43	48.8	13	50.4	30					0.8	0
1920	43	24.7	3	44.4	29			30.9	11		
1925	43	60.9	40	36.3	3			2.8	0		
1928	43	50.6	23	48.3	20			1.1	0		
1933	30	45.9	8	52.6	22	0.7	0			0.8	0
1937	30	46.0	5	52.9	25					1.1	0
1941	30	40.3	4	52.7	23	7.0	3				
1945	30	33.5	0	52.7	28	13.6	2			0.2	0
1949	37	39.2	8	50.9	27	9.7	2			0.2	0

New Brunswick

	total seats	Conservatives vote %	Conservatives seats	Liberals vote %	Liberals seats	Labour / CCF vote %	Labour / CCF seats	United Farmers vote %	United Farmers seats	others and independents vote %	others and independents seats
1903	46	46.3	12	53.1	34					0.6	0
1908	46	51.6	31	45.0	12					3.5	3
1912	48	59.9	46	39.2	2					0.9	0
1917	48	47.9	21	52.1	27						
1920	48	26.3	13	47.0	24	5.1 *(Labour)*	2	20.6	9	1.0	0
1925	48	52.9	37	44.8	11			1.9	0	0.3	0
1930	48	52.3	31	47.7	17					0.0	0
1935	48	40.2	5	59.6	43					0.0	0
1939	48	45.0	19	54.8	29	0.1 *(CCF)*	0			0.3	0
1944	48	40.0	11	48.4	37	11.7	0			0.1	0
1953	37	43.4	12	49.1	23	6.9	2			0.6	0
1956	43	48.6	24	48.2	18	3.0	1			0.2	0
1960	43	48.3	27	42.6	15	8.9	1			0.2	0
1963	43	56.2	39	39.7	4	4.1	0			0.1	0
1967	46	52.8	40	41.8	6	5.2	0			0.4	0
1970	46	46.9	21	46.1	23	6.7	2			0.5	0
1974	46	38.6	12	47.9	31	13.0	3			0.5	0
1978	52	45.8	31	39.4	17	14.4	4			1.2	1
1981	52	47.5	37	33.2	13	18.1	1			2.2	1
1984	52	50.6	42	31.3	6	15.9	3			1.2	1
1988	52	43.5	28	39.6	21	15.8	2			1.5	0
1993	52	31.3	9	49.3	40	17.8	3			0.3	0
1998	52	29.8	14	35.3	19	34.6	19			1.0	0
1999	52	39.2	30	29.8	11	30.0	11			1.0	0
2003	52	36.3	25	31.6	12	31.1	15			1.0	0
2006	52	39.6	23	23.6	9	34.5	20			2.3	0

New Brunswick (cont.)

	total seats	Conservatives vote %	seats	Liberals vote %	seats	NDP vote %	seats	vote %	seats	others and independents vote %	seats
1948	52	31.2	5	57.8	47	6.0	0			5.0	0
1952	52	48.9	36	49.2	16	1.3	0			0.6	0
1956	52	52.2	37	46.1	15					1.7	0
1960	52	46.2	21	53.4	31	*NDP*				0.4	0
1963	52	48.2	20	51.8	32					0.0	0
1967	58	47.1	26	52.7	32	0.2	0	*Parti Acadien*			0
1970	58	48.5	32	48.5	26	2.8	0			0.2	0
1974	58	46.9	33	47.5	25	2.9	0	1.2	0	1.5	0
1978	58	44.4	30	44.3	28	6.5	0	3.5	0	1.3	0
1982	58	47.4	39	41.3	18	10.2	1	0.9	0	0.2	0
1987	58	28.6	0	60.4	58	10.5	0	*Confederation of Regions*		0.5	0
1991	58	20.7	3	47.1	46	10.8	1	21.2	8	0.2	0
1995	55	30.9	6	51.6	48	9.6	1	7.1	0	0.7	0
1999	55	53.0	44	37.3	10	8.8	1	0.7	0	0.2	0
2003	55	45.4	28	44.4	26	9.7	1			0.5	0

Quebec	total seats	Conservatives vote %	seats	Liberals vote %	seats	vote %	seats	vote %	seats	others and independents vote %	seats
1900	74	41.9	7	53.1	67					5.0	0
1904	74	26.7	7	55.5	67					17.8	0
1908	74	39.9	14	53.5	57			2.6	3	4.0	0
1912	81	43.0	16	53.5	63	*Labour*		*Nationalists* 1.0	0	2.5	2
1916	81	35.1	6	60.6	75					4.3	0
1919	81	17.0	5	51.9	74	9.7	2			21.4	0

Year	Seats	*Union Nationale* %	seats	Liberal %	seats	%	seats	%	seats	%	seats
1923	85	39.3	20	51.5	64					9.2	1
1927	85	34.3	9	59.3	74					6.4	2
1931	90	43.5	11	54.9	79					1.6	0
1935	90	18.3	16	46.8	48			*National / Liberal Action* 30.1	26	4.8	0
1936	90	56.9	76	39.4	14					3.7	0
1939	86	39.1	15	54.1	70			4.5	0	2.3	1
1944	91	38.0	48	39.4	37	*Bloc Populaire* 14.4	4			8.2	2
1948	92	51.2	82	36.2	8					12.6	2
1952	92	50.5	68	45.8	23					3.7	1
1956	93	51.8	72	44.9	20					3.3	1
1960	95	46.6	43	51.4	51					2.0	1
1962	95	42.2	31	56.4	63	*RIN*				1.5	1
1966	108	40.8	56	47.3	50	5.6	0			6.3	2
1970	108	19.6	17	45.4	72	*Parti Québécois* 23.1	7	*Créditistes* 11.2	12	0.7	0
1973	110	4.9	0	54.7	102	30.2	6	9.9	2	0.3	0
1976	110	18.2	11	33.8	26	41.4	71	4.6	1	2.0	1
1981	122	4.0	0	46.1	42	49.2	80			0.7	0
1985	122			56.0	99	38.7	23			5.3	0
1989	125			49.9	92	40.2	29			9.9	4[1]
1994	125			44.4	47	44.8	77	*ADQ* 6.5	1	4.4	0
1998	125			43.5	48	42.9	76	11.8	1	1.8	0
2003	125			45.8	76	33.2	45	18.3	4	2.7	0

ADQ = Action Démocratique du Québec

1. In 1989, the four "other" seats were won by the Equality Party.

Ontario	total seats	Conservatives		Liberals		Labour / CCF / NDP		United Farmers / Progressives / Labour–Progressive (communists) / Green Party		others and independents	
		vote %	seats	vote %	seats	vote %	seats	vote %	seats	vote %	seats
1902	98	50.0	48	47.6	50					2.4	0
1905	98	53.4	69	45.8	29					0.8	0
1908	106	56.5	86	40.0	19					1.8	0
1911	106	57.3	83	38.5	22	1.7	1			1.8	0
1914	111	55.3	84	38.6	26	2.4	1			4.8	0
1919	111	34.9	25	26.3	28	11.6	12	22.3	45	4.9	1
1923	111	49.8	75	21.8	14	4.7	4	22.0	17	1.7	1
1926	112	57.6	74	24.6	23	1.3	1	8.5	14	8.0	0
1929	112	58.8	92	32.8	14	1.0	1	4.7	5	2.8	0
1934	90	39.8	17	50.4	69	7.0	1	0.6	1	2.3	2
1937	90	40.0	23	51.6	66	5.6	0	0.5	1	2.3	0
1943	90	35.7	38	31.2	16	31.7	34	0.9	2	0.5	0
1945	90	44.3	66	29.8	14	22.4	8	2.4	2	1.1	0
1948	90	41.5	53	29.8	14	27.0	21	1.0	2	0.7	0
1951	90	48.5	79	31.5	8	19.1	2	0.7	1	0.2	0
1955	98	48.5	84	33.3	11	16.5	3	1.2	0	0.5	0
1959	98	46.3	71	36.6	22	16.7	5	0.2	0	0.2	0
1963	108	48.9	77	35.3	24	15.5	7			0.3	0
1967	117	42.3	69	31.6	28	25.9	20			0.2	0
1971	117	44.5	78	27.8	20	27.1	19			0.6	0
1975	125	36.1	51	34.3	36	28.9	38			0.7	0
1977	125	39.7	58	31.5	34	28.0	33	Green Party		0.8	0
1981	125	44.4	70	33.7	34	21.1	21			0.8	0

1985	125	37.0	52	37.9	48	23.8	25	0.1	0	1.2	0
1987	130	24.7	16	47.3	95	25.7	19	0.1	0	2.2	0
1990	130	23.5	20	32.4	36	37.6	74	0.7	0	5.8	0
1995	130	44.8	82	31.1	30	20.6	17	0.4	0	3.1	1
1999	103	45.1	59	39.9	35	12.6	9	0.7	0	1.8	0
2003	103	34.7	24	46.5	72	14.7	7	2.8	0	1.3	0

Conservatives historically included Conservative independents, Conservative Temperance, and Conservative—Liberals. Likewise, Liberals included Liberal independents, Liberal Temperance, Liberal Prohibitionists, Liberal—Labour, and Liberal Progressives.

Manitoba	total seats	vote %	seats	vote %	seats	vote %	seats	vote %	seats	vote %	seats
		Conservatives		Liberals		Labour / ILP		Farmers / UFM / Progressives		others and independents	
1903	40	50.6	31	44.6	9					4.8	0
1907	41	50.6	28	47.9	13					1.5	0
1910	41	50.9	28	44.3	13					4.8	0
1914	49	46.6	28	42.8	20					10.7	1
1915	47	33.0	5	55.1	40					11.9	2
1920	55	16.9	7	35.9	21	20.8	11	15.8	12	10.6	4
1922	55	16.5	7	24.4	9	16.0	6	32.8	28	10.3	5
1927	55	27.1	15	21.1	7	9.5	3	33.1	29	9.1	1
				Liberal—Progressives		*Labour / CCF*		*Social Credit*			
1932	55	35.5	10	39.6	38	17.0	5			8.0	2
1936	55	28.4	16	36.0	23	12.2	7	9.2	5	14.1	4
1941	55	21.4	15	35.4	27	17.3	3	7.3	3	18.7	7
1945	55	16.3	13	32.9	25	35.3	10	2.1	2	13.5	5
1949	57	20.2	14	40.5	30	25.4	7			13.9	6
1953	57	21.0	12	39.6	33	16.6	5	13.4	1	9.5	6
1958	57	40.5	26	35.0	19	20.2	11	1.8	0	2.6	1
1959	57	46.7	36	30.3	11	22.1	10			0.9	0

Manitoba (cont.)

	total seats	vote %	seats	vote %	seats	vote %	seats	vote %	seats	vote %	seats
				Liberals		NDP					
1962	57	45.2	36	36.4	13	15.3	7	2.5	1	0.6	0
1966	57	40.0	31	33.1	14	23.1	11	3.6	1	0.2	0
1969	57	35.7	22	24.0	5	38.3	28	1.3	1	0.8	1
1973	57	36.7	21	19.0	5	42.3	31	0.4	0	1.6	0
1977	57	48.8	33	12.3	1	38.6	23	0.3	0	0.1	0
1981	57	43.8	23	6.7	0	47.4	34			2.1	0
1986	57	40.6	26	13.9	1	41.5	30			4.0	0
1988	57	38.4	25	35.5	20	23.6	12			2.5	0
1990	57	42.0	30	28.2	7	28.8	20			1.1	0
1995	57	42.9	31	23.7	3	32.8	23			0.6	0
1999	57	40.8	24	13.4	1	44.5	32			1.3	0
2003	57	36.3	20	13.2	2	49.4	35			1.1	0

Note: From 1940 to 1950, the key dividing line in Manitoba politics was between supporters and opponents of a Liberal—Progressive-led coalition. Incumbent coalition candidates, regardless of party, were never challenged by other members of the coalition. The Conservatives were always formally part of this coalition, although there were dissident Independent Conservative candidates in 1941 and 1949—some of whom were elected. The CCF only stayed in the coalition until 1943, thereafter becoming the official opposition. Social Credit candidates ran both for and against the coalition, but only the pro-coalition ones were successful.

The aggregate nature of electoral support was thus as follows:

	total seats	vote %	seats	vote %	seats
		pro-coalition		anti-coalition	
1941	55	82.3	51	17.7	4
1945	55	53.8	43	46.2	12
1949	57	57.2	43	42.8	14

Saskatchewan	total seats	Conservatives vote %	seats	Liberals vote %	seats	Labour / CCF/NDP vote %	seats	Progressives/Farmer–Labour / Social Credit / Western Canada Concept / Saskatchewan Party vote %	seats	others and independents vote %	seats
1905	25	47.5	9	52.2	16					0.3	0
1908	41	47.9	14	50.8	27					1.3	0
1912	53	42.0	7	57.0	45					1.1	1
1917	59	36.3	7	56.7	51	0.8	0			6.2	1
1921	63	7.4	3	52.2	47	3.3	0	7.5	6	29.5	7
1925	63	19.0	3	52.6	51	1.9	1	23.0	6	3.5	2
1929	63	36.4	24	45.9	28	1.2	0	6.9	5	9.6	6
1934	55	26.7	0	48.0	50	0.3	0	24.0	5	0.9	0
1938	52	12.1	0	45.5	38	18.7	10	16.0	2	7.8	2
1944	52	10.7	0	35.4	5	53.1	47	0.1	0	0.7	0
1948	52	9.6	0	32.3	20	47.6	31	8.1	0	2.5	1
1952	53	2.3	0	39.3	11	54.1	42	3.9	0	0.5	0
1956	53	2.0	0	30.3	14	45.2	36	21.5	3	1.0	0
1960	55	13.9	0	32.7	17	40.8	38	12.4	0	0.3	0
1964	59	18.9	1	40.4	32	40.3	26	0.4	0	0.0	0
1967	59	9.8	0	45.6	35	44.3	24	0.3	0		
1971	60	2.1	0	42.8	15	55.0	45			0.1	0
1975	61	27.6	7	31.7	15	40.1	39			0.6	0
1978	61	38.1	17	13.8	0	48.1	44			0.0	0
1982	64	54.1	55	4.5	0	37.6	9	3.3	0	0.5	0
1986	64	44.6	38	10.0	1	45.2	25	0.1	0	0.1	0
1991	66	25.5	10	23.3	1	51.0	55	0.0	0	0.1	0
1995	58	17.9	5	34.7	11	47.2	42			0.2	0
1999	58	0.4	0	20.1	4	38.7	29	39.6	25	1.2	0
2003	58	0.2	0	14.2	0	44.6	30	39.4	28	1.7	0

Alberta	total seats	Conservatives vote %	seats	Liberals vote %	seats	Socialists and Labour vote %	seats	United Farmers of Alberta (UFA) vote %	seats	others and independents vote %	seats
1905	25	37.1	2	57.6	23	3.0				5.3	0
1909	41	31.7	2	59.3	36	1.9	1			6.0	2
1913	56	45.1	17	49.2	39	3.9	0			3.8	0
1917	56	41.8	19	48.1	34	12.3	1			6.2	2
1921	61	11.0	0	34.1	15	7.8	4	28.9	38	13.7	4
1926	61	22.1	5	26.3	7	7.6	5	39.7	43	4.1	1
1930	63	14.9	6	24.6	11	1.7	4	39.4	39	13.5	3
1935	63	6.4	2	23.1	5		0	11.0	0	3.5	0
								Social Credit			
								54.2	56		
						CCF / NDP					
1940	57			0.9	1	11.1	0	42.9	36	45.1	20
1944	57					24.9	2	51.9	51	23.2	4
1948	57			17.9	2	19.1	2	55.6	51	7.4	2
1952	61	3.7	2	22.4	4	14.1	2	56.2	52	3.7	1
1955	61	10.3	4	31.1	15	8.2	2	46.4	37	4.0	3
1959	65	23.9	1	13.9	1	4.3	0	55.7	61	2.2	2
1963	63	12.7	0	20.0	2	9.5	0	54.8	60	3.0	1
1967	65	26.0	6	10.9	3	16.0	0	44.6	55	2.5	1
1971	75	46.4	49	1.0	0	11.4	1	41.1	25	0.1	0
1975	75	62.7	69	5.0	0	12.9	1	18.2	4	1.2	1
1979	79	57.4	74	6.2	0	15.8	1	19.9	4	0.8	0
1982	79	62.3	75	1.8	0	18.7	2	0.8	0	16.3	2
1986	83	51.4	61	12.2	4	29.2	16			7.2	2
1989	83	44.3	59	28.7	8	26.3	16	0.5	0	0.3	0

	total seats	vote %	seats	vote %	seats	vote %	seats	vote %	seats	vote %	seats
1993	83	44.5	51	39.7	32	11.0	0	2.4	0	2.4	0
1997	83	51.2	63	32.8	18	8.8	2	6.8	0	0.4	0
2001	83	61.9	74	27.3	7	8.0	2	0.5	0	2.2	0
2004	83	46.8	62	29.4	16	10.2	4	1.2	0	12.4	1
2004 of which, Alberta Alliance										8.7	1

In 1917, there were also two province-at-large seats for the soldiers' vote.

British Columbia	total seats	Conservatives		Liberals		Socialist Party / CCF		Provincial Party / Social Credit		others and independents	
		vote %	seats	vote %	seats	vote %	seats	vote %	seats	vote %	seats
1900	38	45.0	20	36.6	7	8.0	2	11.1	8	7.3	3
1903	42	46.4	22	37.8	17	8.9	3			7.8	1
1907	42	48.7	26	37.2	13	11.5	2			5.3	0
1909	42	52.3	38	33.2	2	11.1	1			3.0	0
1912	42	59.7	39	25.4	0	1.2	0			3.9	2
1916	47	40.5	9	50.0	36	3.5	0			8.3	2
1920	47	31.2	15	37.9	25	1.3	0			27.4	7
1924	48	29.4	17	31.3	23			24.2	3	13.8	5
1928	48	53.3	35	40.0	12					6.7	1
1933	47			41.7	34	31.5 (CCF)	7			26.7	6
1937	48	28.6	8	37.3	31	28.6	7	1.2	0	4.3	2
1941	48	31.1	12	32.9	21	33.4	14			2.6	1
1945	48	Coalition 55.8	37			37.6	10	1.4	0	5.1	1
1949	48	Coalition 61.4	39			35.1	7	1.7	0	1.9	2

British Columbia (cont.)

	total seats	Conservatives vote %	seats	Liberals vote %	seats	CCF/NDP vote %	seats	vote %	seats	vote %	seats
1952	48	16.8	4	23.5	6	30.8	18	27.2	19	1.7	1
1953	48	5.6	1	23.6	4	30.8	14	37.8	28	2.2	1
1956	52	3.1	0	21.8	2	28.3	10	45.8	39	1.0	1
1960	52	6.7	0	20.9	4	32.7	16	38.8	32	0.8	0
1963	52	11.3	0	20.0	5	27.8	14	40.8	33	0.1	0
1966	55	0.2	0	20.2	6	33.6	16	45.6	33	0.4	0
1969	55	0.1	0	19.0	5	33.9	12	46.8	38	0.1	0
1972	55	12.7	2	16.4	5	39.6	38	31.2	10	0.2	0
1975	55	3.9	1	7.2	1	39.2	18	49.2	35	0.5	0
1979	57	5.1	0	0.5	0	46.0	26	48.2	31	0.3	0
1983	57	1.2	0	2.7	0	44.9	22	49.8	35	1.5	0
1986	69	0.7	0	6.7	0	42.6	22	49.3	47	0.6	0
1991	75	0.0	0	33.2	17	40.7	51	24.0	7	2.0	0
		Progressive Democratic Alliance (PDA)						*Reform Party of B.C. / Unity Party of B.C.*			
1996	75	5.7	1	41.8	33	39.5	39	9.3	2	3.7	0
2001	79			57.6	77	21.6	2	3.2	0	17.6	0
2005	79			45.8	46	41.5	33			12.7	0

of which, *Green Party*

	vote %	seats
1983	0.2	0
1986	0.2	0
1991	0.9	0
1996	2.0	0
2001	12.4	0
2005	9.2	0

Table 6.2. Provincial Election Statistics Since 1900

seats = total seats in the election

Electoral Concentration
ENPP = effective number of parliamentary parties
P 2+ S = number of parties winning 2 or more seats (integer value)
1PSC = one-party seat concentration (percentage of seats won by the largest party in terms of seats)
1PVC = one-party vote concentration (percentage of votes won by this party)
2PSC = two-party seat concentration (percentage of seats won by the two largest parties in terms of seats)

Electoral Competition
SL 1 – 2 (%) = seat lead of largest party (by seats) over second-largest, expressed as a percentage of total seats
ED = electoral decisiveness, whereby HP = hung parliament, EM = earned majority, and MM = manufactured majority
ACCL = total seats won by acclamation (absolute number)

Electoral Bias
DISP = total disproportionality (Loosemore-Hanby index)
SBL = seat bias in favour of the largest party (in terms of seats), calculated as 1PSC – 1PVC

Newfoundland and Labrador	seats	ENPP	P 2+ S	Electoral Concentration			Electoral Competition			Electoral Bias	
				1PSC	1PVC	2PSC	SL 1-2 (%)	ED	ACCL.	DISP	SBL
pre-Federation											
1900	36	1.246	2	88.9	62.9	100.0	77.8	EM		26.0	26.0
1904	36	1.385	2	83.3	60.1	100.0	66.7	EM		23.2	23.2
1908	36	2.000	2	50.0	50.2	100.0	0.0	HP		0.6	-0.2
1909	36	1.670	2	72.2	52.5	100.0	44.4	EM		19.7	19.7
1913	36	2.339	3	58.3	45.5	80.6	36.1	MM		15.5	12.8
1919	36	2.986	3	36.1	37.7	69.4	2.8	HP		10.1	-1.6
1923	36	2.986	3	36.1	48.0	69.4	2.8	HP		12.4	-11.9
1924	36	1.912	3	69.4	57.9	86.1	52.8	EM		15.3	11.5
1928	40	2.730	3	47.5	42.3	77.5	17.5	HP		23.3	5.2
1932	26	1.166	2	92.3	70.8	100.0	84.6	EM	2	21.5	21.5
since Federation											
1949	28	1.537	2	78.6	65.5	96.4	60.7	EM		13.1	13.1

Newfoundland and Labrador (cont.)

	seats	ENPP	P 2+S	1PSC	1PVC	2PSC	SL 1-2 (%)	ED	ACCL.	DISP	SBL
1951	28	1.324	2	85.7	63.6	100.0	71.4	EM	5	22.1	22.1
1956	36	1.246	2	88.9	66.3	100.0	77.8	EM	4	22.6	22.6
1959	36	1.331	3	86.1	58.0	94.4	77.8	EM	1	28.1	28.1
1962	42	1.463	2	81.0	58.7	97.6	64.3	EM	3	22.3	22.3
1966	42	1.153	2	92.9	61.8	100.0	85.7	EM	3	31.1	31.1
1971	42	2.095	2	50.0	51.3	97.6	2.4	HP		3.2	-1.3
1972	42	1.508	2	78.6	60.5	100.0	57.1	EM	1	18.1	18.1
1975	51	2.217	3	58.8	45.5	90.2	27.5	MM		13.3	13.3
1979	52	1.865	2	63.5	50.4	100.0	26.9	EM		13.1	13.1
1982	52	1.352	2	84.6	61.2	100.0	69.2	EM		23.4	23.4
1985	52	1.777	2	69.2	48.6	98.1	40.4	MM		20.6	20.6
1989	52	1.929	2	59.6	47.2	100.0	19.2	MM		12.4	12.4
1993	52	1.536	2	67.3	49.1	98.1	36.5	MM		18.2	18.2
1996	48	1.587	2	77.1	55.1	95.8	58.3	EM		22.0	22.0
1999	48	1.882	3	66.7	49.6	95.8	37.5	MM		17.1	17.1
2003	48	1.767	3	70.8	58.7	95.8	45.8	EM		12.1	12.1

Prince Edward Island

	seats	ENPP	P 2+S	1PSC	1PVC	2PSC	SL 1-2 (%)	ED	ACCL.	DISP	SBL
1900	30	1.724	2	70.0	53.5	100.0	40.0	EM	1	16.5	16.5
1904	30	1.642	2	73.3	54.1	100.0	46.7	EM	2	19.2	19.2
1908	30	1.965	2	56.7	51.6	100.0	13.3	EM	2	5.1	5.1
1912	30	1.142	2	93.3	60.2	100.0	86.7	EM	6	33.1	33.1
1915	30	1.965	2	56.7	50.1	100.0	13.3	EM		6.6	6.6
1919	30	1.385	2	83.3	54.3	100.0	66.7	EM		29.0	29.0
1923	30	1.385	2	83.3	52.3	100.0	66.7	EM		31.0	31.0
1927	30	1.471	2	80.0	53.1	100.0	60.0	EM		26.9	26.9

	seats	ENPP	P 2+S	1PSC	1PVC	2PSC	SL 1-2 (%)	ED	ACCL.	DISP	SBL
1931	30	1.923	2	60.0	51.7	100.0	20.0	EM		8.3	8.3
1935	30	1.000	1	100.0	57.9	100.0	100.0	EM		42.1	42.1
1939	30	1.220	2	90.0	53.0	100.0	80.0	EM		37.0	37.0
1943	30	1.800	2	66.7	51.3	100.0	33.3	EM		15.4	15.4
1947	30	1.471	2	80.0	50.3	100.0	60.0	EM		29.7	29.7
1951	30	1.471	2	80.0	51.6	100.0	60.0	EM		28.4	28.4
1955	30	1.220	2	90.0	55.0	100.0	80.0	EM		35.0	35.0
1959	30	1.642	2	73.3	50.9	100.0	46.7	EM		22.4	22.4
1962	30	1.867	2	63.3	50.6	100.0	26.7	EM		12.7	12.7
1966	32	1.992	2	53.1	50.5	100.0	6.3	EM		2.6	2.6
1970	32	1.358	2	84.4	58.4	100.0	68.8	EM		26.0	26.0
1974	32	1.438	2	81.3	53.9	100.0	62.5	EM		27.4	27.4
1978	32	1.992	2	53.1	50.7	100.0	6.3	EM		2.4	2.4
1979	32	1.822	2	65.6	53.3	100.0	31.3	EM		12.3	12.3
1982	32	1.822	2	65.6	53.7	100.0	31.3	EM		11.9	11.9
1986	32	1.822	2	65.6	50.3	100.0	31.3	EM		15.3	15.3
1989	32	1.133	2	93.8	60.7	100.0	87.5	EM		33.1	33.1
1993	32	1.064	1	96.9	55.1	100.0	93.8	EM		41.8	41.8
1996	32	1.874	2	66.7	47.4	96.3	37.0	MM		19.3	19.3
2000	27	1.077	1	96.3	57.9	100.0	92.6	EM		38.4	38.4
2003	27	1.338	2	85.2	54.3	100.0	70.4	EM		30.9	30.9

Nova Scotia	seats	ENPP	P 2+S	1PSC	1PVC	2PSC	SL 1-2 (%)	ED	ACCL.	DISP	SBL
1901	38	1.111	2	94.7	56.7	100.0	89.5	EM	4	38.0	38.0
1906	38	1.375	2	84.2	53.2	97.4	71.1	EM	2	31.0	31.0
1911	38	1.699	2	71.1	51.1	100.0	42.1	EM		20.0	20.0
1916	43	1.730	2	69.8	50.4	100.0	39.5	EM		19.4	19.4
1920	43	1.904	3	67.4	44.4	93.0	41.9	MM		23.0	23.0
1925	43	1.149	2	93.0	60.9	95.3	90.7	EM		32.1	32.1

Nova Scotia (cont.)	seats	ENPP	P 2+S	1PSC	1PVC	2PSC	SL $_{1-2}$ (%)	ED	ACCL.	DISP	SBL
1928	43	1.990	2	53.5	50.6	100.0	7.0	EM		2.9	2.9
1933	30	1.642	2	73.3	52.6	100.0	46.7	EM		20.7	20.7
1937	30	1.385	2	83.3	52.9	100.0	66.7	EM		30.4	30.4
1941	30	1.625	3	76.7	52.7	90.0	63.3	EM		27.0	24.0
1945	30	1.142	2	93.3	52.7	100.0	86.7	EM		40.6	40.6
1949	37	1.718	3	73.0	50.9	94.6	51.4	EM		22.1	22.1
1953	37	2.022	3	62.2	49.1	94.6	29.7	MM		13.1	13.1
1956	43	2.052	2	55.8	48.6	97.7	14.0	MM		7.2	7.2
1960	43	1.936	2	62.8	48.3	97.7	27.9	MM		14.5	14.5
1963	43	1.203	2	90.7	56.2	100.0	81.4	EM		34.5	34.5
1967	46	1.293	2	87.0	52.8	100.0	73.9	EM		34.2	34.2
1970	46	2.172	3	50.0	46.1	95.7	4.3	HP		3.9	3.9
1974	46	1.899	3	67.4	47.9	93.5	41.3	MM		19.5	19.5
1978	52	2.136	3	59.6	45.8	92.3	26.9	MM		13.8	13.8
1981	52	1.756	2	71.2	47.5	96.2	46.2	MM		23.7	23.7
1984	52	1.494	3	80.8	50.6	92.3	69.2	EM		30.2	30.2
1988	52	2.198	3	53.8	43.5	94.2	13.5	MM		10.3	10.3
1993	52	1.600	3	76.9	49.3	94.2	59.6	MM		27.6	27.6
1998	52	2.946	3	36.5	35.3	73.1	0.0	HP		3.2	1.2
1999	52	2.368	3	57.7	39.2	78.8	36.5	MM		18.5	18.5
2003	52	2.720	3	48.1	36.3	76.9	19.2	HP		11.8	11.8
2006	52	2.677	3	44.2	39.6	82.7	5.8	HP		8.6	4.6

New Brunswick	seats	ENPP	P 2+S	1PSC	1PVC	2PSC	SL $_{1-2}$ (%)	ED	ACCL.	DISP	SBL
1903	46	1.628	2	73.9	53.1	100.0	47.8	EM		20.8	20.8
1908	46	1.910	2	67.4	51.6	95.7	39.1	EM		15.8	15.8
1912	48	1.087	2	95.8	59.9	100.0	91.7	EM		35.9	35.9
1917	48	1.969	2	56.3	52.1	100.0	12.5	EM		4.2	4.2

	seats	ENPP	P 2+S	1PSC	1PVC	2PSC	SL 1-2 (%)	ED	ACCL.	DISP	SBL
1920	48	2.776	4	50.0	47.0	77.1	22.9	HP	2	3.0	3.0
1925	48	1.546	2	77.1	52.9	100.0	54.2	EM		24.2	24.2
1930	48	1.843	2	64.6	52.3	100.0	29.2	EM		12.3	12.3
1935	48	1.229	2	89.6	59.6	100.0	79.2	EM		30.0	30.0
1939	48	1.917	2	60.4	54.8	100.0	20.8	EM		5.6	5.6
1944	48	1.546	2	77.1	48.4	100.0	54.2	MM		28.7	28.7
1948	52	1.210	2	90.4	57.8	100.0	80.8	EM	5	32.6	32.6
1952	52	1.742	2	69.2	48.9	100.0	38.5	MM		20.3	20.3
1956	52	1.696	2	71.2	52.2	100.0	42.3	EM		19.0	19.0
1960	52	1.929	2	59.6	53.4	100.0	19.2	EM		6.2	6.2
1963	52	1.899	2	61.5	51.8	100.0	23.1	EM		9.7	9.7
1967	58	1.979	2	55.2	52.7	100.0	10.3	EM		2.5	2.5
1970	58	1.979	2	55.2	48.5	100.0	10.3	MM		6.7	6.7
1974	58	1.963	2	56.9	46.9	100.0	13.8	MM		10.0	10.0
1978	58	1.998	2	51.7	44.4	100.0	3.4	MM		7.3	7.3
1982	58	1.822	2	67.2	47.4	98.3	36.2	MM		19.8	19.8
1987	58	1.000	1	100.0	60.4	100.0	100.0	EM		39.6	39.6
1991	58	1.536	3	79.3	47.1	93.1	65.5	MM		32.2	32.2
1995	55	1.292	2	87.3	51.6	98.2	76.4	EM		35.7	35.7
1999	55	1.485	2	80.0	53.0	98.2	61.8	EM		27.0	27.0
2003	55	2.070	2	50.9	45.4	98.2	3.6	MM		8.4	5.5
Quebec											
1900	74	1.207	2	90.5	53.1	100.0	81.1	EM	36	37.4	37.4
1904	74	1.207	2	90.5	55.5	100.0	81.1	EM	38	35.0	35.0
1908	74	1.585	3	77.0	53.5	95.9	58.1	EM	6	25.0	23.5
1912	81	1.552	2	77.8	53.5	97.5	58.0	EM	1	24.3	24.3
1916	81	1.159	2	92.6	60.6	100.0	85.2	EM	26	32.0	32.0
1919	81	1.192	3	91.4	51.9	97.5	85.2	EM	45	39.5	39.5

Quebec (cont.)	seats	ENPP	P 2+S	1PSC	1PVC	2PSC	SL 1-2 (%)	ED	ACCL.	DISP	SBL
1923	85	1.607	2	75.3	51.5	98.8	51.8	EM	8	23.8	23.8
1927	85	1.300	2	87.1	59.3	97.6	76.5	EM	12	27.8	27.8
1931	90	1.273	2	87.8	54.9	100.0	75.6	EM		32.9	32.9
1935	90	2.503	3	53.3	46.8	82.2	24.4	MM	3	6.5	6.5
1936	90	1.356	2	84.4	56.9	100.0	68.9	EM		27.5	27.5
1939	86	1.443	2	81.4	54.1	98.8	64.0	EM	1	27.3	27.3
1944	91	2.244	3	52.7	38.0	93.4	12.1	MM		14.7	14.7
1948	92	1.244	2	89.1	51.2	97.8	80.4	EM		37.9	37.9
1952	92	1.642	2	73.9	50.5	98.9	48.9	EM		23.4	23.4
1956	93	1.549	2	77.4	51.8	98.9	55.9	EM		25.6	25.6
1960	95	2.028	2	53.7	51.4	98.9	8.4	EM		2.3	2.3
1962	95	1.830	2	66.3	56.4	98.9	33.7	EM		9.9	9.9
1966	108	2.069	2	51.9	40.8	98.1	5.6	MM		11.1	11.1
1970	108	2.059	4	66.7	45.4	82.4	50.9	MM		21.3	21.3
1973	110	1.159	3	92.7	54.7	98.2	87.3	EM		38.0	38.0
1976	110	2.072	3	64.5	41.4	88.2	40.9	MM		23.1	23.1
1981	122	1.823	2	65.6	49.2	100.0	31.1	MM		16.4	16.4
1985	122	1.441	2	81.1	56.0	100.0	62.3	EM		25.1	25.1
1989	125	1.676	3	73.6	49.9	96.8	50.4	MM		23.7	23.7
1994	125	1.920	2	61.6	44.8	99.2	24.0	MM		16.8	16.8
1998	125	1.934	2	60.8	42.9	99.2	22.4	MM		17.9	17.9
2003	125	1.999	3	60.8	45.8	96.8	24.8	MM		15.0	15.0

Ontario	seats	ENPP	P 2+S	1PSC	1PVC	2PSC	SL 1-2 (%)	ED	ACCL.	DISP	SBL
1902	98	1.999	2	51.0	47.6	100.0	2.0	MM	1	3.4	3.4
1905	98	1.714	2	70.4	53.4	100.0	40.8	EM		17.0	17.0
1908	106	1.448	2	81.1	56.5	99.1	63.2	EM	6	24.6	24.6
1911	106	1.524	2	78.3	57.3	99.1	57.5	EM	17	21.0	21.0

	seats	ENPP	P 2+S	1PSC	1PVC	2PSC	SL 1-2 (%)	ED	ACCL.	DISP	SBL
1914	111	1.593	2	75.7	55.3	99.1	52.3	EM	4	20.4	20.4
1919	111	3.443	4	40.5	22.3	65.8	15.3	HP	4	18.2	18.2
1923	111	2.011	4	67.6	49.8	82.9	52.3	MM	2	17.8	17.8
1926	112	2.023	3	66.1	57.6	86.6	45.5	EM	3	12.5	8.5
1929	112	1.444	3	82.1	58.8	94.6	69.6	EM	8	23.3	23.3
1934	90	1.603	2	76.7	50.4	95.6	57.8	EM		26.3	26.3
1937	90	1.658	2	73.3	51.6	98.9	47.8	EM		21.7	21.7
1943	90	2.832	4	42.2	35.7	80.0	4.4	HP		13.9	6.5
1945	90	1.753	4	73.3	44.3	88.9	57.8	MM		29.0	29.0
1948	90	2.348	4	58.9	41.5	82.2	35.6	MM		18.6	17.4
1951	90	1.284	3	87.8	48.5	96.7	78.9	MM		39.3	39.3
1955	98	1.336	3	85.7	48.5	96.9	74.5	MM		37.2	37.2
1959	98	1.730	3	72.4	46.3	94.9	50.0	MM		26.1	26.1
1963	108	1.780	3	71.3	48.9	93.5	49.1	MM		22.4	22.4
1967	117	2.303	3	59.0	42.3	82.9	35.0	MM		16.7	16.7
1971	117	2.000	3	66.7	44.5	83.8	49.6	MM		22.2	22.2
1975	125	2.925	3	40.8	36.1	71.2	10.4	HP		6.2	4.7
1977	125	2.786	3	46.4	39.7	73.6	19.2	HP		6.7	6.7
1981	125	2.405	3	56.0	44.4	83.2	28.8	MM		11.6	11.6
1985	125	2.774	3	41.6	37.0	80.0	3.2	HP		5.1	4.6
1987	130	1.753	3	73.1	47.3	87.7	58.5	MM		25.8	25.8
1990	130	2.356	3	56.9	37.6	84.6	29.2	MM		19.3	19.3
1995	130	2.135	3	63.1	44.8	86.2	40.0	MM		18.3	18.3
1999	103	2.216	3	57.3	45.1	91.3	23.3	MM		12.2	12.2
2003	103	1.826	3	69.9	46.5	93.2	46.6	MM		23.4	23.4
Manitoba	seats	ENPP	P 2+S	1PSC	1PVC	2PSC	SL 1-2 (%)	ED	ACCL.	DISP	SBL
1903	40	1.536	2	77.5	50.6	100.0	55.0	EM	1	26.9	26.9
1907	41	1.764	2	68.3	50.6	100.0	36.6	EM	1	17.7	17.7

Manitoba (cont.)	seats	ENPP	P 2+S	1PSC	1PVC	2PSC	SL 1-2 (%)	ED	ACCL.	DISP	SBL
1910	41	1.764	2	68.3	50.9	100.0	36.6	EM	1	17.4	17.4
1914	49	2.026	2	57.1	46.6	98.0	16.3	MM	3	10.5	10.5
1915	47	1.358	2	85.1	55.1	95.7	74.5	EM	1	30.0	30.0
1920	55	3.986	4	38.2	35.9	60.0	16.4	HP	3	8.3	2.3
1922	55	3.168	4	50.9	32.8	67.3	34.5	MM	2	18.1	18.1
1927	55	2.689	4	52.7	33.1	80.0	25.5	MM	2	19.6	19.6
1932	55	1.926	3	69.1	39.6	87.3	50.9	MM		29.5	29.5
1936	55	3.505	4	41.8	36.0	70.9	12.7	HP	1	5.8	5.8
1941	55	3.090	4	49.1	35.4	76.4	21.8	HP	16	13.7	13.7
1945	55	3.350	4	45.5	32.9	69.1	21.8	HP	7	14.1	12.6
1949	57	2.823	3	52.6	40.5	77.2	28.1	MM	17	12.1	12.1
1953	57	2.568	3	57.9	39.6	78.9	36.8	MM		18.3	18.3
1958	57	2.803	3	45.6	40.5	78.9	12.3	HP		5.1	5.1
1959	57	2.142	3	63.2	46.7	82.5	43.9	MM		16.5	16.5
1962	57	2.145	3	63.2	45.2	86.0	40.4	MM		18.0	18.0
1966	57	2.540	3	54.4	40.0	78.9	29.8	MM		14.4	14.4
1969	57	2.509	3	49.1	38.3	87.7	10.5	HP		13.7	10.8
1973	57	2.277	3	54.4	42.3	91.2	17.5	MM		12.2	12.1
1977	57	2.007	2	57.9	48.8	98.2	17.5	MM		10.8	9.1
1981	57	1.928	2	59.6	47.4	100.0	19.3	MM		12.2	12.2
1986	57	2.060	2	52.6	41.5	98.2	7.0	MM		16.1	11.1
1988	57	2.779	3	43.9	38.4	78.9	8.8	HP		5.5	5.5
1990	57	2.408	3	52.6	42.0	87.7	17.5	MM		16.9	10.6
1995	57	2.167	3	54.4	42.9	94.7	14.0	MM		19.0	11.5
1999	57	2.029	2	56.1	44.5	98.2	14.0	MM		12.9	11.6
2003	57	1.994	3	61.4	49.4	96.5	26.3	MM		12.0	12.0

Saskatchewan	seats	ENPP	P 2+S	1PSC	1PVC	2PSC	SL 1-2 (%)	ED	ACCL.	DISP	SBL
1905	25	1.855	2	64.0	52.2	100.0	28.0	EM	1	11.8	11.8
1908	41	3.303	2	65.9	50.8	100.0	31.7	EM		15.1	15.1
1912	53	1.354	2	84.9	57.0	98.1	71.7	EM		27.9	27.9
1917	59	1.313	3	86.4	56.7	98.3	74.6	EM	3	29.7	29.7
1921	63	1.755	3	74.6	52.2	84.1	65.1	EM	17	24.4	22.4
1925	63	1.490	3	81.0	52.6	90.5	71.4	EM	8	28.4	28.4
1929	63	2.853	3	44.4	45.9	82.5	6.3	HP		2.7	-1.5
1934	55	1.198	2	90.9	48.0	100.0	81.8	MM		42.9	42.9
1938	52	1.742	4	73.1	45.5	92.3	53.8	MM		28.1	27.6
1944	52	1.210	2	90.4	53.1	100.0	80.8	EM		37.3	37.3
1948	52	1.985	2	59.6	47.6	98.1	21.2	MM		18.2	12.0
1952	53	1.490	2	79.2	54.1	100.0	58.5	EM		25.1	25.1
1956	53	1.871	3	67.9	45.2	94.3	41.5	MM		22.7	22.7
1960	55	1.746	2	69.1	40.8	100.0	38.2	MM		28.3	28.3
1964	59	2.046	2	54.2	40.4	98.3	10.2	MM		13.8	13.8
1967	59	1.933	2	59.3	45.6	100.0	18.6	MM		13.7	13.7
1971	60	1.600	2	75.0	55.0	100.0	50.0	EM		20.0	20.0
1975	61	2.073	3	63.9	40.1	88.5	39.3	MM		23.8	23.8
1978	61	1.672	2	72.1	48.1	100.0	44.3	MM		24.0	24.0
1982	64	1.319	2	85.9	54.1	100.0	71.9	EM		31.8	31.8
1986	64	1.979	2	59.4	44.6	98.4	20.3	MM		14.8	14.8
1991	66	1.393	2	83.3	51.0	98.5	68.2	EM		32.3	32.3
1995	58	1.761	3	72.4	47.2	91.4	53.4	MM		25.2	25.2
1999	58	2.270	3	50.0	38.7	93.1	6.9	HP		14.8	11.3
2003	58	1.998	2	51.7	44.6	100.0	3.4	MM		16.0	7.1

Alberta	seats	ENPP	P 2+S	1PSC	1PVC	2PSC	SL 1-2 (%)	ED	ACCL.	DISP	SBL
1905	25	1.173	2	92.0	57.6	100.0	84.0	EM	1	34.4	34.4

Alberta (cont.)	seats	ENPP	P 2+S	1PSC	1PVC	2PSC	SL 1-2 (%)	ED	ACCL.	DISP	SBL
1909	41	1.290	2	87.8	59.3	92.7	82.9	EM	9	28.5	28.5
1913	56	1.733	2	69.6	49.2	100.0	39.3	MM		20.4	20.4
1917	56	2.063	2	60.7	48.1	94.6	26.8	MM	11	12.6	12.6
1921	61	2.203	3	62.3	28.9	86.9	37.7	MM	2	33.4	33.4
1926	61	1.909	4	70.5	39.7	82.0	59.0	MM		30.8	30.8
1930	63	2.339	4	61.9	39.4	79.4	44.4	MM	4	22.5	22.5
1935	63	1.254	3	88.9	54.2	96.8	81.0	EM		34.7	34.7
1940	57	2.467	1	63.2	42.9	64.9	61.4	MM		20.3	20.3
1944	57	1.245	2	89.5	51.9	93.0	86.0	EM		37.6	37.6
1948	57	1.244	3	89.5	55.6	93.0	86.0	EM		33.9	33.9
1952	61	1.364	4	85.2	56.2	91.8	78.7	EM	1	29.0	29.0
1955	61	2.301	4	60.7	46.4	85.2	36.1	MM		14.3	14.3
1959	65	1.134	1	93.8	55.7	95.4	92.3	EM		38.1	38.1
1963	63	1.101	2	95.2	54.8	98.4	92.1	EM		40.4	40.4
1967	65	1.376	3	84.6	44.6	93.8	75.4	MM		40.0	40.0
1971	75	1.858	2	65.3	46.4	98.7	32.0	MM		18.9	18.9
1975	75	1.177	2	92.0	62.7	97.3	86.7	EM		29.3	29.3
1979	79	1.136	2	93.7	57.4	98.7	88.6	EM		36.3	36.3
1982	79	1.108	2	94.9	62.3	97.5	92.4	EM		32.6	32.6
1986	83	1.724	4	73.5	51.4	92.8	54.2	EM		22.1	22.1
1989	83	1.812	3	71.1	44.3	90.4	51.8	MM		26.8	26.8
1993	83	1.900	2	61.4	44.5	100.0	22.9	MM		16.9	16.9
1997	83	1.603	3	75.9	51.2	97.6	54.2	EM		24.7	24.7
2001	83	1.246	3	89.2	61.9	97.6	80.7	EM		27.3	27.3
2004	83	1.673	3	74.7	46.8	94.0	55.4	MM		27.9	27.9

British Columbia	seats	ENPP	P 2+S	1PSC	1PVC	2PSC	SL 1-2 (%)	ED	ACCL.	DISP	SBL
1900	38	2.798	3	52.6	45.0	73.7	31.6	MM		17.6	7.6

Year											
1903	42	2.267	3	52.4	46.4	92.9	11.9	MM	2	8.7	6.0
1907	42	2.066	3	61.9	48.7	92.9	31.0	MM		13.2	13.2
1909	42	1.215	3	90.5	52.3	95.2	85.7	EM	9	38.2	38.2
1912	42	1.157	1	92.9	59.7	95.2	90.5	EM		33.2	33.2
1916	47	1.602	2	76.6	50.0	95.7	57.4	EM	1	26.6	26.6
1920	47	2.560	3	53.2	37.9	85.1	21.3	MM		16.0	15.3
1924	48	2.749	4	47.9	31.3	83.3	12.5	HP		22.6	16.6
1928	48	1.682	2	72.9	53.3	97.9	47.9	EM		19.6	19.6
1933	47	1.821	3	72.3	41.7	87.2	57.4	MM		30.6	30.6
1937	48	2.141	3	64.6	37.3	81.3	47.9	MM		27.3	27.3
1941	48	2.946	3	43.8	32.9	72.9	14.6	HP		10.9	10.9
1945	48	1.567	2	77.1	55.8	97.9	56.3	EM		21.3	21.3
1949	48	1.466	2	81.3	61.4	95.8	66.7	EM		19.9	19.9
1952	48	3.122	4	39.6	27.2	77.1	2.1	HP		19.1	12.4
1953	48	2.309	3	58.3	37.8	87.5	29.2	MM		20.5	20.5
1956	52	1.663	3	75.0	45.8	94.2	55.8	MM		29.2	29.2
1960	52	2.086	3	61.5	38.8	92.3	30.8	MM		22.7	22.7
1963	52	2.064	3	63.5	40.8	90.4	36.5	MM		22.7	22.7
1966	55	2.190	3	60.0	45.6	89.1	30.9	MM		14.4	14.4
1969	55	1.875	3	69.1	46.8	90.9	47.3	MM		22.3	22.3
1972	55	1.923	4	69.1	39.6	87.3	50.9	MM		29.5	29.5
1975	55	1.950	2	63.6	49.2	96.4	30.9	MM		14.4	14.4
1979	57	1.985	2	54.4	48.2	100.0	8.8	MM		6.2	6.2
1983	57	1.901	2	61.4	49.8	100.0	22.8	MM		11.6	11.6
1986	69	1.768	2	68.1	49.3	100.0	36.2	MM		18.8	18.8
1991	75	1.914	3	68.0	40.7	90.7	45.3	MM		27.3	27.3
1996	75	2.151	3	52.0	39.5	96.0	8.0	MM		14.7	12.5
2001	79	1.052	2	97.5	57.6	100.0	94.9	EM		39.9	39.9
2005	79	1.947	2	58.2	45.8	100.0	16.5	MM		12.7	12.4

Table 6.3. Provincial Electoral Systems Since 1900

Note: M = member; thus 1M = single member district, 2M = two member district, etc.

Newfoundland and Labrador

election(s):	total seats	total districts	of which:	1M	2M
1900–1924	36	18			18
1928	40	37		34	3
1932	26	24		22	2
1949–1951	28	25		22	3
1956–1959	36	35		34	1
1962–1972	42	41		40	1
1975	51	51		51	
1979–1993	52	52		52	
1996–2003	48	48		48	

All members elected by plurality voting.
Labrador did not have a separate seat in pre-1949 Newfoundland.

Prince Edward Island

elections:	total seats	total districts	of which:	1M	2M
1900–1962	30	15			15
1966–1993	32	16			16
1996–2003	27	27		27	

All members elected by plurality voting.
With the abolition of its upper house in 1893, Prince Edward Island instituted a system of dual-member constituencies, with each constituency electing one assemblyman and one councillor. Strictly speaking, these were overlapping rather than true dual-member constituencies, since the assemblyman and councillor were elected on separate one vote ballots and thus did not compete directly against each other. For several decades after its establishment, there was also a suffrage distinction in this system. Specifically, until 1963 only property owners could vote for councillors. Moreover, they could vote for both positions in each and every constituency in which they held property. In any case, there were always fewer voters (and thus votes) in a constituency for the councillor than for the assemblyman. Being elected in a more elitist way (through 1962), councillors arguably inherited the spirit of the old upper house, although in reality there was no major class difference between them and the assemblymen.

Nova Scotia

elections:	total seats	total districts	of which:	1M	2M	3M	4M	5M
1901–1911	38	18			16	2		
1916–1920	43	18			14	2	1	1
1925–1928	43	19			16	2		1
1933–1945	30	26		22	4			
1949–1953	37	32		27	5			
1956–1963	43	40		37	3			
1967–1974	46	43		40	3			
1978–2006	52	52		52				

All members elected by plurality voting.

New Brunswick

election(s):	total seats	total districts	of which:	1M	2M	3M	4M	5M
1903–1908	46	16			7	4	5	
1912–1920	48	17		1	7	3	6	
1925	48	19		3	7	5	4	
1930–1944	48	17		1	7	3	6	
1948–1963	52	17			6	5	5	1
1967–1970	58	22		4	7	6	3	2
1974–1991	58	58		58				
1995–2003	55	55		55				

All members elected by plurality voting.

Quebec

election(s):	total seats	total districts
1900–1908	74	74
1912–1919	81	81
1923–1927	85	85
1931–1936	90	90
1939	86	86
1944	91	91
1948–1952	92	92
1956	93	93
1960–1962	95	95
1966–1970	108	108
1973–1976	110	110
1981–1985	122	122
1989–2003	125	125

All members elected by plurality voting—always in single member districts.

Ontario

election(s):	total seats	total districts	of which:	1M	2M
1902–1905	98	97		96	1
1908–1911	106	102		98	4
1914–1923	111	107		103	4
1926–1929	112	112		112	
1934–1951	90	90		90	
1955–1959	98	98		98	
1963	108	108		108	
1967–1971	117	117		117	
1975–1985	125	125		125	
1987–1995	130	130		130	
1999–2003	103	103		103	

All members elected by plurality voting.

Manitoba

election(s):	total seats	total districts	of which:	1M	2M	4M	10M
1903	40	40		40			
1907–1910	41	41		41			
1914	49	46		43	3		
1915	47	44		41	3		
1920–1945	55	46		45			1
1949–1953	57	47		43	1	3	
1958–2003	57	57		57			

From 1920 through 1945, the 10 member district of Winnipeg used the single transferable vote (STV). Then in 1949 and 1953, the four multimember districts used the single transferable vote (STV). From 1927 through 1953, the single member districts used AV (the alternative vote), that is, a preferential ballot. Otherwise, all members elected by plurality voting.

Saskatchewan

election(s):	total seats	total districts	of which:	1M	2M	3M	4M	5M
1905	25	25		25				
1908	41	41		41				
1912	53	53		53				
1917	59	59		59				
1921–1929	63	60		57	3			
1934	55	52		49	3			
1938–1948	52	49		46	3			
1952–1956	53	49		46	2	1		
1960	55	49		46	1	1	1	
1964	59	52		48	3			1
1967	59	59		59				
1971	60	60		60				
1975–1978	61	61		61				
1982–1986	64	64		64				
1991	66	66		66				
1995–2003	58	58		58				

All members elected by plurality voting.

Alberta

election(s):	total seats	total districts	of which:	1M	2M	5M	6M	7M
1905	25	25		25				
1909	41	39		37	2			
1913	56	55		54	1			
1917	56	56		56				
1921	61	52		49	1	2		
1926	60	52		50		2		
1930–1935	63	53		51			2	
1940–1948	57	49		47		2		
1952–1955	61	50		48			1	1

Alberta (cont.)

election(s):	total seats	total districts	of which:	1M	2M	5M	6M	7M
1959	65	65		65				
1963	63	63		63				
1967	65	65		65				
1971–1975	75	75		75				
1979–1982	79	79		79				
1986–2004	83	83		83				

From 1926 through 1955, the single member districts used AV (the alternative vote), that is, a preferential ballot, while the multimember districts used the single transferable vote (STV). Otherwise, all members elected by plurality voting.

British Columbia

election(s):	total seats	total districts	of which:	1M	2M	3M	4M	5M	6M
1900	38	29		24	3		2		
1903–1912	42	34		31	1		1	1	
1916–1920	47	39		37			1		1
1924–1928	48	40		38			1		1
1933	47	39		34	3	1	1		
1937	48	40		35	3	1	1		
1941–1953	48	41		36	3	2			
1956–1963	52	42		34	6	2			
1966–1975	55	48		41	7				
1979–1983	57	50		43	7				
1986	69	52		35	17				
1991–1996	75	75		75					
2001–2005	79	79		79					

In 1952 and 1953, all districts used AV (the alternative vote), that is, a preferential ballot. In the five multimember districts voters were thus given two or three separate ballots (each with its own list) for each seat. Otherwise, all members elected by plurality voting.

Table 6.4. Canadian Provincial Premiers Since 1900

Newfoundland and Labrador

Pre-Federation

Term of Office	Prime Minister	Party	Sworn in	Age	Constituency	Birthdate
1897–1900	James Spearman Winter	Conservative	Oct 1897	52	Burin	1 Jan 1845
1900–1909	Robert Bond	Liberal	6 Mar 1900	43	Twillingate	26 Feb 1857
1909–1917	Edward Patrick Morris	People's	2 Mar 1909	49	St. John's West	8 May 1859
1918–1919	William F. Lloyd	Liberal	5 Jan 1918	53	Trinity	17 Dec 1864
1919	Michael Patrick Cashin	People's	22 May 1919	54	Ferryland	29 Sept 1864
1919–1923	Richard A. Squires	Liberal	17 Nov 1919	39	St. John's West	18 Jan 1880
1923–1924	William R. Warren	Liberal	24 July 1923	43	Fortune	9 Oct 1879
1924	Albert E. Hickman	Liberal	10 May 1924	48	Harbour Grace	2 Aug 1875
1924–1928	Walter Stanley Monroe	Conservative	9 June 1924	53	Bonavista	14 May 1871
1928	Frederick C. Alderdice	Conservative	27 Aug 1928	55	(in upper house)	10 Nov 1872
1928–1932	Richard A. Squires	Liberal	17 Nov 1928	48	Humber	18 Jan 1880
1932–1934	Frederick C. Alderdice	Conservative (UNP)	June 1932	59	St. John's West	10 Nov 1872

July 1917 – May 1919 National Government coalition
Feb 1934 Commission of Government established

Post-Federation

Term of Office	Premier	Party	Sworn in	Age	Constituency	Birthdate
1949–1972	Joseph R. Smallwood	Liberal	1 Apr 1949	48	Humber West	24 Dec 1900
1972–1979	Frank Duff Moores	Conservative	18 Jan 1972	38	Humber West	18 Feb 1933
1979–1989	A. Brian Peckford	Conservative	26 Mar 1979	36	Green Bay	27 Aug 1942
1989	Thomas Gerard Rideout	Conservative	22 Apr 1989	40	Baie Verte-White Bay	25 June 1948
1989–1996	Clyde Kirby Wells	Liberal	5 May 1989	51	Bay of Islands	9 Nov 1937
1996–2000	Brian Tobin	Liberal	26 Jan 1996	41	The Straits and White Bay North	21 Oct 1954
2000–2001	Beaton Tulk [interim]	Liberal	16 Oct 2000	56	Bonavista North	22 May 1944
2001–2003	Roger Grimes	Liberal	13 Feb 2001	50	Exploits	2 May 1950
2003–	Danny Williams	Conservative	6 Nov 2003	54	Humber West	4 Aug 1950

Prince Edward Island

Term of Office	Premier	Party	Sworn in	Age	Constituency	Birthdate
1898–1901	Donald Farquharson	Liberal	Aug 1898	64	Queens 2nd	27 July 1834
1901–1908	Arthur Peters	Liberal	29 Dec 1901	47	Kings 2nd	29 Aug 1854
1908–1911	Francis L. Haszard	Liberal	1 Feb 1908	58	Queens 4th	20 Nov 1849
1911	H. James Palmer	Liberal	16 May 1911	59	Queens 3rd	26 Aug 1851
1911–1917	John A. Mathieson	Conservative	2 Dec 1911	48	Kings 4th	19 May 1863
1917–1919	Aubin E. Arsenault	Conservative	21 June 1917	46	Prince 3rd	28 July 1870
1919–1923	John H. Bell	Liberal	9 Sept 1919	72	Prince 4th	13 Dec 1846
1923–1927	James David Stewart	Conservative	5 Sept 1923	49	Kings 5th	15 Jan 1874
1927–1930	Albert Charles Saunders	Liberal	12 Aug 1927	52	Prince 2nd	12 Oct 1874
1930–1931	Walter M. Lea	Liberal	20 May 1930	56	Prince 4th	10 Feb 1874
1931–1933	James David Stewart	Conservative	29 Aug 1931	57	Kings 5th	15 Jan 1874
1933–1935	William J.P. MacMillan	Conservative	14 Oct 1933	52	Queens 5th	24 Mar 1881
1935–1936	Walter M. Lea	Liberal	15 Aug 1935	61	Prince 4th	10 Feb 1874
1936–1943	Thane A. Campbell	Liberal	14 Jan 1936	41	Prince 1st	7 July 1895
1943–1953	J. Walter Jones	Liberal	11 May 1943	65	Queens 4th	14 Apr 1878
1953–1959	Alexander W. Matheson	Liberal	25 May 1953	49	Queens 2nd	11 June 1903
1959–1966	Walter R. Shaw	Conservative	16 Sept 1959	71	Queens 1st	20 Dec 1887
1966–1978	Alexander B. Campbell	Liberal	28 July 1966	32	Prince 5th	1 Dec 1933
1978–1979	W. Bennett Campbell	Liberal	18 Sept 1978	35	Kings 3rd	27 Aug 1943
1979–1981	J. Angus MacLean	Conservative	3 May 1979	64	Queens 4th	15 May 1914
1981–1986	James M. Lee	Conservative	17 Nov 1981	44	Queens 5th	26 Mar 1937
1986–1993	Joseph A. Ghiz	Liberal	2 May 1986	41	Queens 6th	27 Jan 1945
1993–1996	Catherine Sophie Callbeck	Liberal	25 Jan 1993	53	Queens 1st	25 Jul 1939
1996	Keith Wayne Milligan	Liberal	10 Oct 1996	46	Prince 2nd	8 Feb 1950
1996–	Patrick George Binns	Conservative	27 Nov 1996	48	Murray River-Gasperaux	8 Oct 1948

Nova Scotia

Term of Office	Premier	Party	Sworn in	Age	Constituency	Birthdate
1896–1923	George H. Murray	Liberal	20 July 1896	35	Victoria	7 June 1861
1923–1925	Ernest Howard Armstrong	Liberal	24 Jan 1923	58	Shelburne	27 July 1864
1925–1930	Edgar Nelson Rhodes	Conservative	16 July 1925	48	Hants	5 Jan 1877
1930–1933	Gordon Harrington	Conservative	11 Aug 1930	47	Cape Breton South	7 Aug 1883
1933–1940	Angus L. Macdonald	Liberal	5 Sept 1933	43	Halifax South	10 Aug 1890
1940–1945	A.S. MacMillan	Liberal	10 July 1940	68	Hants	1 Nov 1871
1945–1954	Angus L. Macdonald	Liberal	5 Sept 1945	55	Halifax South	10 Aug 1890
1954	Harold Connolly	Liberal	13 Apr 1954	52	Halifax North	8 Sept 1901
1954–1956	Henry Davies Hicks	Liberal	30 Sept 1954	39	Annapolis	5 Mar 1915
1956–1967	Robert Lorne Stanfield	Conservative	20 Nov 1956	42	Colchester	11 Apr 1914
1967–1970	George I. Smith	Conservative	13 Sept 1967	58	Colchester	6 Apr 1909
1970–1978	Gerald A. Regan	Liberal	28 Oct 1970	42	Halifax Needham	13 Feb 1928
1978–1990	John M. Buchanan	Conservative	5 Oct 1978	47	Halifax Atlantic	22 Apr 1931
1990–1991	Roger Stuart Bacon [interim]	Conservative	12 Sept 1990	64	Cumberland East	29 Jun 1926
1991–1993	Donald William Cameron	Conservative	9 Feb 1991	44	Pictou East	20 May 1946
1993–1997	John Savage	Liberal	11 June 1993	61	Dartmouth South	28 May 1932
1997–1999	Russell MacLellan	Liberal	18 July 1997	57	Cape Breton North	16 Jan 1940
1999–2006	John Hamm	Conservative	27 July 1999	61	Pictou Centre	8 Apr 1938
2006–	Rodney Joseph MacDonald	Conservative	24 Feb 2006	34	Inverness	2 Jan 1972

New Brunswick

Term of Office	Premier	Party	Sworn in	Age	Constituency	Birthdate
1897–1900	Henry Robert Emmerson	Liberal	29 Oct 1897	44	Albert	25 Sept 1853
1900–1907	Lemuel J. Tweedie	Liberal	31 Aug 1900	51	Northumberland	1849
1907	William Pugsley	Liberal	6 Mar 1907	56	Kings	27 Sept 1850
1907–1908	Clifford William Robinson	Liberal	31 May 1907	40	Westmoreland	1 Sept 1866
1908–1911	John Douglas Hazen	Conservative	24 Mar 1908	47	Sunbury	6 June 1860

Term of Office	Premier	Party	Sworn in	Age	Constituency	Birthdate
1911–1914	James Kidd Flemming	Conservative	16 Oct 1911	43	Carleton	27 Apr 1868
1914–1917	George Johnston Clarke	Conservative	17 Dec 1914	57	Charlotte	10 Oct 1857
1917	James A. Murray	Conservative	1 Feb 1917	52	Kings	9 Nov 1864
1917–1923	Walter E. Foster	Liberal	4 Apr 1917	42	St. John	9 Apr 1874
1923–1925	Peter J. Veniot	Liberal	28 Feb 1923	59	Gloucester	6 Oct 1863
1925–1931	John B.M. Baxter	Conservative	14 Sept 1925	57	St. John and Albert	16 Feb 1868
1931–1933	Charles D. Richards	Conservative	19 May 1931	51	York	12 June 1879
1933–1935	Leonard P.D. Tilley	Conservative	1 June 1933	63	St. John	21 May 1870
1935–1940	A. Allison Dysart	Liberal	16 July 1935	55	Kent County	22 Mar 1880
1940–1952	John B. McNair	Liberal	13 Mar 1940	50	Victoria	20 Nov 1889
1952–1960	Hugh John Flemming	Conservative	8 Oct 1952	47	Carleton	5 Jan 1899
1960–1970	Louis J. Robichaud	Liberal	12 July 1960	34	Kent County	21 Oct 1925
1970–1987	Richard B. Hatfield	Conservative	12 Nov 1970	39	Carleton	9 Apr 1931
1987–1997	Frank J. McKenna	Liberal	27 Oct 1987	39	Miramichi-Bay du Vin	19 Jan 1948
1997–1998	Joseph Raymond Frenette [interim]	Liberal	13 Oct 1997	62	Moncton East	16 Apr 1935
1998–1999	Camille Henri Thériault	Liberal	14 May 1998	43	Kent South	25 Feb 1955
1999–	Bernard Lord	Conservative	21 Jun 1999	33	Moncton East	27 Sept 1965

Quebec

Term of Office	Premier	Party	Sworn in	Age	Constituency	Birthdate
1897–1900	Félix-Gabriel Marchand	Liberal	26 May 1897	65	St. Jean	9 Jan 1832
1900–1905	Simon-Napoléon Parent	Liberal	3 Oct 1900	45	St. Sauveur	12 Sept 1855
1905–1920	Lomer Gouin	Liberal	23 Mar 1905	44	Portneuf	19 Mar 1861
1920–1936	Louis-Alexandre Taschereau	Liberal	8 July 1920	53	Montmorency	5 Mar 1867
1936	J. Adélard Godbout	Liberal	11 June 1936	43	L'Islet	24 Sept 1892
1936–1939	Maurice Duplessis	Union Nationale	26 Aug 1936	46	Trois-Rivières	20 Apr 1890
1939–1944	J. Adélard Godbout	Liberal	9 Nov 1939	47	L'Islet	24 Sept 1892
1944–1959	Maurice Duplessis	Union Nationale	30 Aug 1944	54	Trois-Rivières	20 Apr 1890

Quebec (cont.)

Term of Office	Premier	Party	Sworn in	Age	Constituency	Birthdate
1959–1960	J. Paul Sauvé	Union Nationale	11 Sept 1959	52	Deux Montagnes	24 Mar 1907
1960	J. Antonio Barrette	Union Nationale	8 Jan 1960	60	Joliette	26 May 1899
1960–1966	Jean Lesage	Liberal	5 July 1960	48	Québec-Ouest	10 June 1912
1966–1968	Francis Daniel Johnson, Sr.	Union Nationale	5 June 1966	51	Bagot	9 Apr 1915
1968–1970	Jean-Jacques Bertrand	Union Nationale	2 Oct 1968	52	Missisquoi	20 June 1916
1970–1976	Robert Bourassa	Liberal	29 Apr 1970	36	Mercier (Montreal)	14 July 1933
1976–1985	René Lévesque	Parti Québécois	25 Nov 1976	54	Laurier (Montreal)	24 Aug 1922
1985	Pierre-Marc Johnson	Parti Québécois	3 Oct 1985	39	Anjou (Montreal)	5 July 1946
1985–1994	Robert Bourassa	Liberal	2 Dec 1985	52	Saint-Laurent (Montreal)	14 July 1933
1994	Daniel Johnson, Jr.	Liberal	11 Jan 1994	49	Vaudreuil	24 Dec 1944
1994–1996	Jacques Parizeau	Parti Québécois	12 Sept 1994	64	L'Assomption	9 Aug 1930
1996–2001	Lucien Bouchard	Parti Québécois	29 Jan 1996	57	Jonquière	22 Dec 1938
2001–2003	Bernard Landry	Parti Québécois	8 Mar 2001	63	Verchères	9 Mar 1937
2003–	Jean Charest	Liberal	29 April 2003	44	Sherbrooke	24 June 1958

Ontario

Term of Office	Premier	Party	Sworn in	Age	Constituency	Birthdate
1899–1905	George W. Ross	Liberal	21 Oct 1899	58	Middlesex West	18 Sept 1841
1905–1914	James Pliny Whitney	Conservative	8 Feb 1905	61	Dundas	2 Oct 1843
1914–1919	William Howard Hearst	Conservative	2 Oct 1914	50	Sault Ste. Marie	15 Feb 1864
1919–1923	Ernest C. Drury	United Farmers	14 Nov 1919	41	Halton	22 Jan 1878
1923–1930	George H. Ferguson	Conservative	16 July 1923	53	Grenville	18 June 1870
1930–1934	George S. Henry	Conservative	15 Dec 1930	59	York East	16 July 1871
1934–1942	Mitchell F. Hepburn	Liberal	10 July 1934	37	Elgin	12 Aug 1896
1942–1943	Gordon D. Conant	Liberal	21 Oct 1942	57	Ontario	11 Jan 1885
1943	Harry C. Nixon	Liberal	18 May 1943	52	Brant County	1 Apr 1891
1943–1948	George A. Drew	Conservative	17 Aug 1943	49	High Park	7 May 1894

Term of Office	Premier	Party	Sworn in	Age	Constituency	Birthdate
1948–1949	Thomas L. Kennedy [interim]	Conservative	19 Oct 1948	69	Peel	15 Aug 1879
1949–1961	Leslie M. Frost	Conservative	4 May 1949	53	Victoria	20 Sept 1895
1961–1971	John P. Robarts	Conservative	8 Nov 1961	44	London North	11 Jan 1917
1971–1985	William G. Davis	Conservative	1 Mar 1971	41	Peel North [Brampton]	30 July 1929
1985	Frank S. Miller	Conservative	8 Feb 1985	58	Muskoka	14 May 1927
1985–1990	David Peterson	Liberal	26 May 1985	41	London Centre	28 Dec 1943
1990–1995	Robert Keith (Bob) Rae	NDP	1 Oct 1990	42	York South	2 Aug 1948
1995–2002	Michael Deane Harris	Conservative	26 June 1995	50	Nipissing	23 Jan 1945
2002–2003	Ernie Eves	Conservative	15 Apr 2002	55	Dufferin-Peel-Wellington-Grey	17 Jun 1946
2003–	Dalton James Patrick McGuinty	Liberal	23 Oct 2003	48	Ottawa South	19 July 1955

Manitoba

Term of Office	Premier	Party	Sworn in	Age	Constituency	Birthdate
1888–1900	Thomas Greenway	Liberal	19 Jan 1888	49	Mountain	25 Mar 1838
1900	Hugh John Macdonald	Conservative	8 Jan 1900	49	Winnipeg	13 Mar 1850
1900–1915	Rodmond Roblin	Conservative	29 Oct 1900	47	Woodlands	15 Feb 1853
1915–1922	T.C. Norris	Liberal	12 May 1915	53	Lansdowne	5 Sept 1861
1922–1943	John Bracken	United Farmers	8 Aug 1922	39	The Pas	22 June 1883
1943–1948	Stuart Sinclair Garson	Liberal-Progressive	8 Jan 1943	44	Fairford	1 Dec 1898
1948–1958	Douglas Lloyd Campbell	Liberal-Progressive	7 Nov 1948	53	Lakeside	27 May 1895
1958–1967	Dufferin Roblin	Conservative	16 June 1958	40	Winnipeg South	17 June 1917
1967–1969	Walter Weir	Conservative	25 Nov 1967	38	Minnedosa	7 Jan 1929
1969–1977	Ed Schreyer	NDP	15 July 1969	33	Rossmere	21 Dec 1935
1977–1981	Sterling Lyon	Conservative	24 Nov 1977	50	Charleswood	30 Jan 1927
1981–1988	Howard Pawley	NDP	30 Nov 1981	47	Selkirk-Winnipeg	21 Nov 1934
1988–1999	Gary Filmon	Conservative	9 May 1988	45	River Heights (Winnipeg)	24 Aug 1942
1999–	Gary Doer	NDP	21 Sept 1999	51	Concordia (Winnipeg)	31 Mar 1948

Saskatchewan

Term of Office	Premier	Party	Sworn in	Age	Constituency	Birthdate
1905–1916	Thomas Walter Scott	Liberal	5 Sept 1905	37	Arm River	27 Oct 1867
1916–1922	William M. Martin	Liberal	20 Oct 1916	40	Regina	23 Aug 1876
1922–1926	Charles A. Dunning	Liberal	5 Apr 1922	37	Moose Jaw County	31 July 1885
1926–1929	James G. Gardiner	Liberal	26 Feb 1926	42	North Qu'Appelle	30 Nov 1883
1929–1934	James T.M. Anderson	Conservative	9 Sept 1929	51	Saskatoon	23 July 1878
1934–1935	James G. Gardiner	Liberal	19 July 1934	50	North Qu'Appelle	30 Nov 1883
1935–1944	William J. Patterson	Liberal	1 Nov 1935	49	Cannington	13 May 1886
1944–1961	Thomas Clement Douglas	CCF	10 July 1944	39	Weyburn	20 Oct 1904
1961–1964	Woodrow Stanley Lloyd	CCF	7 Nov 1961	48	Biggar	16 July 1913
1964–1971	W. Ross Thatcher	Liberal	22 May 1964	46	Morse	24 May 1917
1971–1982	Allan E. Blakeney	NDP	30 June 1971	50	Regina Centre	7 Sept 1925
1982–1991	Donald Grant Devine	Conservative	8 May 1982	37	Estevan	5 July 1944
1991–2001	Roy Romanow	NDP	21 Oct 1991	52	Saskatoon Riversdale	12 Aug 1939
2001–	Lorne Calvert	NDP	8 Feb 2001	46	Saskatoon Riversdale	24 Dec 1954

Alberta

Term of Office	Premier	Party	Sworn in	Age	Constituency	Birthdate
1905–1910	Alexander Cameron Rutherford	Liberal	2 Sept 1905	47	Strathcona	2 Feb 1858
1910–1917	Arthur Lewis Sifton	Liberal	26 May 1910	51	Vermillion	26 Oct 1858
1917–1921	Charles Stewart	Liberal	30 Oct 1917	39	Lethbridge	18 May 1878
1921–1925	Herbert Greenfield	United Farmers	13 Aug 1921	51	Peace River	26 Nov 1869
1925–1934	John Edward Brownlee	United Farmers	23 Nov 1925	41	Ponoka	27 Aug 1884
1934–1935	Richard Gavin Reid	United Farmers	10 July 1934	55	Vermillion	17 Jan 1879
1935–1943	William Aberhart	Social Credit	3 Sept 1935	56	Calgary	30 Dec 1878
1943–1968	Ernest C. Manning	Social Credit	31 May 1943	34	Calgary	20 Sept 1908
1968–1971	Harry E. Strom	Social Credit	12 Dec 1968	54	Cypress	7 July 1914

1971–1985	E. Peter Lougheed	Conservative	10 Sept 1971	43	Calgary West	26 July 1928
1985–1992	Donald Ross Getty	Conservative	1 Nov 1985	52	Strathcona West	30 Aug 1933
1992–	Ralph Klein	Conservative	14 Dec 1992	50	Calgary-Elbow	1 Nov 1942

British Columbia

Term of Office	Premier	Party	Sworn in	Age	Constituency	Birthdate
1898–1900	Charles Augustus Semlin	(Conservative)	12 Aug 1898	61	Yale, WR	Oct 1836
1900	Joseph Martin	(Liberal)	1 Mar 1900	47	Vancouver	24 Sept 1852
1900–1902	James Dunsmuir	(Conservative)	15 June 1900	48	South Nanaimo	8 July 1851
1902–1903	Edward G. Prior	(Conservative)	21 Nov 1902	49	Victoria	21 May 1853
1903–1915	Richard McBride	Conservative	1 June 1903	32	Dewdney, then Victoria	15 Dec 1870
1915–1916	William J. Bowser	Conservative	15 Dec 1915	48	Vancouver	3 Dec 1867
1916–1918	Harlan Carey Brewster	Liberal	19 Nov 1916	46	Alberni	10 Nov 1870
1918–1927	John Oliver	Liberal	6 Mar 1918	61	Victoria	31 July 1856
1927–1928	John Duncan MacLean	Liberal	20 Aug 1927	53	Greenwood	8 Nov 1873
1928–1933	Simon Fraser Tolmie	Conservative	21 Aug 1928	61	Saanich	25 Jan 1867
1933–1941	T. Dufferin Pattullo	Liberal	15 Nov 1933	60	Prince Rupert	19 Jan 1873
1941–1947	John Hart	Liberal (Coalition)	9 Dec 1941	62	Victoria	31 Mar 1879
1947–1952	Byron Ingenar Johnson	Liberal (Coalition)	29 Dec 1947	57	New Westminster	10 Dec 1890
1952–1972	W.A.C. Bennett	Social Credit	1 Aug 1952	51	Okanagan South	6 Sept 1900
1972–1975	David Barrett	NDP	15 Sept 1972	41	Coquitlam	2 Oct 1930
1975–1986	William Richards Bennett	Social Credit	22 Dec 1975	43	Okanagan South	14 Apr 1932
1986–1991	William N. Vander Zalm	Social Credit	6 Aug 1986	52	Surrey	29 May 1934
1991	Rita Margaret Johnston	Social Credit	2 Apr 1991	55	Surrey-Newton	22 Apr 1935
1991–1996	Michael Franklin Harcourt	NDP	5 Nov 1991	48	Vancouver-Mount Pleasant	6 Jan 1943
1996–1999	Glen David Clark	NDP	22 Feb 1996	38	Vancouver-Kingsway	22 Nov 1957
1999–2000	Arthur Daniel Miller [interim]	NDP	25 Aug 1999	54	North Coast	24 Dec 1944
2000–2001	Ujjal Dosanjh	NDP	24 Feb 2000	52	Vancouver-Kensington	9 Sept 1947
2001–	Gordon Campbell	Liberal	5 June 2001	53	Vancouver-Point Grey	12 Jan 1948

PART III

Provincial Structures and Processes

CHAPTER 7

Premiers and Cabinets

CHRISTOPHER DUNN

Provincial government is cabinet government. It has sometimes been called "premier's government," but this contention is true only in a limited sense. It is possible to confuse the indisputable fact that premiers are the most important actors and determiners of consensus in provincial cabinets with dominance and "dictatorship." In fact, premiers see their job in the modern cabinet as the establishment of teams, and teams need to be worked with, not dominated. Although premier's government does appear in certain contexts, the move toward the institutionalized cabinet has made the dominant premier pattern not necessarily impossible but harder to achieve. Power and authority are more diffuse today than they have ever been.[1]

The cabinet is the focus and fulcrum of governance in a parliamentary system. The leadership of the legislature and the executive is placed squarely with cabinet. Provincial histories are described, or categorized, in terms of the government of the day and with good reason: the cabinet has the resources to shape the contours of the state and, to some extent, society. Canadian provinces have an array of powers unusually extensive for subnational governments. It is therefore important what provincial cabinets do and how they do it.

This chapter is an introduction to the role of premiers and cabinets and to the basic machinery of cabinet governance. It will investigate the constitutional position of the provincial executive, compare federal and provincial premiers and cabinets, review the design of various provincial cabinets, and describe the various impacts of the "institutionalized cabinet" framework.

The focus here is not only on the premier and cabinet, as the title suggests, but the *central executive*: the collectivity of political and non-political elements of the executive who are engaged in central policy generation and coordination. It can be said to include the cabinet, its committees, the Executive Council Office, the Department of Finance, Treasury Board Secretariat, and other relevant central agencies and central departments.

The Constitution and the Provincial Executive

It is one of the great paradoxes of the Westminster or parliamentary system that the premier (or prime minister) and cabinet exercise enormous power, although they do not exist in a constitutional sense. Their roles have evolved through convention over centuries due to the exigencies of leadership and parliamentary performance in Britain and its former colonies.

To understand cabinet government it is useful to think in terms of dichotomies: first of power and authority, and second of the dignified and efficient executive. It is also helpful to remember that the dichotomies themselves did not always exist. In the era of the autocratic monarch they were unnecessary, since the king exemplified the unity of formal and informal power structures. Over time, as the king's power became constrained by Parliament, it became necessary to distinguish between *authority*, the formal designation of who was enabled to perform public acts, and *power*, the informal political influence which made sure that such acts were performed in the first place. A crude differentiation is to say that authority was possessed by the dignified executive and power was possessed by the efficient executive. This dichotomy between dignified and efficient is the simplest way to understand the structure of the provincial executive. As well, each of the two executives has further subdivisions, as Box 7.1 shows.

Box 7.1. The Provincial Executive

The Dignified Executive	*The Efficient Executive*
Queen	Premier
Lieutenant-Governor	Cabinet
Executive Council	Public Service

There is, in provincial constitutions, a distinction between "cabinet" and "executive council." *The executive council* is the "formal" or "dignified" executive. The Lieutenant-Governor in Council "shall be construed as referring to the Lieutenant-Governor of the Province by and with the Advice of the Executive Council thereof" (section 66, *Constitution Act, 1867*). The *cabinet* is the "effective" executive in that it is the main policy-initiating and administering body and operates according to constitutional conventions which are more or less similar in all Commonwealth countries.

The *Constitution Act, 1867* does not refer to cabinets by name at either the federal or provincial levels, consistent with constitutional convention. It does, however, provide for Executive Councils in Ontario and Quebec (section 63). Since the provinces were being created *de novo*, section 63 specified the composition of the initial cabinets of each: Attorney General, Provincial Secretary, Provincial Treasurer, Commissioner of Crown Lands, and Commissioner of Agriculture and Public Works, with the addition of two more for Quebec, the Speaker of the Legislative Council and the Solicitor General. The Executive Authorities in Nova Scotia and New Brunswick were to continue as they existed at the Union (section 64), an arrangement which was duplicated in later instruments admitting British Columbia, Prince Edward Island, and Newfoundland. Statutes creating Manitoba, Saskatchewan, and Alberta similarly established Executive Authorities in those provinces. Of course, section 92 (1) of the 1867 constitution dealing with amendment of provincial constitutions implied that the composition of the executive councils and indeed the structure of the executive government (save for the office of lieutenant-governor) was a matter of purely provincial jurisdiction. Section 45 of the *Constitution Act, 1982* replaces section 92 (1).

The executive council can be considered the provincial analogue of the Privy Council. "The Queen's Privy Council for Canada" is established by virtue of section 11, "to aid and advise in the Government of Canada." The main difference between federal and provincial executives is that federal ministers do not relinquish membership in the Queen's Privy Council for Canada upon resignation from cabinet, although, for reasons of convention, ex-ministers do not participate in actual executive power. In provinces, membership in cabinet and membership in the executive council are synonymous.

Premiers and Cabinets: Federal and Provincial Comparisons

Many introductions to Canadian politics leave the impression that the federal and provincial cabinets have identical structural and operational elements. While this is basically accurate, there are important nuances. The provincial executives are not miniature versions of their federal counterparts. They are autonomous actors with important traditions and histories of their own. If we overlook this fact, we miss the opportunity to plumb executive governance for comparative insights. First, let us deal with some similarities in cabinet government between the two levels of government.

Federal and provincial similarities

The first area of similarity is the virtually identical conventional and political powers enjoyed by prime ministers and premiers.[2] The premier is the sole interlocutor between cabinet and the lieutenant-governor. This gives him or her the sole ability to choose cabinet ministers and hence to make or break careers, but commonsense parameters are apparent.[3] The premier is the sole architect of the general machinery of the central executive; there may come a day when the cabinet seizes the right to design its own size, committees, central agency support, and procedures, but the contemporary premier reserves executive organization as a personal prerogative. The premier can advise the governor to dissolve or prorogue the provincial legislature. The premier enjoys a privileged relationship with the governing party, since he or she is the dispenser of patronage and the general reason the party is in power in the first place. The premier enjoys a kind of "bully pulpit" with the press—he or she can generally focus attention upon himself or herself to address issues of the day. Thus, the premier, like the prime minister, has at hand the five "P"s of power: prerogative, parliament, party, patronage, and press.

A second area of federal and provincial similarity relates to the conventions of cabinet government. These involve the formation of cabinets, individual responsibility, and collective responsibility.

CABINET FORMATION

Conventions dictate the process of *cabinet formation*. The governor general or lieutenant-governor first appoints a prime minister or premier; the person to choose is evident in the case of a majority government, but in a minority situation, the governor has the right to consult with parliamentary leaders to ascertain which leader is likely to command a durable majority in the House. The prime minister or premier then, by convention, has the sole right to advise the governor on who shall be selected as ministers in the new government.

The general practice, both federally and provincially, is to choose ministers from among those who have been elected to the House, but there are several precedents for appointing ministers who are expected to seek election within a brief delay. Between 1867 and 1984, 76 people entered the federal cabinet who were neither members of Parliament (MPs) nor Senators.[4] Examples from Newfoundland and Quebec will suffice for the provincial case.

In Newfoundland, Joseph R. Smallwood chose the then-unelected Clyde Wells, John Crosbie, and Alex T. Hickman for his cabinet in 1966, and each successfully won seats in the general election of September of that year. In 1971 the mayors of St. John's and Corner Brook, William Adams and Noel Murphy respectively, were elevated to cabinet directly from the mayoralty. Ed Roberts entered the Wells cabinet in February of 1992 and was subsequently elected as member for Naskaupi in June of that year.

The list of people made cabinet ministers before being elected in Quebec is long: Jean Lesage chose Eric Kierans for labour minister; Jean-Jacques Bertrand picked Jean-Guy Cardinal as education minister; Bourassa selected Claude Castonguay to Health and Jean Cournoyer to Labour; and Lévesque made Francine Lalonde the status of women minister. Pierre-Marc Johnson chose four civilians (Louise Beaudoin, Jean-Guy Parent, Lise Denis, and Rolande Cloutier) for his cabinet in 1985.[5]

Regional and gender balance have come to be important considerations in designing cabinets. The convention of sectional or regional representation in the federal cabinet is so basic that it has been called the fundamental characteristic of government in Canada.[6] There is not much formal literature on the matter of regional provincial cabinet balance. However, our research has determined that a similar convention indeed holds provincially. Newfoundland's cabinet is an attempt to balance representation from St. John's/Avalon with southern, eastern, central, and western Newfoundland as well as Labrador. In New Brunswick, there will be attempts to find one-third of the cabinet from the francophone concentrations in the northeast (the Acadian Peninsula), the north shore, the northwest and the eastern shore down to Moncton, and two-thirds representation from the southwestern anglophone counties, as well as from St. John and Moncton. In Ontario, Toronto demands several ministers and smaller cities proportionate representation; the major regions (northeastern, northwestern, and eastern Ontario, as well as the Niagara Peninsula) also require a voice. Ever since the days of Manitoba Premier Duff Roblin, convention demands even balance of urban (Winnipeg and Brandon), rural, and northern representatives in that province, unless a party achieves a stranglehold on some areas, as has been the case with the NDP and the north. Saskatchewan ministers tend to come from Regina, Saskatoon, Moose Jaw, Prince Albert (representing north-central Saskatchewan as well), North Battleford, rural southeastern, east-central, and two other rural ridings.[7] Young and Morley say that for BC premiers constructing cabinets, "there is the fundamental division between the interior and the lower mainland and the finer regional differences among the Cariboo, Kootenays and north coast which cannot be ignored," although the relative weight each is to have has proved flexible.[8]

The gender issue is an emerging organizational factor. Textbooks on Canadian cabinets may one day refer to a convention of gender equality in provincial cabinets, but rules regarding gender representation in council are still in the formative stage. As well, the party recruitment environments which affect the matter differ between regions. However, given the availability of qualified female government caucus members, some premiers are making efforts to achieve numerical gender balance in the cabinet (see Tables 7.1 and 7.2). Table 7.1 shows that once elected as part of the governing caucus in a province, a woman's odds of making it into cabinet are pretty good, at least in this decade. Half the women (8/16) in the Campbell Liberal caucus were in the BC cabinet in 2003; the figures for that year for the governing caucuses of other provinces were Alberta 5/1, Saskatchewan 2/7, Manitoba 3/8; Ontario 6/9, Quebec 7/22; New Brunswick 4/5, Nova Scotia 1/1, PEI 2/6, and Newfoundland 5/7. Yet this tale is marred by the obvious sorry tale demonstrated in Tables 7.2 and 7.3, namely that comparatively few women are elected to legislatures and appointed to cabinet, and the situation has become worse. Most provinces had seen a decrease in the percentage of women members since the last provincial election, and women members make up only one-fifth of legislatures on average. Since 1990, there have been gains in cabinet representation of women, especially in BC, Ontario, Quebec, and Newfoundland, but the progress has been uneven and/or modest. In 1990 there were 33 women in provincial cabinets. In 2004 there were 46.

A related issue has to do with the recruitment of senior women public servants in the central agencies and departments of provincial administrations. There appears to have been progress in this matter. Provinces such as Ontario, Newfoundland, Nova Scotia, and Saskatchewan have appointed women as cabinet secretaries since the 1990s on. In Ontario, senior management positions in

Table 7.1. Women in Federal, Provincial, and Territorial Cabinets (as of 27 January 2005)

Jurisdiction	Government Party	Women Cabinet Ministers/Total Cabinet Ministers	% Women in Cabinet	Women in Government Party Caucus #/Total	% Women in Government Party Caucus
Canada	Liberal	9/38	24%	34/135	25%
BC	Liberal	6/28	21%	15/73	21%
AB	PC	5/24	21%	10/62	16%
SK	NDP	4/17	24%	7/30	23%
MB	NDP	4/17	24%	8/35	23%
ON	Liberal	5/23	22%	18/71	25%
QC	Liberal	7/24	29%	24/76	32%
NB	PC	5/18	28%	8/34	24%
NS	PC	1/15	7%	1/25	4%
NF	PC	4/14	29%	9/34	26%
PEI	PC	2/10	20%	5/23	22%
YT	Yukon Party	1/7	14%	1/11	9%
NWT	N/A	N/A	N/A	N/A	N/A
NU	N/A	N/A	N/A	N/A	N/A
TOTALS	N/A	55/256	21%	140/609	23%

Note: All ministers in cabinet were included in the tabulations.
Source: *Canadian Parliamentary Guide*, 2005. (Figures were as of September 2004, in the *Guide*.)

Table 7.2. Women in Canadian Legislatures: Most Recent Elections as of 5 December 2003

Province/ Territory	Party Elected	Date of Most Recent Election	Number of Members	Number of Women Elected	% of Women Members	% Change Since Last Election
QC	Liberal	2003	125	38	30.4%	7.2%
BC	Liberal	2001	79	18	22.8%	- 3.9%
MB	NDP	2003	57	12	21.1%	- 3.5%
Canada	Liberal	2000	301	62	20.6%	0%
AB	PC	2001	83	17	20.5%	- 6.0%
ON	Liberal	2003	103	21	20.4%	2.9%
SK	NDP	2003	58	11	19.0%	- 3.4%
NF	PC	2003	48	9	18.8%	2.1%
PEI	PC	2003	27	5	18.5%	- 3.7%
YT	Yukon	2002	18	3	16.7%	- 12.7%
NS	PC	2003	52	6	11.5%	1.9%
NB	PC	2003	57	7	12.2 %	- 5.7%
NWT	N/A	2003	19	2	10.5%	0%
NU	N/A	1999	19	1	5.3%	N/A
Totals			1046	212	20.3%	

Sources: Linda Trimble and Jane Arscott, *Still Counting: Women in Politics Across Canada* <http://stillcounting.athabascau.ca/content.php>. The authors used federal, provincial, and territorial websites (downloaded June and August 2001, November 2002); Elections BC, via e-mail, 6 June 2001; Elections Quebec, 14 April 2003.

central agencies are made at four levels: deputy minister (DM), assistant deputy minister (ADM) or equivalent, director, and manager. Between 1996 and 2003 there were 561 women appointed to senior positions in the Ontario Public Service central agencies; this is qualified by the fact that most were at the director (157) and manager (363) levels, with only three at the DM and 38 at the ADM levels.[9] Between 1996 and 2003, Quebec appointed five women at the deputy level and ten at the ADM level in the Ministère du conseil exécutif; as well there were one DM and five ADMs appointed in the Secretariat du Conseil du Trésor.[10] In 1996 there were 233 senior female public service employees (between Management Levels 6 and 12); by 2001 there were 392.[11] There have been 14 DMs in Nova Scotia since 1995; half of these have been in central agency positions like clerk or secretary of/ to of the Executive Council, Deputy Minister to the Office of the Premier, Deputy Minister of Intergovernmental Relations, or Chief Executive Officer of the Office of Aboriginal Affairs.[12] No data were available from other provinces.

INDIVIDUAL MINISTERIAL RESPONSIBILITY

Individual ministerial responsibility holds at both the provincial and federal cabinet level. The concept involves the duty of the minister to lead, to defend, and, if deemed necessary, to resign. The minister is responsible or accountable to the House for the proper leadership of a governmental department. The minister must defend his actions and those of his or her departmental officials and bears

Table 7.3. Number of Women in Cabinet, Out of Total, Canadian Provinces, 1990–2004

	BC	AB	SK	MB	ON	QC	NB	NS	PEI	NF
1990	2/23	3/25	1/20	4/18	11/27	5/30	4/24	0/22	2/11	1/15
1991	9/20	4/27	4/17	3/18	13/27	4/30	6/23	1/17	2/11	1/15
1992	7/20	5/26	5/11	4/18	10/25	4/29	4/18	1/17	2/11	1/15
1993	9/19	3/17	5/18	4/19	11/27	4/29	4/18	3/17	3/11	1/15
1994	7/19	3/17	4/18	4/18	11/27	10/29	5/18	2/17	1/10	2/15
1995	8/19	4/18	6/17	4/18	5/27	5/20	5/21	2/16	1/10	1/13
1996	10/18	4/18	4/15	4/18	5/19	6/22	4/22	2/13	2/10	5/14
1997	5/16	4/19	4/14	3/18	4/20	5/22	4/22	2/17	0/9	4/15
1998–99	6/20	4/21	5/19	3/18	5/24	5/23	4/15	1/12	1/10	4/17
2000	6/21	4/20	7/18	4/15	5/25	9/23	4/15	1/12	1/10	5/18
2001	8/28	4/24	5/18	5/16	5/25	6/29	4/15	1/12	1/10	5/19
2002	9/28	4/24	4/15	5/16	5/25	7/30	4/15	1/14	1/10	4/18
2003	8/28	3/24	5/17	7/18	6/23	8/25	6/18	2/15	2/10	5/14
2004	9/27	5/23	4/17	4/17	5/23	6/25	6/18	1/15	2/10	4/14

Note: Includes premier, ministers without portfolio, associate ministers, ministers of state, government whip if in cabinet, and ministers responsible.

Sources: Correspondences from Cabinet Secretaries; also compiled from *Canadian Parliamentary Guide*, 1980-2004 (Toronto: Globe and Mail Publishing); *Canadian Almanac and Directory*, 1994 and 1995 (Toronto: Canadian Almanac and Directory Publishing Company Limited). These annual surveys may not reflect all variations in cabinet sizes.

full political and legal responsibility for officials' actions regardless of any lack of foreknowledge of them. The minister must resign for a serious breach of ethics or a serious mistake in policy, with the premier, effectively, being the final judge. A special case of individual responsibility involves the culpability of the finance minister for any release of a budget prior to the official budget day, but this convention is as hard to enforce at the provincial level as it is at the federal.

Similar to the federal case, the doctrine of ministerial responsibility has proven to be hard to define in practice. Some situations are more likely to generate successful calls for the resignation of the minister, as Andrew Heard has revealed. Wrong doing by departmental officials and administrative ineptitude appear not to constitute convincing thresholds for ministerial resignation. However, the allegation of conflict of interest or the personal code of ethics of the minister appear to be more formidable reasons.[13]

COLLECTIVE RESPONSIBILITY

Collective responsibility, as Heard reminds us, has three aspects: first, the responsibility of the cabinet to the monarch; second, to itself (through cabinet solidarity and cabinet secrecy); and third, to the elected House.[14] The first is marked when the governor loses confidence in the cabinet and asks it to resign. This, for example, happened in reaction to political corruption in Quebec in 1891 with the Mercier government and in BC in 1903 with the Prior government, and was threatened in Manitoba with the Roblin Government in 1915 unless it appointed a royal commission to investigate the Legislative Building scandal. It did.

In the second sense, provincial cabinets have made significant, if inadvertent, contributions to establishing the parameters of the venerable, once thought absolute, convention of cabinet secrecy in cases like *Smallwood v. Sparling* [1982] and *Carey v. The Queen* [1986].[15] Cabinet documents do not enjoy immunity as a class and must be revealed unless disclosure of them would interfere with the public interest. The Nova Scotia Supreme Court, Appeal Division, maintained in favour of the Donald Marshall Inquiry that cabinet ministers could be compelled to testify about the general nature of discussions in cabinet.[16]

Collective responsibility is as much a provincial convention as it is a federal one. The only difference is that there have been fewer cases of governments losing the confidence of the assembly and, hence, fewer cases about which to theorize and to compare. A notable, somewhat bizarre case was the fall of the Pawley Government in 1988 occasioned by NDP MLA (member of the Legislative Assembly) Jim Walding voting against his own government in a closely balanced budget vote. This example reveals less about collective responsibility and more about the dangers of consistently denying the cabinet ambitions of backbenchers.

The third similarity is that the two levels adopted characteristics of the *institutionalized cabinet* at the same historical junctures. The postwar period in Canadian executive government, especially since the 1960s, has witnessed the replacement of the *unaided cabinet* (sometimes called the departmental cabinet) by the institutionalized (or structured) cabinet. Each of these two cabinet models has recognizable key features,[17] which will be dealt with later in this chapter. One can assign the beginning of the institutionalized categories to the governments of: W.R. (Bill) Bennett (BC), Peter Lougheed (Alberta), T.C. Douglas (Saskatchewan), Duff Roblin (Manitoba), William G. (Bill) Davis (Ontario), the first government of Robert Bourassa (Quebec), Richard Hatfield (New Brunswick), G.I. Smith (Nova Scotia), Alexander (Alex) Campbell (Prince Edward Island), and Frank Moores (Newfoundland). However, the degree to which the cabinets of the various provinces are still institutionalized, or have gone beyond that stage, is now a matter of contention, as this chapter will demonstrate later.

Federal-provincial differences

There are three major dissimilarities between federal and provincial cabinets. They involve the political dynamics arising from the pursuit of politics on a smaller scale.

SIZE OF CABINET AS A CONTROL MECHANISM

One difference is the degree to which the size of the cabinet can be and is used as a *control mechanism* in the provincial context. Federal cabinets regularly comprise around 10 per cent or less of the size of the House, whereas a much larger percentage of the provincial assembly is covered by cabinet membership. If one juxtaposes the cabinet and assembly sizes in Tables 7.4 and 7.5 for various provinces, it will be evident that cabinets may account for from 20 to well over 40 per cent of the size of the legislature. The percentage of the governing caucus covered by cabinet membership is even greater, with often more people in cabinet than there are backbenchers. These two sets of factors give a significant degree of power to the cabinet, and the premier who appoints them, against the backbenchers on both sides of the House.

INTEGRATION OF CAUCUS IN CABINET

A second difference is that provincial cabinets are more likely than a federal one to *integrate the caucus* into a meaningful policy development role. Federal caucuses have traditionally served as the *ex post facto* sounding posts for decisions or directions made by the federal cabinet. This is also true in some provinces, but others—like BC, Alberta, Manitoba, and Ontario—have made significant attempts to involve all the elected governing party members.

In BC in the NDP era, the Government Priorities Committee, which was composed of cabinet ministers and government MLAs, provided advice to full cabinet on policy issues. There was also MLA participation on the cabinet's Planning Board "working groups" on Aboriginal affairs and income security. Working groups were fluid mechanisms, created as needed and ended when needs abated.

In 2001, BC's new Liberal Premier Gordon Campbell, sensing the danger of domination by the Premier's Office, divining a need for policy coherence, and reacting to a surfeit of governing party members (77 in a 79-seat legislature), devised an ambitious system at the centre. It was designed to integrate a trinity of five Cabinet Committees, eight Legislative Committees, and five Government Caucus Committees (GCCs). The five GCCs are composed solely of governing party caucus members, (although ministers must attend them as needed) and are funded under the budget of the Legislative Assembly.[18]

A change to caucus democracy came to Alberta in 1975; before this, cabinet itself had been the prime generator of policy. 1975 was the year of the first big Lougheed landslide (75 of 79 seats) and along with it came a prudential desire for caucus unity. Accordingly, caucus committees were created to assist in the preparation and study of legislation and to hear submissions by interest groups,

Table 7.4. Cabinet Sizes, Canadian Provinces, 1980–2004

	BC	AB	SK	MB	ON	QC	NB	NS	PEI	NF
1980	16	29	20	17	26	26	19	20	10	17
1981	20	29	19	18	27	28	19	20	10	17
1982–83	20	30	16	18	29	27	23	21	10	18
1984	19	30	25	20	29	26	23	23	10	18
1985	19	30	24	19	33	28	21	22	10	19
1986	21	30	19	21	23	28	20	22	10	22
1987	18	25	16	21	21	29	20	21	11	21
1988	16	26	16	19	30	28	21	21	11	20
1989	22	26	16	16	30	25	20	22	10	22
1990	23	25	20	18	27	30	24	22	11	15
1991	20	27	17	18	27	30	23	17	11	15
1992	20	26	11	18	25	29	18	17	11	15
1993	19	17	18	19	27	29	18	17	11	15
1994	19	17	18	18	27	29	18	17	10	15
1995	19	18	17	18	27	20	21	16	10	13
1996	18	18	15	18	19	22	22	13	10	14
1997	16	19	14	18	20	22	22	17	9	15
1998–99	20	21	19	18	24	23	15	12	10	17
2000	21	20	18	15	25	23	15	12	10	18
2001	28	24	18	16	25	29	15	12	10	19
2002	28	24	15	16	25	30	15	14	10	18
2003	28	24	17	18	23	25	18	15	10	14
2004	27	23	17	17	23	25	18	15	10	14

Note: Includes premier, ministers without portfolio, associate ministers, ministers of state, government whip if in cabinet, and ministers responsible.

Source: Correspondence with various premier's offices; *Canadian Parliamentary Guide*, 1980-2004 (Toronto: Globe and Mail Publishing); *Canadian Almanac and Directory*, 1994 and 1995 (Toronto: Canadian Almanac and Directory Publishing Company Limited). These annual surveys may not reflect all variations in cabinet sizes.

who initially made them to cabinet.[19] Government policies would not be implemented over caucus opposition. Occasionally the caucus initiated policies independently.

In 1992 and 1997 Alberta took caucus involvement one step further. Premier Ralph Klein, assuming the reins of power in December of 1992 from fellow Progressive Conservative Don Getty, disbanded 16 cabinet and caucus committees and replaced them with "standing policy committees." Initially four in number, they grew to seven in March 1997, down to five in May 1999, and up to six following the 19 March 2001 provincial election. These committees are hybrids in that they include cabinet members, government caucus members, and occasionally non-MLAs; they are chaired by backbenchers, with ministers as vice-chairs. What is more, the backbench chairs are able to sit at cabinet meetings to represent their committees, and members of the public are able to make

Table 7.5. Size of Canadian Provincial Legislatures (# of members), 1980-2004

	BC	AB	SK	MB	ON	QC	NB	NS	PEI	NF
1980	57[1]	79	61	57	125	110	58	52[2]	32[3]	52
1981	57[1]	79	61	57	125	122	58	52[2]	32[3]	52
1982	57[1]	79	64	57	125	122	58	52[2]	32[3]	52
1983–84	57[1]	79	64	57	125	122	58	52	32[3]	52
1985	57[1]	79	64	57	125	122	58	52	32[3]	52
1986	57[1]	79	64	57	125	122	58	52	32[3]	52
1987	69[4]	83	64	57	125	122	58	52	32[3]	52
1988	69[4]	83	64	57	130	122	58	52	32[3]	52
1989	69[4]	83	64	57	130	122	58	52	32[3]	52
1990	69[4]	83	64	57	130	122	58	52	32[3]	52
1991	69[4]	83	64	57	130	122	58	52	32[3]	52
1992	69[4]	83	64	57	130	122	58	52	32[3]	52
1993	75	83	64	57	130	122	58	52	32[3]	52
1994	75	83	66	57	130	122	58	52	32[3]	52
1995	75	83	66	57	130	122	58	52	32[3]	52
1996	75	83	58	57	130	125	58	52	32[3]	52
1997	75	83	58	57	130	125	55	52	27	48
1998–99	75	83	58	57	103	125	55	52	27	48
2000	75	83	58	57	103	125	55	52	27	48
2001	79	83	58	57	103	125	55	52	27	48
2002	79	83	58	57	103	125	55	52	27	48
2003	79	83	58	57	103	125	55	52	27	48
2004	79	83	58	57	103	125	55	52	27	48

1. Seven ridings are multiple ridings with two members; all others, one member each.
2. One member for each electoral district except in Inverness and Yarmouth, which return two members each.
3. Sixteen elected as councillors and 16 as assemblymen. Each electoral district in the province has two representatives, namely, a councillor and an assemblyman.
4. Seventeen ridings are multiple ridings with two members each; all others, one member each.

representations to the committees, something designed to enhance the populist image of the administration and to remove the "overly secretive and imperial" image of Klein's predecessors.[20] Four coordinating committees were also formed: Agenda and Priorities, Treasury Board, Legislative Review, and Audit Committee. Ministerial policies are sent to Agenda and Priorities, which directs it to the appropriate standing policy committee; the committee's recommendation is approved or disapproved by cabinet (with caucus views considered), and Legislative Review and Treasury Board will devise the statutory and fiscal language, as appropriate, for legislative approval if it is necessary.[21] There are also several "Policy Advisory Committees" chaired by government MLAs who provide advice to departments to which they have been assigned.

In the Manitoba Filmon government (1988-99), the caucus was intimately involved in what used to be deemed strictly cabinet committee business, namely, vetting ministerial policy proposals. A senior Manitoba official says that caucus involvement derived from the premier's experience with minority government in the wake of the 1988 election and the perceived need to maintain caucus unity.[22] The Legislative Review Committee and the Urban Affairs Committee were each composed of ministers and backbenchers, and several other committees have included an MLA or two, officially or unofficially, based on geographic, professional, or related considerations.

The subsequent NDP government institutionalized caucus involvement with a tripartite system involving Cabinet Committees, Government Caucus Committees, and Legislative Committees. The three Government Caucus Committees (GCCs)—Legislative Review Committee, Health and Humanities, and Sustainable Development—do not involve ministers as members. However, ministers and the staff of their departments interact with the GCCs in policy and legislative matters. The Legislative Review Committee reviews and approves draft departmental legislation before it is introduced into the legislature and is often called upon by ministers for policy input. The two other GCCs provide critical assessments of various aspects of their policy areas. All three committees may summon public servants and staff of the Policy Management Secretariat, a central agency, for explanations of policy matters.[23]

The Rae NDP government in Ontario also obscured the line between cabinet and caucus decision-making, apparently with not as much organization and transparency as in Alberta. Determined to follow a consensual form of decision-making, Bob Rae decided late in 1993 to give the NDP caucus a veto over cabinet decisions. Thomas Walkom says the result was that "bureaucrats who had managed to work an issue through cabinet committee, cabinet office, the premier's office, and cabinet itself, now could see their efforts exploded on the caucus-room floor."[24] Under Progressive Conservative Premier Ernie Eves, the cabinet committees included participation by parliamentary assistants. Management Board of cabinet included parliamentary assistants appointed as "advisors," and several were appointed members of the Statutory Business Committee and the policy committees of cabinet. Dalton McGuinty, the new Liberal premier of Ontario announced an even more comprehensive plan for caucus involvement in cabinet[25] when elected in 2003:

> We're moving to make the people's representatives—our MPPs— even more relevant to government. For the first time in Ontario history, every MPP in the government caucus will sit on Cabinet Committees. And those committees will be chaired by non-ministers. In keeping with our parliamentary traditions, decisions will remain with Cabinet. But with this innovation, MPPs will have real, meaningful input into those decisions. When it comes to policy making in our government, there will be no back bench.

The other provinces also had caucus involvement at various points in time. In Saskatchewan's NDP Romanow government there were two government backbenchers on the Planning and Priorities Committee and one on the Legislative Review Committee. In New Brunswick, Progressive Conservative Premier Lord used caucus support committees to generate policy proposals and analysis to the premier and cabinet.[26] PEI adopted a more inclusive cabinet structure in August 2000. It allowed up to two government caucus members to be members of Treasury Board and up to four from caucus to be members of each of the other four cabinet committees. Government caucus members chair three of the cabinet committees.

TYPES OF MINISTERS

Thirdly, there are *different types of ministers* at the federal and provincial level. At the federal level, in Chrétien's time, there was a distinction between the cabinet and the ministry; in the former were the traditional cabinet ministers and in the latter were both the traditional ministers plus "ministers of state." The latter are members of the Privy Council but not of the cabinet—although they could be invited to attend cabinet as circumstances required—and like cabinet ministers are bound by the convention of collective responsibility. They earned three-quarters of the salary of a cabinet minister, and their job was to assist ministers in specific areas of their portfolios. Ministers of state have in fact existed for several decades at the federal level.

In the Martin government, the status of ministers of state was upgraded. The eight ministers of state in Martin's 2003 Cabinet—still eight in the mini-shuffle of January 2005—were accorded full cabinet status and were expected to attend cabinet. Now it was the parliamentary secretaries—26 of them, charged mostly with assisting ministers in parliamentary caucus interface—that were to be not part of cabinet but part of the Privy Council and bound by cabinet secrecy, though attending cabinet only when invited. Previously, of course, the parliamentary secretaries had not been privy councillors. Why the change? The key to understanding the purpose of these latter two positions in the Martin executive, said Leslie Pal, was to see it not in the traditional perspective of creating busywork for restless hands, but as a new manifestation of Ottawa's long preoccupation with horizontal portfolio management.[27] Ministers were to be responsible for new portfolio clusters; ministers of state and parliamentary secretaries had successively more specific designated responsibilities within those clusters.

Provinces have varying arrays of ministers to augment the standard form of departmental minister. Ontario led the way. Premier Bill Davis (Progressive Conservative) created new positions called "provincial secretaries." These were cabinet ministers who were not given line responsibilities but mandated to chair three policy committees, which would coordinate policy in specific sectors and would be aided by small secretariats. The original intent that they be "superministers" with significant authority in cabinet proved to be exaggeratedly optimistic. Liberal Premier David Peterson's government changed the *Executive Council Act* (1990) to allow for the appointment of both portfolio ministers and ministers without portfolio; Peterson had a few ministers without portfolio in his cabinet. NDP Premier Bob Rae expanded upon Peterson's modest example; in 1993, there were seven ministers without portfolio in a cabinet of 27. Walkom, however, alleges that Rae's practice stemmed from a failure of will to downsize the cabinet; instead of firing some ministers, he made them junior ministers drawing their regular salary but unable to attend cabinet except for specific purposes.[28] By the time of Ernie Eve's Progressive Conservative government, the Chief Government Whip was appointed Minister Without Portfolio. Other ministers without portfolio were designated as "associate ministers" with assigned duties and responsibilities with the portfolio of a minister; they were also members of cabinet.[29]

Quebec has had a long history of using ministers of state, or a similar post, to round out the regular cabinet. Their role appears to have changed somewhat since they were inaugurated by Premier René Lévesque. Lévesque devised the Parti Québécois (PQ) government's committee system and placed five ministers of state at their heads. The ministers of state, as well as having their own personal political staff, had associate secretaries-general to aid them. These were appointed officials who, with expert staff, served the policy sector covered by a ministerial committee.[30] The practice was discontinued in 1982.[31] In the Bourassa Liberal government, there were several *ministres d'état*—later called *ministres délégués* or delegated ministers—whose tasks were assigned to them by the premier and cabinet and who received administrative help from the Ministère du Conseil Exécutif (the Quebec version of the Executive Council Office). Such ministers were commissioned for status of women, Aboriginal affairs, electoral reform, and Canadian intergovernmental affairs.[32] There were also associate ministers to assist senior ministers in specified areas.

The Parizeau PQ government backed away from use of non-line ministers. It had only two ministers of state, one for "concerted action" and one for regional development (and the latter is simultaneously the municipal affairs minister and government House leader). There was another innovation, a "minister for restructuring," charged with the coordination of a truly innovative scheme of decentralization of government to 15 areas of the province and aided by as many parliamentary assistants. Even more notable, however, is the fact that the Parizeau cabinet was a "two-tier" one, with some ministers dedicated to ordinary "good government" and the others committed to the process of planning and implementing separation. Lucien Bouchard, however, returned to the old Lévesque model when he formed his government in January 1996. He ended Parizeau's experiment with backbenchers acting as "regional delegates" and returned to a traditional pattern of having cabinet ministers exercise regional responsibilities, assisted by regional parliamentary secretaries. He also created three "superministries" responsible for coordinating government economic, employment, and natural resources policy and entrusted them to senior ministers. Bernard Landry designated some senior ministers as ministers of state, meaning only that they were assisted by junior ministers.[33]

The Charest Liberal government has both traditional and new aspects. There are three types of ministers in Quebec's *conseil executif*: "minister of," "minister for," and "minister responsible for." A "minister of," is an incumbent minister, or what we would call a regular line minister, heading a department, assisted by a deputy minister, and operating under the department's incorporating act. A "minister for" has duties conferred upon him by decree but acts under the authority of an incumbent minister—analogous to ministers of state in English Canada, although the Charest Government does not use that term, as past governments did—unless arrangements for relative autonomy have been reached with the latter. However, two "ministers for"—the Minister for Canadian Intergovernmental Affairs and Aboriginal Affairs and the Minister for the Reform of Democratic Institutions—are autonomous in the performance of their duties and play central roles in Canadian federalism and institutional renewal. They are assisted by senior officials attached to the Ministère du Conseil Exécutif (office of the cabinet); the former is accorded an "associate secretary general" (DM rank), and the latter has an assistant secretary. "Ministers responsible for" are responsible for a sector under section 9 of the *Executive Power Act* and have authority over the deputy minister responsible for the sector in question, as if he were the incumbent minister.[34] Charest has 14 ministers (of 25 in cabinet) "responsible for" 17 regions in the province.

New Brunswick experimented with different types of ministers of state from 1989 to 1999. These ministers, never more than a small percentage of the full cabinet, were considered to have "sunset portfolios." They were appointed for a limited amount of time to accomplish a specific task. They were members of the

Executive Council, but were not ministers as defined in the *Executive Council Act* (section 2) and earned three-quarters of the salary of a cabinet minister. They participated fully in cabinet committees but did not sign cabinet documents; this remained the prerogative of the senior minister with which they were paired. There were 19 ministers of state over the span of the McKenna/Frennette/Thériault era (1987-99): Childhood Services and Mines (1989 to 1991); Mines and Energy (1991 to 1994); Literacy (1991-95); one each for the Electronic Highway, the Family, Youth, and Mines and Energy (1994-95); one each for Mines and Energy, Family and Community Services, Literacy and Adult Education, Intergovernmental and Aboriginal Affairs (1995-97); Quality (1995-99); Mines and Energy plus Rural Development (1997-98); and Tourism and Culture, Youth and Literacy, Seniors (1998-99). The purpose of the innovation was to achieve important public policy objectives while keeping the number of government ministers and departments low. It also served as a method of developing ministerial talent and exposing newer ministers to the cabinet process. There are no ministers of state in the Lord government.

On 5 June 2001, the newly elected Liberal government in BC introduced a cabinet composed of 21 cabinet ministers and seven individuals referred to alternately as "ministers without portfolio" or, in common parlance, "ministers of state." Their titles indicated assignments for Intergovernmental Relations, Early Childhood Development, the Community Charter, Women's Equality, Deregulation, Mental Health, and Intermediate, Long Term and Home Care. They are not assigned their own administrative budget but rather receive a portion of that assigned to a line minister. Accordingly, they do not have to defend budgets in the Estimates process, but sign an Accountability Statement within their assigned minister's service plan (which sets out performance targets and reporting requirements); they may be penalized a 10 per cent salary holdback if they do not achieve results set out by Treasury Board and governed by the *Balanced Budget and Ministerial Accountability Act*. Such a position is useful politically in two ways: it provides work for some of the extremely large BC government caucus (77 of 79 seats) and holds a member of the executive accountable for reaching high-profile campaign promises.

The other provinces have experimented with other forms of minister as well. The Lougheed cabinet in Alberta had the practice of appointing several associate ministers partly as a way of dealing with the overwhelming numbers of members elected under his leadership and partly as way of focusing attention, both ministerial and public, on some aspects of his activist province-building agenda. The Romanow government in Saskatchewan had associate ministers for finance and agriculture and health.

Characterizing Provincial Cabinets

The decades since the 1960s have seen the flourishing of a new type of institutionalized cabinet to replace the unaided cabinet that had prevailed through
most of Canadian history. A new school of thought sees a development beyond
this to the "prime minister-centred cabinet." The features of each of these ideal
types differ significantly, but they may overlap in provincial practice.

The unaided cabinet is simple in structure, with few standing committees, and
features restricted collegiality (that is, limited collective decision-making and
power-sharing as regards departmental policy). The prime minister or premier
is the architect of personnel choice and is usually, but not always, the dominant
politician. There are "central departments": departments which perform service-
wide facilitative and coordinative roles but are headed by a minister other than
the premier. There are few cabinet-level staff. Budgeting has narrow aims—usually fiscal control predominates—and employs narrow means. Planning is seen
as an optional, not essential function of government in nature. The unaided cabinet promotes a decision-making style which features few sources of alternative
advice to cabinet other than DMs. Restricted collegiality is the order of the day.

The institutionalized cabinet, on the other hand, has a complex cabinet structure with many standing committees and expanded collegiality (that is, greater
collective decision-making and power-sharing as regards departmental policy).
The prime minister or premier's role is expanded to include the responsibilities of organizational architect as well as architect of personnel choice. There are
now both central departments and central agencies, the latter being those serv-
ice-wide facilitative and coordinative bodies directly responsible to the prime
minister or premier. Cabinet receives both partisan—"Prime Minister's Office
(PMO) type"—and policy/technocratic—"Privy Council Office (PCO) type"—
input. Cabinet-level staff are relatively numerous. Budgeting features wider aims
and wider means than the control-oriented budget process of the traditional cabinet. Planning is still considered optional by cabinet, but there is generally more
recourse to it. A "planning-budgeting nexus," or explicit link between the two
functions, is common. There are alternative sources of information to cabinet
than the responsible minister and his or her deputy. Decision-making is more
centralized in the structured cabinet, which makes a wider range of decisions,
and central bureaucrats monitor departments to a greater extent. Not surprisingly, there is almost constant tension between the centre and the departments.

The characteristics of the "prime minister-centred cabinet" can be extrapolat-
ed from the work of Donald Savoie, which was premised on the governing style
of Jean Chrétien and, to a lesser extent, Brian Mulroney and Pierre Trudeau.[35]
This type of cabinet features a shift of power from the ministers and their departments towards the centre and, at the centre, away from cabinet and cabinet
committees toward the prime minister and his senior advisors. Central agencies

become extensions of the prime minister, engaged as actors in the policy process, no longer the neutral facilitators of collective decision-making. Prime ministers govern not by comprehensive policy agendas but by "bolts of electricity"—a handful of key objectives that they pursue and push through the system. The priority programs of prime minister, finance minister, and Treasury Board minister—the nominal "guardians" (or protectors of the public purse)—encounter few obstacles. However, those of regular line ministers are subject to the contending wishes of other ministers and the control of the central agencies (that is, the prime minister) in the regular cabinet committee decision-making process. Although Savoie does not emphasize them, there are also fewer cabinet committees—usually four—and some large departments are charged with coordinating aspects of policy.

Of course, the fascinating question is to what extent the prime minister-centred model was rendered of historical interest by Prime Minister Paul Martin. With his arrival, actors in Ottawa had to learn new political ABCs (following "Anybody But Chrétien"), including a less centralized, more inclusive mode of governing. Six qualitative changes were evident. Martin structured more cabinet committees—nine—than Chrétien ever had; gave them important policy and financial management roles; provided for a more horizontal approach to government with cascading minister/ministers of state/parliamentary secretaries responsibilities; included parliamentary secretaries as privy councillors; created new secretariats and roles in the PCO; and sought to dovetail these arrangements with a new democratic action plan for Parliament. This appears to be institutionalization redux.

There were clearly some unaided and institutionalized moments in the evolution of premiers and cabinets, cabinet committees, and central agencies in Canada's provinces. After, there is contention.

Premier, cabinet, and central agencies in historical perspective

Plainly, each province knew an unaided period. The premiers in Canada's unaided cabinets were, for the most part, dominant premiers. They controlled and exploited the levers of power—knowledge, patronage, even strategic departments—in a context of simpler and smaller government. Duplessis's personalized, clientelistic rule, which featured vetting of government contracts and dispensing government largesse on an individual basis, was not the style of a dictator nor a revealing sign of French-Canadian culture, but symptomatic of the nature of the premiership in this period. "It points to the fact that the premier had little to do," Daniel Latouche says, "besides fuss over minor matters and had both the time and the resources to exert a personal control over the administration."[36] W.A.C. Bennett presided over what can only be described as an "imperial premiership" in BC. Major spending decisions were planned and executed not within cabinet but within a tiny circle: the premier, the finance deputy, and the comptroller general. Bennett monopolized financial information and often knew more about a department's finances than did the minister. He also personally controlled special purpose funds which allowed him to sidestep both cabinet and legislative oversight.[37] Joey Smallwood's governing style, at least until the late 1960s, featured an anomalous mixture of the old Newfoundland autocratic prime minister style and a utopian drive towards modernization. He was, Gwyn says, by 1968 "a Maurice Duplessis and a Paul Sauvé combined. If his style, authoritarian and paternalist, was out of date, many of his ideas remained ahead of their time."[38]

Unaided cabinets had a very simple structure and few standing committees other than Treasury Board. The D.L. Campbell cabinet (Manitoba, 1948-58) was typical of its day. Cabinet committees were rarely used. Cabinet was so small (averaging around ten ministers), the workload so reasonable, and the ministers so knowledgeable about the issues that it made little sense to structure committees. Rare exceptions occurred of course: a three-member committee on Red River Flood Relief headed by Campbell was struck in 1950; later the Provincial-Municipal Committee, a quasi-committee of cabinet with cabinet members and mayors on it, was struck. M.S. Donnelly says that previous to 1959 even Treasury Board's activities were modest: "activities that might have been carried out by it were dealt with by the whole cabinet and the board was left with the relatively minor duties of certifying public accounts for presentation to the legislature and serving as a court of appeal on certain decisions of the comptroller-general."[39] Ross Johnson noted that in the Smallwood cabinet, apart from working committees on legislation, routine matters, a largely inactive Treasury Board, and a few *ad hoc* cabinet committees, most policy matters were a matter for full cabinet.[40] In BC Bennett was a one-person *de facto* Treasury Board, the other members of which merely acquiesced to his decisions. Until 1969 there were no other standing committees in that province.

Later, institutionalization was imposed. The premiers of institutionalized cabinets were to prove more collegial, not always as a result of personal choice. Premiers shared power more widely in the institutionalized cabinet.[41] Expanded collegiality expressed itself through the presence of influential priorities and planning committees (or their equivalent) in all provinces except Manitoba by the mid-1990s. These committees characteristically regrouped all the most powerful ministers in cabinet and included the chairs of the standing committees of cabinet. The existence of cabinet committees implies power dispersion as well as functional necessity. The practice of having deputy premiers became a fixture of provincial cabinets in the 1990s, after having started in the central Canadian provinces. Deputy premiers are not merely administrative conveniences, but progressively more institutionalized actors whose presence denotes another power centre in cabinet. The provincial institutionalization of the post progressed to such an extent that by 1996 all but Newfoundland, PEI, and New Brunswick had deputy premiers.

The case was similar at the cabinet committee level. By 1976, Kenneth Bryden found, only in Nova Scotia were there no standing committees of cabinet.[42] He noted underlying similarities from system to system. Where "planning and/or priorities" cabinet committees existed, they were chaired by the premier and usually had a degree of goal-setting power which gave them a significance somewhat approaching "inner cabinet" status. Policy proposals seldom went to full cabinet directly but were vetted through cabinet committees whose decisions were rarely reversed. Planning and priorities committees usually provided guidelines for the expenditure budget process which, along with Finance Department projections, provided Treasury/Management Boards the essential tools for departmental estimate analysis.

The pattern of hierarchical institutionalized cabinet committees described by Bryden has largely continued. In fact, if not in name, coordinating committees set the terms of reference for all other committees to follow. In the 1990s all but Manitoba had some version of the planning and priorities cabinet committee. In BC's Harcourt government, there were only two policy committees—Planning Board and Treasury Board—and working group cabinet committees which reported to Planning Board. In the Rae government in Ontario, there were three coordinating committees—Treasury Board, Management Committee, and Policy and Priorities Board; committee recommendations with financial implications were vetted by Treasury Board before going to full cabinet, and those with policy implications were vetted by Policy and Priorities.[43]

The difference between the 1970s and 1990s was a tendency for diminished numbers of cabinet committees. In BC, Premier Vander Zalm had 12 committees. At the beginning of the Harcourt administration there were eight; in September 1993, the number was further reduced to five. Ralph Klein in Alberta reduced the total number of committees to five, including Treasury Board. In 1990, New Brunswick and Nova Scotia each had five cabinet committees;[44] in 1995 they and PEI got by with only two committees, Policy Board (Policy and Priorities in New Brunswick) and a Board of Management (Treasury Board in PEI). The later Bourassa government in Quebec, like the Lévesque government before it, had several standing (or permanent) committees; the latter covered legislation, regional development, economic development, social development, and Greater Montreal.[45] The Parizeau government reduced the number of committees to four: a (reactivated) priorities committee, the treasury board (retained), the legislation committee (retained), and a special committee for Greater Montreal (*Comité spécial d'initiative et d'action pour le Grand Montréal*).

The era of central departments was the era of the unaided cabinet; the era of central agencies marks the introduction of cabinet institutionalization. It is uncommon, at least in Canadian political science, to draw a distinction between central agencies and central departments. The distinction is useful, however, because of the implications arising from the fact that institutionalized cabinets have both. A cabinet having only central departments such as Finance or Treasury Board Secretariat (TBS) will be subject to the reactive, budget-balancing input of finance officials. When the premier is also finance minister (an unaided cabinet tendency) and TBS becomes, in effect, "the premier's department," the influence of finance officials may be even more magnified.

The introduction of central agencies to operate alongside central departments, and the development of a "PMO/PCO split," or a partisan/technocratic differentiation, in the Executive Council Office,[46] indicate growing institutionalization in the 1970s and 1980s. These developments arose from the particular needs of governments existing in a more complex policy environment and of premiers operating in politically more competitive cabinets.

Premier, Cabinet, and Central Agencies: Current Perspectives

Provincial cabinet studies have traditionally not engendered much in the way of scholarly debate, but lately there has been some disagreement. One area of debate revolves around the degree of institutionalization remaining in provincial cabinets, and the other concerns the relative intensity of premier dominance.

Wrestling with the conundrum of establishing what kind of cabinet now pertains in Canada, Bernier, Brownsey, and Howlett maintain there is not in fact one type:

> The authors writing in this book find evidence of this [institutionalized cabinet] pattern in most jurisdictions. However following upon the insights of Savoie and others looking at the federal level, some have also uncovered evidence of what Keith Brownsey in his study of Alberta cabinets suggests is the emergence of a new fourth stage, the "post-institutional" or "premier-centered" cabinet. In this fourth model, cabinets are often by-passed almost entirely by premiers offices which centralize communications functions and policy development. Central agencies come to serve the premier's office rather than cabinet, per se....[47]

The authors attribute the dividing line between the two types of cabinet as size. The smaller remain institutionalized and the larger become premier-centred. Yet even this generalization is suspect.

On one side are the analysts who adopt what might be called the "Savoie perspective." The evidence on the other side is mixed. Norman Ruff says that BC's Liberal government under Gordon Campbell has a different administrative style than its premier's office-dominated predecessors. "If there is a newly emergent BC administrative style," he says, "it is that of a 'corporate collegiality' facilitated by the shared political mandate which must be referenced by every cabinet member and that in turn informs the sweeping Core Services Review and the rolling three year Strategic Plans begun in 2002." He also notes that there has been a growth of somewhat fragmented central departments and central agencies. Despite this collegial aspect, Ruff saw a counter tendency:

> Beneath its organizational jigsaw, British Columbia had many of the characteristics of what Dunn has described as a post-institutionalized cabinet with an increase in the already considerable concentration of power within the Office of Premier at the expense of Cabinet. The 1996-1999 Premier Clark administration had many post-institutionalized features including a shrunken cabinet and heightened control through his main advisers, his Chief of Staff, his Deputy Minister for Operations and the Communications and Policy Secretariat Deputy Minister. With the exception of an enlarged Liberal cabinet, more recent developments have increased British Columbia's Premier driven "post institutionalization" characteristics. These include several additional emulations of other jurisdictions such as the adoption of the Alberta style three year service plans, core services review, the BC Progress Board and the government-caucus committee structure.[48]

In a similar vein, Keith Brownsey maintains that the institutional cabinet once dominated in Alberta, but its reign was restricted to the eras of Peter Lougheed (1971-85) and Don Getty (1985-92). He reviews a wide array of Alberta government "Standing Policy Committees" (SPCs) coordinated by some committees of cabinet in the administration of Premier Ralph Klein. This would lead most observers to conclude that the power is dispersed widely, but Brownsey maintains that power is centralized under the Agenda and Priorities Committee of cabinet, which is in turn dominated by Premier Klein. Apparently, the ability to set the agenda of the SPCs and to reject departmental policy proposals (or accept and direct them further in the cabinet process) gives it, and the premier, the capacity to dominate.

On the other side are those who hold, albeit with qualifications, to the idea of the persistence of the institutionalized cabinet and/or a relatively collegial premier. Graham White, for example, does not believe in the myth of the autocratic first minister in Canada, especially at the provincial level. He quotes several premiers—Ed Shreyer, Allan Blakeney, Bill Vander Zalm, Glen Clark, Bob Rae, Howard Pawley, John Buchanan—to the effect that they did not permit themselves to attempt autocratic behaviour in cabinet because it was counterproductive. They saw the necessity to persuade rather than dictate to cabinet and to give in to other ministers on some issues in order to save their influence for others. The concept of collegiality can exist within the administration of an influential premier. What some outside observers may see as autocratic behaviour by a first minister may be misleading.

Even Ontario, which the authors give as an example of a premier-centred executive, has in fact oscillated between institutionalized and premier-centred patterns. The determining factor in the Mike Harris years, between June 1995 and March 2002, contends Ted Glenn, was the premier's assessment of the state of the economy and the deficit against the backdrop of his "Common Sense Revolution." When faced with substantial deficits and limited growth (June 1995-May 1996, November 2001-March 2002), the premier downplayed policy; highlighted fiscal control; and opted for the unaided, instrumental cabinet version, with only a Management Board, Policy and Priorities (P&P) Communications Board, and a Statutory Business Committee. When economic growth beckoned (May 1996-May 1999, June 1999-November 2001), combined with increasing demands on government and the intense structural reforms, the institutionalized version predominated. Harris expanded the role of P&P, created five P&P subcommittees, and enhanced the role of the Cabinet Office.[49]

The progressive march towards some kind of institutionalization is hinted at in the list of cabinet committees, in Box 7.2, from the more unaided or unstructured days of Premier Harris's first cabinet to the last Progressive Conservative cabinet under Eves, which had a plethora of cabinet committees.

Box 7.2. Ontario Cabinet Committees, 1995-2003

Harris *1995*	*Harris* *1996*	*Harris* *1997–99*	*Harris* *1999–2002*	*Eves* *2002*	*Eves* *July 2003*
-Policy and Priorities Board (P&P)	-Policy and Priorities Board (P&P)	-Policy and Priorities Board (P&P)	-Priorities, Policy and Communications Board	-Priorities, Policy and Communications Board	-Priorities, Policy and Communications Board
-Management Board	-Management Board	-Management Board	-Management Board	-Management Board	-Management Board
-Legislation and Regulations	-Privatization	-Privatization	-Statutory Business Committee	-Statutory Business Committee	-Statutory Business Committee
	-Financial Planning	-Financial Planning	-Privatization and Superbuild (ad hoc)	-Privatization and Superbuild (ad hoc)	-Privatization and Superbuild (ad hoc)
	-Legislation and Regulations	-Legislation and Regulations			
	P&P Sub Committees:	*P&P Sub Committees:*	*Policy Committees:*	*Policy Committees:*	*Policy Committees:*
	-Restructuring and Local Services	-Policy Coordination	-Health and Social Services	-Health & Social Services	-Health and Social Services
	-Jobs and the Economy	-Who Does What Implementation	-Education	-Education	-Education
	-Federal Provincial Issues	-Jobs and the Economy	-Economic and Resource	-Economic & Resource	-Economic and Resource
		-Federal Provincial Issues	-Justice and Intergovernmental	-Justice & Intergovernmental	-Justice and Intergovernmental
			-Environment	-Environment	-Environment

Source: Cabinet Office, Government of Ontario, September 2003.

Several provincial executives appear to have relative collegiality at work, or at least premiers who do not overwhelm the policy process. Of Quebec, Bernier says, the power of the premier has been seriously attenuated since the 1960s because of the tendency for the governing parties to turn against premiers who are electoral liabilities and for PQ governments to be riven by intra-party and intra-caucus challenges.[50] Lévesque had to struggle to control the PQ; Robert Bourassa in his second era of government was very anti-charismatic. He was followed by the short term of Daniel Johnson. Then Jacques Parizeau spent most of his one year in office preparing for a referendum which he did not see through to the finish. He was succeeded by Lucien Bouchard, who was uninterested in governing outside of crisis circumstances, and finally by Bernard Landry, who faced challenges from strong regional ministers. Charest has had to struggle with a cabinet and caucus unsure of his fiscal policy, divisions that led to the firing recalcitrant Finance Minister Yves Seguin along with two other ministers in February 2005.

The institutionalized cabinet arose in Newfoundland and Labrador in reforms dating back to 1972-73 under Frank Moores, then a new premier. They featured five cabinet committees which have been more or less identical for over 30 years: Planning and Priorities, Economic Policy, Social Policy, Routine Matters/ Appointments, and Treasury Board. The Executive Council Office (ECO) maintains its somewhat quirky but efficient format: there are a Cabinet Secretariat, an Intergovernmental Affairs Secretariat, and a Treasury Board Secretariat, with substantial staff, forming parts of the ECO. The reasons for maintaining this configuration are that the long Progressive Conservative tenure helped solidify the reforms and that later premiers, preoccupied with constitutional and structural reforms, were uninterested in changing them. In addition, the strong premier tradition of Newfoundland was mitigated by the tendency of premiers to lose influence the longer they stayed in office.[51]

Saskatchewan has maintained cabinet institutionalization despite the growing influence of the premier, maintain Rasmussen and Marchildon. It promoted control by planning, rather than by patronage, even under governments of different partisan stripe.

> In the end, Saskatchewan, which began its experience with the institutionalized cabinet quite early and has maintained that structure in various forms for nearly 60 years, has also moved to increase the role of the Premier in executive decision-making.... Yet such developments may have diminished the role of the institutionalized cabinet in Saskatchewan, it has not been entirely sidestepped. The Premier of Saskatchewan may well be more than "the first among equals" but the legacy of the institutionalized cabinet in the province continues to be a powerful presence and is rarely side-stepped in its entirely.[52]

They note that the same "troika" that influenced policy six decades ago has remained in place:

> despite changes in name over time, the three main poles of deci-sion-making influence and fundamental policy direction rested with the three long-term policy, treasury and Crown corporation cabinet committees along with their respective secretariats in the depart-ments of Executive Council, Finance and the Crown Investments Corporation.[53]

My own view is that cabinet dynamics are very much about to-ing and fro-ing. No one actor or set of actors carries the day every day. There is a set of interactions that take place to achieve effect but also to save face if there is a setback at some point. To be certain, on some issues the premier will put his or her foot down, and it is, to be sure, the premier's prerogative to choose the issues on which to domi-nate. However, on other issues, some of the political struggle will be undertaken by proxies. The premier turns to other mechanisms to seek the lost garden of power and authority: strategic roles on committees, central agencies, and officials as sur-rogates. On the other hand, individual ministers have had to seek more subtle ways of exerting influence. They tend to do it by proxy. They request and support meas-ures which give more voice to their departmental officials. One of these measures is the deletion of a control orientation by cabinet and its central agencies.

It appears, then that the characterization of whether or not a cabinet is in-stitutionalized or not is partly a subjective matter. An element of objective measurement—like the number of cabinet committees, the deputy premiers, and the roles of central agencies—might be useful to round out this discussion.

First, consider the list in Box 7.3 of provincial cabinet, caucus, and legisla-tive committees. It shows a significant number of cabinet committees in each province, save for Nova Scotia. This seems to indicate that decision-making is relatively decentralized in the provincial cabinet, at least on the surface. As well, the plethora of caucus committees and caucus/cabinet interface speaks to a fur-ther decentralization of power in the government.

Second, consider that the number of cabinet committees—or their trans-mogrified caucus form—has remained relatively stationary for a decade. Box 7.4 reveals the numbers. They hint strongly at a more collegial central executive.

Third, let us reflect again on the involvement of caucus in the business of gov-erning. This is a quite remarkable development. To some extent it has to do with the overwhelming majorities that happen in some provinces like BC, Alberta, and PEI and the need to keep idle hands busy; however, this does not appear to be the case for Manitoba and Ontario. Instead, the "inclusive cabinet" appears to be gaining strength as a concept. The fact that six provinces instituted task forces on the expansion of various aspects of executive and legislative democracy in the

Box 7.3. Provincial Cabinet, Caucus, and Legislative Committees, 2004

Province	Cabinet Committees	Caucus Committees	Legislative Committees
BC	**5 Cabinet Committees:** -Agenda and Priorities -Core Review and Deregulation -Environment and Land Use -Legislative Review -Treasury Board	**5 Government Caucus Committees** -Communities and Safety -Economy -Government Operations -Health -Natural Resources	**8 Legislative Committees** -Aboriginal Affairs -Crown Corporations -Education -Finance and Government Services -Health -Parliamentary Reform, Ethical Conduct, Standing Orders, and Private Bills -Public Accounts -Legislative Initiatives **5 Special Committees**
AB	**No Cabinet Committees per se, but some "coordinating committees" feature a majority of ministers:** -Agenda and Priorities (7/10 are cabinet ministers, 3 are MLAs) -Treasury Board (7/10 are cabinet ministers, 3 are MLAs) -Legislative Review (6 MLAs, 2 cabinet ministers) -Audit Committee (Minister of Finance, 6 private sector members) The Audit Committee is the only committee with non-MLA members.	**7 Standing Policy Committees:** -Agriculture and Rural Development -Community Services -Education and Training -Financial Planning and Human Resources -Sustainable Development and Environmental Protection -Health Planning -Jobs and Economy	**6 Standing Committees:** -Alberta Heritage Savings Trust Fund -Legislative Offices -Private Bills -Public Accounts -Privileges and Elections, Standing Orders, and Printing -Member Services **7 Select Standing Committees**
SK	**5 Cabinet Committees:** -Treasury Board -Cabinet Committee on Public Sector Compensation -Legislative Instruments Committee -Committee on Planning and Priorities -Crown Investments Corporation Board		**9 Standing Committees:** -Crown and Central Agencies -Economy -Human Services -Intergovernmental Affairs and Infrastructure -Previous Legislatures -Public Accounts -House Services -Private Bills -Privileges
MB	**3 Cabinet Committees:** -Community and Economic Development; -Treasury Board -Healthy Child	**3 Government Caucus Committees:** -Legislative Review	**11 Standing Committees:** -Agriculture -Economic Development -Industrial Relations -Law Amendments

Box 7.3 (cont.)

Province	Cabinet Committees	Caucus Committees	Legislative Committees
MB (cont.)		-Health and Humanities -Sustainable Development	-Municipal Affairs -Private Bills -Privileges and Elections -Public Accounts -Public Utilities and Natural Resources -Rules of the House -Statutory Regulations and Others
ON	**8 Cabinet Committees** -Priorities and Planning Board -Management Board of Cabinet -Legislation and Regulations -Health and Social Services -Education -Economic Affairs -Community Affairs -Federal, Interprovincial, and Municipal Relations	Every MPP in the government caucus will sit on Cabinet Committees and those committees will be chaired by non-ministers. Decisions remain with Cabinet. There is no backbench, per se, Premier McGuinty claims.	**8 Standing Committees:** -Estimates -Finance and Economic Affairs -General Government -Government Agencies -Justice Policy -Legislative Assembly -Public Accounts -Regulations and Private Bills
QC	**5 Ministerial Standing Committees:** -Conseil du trésor -Comité de législation -Comité ministériel du développement social -Comité ministériel de la prospérité économique et du développement durable -Comité ministériel de la citoyenneté et de la culture		**11 Standing Committees** -Committee on the National Assembly -Public Administration -Institutions -Public Finance -Social Affairs -Labour and the Economy -Agriculture, Fisheries and Food -Planning and the Public Domain -Education -Culture -Transportation and the Environment
NB	**6 Cabinet or Executive Committees:** **2 Standing Committees:** -Policy and Priorities Committee -Board of Management **3 ad hoc Cabinet Committees:** -Waste Reduction Cabinet Task Force -Cabinet Committee on NB Power Restructuring, Commercialization and Related Matters -Resource Management Committee (ad hoc)		**8 Standing Committees:** -Privileges -Public Accounts -Private Bills -Crown Corporations -Procedure -Legislative Administration -Law Amendments -Ombudsman **3 Select Committees**

Box 7.3 (cont.)

Province	Cabinet Committees	Caucus Committees	Legislative Committees
NB (cont.)	**1 Executive Committee** (an innovative format which includes the premier, his chief of staff, secretary to cabinet, secretary to Policy and Priorities Committee, president of the Regional Development Corporation, 8 ministers and their deputies, and the deputy minister of Intergovernmental Affairs) -Executive Committee on Economic Competitiveness		
NS	**2 standing cabinet committees** -Treasury and Policy Board of Cabinet replaces the former Priorities and Planning Committee, chaired by the premier -Legislation Committees **Issues committees:** on specific topics of corporate or govemment-wide nature		**10 Standing Committees:** -Special Committee on Assembly Matters -Community Services -Economic Development -Human Resources -Internal Affairs -Law Amendments -Private and Local Bills -Public Accounts -Resources -Veterans Affairs **2 Committees of the Whole:** -Supply -Supply Subcommittee **4 Select Committees**
PEI	**5 Cabinet Committees** -Agenda and Priorities Committee -Treasury Board -Strategic Planning Committee on Economic Policy -Strategic Planning Committee on Community and Social Policy -Legislative Review Committee		**7 Standing Committees** -Agriculture, Forestry, and Environment -Community Affairs and Economic Development -Fisheries, Intergovernmental Affairs, and Transportation -Privileges, Rules, and Private Bills -Public Accounts -Resources -Constitution of Canada
NF	**5 Cabinet Committees:** -Planning and Priorities Committee -Special Committee of Cabinet -Economic Policy Committee -Social Policy Committee -Treasury Board		**5 Standing Committees** -Striking Committee -Public Accounts -Government Services -Resources -Social Services

Box 7.4. Numbers of Provincial Cabinet Committees, 1995-2004

Province	Number of Cabinet committees, 1995	Number of Cabinet committees, 1998	Number of Cabinet and Caucus committees, 2004
BC	4 (and 4 "working groups")	5 (and 3 "working groups")	5
AB	8	10	10
SK	6	9	5
MB	12	7	6
ON	8 (and 2 subcommittees)	4 (and 4 subcommittees)	8
QC	4	7	5
NB	2	2	6
NS	5	1	2
PEI	2	3	5
NF	6	6	5

new millennium is an indication that executive dominance, let alone premier's dominance, is not a popular concept these days.

Fourth, consider the continuing institutionalization of the position of deputy premier. Table 7.6 shows that all but two provinces—the smallest—have such a position and have had for years. (An earlier version of this book shows the names per province going back even further, with a similar conclusion.) This also points to some dispersion of the premier's authority. Table 7.7 demonstrates that the tenure of deputy premiers tends to be as long as, or longer than, that of some premiers, which also serves to strengthen their influence.

Fifth, consider the continuing strength of central agency establishments. Central agencies have never been subject to downsizing, and in fact possess the same relative resources—or even more—than they have for several years. (See Table 7.8 for the tale of central agency funding security.)

Sixth and last, consider what happens to dominant leaders. Chrétien's foray into dominant first minister mode was initially successful, but ultimately it led to his downfall through the opposition of significant numbers of his caucus. This is an object level for other first ministers who would seek to emulate his dominant mode.

The Effects of Premiers and of Cabinet Structure and Operation

One must say at the very least that the literature on provincial cabinets in Canada is underdeveloped. More than a century of the country's existence passed before attention began to focus on provincial and territorial executives, and there remains much to be done in the area. However, what has been done so far can be categorized as falling into two broad categories. One is to see the cabinet as an explanatory variable. The other is to see it as a dependent variable, shaped by various forces.

Table 7.6. Provincial Deputy Premiers, 1994–2004

Year	BC	AB	SK	MB	ON	QC	NB	NS	PEI	NF
1994	Elizabeth Cull	Ken Kowalski	Ed Tchorzewski	James Downey	Floyd Laughren	Monique Gagnon-Tremblay	Marcel Mersereau	J. William Gillis	N/A	Vacant
1995	Elizabeth Cull	Vacant	Dwain Lingenfelter	James Downey	Floyd Laughren	Bernard Landry	Joseph Frenette	J. William Gillis	N/A	Vacant
1996	Dan Miller	Vacant	Dwain Lingenfelter	James Downey	Ernie Eves	Bernard Landry	Joseph Frenette	J. William Gillis	N/A	Vacant
1997	Dan Miller	Vacant	Dwain Lingenfelter	James Downey	Ernie Eves	Bernard Landry	Joseph Frenette	J. William Gillis	N/A	Vacant
1998	Dan Miller	Vacant	Dwain Lingenfelter	James Downey	Ernie Eves	Bernard Landry	Douglas O. Tyler	Vacant	N/A	Vacant
1999	Dan Miller	Vacant	Dwain Lingenfelter	Eric Stefanson	Ernie Eves	Bernard Landry	Dale Graham	Vacant	N/A	Vacant
2000	Joy Macphail	Vacant	Dwain Lingenfelter	Jean Friesen	Ernie Eves	Bernard Landry	Dale Graham	Vacant	N/A	Beaton Tulk
2001	Christy Clark	Shirley McClellan	Clay Serby	Jean Friesen	Jim Flaherty	Pauline Marois	Dale Graham	Vacant	N/A	Beaton Tulk
2002	Christy Clark	Shirley McClellan	Clay Serby	Jean Friesen	Elizabeth Witmer	Pauline Marois	Dale Graham	Vacant	N/A	Beaton Tulk
2003	Christy Clark	Shirley McClellan	Clay Serby	Rosann Wowchuk	Elizabeth Witmer	Monique Gagnon-Tremblay	Dale Graham	Ronald Russell	N/A	Vacant
2004	Christy Clark	Shirley McClellan	Clay Serby	Rosann Wowchuk	Vacant	Monique Gagnon-Tremblay	Dale Graham	Ronald Russell	N/A	Vacant

Table 7.7. Governments in Canadian Provinces, 1995 to Present

Province/Premier	From	To
BC		
Michael Harcourt (NDP)	5 November 1991	22 February 1996
Glen Clark (NDP)	22 February 1996	25 August 1999
Dan Miller (NDP)	25 August 1999	24 February 2000
Ujjal Dosanjh (NDP)	24 February 2000	5 June 2001
Gordon Campbell (Liberal)	5 June 2001	Present
AB		
Ralph Klein (PC)	14 December 1992	Present
SK		
Roy Romanow (NDP)	1 November 1991	8 February 2001
Lorne Calvert (NDP)	8 February 2001	Present
MB		
Gary Filmon (PC)	9 May 1988	21 September 1999
Gary Doer (NDP)	21 September 1999	Present
ON		
Bob Rae (NDP)	1 October 1990	28 June 1995
Mike Harris (PC)	28 June 1995	15 April 2002
Ernie Eves (PC)	15 April 2002	23 October 2003
Dalton McGuinty (Liberal)	23 October 2003	Present
QC		
Jacques Parizeau (PQ)	26 September 1994	29 January 1996
Lucien Bouchard (PQ)	29 January 1996	8 March 2001
Bernard Landry (PQ)	8 March 2001	29 April 2003
Jean Charest (Lib)	29 April 2003	Present
NB		
Frank McKenna (Lib)	13 October 1987	13 October 1997
Joseph Frenette (Lib)	13 October 1997	14 May 1998
Camille Thériault (Lib)	14 May 1998	7 June 1999
Bernard Lord (PC)	7 June 1999	Present
NS		
John Savage (Liberal)	11 June 1993	27 March 1997
Russell MacLellan (Liberal)	27 March 1999	27 July 1999
John Hamm (PC)	27 July 1999	Present
PEI		
Catherine Callbeck (Liberal)	25 January 1993	10 October 1996
Keith Milligan (Liberal)	10 October 1996	18 November 1996
Pat Binns (PC)	18 November 1996	Present
NF		
Clyde Wells (Liberal)	5 May 1989	26 January 1996
Brian Tobin (Liberal)	26 January 1996	16 October 2000
Beaton Tulk (Liberal)	16 October 2000	13 February 2001
Roger Grimes (Liberal)	13 February 2001	6 November 2003
Danny Williams (PC)	6 November 2003	Present

Table 7.8. Amounts Expended on Central Agencies, by Selected Provinces, 1997–98 to 2002–03

BC Public Accounts (in $thousands)
Department Name and/or Specific Section

	1997–98	1998–99	1999–00	2000–01	2001–02	2002–03
Office of the Premier	1,803	1,825	1,376	1,966	2,573	2,672
Cabinet Operations	1,159	957	1,157	1,098	na	na
Treasury Board Staff	8,528	7,243	7,746	11,796	12,294	11,092

AB Public Accounts (in $millions)
Department Name and/or Specific Section

	1997	1998	1999	2000	2001	2002
Dept. of Executive Council	20.9m	13.2m	12.3m	13.2m	na	na
Treasury Board	na	na	na	na	na	na

SK Public Accounts (in $thousands)
Department Name and/or Specific Section

	1997–98	1998–99	1999–00	2000–01	2001–02	2002–03
ECO						
Cabinet Secretariat/Policy and Planning Secretariat	882	950	1,066[1]	1,139	1,208	1,314
Finance: Budget Analysis	3,568	3,865	4,238	3,920	3,783	4,206
Intergovernmental Relations	499	782	586	615	452	533

1. Cabinet Secretariat/Policy and Planning Secretariat name was changed to Cabinet Secretariat/Cabinet Planning Unit beginning in 1999.

MB Public Accounts (in $thousands)
Department Name and/or Specific Section

	1997–98	1998–99	1999–00	2000–01	2001–02	2002–03
Finance:						
Federal-Provincial Relations and Research	1,639	1,770	1,845	2,217	3,509	3,113
Treasury Board Secretariat	2,999	2,916	3,003	4,663	4,789	4,667
Executive Council	3,162	3,461	4,301	3,266	3,279	3,424

ON Public Accounts (in $thousands)
Department Name and/or Specific Section

	1997–98	1998–99	1999–00	2000–01	2001–02	2002–03
Office of the Premier	2,674	2,898	3,201	2,699	2,877	3,754
Cabinet Office	11,572	14,497	14,626	16,306	15,511	17,665
Management Board Secretariat	469,258	689,430	541,609	507,644	563,552	467,374
Ministry of IGA	5,569	4,494	4,138	4,520	4,281	8,877

Table 7.8 (cont.)

QC Public Accounts (in $thousands)
Department Name and/or Specific Section

	1997–98	1998–99	1999–00	2000–01	2001–02	2002–03
Conseil executive (Executive Council)	na	na	180,120	61,180	116,711	115,363
Affaires internationals[1] (International Affairs)	na	na	119,351	102,359	109,498	110,477
Conseil du trésor[2] (Treasury Board)	428,955	na	na	490,973	437,658	450,186

1. Now called Relations Internationales.
2. Now called Conseil du Trésor, et administration gouvernementale.

NB Public Accounts (in $thousands)
Department Name and/or Specific Section

	1997–98	1998–99	1999–00	2000–01	2001–02	2002–03
ECO: Executive Council Secretariat	1,165	2,169	1,565	1,307	1,910	1,732
Department of Finance: Budget & Financial Management Division	920	883	888	891	913	795
Office of the Premier	1,257	1,183	1,610	1,146	1,193	1,151

PEI Public Accounts (in $thousands)
Department Name and/or Specific Section

	1997–98	1998–99	1999–00	2000–01	2001–02	2002–03
Executive Council	1,931	2,094	2,127	2,918	2,918	2,951
Premier's Office[1]	497	553	540	575	582	619
Treasury Board (Provincial Treasury)	16,518	10,609	15,597	16,891	18,248	18,229

1. Premier's Office found under/within Executive Council.

NS Public Accounts (in $thousands)
Department Name and/or Specific Section

	1997–98	1998–99	1999–00	2000–01	2001–02	2002–03
Executive Council Office	441	502	480	464	389	412
Intergovernmental Affairs	406	390	376	977	1,005	1,200
Office of the Premier	688	694	687	673	734	693
Priorities and Planning Secretariat	1,260	1,407	1,402	1,386	2,086[1]	2,257[1]

1. Priorities and Planning Secretariat replaced with Treasury and Policy Board created under the *Government Restructuring Act, 2001.*

Table 7.8 (cont.)

NF Public Accounts (in $thousands)
Department Name and/or Specific Section

	1997–98	1998–99	1999–00	2000–01	2001–02	2002–03
Premier's Office		1,007	1,122	1,169	1,324	1,347
Cabinet Secretariat		2,179	2,156	2,020	2,189	1,743
Treasury Board Secretariat		16,014	14,309	16,998	16,571	17,190
Intergovernmental Affairs Secretariat		1,065	1,391	1,473	1,486	3,138

Note: Data were not available uniformly for all provinces, and for some years.
Source: Provincial Public Accounts; some retrieved from hard copy, some from provincial government websites.

Richard Simeon once famously complained that Canadian academics were focusing attention on the cabinet and central agencies without first establishing that they made any difference.

> Little of the literature seems to try systematically to link some sort set of explanatory variables with some dependent ones; few deal with substance [or] content. Instead we have on the one hand studies which look at a particular institution or process—cabinet, federal-provincial negotiations, the bureaucracy or interest groups—but which simply assume that in some sense they are important variables with an impact on policy. The assumption is seldom tested, and research tends to concentrate on explicating and describing the patterns of interaction within the institution or process....The literature on Congress in the US suffers especially from this malady, as does that on the so-called presidentialization of the prime minister in Canada.

This was a fair assessment at the time. We are now at the point of establishing, at least at the provincial level, that cabinets do make a difference; the interesting point is assessing what the exact nature of the differences are. It would probably be fair to say that the usefulness of the literature is that it yields a number of interesting hypotheses we can use to guide further research. First let us consider premiers and cabinets as independent or otherwise explanatory variables.

Of course one of the most stark notions to emerge is the contention that the first minister affects other institutions and policies by himself—not even in conjunction with cabinet. Donald Savoie's thesis is that "it is important to stress that much of the centre of government belongs to the prime minister and not to ministers, either collectively or as individuals ... the strengthening of the centre of government has not, as was initially envisaged, strengthened the collective decision-making capacity of Cabinet by acting as a counterweight to line ministers and powerful mandarins in line departments."[54] Now for the effects: prime minister-centred government weakened both cabinet ministers as well as line ministers and their departments; it has threatened the power, influence, and even relevance of Parliament; and it has twisted the empowerment movement away from seeking collective goals to seeking individual objectives for the centre of government.[55] This is a tall order for one person, but it is widely believed.

White offers a view of the process effects of provincial cabinets. For him, "size matters." Larger cabinets have a tendency to lead to the creation of a proportionate number of small departments, which in turn leads to "departmentalism," stressing vertical instead of horizontal coordination, providing bureaucrats with incentives to act in proprietorial fashion, and discouraging innovation.[56] The kinds of recruitment patterns for provincial cabinets also matter. They have a higher proportion of political neophytes in them relative to federal ones: White found that between one-quarter and one-third of provincial cabinets in the five decades following the Second World War were composed of ministers with no legislative experience, whereas in federal cabinets the proportion was only about one-seventh. Half the provincial ministers had had no government backbench experience and three-quarters had never sat in the opposition benches.[57] The effects are diminished competence and a tendency by premiers to dominate and disrespect provincial legislatures.

My own view is that we still need research to show some of the realities of the effects of provincial cabinets, especially on the degree of horizontal management that central agencies promote. Departmentalism is another relatively unexplored matter at the provincial level. The growth of concern in the provinces with the viability of their legislatures has to be squared with the frequent charges of executive dominance.

As well, the charge of premier-centred government in the provincial cabinet literature, unlike the scholarship of the federal level, is not substantiated by reviews of the relationship of the finance minister to the first minister, and so we can say relatively less about the provincial situation of dominant premier. J. Stefan Dupré describes the traditional Finance Department: "Long before the rise of the institutionalized cabinet and the coining of the term 'central agency,' Finance Departments stood out as horizontal portfolios whose government-wide scope made them readily available adjuncts of first ministers.[58] What about in the institutionalized and post-institutionalized premier-centred cabinets?

Cabinet Organization as Dependent Variable

We noted that another theme in provincial cabinet studies was to see cabinet organization as a dependent variable, shaped by various forces. The factors influencing each of the various stages of cabinet evolution are diverse, but observers have identified some outstanding ones. Dupré gives the impression that the departmental cabinet was a response to interest group influence (ministers' "portfolio loyalty"—or primary commitment to their departments—derived from the fact that they were judged primarily by departmentally oriented client groups), economic imperatives (in a Keynesian era, government departments and ministers are seen as the most appropriate engines of public sector expansion), and bureaucratic power (federal-provincial officials, bound together in trust networks and supported by powerful finance departments, are influential in policy-making).[59] The institutionalized cabinet had factors relating to both its initiation and its persistence, I have argued. It was initiated due to jurisdiction-specific mixes of factors like ideology, pragmatism, and historical precedent. It persisted because of endogenous factors (like the premier's quest for influence and emulation of predecessors; cabinet's quest for political control, financial control, and decongestion or reducing overload; and ideology and momentum) and exogenous factors (like the wish for policy coherence *vis-à-vis* other governments, political semaphore—signalling of political messages to the public—social science rationalism, and facilitation of interest group input).[60] Savoie gives a complex list of factors influencing the new prime minister-centred governance, but they too can be boiled down into more manageable endogenous and exogenous categories. Exogenous factors are very important: the fear of media criticism, the competitive party system and its tendency to politicize most issues, globalization, and the national unity imperative as a particularly central concern. There are endogenous factors as well, including the first minister's quest for control (by curbing ministerial power) and the wish to reduce overload by reducing the number of effective decision-makers.[61] The factors may be complex, but at least they are an improvement from the older literature in which cabinet organization was said to be simply a response to fear of bureaucratic control or that it arose because of policy interdependencies in an complex world.

There have been changes in provincial cabinets since the 1960s and 1970s. The institutionalized cabinet has affected the traditional authority of premiers within the cabinet. Where once there was (usually) a dominant premier, he or she now shares power among a hierarchy within cabinet, as denoted by the several priorities and planning committees in the various provincial cabinets. The plethora of inroads for caucus member influence on nominal cabinet committees is a sign that the authority of the premier, and for that matter cabinet, is not as unquestionable as it once was. Deputy premiers exercise some power previously exercised by the premier. Even the multiplicity of legislative committees can one day pose a threat to the premier's power.

One must still establish however whether there has been a new development towards a post-institutionalized or premier-centred government. Nonetheless, one can still stay some things. The premier's role has been broadened. Cabinet ministers have a more complex policy environment to navigate. It is not as clear what it means to be in cabinet; the line between cabinet and other actors in the governing caucus has been obscured to some extent. Cabinet secrecy has lost some of its potency with the holding of open cabinet meetings in BC and the expansion of cabinet committee membership in Ontario. The policy process is increasingly, if not exclusively, driven by caucus in BC, Alberta, and Manitoba. Junior cabinet ministers have the ability to check the ministerial prerogative in Quebec. The actors in central agencies and departments have had to be aware of a wider spectrum of political and bureaucratic interests. Those who accuse premiers and cabinets of being the architects of the democratic deficit, similar to dynamics in *fin de siècle* Ottawa, may be misdirected. This may be a miniature revolution in the making, a change in a centuries-old Westminster model, that along with the change in legislatures, means that institutional change of a fundamental nature is in train.

Notes

1. Much is owed to the gracious help of the Cabinet Secretaries/Clerks of the Executive Council across Canada who provided much valuable data for this chapter. I would like to thank Wayne Follett and Dave Patten, my research assistants, for their diligent and resourceful help in this project, and the valuable MUCEP student research project at Memorial University of Newfoundland.
2. There are some commonsense exceptions. One is the prime minister's exceptional ability, exercised through the governor general, to choose senators, although even here the premier could have an analogous power if the legislature chose to create a Legislative Council!
3. The premier must remember the words of Richard Crossman: "The first ten people in Cabinet pick themselves [since] they have got to be there, either because they are indispensable or because they are potential enemies. After that, the PM will draw the teeth from the back benches as far as he can by bringing the talent available into the Cabinet." *The Myths of Cabinet Government* (Cambridge, Mass.: Harvard University Press, 1972) 32. Former Ontario cabinet secretary Ed Stewart has commented on the general accuracy of this principle. The size of cabinet may therefore speak volumes about the relative power of premiers: the larger the cabinet, the more potential enemies defanged.
4. Andrew Heard, *Canadian Constitutional Conventions: The Marriage of Law and Politics* (Toronto: Oxford University Press, 1991) 49.
5. Guy Lachapelle, Gérald Bernier, Daniel Salée, and Luc Bernier, *The Quebec Democracy: Structures, Processes and Policies* (Toronto: McGraw-Hill Ryerson, 1993) 240.
6. J.R. Mallory, *The Structure of Canadian Government*, rev. ed. (Toronto: Gage Publishing, 1984) 89.
7. Allan Blakeney and Sandford Borins, *Political Management in Canada* (Toronto and Montreal: McGraw-Hill Ryerson, 1992) 15.
8. Walter D. Young and J. Terence Morley, "The Premier and the Cabinet," in J. Terence Morley *et al.*, eds., *The Reins of Power: Governing British Columbia* (Vancouver and Toronto: Douglas and McIntyre, 1983) 61–62.
9. Correspondence from Tony Dean, Secretary of the Cabinet, Government of Ontario, 10 September 2003.
10. Correspondence from Georges Riverin, Advisor, Ministère du conseil exécutif, 24 September 2003.

11. Correspondence from Joy Illington, Deputy Cabinet Secretary, Office of the Premier, Government of British Columbia, 4 February 2003. The data base did not indicate how many were in central agencies.

12. Correspondence from Antonette Filmore, Office of the Executive Council, Government of Nova Scotia, 21 February 2003.

13. Heard, chapter 3.

14. Heard 62.

15. *Smallwood v. Sparling* [1982] 2 SCR 686; and *Carey v. The Queen* [1986] 2 SCR 637.

16. Nova Scotia (AG) v. Royal Commission (Donald Marshall Inquiry) (1988) 87 NSR (2d) 183 (NSCA).

17. For a detailed description of the characteristics of the unaided and the institutionalized cabinet, see Christopher Dunn, *The Institutionalized Cabinet: Governing the Western Provinces* (Montreal and Kingston: McGill-Queen's University Press, 1995) chapter 1.

18. Illington. See also Norman J. Ruff, "The West Annex: Executive Structure and Administrative Style in British Columbia," in Luc Bernier, Keith Brownsey, and Michael Howlett, eds., *Executive Styles in Canada: Cabinet Structures and Leadership Practices in Canadian Governments* (Toronto: University of Toronto Press and the Institute of Public Administration of Canada, 2005) 236–38.

19. The Alberta Teachers' Association, *A Guide to Alberta's Twentieth Legislature* (Edmonton: The Association, May 1983) 21.

20. Miro Cernetig, "Backbenchers to sit with Alberta Cabinet," *Globe and Mail*, 10 December 1992.

21. Correspondence from Deborah Owram, Deputy Secretary to Cabinet, Alberta Executive Council, Government of Alberta, 14 February 2003. See also Keith Brownsey, "The Post-Institutionalized Cabinet: The Administrative Style of Alberta," in Bernier, Brownsey, and Howlett, eds., 218–222.

22. Confidential interview.

23. Joan Grace, "Cabinet Structure and Executive Style in Manitoba," in Bernier, Brownsey, and Howlett, eds.

24. Thomas Walkom, *Rae Days: The Rise and Follies of the NDP* (Toronto: Key Porter Books, 1994) 64.

25. This practice was criticized by Nicholas D'Ombrain as an example of some "bizarre results" from some new premiers in Canada "carelessly undermining the convention" of cabinet secrecy. Nicholas D'Ombrain, "Cabinet Secrecy," *Canadian Public Administration* 47,3 (Autumn 2004): 334.

26. Stewart Hyson, "Governing from the Centre, but Not Too Haughtily," in Bernier, Brownsey, and Howlett, eds.

27. Leslie Pal, "Political Carpentry: The New Federal Cabinet and an Integrative Prime Ministership," *Public Sector Management* (Summer 2004): 18–23.

28. Walkom 65.

29. Dean.

30. Alain Baccigalupo, *Les grands rouages de la machine administrative québécoise* (Montreal: Editions Agence d'Arc, 1978) 160–65.

31. Lachapelle, *et al.* 240.

32. Lachapelle, *et al.* 245–47.

33. Luc Bernier, "Who Governs in Quebec? Revolving Premiers and Reforms," in Bernier, Brownsey and Howlett, eds., 136–37.

34. Riverin.

35. Donald Savoie, *Governing From the Centre: the Concentration of Power in Canadian Politics* (Toronto: University of Toronto Press, 1999).

36. Daniel Latouche, "From Premier to Prime Minister: Leadership, State and Society in Quebec," in Leslie A. Pal and David Taras, *Prime Ministers and Premiers: Political Leadership and Public Policy in Canada* (Scarborough, ON: Prentice-Hall,1988) 146.

37. Dunn, *The Institutionalized Cabinet* 207–12.

38. Richard Gwyn, *Smallwood: The Unlikely Revolutionary* (Toronto: McClelland and Stewart, 1968) 279.

39. M.S. Donnelly, *The Government of Manitoba* (Toronto: University of Toronto Press, 1963) 100.

40. Ross A. Johnson, "Cabinet Decision-making Structures: Taking Issues out of Politics?—The Newfoundland Case," paper presented to the annual meeting of the Canadian Political Science Association, Quebec, May 30–June 2, 1976.

41. In some areas, like Atlantic Canada, there are even overtones of the earlier unaided-dominant premier pattern in the midst of an institutionalized cabinet. Jennifer Brown, "Ruling Small Worlds: Political Leadership in Atlantic Canada," in Pal and Taras, eds., 133.

42. Kenneth Bryden, "Cabinets," in David J. Bellamy, *et al.*, eds., *The Provincial Political Systems: Comparative Essays* (Toronto: Methuen, 1976) 319–22; see also Donald M. Jarvis, "Cabinets: Organization," in Donald C. Rowat, ed., *Provincial Government and Politics* (Ottawa: Department of Political Science, Carleton University, 1974).

43. Consistent requests for information from the Harris Government about its cabinet-level organization went unanswered.

44. Dyck 131 and 170.

45. Lachapelle *et al.* 241–44.

46. The term "PMO/PCO Model" is useful in describing provincial central agency roles; as in Ottawa in the 1970s and 1980s, there is a division between Executive Council officials who give partisan political input (the PMO model) and those who give policy and technocratic input (the PCO model).

47. Luc Bernier, Keith Brownsey, Christopher Dunn, and Michael Howlett, "Introduction: Modern Canadian Governance: Politico-Administrative Styles and Executive Organization in Canada," in Bernier, Brownsey, and Howlett, eds., 11.

48. Norman Ruff, "The West Annex: Executive Structure and Administrative Style in British Columbia," in Bernier, Brownsey, and Howlett, eds., 239.

49. Ted Glenn, "The Politics, Personality and History in Ontario's Administrative Style," in Bernier, Brownsey, and Howlett, eds.

50. Luc Bernier, "Who Governs in Quebec? Revolving Premiers and Reforms," in Bernier, Brownsey, and Howlett, eds. 152–153.

51. Christopher Dunn, "The Persistence of the Institutionalized Cabinet: The Central Executive in Newfoundland and Labrador," in Bernier, Brownsey, and Howlett, eds., 73.

52. Ken Rasmussen and Gregory P. Marchildon, "Saskatchewan's Executive Decision-Making Style: The Centrality of Planning," in Bernier, Brownsey, and Howlett, eds., 338–39 in the original ms.

53. Rasmussen and Marchildon 200.

54. Savoie 338. He adds that the Finance and Treasury Board ministers share in the prime ministerial inner circle.

55. Savoie 338–39, 357–59.

56. Graham White, "Adapting the Westminster Model: Provincial and Territorial Cabinets in Canada," *Public Money and Management in Canada* (April–June 2001): 19.

57. Graham White, "Shorter Measures: The Changing Ministerial Career in Canada," *Canadian Public Administration* 41 (1998): 369–94.

58. J. Stefan Dupré, "Reflections on the workability of executive federalism," in R. Simeon, ed., *Intergovernmental Relations* (Toronto: University of Toronto Press, 1985) 4.

59. See Dupré.

60. Dunn, *The Institutionalized Cabinet* 277–85.

61. Savoie 9–11.

CHAPTER 8

Evaluating Provincial and Territorial Legislatures[1]

Graham White

Legislatures are the central democratic institutions in Canada's provinces and territories. Like other Canadian political institutions, however, legislatures have fallen into disrepute, in part because they are widely perceived as unresponsive and unrepresentative. Their activities are seen by many as little more than mindless, futile exercises in partisanship.

Judgements as to provincial legislatures' effectiveness and their realization of democratic ideals depend very much on the criteria brought to bear: Are important policy decisions actually made by legislatures, or are legislatures simply bestowing formal approval on decisions taken elsewhere, for example, in the bureaucracy or the cabinet? Are individual legislators and the legislature as a collectivity representative of the people? Does the legislature provide meaningful accountability for government activities? Is the legislature an effective forum for raising and debating the central issues of the day and for educating the people about them? What role does the legislature play in recruiting political decision-makers? Does the legislature promote or impede the elected government's capacity to establish and to implement its program?

This chapter does not attempt an all-encompassing evaluation of Canadian provincial and territorial legislatures. It does, however, provide a jumping-off point for such analyses by reviewing the basic model to which all provincial legislatures adhere and by examining and attempting to account for some of the more significant differences across provincial legislatures. In doing so, it will not be possible to address all the questions set out above. Instead, the principal focus will be upon the legislatures' role or, perhaps more accurately, their lack of role in policy-making, though issues of representation and accountability will also be considered.

The chapter begins with a discussion of the fundamental similarities among provincial and territorial legislatures and a brief comparison with the House of Commons. Subsequent sections examine the representativeness, size, and party composition of Canadian legislatures. The bulk of the analysis is given over to the legislatures' policy-making capacity, with particular emphasis on their independence from government, their professionalization, and their committee systems.

Provincial Legislatures: Fundamental Similarities

Any comparison of Canadian legislatures must begin with the recognition of their fundamental similarity. Indeed, in terms of basic structure and constitutional principle, they are virtually identical. This reflects not only their common origin in the British (Westminster) cabinet-parliamentary system but also their continued adherence to its constitutional precepts. Variables such as size, party composition, and differences in political culture across provinces and regions—Quebec nationalism, for example, or Western populism—have certainly affected aspects of legislative operations and styles. At root, however, these institutions are fundamentally the same. Some provincial legislatures, such as the Nova Scotia House of Assembly and the New Brunswick Legislative Assembly, predate the House of Commons; others came into existence at or about the same time; still others, most notably in Alberta and Saskatchewan, were created decades later. It is thus not that the national institution, the House of Commons, was copied or set the standard; rather, all Canadian legislatures, Parliament included, adhere without significant deviation to the constitutional system imported to Canada from Britain in the nineteenth century.

Let us proceed to sketch out the basic model of "responsible government" to which all provincial and territorial legislatures conform.

The hallmark of the Westminster system is an effective *fusion of executive and legislative power*. The government—the cabinet—is composed of ministers who are elected members of the legislature. The most fundamental constitutional principle of the Westminster system is that the government retains office only so long as it maintains the "confidence" of the House. This does not mean, as is often thought, that any government defeat is cause for an election or for the government to resign. Governments often lose votes in Westminster systems and suffer nothing more serious than political embarrassment. It is only on basic statements of government policy, most notably the Throne Speech or the budget (the overall budget, not specific items of spending or taxing), or on motions that have been explicitly designated as confidence matters[2] that defeats in the House threaten the life of the government. A government defeated on a confidence matter may seek a dissolution, and thus an election, from the lieutenant-governor, who normally will grant the request (though he or she retains discretion to refuse). This is what occurred in Nova Scotia in 1999 when the MacLellan government lost a vote on its budget. Alternatively, as happened in Ontario in 1985 when the Miller Progressive Conservatives lost a non-confidence vote, the government may resign and the lieutenant-governor offer the reins of power to another party or leader.

Cabinet government under the Westminster system is *collective government*. Cabinet solidarity is, however, not just a strategy for ensuring political survival; it is a constitutional principle. It means that all ministers are responsible for and must support government decisions regardless of whether they personally favour them. Ministers also have individual responsibility to the legislature for the activities of their departments. An important corollary of responsible government is that elected ministers, rather than appointed bureaucrats, answer to the legislature for their departments, taking the blame for problems and the credit for successes. This is key to maintaining the neutrality of the public service. Section 90 of the *Constitution Act, 1867* stipulates that only with the approval of the lieutenant-governor—which in practice means the ministers—may any elected member introduce measures into the legislature calling for the spending of public funds or the raising of taxes (this applies not only to bills, but also to amendments to bills). Thus is power concentrated in the cabinet.

When combined with such strongly entrenched political imperatives of the Canadian party systems as tight discipline and the tendency for party success to turn on leadership rather than policy, these constitutional principles produce *executive-dominated* governments.

Constitutionally, provincial members are free to support or oppose the government as they see fit. In reality, though, the rigid party discipline which dominates every provincial legislature means that party members almost always vote in unison, forming solid and usually unquestioning phalanxes behind their leaders. Legislative politics in Canadian provinces are almost entirely party politics, marked by a primal and relentlessly adversarial division between the government and the opposition. Government and opposition, of course, are defined essentially in terms of parties.

All provincial legislatures, like the House of Commons, thus share the following characteristics: cabinet domination of the policy-making process, to the exclusion of the private members, government as well as opposition; a marked imbalance between the massive resources backing the cabinet (the permanent bureaucracy as well as easy access to funds) and the limited resources available to private members and to the opposition; and debilitating restrictions on the powers of committees to determine public policy or to control government activities. As we shall see, interesting variations do exist among provincial legislatures with respect to these characteristics, but the variations are less important than the fundamental similarities.

Consider the various legislatures' records on government bills and private members' bills. As will be seen in Table 8.2, government bills (those brought forward by cabinet ministers as part of the government's program) stand a very good chance of being passed; the lowest rate was 78 per cent passage in Ontario, and in only three provinces did fewer than 90 per cent of government bills became law.[3] By contrast, private members' bills (those introduced by non-cabinet members) rarely passed; the highest rate of passage was in PEI and Quebec, although the apparently high rate of passage was based on only two or three such bills being passed in a year. In several legislatures, members have effectively given up introducing bills because their prospects are so dismal; instead, they bring forward private members' resolutions, which are statements of opinion, normally carrying no legal force. Table 8.2 also shows that each provincial legislature accords only a few hours a week for private members' business. (In this context, it is worth recalling that constitutional strictures severely constrain the scope of private members' bills; since only ministers can bring forward "money" bills, private members' bills may neither raise taxes nor directly allocate government spending.)

A final important structural similarity among provincial legislatures is that all are *unicameral*, i.e., they have only one House. This distinguishes them from the bicameral federal Parliament, which includes the House of Commons and the Senate. Several of the first provinces to join Confederation initially had bicameral legislatures, with upper houses which were, like the Senate, appointed rather than elected. They generally proved at best benignly useless, at worst obstructionist to the government in the elected lower House, and lacked even the Senate's saving grace of enhancing regional representation. Accordingly, all have been abolished, most within a few decades of their creation, though the Quebec Legislative Council survived until 1968.[4]

The contrast between unicameral and bicameral legislatures, such as Parliament, can be substantial. In recent years, due to shifting party balances, the Senate has on occasion challenged or even defeated parts of the government's legislative program. Yet even when the government party controls both houses, the necessity of Senate approval for legislation and financial measures adds a set of complications and delays unknown in the provinces. Simply put, the legislative process is smoother and faster in the unicameral provincial legislatures.

Beyond the absence of upper houses in provincial legislatures, in all fundamentals the federal Parliament operates according to the same principles as the provincial Houses. Important differences of degree rather than of kind do, however, distinguish the House of Commons from its provincial counterparts. The House of Commons is much larger, has a more complex party system and far more resources (both in absolute and proportional terms), and is substantially more complex (for example, in its elaborate system of committees and its administrative structures) than provincial Houses. But if the resources available to individual MPs, parliamentary committees, and opposition parties are substantially more fulsome in Ottawa than in most provincial Houses, and if procedural mechanisms exist which offer greater opportunity for influencing public policy than in most provincial legislatures—such as open committee mandates and rules more favourable to the passage of private members' bills—it by no means follows that the House of Commons is a more effective institution than its provincial counterparts. Much depends, as noted at the outset, on how one defines "effective." Moreover, the size and complexity of the House of Commons give it a cumbersome, hidebound character that makes genuine change difficult.

Whatever conclusions are drawn about the relative effectiveness of the federal and provincial legislatures and about the specifics of their structures and operations, it is important to reiterate that they are simply variations on the theme of executive dominance. At root their operating principles, the political imperatives faced by their members, the roles the members play, and their capacity to influence policy are very similar.

"Consensus Government" in the Territorial Legislatures[5]

The Yukon Legislative Assembly is essentially a miniature replica of the House of Commons and the provincial Houses, animated by the same party-dominated political dynamics. If anything, partisanship is intensified by the perennially narrow (or non-existent) government majorities. In Nunavut and the Northwest Territories (NWT), however, legislative politics unfold quite differently.

Both adhere to the constitutional precepts of Westminster-style responsible government—confidence votes, cabinet solidarity, and the like—and exhibit familiar procedural trappings, such as Question Period and a neutral Speaker. However, organized political parties are nowhere to be seen. Factions and groupings exist in the legislature, but all candidates, including incumbent members of the Legislative Assembly (MLAs), run as independents. The premier and the cabinet are elected by secret ballot of all MLAs. The premier assigns ministers to portfolios and can reassign and in very unusual circumstances dismiss them, but lacks the dominating control over cabinet enjoyed by provincial premiers. So, too, ministers understand that they owe their positions to their fellow MLAs, not to the premier. Without a supporting phalanx of disciplined backbenchers, cabinet finds itself a permanent minority in the House. Both as individuals and through committees, "ordinary" or "regular" (i.e., non-cabinet) members thus can exercise substantial influence over government and its policies. For example, legislative committees can achieve substantial modifications to government bills and to spending estimates. Cabinet retains extensive power and unquestionably runs the government, but must take other MLAs' views and demands seriously. A good indication of how this dynamic operates is the importance of "caucus," a weekly, closed-door meeting of all MLAs (including the Speaker) where difficult issues are thrashed out and important decisions taken.

Given the territories' demographic make-up (NWT is roughly 50 per cent Aboriginal peoples; about 85 per of Nunavut's population is Inuit), it is not surprising that most MLAs are of Aboriginal heritage. An affinity has often been noted between the so-called "consensus governments" of Nunavut and the NWT and traditional northern Aboriginal decision-making, which rejects majoritarian procedures such as voting as well as unfettered control by strong leaders. At the same time, it is clear that the "consensus governments" are essentially Westminster systems, with intriguing modifications, rather than modern-day versions of traditional Aboriginal political processes.

The absence of parties in Nunavut and the NWT cannot be attributed to a lack of political sophistication or to a primitive state of political development. Despite repeated predictions of its imminent demise, including various stillborn attempts to institute a party system, "consensus government" has persevered in essentially its present form for more than 20 years in the NWT; when Nunavut divided from the NWT in 1999, politicians there explicitly confirmed their support for it. As with any other political regime, consensus government has its strong and weak points. What is significant about the consensus system for our purposes is not whether it is superior to the southern party system but its demonstration of the adaptability of the Westminster cabinet-parliamentary model: provincial legislatures may all be very much of a piece, but not because of any requirement inherent in the principles of responsible government.

Representativeness

The notion of representation in legislatures is multidimensional. It can mean the extent to which the elected members are socially representative, that is, how faithfully legislators' social characteristics—ethnicity, class, sex, age, and the like— mirror those of the population. It can also refer to the legislature's capacity to bring to the attention of government decision-makers the range of ideas and preferences held by the public. Finally, it may mean members' interventions on behalf of individual constituents or groups of constituents in their dealings with government.

In terms of social representativeness, the overall pattern varies relatively little from one province to the next. Members are disproportionately drawn from certain social groups, most notably middle- and upper-middle-class men between 40 and 60 years old with business and professional backgrounds. Other social groupings, such as women, the disabled, the poor, visible minorities, and Aboriginal people are typically underrepresented, often dramatically so.[6] To take a concrete illustration, as Table 8.1 shows, in late 2005 only 156 of 743 provincial and territorial members (21 per cent) were women; in only one jurisdiction (Quebec) did women constitute as much as 30 per cent of the membership. Even these relatively low figures represent a major improvement in recent years, for prior to the 1980s, no provincial House had as many as 10 per cent women, and before the 1970s it was common for provincial legislatures to be entirely male.

Bringing the views of the public to the attention of the legislature and the government requires willingness on the part of legislators as well as suitable structures and procedures. Party discipline certainly inhibits members from publicly voicing criticisms of party policy, though they can be less inhibited behind closed doors in caucus meetings. Legislatures with active and open committee systems offer both individual citizens and organized groups the opportunity to bring forward their views directly. This can be seen most clearly in terms of the committee stage of the legislative process.

In the course of their passage, bills are subject to detailed review and amendment in committee, though this step may be skipped for minor or uncontroversial bills. Committee stage may occur in one of two ways: in the Committee of the Whole, which is essentially the entire membership of the House sitting in the chamber but operating under somewhat more flexible rules than usual; or in a standing committee, a small group of members meeting separately from the House. Procedurally, these routes are effectively equivalent in that they both permit members to discuss the details of proposed legislation and to move amendments. Politically, however, they differ greatly. Committee of the Whole retains much of the theatrical formality of the House, which can significantly inhibit the genuine exchange of ideas. Moreover, only members are permitted to speak, and of course the chamber is immobile.[7] Although grandstanding is not unknown in standing committees, their more intimate scale and format (members remain seated while speaking, for example) make for less bombast and more real discussion. More significantly, standing committees can and do have "witnesses"—experts, public servants, interest group representatives, private citizens—come before them. And in some provinces, standing committees regularly travel to obtain information and to hear from witnesses unable or unwilling to come to the capital to make their views known.

Table 8.2 shows that in several legislatures virtually all government bills receive their detailed study in Committee of the Whole rather than in standing committee. In Nova Scotia, Quebec, Manitoba, Nunavut, and the NWT, standing committees review the bulk of legislation (in Ontario, only about 15 to 25 per cent of government bills go to standing committee, but they tend to be the most significant and controversial ones). Referring a bill to standing committee by no means ensures that the committee will hold public hearings or will travel to gather evidence and opinion on the bill. Table 8.3 shows that only in a few jurisdictions is travel by standing committee a common occurrence (and much of that travel may be unrelated with reviewing legislation). Nonetheless, these are options simply not open in Committee of the Whole.

Size[8]

A legislature's size appears to have greater influence on its operation and performance than any other structural or organizational variable.[9] Canadian provincial Houses range in size from 27 in PEI to 125 in Quebec, though most are between 52 and 83 (see Table 8.1). The territorial assemblies have 18 or 19 members. Even the largest Houses, in Quebec and Ontario, are less than half the size of the House of Commons with its 308 seats.

Several consequences flow from the variations in size among provincial legislatures. Smaller Houses are more likely to be dominated by the executive, because in them the cabinet represents a larger, often much larger, proportion of the government caucus and of the entire House than in larger legislatures. Size greatly affects the scope and effectiveness of committee systems. In small legislatures, with few private members available for committee work, an extensive committee system is simply not possible. For example, in provinces such as Nova Scotia or Manitoba, at most 30 to 40 backbenchers will be available for committee duty, whereas Ontario and Quebec will have 75 to 100 backbenchers who could serve on committees. Moreover, governments in the smaller Houses will be disinclined to permit extensive committee activity because most of the talent in caucus will be in cabinet, so that few able backbenchers are left to protect government interests in committee.[10] Size also affects procedure. Generally speaking, larger Houses require more complex rules and procedures and, as noted above, can support active committee systems (active committee systems offer greater possibilities for detailed scrutiny of spending estimates and of other government policy proposals). Finally, interpersonal dynamics among members are quite different in large and small Houses; cross-party relationships among members can be less hostile and antagonistic in larger legislatures where members get to know one another through committee work.

Public discontent with governmental institutions together with the neoconservative preoccupation with the size of government so prominent in the 1990s led to reductions in the size of legislatures. Saskatchewan reduced its legislature from 66 to 58 members, the PEI House stands at 27 (down from 32 a few years earlier) and the Ontario Legislature, which numbered 130 until 1999, now has 103 members. Such reductions may be symbolically appealing and may score some cheap political points for those who claim credit for them but they are false economies since they produce minimal cost savings, adversely affect members' capacity to serve their constituents, and undercut legislatures' effectiveness.[11]

Party Composition

Although party composition can critically affect legislative activities, provincial legislatures exhibit little variation along this dimension. For one thing, coalition governments—governments in which cabinets are composed of members of more than one party—which were never common, have all but ceased to be part of the Canadian political landscape: Yukon experienced several years of coalition government in the 1990s, but from the 1950s to 1999 no province was governed by a coalition.[12] The Saskatchewan election of that year returned 29 New Democrats and three Liberals, who formed a coalition government, which included two Liberal ministers; the coalition effectively lasted two years.[13]

Of more immediate significance is the continuing primacy of two-party systems, documented by Carty and Stewart in this volume. The snapshot of party standings as of late 2005 presented in Table 8.1 suggests two-party systems as the standard. Several provinces have experienced fleeting episodes of three-party legislatures, for example, New Brunswick and Manitoba in the 1990s, and it is possible that we are witnessing the start of three-party systems in the Nova Scotia Legislature and the Quebec National Assembly; however, over the long term departures from the two-party norm are transitory.[14] In fact, only Ontario has really known a stable three-party system, with three parties regularly capturing a substantial share of the vote and, more important for present purposes, maintaining a significant contingent in the House (in the 1999 election the Ontario NDP was reduced to nine seats; this marked the first time since the 1960s that any of the three Ontario parties had fewer than 16 seats).

Three-party legislatures are subject to minority governments, which, by definition, cannot occur in two-party Houses. Minority governments—in which no party commands a majority of the seats—enhance the policy roles of both the legislature collectively and the members individually. Yet, due to the dominance of the two-party configuration, several provinces (PEI, New Brunswick, Quebec, and Alberta) have never experienced minority government. The three episodes of minority government in the Ontario Legislature in recent decades (1975-77, 1977-81, 1985-87) are thus quite unusual. Not only have these minority periods brought about substantial policy shifts, they have also produced extensive legislative reform.[15]

Even aside from their susceptibility to minority government, legislatures with more than two parties are subject to more complex political machinations than two-party Houses, due to the manoeuvring between the opposition parties. Multi-party Houses differ as well due to their multidimensional political divisions: in a two-party system, all divisions between parties coincide. In situations of three or more parties, by contrast, lines of demarcation may cut across one another: government versus opposition (or "ins" versus "outs") may not be the same as left versus right or as metropolis versus hinterland. This naturally makes for a more complex political situation and can significantly complicate the political calculus facing elected members, voters, and interest groups.

If the number of parties is significant in understanding legislative dynamics, so too is the nature of the parties. In particular, legislatures with strongly ideological parties are qualitatively different from legislatures dominated by middle-of-the-road brokerage parties. The most obvious contrast is between the legislatures of Atlantic Canada, where parties are principally distinguished by their status as "ins" or "outs" and the ideologically polarized legislatures of the West. The presence or absence of a substantial NDP contingent in the House is often an indicator of ideological polarization; however, language-based parties such as New Brunswick's Parti Acadien and Confederation of Regions Party can occasionally mar the symmetry of the ins/outs brokerage parties pattern and reveal a different form of polarization. Legislatures with ideological parties tend to focus attention on fundamental questions such as the role of the state in the economy, the distribution of wealth and power in society, and the entitlements and responsibilities of the individual vis-à-vis the state. Legislatures dominated by less ideological brokerage parties devote greater attention to issues of government competence, honesty, and integrity.

Provincial Legislatures' Policy-Making Capacity

Within the constraints of the Westminster system, important variations can be identified in provincial legislatures' capacity to develop and to influence public policy. Three interrelated sets of variables directly affect this capacity: independence from government, professionalization, and committee effectiveness.

In all three areas, significant change is evident over the past two decades. Indeed, in terms of policy-making capacity, almost all significant enhancements in provincial legislatures' influence over public policy this century have occurred since the mid-1970s.[16] Sorting out the sources and processes of reform across the provincial legislatures is beyond the scope of this chapter, although a common pattern can be identified in several provinces. Long pent-up pressures for change have given rise to an important, initial set of reforms. These reforms demonstrated the possibility and the advantages of moving away from long-established practices, but typically failed to satisfy members' demand for genuine, far-reaching change. The upshot has been steady, if intermittent, reform of practices and structures—more tinkering than overhauling.

Independence from government

The notion that the legislature might be independent from the cabinet, which forms part of the legislature, is at first blush a curious one. Constitutional theory holds that cabinet must be responsible to the legislature and, indeed, dependent on it. Political reality, of course, is quite different: as noted above, party discipline, the growth of the size and the scope of the state, and other factors have made for cabinet domination of provincial legislatures. Accordingly, in order for private members, be they government or opposition, to influence policy, the legislature must enjoy some independence from cabinet. The primary determinants of a legislature's independence are its members' attitudes and behaviour, most notably their willingness to stand up for themselves and to exercise the powers available to them. At the same time, though, certain structural and procedural arrangements can enhance legislative independence.

As discussed below, effective legislatures require resources in the form of staff support, library and computer facilities, constituency offices, and the like. These can be costly undertakings for which the public holds the government responsible. Moreover, many of these resources will be used to review and to criticize the government. Governments thus have a strong interest in retaining control over the process for allocating resources and facilities to legislatures.

In recent years, all provincial and territorial legislatures have established Boards of Internal Economy to determine their budgets and to oversee their administration. In all instances, governments retain numerical control over these important bodies, which meet in private. However, all provinces now include representatives of opposition parties, and often of government backbenchers, on their boards.[17] This is a decided improvement over the previous arrangements, which saw decisions on legislative funding made exclusively by cabinet and the special requirements and status of the legislature frequently ignored. Moreover, responsibility for personnel decisions and other administrative matters pertaining to the legislature are increasingly being taken away from government departments (which are headed by ministers), and vested in the Speaker, who embodies legislative neutrality and independence.

The practical consequences of this growing administrative independence depends heavily on how truly independent the Speaker is. Though the cast of mind of the person chosen as Speaker is obviously critical, procedural and political changes over the past few years have served to enhance the Speaker's independence. Until recently, provincial speakerships were given out by premiers, often as consolation prizes for members who had not made it to cabinet, and it was common for Speakers to be subsequently appointed to cabinet. Needless to say, such practices undermined both the reality and the perception of the Speaker's independence. In 1986 the House of Commons became the first Canadian legislature to elect its Speaker by secret ballot, and all provinces, plus the NWT and Nunavut, have followed suit. Together with the decreasing tendency of premiers to appoint Speakers to cabinet, this reform has enhanced the Speakers', and thus the legislatures', independence.

A small but nonetheless significant sign of movement toward legislative independence is the growing recourse to legislative committees for the appointment of neutral legislative officials such as the clerk, the ombudsman, and the provincial auditor. In several legislatures, all-party committees now make the effective decisions on such key appointments (though a motion and vote in the House is usually necessary to formalize the decision). Until recently, cabinet decided on these important staffing matters, and while care was usually taken to avoid partisan or political taint, transferring this task to a legislative committee, with representation from both sides of the House, clearly enhances legislative autonomy.

Such advances have not fundamentally altered the overall pattern of executive dominance, but along with the growing professionalization of provincial legislatures, they have shifted the balance somewhat toward effective legislatures.

Professionalization

Legislative professionalization refers to a set of attitudes and procedural/administrative arrangements supporting elected members' capacity to carry out their duties. One writer simply notes that professionalization "is aimed at making the institution of the legislature more effective."[18] Among the indicators of legislative professionalization are adequate levels of pay, based on the presumption that

elected life is a full-time calling; sufficient professional staff support, research facilities, and the like; and legislative sessions of reasonable duration. All of this may
seem unexceptional, yet just two or three decades ago, all provincial legislatures
lacked even the rudiments of professionalization. Members were badly paid, requiring them to hold virtually full-time jobs while serving in the legislature. This
was possible because the legislature was only in session a few weeks each year. If
they were lucky, members might share a cramped office in the legislative building
while the House was sitting and have access to a pool of stenographers to type
their letters. Beyond that, members had virtually no staff resources or facilities to
assist them in their duties.

In recent years, however, the trend has unmistakably been toward enhanced
professionalization, especially in larger provinces. Improvements in professionalization are directed at least as much to assisting members in their role
of constituency politician as in enhancing their law-making capacity. Personal
staff for members and publicly funded constituency offices give incumbents an
electoral advantage, but their real significance lies in how these additions have
improved members' capacity to represent their constituents. Nor do the accoutre-
ments of greater professionalism necessarily guarantee re-election for members
fortunate enough to enjoy them; indeed, Gary Moncrief's research suggests just
the reverse. Moncrief has demonstrated that the provincial legislatures with the
lowest rates of professionalism also had the lowest rates of electoral turnover of
members.[19] He also showed that the rate of electoral defeat for provincial members increased from the 1960s to the 1990s.[20]

Legislatures can hardly be professional or effective if most of their members
only serve on a part-time basis. And since few members are sufficiently wealthy
or public-spirited to work full-time on their legislative duties for part-time pay,
it is important that they receive adequate compensation. Table 8.1 provides information on the pay rates of members in provincial and territorial legislatures
as of 2005.[21] Many members receive additional payments for holding special
legislative offices; party leaders, speakers, and ministers may receive as much
as $30,000 to $40,000 extra, but lesser figures such as party whips, committee
chairs, and parliamentary assistants (most of whom are on the government side)
may receive several thousand dollars as well.[22] The pay for MLAs in Nunavut
and the NWT may seem extraordinarily generous but must be understood in the
context of the very high living costs which characterize the Arctic.

Since most provincial members earn over $75,000 a year, sometimes well over
(Table 8.1), they may not be in need of tag days, but neither are they particularly
well paid. For established professionals and businesspeople, becoming a provincial member often entails a dramatic drop in pay. Whether legislators are over or
underpaid is not the issue here; what is significant is that most are paid enough
to be able to devote full-time—many would say more than full-time—attention
to their jobs.

Elected members need a substantial amount of time away from the provincial or territorial capital, when their legislatures are not in session, to attend to their ridings and to keep in touch with their constituents. Nonetheless, it is also important that legislatures meet for extended periods and offer their members sufficient time and opportunity to become thoroughly enmeshed in their provinces' affairs. Most Houses meet between 50 and 70 days a year (see Table 8.2). Depending on whether they sit four or five days a week, this means that they are in session roughly three to five months a year. Whether this is enough time for adequate scrutiny of the government and for debate on important public policy issues is hard to say in the abstract, but it is clearly not excessive. Significantly, the trend has in recent years been towards shorter legislative sessions.[23]

Making best use of legislative time depends very much on the services and resources available to the members. Without good access to information and staff to assist in compiling and analyzing information, members are in no position to influence complex government policy. Moreover, staff are necessary to assist members in dealing with their constituency casework (their "ombudsman" or "social-worker" function). Otherwise, the endless requests for information or help that members receive from constituents would leave no time for the background work that involvement in public policy entails.

The level and nature of services and resources available to provincial members varies a good deal. In the larger, wealthier provinces like Ontario and Quebec, members each have three or four personal staff, publicly funded constituency offices, access to non-partisan professional expertise through their legislative libraries and clerk's offices, and extensive political assistance through caucus support groups (which provide research, advice on dealing with the media, outreach services, and the like). In other legislatures, members are not nearly so well served; members often find themselves sharing staff and on their own for many of their research needs. The legislative libraries and clerk's offices across Canada are uniformly staffed with exceptionally competent, hard-working people, but in many legislatures they are simply too hard-pressed to meet all the demands for assistance that members might make of them. Even allowing for the differences in size of their Houses, for example, the seven people in the New Brunswick Legislative Library cannot possibly offer their MLAs the services that Ontario members of the Provincial Parliament (MPPs) receive from the 68 staff in the Ontario Legislative Library.

A rough idea of the level of services available to members can be gleaned from Table 8.1, which shows the 2005-06 budget for each legislature (both in absolute terms and in expenditure per member) and the number of full-time staff (partisan and non-partisan) employed there in 2002.[24] Such figures are by no means foolproof guides to the professionalization or effectiveness of provincial legislatures. For example, the fact that members in Quebec have on average more than 60,000 constituents and their Ontario counterparts have 121,000 means that they require substantially more staff support to deal with casework than do members in the Atlantic provinces and in Saskatchewan and Manitoba, where constituencies average between 10,000 and 20,000 people. Nonetheless, the differences are quite staggering, with Ontario and Quebec spending several times the amount of money per member—just over $1 million annually for Ontario—as other provinces.[25] Similarly, staff levels vary dramatically, with some legislatures' staff numbering in the dozens and others in the hundreds.

Spending money on legislatures and providing staff for members will not guarantee their effectiveness. Yet professional, well-served members are not easily satisfied with a subservient policy role in which they must support party positions over which they have little influence. With resources and opportunities at their disposal, they expect to affect policy, not as mavericks opposing or obstructing their parties, but as active contributors to the policy process. Staff and services may not be sufficient for effectiveness, but they are surely necessary, and the evidence clearly shows that many provincial members are only minimally served. Little wonder, then, that executive dominance is so widespread in Canadian provincial legislatures.

Nor are legislatures' capacity to challenge their executives improved when their resources are diminished. During the 1990s legislative budgets were held constant or shrank in most provinces. While legislatures cannot expect to be exempt when cutbacks are the order of the day in the public sector, they make easy targets for knee-jerk funding reductions that may ultimately prove to be false economies. The old adage that "you get what you pay for" applies no less to legislatures than to anything else.

Committees

Legislative committees offer the best opportunity for members to become knowledgeable about specific aspects of public policy, so that they may hold government accountable for its actions as well as influence the policy process. As the earlier discussion of the political consequences of reviewing legislation in Committee of the Whole or in standing committee suggests, committees have several advantages over House proceedings: they have the time to deal in depth with specific issues or policy questions as well as the small membership to allow full participation by all members; they can operate in a less adversarial, less politically charged format; they can travel to collect information and hold hearings to solicit public opinion; they can summon expert witnesses to discuss policy matters with them; and they can call on professional staff support to guide and supplement their work in ways that are not possible in the House.

These, however, are only potential advantages, realized only to limited degrees in Canadian provincial legislatures. Again, a critical dynamic is the wish of the cabinet to retain its dominance. Ministers do not wish to see independent, effective committees with substantial opposition representation challenging their power or causing political difficulties for them. (They may, as in Alberta, be amenable to active government caucus committees[26] or to extensive participation in cabinet committees by government backbenchers.) Provincial legislative committees may thus be hamstrung by restrictive procedures and lack of staff support or, at a more basic level, by government reluctance to sanction active committees. A telling illustration of this last point is the fact that until recently the Agriculture Committee of the Saskatchewan Legislature had not met for decades. This was sometimes explained on the grounds that agriculture in Saskatchewan is too important to be left to a committee, an argument that conveniently ignores the advantage to the cabinet in preventing a committee from holding hearings and traveling the province to review the government's agriculture policy.

Legislative committees are in certain ways microcosms of the House. Most notably, they include representatives of all major parties, in rough proportion to their numbers in the House (one important consequence of which is that government members outnumber the opposition of committees under majority governments but not in minority settings). Table 8.3 presents information on provincial legislative committees. The number of standing (permanent) committees in each legislature is shown, but since wide variation exists in their level of activity, it also shows how many are active or moderately active.[27] In Quebec, Ontario, Nunavut, and the NWT almost all committees are active, but elsewhere half or more of the standing committees are largely or entirely inactive. In BC, as in Alberta, only one committee exhibits significant levels of activity (doubtless, this is related to the lopsided majorities in these Houses when the data on committee activity were gathered—in Alberta the opposition numbered only 21 of 83 MLAs; in BC it was weaker still, three of 79).

Table 8.3 also shows the number of members who sit on standing committees, the extent to which they travel outside the capital for meetings (usually for public hearings), and their normal staff resources. The line of the table setting out committee staff, however, tends to underestimate differences. In the smaller provinces, for example, one clerk (who attends primarily to administrative matters) may have responsibility for several committees, whereas each major committee in Ontario and Quebec, will have its own clerk. Similarly, only in the three largest provinces—BC, Quebec, and Ontario—and the territories with "consensus government" can committees count on having expert research staff assigned to them; elsewhere, research for committees is either limited or non-existent.

In addition to standing committees, provincial and territorial assemblies utilize special (sometimes called "select") committees for specific inquiries or studies of limited duration. Recent examples include Nova Scotia's Special Committee on Fire Safety, Ontario's Select Committee on Alternate Fuel Sources, the Saskatchewan Special Committee on the Abuse and Prevention of Exploitation of Children, and BC's Special Committee on Information Privacy in the Private Sector. These committees are typically among the most effective in influencing policy because they have precise mandates and more extensive staff resources and also because their very existence signals the government's interest in receiving advice and recommendations on a particular set of issues. And, as the illustrations suggest, these committees are often asked to examine and report on issues that are not inherently partisan in nature. In turn, members recognize that such committees represent a genuine opportunity to contribute to policy development and thus take them more seriously, reining in their partisan stridency. As the table demonstrates, special committees are more likely to travel either within the province/territory or further afield to seek information and opinion related to their mandates.

Active committees, even those that can call on professional staff, are by no means effective committees. Indeed, it is not unknown for governments to establish time-consuming but largely pointless committee tasks to keep their own backbenchers from getting underfoot. In order to be effective, committees, like their parent legislatures, must enjoy some independence from government, an independence largely determined by the attitudes and behaviour of members.

Yet procedural arrangements can also be of moment. For example, putting ministers on legislative committees severely undercuts their independence; this once common practice has been all but abandoned in most legislatures. However, another practice which severely restricts committee independence remains the norm in most provincial legislatures. In six of the ten provincial Houses and in the Yukon, other than one or two specialized committees such as Public Accounts or Regulations, committees are only empowered to deal with matters referred to them by the House (see Table 8.3). In other words, committees cannot decide, on their own, to conduct policy studies or enquiries; they require government approval, which cabinets may be reluctant to grant. Giving committees formal control over their own agendas does not, of course, ensure that they will be active, effective committees supplementing or challenging the cabinet's policy role. Except in minority situations, the government party enjoys numerical control of committees and can thus constrain impulsive or threatening committee initiatives. Still, cabinet's capacity to block committee enquiries from taking place, regardless of what their own committee members want, substantially lessens the prospects for effective committees. In short, this apparently obscure procedural issue holds the potential for significantly enhanced committee autonomy and effectiveness.[28]

Committees can play a crucial accountability role. Question Period may be explosive and dramatic, but committees can scrutinize political decisions and administrative processes in far more detail and in a less adversarial manner than is possible in the politically supercharged atmosphere of the House. In addition, committees (unlike the House) can and do call appointed officials before them, and thus contribute to holding the bureaucracy answerable.

All provinces except Quebec have active Public Accounts Committees (PACs). These committees, which in every instance are chaired by opposition members, are usually among the better staffed committees (in Newfoundland and Labrador, for example, the PAC is the only committee with research support). Moreover, PACs are assisted by the provincial auditor, an independent legislative official whose professional staff investigate and make public reports on efficiency and effectiveness of government spending. Though PACs often fall into partisan bickering, opt to pursue flashy but insubstantial issues, or are reined in by uncooperative government members, they nonetheless represent a significant force for accountability. In this respect, as is generally the case with legislative mechanisms for promoting government accountability, the actual record of what a committee accomplishes—which may be quite limited—is often less important than the *threat* of what it might do. Like the driver who obeys the speed limit because there *might* be a radar trap around the next bend, governments are concerned to avoid improper or unwise actions not because PACs (or opposition members) are likely to find out about them and cause political embarrassment, but because they *might* find out and create problems.

PACs usually enjoy very wide terms of reference, which usually extend to the myriad semi-independent agencies, boards, and commissions found in every jurisdiction. Several provinces, such as New Brunswick, Ontario, and Saskatchewan, have established specific legislative committees to review the operations and finances of major Crown corporations, if not the entire range of government agencies. Elsewhere, in Quebec, Nunavut, and the NWT, all committees are empowered to review the Crown corporations and agencies which fall under the subject areas the committees cover (see the line of Table 8.3 on ABCs—agencies, boards, and commissions).

PACs and committees that review Crown corporations and agencies can and do enhance accountability. However, legislatures fail miserably in their scrutiny of regulations (also called delegated legislation). Much of the work of contemporary governments goes on through such regulations, which carry the force of law but do not require approval of the legislature.[29] Most provinces have no committees empowered to consider regulations (Manitoba has a Statutory Regulations and Orders Committee, but it has not met since 1972 to deal with regulations). Even where such committees do exist, they confine their attention to narrow technical and legal issues about the scope of regulations; they may not assess the merits of the policies being set by regulation. Committees in Quebec, Nunavut, and the NWT can delve into the policy substance of regulations but don't often do so.

Similarly, the vast number of government appointees to boards and agencies also escape legislative scrutiny in all legislatures save those of New Brunswick, Nova Scotia, Ontario, and the Yukon where, as in Ottawa, committees can and do call prospective appointees before them. The Ontario experience in this area is mixed,[30] but at least the procedural mechanism is in place for the legislature to review government appointments.

Conclusion

Two contradictory tendencies are evident from this chapter. On the one hand, Canada's provincial and territorial legislatures exhibit substantial variation on a range of characteristics—size, resource levels, committee operations, and procedural practices. The time allotted to Question Period, for example, ranges from 15 minutes a day in BC to an hour in Ontario. To take another important illustration, the extent to which cabinet cuts off debate on contentious issues by imposing closure (immediate end to debate) or time allocation (ending debate within a short period) ranges widely: as Table 8.2 shows, in several legislatures use of these devices is unknown, whereas under the Harris government it had become routine in Ontario—on average 17 times a year. On the other hand, while these and other variations in legislative operations are worth knowing about, such differences in rules and practices do not in the end make for significantly different legislative processes or politics. Aspects of provincial legislatures which may produce important differences are size and party composition, autonomy from government, extent of professionalization, and structure and operation of the committee system. Yet even these are essentially variations on the same Westminster cabinet-parliamentary, responsible government theme.

Within this defining Westminster framework, however, important variations across provincial legislatures are evident. No single factor accounts for all of them. Size, wealth, and resources clearly accord the Ontario and Quebec legislatures advantages not enjoyed by other provincial parliaments, yet repeated minority government episodes (which in turn reflect its unique party system) also stand as key catalysts in shaping Ontario's legislature. And of course, we have the "consensus'" legislatures in Nunavut and the NWT. The lesson from these bodies is not that provincial legislatures should abandon political parties or that they should emulate Aboriginal decision-making models, but rather that the Westminster system of responsible government is far more adaptable than is often thought. If provincial legislatures sometimes seem impervious to genuine reform, this is not due to inherent rigidities in the Westminster system—which can in fact exhibit remarkable flexibility—but because cabinets are notoriously unwilling to give up any of their extensive powers and because too many members are unwilling or unable to imagine alternatives to the prevailing political order.

Like any other human construct, the Westminster cabinet-parliamentary system involves trade-offs. Its strong, unified executive with its capacity to quickly put in place decisive, coherent public policy and its clear accountability trail permitting voters to pass judgement on government decision-makers come at the cost of limited independent policy-making capacity for the legislatures and severe constraints on the ability of individual members to influence policy. Still, the Westminster system need not entail the suffocating party discipline and the attendant policy enfeeblement that characterizes Canadian provincial legislatures.

Much scope exists within the current system for enhancing the contributions that individual members and the opposition can make to the governing process.

Moreover, Westminster constitutional precepts are consistent with many possibilities for democratizing reforms, be they improvements in services and funding for members or more far-reaching structural reform. For example, adopting a proportional representation electoral system (as New Zealand did in the 1990s) is entirely compatible with Westminster principles as is the dual member constituency approach (one male member and one female member) proposed for the Nunavut Legislature in order to guarantee equal representation of men and women among elected members.[31]

Although some provinces have made more progress than others, the general trend over the past decade or two has been toward more effective provincial and territorial legislatures. Members are better paid and have call on more extensive resources; procedural and administrative advances have enhanced provincial legislatures' independence from government and their overall capacity to influence public policy, to hold the government accountable, and to represent the people. These advances have not, however, reversed the underlying cabinet domination of provincial legislatures in any fundamental way. The provincial and territorial legislatures are indeed our central democratic institutions, but their effectiveness along many dimensions—not least in safeguarding and strengthening democracy—leaves much to be desired.

Notes

1. Most of the statistical data, and a good deal of the qualitative data, for this chapter was acquired through the good offices of the provincial legislative clerks, who responded with dispatch and thoroughness to a detailed questionnaire. Without this assistance, this chapter would not have been possible. To all, many thanks.
2. For example, a motion might include some variation on the formula "... the government no longer enjoys the confidence of the House...," or the government might publicly declare, in advance of a vote, that it considers the vote a matter of confidence.
3. Few, if any, government bills were defeated; typically, those that failed to pass were bills on which the government changed its mind or ran out of legislative time.
4. Edmond Orban, "La fin du bicaméralisme au Québec," *Canadian Journal of Political Science* 2 (1969): 312-26.
5. On "consensus government," see Graham White, "Westminster in the Arctic: The Adaptation of British Parliamentarism in the Northwest Territories," *Canadian Journal of Political Science* 24 (September 1991): 499-523; and "And Now for Something Completely Northern: Institutions of Governance in the Territorial North," *Journal of Canadian Studies* 35 (Winter 2000-01): 80-99; see also Kevin O'Brien, "Some Thoughts on Consensus Government in Nunavut," *Canadian Parliamentary Review* 26 (Winter 2003-04): 6-10.
6. For a statistical overview of the social characteristics of federal, provincial, and territorial members, see Donley T. Studlar, *et al.*, "A Social and Political Profile of Canadian Legislators, 1996," *Journal of Legislative Studies* 6 (Summer 2000): 93-103.

7. Chambers are not universally immobile. The Nunavut Legislature continues the tradition established by the NWT (but abandoned in the early 1990s) of every year holding several weeks of House sittings in communities distant from the capital.

8. For a fuller account of the significance of legislatures' size, see Graham White, "Big is Different from Little: On Taking Size Seriously in the Analysis of Canadian Governmental Institutions," *Canadian Public Administration* 33 (1990): 527-34.

9. Ronald D. Hedlund, "Organizational Attributes of Legislatures: Structures, Rules, Norms, Resources," *Legislative Studies Quarterly* 9 (1984): 89-103.

10. The numbers problem could be (and occasionally is) partially alleviated in small houses by having ministers serve on committees, but this can severely undercut committee independence and effectiveness.

11. Emery Barnes, *et al.*, "The Size of Legislatures: Perspectives on Provincial Assemblies," *Canadian Parliamentary Review* 18,1 (1995): 2-8.

12. The Ontario Liberal-NDP *Accord* in 1985-87 was often incorrectly described as a coalition; the NDP agreed to support the Liberal government, subject to certain conditions, but had no representatives in cabinet.

13. In 2001, the two ministers who had been elected as Liberals decided to sit as independents, having been disavowed by the Leader of the Saskatchewan Liberal Party. Although they remained in office, cabinet could no longer be said to include ministers from more than one party.

14. Since the 1960s, Quebec has experienced the rise and demise of several parties, such as the Parti Québécois, the Action Démocratique, the Union Nationale, and the Créditistes. On various occasions, three parties have attained significant representation in the National Assembly, but none of these configurations lasted more than one or two elections.

15. Graham White, *The Ontario Legislature: A Political Analysis* (Toronto: University of Toronto Press, 1989) chap. 9.

16. The capacity of individual members and of the legislatures collectively to influence policy was often substantial in the nineteenth century before party lines solidified and strict party discipline came to dominate and before the growth of the state and associated processes rendered policy-making so complex and specialized. By the First World War, however, the legislatures' policy-making capacity had been severely curtailed as executives grew increasingly dominant.

17. For details on the composition and activities of Boards of Internal Economy, see Robert J. Fleming and J.E. Glenn, eds., *Flemings Canadian Legislature 1997* (Toronto: University of Toronto Press, 1997) 131-34.

18. Gary Moncrief, "Professionalism and Careerism in Canadian Provincial Assemblies: Comparisons to U.S. State Legislatures," *Legislative Studies Quarterly* 17 (1994): 34.

19. Moncrief, "Professionalism" 40.

20. Gary Moncrief, "Terminating the Provincial Career: Retirement and Electoral Defeat in Canadian Provincial Legislatures, 1960-1997," *Canadian Journal of Political Science* 31 (June 1998): 359-72.

21. Data from Legislative Assembly of Alberta, "Member Indemnity and Expense Allowance Comparisons (Updated April 2005)"; available at <http://www.assembly.ab.ca/lao/hr/MLA/mem_indemnity_comparisons2005.htm>. With members in most jurisdictions receiving tax-free allowances in addition to their regular salary, their effective rate of pay can be substantially higher than the basic salary. The "effective rate of pay" indicated in the table thus includes the basic indemnity plus 167 per cent of any tax-free allowance. This calculation reflects the fact that at a 40 per cent

marginal tax rate (some provinces have slightly higher rates) $1.00 not subject to tax is equivalent to $1.67 which is taxable. In Newfoundland and Labrador, for example, the effective pay of members of the House of Assembly is $86,681 ($47,238 basic indemnity plus 167 per cent of the $23,619 tax-free allowance).

22. Members in most provinces also receive a wide range of allowances for the extraordinary expenditures that elected office can entail, such as for travel or for maintaining an additional residence. By and large, however, members pocket little of this money; most, if not all, goes to reimburse members for their expenses. An important exception is Nunavut, where various allowances mean that MLAs' effective pay is over $100,000 a year; see Jim Bell, "How much money does your MLA make?" *Nunatsiaq News*, 9 December 2005: 3.

23. A comparison of the data in Table 8.2 with similar data covering the years 1990-95 reveals that in only two of ten provinces did the legislatures sit more often in 1997-2002 than they had in the earlier period. Overall the provincial average declined from 71.4 days a year to 61.9 days a year, and even this understates the change, since PEI increased from 27 to 55 days a year; if PEI is excluded, the decline is 76.3 to 62.5 days a year. In three provinces (Newfoundland, Manitoba, and Alberta), the decline was more than 20 days a year. See Graham White, "Comparing Provincial Legislatures," in Christopher Dunn, ed., *Provinces* (Peterborough, ON: Broadview Press, 1996) 214, Table 2.

24. These financial and staffing figures all exclude independent (non-government) offices which report to the legislature, such as provincial auditors, ombudsmen, and information and privacy commissioners.

25. The figures in the table pertaining to budget are not precisely comparable, since for the largest legislatures they include some overhead expenses that in other provinces are not counted among legislative expenses. If precise dollar amounts may not be comparable, however, certainly the orders of magnitude of differences are.

26. Frederick C. Engleman, "The Legislature," in Allan Tupper and Roger Gibbins, eds., *Government and Politics in Alberta* (Edmonton: University of Alberta Press, 1992) 152-53.

27. These judgements are those of the Clerks of the House, who were asked to categorize each committee as follows: active—average of one or more meeting a week while the House is in session; moderately active—one to three meetings a month; inactive—less than one meeting a month; paper existence only—rarely if ever meets.

28. In a minority setting, this power can become very significant, for while the cabinet's procedural mechanisms for restraining active committees via House orders remain in force, without a numerical edge the government effectively loses control over committees that have the capacity to set their own agendas.

29. Typically, when the legislature passes a bill, it authorizes cabinet to make regulations which contain implementation details; in so doing the legislature loses all control of the process. An example of the use of regulations would be in setting welfare rates: the legal framework for a province's welfare system would be established by passage of a bill through the legislature, but specific rates of payments and conditions would be determined by the cabinet through regulation.

30. Valerie Moores and Heather Plewes, "The Ontario Legislature's Appointments Review Process," in Graham White, ed., *Inside the Pink Palace: Ontario Legislature Internship Essays* (Toronto: CPSA/Ontario Legislature Internship Programme, 1993).

31. Lisa Young, "Gender Equal Legislatures: Evaluating the Proposed Nunavut Electoral System," *Canadian Public Policy* 23 (1997): 306-15.

Table 8.1. Selected Characteristics of Provincial and Territorial Legislatures[1]

	NF	PEI	NB	NS	QC	ON	MB	SK	AB	BC	NU	NWT	YT
Size	48	27	55	52	125	103	57	58	83	79	19	19	18
Party	PC 34 Lib 11 NDP 2	PC 23 Lib 4	PC 28 Lib 26	PC 25 NDP 15 Lib 10	Lib 72 PQ 44 AD 5	Lib 71 PC 24 NDP 8	NDP 34 PC 20 Lib 2	NDP 30 Sask 28	PC 61 Lib 17 NDP 4	Lib 46 NDP 33	No parties	No parties	Yuk 11 NDP 5 Lib 2
Population/ Member	10,750	5,111	13,672	18,019	60,784	121,757	20,666	17,137	36,921	53,848	1,578	2,263	1,722
Women (#)	10	6	8	8	40	23	13	11	13	17	2	2	3
Women(%)	21	22	15	16	32	23	23	19	26	22	11	11	17
Budget ($M)	10.5	3.2	10.7	17.1	94.8	105.4	16.5	19.4	42.7	51.2	11.8	14.4	4.0
Budget/ member ($000)	219	119	194	329	758	1023	289	334	514	648	621	757	210
Effective pay ($000)	86.6	55.3	78.3	62.5	101.2	85.2	65.5	75.5	83.0	75.1	68.2	99.1	68.9
Full-time staff (partisan)	57	11	65	25	300	600	27	84	125	200	29	30	8
Full-time staff (non-partisan)	20	6	43	35	548	384	38	75	80	140	29	32	6

Notes: Lib - Liberal   PQ - Parti Québécois   Yuk - Yukon Party   PC - Progressive Conservative
AD - Action Démocratique   NDP - New Democratic Party   Sask - Saskatchewan Party   AA - Alberta Alliance
1. Data are for December 2005, except staff numbers, which are for 2002.

Table 8.2. Selected Indicators of Legislative Activity and Procedure

	NF	PEI	NB	NS	QC	ON	MB	SK	AB	BC	NU	NWT	YT
Sitting Days/year	60	55	50	67	67	80	71	61	51	67	46[4]	50	60
Sitting Hours/week	15	16	25	40	18/40[3]	31	20	20-24	25	28	22	22	20
PM Bus Hours/week	2	4	4	2[2]	2	2	4	3	3.5	2	NA	NA	2
Gov't Bills (#)	49	43	66	35	75	39	53	66	36	45	16	34	25
Gov't Bills (%)	92	93	99	88	87	78	98	100	95	96	94	97	97
PM Bills (#)	0	2	1	1	3	5	2	.2	3	1	?	.5	.2
PM Bills (%)	–[1]	50	33	5	50	6	33	<1	12	11	?	100	25
Gov't Bills to committee	rarely	<10	0	100	95	15-25	92	0	0	0	100	95	0
Estimates to committee	80	0	0	50	?	100	0	5	0	0	?	100	0
Closure/Time Alloc	5	0	0	0	4	17	0	0	3	.2	0	0	0

NA = not applicable   1. = none introduced   2. = opposition time   3. = ordinary/intensive   4. = 2000, 2001 only
PM Bus = private members' business   PM Bills = private members' bills

Notes: Other than the rows indicating the frequency with which government bills and estimates are reviewed in standing committees, the information in this table is based on the average over the period 1997–2002. "Gov't Bills (#)" indicates the number of government bills introduced per year, "Gov't Bills (%)" indicates the percentage of government bills passed per year; the next two rows indicates the same information for private members' bills (PMB).

Table 8.3. Selected Characteristics of Legislative Committees

	NF	PEI	NB	NS	QC	ON	MB	SK	AB	BC	NU	NWT	YT
Standing committees	8	9	6	10	11	8	11	14	6	4	5	4	5
Active/ mod active	4	4	3	6	10	7	8	6	1	1	4	3	0
Size Standing	5-7	4-6	9-14	9-10	10-18	8-10	11-12	7-10	9-21	9-11	5	5-11	4-7
Ad hoc/ special	occ	rare	common	occ	rare	occ	rare	common	occ	common	occ	common	rare
Standing Travel	occ	occ	occ	rare	rare	common	occ	occ	rare	common	common	common	rare
Special Travel	occ	occ	common	common	rare	common	rare	occ	occ	common	common	common	occ
Staff	clerk	clerk	clerk	clerk	clerk + researcher	clerk + researcher	clerk	clerk	clerk	clerk + researcher	clerk + researcher	clerk + researcher	clerk
Control own agenda	N	Y	N	N	Y	Y	N	N	Y	N	Y	Y	N
Review delegated leg	N	N	N	N	Y (all)	Y	Y	Y	N	N	Y (all)	Y(all)	Y
Review ABCs	N	N	Y	Y	Y (all)	Y	Y	Y	N	Y	Y (all)	Y(all)	Y
Review appointments	N	N	Y	Y	N	Y	N	N	N	N	N	N	Y

Notes: ABCs: agencies, boards, and commissions   occ: occasional

CHAPTER 9

Court Systems in the Provinces[1]

CARL BAAR

Courts are fundamental elements of legal authority in Canada. They are also an essential part of the governing institutions in every province and territory. The administration of justice has been a provincial responsibility under the original terms of the *Constitution Act, 1867*.[2] Yet at the same time the courts, at the centre of the justice system, are disengaged from provincial political life.

Of course they are, you might respond. That's the whole point of having courts. While they are public institutions supported by taxpayers' money, they are supposed to stand apart from politics and apart from the government of the day. The courts' job is to make independent and impartial judgements about how laws and legal principles apply in specific cases. Courts must be independent of the provincial government, because that government is the most frequent litigator in the courts—prosecuting criminal cases; seeking child protection orders; and defending administrative decisions by labour boards, human rights tribunals, and environmental agencies against legal attack.[3]

While these responsibilities set the courts apart, political scientists also argue that they have placed the courts at the centre of some of the most important political disputes within the provinces—the status of official languages in Quebec and Manitoba, the rights of Aboriginal peoples in BC, the legality of restrictions on abortion in Nova Scotia, and the rights of same-sex couples in Ontario. While courts are involved in these matters in a different way than other institutions of the state, using different procedures, style, and language, they still make authoritative decisions that produce winners and losers and that carry the full sanctioning authority of the state. In this broader sense, courts are definitely political.[4]

This chapter will look at provincial court systems from a political perspective. It will take two contrasting approaches. First, it will argue that Canadian provincial court systems are not only disengaged from the central processes of provincial politics, but are disengaged to a greater extent than the courts in other federal systems. This greater degree of disengagement will be explained in terms of the distinctive organization of Canadian provincial courts and the broad authority of the Supreme Court of Canada.

Second, this chapter will argue that the provincial court system's disengagement requires that its political dimensions be examined separately, by looking at the areas in which the courts are normally asked to exercise their authority and analyzing their roles in those terms. Therefore, the authoritative role of provincial trial and appellate courts in criminal, civil, and family matters (the three major types of court work) and the advocacy role of the judiciary as an interest group in provincial politics will be examined.

Provincial Courts and Provincial Public Policy

The interplay of cabinet, legislature, bureaucracy, parties, and interest groups is the stuff of public policy literature in the provinces. The courts are frequently in the news, as a notorious trial unfolds or a controversial judgement is released, but their work less frequently intersects with the policy matters that drive provincial politics.

The courts do become a part of the policy process when they are asked to evaluate a policy embodied in legislation or in administrative rulings. A provincial government can ask the highest court in the province—universally titled the Court of Appeal[5]—to rule on the validity of a law before it takes effect. This procedure is called a reference. Reference cases are few in number; years may go by without one. But the cases that have occurred are among some of the most important in Canadian history and affect the terms of future policy debate. Private citizens and corporations can also ask the courts to rule on the validity of a provincial law or regulation once it is enacted, but can do so only in the context of an action already before the courts. For example, private parties can defend themselves by arguing that the law or regulation should not be used against them—perhaps because it violates the *Charter of Rights and Freedoms* or is beyond the constitutional authority of the federal or provincial government, but more commonly because it has been interpreted incorrectly or too broadly, or because there is insufficient evidence to reach a finding of guilt or liability.

In this context, court decisions on the legal or constitutional validity of government policies, although infrequent, have a significant impact. But when they do, they are more likely to be appealed to the highest court in the land, the Supreme Court of Canada, whose nine members sit only in Ottawa. This is because the Supreme Court of Canada is the final authority for the interpretation of all laws in Canada, including provincial law. In this process, provincial trial courts and courts of appeal are only the preliminary stages in applying and interpreting the law.

This situation need not occur in a federal system. In the US, the highest court in a state is the supreme authority on the interpretation and application of state law. True, the US Supreme Court often deals with the constitutionality of state laws, but this is because a constitutional challenge requires the interpretation and application of the federal American constitution. American state courts over the past generation have learned that if they base their decisions on interpretation of their state constitutions, their decision is binding, because the US Supreme Court has no authority to second-guess the state's highest court on matters of state law.[6]

American state courts have not always been the final interpreters of the meaning and application of state law. Until 1938,[7] a federal judge asked to apply state common law to a dispute within the jurisdiction of federal courts (because the dispute was between citizens of different states) could give his own interpretation of that law, regardless of interpretations by the state's highest court. That authority, affirmed by the US Supreme Court in 1842,[8] allowed the development of a parallel system of federal common law. As a result, the law that applied to a dispute depended upon which court heard the case. After decades of criticism, the Supreme Court finally agreed to be bound by state court interpretation of state law.

The approach of the Canadian courts and legal system differs from the approach of their American counterparts in two ways. First, there is no set of parallel federal courts in Canada with overlapping jurisdiction in cases involving citizens of different provinces. An Ontario resident involved in an accident in Quebec could sue or be sued in the courts of Quebec; an Illinois resident involved in an accident in Michigan could sue or be sued in either the Michigan state courts or the American federal district court in Michigan.[9] In this sense, our court organization is more unified than that in the US. Second, the interpretation of Quebec law by Quebec courts—or Ontario law by Ontario courts, or Newfoundland law by Newfoundland courts—is subject to review by the Supreme Court of Canada. The Supreme Court of Canada is therefore the final judge of all laws, federal and provincial. In this sense, our legal system is also more unified.

Thus, in constitutional and political terms, our highest national court has more authority within the Canadian federal system than the US Supreme Court has within the American federal system. The Supreme Court of Canada, for example, is the final interpreter of the meaning and application of the provisions of the Quebec Civil Code, even though only three of the nine justices of that court must be members of the Quebec Bar. While we usually think of Canadian provinces having more autonomy and power within our federal system than states have in the American federation, the role of the Supreme Court of Canada in interpreting provincial law is an important exception. Thus, for example, the Louisiana courts are the final interpreters of that state's system of civil law (Louisiana is the only civil law jurisdiction in the US), but the Quebec courts are not the final interpreters of that province's Civil Code.

The Supreme Court of Canada has more real power in the Canadian legal system than the US Supreme Court has over the American legal system for another simple reason: the country's size. The US has ten times the population and five times the number of federal units that we have in Canada. As a result, our Supreme Court, which has the same number of judges as its American counterpart and often sits in panels of five and seven justices (the US Supreme Court sits only with a full bench of nine), has the potential to—and does—address a much larger proportion of the country's legal issues.[10] To the extent that the Supreme

Court of Canada decides major issues of provincial law, it can limit the discretionary role of provincial trial and appeal courts.

In reality, the Supreme Court of Canada rarely decides private disputes and is in a position to review only a small percentage of the decisions made by provincial courts of appeal. Decisions of those courts are likely to be final in most cases. However, only a small proportion of provincial appeals raise new legal issues, so the Supreme Court of Canada is still in a position to exercise its authority—for example, where provincial interpretations of law conflict from one court to another.[11]

Ironically, then, the very importance of the Supreme Court of Canada, both because of its authority as final arbiter of all federal and provincial law and because of its ability and willingness to address undecided legal questions, reduces the political role of provincial court systems. By its very willingness to intervene, the Supreme Court of Canada increases the provincial courts' disengagement from provincial politics. Other characteristics of court organization reinforce this disengagement.

Selection and remuneration of judges

The judges on provincial courts of appeal and provincial superior trial courts are selected by the federal government, not the provinces, a procedure required by section 96 of the *Constitution Act, 1867*. This provision does not ensure that the selection of judges is free from partisan considerations (some historical speculation suggests that section 96 originated from the fears of some framers that their patronage would slip away). It does decrease the likelihood that those who have political connections when they go on the bench will have links to the provincial party in power.[12] In contrast, American state judges are either selected by the state governor or elected by the state's voters, sometimes on a nonpartisan ballot but often as part of a party's slate of candidates.

Furthermore, section 96 provides that the salaries and expenses of federally appointed superior court judges will be paid by the federal government. While judges' salaries have often been the source of disputes between the judiciary and government, section 96 means that lobbying activity for superior court salary increases is directed to the federal government, not to the provinces. This has not only decreased the off-the-bench contact between provincial governments and section 96 judges (both in appellate and trial courts), it has also meant that there has been a wide (and until recent years, a growing) salary gap between section 96 judges and the provincially appointed (and provincially compensated) judges who usually sit on high-volume criminal courts. Section 96 judges receive $224,200 per year,[13] while provincially appointed judges' annual salaries range from $159,181 in Newfoundland to $213,630 in Ontario. The conflicts between provincially appointed judges and the provincial governments that pay their salaries became so heated by the 1990s that the judges themselves brought a series of legal actions that resulted in a broad and controversial decision of the Supreme Court of Canada in 1997 ordering provincial governments to set up independent compensation commissions to set judicial salaries.[14] This legally far-reaching and procedurally innovative decision, an attempt to move salary determination out of the partisan arena, has in fact created more tensions between judiciaries and provincial governments in the years since 1997. Perhaps in an effort to defuse these conflicts, the Supreme Court in summer 2005 gave provincial governments more leeway to modify recommendations of the independent commissions than provincial courts of appeal had previously allowed.[15]

For most of its history, Canada was unique among federal systems in requiring that its provincial judges be appointed by the federal government. For example, Australia's 1901 Constitution followed the American model and placed appointing power in the state rather than commonwealth governments. The only federation to adopt the Canadian model was India. Its 1949 Constitution consciously followed the Canadian pattern, with the central government appointing state High Court (superior court) judges; Indian constitution-makers were apparently motivated by the desire to place political control over appointments at the centre and to reduce the ability of state politicians to influence these appointments.[16]

Legal cultural norms

Canadian legal culture has encouraged disengagement from provincial politics. Canadian judges traditionally followed the English pattern rather than the American, defining their role narrowly as responding to legal questions in the cases before them and hesitating to rewrite statutes passed by elected legislative bodies. This role definition, or legal cultural norm, traditionally kept provincial courts out of the headlines but did not make them politically neutral. Historically, disengagement achieved by deference to government made the courts' impact highly conservative by reinforcing public authority against citizen challenges. It is this deferential conservatism that has been changed since 1982 by the *Charter of Rights and Freedoms*. However, it was the Supreme Court of Canada rather than the provincial appeal courts that led the way in Charter activism during its first decade; rights claimants won 33 per cent of the cases before the Supreme Court of Canada as against 26 per cent in provincial courts of appeal.[17] In the 56 cases in which a provincial court of appeal was reversed, 33 were in favour of the rights claimant (56 per cent) and 19 against (32 per cent). Only in the Quebec and Saskatchewan Courts of Appeal were Charter claimants more successful than in the Supreme Court.[18]

The influence of the federal government

The federal government retains other powers over provincial court operation that reduce the ability of provincial governments unilaterally to alter court organization and procedure. Thus, a wide range of court reform proposals desired by provincial governments require concurring legislation by the federal Parliament, increasing the incentive for section 96 judges to lobby federal officials to stop provincial legislation. Provincial government anti-crime initiatives are limited by the fact that criminal law and procedure are federal responsibilities under section 91(25) of the *Constitution Act, 1867*. Thus, for example, provincial governments can organize and administer criminal courts under section 92(14) but cannot set statutory time standards in criminal cases. For several years in the early 1980s, the Nova Scotia government wanted to abolish grand juries (every other province had previously done so), but the federal government, pressed with other priorities, did not pass the necessary enabling legislation.

In summary, the role of the Supreme Court of Canada combines with federal control over judicial appointments to the superior and appellate courts, federal power over criminal procedure, and a traditional legal culture to disengage provincial courts from the day-to-day world of provincial politics and public policy. At the same time, this disengagement invites the researcher to examine the legal life of provincial courts from a fresh perspective.

The Politics of Provincial Judicial Decision-Making

While trial and appeal courts in the provinces are subordinate to the Supreme Court of Canada on the most controversial and fundamental legal issues that are brought to the judiciary for resolution, most of the courts' day-to-day work is done apart from the spectre of Supreme Court review. The Supreme Court accepts only a small number of cases for review each year, only around 100 from across the country, while the ten provincial appeal courts hear thousands of cases each year, and provincial trial courts deal with many times more. Furthermore, appeal courts rule only on legal issues arising in cases decided in trial courts, even though many of the most important decisions made by trial court judges involve the interpretation of factual evidence. Finally, the overwhelming majority of cases that are brought to trial courts in Canada and in other countries are never actually tried. Most cases reach a disposition without trial, either because the parties have reached an agreement prior to trial (sometimes even on the day of trial), or because the party that brought the case does not proceed (the crown may drop criminal charges or a plaintiff may discontinue a civil claim), or the party against whom the claim is made (the defendant) does not respond (many divorces and civil debt actions are uncontested).

While a great deal of this judicial work is predictable in its outcome, and disengaged from political issues before the provincial government, it retains important political dimensions. Its very predictability reinforces the authority of the state and the law. A large number of civil cases involve banks and corporations suing to collect money owed by members of the public (e.g., mortgage foreclosures, debt collection), and many of those are handled by default judgements in which the court "rules" in favour of the bank or corporation when the debtor does not file a defence against the claim. In the process, courts serve an important economic and social function every day in every province, one that businesses rely on and social critics might see as the use of public authority to maintain private economic power.

At the same time, many routine judicial proceedings involve the exercise of discretion by judges and court officials.[19] This is particularly evident in criminal proceedings. While most criminal matters are not decided at trial—typically, an accused pleads guilty or a Crown prosecutor declines to proceed with charges—judges must still decide what sentence to impose and must still make a variety of preliminary decisions that have important effects on the accused and the community. For example, should an accused person be held in custody prior to trial, or should the person be released on bail?

In short, understanding the political dimension of provincial courts requires an understanding of their day-to-day work. Courts today usually classify their work under three headings: criminal matters, civil matters, and family matters. The term "matters" is used instead of "cases" because a judge sitting in court on any given day is as likely (or more likely) to be hearing a preliminary motion in a case, or deciding whether a case should proceed or be adjourned to a later date, as presiding at a trial. At this point, a summary of the work of trial court judges is appropriate.

CRIMINAL MATTERS:

- Presiding at preliminary proceedings; for example, first appearances, bail hearings, bail reviews, scheduling and pretrial conferences, preliminary inquiries.
- Accepting pleas of guilty made by persons accused of summary conviction offences (less serious offences normally punishable by a maximum of six months in custody,[20] analogous to misdemeanors in American criminal law) and indictable offences (serious criminal offences, with maximum liability for punishment set in the Criminal Code of Canada; analogous to felonies in American criminal law);[21] trying summary conviction offences and indictable offences.
- Trying indictable offences before a jury when the accused elects to be tried by jury (except in murder cases,[22] where a jury is required).
- Sentencing accused persons who plead guilty to or are found guilty of an offence; prescribing treatment as a condition of sentence.

CIVIL MATTERS:

- Trying disputes between private parties, primarily dealing with liability of a defendant to the plaintiff, and the amount (quantum) of money that is owed to the plaintiff once liability has been established.

- Conducting pretrial conferences in these disputes.
- Hearing motions seeking particular orders at any time between the initiation of a civil action and its resolution by settlement or trial.

FAMILY MATTERS:

- Dealing with issues arising from the breakdown of family relationships, including divorce, division of property, custody and access, and support and maintenance. These issues are dealt with in a variety of proceedings—trials, pretrials, motions, and mediation-based alternatives.
- Hearing matters involving child protection, typically actions brought by public authorities to remove children from the parental home and place them "in care."

While most trial court work falls in one of these three categories, not all of it does. For example, matters involving young offenders are heard along with family matters in some provinces and criminal matters in others. Furthermore, a variety of trial court work is done by judges in some provinces and quasi-judicial officers in other provinces. In this category are so-called "provincial offences," principally violations of traffic laws, liquor regulations, and municipal by-laws but extending to other offences under provincial law, for example, environmental offences.[23] One particular class of quasi-judicial officers, justices of the peace, not only handle provincial offences but have expanded into an increasingly wide range of Criminal Code matters, particularly in Alberta and Ontario. On the civil side, a number of provinces allow civil disputes involving less than a certain amount of money (now as high as $10,000) to be tried by lawyers who work as part-time "deputy judges" or by full-time hearing officers (who may or may not be lawyers).[24]

Appeal courts in each province hear cases in all of these areas, but their work is fundamentally different. They hear only legal arguments, not sworn testimony. Witnesses do not appear; appeal courts must rely on the evidence contained in the transcript of the proceedings at trial. In the process, however, appeal court judges, usually sitting in panels of three, deal with issues in all areas of the law. Furthermore, appeal courts can consider not only a request to overturn a criminal conviction or a civil damage award, but also whether the resulting sentence or financial award is too high or too low.

Canadian appeal courts are more constrained than their counterparts in continental Europe or Latin America. Those courts can call and examine witnesses who appeared at the original trial. Conversely, Canadian appeal courts have more discretion than their American counterparts. As a rule, appeal courts in American states cannot increase or decrease the sentences given by trial courts in criminal cases.

The trial court judges who hear civil, criminal, and family matters in Canadian provinces and territories include both generalists and specialists. The superior courts, whose judges are appointed and paid by the federal government, are primarily generalists. The courts on which they sit have a caseload that is predominantly civil, but in the larger centres there is sufficient criminal and family law work that superior court judges may sit for extended rotation on those cases. As shown in Table 9.1, superior courts vary in name: the Supreme Court (BC, Nova Scotia, Yukon, and NWT), the Supreme Court (Trial Division) (PEI and Newfoundland), Court of Queen's Bench (Alberta, Saskatchewan, Manitoba, and New Brunswick), cour supérieure (Quebec), and Superior Court in Ontario. Even when superior court judges serve for long periods on a rotation, or handle almost entirely civil cases, they pride themselves on having the skills to work as generalists in an age of specialization.

Table 9.1. Canadian Provincial and Territorial Trial Courts

Province	Superior Court	Other Sec. 96 Courts	Provincial Court
BC	Supreme Court	NA	Provincial Court
AB	Court of Queen's Bench	Surrogate Court	Provincial Court
SK	Court of Queen's Bench Unified Family Court	Surrogate Court Provincial Court	
MB	Court of Queen's Bench *Trial Division *Family Division	NA	Provincial Court
ON	Superior Court	Unified Family Court	Ontario Court of Justice
QC	La Cour supérieure	NA	Cour du Québec *chambre civile *chambre criminelle et pénale *chambre de la jeunesse *chambre administrative *Cours municipales
NB	Court of Queen's Bench *Trial Division *Family Division	NA	Provincial Court
NS	Supreme Court	Supreme Court (Family Division)	Provincial Court
PEI	Supreme Court (Trial Division)	NA	Provincial Court
NF	Supreme Court (Trial Division)	Unified Family Court	Provincial Court
YT	Supreme Court	NA	Territorial Court
NWT	Supreme Court	NA	Territorial Court
NU	Nunavut Court of Justice	NA	NA

NA= Not applicable

Each province also has a provincial court (called the Ontario Court of Justice and the Cour du Québec in those provinces) staffed by provincially appointed judges. Provincial courts are the descendents of Magistrate's Courts that existed from before Confederation until the 1970s for the purpose of trying minor criminal offences, small claims, and family disputes that involved women and children but little money. Over time, these courts grew in importance and were transformed into fully professional courts with broad powers.[25] For example, provincial court judges not only try all summary conviction offences, but also try most indictable offences (with the consent of the accused). The growing importance of the provincial courts has meant that in most provinces, half or more of the trial court judges are provincial rather than federal appointees. Of the 1,601 trial judges shown by province in Table 9.2, 937 are provincially appointed, compared with 664 federally appointed.[26] This is not the picture that the framers of section 96 would have envisioned in the 1860s. Despite these changes, however, differences in salary and status between the "section 96 judges" and the provincially appointed judges remain.

Work styles of the two groups of trial judges also differ. Provincial court judges generally specialize. In New Brunswick and much of Nova Scotia, they hear only criminal matters. In turn, Ontario Court of Justice judges have jurisdiction in criminal and family matters, but in all but the smallest court centres some judges are identified as family court judges and others as criminal court judges. Even in Quebec, which has enlarged the jurisdiction of the Cour du Québec so that superior court judges appointed by Ottawa have a smaller role in the legal life of the province, provincially appointed judges are specialists. There are separate divisions in the Cour du Québec where one group of judges hears criminal cases, another hears civil cases, and a third sits in the Youth Court (Chambre de la jeunesse).

The high degree of specialization encourages provinces to select for appointment as judges those lawyers with specialized experience. The development of provincial judicial councils and appointment review bodies may reinforce this tendency, even as those bodies reduce the ability of provincial governments to use judicial appointments to reward political allies. At the same time, appointing experienced counsel to courts with extensive jurisdiction over criminal matters can mean appointing lawyers who, having spent their careers as Crown prosecutors, have developed knowledge and perspectives about criminal behaviour that may affect how they interpret the evidence presented in each specific case.

The effects of specialization are sometimes seen in how discretion over sentencing is exercised. In a number of provinces, anecdotal evidence[27] suggests that sentences given in provincial courts are not generally as onerous as those given in superior courts for similar offences. Provincial court judges, even if they had served as Crown attorneys and argued in court for more severe sentences, tend to view sentencing in terms of the large number and variety of offenders who appear before them. Sentences at the high end of the normal range tend to be reserved for repeat offenders and particularly egregious acts. For example, how severe was the assault? How large was the fraud? How helpless was the victim? Under these conditions, provincial court judges who sit full time on criminal matters may not mete out sentences as severe as those of superior court judges who see fewer cases.

Furthermore, many more criminal cases in provincial court end with a plea of guilty rather than a judgement at trial, and when an accused pleads guilty, legal arguments focus on sentence, and defence counsel emphasize grounds for

Table 9.2. Number of Federally Appointed and Provincially Appointed Judges in Office, by Type of Court, by Province, 2004

Province/ Territory	Court of Appeal Judges	Superior Court Judges	Other S. 96 Judges	Provincial Court Judges
BC	15	82	0	157
AB	13	61	0	108
SK	9	31	0	45
MB	7	31	0	38
ON	18	201	29	238
QC	20	141	0	262
NB	6	22	0	26
NS	8	25	8	32
PEI	3	5	0	3
NF	6	20	0	24
YT	—	2	0	2
NWT	—	3	0	2
NU	—	3	0	0
TOTALS	105	627	37	937

Notes: The number of court of appeal and superior court judges is current as of 1 November 2004. Note that the figures exclude supernumerary judges, who have elected to sit on a part-time basis once they have become eligible for a full pension (but prior to the compulsory retirement age of 75). There are currently 22 supernumerary judges on the courts of appeal and 167 on the superior courts, for a total of 958 sitting section 96 judges.

Figures for the three territories (Yukon, Nunavut, and NWT) do not include figures for court of appeal. In all three jurisdictions, appellate panels are composed of judges from outside the territories. For example, the Yukon Court of Appeal is made up of judges from the BC Court of Appeal, and the NWT Court of Appeal is made up of judges from the Alberta Court of Appeal.

Figures for "other Section 96 Judges" include 29 Family Court Judges in Ontario and eight Family Division Judges in Nova Scotia.

The number of provincially appointed judges is current as of 15 December 2003. Figures do not include per diem judges and also exclude full-time as well as part-time Municipal Court judges in Quebec.

Sources: For federally appointed judges: Office of the Commissioner for Federal Judicial Affairs, Ottawa, "Number of Judges on the Bench as of November 1, 2004," 2 pp. For provincially-appointed judges: *Canada Law List 2004.*

leniency. The plea of guilty itself becomes an argument that the accused person has accepted responsibility and has taken the first step to rehabilitating himself or herself. If the accused has a job, defence counsel would argue that the public interest is not served by a term in custody; if the Crown prosecutor insists on a custodial sentence, he or she might agree to a term of less than three months so that the time could be served on weekends.

The guilty plea process can reinforce the sentencing differences between provincial court judges and superior court judges. The likelihood of a higher sentence is so much a part of the legal culture in Quebec that lawyers there say that accused persons pay an "assize tax" when they elect to go before a superior court judge and an "amusement tax" when they go to trial rather than enter a plea of guilty.[28]

Traditionally, this was not the case in Ontario and BC. But the fact that section 96 judges in those provinces were not stricter in their sentences meant that defence counsel faced with a "hawk" in provincial court could recommend that their client elect to be tried in the superior court. Later, when the superior court trial date arrived, the accused could enter a plea of guilty and receive a lighter sentence than he or she would have received in provincial court, as well as spending several additional months out of custody before serving that sentence. The fact that this sort of "judge shopping" (or, more properly, forum shopping) occurs is another reminder of how much discretion judges have over sentencing in criminal cases.

Since 1990, changes in the pattern of elections by accused persons have been reported in Ontario, BC, and Nova Scotia.[29] As shown in Table 9.3, these three provinces were the last in Canada to move from having two section 96 trial courts (a province-wide superior court and a set of county and district courts with judges residing in local counties and districts) to having a single superior court. After merger, the number of federally appointed judges assigned to try criminal cases in Toronto, Vancouver, and Halifax increased to the point where defence counsel were not as certain what sentences could be expected. Without the level of predictability that existed in the past, counsel hesitated to recommend that their clients elect to go from provincial court to the section 96 court. At the same time, the addition of a new generation of provincial court judges screened by advisory bodies has increased the confidence of defence counsel in that bench. These changes, taken together, have further reduced the criminal caseload of section 96 courts.

While sentencing variation is the most commonly acknowledged effect of discretion possessed by trial judges, examples occur in other fields of law as well. In family matters, a petition for divorce is unlikely to be rejected, but the terms of a divorce or separation may be highly contentious. The amount of financial support ordered by judges for the children of the marriage may vary. Even more important, the enforcement of child support varies widely from court to court and from judge to judge. Some judges actively intervene to ensure that a court order to pay support is respected. Others are uneasy, fearing that the intervention makes it difficult to appear neutral if the judge appears to be prosecuting the party that has not paid the support (usually the father).[30] Even if the judge is prepared to enforce support vigorously, if the administrative apparatus of the court is not equipped to monitor payment and nonpayment, the case may not come before the judge until several weeks or even months of arrears have accumulated. At that point, some judges will waive payment of arrears once the paying party agrees to resume payments. Once discretion is exercised in this manner, the paying party may see it to his advantage to default again.

In civil matters, the most frequently tried cases in most superior courts are tort cases (covering negligence and other legal wrongs), the largest category of which are motor vehicle accidents. The dispute may centre on whether the defendant is liable to pay damages to the plaintiff but often focuses on the quantum of damages—that is, how much money should the defendant pay to the injured party? How serious or permanent are the injuries? How can pain and suffering

Table 9.3. Court Reorganization in Canadian Provinces: Merger of Superior and County/District Courts, Creation of Provincial Courts from Magistrate's Courts, and Unification of Family Courts

Province	Merger of Superior and County/District Courts	Creation of Provincial Court	Unification of Family Court
BC	1989	1969	NA
AB	1978	1971	NA
SK	1980	1978	1978–94[1]
MB	1983	1972	1983
ON	1989	1968	1976–95[2]
QC	NA[3]	1965	NA
NB	1979	1959	1978–81[4]
NS	1992	1976	1999[5]
PEI	1975	1975	1975
NF	1984	1974	1977[6]

Notes: Years indicate when statute received royal assent, not necessarily when the reorganization was implemented. For example, the merger statute in New Brunswick, passed in 1978, provided an effective date of 4 September 1979; the 1989 BC merger statute set 1 July 1990; and the 1998 statute creating the Supreme Court (Family Division) in Nova Scotia was proclaimed 6 April 1999. Most statutes did not designate specific effective dates.
1. 1978 statute for Saskatoon only; 1994 legislation authorized province-wide implementation.
2. 1976 statute for Hamilton only; 1994 legislation authorized province-wide implementation that began with four additional locations in 1995 and still covers less than half the province.
3. Quebec was the only province never to have a system of county or district courts.
4. Authorized in Fredericton, 1978; province wide in 1981.
5. Not yet implemented province wide.
6. St. John's only.

be translated into dollar terms? In these cases, the insurance companies who normally retain counsel for the defendants will argue for lower awards. The range available to the judge can be substantial, and just as there are judges who may be termed hawks or doves (or even "marshmallows") in criminal sentencing, so there are judges who are seen as more sympathetic to the defence or the plaintiffs in personal injury cases. The fact that the largest and most prestigious law firms in large cities tend to handle more cases for insurance companies than for individual plaintiffs, and the search for excellent judges may lead appointing authorities to those firms, may have the potential to build in a pro-defence orientation in large urban superior courts.

Sometimes, the best way to understand the political role of trial courts is to look at the cases in which the range of discretion used in practice is very narrow. For example, if a criminal court always followed the recommendation of the Crown prosecutor when awarding sentences, the court's role in reinforcing law enforcement would be dominant. If a family court always followed the recommendations of child protection agencies who sought to place children "in care" outside their family, the court might rightfully be seen as an extension of the provincial child welfare apparatus. Small claims courts whose workload is dominated by requests for default judgement by creditors against debtors may come to be seen as providing a low-cost debt collection service for the business community. Whether these patterns and perceptions are valid requires empirical research, either through observation in court[31] or research in case files.[32] Legal research can only tell us the range of options available to someone pursuing or responding to a legal claim. An understanding of who brings legal claims and what normally happens to those claims takes us beyond legal research, just as the student of provincial legislatures must go beyond the rules of parliamentary procedure to observe what a legislature actually does and to analyze its role in a democratic polity.

The Interest Group Politics of the Judiciary

While judges have authority in the courtroom, the organization and administration of their courts is a provincial legislative responsibility. In every province, that responsibility has been delegated to a department of government, despite persistent recommendations that it would be more consistent with principles of judicial independence for administrative authority to be delegated to the judiciary itself.[33] As a result, court reforms cannot be initiated by judges but can only be suggested by them. Conversely, government initiatives may give rise to opposition from the courts. Given the overlapping involvement of federal and provincial governments through sections 91, 92, and 96, the court reform process is particularly complex, and the opportunities for judicial advocacy are numerous despite the culture of restraint that keeps judges away from the most visible seats in the political arena.

Consider two of the most contentious reforms in court organization: the unified family court and the unified criminal court. Proposals to unify family courts have been made for over three decades as a way to ensure that members of the public who must go to court in family disputes can be served more effectively. However, these proposals have been delayed by federal-provincial differences unknown in other federations. Until 1975 in every province, divorce proceedings and division of marital property took place in a superior court, while issues of custody and access, enforcement of child support, and child protection and child welfare were handled in provincial courts by family court judges appointed and paid by the provincial government. Initially, some provincial governments favoured placing all the jurisdiction over family matters in the family courts, not the superior courts, but the Supreme Court of Canada had held similar initiatives unconstitutional, reasoning that section 96 prevents provincial legislatures from reducing the jurisdiction belonging to superior court judges at the time of confederation.[34] Some provinces then supported placing all jurisdiction over family matters in the superior court, but this required concurrent legislation by the federal government to authorize paying the salaries of the additional federally appointed judges. As a result, PEI, with its small population, was the first to implement a province-wide unified family court (see Table 9.3). Four provinces followed with pilot projects in the late 1970s, but they were confined to a single city in each province. Manitoba and New Brunswick both moved to a province-wide unified family court in the early 1980s, but Ontario's plans were delayed in part because the province wanted a voice in the appointment of the unified family court judges. (It is perhaps not a coincidence that Ontario's provincial government was Progressive Conservative when the federal government was Liberal, and later was Liberal when the federal government was Progressive Conservative.) Alberta has thoroughly studied family court unification, but recommendations to move to that model have been caught in more recent efforts to unify criminal courts.

Criminal court unification proposals reflect another split in jurisdiction. Only superior court judges preside at all jury trials, but most criminal offences are dealt with in provincial courts staffed by provincially appointed judges. Provinces argued that expense and complexity would be reduced if all criminal matters were dealt with in a single court. New Brunswick made the first proposal in 1981, but it was unanimously rejected by the Supreme Court of Canada because it placed all criminal jurisdiction in courts staffed by provincially appointed judges, again in violation of section 96.[35] (Earlier, the New Brunswick Court of Appeal had unanimously approved the proposal.)[36] By 1990, the provincial attorneys-general unanimously supported placing all criminal cases in superior courts staffed by federally appointed judges.[37] This proposal was supported by the Canadian Association of Provincial Court Judges, whose membership—provincially appointed judges—served to gain more prestige and higher salaries from the change.[38] However, the proposal ran into opposition from the superior court judges, who feared they would be inundated by high volumes of routine criminal work. The federally appointed judges urged the federal government not to pass the legislation necessary to put the provincial proposals into effect, and the federal government, seeing how much judicial salary money would be required to implement the plan, backed away. Five years after the unanimous 1990 resolution, only New Brunswick was still considering the proposal.[39] In the meantime, the salary increases awarded to provincially appointed judges have led some provincial governments to shift routine criminal work to lower paid (and less securely tenured) judicial officers, principally Justices of the Peace.[40]

These examples illustrate the complex political processes that surround efforts to reform court operations and show the judges' direct involvement in some of those processes. At the same time, because provincial governments, unlike Australian or American state governments, lack exclusive control over the organization of and procedure in their courts, the judges frequently direct their efforts toward the federal government. Another common strategy of judges' groups is to seek support from the organized bar. When support began growing among

Table 9.4: Titles of Judges and Quasi-Judicial Officers in Canadian Provinces

Province	Federally Appointed Judges	Provincially Appointed Judges	Quasi-Judicial Officers
BC	Justice	Judge	Justice of the Peace Registrar Referee
AB	Justice	Judge	Justice of the Peace Commissioner Master
SK	Justice	Judge	Justice of the Peace
MB	Justice	Judge	Magistrate Hearing Officer Justice of the Peace
ON	Justice	Justice	Justice of the Peace Deputy Judge Assessment Officer Case Management Master Referee
QC	juge	juge	juge de paix
NB	Justice	Judge	NA
NS	Justice	Judge	Justice of the Peace Small Claims Adjudicator
PEI	Justice	Judge	Justice of the Peace
NF	Justice	Judge	Justice of the Peace

provincial attorneys-general for a unified criminal court, the Canadian Bar Association set up a special task force—headed by a well-respected supernumerary (partially retired) judge of the BC Court of Appeal. Its report recommended against creation of unified criminal courts.[41]

Controversy a decade ago over the need to improve gender equity in the legal and judicial systems disrupted traditional alliances between bench and bar. Reports on gender equity and gender bias were produced by task forces appointed by lawyers' groups, including provincial law societies in BC and Ontario and the Canadian Bar Association nationally.[42] *Touchstones for Change*, the Report of the CBA Task Force headed by retired Supreme Court Justice Bertha Wilson, provoked lively debate not only about the extent of gender bias in the legal system but about the appropriateness of using compulsory judicial education courses and revamped disciplinary processes to address the issue. Criticism by the Canadian Judges Conference, a voluntary association of federally appointed judges, succeeded in delaying action on Wilson Report recommendations.

While gender bias continues to be a basis for complaints against sitting judges, the context has changed from the 1990s to the current decade. Thus, while the Canadian Judicial Council (a statutory body made up of federally appointed chief justices), which hears complaints against section 96 judges, reported that 18 of the 172 complaint files that it closed in the 2001-02 fiscal year alleged gender bias, all 18 complaints were made by men. The examples given in the Council's *Annual Report* for that year indicate that complaints typically involved adverse decisions in family law cases. Thus one complainant's allegations were subject to "careful review," but a number of other complainants' allegations were not pursued because the appropriate remedy was an appeal.[43]

The impact of gender equity concerns has also been reflected in the changing composition of the Section 96 courts, as shown in Table 9.5. The number of women justices in provincial courts of appeal has gone from 28 in 1995 to 42 in 2004, a 50 per cent increase, and the number of women justices sitting in superior trial courts has virtually doubled in that period (from 111 to 219). The overall percentage of women serving as section 96 judges has increased from 15 per cent to 27 per cent. While this percentage is still well below full equality, it should be noted that Table 9.5 includes supernumerary judges, all over 65, and they are overwhelmingly male.

Variations are still visible from province to province, but in only one court do women make up a majority: the Alberta Court of Appeal (eight of 14 justices), and in only one court are women numerically equal: the Nova Scotia Court of Appeal (five out of ten justices). One must note that these are the only two instances in which women have served as chief justices of a province, in each case for an extended period of time, thus suggesting that while the appointment of judges is an executive responsibility, the head of the provincial judiciary can be influential in shaping the composition of the bench.

Table 9.5: Gender Breakdown of Federally Appointed Judges, by Court, 1995 and 2004

Court and Year	Male	Female	Total	Percent Female
Courts of Appeal, 1995	99	28	127	22%
Courts of Appeal, 2004	85	42	127	33%
Superior Courts, 1995	673	111	784	14%
Superior Courts, 2004	612	219	831	26%
Totals, 1995	772	139	911	15%
Totals, 2004	697	261	958	27%

Note: These figures include supernumerary judges, who have elected to sit on a part-time basis once they have become eligible to retire on a full pension. Excluding the supernumeraries (149 in 1995 and 167 in 2004) would increase the percentage of women in both years.

Source: For 1995 figures: Judicial Affairs Unit, Department of Justice Canada, Ottawa. For 2004 figures: Office of the Commissioner for Federal Judicial Affairs, Ottawa, "Number of Judges on the Bench as of November 1, 2004."

This brief survey of court reform issues is not definitive but should illustrate how judges and judges' organizations participate in the change process, propounding their own points of view about legislation and executive action put forward in the name of court improvement.

Conclusion

The purpose of this chapter has been to examine the political role of court systems in the provinces. It has deliberately been more interpretive and less descriptive. A proper understanding of provincial court systems from a political science perspective, argues this chapter, requires first an understanding of their disengagement from partisan political life of the provinces and secondly a reconsideration of the nature and political significance of the normal work of provincial trial and appeal courts.

Notes

1. The author wishes to acknowledge the assistance of Professor Ian Greene of York University and Alison Brierly, his research assistant.
2. *Constitution Act, 1867*, section 92(14).
3. Government is a party in every criminal case but in only a small percentage of civil cases. Note however that a major Ontario report on civil justice still argued that "the Attorney General, and other government ministries and agencies, are major civil litigants in the courts." See *Civil Justice Review: First Report* (Toronto: Ontario Civil Justice Review, March 1995) 116.
4. See generally Peter H. Russell, *The Judiciary in Canada: The Third Branch of Government* (Toronto: McGraw-Hill Ryerson, 1987).
5. Except in Newfoundland and PEI, where it is the Appeal Division of the provincial Supreme Court. For an overview of all Canadian appellate courts, see Ian Greene

et al., *Final Appeal: Decision-Making in Canadian Courts of Appeal* (Toronto: James Lorimer, 1998).

6. For case studies of judicial politics in three states, see G. Alan Tarr and Mary Cornelia Aldis Porter, *State Supreme Courts in State and Nation* (New Haven, CT: Yale University Press, 1988).

7. *Erie Railroad Co. v. Tompkins*, 304 US 64 (1938).

8. *Swift v. Tyson*, 16 Pet. 1 (1842).

9. The American federal court has jurisdiction when a citizen of one state sues a citizen of another state; cf. US Constitution, Art. III, s. 2. This is known as "diversity of citizenship" or simply "diversity" jurisdiction.

10. While the US Supreme Court disposes of an enormous number of appeals every year, most are simply denied a hearing on the merits. In its 2003 term, that court disposed of 7,779 appeals, but only 133 on the merits and only 78 with full opinions (see *Harvard Law Review* 118 [2004]: 504–06). Over the previous ten years, disposals ranged from 6,597 (1995) to 8,342 (2002), while dispositions on the merits declined to a ten-year low in the 2003–04 term—less than 2 per cent of the total (see *Harvard Law Review* 118 [2004]: 510 at 514). In Canada, petitions for leave ranged from 456 to 653 per year in the past ten years, with just under 11.5 per cent and 12.9 per cent granted in the two most recent years for which figures are available. See the annual figures in *Supreme Court Law Review*, most recently at 26 SCLR (2d) (2004): 568ff.

11. For data on the workloads of Canadian appeal courts, see Greene *et al.*, Table 3.1, p. 45.

12. Provincial political links have not been eliminated. In some instances, the party in power federally also governs the province; in other instances, federal appointing authorities may defer to the wishes of provincial governments or provincial ministries of the attorney-general and choose judges from among those with partisan or bureaucratic links to the provincial government.

13. The Chief Justices and Associate Chief Justices receive $245,600. These salaries are in effect from 1 April 2005, until 31 March 2006 and are currently subject to annual adjustment. Section 96 judges' salaries remained unchanged from 1 April 1992, until 31 March 1997, when they stood at $155,800 and $170,600.

14. See PEI Reference, [1997] 3 SCR 3.

15. See the *Remuneration Commissions Decision*, 2005 SCC 44, allowing appeals from three provinces (New Brunswick, Ontario, and Alberta) and modifying a judgement from the Quebec Court of Appeal.

16. Note, however, that in contrast to Canada, India's judiciary today is highly politicized and highly interventionist, more so perhaps than any other in the world. See Carl Baar, "Social Action Litigation in India: The Operation and Limits of the World's Most Active Judiciary," *Policy Studies Journal* 19 (Fall 1990): 140–50; and the writings of Upendra Baxi and Rajeev Dhavan.

17. F.L. Morton, Peter H. Russell, and Troy Riddell, "The *Canadian Charter of Rights and Freedoms*: A Descriptive Analysis of the First Decade, 1982–1992," *National Journal of Constitutional Law* 5 (November 1994): 10.

18. Morton *et al.* 11. The totals in their Table 9.4 were adjusted to exclude the Federal Court of Appeal.

19. These court officials include quasi-judicial personnel such as justices of the peace, hearing officers, clerk/registrars, and assessment officers; see Table 9.4. Their functions vary from province to province, but generally include, among other things, trial of highway traffic and liquor offences, approval of search warrants, and review of a lawyer's bill to determine how much the client must pay.

20. In 1995, a little-noticed bill in the federal Parliament, C-42, changed over a century of Canadian practice, raising the maximum sentence for four frequently charged summary conviction offences from six to 18 months. The legislation was designed to result in fewer jury trials, particularly in sexual assault prosecutions.

21. There are a number of criminal offences that are termed "hybrid offences" because the Crown can choose the mode of trial. If the offence is prosecuted as a summary conviction, the maximum penalty is six or 18 months (depending on the offence), and no jury trial is available. If the offence is prosecuted as an indictable offence, the maximum penalty is as long as the Criminal Code allows, and the accused can elect to be tried by judge and jury.

22. And in "a clutch of somewhat exotic offences" that are rarely prosecuted. See Perry Millar and Carl Baar, *Judicial Administration in Canada* (Kingston and Montreal: McGill-Queen's University Press, 1981) 78.

23. Since criminal law is a federal responsibility, any provincial law whose violation can result in a fine or jail term is called an "offence" rather than a "crime."

24. See Carl Baar, "The Problematic Growth of 'People's Justice,'" *The National* (June/July 1995): 16–22.

25. For a brief historical overview, see Carl Baar, "Trial Court Reorganization in Canada: Alternative Futures for Criminal Courts," *Criminal Law Quarterly* 48 (2003): 110–18.

26. Even with the addition of 167 supernumerary (partially retired) superior court judges, a majority of trial judges are provincial appointees.

27. Based on interviews by the author over a 20-year period covering most jurisdictions in Canada.

28. See Carl Baar, *One Trial Court: Possibilities and Limitations* (Ottawa: Canadian Judicial Council, 1991) 107.

29. Based on interviews by the author with judges, trial coordinators, and lawyers.

30. See Ellen Baar and Dorathy Moore, "Ineffective Enforcement: The Growth of Child Support Arrears," *Windsor Yearbook of Access to Justice* 1 (1981): 94–120.

31. For an example of systematic observation, see Maureen Mileski, "Courtroom Encounters: An Observation Study of a Lower Criminal Court," *Law and Society Review* 5 (May 1971): 473–538.

32. See John Twohig *et al.*, "Empirical Analyses of Civil Cases Commenced and Cases Tried in Toronto 1973–1994," in Ontario Law Reform Commission, *Rethinking Civil Justice*, Vol. 1 (Toronto: Publications Ontario, 1966) 77–181, esp. 10–34; and Baar and Moore. For an earlier American study, see Craig Wanner, "The Public Ordering of Private Relations, Part One: Initiating Civil Cases in Urban Trial Courts," *Law and Society Review* 8 (Spring 1974): 421–40, and "The Public Ordering of Private Relations, Part Two: Winning Civil Cases," *Law and Society Review* 9 (Winter 1975): 293–306.

33. See Jules Deschênes, *Maître chez eux/Masters in their own house* (Montreal: Canadian Judicial Council, 1981); Millar and Baar, ch. 3; Joint Committee on Court Reform, Canadian Bar Association-Ontario, "Report on Ontario Court Administration: Submission to the Attorney General of Ontario" (June 1992); and generally, Martin Friedland, *A Place Apart: Judicial Independence and Accountability in Canada* (Ottawa: Canadian Judicial Council, May 1995), ch. 9. Late in 2005, the Canadian Judicial Council approved a new and wide-ranging report on alternative models of court administration that expands this discussion still further.

34. *Re B.C. Family Relations Act*, [1982] 1 SCR 62; *Re Residential Tenancies Act* [1981] 1 SCR 714; *Labour Relations Bd. (Sask.) v. John East Iron Works*. But cf. *Re Adoption*

Act [1938] SCR 398; see generally Peter W. Hogg, *Constitutional Law of Canada*, 4th ed. (Scarborough, ON: Carswell, 1999), ch. 7. Since superior courts had exclusive jurisdiction over property matters at the time of Confederation, this reasoning would make it impossible for a provincially appointed judge to be given authority to divide marital property.

35. *McEvoy v. Attorney General of New Brunswick and Attorney General of Canada* [1983] 1 SCR 704, 148 DLR(3d) 25.

36. *Reference Re Establishment of a Unified Criminal Court of New Brunswick* (1981), 62 CCC (2d) 165.

37. Cf. Carl Baar, *One Trial Court*, 2.

38. The association's support was not conditioned on its members being appointed to the new court by the federal government, and Canadian Association of Provincial Court Judges has maintained its support of a unified criminal court even when proposals might phase out some of its members' positions.

39. See *A Proposal by the Department of Justice, Province of New Brunswick, for a Unified Criminal Court: Consultation Document* (Fredericton, May 1994). By June 1995 the proposal had been modified further to a one-city pilot project. For a similar history, examine the effort by the federal Department of Justice in the early 1980s to amend section 96 to allow provinces more discretion to expand the jurisdiction of provincial administrative tribunals.

40. See Table 9.4 for the titles of various judges and judicial officers in the provinces.

41. Canadian Bar Association Task Force, *Court Reform in Canada* (Ottawa: Canadian Bar Association, August 1991).

42. Law Society of British Columbia Gender Bias Committee, *Gender Equality in the Justice System* (Vancouver: Law Society of British Columbia, 1992), esp. ch. 4; Law Society of Upper Canada, *Transitions in the Ontario Legal Profession* (Toronto: Law Society of Upper Canada, May 1991); Canadian Bar Association Task Force on Gender Equality in the Legal Profession, *Touchstones for Change: Equality, Diversity and Accountability* (Ottawa: Canadian Bar Association, August 1993) esp. ch. 10.

43. Canadian Judicial Council, *Annual Report 2001–02* (Ottawa) 15–17. Also available on the Council's web site: <http://www.cjc-ccm.gc.ca>.

CHAPTER 10

Intergovernmental Relations from the Local Perspective[1]

RICHARD TINDAL AND SUSAN NOBES TINDAL

Local governments must get beyond the limiting mindset that they are but constitutional orphans who must constantly plead for better treatment from the provincial (and federal) government. They need to recognize their growing importance, convey that reality more forcefully to their local communities, and build their strength upward from that local foundation.

Introduction

The examination of intergovernmental relations usually begins with the traditional hierarchical approach, tracing municipal relations upward—to the province, the federal level, and even the international sphere. While these relationships are essential to an understanding of municipal operations and their scope and constraints, they certainly do not tell the whole story. Viewing municipalities through only the constitutional lens presents a limited and, in some respects, distorted picture.

Intergovernmental relations involving local governments usually focus on relations with the provincial government. This is understandable, since local governments lack any recognition in the Constitution of Canada and are simply one of the powers given to the provinces to exercise as they see fit. Over the years, there have been many complaints about the nature of the local-provincial relationship, as well as some moderately encouraging developments more recently. While these matters will be addressed first, relations between local governments and the federal government are also important—in spite of the Constitution— and these have also been going through problems and changes. Broadening our perspective even further, local governments are also involved in international relationships of growing significance, as a result of globalization and the international agreements and organizations associated with it. However, as discussed in the concluding section, local governments must not let themselves be defined by, and limited to, these formal hierarchical relationships.

The Provincial-Local Relationship

The evolution of provincial-local relations in Canada has involved, for the most part, a pattern of increasing provincial supervision, influence, and control. Departments of municipal affairs were established by the beginning of the twentieth century in a number of provinces "to give leadership and guidance in municipal development and to provide for the continuous study of the problems of municipalities."[2] The Depression of the 1930s and attendant municipal defaulting on financial obligations led in several provinces to the establishment (or strengthening) of municipal departments and municipal boards exercising a variety of supervisory powers in relation to local government.

The period following the Second World War brought a further increase in provincial supervision and control, largely because of growing service demands on local government arising from the extensive urbanization of the time. As the revenues from the real property tax became less and less adequate to finance the growing expenditures of municipal government, the provinces increased their financial assistance. Most of this increased assistance, however, was in the form of conditional grants. By attaching conditions, provinces attempted to ensure that certain services were provided to at least a minimum standard regardless of the varying financial capacities of their individual municipalities. But as municipalities participated in more of these shared cost programs, their local expenditures increasingly reflected provincial priorities.

In some instances, provincial intervention was even more direct, with the provincial government taking over all or partial responsibility for functions traditionally exercised by the local level on the grounds, often quite valid, that the function had outgrown local government—or at least its limited boundaries—and now had much wider implications. Especially during the first half of the twentieth century, this pattern of responsibilities shifting upward to more senior levels occurred with respect to such matters as roads, assessment, the administration of justice, education, public health, and social services. A related development in some of the provinces saw the establishment or enlargement of a number of intermunicipal special purpose bodies that were ostensibly part of the local government structure and yet came under increasing provincial influence and control. Here again there was a valid concern on the part of the province about minimum standards in such areas as health and education, but the end result was a further weakening of municipal government in relation to the provincial level. As one analyst saw it:

> The succession of efforts to enlarge local administrative structures in education, public health, welfare, and toward regional municipalities has simply reduced the number of units confronting the provincial administrator at any one time.... The taxpayer's dollar has been the fulcrum of power for the bureaucrat to use in organizing things, ostensibly for the citizen's benefit but inevitably for the bureaucrat's benefit as well.[3]

By the 1960s, then, local governments had been subjected to three decades of developments that undermined their operating independence and brought them increasingly into the orbit of the senior levels of government.

Box 10.1. Three Decisive Decades

1. As a result of the Depression of the 1930s, municipalities experienced increased provincial surveillance over their financial activities and lost their historical place in the social services field to the provincial and federal governments.
2. During the 1940s, massive centralization occurred because of the war effort. As part of the tax-rental and then tax-sharing agreements brought on by the wartime emergency, municipal governments were squeezed out of such fields as income tax and sales tax, and confined to their historical dependence upon the real property tax as their main source of revenues.
3. By the 1950s, the greatly increased demands of the post-war period resulted in further provincial and federal encroachment on the operations of local government.

Even where municipalities retained some jurisdiction over traditional functions, they found themselves increasingly entangled with the senior levels of government. To a considerable extent this intertwining of activities was inevitable, reflecting the interdependence of the programs and policies of all three levels of government. As O'Brien points out, the various functions have become interrelated in ways that would require intergovernmental activity even if they were all parcelled out in separate pieces to one level only—which they aren't and can't be (and arguably shouldn't be, as discussed later in this chapter):

> The line between health and welfare is not always easy to find. Welfare and social housing are part of one policy. Housing density depends on transit or the automobile. The latter affects the environment and depends on energy policy. Add the need for planning and financing and there is no escaping the fact that governance in our society requires a lot of communication among governments at various levels.[4]

Disentangling or downloading?

Notwithstanding the inevitability of overlap, the past few decades have seen a number of provincial initiatives to reallocate and disentangle responsibilities. While the New Brunswick changes go back to the 1960s and the first Quebec initiative to 1980, the 1990s saw major initiatives in Ontario and Quebec. The added incentive during this past decade was the increased fiscal restraint facing provinces, partly as a result of cuts in federal transfers to them. Reducing the duplication and overlap in provincial and municipal service delivery was seen as a way of cutting costs. It was also felt that the entanglement of service responsibilities obscured lines of responsibility and reduced political accountability, thereby removing or weakening the pressure on governments to strive for more efficient service delivery.[5]

The approaches taken in the various provinces, the underlying objectives, and the results achieved have all varied widely, as will be seen from the descriptions that follow. It will also be apparent that a number of the more recent initiatives seem to be more concerned with downloading than disentangling and that some result in arrangements that are at least as entangled as before.

THE NEW BRUNSWICK EXPERIENCE

The earliest initiative, and one of the most substantial, began with the Byrne Commission of 1963 and led to the 1967 Program for Equal Opportunity. On the basis of the Commission's identification of services appropriate for the provincial and local levels, the New Brunswick government took over responsibility for the administration of justice, welfare, and public health, and financial responsibility for the provision of education. Property assessment and property tax collection also became provincial responsibilities. The primary objective of achieving greater equity in services was achieved, but the extent of the provincial takeover of formerly local responsibilities, and the fact that the province replaced municipalities in providing services in rural New Brunswick, caused many to worry that the improvement had been achieved at the price of municipal government.

THE QUEBEC EXPERIENCE

The Quebec government undertook a significant realignment of responsibilities and financing in 1980. School board revenues from property taxes were substantially reduced, and their revenues from provincial transfers were increased. To offset its increased costs for education, the province also significantly reduced its transfer payments to municipalities, thereby increasing municipal reliance on the property tax.[6] As a result, the share of school board expenditures financed by provincial transfers increased from 60 per cent to 93 per cent between 1969 and 1989. Even more dramatic, with these changes Quebec municipalities were meeting 96 per cent of the cost of local services through their own fees, charges, and local taxes,[7] a degree of fiscal autonomy not approached in any other province.

Two further changes were introduced at the beginning of the 1990s, prompted by the provincial government's concern about its growing expenditure burden and its perception that the revenue-raising potential of the property tax had not yet been fully tapped. In 1990 the province transferred to Quebec school boards the expense of maintaining school facilities while authorizing the boards to levy a property tax (to be collected by municipalities) covering up to 10 per cent of their expenditures.[8] The result was to reduce the share of provincial funding of school board operations to about 88 per cent.[9] The following year the Quebec government introduced changes that shifted to municipalities greater responsibility and financing obligations for public transit, roads, and policing. Both of these changes were seen as an attempt by the province to shift back to the property tax the burden for financing some of the expenditures that had been assumed by the 1980 reforms—a move strongly opposed by the Quebec Union of Municipalities.[10]

THE NOVA SCOTIA EXPERIENCE

The disentanglement process in Nova Scotia arose out of a provincial initiative that was originally focused on reducing the number of municipalities in the province. The *Task Force on Local Government*, which reported in April 1992, called for a major restructuring of municipal government in the five most urbanized areas of the province. It also cited the position of the Union of Nova Scotia Municipalities that:

> Property services should be supported by property taxes and delivered by municipal government. People services are the responsibility of the provincial government and should be financed by general provincial revenues. Both orders of government should continue efforts to reallocate the delivery and financing of services recognizing this basic principle.[11]

The report also reflected the position of the municipal association in calling for any reallocation of services to be revenue-neutral, meaning that neither the provincial nor the local level would be better or worse off financially as a result of the changes.

More specifically, the task force proposed that rural municipalities would have to start providing their own policing and roads (as urban municipalities had been doing) and that the province would take over the municipal share of the administration and financing of general welfare assistance.[12] In one of several parallels with the Ontario experience (described below), these disentanglement proposals caused greater concern among rural municipalities than urban. The urban municipalities have larger social assistance obligations (which the province would assume) and they were already paying their own way with regard to policing and roads.

The Liberal government elected in 1993 adopted the principle of service exchange proposed in the 1992 task force report. The province would provide a five-year period of transition payments during which time municipalities would "be relieved of responsibility for social welfare services and contributions to the cost of correctional services." To offset this shift and to maintain the fiscal neutrality of the swap, rural municipalities would take over the costs of policing and residential streets (services already being paid for by urban municipalities). But as these changes were being implemented, the province became increasingly preoccupied with deficit reduction. As a result, it capped the amount available for equalization payments to financially weak municipalities, causing particular hardship to a number of coastal towns formerly dependent on the ground fishery.[13]

More generally, an analysis by Vojnovic finds that while the service swap in Nova Scotia was intended, in part, to assist financially distressed municipalities, it resulted in an increased financial burden for some of the fiscally weakest municipalities. In his view:

> The overwhelming emphasis on maintaining a revenue-neutral exchange between the province and the municipalities, and ensuring a government structure where one level of government provides a single public service or governance function, redirected the attention of the province and the municipalities away from the basic distributional aspects of the reform.[14]

Poel points out that the services swap was not as straightforward and clearcut as originally intended.[15] The municipal and provincial levels continued to exercise a degree of shared responsibility with respect to bridges, some social services, and correctional services. In addition, the development of provincial solid waste resource regions across the province involved a combination of provincial policies and performance targets and municipal responsibility for operations—providing another example of the difficulty of distinguishing between general and local services.

In April 1998, the province and the Union of Nova Scotia Municipalities signed a memorandum of understanding under which the municipal contribution to social service costs was phased out between 1998-99 and 2002-03. A comprehensive review of roles and responsibilities was initiated, the first phase of which involved the identification of issues affecting the provincial-local relationship. One of the concerns expressed by municipalities was that they should have more say with respect to services for which they have a financial responsibility. For example, rural municipalities complained that service standards, the level of police service, and RCMP budgets are set by the federal and provincial governments, but funded by municipalities. Similarly, it was argued that if municipalities are required to contribute to the cost of roads, they should have some say about roads standards, presently determined by the province.[16]

ONTARIO'S DISENTANGLEMENT EXPERIENCE

Social services figured prominently in the reallocation of responsibilities in New Brunswick and Nova Scotia, and it was also social services that launched disentanglement in Ontario.[17] The *Report of the Provincial-Municipal Social Services Review* recommended in 1990 that Ontario follow the lead of most other provinces and take complete responsibility for the cost of social assistance. The province agreed with this shift in principle but was not prepared to absorb the approximately $800 million in extra costs that this would entail. A follow-up study examined the entire division of powers between the provincial and local level and recommended that (1) functions should be assigned clearly and unambiguously to one level to the extent possible, and (2) financial relationships should be simplified so that the province would continue to provide conditional grants to municipalities only in areas where there is a legitimate provincial interest.

The 1991 report[18] resulting from this study prompted the newly elected NDP government to invite the Association of Municipalities of Ontario to participate in a joint examination of possible service reallocation with the objectives of creating better, simpler government; improving the efficiency and effectiveness of services to the public; clarifying which level of government is responsible for what services; and improving financial accountability and fiscal management.[19] A key guiding principle was that the exercise had to be fiscally neutral—echoing the guiding principle of revenue neutrality that was to guide Nova Scotia's deliberations. A draft agreement was reached in January 1993, under which the province would assume responsibility for general welfare assistance in return for the municipal level assuming greater responsibility in connection with roads, paying for property assessment services, and receiving reduced provincial grants (to achieve the fiscal neutrality objective). Small and rural municipalities were not comfortable with the proposed roads for welfare swap, given that roads constituted their primary function and expenditure. In any event, the tentative agreement fell apart when the province, in response to its growing deficit and debt problems, introduced a social contract and expenditure control program that included major cuts in transfer payments to the local level.

Disentanglement returned, albeit with some important changes in approach and emphasis, following the election of the Progressive Conservative (PC) government in June 1995. A *Who Does What* panel, chaired by former Toronto mayor David Crombie, was appointed on 30 May 1996 to begin a complete overhaul of who does what in the delivery and funding of many government services. The stated goal of the panel was "to ensure the very best service delivery by reducing waste, duplication and the overall cost of government at the provincial and local government levels."[20] The panel's recommendations culminated in a summary report in December 1996, which largely followed the services to property versus services to people distinction cited earlier in the Nova Scotia exercise. It called for increased municipal responsibility with respect to roads, transit, ferries, airports, water and sewer systems, and policing, and increased provincial responsibility for social services (notably social assistance and child care) and education.

The Ontario government's response, in January 1997, was a proposed realignment of responsibilities that ignored the recommendations of *Who Does What* in several key respects. In particular, the province proposed to download to municipalities increased responsibility for a number of social programs, including public housing, public health, homes for special care, long term care, and general welfare assistance. In return, the province would assume all of the education costs previously borne by residential property tax payers. The nature and speed of the government's response suggested that it had been pursuing its own internal agenda, while using the *Who Does What* panel almost as a front or diversion. That agenda, it seemed, was to gain full control of education decision-making in Ontario.[21] Subsequent events (discussed below) support this interpretation.

In the face of widespread criticism and evidence that the proposed service swap was not fiscally neutral, the province accepted a number of modifications that arose from joint discussions with the Association of Municipalities of Ontario. Central to the new agreement was the fact that residential property tax payers would continue to pay half of the education costs they had been financing (about $2.5 billion), but with the province now responsible for setting the education tax rate. With the money saved from not taking over all of the education financing from residential property tax payers, the province found itself able to retain a number of responsibilities relating to social programs (such as long term care and homes for special care) that were to be shifted to the local level. However, it still transferred additional responsibilities and/or costs relating to a number of social programs (including public housing, public health, land ambulances, and general welfare assistance), along with public transit, policing (in rural areas), and water and sewer systems (although after the Walkerton water tragedy[22] provincial financial support for these latter services was increased).

While these changes represented a number of concessions that the province had earlier indicated it was not prepared to contemplate, statements from the premier and the minister of municipal affairs suggested that they were quite satisfied with these changes, which still met their objectives. Interestingly, the minister, in a statement to the legislature on 1 May 1997, when he introduced these changes, explained that the first priority of the whole exercise had been "to reduce taxes by ending the spiralling costs of education in this province."

Effective 1 January 1999, the province agreed to share half of the municipal costs for public health and land ambulances, in part to ensure provincial standards in the delivery of these services. Since provincial grant support was adjusted to reflect this change, there was no net financial gain for municipalities. But the initiative may indicate some provincial sensitivity to the complaint that municipalities should not have to pay for services whose standards are set by the province. This is essentially the same complaint about violation of "pay for say" noted above with respect to Nova Scotia municipalities. Before leaving this section, we should note that the province has dropped the use of the "who does what" terminology—notwithstanding the contribution of the Crombie panel of the same name—and now insists upon referring to this whole exercise as a local services realignment or LSR.

Disentanglement potential and pitfalls

Those who propose the disentanglement of provincial and local responsibilities cite a number of advantages. These include simplified arrangements, less overlap and regulation from above, and increased local autonomy. It has also been suggested that the local level will be left with clearly assigned services and access to sufficient revenues to carry these out, which would enhance public accountability and lead to more citizen involvement in government. This is an impressive list of advantages, but the provinces have been less than precise or consistent in the approach used to achieve them, especially on the basis on which powers would be divided between the provincial and local level.

THE RATIONALE FOR SERVICE ALLOCATION

When municipal institutions were established, their limited role consisted mainly of providing services to property financed, quite logically, by a tax on property. The property tax came under increasing criticism as the twentieth century advanced not only because it was no longer adequate to generate all of the revenues required but also because it was seen as no longer appropriate to finance the services to people that were becoming part of municipal operations. Those looking for a rationale for a new distribution of provincial and municipal responsibilities often seized upon this services to property versus services to people distinction for their purposes. They argued that services to people should be handled by the provincial level. They pointed out that services such as education provided benefits well beyond the boundaries of any one municipality and should be financed appropriately. They also noted that social services involve an income redistributive function tied to broad provincial (even national) standards and objectives, should not be open to local variation, and, as a result, were not appropriate for local administration.

These distinctions have been used, at least in part, in several studies related to disentanglement, including New Brunswick's Byrne Commission (1963), the Michener Commission in Manitoba (1964), the Graham Commission in Nova Scotia (1974), and Ontario's *Who Does What* panel (1996). For example, the Graham Commission contended that municipal responsibilities should be divided into two groups: "... local services, which are of primarily local benefit or which might best be provided by municipal government, and general services, which are of more general benefit to the province or which the province might best provide."[23] A similar distinction underlies the services swap in Nova Scotia.

Cameron is critical of this approach, which suggests that municipal responsibilities don't extend beyond the provision of services, however defined, and therefore ignores the representative and political role of municipal government. Second, he finds the allocation of responsibilities arbitrary and likely to result in a municipal system that is responsible only "for that which is unimportant or inexpensive." [24] Sancton is critical of disentanglement's underlying rationale that municipalities should concentrate on those responsibilities that are inherently local, an approach which he suggests inevitably means a narrower range of municipal functions. He describes the faulty assumption made by advocates of disentanglement as follows:

> To base municipal government's existence on a mission to concern itself with inherently local issues is to insure its quick death. Does anyone really believe that there are *any* issues which are still inherently local? [25]

Sancton points out that there are provincial rules and regulations in place for almost any municipal function that one can cite[26] and notes as examples garbage disposal and sewers—once thought of as local matters. Indeed, he has demonstrated elsewhere that even metropolitan and regional governments have not been able to handle functions such as public transit, water supply, and garbage disposal, which have increasingly come under provincial jurisdiction.

If, we argue, municipalities are to act as a political mechanism through which a local community can express its collective objectives, then it is essential that they be involved in as many activities as possible that are of interest and concern to the local community. This means expanding, not reducing, their sphere of influence. It means becoming (or staying) involved in functional areas in which the municipalities cannot expect to be autonomous. As Sancton wryly observes: "If municipal politicians are not interested in *all* government policies that affect their community, they can hardly complain if many in the community are not interested in municipal government."[27]

Even viewed only from the narrow perspective of services and their delivery, it can be argued that disentanglement efforts are misguided and are as likely to reduce efficiency as to increase it.[28] When a responsibility is shared by more than one level of government, it should not automatically be assumed that this arrangement represents wasteful duplication. It may, but it might also represent a logical and beneficial division of responsibility that is much more likely to generate economies of scale and operating efficiency than would arise from consolidating total responsibility for the function in question at one level only.

CONTRASTING SERVICE REALLOCATIONS

It is instructive to examine the markedly different approaches taken in New Brunswick and Ontario. Under the Program for Equal Opportunity, the New Brunswick government took over responsibility for the administration of justice, welfare, and public health, as well as financial responsibility for the provision of education. These were services to people, not to property, and they were viewed as general or universal services, not local ones, so the shift in responsibilities to the province was consistent with the criteria usually cited as a rationale for service reallocation. As noted above, however, these changes—coupled with other reforms that saw the province abolish rural counties and take over direct provision of some services to rural areas—led to criticisms that the Program for Equal Opportunity had diminished the role of municipal government in New Brunswick.

In contrast, the Ontario experience seems to represent the other extreme in service reallocation. Instead of the province retaining, or even assuming greater responsibility for, various social programs—as has been the pattern in other jurisdictions and was recommended in a series of previous Ontario studies including those of the *Who Does What* panel—the province downloaded to local governments more responsibility and costs with respect to a number of social programs (social assistance, social housing, and public health in particular). These actions were completely at odds with the criteria and rationale generally accepted as appropriate for service reallocation.

Nor can the nature and scope of the downloading in Ontario be explained or justified by the principle of subsidiarity that has gained prominence in recent years. That principle proclaims that responsibilities should rest at the lowest level *capable of providing them*. While the notion of subsidiarity can be traced back to the writings of Aristotle,[29] it has come to the forefront in connection with the debate about how responsibilities would be assigned within the European Union. The principle of subsidiarity has been cited in numerous studies, including the Golden Report on the Greater Toronto Area (GTA).[30] It is our contention, however, that the Ontario government has downloaded responsibilities that are beyond the capability of the municipal system. Moreover, to overcome this problem, the government also embarked on a very aggressive campaign to force amalgamations, with the intention of creating large enough units to be able to handle this download. In our view, these actions seriously distort what was intended by the concept of subsidiarity. As Courchene has pointed out, "there is a flip side to the principle of subsidiarity," which means that where externalities and spillovers exist, policy areas should be transferred upward to the jurisdictional level that can internalize these spillovers.[31]

Because the Ontario government downloaded inappropriate responsibilities, ones that are of wider than local significance, it has been obliged to introduce or expand the standards that must be maintained with respect to many of these services. This is evident from the provincial requirements that now exist with respect to the provision of such services as public health, social housing, and water and sewage services. Ironically, the result is that provincial and local entanglement has been increased, not decreased.

It should be noted that not all Ontario municipalities object to the increased responsibilities that have been downloaded to them. Differences in rural and urban views are evident, just as they were at the time of the previous disentanglement exercise at the beginning of the 1990s. Small and rural municipalities, which are heavily represented in the Association of Municipalities of Ontario, generally support the services to property versus services to people distinction and have been opposed to the downloading of social programs. However, the regional governments and a number of the large cities recognize the importance of social programs as a way of "connecting to diverse communities and promoting quality of life" and they also recognize that the quality of life in urban areas is "the key instrument of economic development in a global economy."[32] Accordingly, they are interested in the possibility of greater responsibility for social programs, *if* commensurate financial resources are also provided—a condition that they would argue has not been met.

THE FISCAL NEUTRALITY FIXATION

The preoccupation with ensuring that any service reallocation was fiscally neutral seriously compromised the whole exercise. A true disentanglement exercise would determine what services were best handled by what level of government and would then shift them accordingly, *regardless* of the financial impact. There would be "winners" and "losers" between levels of government, but since there is only one set of taxpayers in Canada (as governments are fond of repeating), then the overall impact would balance out. If provincial costs went up as a result of a service swap, then municipal costs would go down by a corresponding amount, and the total provincial and municipal taxes paid should remain about the same.

Whatever superficial logic this theoretical argument has, it totally ignores political reality. It matters greatly to governments which level is perceived as spending more or less—especially in the current climate. As a result, the disentanglement exercises of the 1990s have had as an overriding objective the achievement of fiscal neutrality—a pledge that neither level of government will be better or worse off financially as a result of any service swap. The requirement of this objective is understandable to a point, but it effectively destroys the disentanglement exercise. One cannot shift functions to the level where they most logically belong; one must manipulate the final service swap in such a way as to balance the books.

The extent to which this financial requirement can distort disentanglement is painfully apparent in the Ontario experience. The province was determined to take over responsibility for education in order to cut back on what it regarded as excessive spending by school boards. The same logic that made education an appropriate provincial responsibility also extended to other social programs such as social assistance and social housing. But taking over all of these services would have meant an increase in provincial costs and a decrease in municipal costs.

Instead, the combined forces of the fiscal neutrality pledge and the provincial government's own financial and tax-cutting priorities reduced the disentanglement exercise to "basic arithmetic." Since the province wanted education, it needed to download enough other services to offset that cost. This largely explains why social housing, which wasn't part of the *Who Does What* panel's deliberations, got tossed into the mix.[33]

Ultimately, it may be that efforts at disentanglement are not only flawed in ways described above, but pointless or inappropriate. The needs of citizens may best be addressed by more than one level of government. For example, "acknowledging the legitimate local interest in human-service delivery, while retaining responsibility for income redistribution at the provincial level, would contribute to recognition of the diversity of circumstances and needs across communities and affirm a vital role for local governments in the social domain."[34] In addition, as argued above, having different aspects of a responsibility handled by more than one level of government may be the best way to achieve economies of scale rather than being wasteful duplication.

The changing provincial-local financial relationship

Disentanglement, of a sort, is also occurring with respect to intergovernmental financial relations. It has been driven and shaped by the deficit and debt reduction measures that preoccupied the senior levels throughout the 1990s. In what has been characterized as an era of fend-for-yourself federalism, the federal government reduced its transfers to the provinces, while softening the blow by making them less conditional. The provinces responded in kind, with respect to their financial assistance to municipalities. The result, in Brodie's colourful language, has been a kind of "demolition derby—a scurry of fiscal off-loading onto newly designated 'shock absorbers.' "[35]

If this trend continues, municipal governments will find themselves (whether willingly or not) with greater financial independence. They are being required to find a growing portion of the funds they need from their own revenue sources, much as they had to do in the early years of their existence. Transfer payments represented only 14 per cent of municipal revenues in 2001, while the property tax had increased to 52 per cent of the total as it expanded in an attempt to make up the shortfall. Given their growing dependence on the property tax, municipalities are very concerned about provincial encroachment into this tax field—to fund provincial responsibilities with respect to education and social programs.

The changing legal relationship

Unlike provincial and federal governments, local governments were not given any guaranteed right to exist under Canada's Constitution, but were simply identified as one of the responsibilities that provinces could exercise. In response, provincial governments passed legislation that provided for the kinds of municipalities that could be incorporated and their governing structures, functions, and financial resources. These statutes were traditionally very prescriptive in nature, detailing what municipalities could do—and often how they could do it—in what was often described as a "laundry list" approach. The courts usually took the position that if a provincial legislature had specified some items, then anything not specified was not intended. As a result, if municipalities could not find express legal authority for an action, they could not undertake it—or would face the risk of a court challenge (usually successful) if they proceeded in the absence of such express authority.

This very narrow scope for municipal action reflected "Dillon's Rule," as set down by Iowa Supreme Court Judge John F. Dillon in the 1860s, who equated municipalities with business corporations, both of them limited to the powers expressly granted through their incorporation.

Box 10.2. Dillon's Rule

A municipal corporation possesses and can exercise the following powers and no others: first, those granted in express words; second, those necessarily implied or necessarily incident to the power expressly granted; third, those absolutely essential to the declared objects and purposes of the corporation – not simply convenient but indispensable; and fourth, any fair doubt as to the existence of a power is resolved by the courts against the corporation.

Source: John F. Dillon, from an 1868 decision in *Merriam vs. Moody's Executors*, as quoted in Harold Wolman and Michael Goldsmith, *Urban Politics and Policy: A Comparative Approach* (Oxford: Blackwell, 1992) 72.

A contrasting approach is that of "home rule," which is common in the western US and which essentially provides that municipalities can do anything that is not explicitly prohibited by state (or provincial) legislation, instead of only what the legislature specifically authorizes.[36] While the contrasting approaches associated with these two rules provide a useful spectrum along which to measure efforts to reform municipal legislation in Canada, the contrast between them should not be exaggerated. The reality, as depicted in Figure 10.1, is that between these two extremes lies a "mushy middle" in which the scope for municipal action is greater than Dillon's Rule would suggest and less than home rule would imply.[37] We will return to this point toward the end of this chapter.

Municipal governments and their associations, notably the Federation of Canadian Municipalities (FCM), have long lobbied for some constitutional recognition that might provide them with at least a degree of protection from arbitrary provincial actions. However, these requests have fallen on deaf ears. Municipal governments were ignored in both the Meech Lake and Charlottetown

Figure 10.1. The Scope for Municipal Action

Home Rule   Mushy Middle   Dillon's Rule

constitutional accords and they were also left out of the 1982 *Constitution Act* that repatriated the Constitution. Given the widespread feeling that the country has wasted too many years in divisive and ultimately futile attempts to bring about constitutional change, few now seem interested in pushing constitutional recognition for municipalities. In any event, L'Heureux[38] and Cameron both argue that it would be more realistic and appropriate to protect municipal interests by way of provincial constitutions. In Cameron's words:

> Municipalities have no place in a federal constitution, at least not beyond the present references which consign them to provincial jurisdiction. Any further reference could only serve to remove decisions about the provincial-municipal division of power to extra-provincial constitutional processes. Any direct participation by municipalities in the federal-provincial constitutional process could only occur at the price of their becoming special interest groups. [39]

Since the beginning of the 1990s, municipal associations in a number of provinces have pushed for some form of provincial charter that would recognize the existence of a separate level of municipal government. The Union of British Columbia Municipalities (UBCM) called for a charter or bill of rights in 1991, followed by similar demands from the Union of Nova Scotia Municipalities (UNSM) in 1993 and the Association of Municipalities of Ontario (AMO) in 1994. The lobbying by the associations seemed to have an impact, since most provinces over the past decade have enacted new legislation that reflects—to varying degrees—the changes being sought.

A more positive legislative framework?

The first breakthrough came with Alberta's *Local Government Act* of 1994, and the most recent initiative is also found in Western Canada, with BC's community charter legislation that came into force on 1 January 2004. In the intervening decade, positive legislative changes were also enacted in most other provinces, notably Saskatchewan, Manitoba, Ontario, Nova Scotia, and Newfoundland. These changes usually incorporated some combination of the following key features:

1. the provision of natural person powers;
2. authorization to act within broad spheres of jurisdiction;

3. a commitment to advance consultation;
4. a requirement for municipal approval before certain actions (notably amalgamation) could proceed; and
5. a commitment to provide resources commensurate with the municipal responsibilities being allocated.

While the last three points are self-explanatory, the significance of the first two features is explained in Box 10.3.

Box 10.3 Key Concepts in New Municipal Legislation

Natural person powers	Vesting municipalities with natural person powers gives them a general authority to do those things that a person can do—such as hiring and dismissing staff, contracting for services, purchasing land or buildings, or selling or otherwise disposing of assets. These are things that municipalities have always done, but they had to find express authority in statutes before taking any such actions. While granting natural person powers gives municipalities greater flexibility, no additional powers are conveyed with this designation. Rather, the natural person powers are used as a tool for implementing the responsibilities otherwise assigned to municipalities.
Spheres of jurisdiction	Spheres of jurisdiction (or spheres of authority) authorize municipal action on the basis of broad and general categories. They provide an alternative to allocating powers to municipalities by itemizing specifically what they can do—as in the previously cited laundry list approach. The problem with such a list is that anything not mentioned, even inadvertently, is likely to be ruled beyond municipal jurisdiction on the grounds that if the provincial government had intended such a matter to be assigned, it would have been specified. Assigning broad spheres of jurisdiction is supposed to give municipalities greater flexibility and discretion. However, the scope of these spheres is constrained by limits that may be provided elsewhere in provincial legislation, and there are also some subjects that are not covered by the spheres and are addressed separately and in a more prescriptive fashion.

Alberta's *Local Government Act* was the first to give municipalities natural person powers and it also gave them general bylaw-making authority similar to spheres of jurisdiction. But many municipal powers still require provincial approvals and nothing in the act requires the province to consult with municipalities. One analysis points out that within six months of the act coming into force several hundred amendments were enacted.[40] The flow of amendments has continued in the years since, leading to some concern that their cumulative impact will be to undermine the freedom and flexibility originally intended for this legislation.[41]

Saskatchewan passed a new *Cities Act* in July 2002, modeled upon similar legislation in other provinces and giving municipalities natural person powers and two broad areas of authority to pass bylaws for the "peace, order and good government of the city" and for "the safety, health and welfare of the people and the protection of people and property."[42] The act also gives cities the authority to levy additional property taxes to pay for a specific service or purpose. There are also some new public accountability provisions that balance the increased autonomy and flexibility for cities with requirements to involve and inform the public of decisions.

Manitoba passed a *Municipal Government Act* in October 1996, but it limits municipal discretion to a narrower range of permissive powers than the Alberta legislation, and it does not give them natural person powers. However, one recent analysis points out that the new act has eliminated many of the detailed instructions that used to severely constrain municipal operations. It also concludes that the new provisions encouraging contracting for services are intended to create a more competitive atmosphere in which market pressures will bring about greater collaboration and integration in service delivery (without the need for the municipal restructuring for which there has been strong public opposition in the province) and expresses some reservations about the implications of relying on this type of market model.[43]

This new *Municipal Act* does not apply to the City of Winnipeg, which has had its own charter since its formation in 1972. That charter was amended in 1998 but mainly in connection with some internal restructuring relating to the council and senior administration. However, a new *City of Winnipeg Charter Act* was enacted in 2002 (effective January 2003), partly to incorporate or keep up with the changes that had appeared in the 1996 general municipal legislation. The new act combines large numbers of previously detailed and scattered powers into 14 broad spheres of authority and also gives Winnipeg natural person powers.[44] However, the analysis previously cited finds that natural person powers are limited to a brief reference at the beginning of the Act, which otherwise deals with the more traditional corporate powers, and it suggests that over time the concept of natural person powers may contain "more politics and public relations than legal substance."[45]

Ontario's new *Municipal Act* was passed in December 2001 and took effect on 1 January 2003. It authorizes municipalities to exercise natural person powers and governmental powers within ten general spheres of jurisdiction. In what has been a fairly common pattern, the legislation combines increased municipal powers with greater accountability and reporting requirements. The new act endorses the principle of ongoing consultation with municipalities in relation to matters of mutual interest, and a memorandum of understanding has been signed by the province and the Association of Municipalities of Ontario (in December 2001) setting out these consultation arrangements.

Nova Scotia amended its *Municipal Government Act* in December 1998. The new legislation does not give municipalities natural person powers or broad spheres of jurisdiction, continuing instead the traditional approach of giving municipalities a list of specific powers. But it does provide somewhat more autonomy by reducing the number of provincial approvals relating to financing and bylaws. In addition, the act provides that the provincial government must give municipalities 12 months notice of any initiatives that may affect municipal finance.[46]

The Government of Newfoundland and Labrador enacted a new *Municipalities Act* in May 1999 that has been described as "one of the most modern of Municipal Acts in Canada, offering more opportunity for flexibility and autonomy within a framework of municipal self-government."[47] It provides for the province to consult with the mayor of a city before it enacts or amends legislation or makes regulations or policies that affect the city. According to Lidstone, "although the legislation eliminates may of the paternalistic, centralized controls under the current legislation, the greater autonomy, flexibility and powers are combined with increased requirements for accountability, transparency and public participation."[48]

Turning finally to BC, there has been a series of positive legislative changes. These began with *Municipal Act* revisions in 1998, in an amending bill which incorporated by reference BC's protocol of recognition signed by the province and the UBCM two years earlier. The act was renamed the *Local Government Act* in June 2000, with amendments that facilitated public private partnerships and provided more flexible revenue-raising authority for municipalities.

Most attention, however, has been focused on the new community charter legislation that recently appeared in BC. A *Community Charter Council Act* was passed in August 2001, providing for the appointment of a Community Charter Council (of provincial and local representatives) to oversee the preparation of community charter legislation governing municipalities.[49] That legislation was passed in April 2003 and came into effect January 2004. Its key features include:[50]

- recognition of municipalities as an "order of government" within their jurisdiction;
- requirement of provincial consultation prior to changes in the act or to provincial grants to municipalities;
- provision for consultation agreements between the provincial government and the UBCM on matters of mutual interest;
- provision of a dispute resolution process, including binding arbitration where all parties to a dispute choose this method;
- provision that municipal amalgamations cannot proceed unless approved by a vote in the affected jurisdictions;
- provision of natural person powers;

- provision of power to provide any service that the council considers necessary or desirable;
- provision of autonomous or concurrent authority (with the province) to regulate, prohibit, or impose requirements in relation to 13 broad spheres of authority in which municipalities typically operate; and
- new accountability requirements including an annual municipal report and a public meeting to present this report.

The new community charter has been characterized as the most empowering local government statute in Canada. In a recent report card on municipal legislation, the BC legislation ranks second only to the new Winnipeg Charter (phase two) and well ahead of the other legislation enacted across Canada over the past decade.[51] However, Smith and Stewart have a number of reservations about the community charter legislation.[52] They note, for example, that it continues both the province's authority to impose limits on municipal property tax increases in particular circumstances and the commitment to "work toward the harmonization of provincial and municipal enactments, policies, and programs,"[53] and they wonder how this latter provision will work in those instances where a municipality wishes to pursue a unique approach.

Smith and Stewart are particularly critical of the legislation's failure to address municipal accountability, which, in their view, requires such responses as electoral financing reform and the removal of such barriers to electoral participation as at-large elections in large municipalities, including Vancouver. They do not find the call for annual reports and public meetings an adequate means of strengthening accountability. Indeed, these mechanisms reflect a corporate model of accountability that does not seem particularly applicable to the municipal government sphere.[54] Carrel is very concerned about measures in the charter legislation that would structure local government on the corporate model and dismisses the new annual report requirement as a very inadequate tool for accountability. In his view, "to set up the annual report as the principal tool of accountability and citizen involvement is an open invitation to accepting justification, white wash and obfuscation as a substitute for accountability."[55]

Significance of the legislative reforms

The key features of the reforms, not found in all provinces, are the provisions for natural person powers, more general municipal authority within broad spheres of jurisdiction, and a commitment to advance consultation with municipalities. These changes are most welcome, although in several instances (notably BC, Saskatchewan, and Ontario) they are accompanied by new requirements presented as enhancing the accountability of municipal governments. In the case of Ontario, at least, there are concerns that these requirements may increase the accountability of municipalities to the province rather than necessarily to their local electorates.

It is also clear that the new legislation is being used in some provinces to further ideological leanings of the provincial governing parties. As noted above, Piel and Leo describe the promotion of partnerships and the market model in Manitoba, and this theme is also reflected in the legislation in BC and Ontario. A business or corporate emphasis is also evident in provisions for accountability in the legislation in both those provinces, with efficiency and effectiveness measures and annual reports and meetings advocated more than provisions to strengthen local democracy.

While the new legislative initiatives are generally positive and a welcome step in the right direction, they do not protect municipalities from adverse actions being taken by their provincial governments. For example, the same year (1996) that BC introduced its Recognition Protocol, the province also unilaterally eliminated municipal grant guarantees, reduced grants, transferred major highway responsibilities, and closed local courthouses—all without any real consultation with municipalities.[56] As noted earlier, Alberta and Ontario introduced their new municipal acts during times when they were also curtailing, or had curtailed, their provincial grant support.

Yet municipalities need expanded, not reduced, financial resources if they are to have the capacity to take action on behalf of their residents—whatever their legislation may allow. In that regard, consider LeSage's observation that Alberta municipalities have approached "with kid gloves" the natural person powers and spheres of jurisdiction allocated to them, with the result that, by anecdotal accounts, the general exercise of municipal affairs in Alberta is not much different than it was under the previous act. The prevailing view is that smaller municipalities do not have the resources to take advantage of the legislation and that larger municipalities are being cautioned by their legal advisors about the legal risks to which they might expose themselves.[57] Andrew also notes that cuts in provincial grants compromised the potential of the new municipal legislation and states that " it is not at all clear that the legislation has made any difference to municipal behaviour in Alberta."[58]

The new *Municipal Act* in Ontario endorsed the principle of ongoing consultation with municipalities in matters of mutual interest, and a memorandum of understanding was signed by the province and the Association of Municipalities of Ontario (in December 2001) setting out these consultation arrangements. Yet the campaign platform released by the ruling PCs in mid-2003 contained a proposal that any future tax increases by Ontario municipalities would have to be approved in a local referendum.[59] There was no consultation with the Association of Municipalities of Ontario about this proposal, which would have constituted an unprecedented intrusion into municipal decision-making. This example reminds us that whatever new legislation may be introduced, the provincial-local relationship is still very much one of superior-subordinate, and municipalities still remain vulnerable to capricious actions taken by their provincial governments. This does not mean that an improved legislative framework is not worth pursuing, just that, if achieved, it will not alter the underlying imbalance in the distribution of power and authority.

It must also be remembered that the potential of these various initiatives to improve municipal legislation is somewhat dependent on the interpretations given by the courts. One of the early examples saw the Alberta Court of Appeal quash a Calgary bylaw that limited the number of taxi licences. The court found that while the old legislation had expressly conferred a power to limit the number of taxi licences, this power was not found in Alberta's landmark 1994 legislation, and Calgary's bylaw, therefore, lacked specific authorization. This decision was clearly inconsistent with the notion that municipalities should be able to take action within broad spheres, but on appeal the Supreme Court of Canada held that the spheres of jurisdiction and governmental powers given to Alberta municipalities provided the authority to limit taxi licences without further, more specific authorization.[60]

Pursuing individual city charters

Paralleling the demand for more permissive provincial legislation for local governments in general has been a growing demand that Canada's largest cities receive individual charters that would set out responsibilities appropriate to their size, resources, and importance. Having specific charters is not a new idea, of course, as indicated below.

Box 10.4. Charter Cities in Canada

Saint John	Incorporated by royal charter in 1785. City has natural person powers. The charter is exclusive of generally applicable municipal legislation unless there is a conflict with provincial statutes.
Vancouver	Charter dates from 1886 and is the exclusive authority except for a few provisions from generally applicable municipal legislation.
Montreal	Original charter dates from 1890s. New "city contract" entered into between province and new city of Montreal in June 2002 in support of the city charter.
Winnipeg	Charter dates from the amalgamation that created the city in 1972. Major revisions effective 2003 to provide greater autonomy, are in line with changes in new Municipal Act of 1996.

Conspicuous by their absence from this list of charter cities are Calgary, Edmonton, and Toronto (especially). Toronto, among others, argues that it is quite distinct from most other municipalities in Canada and needs special governing arrangements that can be best provided by having its own charter.[61] A model framework for a city charter was adopted by the Big City Mayors Caucus of the FCM on 30 May 2002.[62] A year later, the first official summit of the Creative Cities Coalition was held just prior to the FCM's annual conference, and it is continuing the campaign to get provinces to adopt the standardized city charter.[63]

Treating different classes of municipality differently may seem arbitrary and could be seen as an implied criticism of those municipalities excluded from charter status. On the other hand, it can also be argued that such an approach could be beneficial for the small and rural municipal governments that make up the vast majority of Canada's municipalities. They often feel that policies are enacted to address concerns of the larger centres, without sufficient regard to how appropriate such policies may be for them and their much different needs and conditions. If the needs of the largest cities can be handled through separate charters for them, then it may be possible to develop general municipal legislation that is more suitable for the smaller and more rural municipalities to which it will apply. For this reason, some feel that "a charter for cities achieves a balance between a group of municipalities that needs more enabling power (cities) and those that are content with the status quo (smaller communities)."[64] If we can countenance asymmetrical federalism at the federal and provincial levels, it would not seem unreasonable for us to consider comparable arrangements between provinces and their widely varied municipal governments.

The Federal-Local Relationship

While local governments do not have any direct link with the federal government according to the Constitution, nothing could be further from the truth. Federal programs and policies have long had a major impact on local government operations. There is no better example than the federal contribution, through financial assistance for housing, to low density sprawl and all of its associated municipal servicing problems. Decisions by the Department of Transport concerning rail services have had a critical impact on the economic vitality of communities, as have various industrial incentives and other programs offered by the federal government. Immigration policy is another federal responsibility that affects municipalities, dramatically so in the case of Canada's largest urban centres. But as Frisken notes, "federal immigration policy makes little attempt to ease the strains imposed on cities or city neighbourhoods by large influxes of new immigrants...."[65] Consider the case of Toronto, which received more than 30 per cent of immigrants and refugee claimants during the 1990s, which pays out $30 million annually for refugee claimants alone (for social assistance, housing, and health services), and which has refugee claimants occupying 10 per cent of the space in its emergency hostels on any given night. If the federal government wants an open door policy for refugee claimants, why should the cost of looking after them fall mainly on the residents of Toronto and other urban centres such as Montreal and Vancouver?[66]

These examples should suffice to demonstrate that a kind of federal-local relationship existed long before it was given any formal recognition during the 1970s. Indeed, one study found that by the late 1960s, "more than 117 distinct programs administered by 27 departments in Ottawa influenced metropolitan development plans."[67] In almost every case, however, the federal programs were introduced without regard to their impact on the local level. Municipalities had no opportunity for advance consultation and little hope of obtaining adjustments after the fact. In many cases, the varied federal initiatives were not even coordinated with each other.

The once (and future?) MSUA

By the end of the 1960s, however, two major factors combined to produce strong pressure for a closer and more formalized federal-local relationship. First, there was a growing municipal interest in the possibility of increased federal funds being made available to deal with major service demands, especially in urban areas. Second, there was a growing federal appreciation that, because of the large number of Canadians living in urban areas, the ability of municipal governments to meet their needs was of more than local, or even provincial, interest. A federal task force on Housing and Urban Development was appointed in mid-1968, and its report recommended a greatly expanded federal role. After some delays, during which the head of the task force (Minister of Transport Paul Hellyer) resigned from the cabinet in protest, the government acted by establishing a Ministry of State for Urban Affairs (MSUA). As recommended by the task force, the new ministry was not to be a traditional operating department but was to concentrate on developing policy and coordinating the projects of other departments. Also emphasized was the need to increase consultation and coordination among all three levels of government in dealing with the challenges of urbanization.

The new ministry began with ambitious objectives considering "the absence of any authority with which to control the legislative or spending proposals of other agencies."[68] One analysis observed that "it was created as a new David without a sling; the new ministry of state could fulfill its mission only with mutual trust and goodwill."[69] These commodities turned out to be in short supply, and none of the approaches it attempted had much success. A closer look at these approaches seems timely, given that the federal government has, in effect, appointed ministers with responsibility for urban Canada in the Martin government (Minister of State for Infrastructure and Communities) and the Harper government (Minister of Transport, Infrastructure and Communities).

Initially, in an attempt to gain credibility, "MSUA offered to represent the interests of municipalities and provincial governments in discussions with other federal agencies."[70] But this role brought it into direct confrontation with other federal agencies and little was accomplished. By 1972 MSUA had adopted a new strategy—it would promote coordination by arranging meetings among representatives of all three levels of government and the various federal ministries whose programs affected urban areas. This approach had already been advocated by the Canadian Federation of Mayors and Municipalities (now the FCM), and partly through its efforts the first ever national tri-level conference was held in Toronto in November 1972. The fact that the municipal level was represented in its own right was something of a breakthrough, but the extent to which the conference might be considered a success depends upon the expectations of those participating in it. A Joint Municipal Committee on Intergovernmental Affairs presented several well-researched papers, but little progress was made because of the uncompromising attitude of the provinces, especially Ontario.[71]

A second national tri-level conference was held in Edmonton in October 1973. It was decided to undertake a study of public finance with particular reference to the adequacy of municipal revenue sources, a development seen optimistically as "the first important piece of firm evidence of the success of the tri-level process."[72] But delays in launching the Tri-Level Task Force on Public Finance led to the third tri-level conference being postponed—forever, as it turned out.

With the national tri-level conferences stalled by provincial intransigence, MSUA adopted another strategy. It attempted to move from persuasion to power, which it sought through the Canada Mortgage and Housing Corporation (CMHC), which controlled major expenditures. Here again, however, successes were limited, and by 1975 there was "a state of open warfare between MSUA and CMHC."[73] Within 18 months the MSUA personnel were cut by 40 per cent.

MSUA adopted yet another approach at this point. It made no effort to initiate meetings, but let it be known that it would organize them if requested. "MSUA thus evolved from an agency that had flirted with the imposition of policy to an urban consultant active only on invitation." This final phase of MSUA activity was received more favourably, largely because of its much more modest mission, not because of any real support. By the spring of 1979 it had fallen victim to the politics of austerity. "Total savings would be less than $4 million (perhaps closer to $500 000), but the public would be impressed by a government prepared to abolish a whole ministry in the name of fiscal responsibility."[74] Lacking the clout that comes with specific program responsibilities, regarded with suspicion by federal bodies protecting their turf, and disliked by provincial governments also protecting their (municipal) turf, MSUA never really had a chance.

The death of MSUA did not in any way signify the end of tri-level relations in Canada. In fact, the federal influence may have been greater during the 1980s, as evidenced by major development projects in almost all of Canada's major metropolitan areas. Some of these projects (such as Harbourfront in Toronto and the Rideau Centre in Ottawa) were the result of election promises, while others reflected the regional influence of a member of the cabinet—such as the Winnipeg

Core Area Initiative promoted by Lloyd Axworthy.[75] Whatever their impetus, these projects demonstrated the continuing significance of the federal presence in urban Canada.

However, with the demise of the MSUA, federal policies continued to appear without much regard to their urban impact, leading one analysis to conclude that "[f]ederal initiatives in the cities have been not only incoherent and irrational, often they have been inconsistent and unequal."[76] Yet there has never been a greater need for coherent urban policies. As one recent analysis points out, Canada faces the likelihood of "a permanent set of place-based winners and losers." According to this analysis, the settlement pattern of those who immigrate to Canada is helping to create one set of places that exhibits social diversity and rapid growth, while other places are growing slowly, if at all, are socially homogenous, and have an aging population. As a result, Canada's complex policy challenge is how to manage growth and also plan for decline, while adapting to heterogeneity and an aging population.[77]

The 1980s and 1990s saw repeated calls for a tri-level approach to infrastructure financing. The election of the Liberals in 1993 led to a *Canada Infrastructure Works* program under which the federal level provided $2 billion over a two-year period, matched by similar amounts from the provinces and municipalities. Over the past few years, however, a series of developments brought the financial challenges facing Canadian cities much more to the forefront and increased the pressure on the federal level to assume a more active role.

In the midst of this flurry of reports and demands for action, the federal government established, in May 2001, a Prime Minister's Caucus Task Force on Urban Issues (chaired by Judy Sgro) to examine the challenges and opportunities facing Canada's urban regions. It issued an interim report in April 2002 and a final report in November 2002.[78] The findings and recommendations provide a striking parallel with the Hellyer Task Force of 30 years earlier. The Sgro reports emphasized the growing urbanization of Canada and the importance to the national economy of vital urban regions. As major pillars of a new urban strategy for Canada, the reports called for long term funding for affordable housing, transit/transportation, and sustainable infrastructure. A key recommendation is the appointment of a cabinet minister with responsibility for developing Canada's urban strategy and implementing an action plan to ensure that the voices of urban regions are heard.

Early indications were not especially encouraging, notably the fact that both the finance minister (John Manley) and the prime minister rejected the idea of transferring federal tax resources (such as a portion of gas taxes) to aid the cities.[79] However, Paul Martin's Liberals campaigned in 2004 on a vague promise to share gasoline taxes with the municipal level. In September 2004, Canada's "big city mergers" (now ten in number) proposed a formula to Ottawa for allocation of gas tax revenues, but Ottawa demurred, saying that would result in a $10 billion commitment by 2007. Instead, Budget 2005 announced a five-year, $5 billion gas tax sharing plan. As for the recommendations calling for new federal money for housing, transportation, and infrastructure, they will have to compete with other pressing financial demands on the federal government—notably health expenditures in the aftermath of the Romanow Report on the future of Canada's health care system. It is also unclear at this point how a new minister with responsibility for developing an urban strategy would avoid the infighting and fate that befell a very similar initiative in the form of the Minister of State for Urban Affairs.

While most attention has focused on the amount of federal financial assistance that may flow to cities as a result of the Sgro reports, a recent analysis by

---

Box 10.5. Cities to the Forefront

In March 2001 the Federation of Canadian Municipalities (FCM) released its second report on the quality of life in urban Canada, which found that poverty and income inequality had continued to expand in large urban communities since the first study in 1999.[1]

A May 2001 research paper from the FCM found that European and American governments were investing powers and financial resources in their cities at a much greater rate than is happening in Canada.[2]

May 2001 saw a historic meeting of the mayors of Vancouver, Calgary, Winnipeg, Toronto, and Montreal, a group that has become known as the C5. Discussions emphasized that far more revenues flow out of Canada's largest cities (in the form of taxes collected by the senior levels of government) than flow back into them. A prime example cited was the fact that "$4 billion in motor fuel taxes is going out of cities across Canada to the federal government, and less than 3.5% of that money is reinvested back in the cities that generated it in the first place."[3]

The Toronto Board of Trade picked up on this theme in its June 2002 report *Strong City: Strong Nation*, in which it contended that in 2000 there was a net outflow of $9 billion from Toronto to the provincial and federal governments – with the bulk of it ($7.6 billion) going to the federal level.

An April 2002 report from the TD Bank concluded that Canada's cities were at a disadvantage because of lack of access to revenue streams other than the property tax.[4]

---

1. Federation of Canadian Municipalities, *Quality of Life in Canadian Communities, 2001 Report* (Ottawa: FCM, 27 March 2001). This report is available at the CFM's web site at <http//www.fcm.ca>, accessed 12 December 2002.

2. Federation of Canadian Municipalities, *Early Warning: Will Canadian Cities Compete?* (Ottawa: FCM, May 2001); <http//www.fcm.ca>, accessed 12 December 2002.

3. Remarks by Winnipeg mayor Glen Murray at the first C5 meeting on 25-26 May 2001, Winnipeg, as reported in *Ideas That Matter* 2,1 (Owen Sound, ON: The Ginger Press, 2001).

4. TD Economics Special Report, *A Choice Between Investing in Canada's Cities or Disinvesting in Canada's Future* (22 April 2002).

Wolfe provides a much broader (and more insightful) perspective. She finds that the task force was too preoccupied with building cities to compete in the global economy to the neglect of other important issues and considerations. There was no discussion, for example, of the extent to which the cities are being shaped by corporate agendas, the way big box stores "drain traditional business districts, and turn the city inside out." She also finds that the task force ignored the nature of civic life and how it is changing, and had little to say about poverty problems and the widening income gap between rich and poor. Nor did the task force reports address urban distributional problems, as reflected in the increasing concentration of population in a few major urban areas and slow population and economic growth in much of the rest of the country. Echoing the already noted views of Bourne and Simmons, Wolfe argues that "[b]urgeoning metropolitan areas, medium-sized centres with a viable economy, and declining towns require very different policy responses." [80]

Whatever form it takes, federal involvement with the municipal level, and especially with Canada's major cities, has been extensive for some time and will continue to be. Bradford argues that the pivotal role of cities in determining the quality of national life demands close collaboration among all levels of government. In his view:

> The issue is not simply one of helping municipalities cope with their responsibilities but, equally, one of ensuring that macro-level policy interventions of upper level governments are sufficiently informed by the locality's *contextual intelligence* to work effectively.[81]

While the federal government has to be sensitive to provincial jurisdiction over municipalities, this constitutional reality should not be used as an excuse for federal inaction. "Whether the federal government is to be involved or excluded from new governance patterns will depend on political choices, not constitutional formalities."[82] In support of this position, Jane Jacobs and Alan Broadbent gave the federal government a list of more than a dozen actions that it could take without "violating the federal-provincial balance"—suggestions that ranged from tax deductions of transit passes provided by corporations to employees, to full rebating of the GST for rental projects, to a per capita settlement payment that follows refugees and immigrants where they move in Canada, based on an index of costs in various cities.[83]

International Relations

In addition to relations with the provincial and federal governments, there is a growing appreciation that municipalities are also affected, directly and indirectly, by the globalization of the economy and the international organizations and agreements related to that process. What is less clear is whether the overall impact of these developments on municipalities will be positive or negative.

The negative or pessimistic view is that globalization has increased the power of private capital and that municipal governments have no choice but to implement the prevailing neoliberal free market agenda.[84] Municipalities now have reduced bargaining power in dealing with developers, and Leo comments that "mobile companies often call the tune in their dealings with local governments, and, in the process, they can cancel development plans, zoning rules, building code regulations, and even the taxes that are levied to support the city's services."[85]

There is also growing evidence of the extent to which municipalities (as well as provincial and federal governments) are constrained by such factors as the North American Free Trade Agreement (NAFTA) and the World Trade Organization (WTO). For example, NAFTA created extensive rights for foreign firms to sue governments under a very broadly defined category of expropriation. In 2001 a BC Supreme Court Justice reviewed the decision of a NAFTA Tribunal that had ruled that American toxic waste firm Metalclad had to be compensated for a number of actions taken by the federal, state, and local governments in Mexico. He stated that:

> In addition to the more conventional notion of expropriation involving a taking of property, the Tribunal held that expropriation under the NAFTA includes covert or incidental interference with the use of property that has the effect of depriving the owner, in whole or in significant part, of the use or reasonably-to-be-expected economic benefit of the property. This definition is sufficiently broad to include a legitimate rezoning of property by a municipality or other zoning authority.[86]

According to Lidstone, "Metalclad is a wake-up call for municipalities throughout North America." He also points out that the General Agreement on Trade in Services (GATS) expressly applies to services provided by or on behalf of municipalities and requires the federal government to ensure that local authorities fulfill the obligations and commitments made by the federal government. From the way services are defined under the GATS, Lidstone concludes that public-private partnerships, contracting out, design-build arrangements, and privatization would be subject to the GATS provisions.[87] In this regard, the Greater Vancouver Regional District dropped plans to construct a water filtration plant under a $400 million public-private partnership plan because it could not receive satisfactory assurances about the possible risk of losing control of this plant in the future from trade challenges under the NAFTA and GATS provisions.[88] Another analysis also sounded a caution about the GATS, pointing out that it adversely affects the ability of municipal governments to supply and regulate basic services such as water and sewage services, waste management, transportation services, public transit, road building, land use planning, and library services.[89]

Globalization has had quite an impact on the local level in an indirect way through the pressure that it has placed on senior levels of government to scale back and downsize their operations in support of the more competitive atmosphere demanded by the international marketplace. One of the primary ways that they have made this adjustment is by shifting responsibilities and costs downward, where they have ultimately landed in the laps of local governments.

Local governments are also affected by the fact that globalization and international trade rules and regulations now make it almost impossible for senior governments to pursue the kinds of regional policies that used to be provided in support of have-not areas; such policies would almost certainly be challenged at the WTO as unfair trade practices.[90] The result is that local economies face increasingly stiff competition—from virtually anywhere in the world—and must respond without at least some of the provincial and federal government supports that used to exist.

Globalization has had a positive impact in making cities and city-regions increasingly important as key players in the world economy. But does it follow that the municipalities within these urban areas have also become more important? Not necessarily, one would think, given the municipal limitations that have been frequently cited. However, Courchene seems to have no doubts about the positive future for cities. As he sees it, "the issue is not so much *whether* they will be able to extricate themselves from their current 'constitution-less' status as wards of their respective provinces, but rather *how* they will increase their autonomy and forge more formal linkages with both levels of government."[91] For this to happen, cities need to stop thinking of themselves only in constitutional terms, as creatures of the province.

Concluding Comments

We have noted that Smith and Stewart have identified a mushy middle that may characterize more accurately where municipalities operate—or at least where they have the potential to operate—than the supposedly precise locations defined by Dillon's Rule and home rule. In support of their contention, they provide three examples of the capacity of local governments to act "*despite constitutional and statutory inferiority.*" The first case describes how the City of Vancouver led the way in intergovernmental dealings in pursuit of a new approach to drug treatment that emphasizes harm reduction. Vancouver's decision to hold a referendum on Canada's bid to hold the 2010 Winter Olympics in that city is the basis for the second case study. It reveals how the city used bargaining leverage that it enjoyed temporarily (while there was uncertainty about how much the newly elected mayor and council might oppose the Olympic bid) to gain some concessions from both the province and the federal government. The last example describes global activities by Vancouver such as twinning (with Odessa in the Soviet Union in 1944) and declarations of peace, anti-war, and making the city a nuclear weapons free zone—all done without any formal authority and sometimes in conflict with senior government authorities.[92] To some extent, Vancouver seems to embrace the oft-quoted Nike slogan "Just Do It."

Another way of looking at municipal relationships is provided by Leo and Mulligan, who suggest that instead of focusing on which functions are, or should be, assigned to particular levels of government (as was the approach of the disentanglement exercises described above), we need to recognize that more than one level of government is quite appropriately involved with different aspects of the same function. They see a role for the federal government in setting broad policy objectives, while lower levels of government work out how these objectives can best be met in different areas of the country. To illustrate this point, they describe national policies and programs relating to immigration, welfare, and affordable housing and show how these issues have their own particular features in Winnipeg and benefit from distinctive local applications. They call for a new approach to governance in the twenty-first century based on "an acceptance of the declining power of the national state, the reduction in its role from interventionist programme-provider to supporter of programmes driven by the local and provincial level, and thereby the elevation of local governments and community groups to a more central role in the formulation of both economic and social policy."[93]

If more local governments are to take the initiative by moving toward the mushy middle or by fine-tuning the local application of senior government programs, they need to stop seeing their roles and potential through the perspective of only the constitutional lens. That cities need to become much more assertive is a theme which has been advanced by several others as well. Jane Jacobs delivered this message at the first meeting of the C5, and her words merit repeating at some length.

> I think you have an ingrained mindset of dependency and that this is going to be the hardest thing for you to overcome.... You must somehow gather your self-esteem not to be apologetic about yourselves. Certainly the country needs to be educated about how important the cities are. But if the cities themselves don't believe it or are apologetic about it, or are afraid to bring it up, even aggressively, the education of the country and the understanding of what really is necessary and what ails us, is never going to come about.[94]

Andrew advances a similar argument after expressing a number of concerns about the approach that federal and provincial governments have been taking to the needs of the cities. She finds that the federal government seems to lack an understanding of the role and importance of large cities in the global economy and that provincial governments have been either ineffective or even anti-urban. She calls for a broader perspective that focuses on urban governance rather than urban government, therefore providing the opportunity for municipalities to link with the many other organizations and interests that can strengthen the response to the challenges in our urban areas—an approach quite similar to that advocated by Leo and Mulligan above.

According to Andrew, the future of local governments depends more on their actions than on some constitutional breakthrough. In her words: "City governments will not become more effective actors through provincial or federal recognition or power-sharing arrangements; rather, they can become more effective through their creation of more inclusive urban governance regimes." Her concluding observation, reminiscent of the above-noted advice of Jane Jacobs, is: "We should not ignore our cities, but this will happen only when they demonstrate to us and to the other levels of government that we cannot ignore them."[95]

Notes

1. This chapter was originally published in C. Richard Tindal and Susan Nobes Tindal, *Local Government in Canada*, 6th ed. (Toronto: Nelson Thomson Learning, © 2004) and is reprinted with the permission of Nelson, a division of Nelson Thomson Learning: <www.thomsonrights.com>. Fax (800) 730-2215.

2. K.G. Crawford, *Canadian Municipal Government* (Toronto: University of Toronto Press, 1954) 345. Chapter 17 of this text provides a good description of the historical evolution of provincial-local relations.

3. Vernon Lang, *The Social State Emerges in Ontario* (Toronto: Ontario Economic Council, 1974) 61.

4. Allan O'Brien, "A Look at the Provincial-Municipal Relationship," in Donald C. MacDonald, ed., *Government and Politics of Ontario* (Toronto: Van Nostrand Reinhold, 1980) 167.

5. Igor Vojnovic, "The Fiscal Distribution of the Provincial-Municipal Service Exchange in Nova Scotia," *Canadian Public Administration* (Winter 1999): 512–13.

6. F. Vaillancourt, "Financing Local Governments in Quebec: New Arrangements for the 1990s," *Canadian Tax Journal* 40,5 (1992): 1123–39.

7. Canadian Urban Institute, *Disentangling Local Government Responsibilities—International Comparisons* (Toronto: Canadian Urban Institute, January 1993) 27.

8. This view is frankly expressed by Claude Ryan, Minister of Municipal Affairs, in a 14 December 1990 statement, *The Sharing of Responsibilities Between The Government and Municipalities: Some Needed Adjustments*.

9. Vaillancourt 1137.

10. Katherine A. Graham, Susan D. Phillips, and Allan M. Maslove, *Urban Governance in Canada* (Toronto: Harcourt, Brace, 1998) 72.

11. Report to the Government of Nova Scotia, *Task Force on Local Government* (April 1992) 11.

12. Allan O'Brien, *Municipal Consolidation in Canada and Its Alternatives* (Toronto: ICURR Press, May 1993) 18.

13. Kell Antoft and Jack Novack, *Grassroots Democracy: Local Government in the Maritimes* (Halifax: Dalhousie University, 1998) 11, 12.

14. Vojnovic 516.

15. This discussion is based on Dale H. Poel, "Municipal Reform in Nova Scotia," in Joseph Garcea and Edward LeSage, eds., *Municipal Reform in Canada: Dynamics, Dimensions, Determinants* (Toronto: Oxford University Press, 2005).

16. These examples are from Richard Ramsay, *Report to the Union of Nova Scotia Municipalities and the Department of Housing and Municipal Affairs* (23 October 1998): 8.

17. The summary which follows is based on David Siegel, "Disentangling Provincial-Municipal Relations in Ontario," *Management* (Toronto: Institute of Public Administration, Fall 1992).

18. *Report of the Advisory Committee to the Minister of Municipal Affairs on the Provincial-Municipal Relationship* (Hopcroft Report), Toronto (January 1991).

19. Ian Connerty, "Disentanglement: Changing the Provincial-Municipal Balance," *Municipal Monitor*, Association of Municipal Managers, Clerks and Treasurers of Ontario (October 1992): 182.

20. According to Ministry of Municipal Affairs and Housing, *News Release*, 14 August 1996.

21. These observations, with which we concur, are made by, among others, Katherine A. Graham and Susan D. Phillips, "Who Does What in Ontario: The Process of Provincial-Municipal Disentanglement," *Canadian Public Administration* (Summer 1998): 186–87.

22. Seven people died in the small community of Walkerton in 2000, and many more became seriously ill, as a result of a contaminated water supply caused by a mixture of improper local operating procedures and inadequate provincial supervision and inspection. The report of the Walkerton water inquiry is available at <http://www.attorneygeneral.jus.gov.on.ca/english/about/pubs/walkerton/>, accessed 27 July 2003.

23. *Royal Commission on Education, Public Services, and Provincial-Municipal Relations, Report*, Vol. 2 (Halifax: Queen's Printer, 1974) 3: 22.

24. David Cameron, "Provincial Responsibilities for Municipal Government," *Canadian Public Administration* (Summer 1980): 222–35.

25. Andrew Sancton, "Provincial-Municipal Disentanglement in Ontario: A Dissent," *Municipal World* (July 1992): 23.

26. Andrew Sancton, "Canada as a Highly Urbanized Nation," *Canadian Public Administration* (Fall 1992): 281–316.

27. Sancton, "Provincial-Municipal Disentanglement" 24.

28. Tindal and Tindal, Ch. 5.

29. Alan Norton, *The Principle of Subsidiarity and its Implications for Local Government* (Birmingham: Institute of Local Government Studies, 1992) 6–11.

30. Report of the GTA Task Force, *Greater Toronto* (January 1996): 163.

31. Thomas J. Courchene, *A State of Minds* (Montreal: Institute for Research on Public Policy, 2001) 26.

32. Graham and Phillips 194 and 205.

33. Graham and Phillips 187.

34. Graham and Phillips 205.

35. Janine Brodie, "Imagining Democratic Urban Citizenship," in Engin Isin, ed., *Democracy, Citizenship and the Global City* (London: Routledge, 2000) 120.

36. Robert L. Bish and Eric Clemens, *Local Government in British Columbia*, 3rd ed. (Richmond: University of British Columbia Municipalities, 1999) 18.

37. Patrick J. Smith and Kennedy Stewart, "Beavers and Cats Revisited, Creatures and Tenants vs. Municipal Charter(s) and Home Rule, Has the Intergovernmental Game Shifted?" paper prepared for the Municipal-Provincial-Federal Relations Conference, Institute of Intergovernmental Relations, Queen's University, 9–10 May 2003; available at <http://www.iigr.ca>, accessed 25 May 2003.

38. Jacques L'Heureux, "Municipalities and the Division of Power," in Richard Simeon, Research Coordinator, *Intergovernmental Relations*, Vol. 63, Royal Commission on the Economic Union and Development Prospects for Canada (Toronto: University of Toronto Press, 1985).

39. Cameron 222–35.

40. Kristen Gagnon and Donald Lidstone, *A Comparison of New and Proposed Municipal Acts of the Provinces*, paper presented at the annual conference of the Federation of Canadian Municipalities, 1998: 22.

41. Edward LeSage, *Municipal Reform in Alberta: A Review of Statutory, Financial and Structural Changes Over the Past Decade*, paper presented at the Canadian Political Science Association annual meeting, Quebec City, 28 May 2001: 8. Much of this paper has been incorporated into the Alberta chapter of Garcea and LeSage.

42. Saskatchewan Ministry of Government Relations and Aboriginal Affairs, *The Cities Act—An Introduction*, available from <http://www.municipal.gov.sk.ca>, accessed 15 March 2003.

43. Mark Piel and Christopher Leo, "Governing Manitoba's Communities: Legislative Reform in the 1990s and Beyond," Garcea and LeSage.

44. *City of Winnipeg Charter Act* (Bill 39), SM 2002, c. 39.

45. Piel and Leo.

46. Department of Housing and Municipal Affairs, "Municipal Legislation Gets Makeover," 27 October 1998.

47. Federation of Canadian Municipalities, *Early Warning: Will Canadian Cities Compete?* (May 2001): 7.

48. Donald Lidstone, "A Comparison of New and Proposed Municipal Acts of the Provinces: Revenues, Financial Powers and Resources," prepared for the 2001 annual conference of the Federation of Canadian Municipalities, 27 May 2001.

49. British Columbia Minister of State for Community Charter, *The Community Charter: A Discussion Paper*, October 2001.

50. Ministry of Community, Aboriginal and Women's Services, *Highlights Community Charter*, available at <http://www.mcaws.gov.bc.ca>, accessed 30 May 2003.

51. Donald Lidstone, "Municipal Acts of the Provinces and Territories: A Report Card," prepared for the "Future Role of Municipal Government" forum held during the annual conference of the Federation of Canadian Municipalities, 1 June 2003.

52. The discussion that follows is based on Smith and Stewart 18–19, and Kennedy Stewart and Patrick Smith, "Community Charter," *Vancouver Sun*, 15 March 2003.

53. Bill 14, *The Community Charter*, "Principles of the Provincial-Municipal Relationship," Part 1, Sec 2.

54. Peter Kenward, *The British Columbia Community Charter—What Is Going On, and What Does It Mean For You?*, McCarthy Tétrault, October 2001, available at <http:??www.mccarthytetrault.ca>, accessed 15 November 2001.

55. André Carrel, "The Community Charter: Strengthening or Weakening the Citizen Voice at City Hall?" Langora College Continuing Studies, 10 May 2002.

56. Lidstone, "A Comparison of New and Proposed Municipal Acts, 2001" 6.

57. Edd LeSage, presentation at workshop, "New Community Charter in British Columbia," 14 June 2002, Local Government Institute, University of Victoria.

58. Caroline Andrew, "Globalization and Local Action," in Timothy L. Thomas, ed., *The Politics of the City* (Toronto: ITP Nelson, 1997) 143.

59. See Policy Paper "A Fair Deal for Municipalities," which is part of *The Road Ahead*, the PC campaign platform for 2003, available at <http://www.ontariopc.com>, accessed 10 June 2003.

60. See *United Taxi Drivers' Fellowship of Southern Alberta v. Calgary (City)*, [2004] SCJ No. 19 (2004), 46 M.P.L.R. (3d) 1 (S.C.C.), a decision available at <http://www.canlii.org/ca/cas/scc/2004/2004scc19.html>.

61. For a series of articles relating to this issue, see Mary W. Rowe, *Toronto: Considering Self-Government* (Owen Sound, ON: The Ginger Press, Inc., 2000).

62. Available from the FCM web site at <http://www.fcm.ca>, accessed 2 May 2003.

63. Details on that first conference, hosted in June 2003 by the City of Winnipeg, are available at <http://www.winnipeg.ca/interhom/mayors_office/creativecities/home.html>, accessed 12 June 2003.

64. Denis Wong, *Cities at the Crossroads: Addressing Intergovernmental Structures for Western Canada's Cities* (Calgary: Canada West Foundation, August 2002) 9, available at <http://www.cwf.ca>, accessed 14 April 2003.

65. Frances Frisken, "Introduction," in Frances Frisken, ed., *The Changing Canadian Metropolis*, Vol. 1 (Toronto: Canadian Urban Institute, 1994) 19.

66. Statistics from Michael Valpy, "Constitution Makes it Easy to Push Toronto Around," *Toronto Star*, 13 October 1999.

67. Elliot J. Feldman and Jerome Milch, "Coordination or Control? The Life and Death of the Ministry of Urban Affairs," in Lionel D. Feldman, ed., *Politics and Government of Urban Canada* (Toronto: Methuen, 1981) 250.

68. Cameron 245.

69. Feldman and Milch 254.

70. Feldman and Milch 255.

71. For an assessment of this first conference, see Queen's University, Institute of Local Government and Intergovernmental Relations, "The Tri-Level Conference—The Morning After," *Urban Focus* 1,2 (January–February 1973).

72. *Urban Focus*, 2,1 (November–December 1973).

73. Feldman and Milch 257–58.

74. Feldman and Milch 260.

75. Caroline Andrew, "Federal Urban Activity: Intergovernmental Relations in an Age of Restraint," in Frisken 430.

76. Feldman and Milch 263.

77. Larry Bourne and Jim Simmons, "New Fault Lines? Recent Trends in the Canadian Urban System and their Implications for Planning and Public Policy," *Canadian Journal of Urban Research* 12,1 (Summer 2003): 40 and 32.

78. Both reports are available at <http://www.liberal.parl.gc.ca/urb>, accessed 15 February 2003.

79. Graham Fraser, "PM Won't Aid Cities with Tax Revenue," *Toronto Star*, 12 June 2002.

80. Jeanne M. Wolfe, "A National Urban Policy for Canada? Prospects and Challenges," *Canadian Journal of Urban Research* 12,1 (Summer 2003): 11, 12.

81. Neil Bradford, *Why Cities Matter: Policy Research Perspectives for Canada* (Ottawa: Canadian Policy Research Networks, Discussion Paper No. F\23, June 2002), available at <http://www.cprn.org>, accessed 20 May 2003; emphasis in the original.

82. Jane Jenson and Rianne Mahon, *Bringing Cities to the Table: Child Care and Intergovernmental Relations* (Ottawa: Canadian Policy Research Networks, Discussion Paper No. F\26, 2002): 20, available at <http://www.cprn.org>, accessed 20 May 2003.

83. Alan Broadbent, *The Place of Cities in Canada: Inside the Constitutional Box and Out* (Ottawa: Caledon Institute of Social Policy, June 2002) 4.

84. For example, see Gary Teeple, *Globalization and the Decline of Social Reform* (Toronto: Garamond Press, 1995).

85. Christopher Leo, "Planning Aspirations and Political Realities," in Edmund P. Fowler and David Siegel, eds., *Urban Policy Issues* (Toronto: Oxford University Press, 2002) 223.

86. Supreme Court of British Columbia, "Reasons for Judgment of the Honourable Mr. Justice Tysoe, *United States of Mexico v. Metalclad Corporation*, May 2, 2001," as quoted in Ellen Gould, *International Trade and Investment Agreements: A Primer for Local Governments* (Richmond: Union of British Columbia Municipalities, June 2001).

87. Lidstone, "A Comparison of New and Proposed Municipal Acts, 2001" 11.

88. See *GRVD Decides Against Design-Build-Operate Arrangements for Construction Drinking Water Filtration Facilities*, GVRD Press Release, 29 June 2001; and Murray Dobbin, "Municipalities Take on Ottawa's Trade Agenda," *National Post*, 17 September 2001.

89. Michelle Swenarchuk, *From Global to Local: GATS Impacts on Canadian Municipalities* (Ottawa: Canadian Centre for Policy Alternatives, May 2002) v.

90. Christopher Leo, with Susan Mulligan, "Rethinking Urban Governance in the 21st Century," paper presented at the Canadian Political Science Association conference, Halifax, May 2003: 9.

91. Courchene 277 [emphasis in the original].

92. Smith and Stewart 19–25 [emphasis in the original].

93. Leo and Mulligan 11–17.

94. Quoted in Max Allen, ed., *Ideas That Matter: The Worlds of Jane Jacobs* (Owen Sound, ON: Ginger Press, 1997) 20.

95. Caroline Andrew, "The Shame of (Ignoring) the Cities," *Journal of Canadian Studies* (Winter 2001): 109, 110.

CHAPTER 11

A Nutshell Reminder of the Evolution of Canada's Territories[1]

GREGORY TARDI

The Significance of the Territories

It is not a coincidence that the expression "The True North, Strong and Free" is included in Canada's national anthem. Its use is as reflective, domestically, of the significance of the territories which comprise the sizeable northern portion of the country as it is, internationally, of the northerly nature of the entire country on the world stage. While the part of Canada that is organized in the territorial, rather than the provincial, form of government carries relatively little weight in national politics, law, and society, it has been, and continues to be, of enormous geopolitical significance to the country. The North, comprising the territories, is also an indelible part of the Canadian socio-political psyche.

Canada's three northern territories, Nunavut, the Northwest Territories, and the Yukon, are the modern successor jurisdictions to the lands of the Hudson's Bay Company, known as Rupert's Land, and to those of the original North West Company. The Hudson's Bay Company, which was granted its royal charter on 2 May 1670[2] by King Charles II, was an instrument of British mercantilism and colonization. This form of corporate colonial development was consistent with both British and French royal practice in the seventeenth century. For example, the East India Company had been established for similar purposes as early as 1600. Likewise, on 29 April 1627, the Compagnie des Cent Associés was constituted[3] for development and local governance in New France by Cardinal Richelieu on behalf of King Louis XIII. Of all the mercantilist companies, the Hudson's Bay Company holds the record for longevity and over its lifetime achieved the most in terms of imperial designs of both its royal incorporators and its founding and funding merchants. This company merged with the North West Company in 1821 and carried on its exploration, development, and exploitation of Canada's northern and western lands until Confederation in 1867.

The key to understanding the contribution of the geographic landmass of Rupert's Land and the North-West Territory[4] to making Canada a viable and successful country lies in the political legal instruments of Confederation. In the *Québec Resolutions* adopted in October 1864 by the Fathers of Confederation, the second resolution included reference to the admission into the eventual union of the British-controlled areas of North America that would be contiguous to, or otherwise outside of, Canada:

> 2. In the Federation of British North American Provinces, the system of Government best adapted under existing circumstances to protect the diversified interest of the several Provinces, and secure efficiency, harmony and permanency in the working of the Union, would be a general Government, charged with matters of common interest to the whole country; and Local Governments for each of the Canadas, and for the Provinces of Nova Scotia, New Brunswick and Prince Edward Island, charged with the control of local matters in their respective sections. Provision being made for the admission into the Union, on equitable terms, of Newfoundland, the North-West Territory, British Columbia and Vancouver.[5]

Resolution 69 went on to underline the importance of this link:

> 69. The communications with the North-Western Territory, and the improvements required for the development of the Trade of the Great West with the Seaboard, are regarded by this Conference as subjects of the highest importance to the Federated Provinces, and shall be prosecuted at the earliest possible period that the Finances will permit.[6]

These preliminary intentions were reflected and confirmed in s. 146 of the *Constitution Act, 1867*, which provides, *inter alia*, that:

> 146. It shall be lawful for the Queen, by and with the Advice of Her Majesty's Most Honourable Privy Council, ... and on Address from the Houses of Parliament of Canada to admit Rupert's Land and the North-western Territory, or either of them, into the Union, on such Terms and Conditions in each Case as are in the Addresses expressed and as the Queen thinks fit to approve, subject to the Provisions of this Act; and the Provisions of any Order in Council in that Behalf shall have effect as if they had been enacted by the Parliament of the United Kingdom of Great Britain and Ireland.[7]

This constitutional text clearly demonstrates that the 1867 confederators were as expansionist in respect of Canada as the British monarchy and its mercantilist allies had been two centuries earlier. The Fathers of Confederation held an undisguised continentalist dream for British North America. There was much more involved, however, for Canada to admit Rupert's Land and the North-West Territory than mere extension of boundaries. First, these areas constituted the land bridge between the original four provinces of the Canada of 1867 and BC and Vancouver Island, which by then were much more advanced than the lands of the Hudson's Bay basin and the prairies and with which Canada wanted to unite. From this perspective, if the northwestern lands were not included in Canada, union with the colonies on the west coast of the continent would be meaningless.

Even more significantly, from the Canadian as well as the British perspective, Rupert's Land and the North-West Territory constituted the only feasible bulwark against the "manifest destiny" expansionism of the US. In 1865, the end of the Civil War left the US far more politically and economically advanced, more densely populated, and more consciously expansionist than were the British colonies in the Maritimes and the St. Lawrence Valley. The American advance westward and northward seemed determined to proceed, despite the formalization of the international boundary from the Lake of the Woods all the way to the Pacific coast.[8] The impression of potential encroachment on British Canada was heightened by the American purchase of Alaska from the Russian Empire on 20 June 1867.

In sum, without the areas which comprised Rupert's Land and the North-West Territory, Canada would have remained a small country wedged between the Great Lakes and the northern Atlantic seaboard.

Admission into Canada

The transfer of jurisdiction over Rupert's Land and the lands which had earlier been held by the North West Company, and the incorporation of this combined area into Canada required both imperial and Canadian legislative instrumentation. As early as 13 months after Confederation, that is, on 31 July 1868, Britain's Parliament enacted the *Rupert's Land Act, 1868*,[9] which vested in the Hudson's Bay Company authority to surrender its royal charter and in Her Majesty the power to accept such a surrender, all subject to the approval of the Parliament of Canada. This statute also authorized the monarch to declare by Order in Council that Rupert's Land should, thenceforth, be part of Canada. The matching Canadian legislation was the *Temporary Government of Rupert's Land Act, 1869*,[10] assented to on 22 June 1869. This was the origin of the present-day *Northwest Territories Act*.[11] The 1869 Act was the federal statute which established the Northwest Territories (NWT) as a modern territorial jurisdiction within Canada; it left the local public administration in place but made possible the transfer of governance responsibilities of those earlier local authorities from the Hudson's Bay Company to the Government of Canada. It further provided for the appointment of a lieutenant-governor, as in each of the provinces, and enabled the establishment of a

Council. It also affirmed the continuation of the pre-admission legal system in force in Rupert's Land and the North-West Territory. These provisions laid the foundations of the NWT's current governmental and legal regime. The 1869 *Act* declared that it was a temporary measure, but its effect would in fact continue to be extended over time by subsequent legislation.

On 12 May 1870, another federal statute, the *Manitoba Act, 1870*,[12] received royal assent. This law anticipated that the British authorities would use the power granted to them in the *Rupert's Land Act, 1868* and provided that a new province was to be carved out of the territories eventually to be transferred to Canada. Indeed, on 23 June 1870, the British authorities made the *Rupert's Land and North-Western Territory Order*,[13] by which Rupert's Land and the North-West Territory was in fact admitted into Canada. The effect of the *Order* was thus not only to increase the geography of Canada severalfold to, effectively, continental proportions, but also to bring into existence Manitoba as the fifth province, although at that time with a much smaller area than it has today.

These initial instruments were to serve as the cornerstones for the territorial part of Canada. Over the next several years, they needed clarification, precision, and adjustment. By the *British Columbia Boundaries Act, 1863*,[14] the northern and eastern boundaries of that colony had been settled by the British Parliament. Considering that the exact westerly and northwesterly boundaries of Rupert's Land and the North-West Territory had not earlier been defined, this imperial statute had the effect of delimiting the area that was intended by the British and Canadian legislation regarding the admission of territories into Canada.

In the 1873 federal statute with the cumbersome title of *An Act to Amend the Act to Make Further Provision for the Government of the Northwest Territories*,[15] the Parliament of Canada assimilated the NWT legal system to that of then existing provinces by restricting the legislative jurisdiction of the NWT Territorial Council, by subordinating territorial laws to federal ones, and by extending over the NWT the federal power of disallowance of provincial or territorial legislation, derived from s. 56 of the *Constitution Act, 1867*.

The *Act respecting the Administration of Justice and for the Establishment of a Police Force in the North-West Territories*[16] was to make an institutional contribution not only to the territories but to all of Canada, in that it was the instrument that established the North-West Mounted Police, the predecessor force to the Royal Canadian Mounted Police.

Chapter 25 of the federal statutes of 1880 contained the first consolidation of legislation regarding the NWT. By then, there was nothing temporary or partial in the legislative scheme applicable to the northern parts of Canada, or in the general pattern of governance of the NWT, based principally on federally mandated powers.

To complete the entire process of the territories' admission into Canada, on 31 July 1880, it was necessary for Queen Victoria to make the *Adjacent Territories*

Order.[17] The northerly extent of Rupert's Land and the North-West Territory had never been defined or charted with any degree of certainty. Moreover, possession of, and sovereignty over, the Arctic islands north of the Canadian mainland had never been fully determined or asserted. By this *Order*, all of British North America other than Newfoundland was annexed into Canada. The precise boundaries between Labrador, as part of Newfoundland, and Canada would not be settled until 1927, but by then this international boundary was to involve only Quebec, not the NWT, as the territories no longer included lands contiguous to Labrador.

It was thus in 1880 that the NWT, as part of Canada, reached its geographic zenith.

That part of the admission of the territorial lands which occurred in 1869-70, and in which there was an apparent leap-frogging between the incorporation of Rupert's Land and the North-West Territory into Canada as the NWT and the carving out of Manitoba as a province, raises the most fundamental questions this essay can address: what is the difference between a province and a territory, and why do different land areas become one type of jurisdiction or the other?

There can be no single, comprehensive reply applicable to all of Canadian history in this regard. Nevertheless, we may contrast the political legal attributes of provinces such as the ones in existence at the establishment of Confederation and some thereafter, with territories subsequently admitted or annexed. The four constituent provinces, as well as PEI, BC, and Newfoundland, could all claim to have, *mutatis mutandis* as subnational jurisdictions, most of the characteristics required for the recognition of a state in modern public international law. Each of them had a determined territory and a population, as well as a government. Of course, none of them had, nor as parts of the British Empire did they have the right to have, the last of the criteria of statehood in modern international law, namely, the capacity to engage in or to conduct international relations. The important element to note, however, is that these jurisdictions were suitable for provincial status because of their state of development.

By contrast, Rupert's Land and the North-West Territory had a large, not to say enormous, and not precisely delimited area; an extremely sparse and fluid population; vast distances not only from the centres of government, law, and commerce, but also from each other within the territorial lands; and a harsh geography that made transportation, communications, and public administration difficult. Equally significantly, while the territories were endowed with vast natural resources, they had no genuine economic base with which to tap into them so as to induce development and growth of population. The conclusion to be derived from the combination of these characteristics is that the criterion of distinction between provinces and territories is that of viability. As a comprehensive unit, the NWT, at its admission into Canada, could not yet be viable enough to achieve provincial status.

In the federal scheme of the Constitution designed in 1867, especially in respect to the division of legislative jurisdictions in ss. 91 and 92, provinces had a form of local and legislative sovereignty. Territories, by contrast, had only a much more limited form of local autonomy, with the remaining powers and the financing of government exercised from the federal level in Ottawa.

The carve-out of Manitoba from the NWT in 1870 provides the first example of several similar processes which would later occur in Canadian political legal history. Where and when an economic base was locally alleged or perceived by the federal authorities to have arisen within the territories, the relevant part of the territories would be carved out, either to form a new territory or to be elevated to provincial status, depending on the circumstances. This would be the vital force at play, notably in the establishment of the provinces of Alberta and Saskatchewan. However, it is necessary to remember that Canadian history has been determined as much by socio-political will and desire as by economic, political, and legal reality. Thus, where and when the community of interests was locally alleged to have arisen by a part of the territorial population, or was perceived by the federal authorities, a similar carve-out was arranged. This, in turn, was the vital force at play in the establishment of Nunavut.

Progressive Fragmentation

The jurisdictional landscape of Canada's north and northwest is marked, from Confederation until the present, by the elevation of some territorial lands to provincial status, by the attachment of other territorial lands to existing provinces, and by the separation of parts of the NWT, as they were constituted in 1870, into separate territories. In addition, the NWT itself was, at times, divided into districts which can best be characterized as autonomous administrative units within the NWT.

The establishment of Manitoba as a province had, chronologically, been the first step in this evolution. Through a series of extensions in 1881,[18] 1912[19] and 1930,[20] this province came to achieve its present configuration.

At the time of Confederation, the Province of Ontario had but a portion of its present-day geography, and the lands to the north and northwest of what we now know as southern Ontario, all the way to Manitoba, were part of the NWT. At times, both Manitoba and Ontario laid claim to overlapping parts of this area. Ontario's area was extended by the transfer to it of territorial lands contiguous to its original area in 1889[21] and again in 1912.[22] Considering the conflicting claims with Manitoba, the boundary between these provinces also needed to be defined.[23]

In similar fashion, the Province of Quebec was extended northward and in a northwesterly direction by gradual incorporation into it of the entire Ungava Peninsula, first in 1898[24] and later in 1912,[25] all at the expense of the NWT.

In conjunction with the gold rush in Canada's far northwest and in order to avoid border difficulties with the American territory of Alaska, the most northwesterly part of the NWT was made into a separate Yukon Territory in 1898.[26] During the federal general election campaign of 1979, the PC Party, under the leadership of Joe Clark, made a campaign promise to transform the Yukon from a territory into a province. Part of the credit for this idea may be attributed to the then federal MP for the electoral district of Yukon, Erik Nielsen, who was also deputy leader of the PCs. While the party succeeded in forming the government after that election, it was so short-lived that the elevation of the Yukon to provincehood did not have time to mature. The proposal has not been seriously revived since.

By 1905, Canadian immigration policy and the development of agriculture had attracted a sufficient population to the area of the NWT east of BC and west of Manitoba for these lands to be able to aspire successfully to provincial status. Thus, the provinces of Alberta[27] and Saskatchewan[28] were created by federal statute out of what had until then formed part of the NWT. By this point in the development of Canada, the territorial form of government was indeed restricted to Canada's northwest.

The most recent jurisdictional change in the NWT occurred over the course of the 1990s. Culminating roughly a quarter century of land claims negotiation, plebiscites, and public law and public administration planning, Nunavut was separated from the NWT and established as a separate territory. The major purpose for this change was to endow the Inuit of the Eastern Arctic, at their request, with a jurisdiction and a governmental entity in which they could be majoritarian. The foundation of this change was the federally enacted *Nunavut Act*.[29]

Modern Characteristics

Several aspects underlying public life in the territories are still very similar to the ones which prevailed at the time of Confederation. There is still an insufficient population base and an inadequate level of economic activity to render government and politics self-sustaining to the point of autonomy. The financial assistance of the federal government is still required in order to enable territorial public authorities to function. With such funding comes a certain degree of political control.

However, through all the jurisdictional changes, economic development, and rise in population, even if these latter trends have been gradual and limited, public life in the territories has not been static. Bearing proportions in mind, each of the three northern territories is a microcosmic Canadian-style democracy, and each has its specificities.

Governance in Nunavut, the NWT, and the Yukon is based on unicameral legislative assemblies. Interestingly, in Nunavut and the NWT, there are no political parties. This considerably alters the notion of governments being responsible to the legislatures and effectively reduces the possibility of governments being defeated on issues of confidence. Rather, majorities are formed by consensus around diverse issues, and support of the governing coalition is constantly fluctuating. As in the rest of Canada, democratic governance is based on the rule of law. At the federal level, each territory is represented in the Parliament of Canada by one member of the House of Commons and by one senator. Each territory has its particular legal system that blends statutes and Anglo-Canadian common law with customary Aboriginal legal elements. Each also has an independent judiciary and a self-regulating bar.

Each of the territories devotes particular attention to local issues which blend politics, public administration, and the legal regime.

The first Legislative Assembly of Nunavut was elected on 15 February 1999. It is comprised of 19 members, representing a population that currently stands at 30,000.[30] In various jurisdictions throughout Canada, there is discussion of whether election dates fixed in advance are compatible with the Westminster model of parliamentary democracy. In Nunavut, ahead of all other provinces and territories, the authorities came to an affirmative conclusion. They thus determined that the second general election should take place on 16 February 2004. The current legislature, the second of that jurisdiction, was in fact elected on that date. A lone candidate was acclaimed in one electoral district. In the other 18, the average number of eligible voters was an astoundingly low 573. The most populous of these electoral districts had 947 listed electors, while the least populous, that named Hudson Bay and comprising essentially the Belcher Islands off the northwest coast of Quebec, counted only 307 voters. The premier of Nunavut is Paul Okalik, who has represented the electoral district of Iqaluit West since 1999.

In addition to the local reflection of national political issues, the hottest current topic of public controversy relates to the shrimp fishery. In respect to the deep sea waters adjacent to the east coast of Baffin Island—that is, for the Canadian portion of the Davis Strait between Canada and Greenland—the federal Department of Fisheries and Oceans has allocated quotas which territorial fishers and the territorial authorities consider inadequate. The governments of the Atlantic Provinces and of Quebec have expressed support for the Nunavut position in this matter. The conflict may indicate that in the relations between the federal and other governments, the distinction between provincial and territorial status diminishes. Federalism implies contention between national and local views, whatever the form of the local government.

The NWT is the most populous of the territories, with 43,000 inhabitants, according to the most recent postcensal estimates of Statistics Canada, done in 2005. Its Legislative Assembly, like that of Nunavut, consists of 19 single-member constituencies. The first general election following the separation of Nunavut from the NWT was held on 6 December 1999, after an adjustment period of eight months. The most recent general election, to constitute the fifteenth Legislative Assembly, was held on 24 November 2003. The current premier is Joseph Handley, who was acclaimed in the electoral district of Weledeh.

In this jurisdiction, the most immediate and noteworthy topic of public policy is the development of comprehensive agreements for land claims and self-government. These are usually tripartite negotiations involving federal and territorial authorities with Aboriginal groups, which can lead to instruments with quasi-constitutional status. They bring fundamental reform to the nature of local governance for the Aboriginal peoples implicated. At present, discussion toward the Dogrib (Tlicho) Agreement, the Delta-Beaufort Agreement involving both Gwitchen Indians and Inuvialiut peoples, and the Decho Agreement, relating to the Fort Simpson area, are most prominent.

Also noteworthy is the devolution of resources from the control of the government of Canada to that of the NWT. The territorial government is not vested with proprietary rights to the NWT's subsoil and therefore has difficulty regulating the oil and gas industry, the gold mining, and the diamond extraction sector of the economy. The territories' position is that if, based on federal-territorial discussions, it could secure the rights necessary to foster the NWT's development, the jurisdiction's economy could evolve more rapidly, inducing evolution of the rest of its public life. Current developments of significance to the NWT's economy are the recent opening of new diamond mines and the renewed prospect for the construction of a pipeline along the Mackenzie Valley.

The issue of constitutional evolution is also rather prominent in the NWT. Reformist ideas such as guaranteed Aboriginal representation in the Legislative Assembly and different rules for deciding on different issues in the Assembly are being discussed.

The Yukon Territory is the jurisdiction within Canada furthest away from the political centre at Ottawa and from the economic hub in Toronto. It has 31,000 inhabitants according to the 2005 estimates of Statistics Canada. This is less than 1/1000 of the overall population of Canada, and yet its democratic life is well developed. The Legislative Assembly constituted from 18 electoral districts, was last elected on 4 November 2002. Yukon legislatures usually last three to four years. In this political system, the Yukon Party forms the current government, and it is opposed by the Yukon Liberal Party and the Yukon NDP. The premier is Dennis Fentie, who represents the electoral District of Watson Lake.

The major focuses of political attention are, perhaps not surprisingly in light of the similarity of issues across the North, the devolution to the territorial authorities of control over resources and the slow evolution of the form of government. The Yukon seems to have no current interest in achieving provincial status. This is particularly true because a shift in that direction would imply a loss of federal subsidies in favour of less generous transfer payments. However, the desire for greater local latitude of governmental action is real.

Political life throughout the territories is often as lively as it is in southern Canada. Indeed, many of the current issues of public debate are recognizable to other Canadians. A document issued in 1999 by then Premier Jim Antoine of the NWT, entitled "Agenda for the New North: Achieving our Potential in the 21st Century," provides a good example of this. Under the rubric of "A Shared Vision of Our Future," the premier indicated the following plan:

> A SHARED VISION OF OUR FUTURE
> To move together towards a prosperous and secure future for all residents of the Northwest Territories, we need to agree on and be guided by a shared vision of our future.
>
> We propose a vision that includes:
> A system of government that respects the collective rights of Aboriginal peoples and the individual rights of all Northerners.
> Northerners taking greater control of their future and becoming more responsible for their own well being.
> Modern health care, education, housing and social programs that are provided by and for Northerners.
> Sustainable development of the north's economic potential in a way that benefits all Northerners.
> Greater Aboriginal representation in the workforce and economy.
> Healthier, more self-reliant individuals, families and communities.
> Less dependence on federal transfer payments.
> A strong unified territory, taking its place in the federation and contributing to the prosperity of Canada.[31]

Going beyond these generalities, however indicative they may be, current issues of political controversy common to the territories include health care and the governmental response to the recommendations of the Romanow Report[32] with special emphasis on the health care needs of Aboriginal populations, education including legal education for Aboriginal peoples, gun control, land claims, relations between Aboriginal and non-Aboriginal communities, governmental support for economic development, and measures to promote higher employment.

The administrations of the three northern territories recognize that their conditions of public life and governance are both specific within the Canadian experience of democracy and common across the north in many respects. In order to highlight these commonalities, the northern premiers organized a first regional heads of government meeting on 3 September 2003, in Cambridge Bay, Nunavut. They used the occasion to subscribe to a *Northern Cooperation Accord*, declaring their intent to promote intergovernmental cooperation on matters of mutual concern and interest. In particular, they adopted the following mechanisms of cooperation.

3. MECHANISMS TO PROMOTE COOPERATION AND INFOR-
MATION SHARING

3 (1) The Three Governments intend to enable or promote:

    a) the enhancement of working relationships at both the po-
litical and official level;

    b) the development and advancement of a common agenda
on matters of mutual concern and interest;

    c) the sharing of information relevant to such matters of mu-
tual concern and interest;

    d) the fostering of economic opportunities;

    e) the maximization of benefits for northern people; and

    f) the provision of mutual support in matters of regional, ter-
ritorial, national and international interest.[33]

Although the Accord included a plan for the premiers to meet yearly, they specifically avoided creating legal obligations or imposing financial burdens on their respective governments through these mechanisms. It therefore remains to be seen whether the intended cooperation will materialize in terms of public administration or remain a statement of intent.

Constitutional Evolution

The political legal issue which, ultimately, underlies and colours all others is territorial constitutional development, along with assuring a sufficiently serious role for the territories within Canada. At the time of the enactment of the *Constitution Act, 1982*, federal and provincial authorities did give some thought to the future of the territories. The only textual reflection of that planning, however, was in terms of the possible extension of existing provinces into the territories or the establishment of new provinces, presumably out of territorial lands.

42. (1) An amendment to the Constitution of Canada in relation to the following matters may be made only in accordance with subsection 38 (1):

...

    (e) the extension of existing provinces into the territories; and

    (f) notwithstanding any other law or practice, the establish-
ment of new provinces.[34]

The sense of these paragraphs is that either course of action would require use of the 7/50 constitutional amendment formula, meaning that any constitutional amendment aimed at achieving one of these plans would have to receive the authorization of the Senate, the House of Commons, and the legislative assemblies of at least two-thirds of the provinces, representing at least 50 per cent of the population of all the provinces. The unilateral federal carving out of Nunavut from the NWT, even if it was done with the consent of the people of Nunavut while they still formed part of the NWT population, was possible only because the constitutional provisions referred to here do not address the issue of the creation of a new territory.

At present, it seems unlikely that any other territory will be legislated into existence, and the extension of provinces into territorial lands is not on the horizon. Consequently, the focus of political legal development is devolution, the progressive transfer of powers from the federal to the territorial level. This can be done by each territorial legislature's enactment of legislation which mirrors earlier federal statutes. This method was used, for example, with the mining legislation that the Yukon enacted, effective 1 April 2003, territorial statutes to replace what had been the earlier federal *Yukon Placer Mining Act* and the *Yukon Quartz Mining Act*. Alternatively, devolution can be achieved where federal authorities make legislative jurisdiction available to a territory, such as was done in the case of the Yukon's enactment of the *Yukon Oil and Gas Act*.[35]

The territories are participants in the ebb and flow of Canadian governmental, political, and legal life even though they may not be fully autonomous and have fewer legislative competencies and administrative rights and obligations than provinces. Their main advantage is their still enormous potential wealth, which will be developed only with sufficient immigration and investment. Their principal disadvantage is that, until they achieve a genuine level of viability based on a combination of demographic, economic, governmental, political, and legal factors, they will not have the autonomy necessary to control their own political destinies within the federation.

Is the elevation of any territory to provincial status sound public policy, and is it foreseeable? The proposal by the Clark government to transform the Yukon Territory into a province evaporated with its loss of power, and no other arose for over two decades.

The most recent federal attention to the constitutional evolution of the north has come from the government of Prime Minister Paul Martin in the fall of 2004. As a prelude, on 26 October 2004, the prime minister announced a new Equalization and Territorial Financing Formula to assist poorer jurisdictions, including all three territories, in meeting their commitments to strengthen the health care system.[36]

Then, in a somewhat surprising fashion, while on a diplomatic and commercial trip in Brazil, on 22 November 2004, the prime minister voiced publicly the idea of gradual territorial evolution toward provincehood.[37] The reason and timing of this rather indirect announcement policy relate far less to the progress or viability of the North within Canada than to the overall national interest and the perceived threat to Canadian sovereignty from the northerly military and economic activities of other countries, in particular the US.

> And, just a week before U.S. President George W. Bush visits Ottawa, he [Paul Martin] also declined to point the finger at the U.S. refusal to recognize Canadian sovereignty over the Arctic as the reason for his concern.
>
> "There are other countries. I'm not going to name countries. I'm just telling the world, the Arctic is Canadian territory, and we will exercise our sovereignty."[38]

The announcement gave rise to much speculation concerning the domestic impact of the proposal. Commentators praised the economic benefits of provincehood on northern citizens' equality of access to the services provided in other parts of the country and the advancement it would mean in terms of governance. The process of converting territories into provinces also raised sober second thoughts, however. It cannot be accomplished without constitutional amendment. That, in turn, would revive two inextricably related issues. The first is the permanent question of the balance within Confederation. Provincial status for the territories through constitutional amendment could be successfully accomplished only, informed observers presume, if it did not lead to a diminishing of the relative institutional and social weight of Quebec as part of the country. Moreover, a reopening of the constitutional negotiation process at this time would inevitably entail dealing with whatever other issue was timely at the moment. Currently, that is the reform of the Senate to make it at least an elected body, if not to also endow it with the other two "e" qualities, making it also equal and effective. In sum, Martin's plan may be characterized as being premature.

Whether in domestic terms as an historical, economic, and political complement to the ten provinces, or internationally as a geo-strategic foothold at the top of the world, the North is a vital component of Canada as well as an integral part of this country on the world stage.

Notes

1. The views expressed here are exclusively those of the author and are entirely non-partisan. This article was prepared as a scholarly paper, not on behalf of the House of Commons, its members or its administration.
2. The best source of information about the history of the Hudson's Bay Company is <http://www.gov.mb.ca/chc/archives/hbca/about/holdings/text.html>.
3. Jacques-Yvan Morin and José Woehrling, *Les Constitutions du Canada et du Québec du Régime Français à nos Jours* (Montreal : Les Éditions Thémis, 1992) 581.
4. This is the pre-Confederation designation and spelling. The same area later became known as the Northwest Territories.

5. The Quebec Resolutions are online at the site of the National Library of Canada, <http://www.nlc-bnc.ca/2/18/h18-245-e.html>; accessed 30 August 2003.

6. Quebec Resolutions.

7. R.S.C. 1985, App. No. 5, s. 146.

8. Treaty between Britain and the US (Oregon Boundary), Washington, 15 June 1846; commonly designated the Oregon Treaty.

9. 31-32 Vict., c 105 (UK) and R.S.C. 1985, App. No. 6.

10. 32-33 Vict., c. 3.

11. R.S.C. 1985, c. N-27.

12. R.S.C. 1985, App. No. 8.

13. R.S.C. 1985, App. No. 9.

14. 26-27 Vict., c. 83 (UK).

15. 36 Vict., c. 34.

16. 37 Vict., c. 22.

17. R.S.C. 1985, App. No. 14.

18. *Manitoba Boundaries Extension Act*, S.C. 1881, c. 14.

19. *Manitoba Boundaries Extension Act, 1912*, S.C. 1912, c. 32.

20. *Manitoba Boundaries Extension Act, 1930*, S.C. 1930, c. 28.

21. *Canada (Ontario Boundary) Act, 1889*, R.S.C. 1985, App. No. 16.

22. *Ontario Boundaries Extension Act*, S.C. 1912, c. 40.

23. *Manitoba Boundaries Extension Act, 1912; Ontario Boundaries Extension Act Amendment*, S.C. 1950, c. 16; and *Ontario-Manitoba Boundary Act, 1953*, S.C. 1953-54, c. 9.

24. *An Act Respecting the North-western, Northern and North-eastern Boundaries of the Province of Quebec*, S.C. 1898, c. 3.

25. *Quebec Boundaries Extension Act, 1912*, S.C. 1912, c. 45.

26. *Yukon Territory Act, 1898*, R.S.C. 1985, App. No. 19.

27. *Alberta Act, 1905*, R.S.C. 1985, App. No. 20.

28. *Saskatchewan Act*, 1905, R.S.C. 1985, App. No. 21.

29. The *Nunavut Act* was enacted as S.C. 1993, c. 28, but it came into force, creating the Nunavut Territory, on 1 April 1999.

30. Quarterly demographic statistics, as of April 2003. See Statistics Canada, Catalogue No. 91-002, 17, 1: 6, Table 1.

31. Jim Antoine, *Agenda for the New North: Achieving our Potential in the 21st Century* (1999).

32. Roy Romanow, *Building on Values: The Future of Health Care in Canada* (Ottawa: Royal Commission on the Future of Health Care in Canada, November, 2002).

33. *Northern Cooperation Accord*, 3 September 2003, s. 3.

34. *Constitution Act, 1982*, s. 42, R.S.C. 1985, App. No. 44.

35. R.S.Y., c. 162.

36. "Prime minister announces new equalization and territorial funding formula framework" (26 October 2004), <http://www1.pm.gc.ca/eng/news.asp?id=300>; accessed 23 November 2004.

37. "Northern territories (eventually) to be given provincial status," CBC News Online (22 November 2004), <http://www.cbc.ca/story/canada/national/2004/11/22/provinces 041122.html>; accessed 23 November 2004.

38. "Martin signals provincial status for North," GlobeandMail.com (23 November 2004), <http://www.theglobeandmail.com/servlet/story/RTGAM.20041122.wmarty 1123/BNPrint/>; accessed 23 November 2004.

PART IV

Provincial Political Economies

CHAPTER 12

De-Mythologizing Provincial Political Economies

The Development of the Service Sectors in the Provinces 1911–2001

MICHAEL HOWLETT

Introduction: The Political Economy of Provincial Politics

As the chapters by David Foot, Nelson Wiseman, and others in this volume attest, the background conditions under which provincial politics play out are affected by a diverse range of phenomena. These include the common sets of ideas provincial citizens hold about such things as the nature of justice, fairness, and "good government" as well as the basic characteristics of the population, including its age structure and other demographic variables. These conditions help identify some of the issues which a populace will find important—such as pensions and health care for an aging populace or schools and education for a younger one—as well as how they will tend to respond to these issues—in an authoritarian or egalitarian way, by the use of market-based devices or more supportive of government provision of goods and services to the public.

However, these are not the only background conditions that help to structure political life. Another set of such conditions relates to the "political economy" of a polity, that is, to the nature of its economy and to the types of relations existing between and among citizens as they earn a living.[1] Political economic realities shape the occupational structure of a jurisdiction, influence demographic variables such as the urban and rural structure of the population, affect the ability of different groups in the population to carry out their wishes and ensure government policies reflect their values and aspirations, and have a very important impact on the types of issues which are considered important by the population and, hence, form the government agenda in democratic polities.[2]

As a result, the analysis of any polity, be it an international regime, a domestic nation or a subnational government like a province or a municipality, includes the analysis of that polity's political economy. How a provincial economy is structured, how or to what extent it is tied to international trade regimes, whether it is stable or prone to boom and bust cycles, whether it is wealthy or poor as a whole, and whether or not its wealth or poverty is distributed equally or unequally, and many other aspects all have a significant impact on the political life of that polity.[3]

In this book, most of the chapters deal with elements of questions about how provinces are organized politically and whether or not they have effective state institutions capable of adequately anticipating or responding to the needs of their citizens. This chapter helps to set the stage for discussions of many of these elements by outlining the nature of the provincial political economies, how they have changed over time, and what implications those changes have had, and continue to have, for provincial political life.

The Myths and Realities of Provincial Political Economy

Studies of provincial politics have tended to stress the differences that exist between Canada's ten provinces. This was true of the first major studies of the provinces conducted by Adam Shortt and William Doughty at the beginning of the twentieth century[4] and remains true of many present-day studies. While it is true that the provinces have very different histories of settlement and expansion, comparative provincial studies that emphasize the differences tend to overshadow or downplay the extent to which they are similar and, as this chapter will argue, the extent to which they have been growing increasingly similar over the course of Confederation.

Many people's perceptions of Canada's provinces centre around a common myth or stereotype which very often has an important political economic dimension. Usually this stereotype is found in the minds of "outsiders" or non-residents of the province concerned, although sometimes it is also shared by substantial portions of the provincial population. Myths contribute in many ways, often virtually unconsciously, to the public discourse on the provinces in Canada and form an important part of the attitudes and approaches commonly espoused to resolve various provincial problems.

Unfortunately, while some of these myths were accurate in past times, virtually none are now. As such, the attitudes and approaches to provincial problems they inculcate, as a result, can do more to exacerbate problems than cure them. However, they are continuously reinforced by references to them in popular accounts such as newspapers, television, and radio reporting, which remain the most important sources of the very limited knowledge most Canadians have about the provinces.[5] A political economic analysis of the provinces, focusing on the changing nature of their occupational structures, helps to show that the provinces have undergone a profound modernization process since their entry into Confederation, a process which shares at the subnational level many of the characteristics of the modernization process found in most Western industrial states.

This section examines these myths of provincial politics and evaluates them in the light of the actual pattern of development of the provincial economies. In doing so, each province is examined at three key points in time for which comparable data is available—1911, at the end of the period of change brought about by Confederation in 1867 but just before the changes brought into place by the First World War; 1951, after the entrance of Newfoundland in Confederation and the restructuring brought about by the Second World War; and 2001, 50 years later, in order to demonstrate the trends and changes in provincial political economies as they have attained their modern shape (see Table 12.1).

Table 12.1. Sectoral Pattern of Provincial Economies 1911–2001

	Primary			Secondary			Tertiary		
	1911	1951	2001	1911	1951	2001	1911	1951	2001
NF	84.0	46.2[1]	7.9	11.9	6.5[1]	14.7	4.1	47.3[1]	73.0
PEI	66.2	44.4	11.5	10.3	12.6	17.7	23.4	42.9	69.9
NS	48.3	23.1	5.1	15.2	19.2	16.7	15.2	19.2	75.6
NB	44.9	28.0	5.8	14.6	17.9	18.7	0.4	54.0	72.9
QC	35.9	16.9	3.0	22.7	28.7	22.3	41.3	54.4	71.5
ON	34.1	13.0	2.0	23.0	29.6	23.8	42.8	57.4	72.0
MB	40.1	26.1	6.5	14.4	18.6	17.6	45.4	55.3	74.6
SK	65.2	49.8	14.3	7.5	8.4	11.7	27.3	41.8	72.3
AB	54.0	35.5	9.9	10.6	14.5	16.9	35.4	49.9	72.0
BC	27.3	13.6	3.8	19.4	23.4	16.1	53.3	63.0	77.7

1. Figures are estimates for 1948 on basis of 1945 Newfoundland Census.
Sources: Newfoundland, Census of Newfoundland and Labrador, 1911 (St. John's: King's Printer, 1914) Table I, Section C; Canada, Newfoundland: An Introduction to Canada's New Province (Ottawa: Department of External Affairs, 1950) 113; Canada, Statistics Canada, ESTAT Database—Table 282-0008 Labour Force Survey Estimates (LFS) by North America System (NAICS), Sex, and Age Group, Annual, 200a; available at <http://estat.statcan.ca>; Canada, Dominion Bureau of Statistics, Ninth Census of Canada 1951—Volume IV: Labour Force—Occupations and Industries (Ottawa: Queen's Printer, 1953) Table 2.

Newfoundland: The fishing economy

The pre-eminent myth concerning the economy of Newfoundland and Labrador centres on the idea of the province as relying on the fishery for its economic well-being.[6] While this was true for several centuries,[7] it has become less and less of a reality.[8]

Although Newfoundland was late in modernizing and had a very high percentage of its labour force employed in the fishery as late as 1911, soon afterwards the efforts of it governments to diversify the economy began to bear fruit. Just prior to the First World War, the province experienced a rapid growth in forest-related activities with the creation of a pulp and paper complex at Grand Falls.[9] These activities continued into the 1920s and 1930s with the expansion of the provincial mineral sector and plans for large-scale development in Labrador.[10]

Following Confederation many of these plans were realized, such as the massive hydro-electricity development at Churchill Falls, and when the fishery finally collapsed in the early 1990s the effects of this, although severe, were partially offset by the existence of energy mega-projects such as Hibernia.[11]

As the figures in Table 12.1 show, Newfoundland had a very high proportion of its workforce in the primary sector in 1911. Although there is some difficulty comparing these figures compiled under the Newfoundland census with those compiled under a different system in Canada following Confederation in 1949, it is safe to say that employment in the fishery was a mainstay of the provincial economy.

By 1951, this had changed as approximately the same number of people were employed in a variety of tertiary activities as in the primary sector, which now included the much expanded forestry and mining sectors. By 2001, even with the increases caused by Hibernia and other offshore oil and gas developments, the primary sector accounted for only 8 per cent of total employment with a much expanded secondary manufacturing and construction sector (15 per cent) but a dominant service sector (73 per cent).[12]

Prince Edward Island: The myth of the garden

In PEI the predominant myth is of the province as an agrarian rural paradise.[13] This is the "myth of the garden," of PEI as home to the sorts of prosperous and educated farmers portrayed in Lucy Maud Montgomery's novel *Anne of Green Gables* and its successful television and film adaptations.

It is, in fact, hard to determine if this period of paradisiacal pastoral pleasure ever existed. Up until Confederation with Canada in 1873, the predominant issue on the island was the absentee landownership resulting from its sale to 67 landowners in England in July 1767 and the desire of farmers to cease paying "quitrents" to these foreign landlords. After Confederation the government of Canada loaned the island government enough funds to purchase and redistribute the farmland.[14]

So if an idyllic age of prosperous farmers existed, it could have occurred only after 1873, by definition. Although their relative level of prosperity is another issue, it is fair to say, however, that the province was dominated by agricultural activities at the turn of the twentieth century.

While this domination declined after 1911, it was still substantial in 1951 when about 45 per cent of the population still worked on farms. However, there is little doubt that any "golden age" of the garden had ended by this time, as the average per capita income in the province had fallen to very low levels *vis à vis* the rest of the provinces. Considered a basket case rather than a breadbasket by the federal government, by 1965 efforts to resurrect the province led to the creation of a modern tourism industry through the 15-year Comprehensive Economic Development plan (CED) signed by the federal and provincial governments.[15]

By 2001, as a result of this and other efforts on the part of both governments, the provincial social and economic structure had changed dramatically to the point where now less than 12 per cent of the populace works in the primary sector and 70 per cent in the service sector. In 2001 more people worked in the retail trade and government service industries than in agriculture, and the province had joined the mainstream in Canada.

Nova Scotia: The Golden Age of wind and sail

Nova Scotia is often portrayed as the major loser in Confederation. In many minds, the province had entered into a Golden Age of wind and sail in the second half of the nineteenth century, epitomized by the schooner *Bluenose* portrayed on the Canadian dime, and has declined ever since, at least partially due to the Confederation arrangement itself.[16]

This thesis comes in two forms. On the one hand, authors such as Forbes and Saunders have contended that the decline was due to federal government policies, such as the setting of maritime freight rates and banking policy, which favoured central Canadian manufacturing and financial development over that of the Maritimes and especially Nova Scotia. Others, however, argued that the transition resulted from a shift in technology as the economy based on "wood and wind" which favoured the Maritimes was replaced by one based on "iron and steel" which favoured Central Canada.[17]

Both theses presuppose a time when Nova Scotia had a high proportion of its population engaged in secondary and tertiary activities such as manufacturing and transportation. However, if there was such a time, it certainly lapsed close to 100 years ago, as the twentieth century began with a high proportion of the Nova Scotia populace engaged in primary activities, especially agricultural pursuits.[18]

As the data in Table 12.1 show, the province underwent not a transition from manufacturing to primary employment in the last century, but one from primary employment to tertiary. This process was underway between 1911 and 1951 when primary employment dropped by half and accelerated between 1951 and 2001 when employment in that sector fell almost 80 per cent. During this period, tertiary employment quadrupled to the point where now just under three out of four members of the provincial labour force are employed in service sector activities.[19]

New Brunswick: Appalachia North or the politics of backwardness

New Brunswick is often thought of outside its provincial borders as the most rural and backward of the Canadian provinces—as a kind of northern extension of Appalachia in the US.[20] This is primarily due to the province's dependence in the eighteenth and nineteenth centuries on forestry, farming, and fishing activities, none of which was entirely successful or prosperous.[21]

Once again, however, if this stereotype ever had some base in reality,[22] it has disappeared as the province moved into the modern era post-1960.[23] Although the province continues to have important forest- and agricultural-based industries, these are of a hi-tech nature (pulp and paper, frozen foods, etc.)[24] More recently the province has attracted attention by luring sophisticated telephone calling-centre operations to its state-of-the-art digital telephone system.[25]

As Table 12.1 shows, the primary sector declined rapidly in significance in New Brunswick between 1911 and 1951 and continued to decline through 2001. Like Nova Scotia and the rest of the Maritime provinces, by 2001 New Brunswick had developed a fully fledged service sector economy employing 73 per cent of its workers.[26]

Quebec: The politics of defensive nationalism

The dominant myth outside Quebec, perpetuated by a fascinated English-Canadian media, is that Quebec provincial politics is obsessed with the national question.[27] While there is some truth to this myth, it is important to note the fashion in which Quebec nationalism has evolved over the years.

As Quinn has argued, at the turn of the twentieth century, Quebec nationalism was "defensive" in nature, promoted by a small oligarchy of church and government officials with the aim of protecting the French language and Catholic faith from the dual threats of secularization and Anglicization.[28] While this form of nationalism was significant right through the Second World War and gave Quebec a distinctive hue and cast within the Canadian federation (for example, a separate labour movement), it was this *ancien régime* embodied in *Duplessisme* which was cast aside by the *révolution tranquille* in the 1960s and 1970s.[29]

By the time the nationalist movement produced the Parti Québécois government of René Lévesque in 1976, it was of a less defensive and inward-looking nature, supported not by rural farmers and workers as had been the case in the past, but by elements of the urban middle and working classes.[30]

Thus it must be remembered that in the case of Quebec, nationalism is not simply a "political" movement, but a "political economic" one.[31] The nature and consequences of nationalism have changed and adapted as the province has gone through the same type of overall pattern of change as has the rest of the provinces, moving into the modern service sector era between 1951 and 2001.[32]

This pattern is set out in Table 12.1. As these figures show, by 1911 Quebec already had a very low level of primary sector employment by Canadian standards. It boasted the largest metropolis in Canada in Montreal and had begun to develop a sizable manufacturing centre in that city. The decline of the rural areas of the province continued through the Second World War which boosted the fortunes of Montreal and manufacturing.[33]

Although the manufacturing centre declined after 1951, with serious consequences for the economic health of many urban centres in the province, the decline was nowhere near as steep as that of rural Quebec. Rural-based primary sector employment plummeted to only 3 per cent of the provincial labour force.

By 2001 Quebec, like the Maritime provinces, had generated a modern, urbanized, service sector economy, and the nature of Quebec nationalism had changed dramatically.

Ontario: The smug and stable province

Ontario has a reputation outside its borders as a big, bland powerhouse. Smug and stable, it is alleged to have dominated and prospered throughout Confederation, often at the expense of other regions and provinces.[34] While the question of Ontario's dominance within Confederation is another matter,[35] there is little question that the province is the largest in Canada by virtually any measure one chooses to use. It now has a GDP roughly equal to that of the immediate post-Second World War Canada and remains the largest in terms of population by almost one-third more than its nearest rival, Quebec.

The mythopaeic elements of the popular position of Ontario stems not from the concerns about power and size but with the idea that the province is by nature smug and stable. Once again, as in Quebec, this myth has some element of truth, as it refers at one level to the extended period in office of the Conservative Party (1943-1985).[36] However, it should be remembered that this long period of one-party tenure was preceded by the election of the first radical farmers' party government in Canada[37] and ended with a coalition Liberal-NDP regime and ultimately the election of only the fourth provincial NDP government in Canadian history in 1991. This, in turn, was followed by alternating Progressive Conservative and Liberal regimes.[38] Even during the 42 years of Conservative rule, it should also be noted that this era began with a minority government under George Drew and ended with minority and slim majority governments under Bill Davis and Frank Miller in the 1970s and 1980s.

Nevertheless, it is true that Ontario underwent the least severe dislocations of any provincial government in the twentieth century. As Table 12.1 shows, primary employment had already dropped to about one-third of the labour force by 1911 in Ontario, a figure most other provinces did not reach until after the Second World War.

Manufacturing employment has been relatively stable, while service sector employment has grown, although it was already high in 1911 at over 40 per cent. For the most part the recent politics of the province have centred on service sector issues, although much attention has been paid to the decline in manufacturing employment which has occurred since 1951.[39]

Manitoba: The farmer province

Manitoba is often viewed from outside as a "typical" prairie province, that is, as a farming province with a grain export-based economy.[40] Such a vision, however, does not do justice to the pivotal role Manitoba played in the development of Western Canada, both as a transportation centre and a hub for such activities as meat packing and manufacturing.[41]

As the figures in Table 12.1 reveal, Manitoba in 1911 had less of its labour force employed in the primary sector than did the Maritime provinces and only slightly more than Ontario and Quebec. While the percentage employed in manufacturing and construction remained low, that in the tertiary sector (including transportation) was higher than in the two central Canadian provinces.

The myth of the farmer province, in fact, applies only to the period from 1911-51 when the percentage of the population employed in primary sector occupations fell, although not as rapidly as in the rest of Canada. It is important to recall, however, that even in this period, farming was not responsible for all primary sector employment. For instance, the federal government developed the first pulp and paper mill on lands under its own control at Pine Falls and attempted to develop a freshwater fishery on the great lakes of the province's interior. The provincial mineral industry also expanded to take advantage of the rich ore deposits found in the mid-north and northern regions of the province, and successive provincial governments embarked on massive hydro-electric projects in the northern regions.[42]

By the 1970s the myth was already out of date[43] and by 2001, of course, there was no substance to it whatsoever, as the province had less than 7 per cent of its workforce employed in primary occupations and three out of every four workers was employed in a service sector occupation.

Saskatchewan: Agrarian socialism

Saskatchewan has often been discussed as the home of socialism or social democracy in Canada. Unlike its European equivalents, however, it is important to recognize that this socialism has been a farmer-based, populist type of social democracy with its roots in the farming economy and not the manufacturing sector as was the case in most European countries.[44] As the significance of the primary sector waned over the course of the latter half of the twentieth century, however, so have the fortunes of Saskatchewan's social democratic NDP governments, which now rule only with the support of the provincial Liberal Party.[45]

As the figures in Table 12.1 show, within Canada Saskatchewan has historically had the highest percentage of its labour force employed in the primary sector. Just after the province's creation in 1905 over 65 per cent of the labour force was employed in the primary sector, almost all of which involved agricultural activities. By 1951 this figure had declined, but still just under one-half of all workers were employed in this sector.

The province underwent a fairly rapid process of change, however, between 1951 and 2001 as primary employment dropped by almost 75 per cent. Still, almost one in seven members of the provincial labour force continue to work in this area. While this lends some credence to one part of the myth of agrarian socialism,[46] it is important to remember that, although primary sector employment is high by Canadian standards, a larger percentage of the population now works in the service sector than did in the primary sector at its height in 1911.[47]

Alberta: A province unlike all the others

The central myth of Alberta is that it is an unusual province with a whole series of peccadilloes making its political life unique.[48] The classic analysis in this mode was made by C.B. MacPherson in 1962 when he argued that the unique class structure of the province lent itself to the election of one-party governments in a system he labeled as "quasi-party." Others continued to assert throughout the 1970s and 1980s that the province's oil wealth continued to contribute to its unique status in Confederation.[49]

These analyses, however, tend to focus upon only a single aspect of the province's political or economic make-up in reaching their conclusion—either the penchant of provincial voters to return one party to office for multiple terms and then replace that party with another, and often new, opponent, or the boom-and-bust nature of the oil and gas industry.[50] An analysis taking into account a longer term historical perspective and assessing the overall structure of the provincial economy reaches a different conclusion.

Such an analysis reveals that Alberta historically has had a relatively diversified economy. As Table 12.1 shows, employment in the primary sector as early as 1911 did not reach the heights that it did in Saskatchewan, where farmers returned traditional parties to office until the election of the CCF in 1944. It should also be recalled that Alberta had a large mineral and forest sector compared to the other Western provinces and that its agrarian sector featured cattle-raising and other activities besides grain production. It also reveals a large decline in primary employment by 1951, despite the creation of the provincial oil and gas industry following strikes in Turner Valley after the First World War and at Leduc in central Alberta in 1947.

By 2001 the province still had a large primary sector by Canadian standards, in part at least due to efforts by the provincial government in the late 1980s to promote a large new forest industry in the province,[51] but like all of the other provinces, it was dominated by service sector occupations. As a result, its political issues were those typical of such economies, notably the mix of public and private services, deficit reduction, health care, the environment, and the like.[52]

British Columbia: The politics of exploitation

In BC the predominant myth centres on the province as a resource hinterland whose wealth revolves around the exploitation of natural resources, especially forestry but also fisheries and mining.[53] This myth had a firm basis only in the very early years of the province,[54] but it is perpetuated by every headline setting out the latest conflict between loggers and environmentalists in the province. Notwithstanding its popularity, however, it is a myth with very little foundation in fact.[55]

As Table 12.1 reveals, BC has always been unique in Canada due not to its "dependence" on resources but to the very large component of the labour force employed in the service sector. This reflects the significant role played by transportation activities in the province's history from its entry into Confederation as the terminus of the trans-Canada Canadian Pacific Railway (and the later addition of the Canadian Northern and Grand Trunk Pacific railways) to the vital role played by the Port of Vancouver in the export of all kinds of goods produced in the interior of the country.

As early as 1911, over one-half of BC's labour force already was employed in service sector activities. Even during the first major forest sector boom after 1911, primary sector employment declined as the sawmill and pulp and paper boom spurred the growth of the secondary, or manufacturing, sector.

Between 1951 and 1911 as mechanization overtook the logging and fishing activities, the primary sector declined even further to the point where only just over 6 per cent of the provincial labour force is now employed in these activities.[56] By 2001 service sector activities accounted for more than three out of every four jobs in the province, the highest level in Canada.[57]

The General Pattern of Provincial Economic Development

The case-by-case examination of the record of change in the provincial economies undertaken above reveals that despite a range of popular mythologies that tend to focus on the idiosyncrasies of each province's political and economic origins, the general pattern of provincial economic development has been one in which the differences between provincial political economies have gradually eroded to the point where all are now heavily dependent on service sector activities for employment and growth.

The average pattern in Canada has been for employment in the primary sector to decline by almost half between 1911 and 1951 and then by more than half again in the period 1951-2001. While manufacturing employment tended to grow by one-quarter in the 1911-51 period, average growth in this sector in 1951-2001 was zero. Service sector growth, however, was rapid in the period from 1911 to 1951, when it grew by over 40 per cent, and in 1951-2001, when it grew by almost the same amount again.

While not all the provinces have undergone exactly the average process of change, all have moved to the point where they currently have very similar socio-economic structures, something they have not had in common since the middle of the nineteenth century when all were completely dependent on agricultural and resource-based activities.[58] By 1991 the ten provinces differed by just over 5 per cent in terms of their dependence on service sector activities, ranging from a "low" of over 68 per cent in PEI and Saskatchewan to a "high" of over 74 per cent in Nova Scotia and BC.

Modernization and the Political Economy of Provincial Service Sector Growth

What have been the political consequences of this modernization process? Somewhat surprisingly, very little information exists on the subnational modernization process, despite volumes having been written on development at the national, international, regional, and community levels. For the most part the literature tends to assume that subnational developmental processes are scale images of larger national processes. Although staples theorists and others in Canada have been very sensitive to the differential regional consequences of development,[59] even they have tended to ignore the similar provincial paths of change and their transformation into modern service sector economies.

The key point in much recent work on development has been to try to avoid the error of assuming that economic changes such as technological advances, or social changes such as an aging demographic structure, *automatically* translate into more or less predictable political changes. Rather, the argument being made is that politics is about *both* shaping and responding to issues and concerns of the public and special interests in society. While very large-scale economic and social changes can affect the discourse or conception of what must be responded to or shaped,[60] the discourse itself is a result of past and present political practice and plays an important role in determining the outcome of change.

In the context of Canada's provinces, the major changes set out in this chapter are economic. They have been accompanied by substantial social changes, including massively increased literacy, per capita incomes and educational levels of the population, and the secularization of provincial society. The discourse in which these changes have occurred is that of the liberal democratic state, in which the state has been placed at the service of individual rights and freedoms, autonomy, and market exchange.

One of the results of these economic and social changes at the provincial level, when filtered through the prevailing political discourse, has been the large-scale expansion of the provincial state and the creation of miniature welfare states in each province.[61] As the figures in Table 12.2 show, by the year 2001 provincial governments alone spent on average 20 per cent of the provincial gross domestic product (GDP). That is, almost one out of every five dollars generated in the provinces in a calendar year was spent by the public sector. Of this, almost two-thirds was spent in the three areas which comprise the "classical" welfare state: education, health care, and social services. These figures do not include expenditures by closely related provincial agencies such as Crown corporations, municipalities, hospitals, and universities which, when added to these totals, raises the average percent of GDP accounted for by provincial governments to approximately 50 per cent.[62]

Table 12.2. Public Sector Spending by Province, 2001

		($ millions)				
	GDP	Total Govt. Expend- itures	Health, Education, Social Services Expenditures	Total Expend- itures as % GDP	HESS Expend- itures as % GDP	HESS Ex- penditures as % Total Govt. Expenditures
NF	13,000	4,038	2,477	31.1	19.1	61.3
PEI	3,174	998	553	31.4	17.4	55.4
NS	23,368	5,767	3,621	24.7	15.5	62.8
NB	18,739	5,404	3,118	28.8	16.6	57.7
QC	216,988	53,770	34,261	24.8	15.8	63.7
ON	430,957	67,158	47,052	15.6	10.9	70.1
MB	33,305	8,099	5,079	24.3	15.2	62.7
SK	30,836	6,884	4,199	22.3	13.6	61.0
AB	123,955	20,765	13,477	16.8	10.9	64.9
BC	125,534	26,809	19,078	21.4	15.2	71.2
Total	1,019,856	199,692	132,915	19.6	13.0	66.6

Source: Statistics Canada website:
<http://www.statcan.ca/english/Pgdb/Economy/Economic/econ50.htm> and
<http://www.statcan.ca/english/Pgdb/State/Government/govt08a.htm>.

This growth in public services is one of the major components of the overall increase in the service sector in all the provinces noted above. Two other phenomena account for virtually all the rest of the growth.[63]

One is the replacement of in-house production in firms by contracting out to other firms. This phenomena of increased specialization and division of labour in private companies is not new but has progressed to the point where, for example, automobile manufacturing companies now contract out virtually all of their financial and manufacturing activities, remaining as essentially final assembly and product producers and marketers. In most cases the contracting firms are much smaller than their predecessors, resulting in the appearance of growth in small business employment. These companies are much more vulnerable to economic fluctuations than large multinationals and their employees even more so.

A second factor which also relates to the growth of small business, but has a more dramatic day-to-day impact on the life of families and communities, is the commercialization of former "household" tasks such as day care, cleaning, haircuts, and food preparation. These activities have gradually come to be performed in the private small business sector. Although this transition has positively affected many households in that this work, traditionally undertaken by unpaid women, has been removed from the sphere of the family, the resulting private sector jobs tend to be low paid and, even in the private sector, predominantly female. The net effect of this is the creation of a large, usually low paid, and often part-time female labour force.[64]

These three activities—growth in the public sector, contracting out of elements of the manufacturing process, and commercialization of personal services—account for much of the growth in service sector employment noted above.

The Political Consequences of Service Sector-Based Provincial Political Economies

Not surprisingly given political economic theory, the changes outlined above in provincial occupational and social structures that have resulted in a transition to a service sector political economy have also generated several issues which have come, in one form or another, to dominate contemporary provincial political agendas.[65]

First, all of Canada's jurisdictions face several key gender issues. The movement of women into the service sector workforce in both the public and private sector has raised a whole host of issues related to the issue of gender equality, including demands for increased government action to ensure pay equity, an end to on and off the job sexual harassment, and the provision of high quality and accessible childcare for working families.

Second, each of Canada's provinces face many issues related to the growth of the small business sector and the critical role it plays in employment creation and destruction. While small businesses can be successful, they often require either explicit subsidies, such as low interest loans, or implicit subsidies, such as low minimum wage or low corporate tax rates, in order to successfully survive their start-up period. Despite the best intentions of their owners, such firms are inherently unstable and have a high failure rate, with negative consequences not only for the owners but for employees faced with real or anticipated job losses. If these problems are not going to have an overall negative effect on the economy in terms of lowering consumption rates, governments are faced with offsetting the costs of unemployment through various unemployment or social insurance schemes. Small businesses also rarely have the wherewithal required to train their workers, meaning that states must also pick up an increasing amount of the responsibility and cost for education, training, research, and development.

Both of these problems relates to a third: the issue of increasing government spending.[66] Whether this spending is funded through increased tax revenues or through deficit financing brings another problem to bear on governments: the reactions of taxpayers and lenders. However, the ultimate concern is not with how to finance increased government expenditures, but how and why the economies and societies of the provinces are developing so as to further both the need and demand for increased public services. How such needs are to be reconciled with taxpayers' concerns over government budgetary deficits and debt loads has been one of the most challenging and politically salient issues of contemporary provincial politics.[67]

Conclusion

This chapter has demonstrated that many of the stereotypes and myths of provincial politics have their origins in earlier periods of provincial history when provincial political economies were challenged by the realities of primary sector production. These myths have become increasingly dated, however, as the provinces have been transformed into very similar service sector economies. All of the provinces now have highly developed service sector political economies with approximately 70 per cent of the populace employed in a range of "tertiary" occupations.

In the past, most Canadian provinces were heavily reliant upon production from the *primary* sector of the economy, that is, from the essentially unprocessed natural resource or "staples" exports of fish, forest products, minerals, wheat, and energy products, which fueled much of Canada's growth in the late nineteenth and early twentieth centuries.[68] While in some provinces at various points in time upgrading natural resources into various kinds of finished products generated substantial employment and economic activity in the *secondary* or manufacturing sector of the economy,[69] by the late twentieth century all of the provinces had developed economies in which at least two out of every three gainfully employed person worked not in resource extraction or manufacturing but in a wide variety of tertiary or *service* sector occupations.[70]

While the service sector is an admittedly very loose category encompassing activities from construction and transportation to government administration and a host of commercial and personal services, as an occupational category it has several features which set it apart from the primary and secondary sectors and which have a significant impact on the day-to-day life of provincial residents. Unlike the primary sector, for example, service sector employment tends to be highly urbanized and to require some basic formal education. Unlike the manufacturing sector, it tends to be scattered in multiple small job sites, thus lacking the concentration in the workplace that allowed for the successful trade union organization characteristic of Canada's factories and resource towns in earlier periods. As this chapter has shown, many salient political issues in contemporary society are now framed by the particular characteristics of service sector occupations.

The implications for provincial politics of these converging service-driven political economies are manifold. High among them are: (1) the high salience of public sector issues such as public servant compensation levels and government deficits and spending practices; and (2) the high salience of service sector issues including those related to gender, part-time work, and family disruptions associated with jobs in the "new" economy.

Despite the ample empirical evidence concerning this transition from primary resource dependence to service sector activities over the course of the twentieth century, however, many students of provincial politics continue to cling to out-dated or purely mythological conceptions of provincial political economic life.[71] While there is no question that students of Canadian provincial politics should be aware of the historical nature and origins of the myths surrounding provincial political life, they should not let those myths blind them to the realities of contemporary Canadian provincial political economies. If the development of political institutions and the evolution of provincial public polices is to be properly understood, a grasp of the basic fundamentals of provincial political economy is essential.

Notes

1. William Carroll, "The Political Economy of Canada," in J. Curtis and L. Tepperman, eds., *Understanding Canadian Society* (Toronto: McGraw-Hill Ryerson, 1988).

2. Adam Przeworski, *The State and the Economy under Capitalism* (Chur, Switzerland: Harwood, 1990).

3. M. Howlett, A. Netherton, and M. Ramesh, *The Political Economy of Canada: An Introduction* (Toronto: Oxford University Press, 1999).

4. A. Shortt, and A.G. Doughty, eds. *Canada and Its Provinces* (Toronto: Glasgow Brook and Company, 1914).

5. Paul Howe, "Name That Premier: The Political Knowledge of Canadians, Past and Present," paper presented to the annual general meeting of the Canadian Political Science Association, Toronto, 2002.

6. S.J.R. Noel, *Politics in Newfoundland* (Toronto: University of Toronto Press, 1971).

7. James Hiller and Peter Neary, eds., *Newfoundland in the Nineteenth and Twentieth Centuries: Essays in Interpretation* (Toronto: University of Toronto Press, 1980); D.W. Prowse, *A History of Newfoundland From the English, Colonial, and Foreign Records* (London: Macmillan, 1895).

8. R.A. MacKay and S.A. Saunders, *Newfoundland Economic, Diplomatic and Strategic Studies* (Toronto: Oxford University Press, 1946); James Hiller and Peter Neary, eds., *Twentieth-Century Newfoundland: Explorations* (St. John's: Breakwater, 1993).

9. David Alexander, *Atlantic Canada and Confederation* (Toronto: University of Toronto Press, 1983); Raymond B. Blake, *Canadians at Last: Canada Integrates Newfoundland as a Province* (Toronto: University of Toronto Press, 1994).

10. Valerie A. Summers, *Regime Change in a Resource Economy: The Politics of Underdevelopment in Newfoundland Since 1825* (St. John's: Breakwater, 1995).

11. Douglas M. Brown, "Sea-Change in Newfoundland: From Peckford to Wells," in R.L. Watts and D.M. Brown, eds., *Canada: The State of the Federation 1990* (Kingston: Queen's University Institute of Intergovernmental Relations, 1990); Robert Paine, *Ayatollahs and Turkey Trots: Political Rhetoric in the New Newfoundland—Crosbie, Jamieson and Peckford* (St. John's: Breakwater, 1981); Valerie A. Summers, "Newfoundland: Resource Politics and Regime Change in the Federal Era, 1949–1991," in K. Brownsey and M. Howlett, eds., *The Provincial State: Politics in Canada's Provinces and Territories* (Toronto: Copp Clark Pitman, 1992) 9–31.

12. James Overton, "Towards a Critical Analysis of Neo-Nationalism in Newfoundland," in R.J. Brym and R.J. Sacouman, eds., *Underdevelopment and Social Movements in Atlantic Canada* (Toronto: New Hogtown Press, 1979) 219–50.

13. David A. Milne, "Prince Edward Island: Politics in a Beleaguered Garden," in Brownsey and Howlett, eds., *The Provincial State* 31–56; V. Smitheram, D. Milne, and S. Dasgupta, eds. *The Garden Transformed: Prince Edward Island 1945–1980* (Charlottetown: Ragweed Press, 1982).

14. Errol Sharpe, *A People's History of Prince Edward Island* (Toronto: Steel Rail Publishing, 1976); J.M. Bumsted, *Land, Settlement, and Politics on Eighteenth Century Prince Edward Island* (Montreal and Kingston: McGill-Queen's University Press, 1987); D.C. Harvey, "Early Settlement Conditions in Prince Edward Island," *Dalhousie Review* 11 (1932): 448–61.

15. Canada, *Development Plan for Prince Edward Island: A 15-year Federal-Provincial Program for Economic Expansion and Social Adjustment* (Ottawa: Department of Regional Economic Expansion, 1969).

16. L.G. Barrett, "Perspectives on Dependency and Underdevelopment in the Atlantic Region," *Canadian Review of Sociology and Anthropology* 17,3 (1980): 273–86; James Bickerton, *Nova Scotia, Ottawa, and the Politics of Regional Development* (Toronto: University of Toronto Press, 1990); Philip J. Wood, "Nova Scotia: Social Structure and Politics," in Brownsey and Howlett, eds., *The Provincial State* 57–80; and James Bickerton, "Nova Scotia: The Politics of Regime Change," in K. Brownsey and M. Howlett, eds., *The Provincial State in Canada: Politics in the Provinces and Territories* (Peterborough, ON: Broadview Press, 2001) 49–75.

17. T.W. Acheson, "The National Policy and the Industrialization of the Maritimes, 1880–1910," *Acadiensis*. 1 (1972); E.R. Forbes, *The Maritime Rights Movement 1919–1927* (Montreal and Kingston: McGill-Queen's University Press, 1985); S.A. Saunders, *The Economic History of the Maritime Provinces* (Saint John: Acadiensis, 1984).

18. Colin Howell, "The 1900s: Industry, Urbanization and Reform," in E.R. Forbes and D.A. Muise, eds., *The Atlantic Provinces in Confederation* (Toronto: University of Toronto Press, 1993); Nova Scotia, *Report of the Royal Commission on Provincial Development and Rehabilitation* (Halifax: King's Printer, 1944); Phillip A. Buckner, "The 1860s: An End and a Beginning," in P.A. Buckner and J.G. Reid, eds., *The Atlantic Region to Confederation: A History* (Toronto: University of Toronto Press, 1994) 360–86.

19. Michael Earle, ed., *Workers and the State in Twentieth Century Nova Scotia* (Fredericton: Gorsebrook Research Institute of Atlantic Canada Studies, 1989); Barbara Jamieson, ed., *Governing Nova Scotia* (Halifax: Dalhousie University School of Public Administration, 1984).

20. Hugh Mellon, "New Brunswick: The Politics of Reform," in Brownsey and Howlett, eds., *The Provincial State* 81–112; and Hugh Mellon, "The Challenge of New Brunswick Politics," in Brownsey and Howlett eds., *The Provincial State in Canada* 75–110. See also Hugh Thorburn, *Politics in New Brunswick* (Toronto: University of Toronto Press, 1961); Stephen H. Ullman, "Political Disaffection in the Province of New Brunswick: Manifestations and Sources," *American Review of Canadian Studies* (Summer 1990): 151–77; R.A. Young, "'and the people will sink into despair': Reconstruction in New Brunswick, 1942–52," *Canadian Historical Review* 69,2 (1988): 127–66.

21. W.S. MacNutt, *New Brunswick: A History 1784–1867* (Toronto: Macmillan, 1963); Graeme Wynn, *Timber Colony: A Historical Geography of 19th Century New Brunswick* (Toronto: University of Toronto Press, 1981); T.W. Acheson, "New Brunswick Agriculture at the End of the Colonial Era: A Reassessment," *Acadiensis* 22, 2 (1993): 5–26.

22. Arthur T. Doyle, *Front Benches and Back Rooms: A Story of Corruption, Muckraking, Raw Partisanship and Intrigue in New Brunswick* (Toronto: Green Tree Publishing, 1976); Calvin A. Woodward, *The History of New Brunswick Provincial Election Campaigns and Platforms 1866–1974* (Toronto: Micromedia, 1976).

23. Mellon; James L. Kenny, "'We Must Speculate to Accumulate!': Mineral Development and the Limits of State Intervention, New Brunswick, 1952–1960," *Acadiensis* 23,2 (1994): 94–123.

24. Michael Jenkin, *The Challenge of Diversity* (Ottawa: Science Council of Canada, 1983).

25. Donald J. Savoie and Ralph Winter, eds., *The Maritime Provinces: Looking to the Future* (Moncton: Canadian Institute for Research on Regional Development, 1993).

26. See Donald J. Savoie, *Pulling Against Gravity: Economic Development in New Brunswick During the McKenna Years* (Montreal: IRPP, 2001).

27. A.G. Gagnon and M. Montcalm, *Quebec: Beyond the Quiet Revolution* (Toronto: Nelson, 1990). See also Claude Jean Galipeau, "Quebec: Le Contre-Courant Québécois," in Brownsey and Howlett, eds., *The Provincial State* 113–46; K. McRoberts and D. Postgate, *Quebec: Social Change and Political Crisis* (Toronto: McClelland and Stewart, 1980); and Luc Bernier "The Beleaguered State: Quebec at the End of the 1990s," in Brownsey and Howlett, eds., *The Provincial State in Canada* 139–62.

28. Herbert Quinn, *The Union Nationale: Quebec Nationalism From Duplessis to Quebec's Quiet Revolution* (Toronto: University of Toronto Press, 1979); Bernard L. Vigod, *Quebec Before Duplessis: The Political Career of Louis Alexandre Taschereau* (Montreal and Kingston: McGill-Queen's University Press, 1986).

29. Paul Bouchard, *La Province de Quebec sous l'Union Nationale: 1936–1939; 1944–1956* (Quebec: Ateliers de l'action sociale, 1956).

30. Richard D. French, "Governing Without Business: The Parti Quebecois in Power," in V.V. Murray, ed., *Theories of Business-Government Relations* (Toronto: Trans-Canada Press, 1985) 159–80: R. Hudon, "The Parti Quebecois in Power: Institutionalization, Crisis Management and Decline," in H. Thorburn, ed., *Party Politics in Canada* (Scarborough: Prentice Hall, 1985) 220–33.

31. Richard Handler, *Nationalism and the Politics of Culture in Quebec* (Madison, WI: University of Wisconsin Press, 1993).

32. Guy Lachapelle, et al., *The Quebec Democracy: Structures, Processes and Politics* (Toronto: McGraw Hill, 1993).

33. As well as separatist sentiments. See Marc V. Levine, *The Reconquest of Montreal: Language Policy and Social Change in a Bilingual City* (Philadelphia, PA: Temple University Press, 1990); and especially Pierre Vallieres, *White Niggers of America* (Toronto: McClelland and Stewart, 1971).

34. Keith Brownsey and Michael Howlett, "Ontario: Class Structure and Political Alliances in an Industrialized Society," in Brownsey and Howlett, eds., *The Provincial State* 147–74; Donald C. MacDonald, ed., *Government and Politics of Ontario* (Toronto: Macmillan, 1985); H.V. Nelles, "Red Tied: Fin de Siècle Politics in Ontario," in M. Whittington and G. Williams, eds., *Canadian Politics in the 1990s* (Toronto: Nelson, 1990) 76–97: K.J. Rea, *The Prosperous Years: The Economic Years: The Economic History of Ontario 1939–75* (Toronto: University of Toronto Press, 1985); Graham White, ed., *The Government and Politics of Ontario* (Toronto: Nelson, 1990); F.F. Schindeler, *Responsible Government in Ontario* (Toronto: University of Toronto Press, 1969).

35. Christopher Armstrong, *The Politics of Federalism: Ontario's Relations with the Federal Government 1867–1941* (Toronto: University of Toronto Press, 1981).

36. Although long, this record of 42 years in government is second to that of the Liberal Party in Nova Scotia at the turn of the twentieth century. See Roger Graham, *Old Man Ontario: Leslie M. Frost* (Toronto: University of Toronto Press, 1990); Allan Kerr McDougall, *John P. Robarts, His Life and Government* (Toronto: University of Toronto Press, 1986).

37. Charles M. Johnston, *E.C. Drury: Agrarian Idealist* (Toronto: University of Toronto Press, 1986); Peter Oliver, *G. Howard Ferguson: Ontario Tory* (Toronto: University of Toronto Press, 1977).

38. Thomas Walkom, *Rae Days: The Rise and Fall of the NDP* (Toronto: Key Porter, 1994).

39. Daniel Drache, "The Way Ahead for Ontario," in D. Drache, ed., *Getting on Track: Social Democratic Strategies for Ontario* (Montreal and Kingston: McGill-Queen's University Press, 1992) 217–37; Bob Rae, *Ontario's Challenge* (Kingston: Industrial Relations Centre, Queen's University, 1992); and Robert MacDermid and Greg Albo, "Divided Province, Growing Protests: Ontario Moves Right," in Brownsey and Howlett, eds., *The Provincial State in Canada* 163–202.

40. Alex Netherton, "Manitoba: The Shifting Points of Politics: A Neo-Institutionalist Analysis," in Brownsey and Howlett, eds., *The Provincial State* 175–206; Paul Phillips, "Manitoba in the Agrarian Period: 1870–1940," in J. Silver and J. Hull, eds., *The Political Economy of Manitoba* (Regina: Canadian Plains Research Centre, 1990) 3–24; Nelson Wiseman, *Social Democracy in Manitoba* (Winnipeg: University of Manitoba Press, 1983).

41. Cy Gonick, "The Manitoba Economy Since World War II," in Silver and Hull, eds., 25–48; John Kendle, *John Bracken: A Political Biography* (Toronto: University of Toronto Press, 1979); Arthur Morton, *History of Prairie Settlement* (Toronto: Macmillan, 1938).

42. Alex Netherton, "Manitoba: The Shifting Points of Politics: A Neo-Institutionalist Analysis," in Brownsey and Howlett, eds., *The Provincial State* 175–206.

43. James A. McAllister, *The Government of Edward Schreyer: Democratic Socialism in Manitoba* (Montreal and Kingston: McGill-Queen's University Press, 1984).

44. Christopher Dunn and David Laycock, "Saskatchewan: Innovation and Competition in the Agricultural Heartland," in Brownsey and Howlett, eds., *The Provincial State* 207–42. See also Ken Rasmussen, "Saskatchewan: From Entrepreneurial State to Embedded State," in Brownsey and Howlett, eds., *The Provincial State in Canada* 241–76.

45. Vernon Fowke, *The National Policy and the Wheat Economy* (Toronto: University of Toronto Press, 1957); Vernon Fowke, *Canadian Agricultural Policy: The Historical Pattern* (Toronto: University of Toronto Press, 1978).

46. S.M. Lipset, *Agrarian Socialism: The Co-operative Commonwealth Federation in Saskatchewan—A Study in Political Sociology* (Berkeley, CA: University of California Press, 1959). Some vestiges of this tradition still exist in Saskatchewan's penchant for voluntarism and civic pride of which it has the highest levels in Canada. See Paul B. Reed and L. Kevin Selbee, "Canada's Civic Core: On the Disproportionality of Charitable Giving, Volunteering and Civic Participation," *Isuma* 2,2 (2001): 28–33.

47. It should also be recalled that simply having a large agricultural community in no way ensures that the political complexion of that community will be socialist. Other provinces with large agricultural communities (such as PEI in the modern era or most of the other provinces in earlier eras) never elected socialist or social democratic governments.

48. David Leadbetter, "An Outline of Capitalist Development in Alberta," in D. Leadbetter, ed., *Essays on the Political Economy of Alberta* (Toronto: New Hogtown Press, 1984) 1–76; C.B. MacPherson, *Democracy in Alberta* (Toronto: University of Toronto Press, 1962); Peter J. Smith, "Alberta: A Province Just Like Any Other?," in Brownsey and Howlett, eds., *The Provincial State* 243–64; Allan Tupper and Roger Gibbins, eds., *Politics in Alberta* (Edmonton: University of Alberta Press, 1992); and Peter J. Smith, "Alberta: Experiments in Governance—From Social Credit to the Klein Revolution," in Brownsey and Howlett, eds., *The Provincial State in Canada* 277–308.

49. J. Richards and L. Pratt, *Prairie Capitalism: Power and Influence in the New West* (Toronto: McClelland and Stewart, 1977).

50. John J. Barr, *The Dynasty: The Rise and Fall of Social Credit in Alberta* (Toronto: McClelland and Stewart, 1974).

51. Ian Urquhart and Larry Pratt, *The Last Great Forest: Japanese Multinationals and Alberta's Northern Forests* (Edmonton: NeWest Press, 1994).

52. See Mark Lisac, *The Klein Revolution* (Edmonton: NeWest Press, 1995); and Ian Urquhart, ed., *Assault on the Rockies: Environmental Controversies in Alberta* (Edmonton: Rowan Books, 1998).

53. E.R. Black, "British Columbia: The Politics of Exploitation," in R.A. Shearer, ed., *Exploiting Our Economic Potential: Public Policy and the British Columbia Economy* (Toronto: Holt Rinehart and Winston, 1968) 23–41.

54. Martin Robin, *The Rush for Spoils: The Company Province 1871–1933* (Toronto: McClelland and Stewart, 1972).

55. Michael Howlett and Keith Brownsey, "The New Reality and the Old Reality: Party Politics and Public Policy in British Columbia 1941–1987," *Studies in Political Economy* (1988); Michael Howlett and Keith Brownsey, "British Columbia: Public Sector Politics in a Rentier Resource Economy," in Brownsey and Howlett, eds., *The Provincial State* 265–96; and Michael Howlett and Keith Brownsey, "British Columbia: Politics in a Post-Staples Political Economy," in Brownsey and Howlett, eds., *The Provincial State in Canada* 309–34.

56. T.J. Barnes and R. Hayter, "Economic Restructuring, Local Development and Resource Towns: Forest Communities in Coastal British Columbia," *Regional Studies* 26 (1992): 647–63.

57. Rennie Warburton and David Coburn, eds., *Workers, Capital and the State in British Columbia: Selected Papers* (Vancouver: University of British Columbia Press, 1988); R. Warburton and R. Coburn, "The Rise of Non-Manual Labour in British Columbia," *BC Studies* 59 (1983): 5–27.

58. W.T. Easterbrook and H.G.J. Aitkin, *Canadian Economic History* (Toronto: Macmillan, 1956).

59. M. Howlett and M. Ramesh, *The Political Economy of Canada: An Introduction* (Toronto: McClelland and Stewart, 1992).

60. Stephen Hilgartner and Charles L. Bosk, "The Rise and Fall of Social Problems: A Public Arenas Model," *American Journal of Sociology* 94,1 (1981): 53–78; Burkhart Holzner and John H. Marx, *Knowledge Application: The Knowledge System in Society* (Boston, MA: Allyn and Bacon, 1979); David A. Rochefort and Roger W. Cobb, "Problem Definition, Agenda Access, and Policy Change," *Policy Studies Journal* 21,1 (1993): 56–71; Deborah A. Stone, *Policy Paradox and Political Reason* (Glenview, IL: Scott, Foresman, 1988); Deborah A. Stone, "Causal Stories and the Formation of Policy Agendas," *Political Science Quarterly* 104,2 (1989): 281–300.

61. J.A. McAllister, "Fiscal Capacity and Tax Effort: Explaining Public Expenditures in the 10 Canadian Provinces," paper presented to the annual meeting of the Canadian Political Science Association, Guelph, ON, 1984.

62. I.D. Horry and M. Walker, *Government Spending Facts* (Vancouver: Fraser Institute, 1991).

63. Herbert G. Grubel, ed., *Conceptual Issues in Service Sector Research: A Symposium* (Vancouver: Fraser Institute, 1987); Herbert G. Grubel and Michael A. Walker, *Service Industry Growth: Causes and Effects* (Vancouver: Fraser Institute, 1989); Richard B. McKenzie, "The Emergence of the 'Service Economy': Fact or Artifact," in Grubel, ed. 73–97.

64. Morley, Gunderson, Leon Muszynski, and Jennifer Keck, *Women and Labour Market Poverty* (Ottawa: Canadian Advisory Council on the Status of Women, 1990); and Leah F. Vosko, *Temporary Work: The Gendered Rise of a Precarious Employment Relationship* (Toronto: University of Toronto Press, 2000).

65. Harold Chorney and Phillip Hansen, "Neo-Conservatism, Social Democracy, and 'Province-Building': The Experience of Manitoba." *Canadian Review of Sociology and Anthropology* 22,1 (1985): 1–29.

66. Canadian Tax Foundation, *Provincial and Municipal Finances 1991* (Toronto: Canadian Tax Foundation, 1991); Irene Ip, "An Overview of Provincial Government Finance," in M. McMillan, ed., *Provincial Public Finances*, (Toronto: Canadian Tax Foundations, 1991).

67. See Christopher J. Bruce, Ronald D. Kneebone, and Kenneth J. McKenzie, eds., *A Government Reinvented: A Study of Alberta's Deficit Elimination Program* (Toronto: Oxford University Press, 1997); and Paul Boothe and Bradford Reid, eds., *Deficit Reduction in the Far West: The Great Experiment* (Edmonton: University of Alberta Press, 2001).

68. Harold A. Innis, "Significant Factors in Canadian Economic Development," *Canadian Historical Review* 18,4 (1937): 374–84; Arthur Lower, *The North American Assault on the Canadian Forest: A History of the Lumber Trade Between Canada and the United States* (Toronto: Ryerson, 1938); M.H. Watkins, "A Staple Theory of Economic Growth," *Canadian Journal of Economics and Political Science* 29,2 (1963): 141–58.

69. G.W. Bertram, "Historical Statistics on Growth and Structure of Manufacturing in Canada, 1870–1957," paper presented to the Canadian Political Science Association, Conference on Statistics, Ottawa, 1962.

70. David A. Warton, "The Service Industries in Canada 1946–1966," in V.R. Fuchs, ed., *Production and Productivity in the Service Industries* (New York: Columbia University Press, 1969).

71. On the detrimental aspects of conventional stereotypes see for example, R.A. Young, "Teaching and Research in Maritime Politics: Old Stereotypes and New Directions," *Journal of Canadian Studies* 21,2 (1986): 133–56; and E.R. Forbes, ed., *Challenging the Regional Stereotypes: Essays on the 20th Century Maritimes* (Fredericton: Acadiensis Press, 1989).

CHAPTER 13

Balancing Autonomy and Responsibility

The Politics of Provincial Fiscal and Tax Policies

GEOFFREY E. HALE

Money is, with propriety, considered as the vital principle of the body politic; as that which sustains its life and motion and enables it to perform its most essential function. A complete power, therefore, to procure a regular and adequate supply of revenue, as far as the resources of the community will permit, may be regarded as an indispensable ingredient in every constitution.[1]

Canada's ten provinces wield greater power and discretion through the working of their fiscal and tax policies than do the subnational governments of almost any other federal system of government. Provincial and territorial governments have accounted for a larger share of total government spending than the federal government since the early 1990s. Since the mid-1990s, provinces have also raised a larger overall share of public sector revenues than the federal government.

However, these figures conceal considerable differences in the political priorities which guide tax and spending decisions in individual provinces, the level of **fiscal autonomy**—the capacity of provinces to finance their activities and the degree to which they can exercise discretion in choosing how to do so—and the relative dependence of provincial governments on federal transfers and other policies.

This chapter examines the major internal and external factors that affect the fiscal autonomy and capacity of Canadian provinces. These factors include their economic structures, political cultures, and the impact of ongoing changes to fiscal federalism—matters largely beyond the control of individual governments, at least in the short run. However, they also include specific choices made by individual governments: past and present political priorities, administrative decisions, and the steps taken in areas within provinces' jurisdiction to manage the economic shocks of recent years and to promote greater fiscal and economic sustainability in future.

This chapter has three main sections. It begins by examining the major structures and components of provincial fiscal and tax policies. It considers several major factors that have shaped the evolution of provincial fiscal and tax policies and the effects these trends have had on provinces' abilities to manage their own fiscal priorities when they choose to do so—a key element of fiscal autonomy. The varying levels of provincial public services and the choices made by provinces to finance these services reflect both the widely different political cultures and priorities of individual provinces and the effects of transfer federalism on spending levels in different provinces.

The second section addresses the structures and politics of **fiscal federalism**—the structures and processes for sharing revenues and spending responsibilities between different levels of government. Constitutional precedents, court decisions, the willingness of provincial premiers to defend provincial powers against federal encroachment, the relative solvency of both levels of government, and the relevance of regional issues to federal policies and priorities have all played major roles in the evolution of the fiscal balance of powers between federal and provincial governments.

The third section outlines the evolution—and growing diversity—of provincial fiscal and tax policies in recent years in response to changes in the political and economic environments. It outlines the resort of some provinces to **fiscal rules** to help provinces adapt to economic fluctuations and exercise greater political discretion in setting priorities. It also summarizes current debates over **fiscal imbalance** and **fiscal sustainability** as federal and provincial governments continue to spar over tax and spending priorities, and the widely differing capacities of Canada's provinces to finance comparable levels of public services.

Box 13.1. Introduction to "Fiscalese": A Note on Terminology

As with "legalese," it is easier to understand taxation and public finance issues if one develops a working knowledge of "fiscalese." The federal Department of Finance maintains a fairly thorough glossary of technical and organizational terms related to tax and transfer system, fiscal and economic policy issues on its website at <http://www.fin.gc.ca/gloss/gloss-e.html>.

A glossary at the end of this chapter defines some of the more important terms contained herein.

Balanced budget legislation	Benefit-related taxation
Budget surplus	Budget deficit
Contingency funds	Cost recovery
Debt	Debt service charges
Effective income tax rate	Expenditure-driven budgeting
Federal-provincial tax collection agreement	Federal spending power
	Fiscal autonomy
Fiscal capacity	Fiscal federalism
Fiscal illusion	Fiscal imbalance
Fiscal rules	Fiscal sustainability
Marginal income tax rate	Net debt
Own-source revenues	Payroll taxes
Political Business Cycle	Progressive tax rate structure
Proportional tax rate structure (also "progressivity")	Revenue-driven budgeting
	Stabilization funds
Vertical fiscal imbalance	

The Structures of Provincial Public Finance

Governments typically outline their major policy priorities—particularly how they intend to raise and use taxpayers' money through various forms of taxation and spending—in annual budget speeches made by federal and provincial ministers of finance. However, the vast size and scope of government activities means that most budget speeches involve relatively modest changes to existing policies and programs. The main fiscal building blocks for public sector budgets remain relatively consistent from year to year, although accumulated changes may result in bigger shifts in the overall size and distribution of government revenues and spending priorities over time.

Provincial budgets involve the interaction of six major factors, all of which vary to some degree between provinces. These are:

1. own-source revenues: revenues generated by provincial governments under their own constitutional and legislative authority;

2. direct provincial spending: spending by provincial governments on the provision of goods, services, and transfers to individuals and businesses (not including transfer payments to other levels of government);

3. transfers from other levels of government: primarily conditional and unconditional grants from the federal government;

4. transfers to other levels of government: primarily transfers to municipal governments and school boards;

5. debt service changes: interest payments on the provincial debt (not including those of commercial Crown corporations); and

6. net fiscal balance: the overall balance between annual revenues and spending.

We will now examine each of these factors and their importance both in shaping and reflecting provincial budgetary and tax policies.

1. Own-source revenues

Provincial governments have constitutional rights to raise revenues from a variety of sources, many of which are shared with the federal government. Major sources of provincial revenues include:

- personal and corporate income taxes;
- general sales taxes (levied on a wide range of goods and, sometimes, services);
- sales taxes on specific products such as alcohol, tobacco, and gasoline;
- profits from provincial liquor and gambling monopolies;
- payroll and social insurance taxes, usually to finance provincial health insurance and social insurance programs such as Workers' Compensation;
- taxes on property and other forms of capital;
- income from the sale of licences and permits to individuals and businesses;
- income from the sales of other goods and services; and

- "investment income," primarily from natural resource revenues and provincial investment funds.

Both the wide differences among provinces in levels and types of economic activity and policy choices of individual governments make it difficult to speak of a
"typical province" in describing provincial revenue sources. Table 13.1 summarizes major sources of income for Canada's ten provinces in 2003-04, measured
on a "financial management system" basis to standardize variations in accounting methods.

Provincial tax bases and the levels of revenue extracted from them reflect
both the economic structures of individual provinces and deliberate political
choices made by governments. These choices include the tax rates for individuals
and corporations; the decision to shift a larger portion of the tax burden from
income to consumption taxes (or vice versa) or to provincial liquor and gambling revenues; and the degree to which certain government activities should
be largely self-funding, either through **benefit-related taxation** or their delivery
through arms-length Crown corporations and agencies. The greater the number
of revenue sources, the less vulnerable governments become to a public backlash
against excessive tax rates on any one form of economic activity.

PERSONAL INCOME TAXES

Personal income taxes (PITs) are the largest single revenue source for both levels
of government and eight of ten provinces (except Alberta and PEI).[2] Specific PIT
revenue shares vary widely across provinces. PITs accounted for 38 per cent of
provincial revenues in Quebec, which collects its own personal income taxes,
33 per cent in Nova Scotia, and between 19 and 32 per cent in other provinces.
Until 2001, provincial income taxes in all provinces except Quebec were levied
as a percentage of federal income taxes payable. Since then, provinces have established their own tax rate structures, with varying degrees of **progressivity** as
income rises.

Two major factors account for these variations: the relative affluence of a
province's citizens and the political choices of their governments. Income taxes
paid tends to increase with levels of employment and income. Average family
incomes in 2002 ranged from $55,400 in Newfoundland and Labrador (hereafter
referred to as Newfoundland), 24 percent below the national average of $73,200
to $81,400 in Ontario—11 percent above the national average.[3]

Federal and most provincial income taxes have a **progressive tax rate structure** which provides for higher tax rates for individual taxpayers as their taxable
incomes increase. Appendix 13.1 summarizes 2005 **marginal income tax rates**—
the tax rate levied on each additional dollar of income earned—by province and
territory. However, since federal and provincial tax systems also provide for a
variety of income tax deductions and credits to accommodate a variety of discretionary and non-discretionary expenses faced by taxpayers, it is often more

Table 13.1. Provincial Own-Source Revenues 2003–04

Financial Management System

	All provinces, territories	NF	PEI	NS	NB	QC	ON	MB	SK	AB	BC	Terri- tories
Income taxes[1]	34.7%	33.4%	29.5%	36.6%	27.6%	40.0%	38.7%	32.6%	25.3%	27.8%	24.4%	-33.3%
Consumption taxes[2]	29.5%	40.0%	41.7%	38.2%	34.9%	26.8%	36.1%	30.4%	28.2%	13.2%	29.9%	43.3%
Property, related taxes[3]	4.7%	0.3%	7.7%	1.7%	9.4%	3.6%	3.4%	5.8%	10.5%	5.0%	9.2%	7.6%
Other taxes[4]	8.3%	3.9%	4.2%	3.6%	3.4%	12.9%	9.1%	7.4%	7.4%	4.3%	2.5%	10.5%
Health and drug insurance premiums	1.6%	0.0%	0.0%	0.2%	0.0%	1.3%	0.0%	0.0%	0.0%	4.1%	5.7%	0.0%
Contributions to social security plans[5]	3.8%	6.0%	3.6%	3.4%	3.4%	3.6%	4.3%	2.3%	2.7%	4.2%	4.2%	10.0%
Sales of goods and services	3.7%	5.2%	8.0%	7.6%	4.3%	4.0%	3.7%	3.2%	5.9%	1.9%	2.8%	32.9%
Investment income[6]	13.5%	7.5%	5.1%	8.5%	16.7%	7.3%	4.4%	18.1%	24.3%	40.5%	20.7%	28.6%
Other own-source revenues	0.3%	0.3%	0.2%	0.1%	0.3%	0.4%	0.3%	0.2%	0.4%	0.2%	0.5%	1.0%
Total own-source revenues	100.0%	100.0%	100.0%	100.0%	100.0%	100.0%	100.0%	100.0%	100.0%	100.0%	100.0%	100.0%

1. Personal and corporate income taxes.

2. General and goods-specific sales taxes (e.g., alcohol, tobacco, gasoline), plus remitted liquor and gambling profits.

3. General property taxes allocated at discretion of provinces; land transfer taxes; capital taxes on corporations.

4. Payroll taxes, often used to finance health and/or education, motor vehicle licences, natural resources taxes; insurance premium taxes; liquor and other licences and permits; business fines, penalties and donations.

5. Contributions to Workers' Compensation Boards, non-autonomous pension plans, and other social insurance plans.

6. Natural resource royalties; remitted profits of government enterprises; interest and other investment income.

Source: Statistics Canada, Public Sector Statistics, Cat. #68-213, 32-33 (Ottawa: Statistics Canada, 2004); author's calculations.

useful to compare **effective tax rates**—the percentage of total personal or family income paid in taxes.

Quebec and three of the Atlantic Provinces have the most sharply progressive income tax systems, with relatively high taxes on lower income families and top tax rates taking effect on individual incomes between $55,000 and $65,000. Alberta imposes a proportional (or single-rate) tax of 10 per cent for all residents on taxable income over a relatively high threshold of $14,523 in 2005. Combined federal-provincial marginal tax rates on individuals with taxable incomes of $35,000 vary between 25.15 per cent (Ontario) to 32.16 per cent (Newfoundland). Top combined marginal rates vary from 39 per cent in Alberta to 53 per cent in Quebec. However, wide differences exist between provinces in levels of tax-exempt income, tax credits, or income supplements paid to low income families, and the incomes at which top tax rates are applied.

CONSUMPTION AND OTHER TAXES

As noted in Table 13.1, consumption taxes on a variety of products and services are the second largest set of provincial revenue sources. Most provinces, except for Alberta, levy general sales taxes either on retail sales or in conjunction with the federal Goods and Services Tax (GST).[4] Provinces also enjoy substantial revenues from taxes on alcohol, tobacco, and gasoline, as well as profits from liquor and gambling businesses that serve as *de facto* consumption taxes. Consumption taxes tend to account for a higher share of government revenues in Ontario and Atlantic Canada (35 to 42 per cent in 2003-04), and a lower share in Quebec and Western Canada. The latter tend to generate a larger share of their revenues from social insurance taxes and natural resource royalties. During the 1990s, most provinces exploited their monopoly over the marketing of liquor and gambling to finance deficit reduction and, later, tax reductions in other areas.

For example, Alberta, Saskatchewan, and BC all have relatively high levels of resource revenues, particularly from oil and gas. This dependence can be a two-edged sword when global energy prices drop unexpectedly, leaving energy-producing provinces at risk of significant budget deficits. As noted later in this chapter, sharp year-over-year increases in provincial resource revenues often result in reduced federal equalization payments. Ontario and Alberta have the largest concentrations of corporate head offices and business profits, enabling them to generate much higher corporate income tax (CIT) revenues than other provinces, at least during periods of relative prosperity.

In recent years, several provinces have centralized control over the funding of primary and secondary (K-12) education, along with responsibility for the collection of all or part of property tax revenues traditionally collected by local school boards.[5] Most provinces also derive substantial incomes from the sale of goods and services, often through Crown corporations, and other investments.

As a result, the variety and complexity of provincial tax systems suggest that the fairest way of making interprovincial comparisons is to calculate the total tax cost across provinces for taxpayers in comparable circumstances. Table 13.2 indicates the range of **effective tax rates** paid by representative lower, middle, and upper income families across Canada and shows that the percentage of total income paid in five major provincial taxes varied sharply between provinces in 2004. Although these estimates do not permit an exact comparison among all income groups, they indicate that families earning about $30,000 a year pay a larger proportion of their total incomes in the five major taxes than families earning $60,000 (slightly above the national median family income) in eight out of ten provinces, with Alberta and Quebec the exceptions. Effective tax rates for families earning $90,000 are marginally higher than those for families earning $60,000 in six provinces, at least one to two percentage points higher in three—Manitoba, New Brunswick, and Quebec—and somewhat less in BC (see Appendix 13.2.) The overall impression of this analysis is that the regressive effect of payroll, sales, and property taxes in most provinces largely, if not completely, offsets the effects of progressive income tax rate structures. Ironically, the two exceptions to this pattern are low-tax Alberta, which adopted a proportional or single-rate tax system in 2001, and high-tax Quebec.

Table 13.2. Effective Tax Rates Vary Widely Across Provinces

Two-income family of four earning:	Lowest effective tax rate	Median	Highest effective tax rate
$30,000	5.0% (AB)	13.3% SK/NS	17.0% (MB)
$60,000	9.2% (AB)	11.7% SK/PEI	17.2% (QC)
$90,000	9.3% (AB)	12.4% ON/NS	19.3% (QC)

Source: author's calculations, based on comparisons from 2004-05 BC budget, based on combination of personal income taxes (less child benefits); sales, fuel, property, and payroll taxes; and health premiums.

However, perhaps the most significant political choice governments make is that between **revenue-driven budgeting**—the decision to base provincial spending priorities and decisions on available and projected revenues—and **expenditure-driven budgeting**—deciding what levels of services and transfers they wish to provide and adjusting revenue and borrowing decisions in response to these targets.

2. Direct provincial spending

Provincial and territorial governments spent $258.0 billion in 2003-04, including transfers to other governments—about 55 per cent of total government spending in Canada—as measured by Statistics Canada's Financial Management System.[6] Spending on health care accounts for the largest (and fastest growing) share of provincial spending at an average of 33 per cent, followed by education (20 per cent), social services (16 per cent), and interest payments on provincial debts (11.3 per cent). However, these proportions vary widely from province to province. Table 13.3 summarizes the distribution of spending, by sector, in each province for the 2003-04 fiscal year.

Another way to compare provincial spending levels is to examine per capita spending levels (adjusted for differences in population) in each province. Table 13.4 compares provincial spending per capita overall and in each of the four biggest areas of provincial spending. Per capita interprovincial spending variations are greatest when comparing interest charges on provincial debts, which range from 25.4 per cent of the national average in Alberta to 151.6 per cent in Manitoba. Debt charges also accounted for a significantly higher than average share of provincial spending in Nova Scotia, New Brunswick, and Quebec in 2003-04. Alberta's decision to use most of its surpluses to pay off debt after balancing its budget in 1993-94 has allowed it to redirect resulting savings towards increased spending and lower taxes in recent years.

The smallest variation is found in per capita health spending, which ranges from 115.2 per cent of the national average in Newfoundland to 95.4 per cent in Ontario. The varying sizes of local government sectors across Canada (and the degrees to which municipal government activities are financed by provincial governments) tend to further complicate interprovincial comparisons of the size of governments.

Variations in provincial spending levels and priorities are shaped by several factors, including a province's political culture and the environment for party competition, the relative availability of federal transfers, and overall debt load relative to population and provincial incomes.

Overall levels of public spending tend to be higher in provinces with a history of social democratic governments favouring high levels of government intervention and income redistribution. These factors contribute to relatively higher per capita spending levels in provinces such as Quebec, Newfoundland, Saskatchewan, Manitoba, and, during the 1990s, BC. Public expectations of activist governments tend to encourage higher spending levels by small-c conservative governments in these provinces as well.

Overall spending levels, adjusted for differences of population, range from 8 to 23 per cent over the national average in four of the five provinces with higher levels of dependence on federal transfers: Manitoba, New Brunswick, PEI, and Newfoundland. However, these higher spending levels are offset in New Brunswick, PEI, and, to a lesser degree, Manitoba, by provincial policies which contribute to much lower levels of local government spending.

3. Transfers from other levels of government

Historically, federal transfer payments to the provinces to compensate for differences in levels of provincial economic development and **fiscal capacity**—the

Table 13.3. Distribution of Provincial Spending, 2003–04

	All provinces, territories	NF	PEI	NS	NB	QC	ON	MB	SK	AB	BC
Total expenditures	100.0	100.0	100.0	100.0	100.0	100.0	100.0	100.0	100.0	100.0	100.0
Health	32.9	30.7	29.1	35.4	30.7	28.3	36.5	31.5	30.2	32.7	36.2
Education	20.0	21.8	20.7	19.1	21.1	19.8	18.6	17.3	15.7	25.3	22.0
Social services	16.0	13.0	9.9	11.8	11.1	17.6	16.9	15.2	13.8	15.6	14.4
Debt charges	11.3	12.5	9.9	17.6	14.5	13.9	11.8	15.7	11.4	2.9	8.2
Resource conservation and industrial development	4.9	3.2	9.5	3.4	3.8	5.1	2.3	4.5	12.1	10.4	5.7
Transportation and communication	4.2	7.2	8.0	3.5	8.6	3.8	3.4	3.4	4.1	4.3	5.6
Protection of persons and property	3.9	4.5	3.3	4.0	3.0	3.5	4.3	4.1	4.2	2.8	3.7
General government services	1.8	2.0	4.8	0.9	1.6	2.2	1.4	2.1	2.0	1.5	1.4
Other spending	5.1	5.1	4.9	4.1	5.6	5.7	4.9	6.2	6.5	4.6	2.8

Source: Statistics Canada, *Public Sector Statistics*, Cat. # 68-213 (Ottawa: Statistics Canada, July 2004) 32–33; author's calculations.

Table 13.4. Provincial Government Spending Per Capita, 2003–04

vs. National Average	All provinces, territories ($ per capita)	NF	PEI	NS	NB	QC	ON	MB	SK	AB	BC
Total expenditures	7330.1	123.4	113.6	95.0	107.8	114.5	86.1	108.7	110.1	98.3	100.9
Health	2411.8	115.2	100.4	102.3	100.7	98.6	95.4	104.0	101.1	97.7	111.0
Education	1467.9	134.0	117.2	90.9	113.6	113.2	79.9	94.0	86.3	124.1	110.8
Social services	1170.7	113.7	70.4	70.4	75.1	125.9	91.2	103.4	94.9	95.9	90.9
Debt charges	825.6	136.8	99.8	148.7	138.5	141.6	89.9	151.6	111.6	25.4	73.6
Local government spending per capita	2598.9	54.9	42.0	66.2	49.4	87.6	110.5	75.5	97.1	89.5	73.3
Provincial and local gov't spending/capita	9929.0	105.5	94.8	87.5	92.5	107.5	92.5	100.0	106.7	96.0	93.7

Source: Statistics Canada, *Public Sector Statistics*, Cat. # 68-213 (Ottawa: Statistics Canada, 2004); author's calculations.

relative ability to raise revenues—have accounted for between 15 and 20 per cent of overall provincial revenues.

However, there are major differences in relative levels of provincial dependence on federal transfers between the so-called "have" provinces of Ontario and Alberta; "have less" provinces, such as Quebec, BC, Saskatchewan, and Manitoba; and the traditionally "have not" provinces of Atlantic Canada. Larger provinces tend to enjoy a greater range of fiscal options than smaller ones, reflecting their larger populations, more diversified economies, and the broader and deeper tax bases that go with them. These disparities are reflected in the fact that five provinces still depend on Ottawa for more than 30 per cent of their revenues. This dependence contributes to a continuing federal role in provincial finances and priorities through transfer programs and the unilateral exercise of the **federal spending power**.

Table 13.5 notes the fluctuation of federal transfers as a share of provincial revenues since the early 1980s. Combined with the rapid growth of provincial revenues during the mid-1990s, federal transfers dropped from 22.7 per cent of total provincial revenues in 1992-93 to 14.9 per cent in 1997-98, before rebounding to 18.2 per cent in 2003-04. The major structures of **fiscal federalism**—the interaction of federal and provincial powers and policies on issues of taxation and spending activity—will be discussed later in this chapter.

Table 13.5. Transfer Federalism and Provincial Income

	1982–83	1992–93	1997–98	2003–04
All provinces, territories	22.6%	22.7%	14.9%	18.2%
NF	49.8%	47.0%	52.1%	38.5%
PEI	50.0%	42.6%	37.1%	38.4%
NS	45.9%	40.5%	43.3%	34.9%
NB	45.4%	43.4%	37.2%	35.3%
QC	26.1%	21.6%	14.1%	18.1%
ON	17.8%	18.1%	9.7%	14.5%
MB	38.1%	38.7%	32.8%	34.4%
SK	15.2%	29.8%	10.7%	15.8%
AB	10.6%	17.2%	6.7%	11.3%
BC	15.8%	14.9%	9.1%	13.4%

Source: Canada, *Fiscal Reference Tables* (Ottawa: Department of Finance, October 2004); author's calculations.

4. Transfers to other levels of government

Under Canada's Constitution, local governments such as municipalities and school boards are "creatures of the provinces," with legal authority and responsibilities assigned under provincial legislation. These arrangements vary too widely between provinces to be described in detail here.

As noted in Table 13.4, local governments play a much more limited role—and account for much smaller levels of spending—in the four Atlantic Provinces, Manitoba, and BC, than they do in Ontario or Saskatchewan. Transfers from other governments (mainly provincial) averaged about 22.5 per cent of local revenues in 2003.[7]

Most provinces took greater responsibility for financing primary and secondary education during the 1990s. Six—BC, Alberta, Manitoba, Ontario, New Brunswick, and PEI—levy province-wide property taxes to pay a portion of these costs, resulting in much diminished autonomy for local school boards.[8]

However, several provinces also offloaded significant responsibilities to municipalities during the 1990s, contributing to sharp increases in local taxation and user fees for municipal services. These practices reflected a general trend towards the commercialization of public services which lend themselves to greater or lesser degrees of **cost recovery** from citizens as consumers, based either on prices related to costs of production or collected through various forms of **benefit-related taxation**.

5. Debt and related interest costs

Provincial tax and spending decisions are not just the product of current political choices. They also reflect the legacy of past decisions, particularly, the cumulative impact of provincial **debt** and related interest payments on provincial budgets. The larger the share of provincial revenues or spending accounted for by **debt service charges**—the cost of interest payments on public debt—the more that governments face the trade-offs of having to increase taxes or reduce spending on current public services. Governments whose debts grow faster than the economy that supports them over an extended period run the risk of not being able to sustain existing levels of public services.

Provinces with steadily growing populations, such as Ontario and BC, have the capacity to carry higher debt loads to finance the construction of public infrastructure, including schools, hospitals, roads, transit systems, sewers, and parks. Demand for these services is driven in part by population growth.[9] For provinces with stable or stagnant populations, increased debt loads may simply defer taxation to pay for current services. This problem is compounded for provinces, such as Newfoundland or Saskatchewan, whose populations have declined in recent years or whose labour forces are expected to shrink as the "baby boom" generation approaches retirement after 2010.

The high deficits of the early 1990s resulted in sharp increases in provincial debts. The average provincial **net debt** per capita—the value of provincial government debts minus assets for each resident—increased by an average of 60 per cent between 1992 and 1997, before declining slightly in the late 1990s. Appendix 13.3 outlines changes in levels of provincial net debt (liabilities minus provincial assets) relative to population and overall provincial levels of indebtedness in the

1990s. These levels range from more than $16,000 per Newfoundlander and just under $12,000 in Nova Scotia and Quebec to about $3,800 in BC and net *assets* of $3,279 in Alberta.

Some governments have responded to this problem by resorting to dubious bookkeeping methods, such as shifting debt to Crown corporations without taking the necessary steps to generate new revenues or to reduce their operating losses. However, some exercised considerably more fiscal discipline than others. Alberta used its energy windfalls of the mid- and late-1990s to pay down its net debt, so that the value of its assets is now greater than the debt accumulated to pay for them. Saskatchewan also experienced a significant fiscal turnaround during the 1990s by balancing annual budgets and selling off assets in some of the province's Crown corporations to pay down debt. However, several provinces continue to experience significant debt challenges limiting their capacity to maintain or expand public services, particularly Newfoundland, Nova Scotia, and Quebec.

6. Net fiscal balance

All the factors discussed above contribute to the government's annual **budget surplus** or **deficit**—the excess or shortfall of revenues compared with expenditures in its annual financial statements. Governments' commitments to balanced budgets have taken on increased political and symbolic importance in recent years as most governments struggled to reduce large-scale deficits, usually through some combination of increased revenues and reduced spending.

Requiring balanced budgets as a matter of law or policy provides a relatively simple, symbolic "bottom line" that governments can use to demonstrate good management skills with taxpayers' money—or at least the capacity to "live within their (citizens') means." The reality, as with many issues, is a lot more complicated, particularly as balanced budget rules can encourage governments to use creative accounting procedures and other forms of **fiscal illusion** to achieve desired results.

Although balanced budgets may be symbolically important—and their absence, particularly in the form of chronic deficits, can reduce the political choices available to governments and their citizens over time—perhaps the most important effect of a balanced budget policy is to impose discipline on governments by forcing them to set clear tax and spending priorities and to justify those priorities to their citizens. These issues will be addressed later in the chapter in discussions of fiscal rules and the federal-provincial debate over "fiscal imbalance."

The Politics of Fiscal Federalism

Fiscal and tax policies do not occur in a vacuum. On one level, they are a by-product of the constitutional authority shared between governments in Canada's federal system, court decisions which have extended or constrained the exercise of that authority, the past actions and commitments of governments, and the public expectations they have helped to create. On another, they reflect the ability of governments to promote a healthy and growing economy that can expand their **fiscal capacity**—the ability of governments to finance, expand, and maintain valued public services—without undermining the living standards of their citizens.

This section examines the institutional context for provincial fiscal and tax policies and the system of fiscal federalism with which it is inextricably entwined. It also addresses three major elements of Canada's system of **fiscal federalism**— the structures and processes for sharing revenues and spending responsibilities between different levels of government:

1. the division of taxation and spending powers under the *Constitution Act* of 1867 and subsequent amendments;
2. the major structures and processes of transfer federalism, including federal equalization payments and other cash transfers to provinces and territories; and
3. the federal-provincial tax collection agreements, including provisions for "tax point transfers" as an alternative approach to revenue sharing.

1. Constitutional issues and competing visions of federalism

Canada's 1867 constitution, as interpreted by the courts, acknowledges the provincial governments as sovereign equals to the federal government with a broad range of legislative competence. A broad interpretation of provincial powers over "property and civil rights" in section 92(13) of the *BNA Act*, along with ownership of natural resources and public property noted in sections 109 and 117 and reinforced in section 92A, gives the provinces broad powers over economic development.[10] Section 92(2) gives provinces the authority to raise "Direct Taxation within the Province in order to raise Revenue for Provincial Purposes." Provincial governments have primary jurisdiction over hospitals, charitable and social services, education, intraprovincial transportation (i.e., highways), municipal institutions, and other major spending fields.[11] However, the federal government may influence provincial priorities through its use of the **federal spending power**—its capacity to make spending decisions in areas of provincial jurisdiction and to set conditions on its transfers to other levels of government.

While the federal government may "raise money by any mode or system of taxation" under section 91(3), the provinces' power to impose direct taxes under section 92(2) entitles them to levy income and sales taxes on individuals, businesses, and other legal persons. Other provincial taxing powers derive from section 92(5), relating to "the management and sale of the public lands belonging to the province and of the timber and wood thereon," and a wide variety of licence fees under section 92(9). Under section 125, "no lands or property belonging to Canada or any province shall be liable to taxation." This section precludes one level of government from taxing another. As a result, most major sources of revenue are shared by both senior levels of government. The federal government collects between 60 and 70 per cent of personal and corporate income taxes, while over half of consumption tax revenues, both general and targeted sales taxes, are collected by the provinces.[12] However, the overall ratio of provincial/local own-source revenues to federal revenues has fluctuated around 55/45 since 1978 (56/44 in 2003-04).[13]

The evolution of fiscal federalism since the 1940s has often reflected the efforts of federal and provincial politicians to work around formal constitutional structures in response to competing political priorities and visions of Canada as a political community—or "community of communities." Banting and Boadway have suggested three broad approaches to the politics of federalism as they related to the sharing of fiscal and social responsibility among Canadians.[14]

The first approach is based on a "predominantly Canada-wide sharing community."[15] This outlook gives a dominant position to the federal government in "ensur(ing) that important social programs (are) available in all provinces and territories on fairly comparable terms" through the use of a variety of policy tools.[16] The practical effect of this approach is to subordinate provincial priorities to federal ones and increase provinces' fiscal dependence on the federal government.

This approach has considerable support in provinces that already have relatively high levels of fiscal dependence on Ottawa, as long as safeguards are in place to maintain existing rates of growth in federal subsidies over the medium and long term. Subsidy dependence tends to reinforce incentives for provincial politicians to increase spending on services provided to their own citizens, while enabling them to shift a larger share of the responsibility for raising revenues to the federal government when the time comes to pay for that spending.

The "Canada-wide sharing approach" is consistent with the idea of "expenditure-driven budgeting," but only if there is a consensus between federal and provincial governments on fiscal and social policy priorities and constraints. Provinces cannot expect to set spending levels independently of revenues, with Ottawa making up the difference, unless they are prepared to concede much greater federal influence over their fiscal priorities and decisions. Similarly, the federal government cannot expect to shape provincial priorities through its manipulation of the terms of shared-cost programs and then unilaterally withdraw from medium-term commitments when circumstances change. The failure of both levels of government to address these contradictions directly led to unilateral policy changes and efforts at political "blame-shifting" by both levels of government during the 1980s and 1990s.

The second approach suggests a "predominantly provincial sharing community." It emphasizes both federal traditions of equal and autonomous provincial communities with a capacity for self-government and the direct accountability of provincial governments to their own citizens rather than to a federal paymaster. Ottawa's role is limited to equalizing provincial fiscal capacities and to promoting reduced barriers to mobility between provinces by individual Canadians. Noel has noted that this approach can incorporate more extensive or limited approaches to income redistribution through the expansion or targeting of welfare state programs, depending on the political orientation of individual governments.[17]

However, while this approach offers provinces greater potential autonomy, it also forces them to accept full political responsibility for the fiscal outcomes of their own decisions. Historically, both federalist and sovereignist governments in Quebec have been willing and anxious to accept that responsibility, while at the same time demanding that Ottawa "vacate" some of its taxing authority in order to help them do so. Unilateral changes to federal transfer policies have also contributed to support for a more decentralized approach to fiscal federalism in Ontario and Alberta, whose taxpayers have long subsidized federal transfers to other provinces. However, in practice, the heavy dependence of most "have less" provinces on federal transfers has prevented the emergence of an interprovincial consensus on greater fiscal decentralization.

The third approach is a "dual sharing community." Federal and provincial governments share responsibility for financing and providing services while allowing for variations in provincial priorities and approaches to service delivery. This approach allows governments to combine some of the benefits of the other two alternatives, although at the risk of periodic federal-provincial bickering. The practical result is that the ratio between provincial/local and federal spending in Canada has been roughly 60/40 for most of the period since 1971 (62/38 in 2001).[18] Both levels of government have sought to manage the relationship in ways that are calculated to give them greater fiscal discretion, often at the expense of the other.[19]

The constitutional division of powers, and the "fiscal gap" between federal and provincial spending and revenue levels resulting from the ways in which it has been applied in practice, has several practical implications for provincial governments. Some system of federal-provincial transfers is necessary to enable provinces to provide roughly comparable levels of public services to Canadians while allowing them to answer to their own citizens when balancing tax and spending decisions and setting priorities. Provincial acceptance of federal involvement in areas of provincial jurisdiction—and with it a greater influence over provincial policies and priorities—is directly linked to the growth of cash transfers with overall levels of public spending.

Some degree of tax policy coordination is also necessary if Canadians are not to be subject to conflicting tax rules imposed by competing governments. Ottawa has been also forced to accommodate Quebec's determination to exercise full control over tax and spending policies within its constitutional jurisdiction while exploiting political differences among other provinces in order to preserve and expand its own role in delivering social policies. These factors have influenced the evolution of fiscal federalism and the mix of policy instruments used to bridge the fiscal gap between provinces' spending responsibilities and their capacity (or willingness) to raise revenues.

2. The evolution of fiscal federalism

Following the Second World War, the federal government used the growth of transfer federalism to foster the growth of the welfare state in Canada and to make it serve national policy objectives through the use of conditional grants for the funding of shared-cost programs. The federal government would establish programs to provided provinces with matching grants for provincial programs meeting federal social policy objectives.

The rising cost of these programs, along with rising federal deficits, led Ottawa to rethink this approach during the late 1970s. After 1977, it transferred more taxing powers to the provinces while capping transfer payments at the rate of growth of the economy. Matching grants were largely replaced by "block funding" of provincial programs. These changes were intended to give the provinces greater discretion in setting priorities and managing programs. They also enabled Ottawa to limit the rate of growth in its transfer payments and to impose conditions at the margin from time to time through such instruments as the *Canada Health Act*. However, while most provinces consistently reported small surpluses or deficits during the 1980s, the federal deficit ballooned to record levels.

Inevitably, the federal deficit reduction campaign of the mid-1990s involved major reductions to intergovernmental transfers. Cuts in cash transfers totaled about 25 per cent between 1995 and 1998. While these cuts have been largely restored, the adequacy and predictability of federal transfers to the provinces are the source of constant bickering between the two levels of government. Table 13.6 outlines the composition of major federal transfers to provinces and territories and their growth since 1998.

Since 1957, the federal government has provided a formal system of **equalization payments** to most provinces, which are intended to offset provincial fiscal disparities with no political strings attached. As such, they are known as "unconditional transfers" because provincial governments can spend the money as they see fit. This formula is reviewed every five years by the federal government, following discussions with the provinces. At present, equalization is based on a complex formula using revenues from 33 separate sources at standardized rates.[20] This process allows the formula to take into account variations in revenue-raising ability, ranging from variations in relative levels of personal income, business profits, resource taxes and royalties, individual tax rates, and other economic factors. Equalization payments totaled more than $9 billion in 2004-05. Eight provinces—Ontario and Alberta excepted—have typically been in receipt of equalization payments in recent years, although payments to British Columbia and Saskatchewan may be reduced substantially during periods of high prices for provincial resources.

Table 13.6. Major Federal Health and Social Transfers, 1993–94 to 2007–08

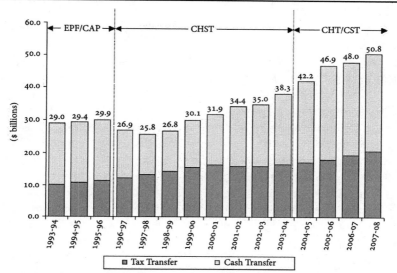

Note: Includes funding provided under the Canada Health and Social Transfer (CHST) and its successors, the Canada Health Transfer (CHT) and the Canada Social Transfer (CST), as well as cash increases to the CHST/CHT/CST base for health, early childhood development, and early learning and child care. Also includes the 2003 and 2004 CHST supplements, the Health Reform Transfer (which will be rolled into the CHT in 2005-06, subject to passage of authorizing legislation), and the CHT increases from the 10-Year Plan to Strengthen Health Care (subject to passage of authorizing legislation). Excludes targeted health funding provided under the Diagnostic/Medical Equipment Fund, Public Health and Immunization Fund, and funding for wait times reduction and medical equipment in the 10-Year Plan to Strengthen Health Care.
Source: Canada, "Total Federal Support for Health, Post-Secondary Education, and Social Assistance and Social Services (2004-05)" (Ottawa: Department of Finance, October 2004).

Federal equalization policies were destabilized in 2005 by *ad hoc* agreements made with individual provinces to address their complaints about the system's impact on provincial finances and economic prospects. Of particular concern are the interaction between equalization and provincial non-renewable resource royalties, and Ontario's claims that its residents are carrying a disproportionate share of the costs of fiscal federalism. The federal government has appointed an Expert Task Force to review these issues. It will report following the 2006 federal election.

Other transfer payments are subject to different levels of conditionality. The Canada Health and Social Transfer (recently divided into separate Health and Social Transfers, ostensibly for reasons of greater transparency) are block grants which replaced previous unconditional transfers in 1995. These programs have been revised in recent years to provide equal per capita federal transfers to each province when both cash and tax transfers are included.[21] The federal government has also negotiated bilateral transfer agreements with individual provinces in recent years on issues ranging from the funding of specific infrastructure projects to labour market training and immigrant integration programs.

CHST cash transfers totaled $23.5 billion in 2004-05 and are scheduled to increase steadily in coming years. Ottawa also makes a number of smaller, specific purpose transfers, subject to periodic review, ranging from support for minority language education to the funding of legal aid and financing of provincial infrastructure projects. These transfers totaled about $3.5 billion in 2003-04.[22]

Federal transfers have enabled "have less" provinces, particularly in Atlantic Canada, to provide much higher levels of public services than would otherwise have been possible given the significantly lower per capita incomes of their citizens and their correspondingly lower fiscal capacity.

Table 13.7 compares personal incomes, own-source and total revenues, and spending for each province, adjusted for differences in population. Except for Nova Scotia, per capita provincial spending in the five have-least provinces is 8 to 23 per cent *higher* than the national average, even though their provincial economies offer less potential to raise revenues from their own citizens. This is reflected in per capita revenues ranging from 4 per cent (Manitoba) to 17 per cent (PEI) *below* the national average.

The redistributive effects of transfer federalism are reinforced by those of Canada's personal income tax system. Variations in after-tax incomes between "have" and "have less" provinces tend to be considerably lower than those in GDP per capita, except for the energy-producing provinces of Newfoundland and Saskatchewan. For example, personal after-tax incomes in the three Atlantic

Table 13.7. Provincial Revenues and Spending, Adjusted for Population

	Personal income per capita 2003	Per capita own-source revenue	Total per capita revenue	Total per capita spending
			—2003–04 (FMS) —	
	Canadian average = 100			
All provinces	100.0	100.0	100.0	100.0
NF	83.7	87.7	119.6	123.4
PEI	82.5	82.5	108.0	113.6
NS	91.0	84.7	102.2	95.0
NB	86.6	89.0	109.8	107.8
QC	93.6	115.8	114.2	114.5
ON	105.7	86.2	82.9	86.1
MB	91.9	95.6	110.4	108.7
SK	87.2	111.9	110.5	110.1
AB	115.3	125.8	116.8	98.3
BC	94.5	100.1	95.3	100.9

Source: Statistics Canada, *Provincial Economic Accounts*, 2003 preliminary estimates, Cat. 13-213 (Ottawa: Statistics Canada, April 2004) 394; Statistics Canada, *Public Sector Statistics*, Cat # 68-213 (Ottawa: Statistics Canada, July 2004) 32-33; author's calculations.

provinces ranged from 84 to 91 per cent of the national average in 2002, despite provincial per capita GDPs ranging between 73 and 80 per cent.[23]

3. Federal-provincial tax coordination

Although seven provinces introduced personal income taxes between 1876 and 1939, and the federal government did so in 1917, there was no formal provision for the coordination of tax rules or rates before 1941, when the federal government took over responsibility for personal, corporate income, and inheritance taxes as an emergency wartime measure. Ontario and Quebec resumed their collection of corporate income and inheritance taxes in 1947. Provincial pressures for increased "tax sharing" led to a gradual decentralization of powers over taxation, culminating in the **federal-provincial tax collection agreement** (TCA) of 1962.[24]

To avoid double taxation and conflicting tax rules between the two levels of government, the federal-provincial tax collection agreements in place since 1962 have enabled Ottawa to administer the personal income tax system for nine provinces and the corporate income tax system on behalf of seven provinces, based on a common **tax base** (definition of taxable income). Between 1992 and 2001, participating provinces levied their PITs as a percentage of federal taxes payable by individual taxpayers, although most provinces introduced a number of variations during that period. Provinces were somewhat limited in their flexibility to set tax rates, although most introduced a variety of surtaxes, tax credits, and supplemental flat taxes during the 1980s and 1990s to increase revenues and give themselves greater policy discretion over effective tax rates at different levels of income.

Changes to the federal-provincial tax collection agreements introduced in 2001 gave provincial governments significantly greater latitude in setting their own tax rates and in adapting elements of their tax structures to their own political and economic priorities. The combined effect of these realities, reinforced by efforts of most governments to regain control over their finances and balance their budgets during the 1990s, has been described as the "provincialization of the Canadian fiscal system."[25]

Reflecting the determination of its provincial government to defend its constitutional jurisdiction and set its own policy priorities, only Quebec collects its own personal and corporate taxes based on separate definitions of income. As a result, residents of Quebec submit separate tax forms to Ottawa and Quebec City. Ontario and Alberta administer their own corporate tax systems, which tend to parallel federal rules. Since Quebec decided to opt out of a number of federal transfer programs to the provinces during the 1960s, preferring to create and pay for its own programs instead, the federal government gives Quebec-based taxpayers a 16.5 per cent "**tax abatement**" to compensate for the resulting higher tax levels in that province.

Another form of tax abatement are the "tax transfers" provided by Ottawa to the provinces since 1977 as compensation for reductions in the rate of growth of federal transfer payments. In effect, the federal government agreed to reduce its personal and corporate income tax rates to enable provinces to raise more tax revenues to finance their own services and to reduce their relative dependence on federal transfers. As a result, most larger provinces have been able to finance the bulk of their spending requirements from their own-source revenues. The federal Department of Finance estimated the total value to the provinces of these tax transfers at $17.5 billion in 2003-04 compared with $20.8 billion in cash transfers under the largest federal transfer program.[26]

When the federal government converted its manufacturers' sales tax into the GST in 1989-90, it invited other provinces to enter into a comparable tax harmonization and collection agreement covering sales taxation. Although three provinces—Newfoundland, Nova Scotia, and New Brunswick—entered a "harmonized sales tax" (HST) agreement with Ottawa in 1996, and Quebec has set up a comparable tax, most other provinces continue to levy their retail sales taxes on a variety of consumer goods and services.[27]

Balancing Budgets or Passing the Buck: The Politics of Provincial Public Finance

Provincial finances have been on a provincial roller-coaster since the early 1990s. Collectively, the provinces balanced their budgets during the late 1980s and at the turn of the century, although there are wide variations between provinces and in cumulative year-to-year fiscal positions.

Deficits in several provinces reached record levels during the recessions of the early 1990s. Provincial deficits averaged a record 18.1 per cent of revenues in 1992, as noted in Table 13.8, with five provinces reporting deficits over 10 per cent of revenues. However, while some provinces—particularly Alberta, Saskatchewan, and Manitoba—took early and decisive actions to balance their budgets, several others continued to run sizeable deficits into the late 1990s.

The easing of fiscal pressures and the restoration of federal transfer payments since 1998 has led to a relaxation of spending discipline in most provinces, with the significant exception of BC, whose Liberal government set out to make major reductions in the size of that province's public sector after 2001. Eight provinces had drifted back into deficits by 2003-04, despite balanced budget laws and other fiscal rules introduced during the 1990s to avoid such problems under normal circumstances. However, seven provinces (excepting Ontario, Newfoundland, and PEI) reported surpluses or balanced budgets for 2004-05.

We will now look at the fiscal performance of provincial governments in recent years, considering the role and limitations of fiscal rules in contributing to the sustainability of provincial public finances. In conclusion, we will review the current debate over "fiscal imbalance" and its implications for the sustainability of provincial public services.

Provincial fiscal performance: All over the map

Ultimately, provinces are sovereign governments with varying degrees of capacity to manage their own finances. Wealthier, more economically diversified provinces typically have more choices and greater fiscal capacity than poorer ones, though the examples of BC and Ontario during the 1990s show that such inherent fiscal advantages can be squandered.

The ultimate evaluation of fiscal performance in a democracy is the capacity of governments to grow their economies in ways that enable them to provide the services that citizens want (and are willing to pay for) and that can adapt with changes in broader economic circumstances and societal expectations.

Fiscal capacity can also be restored as a result of deliberate policy choices, although the examples of neighbouring Alberta and Saskatchewan during the 1990s demonstrate that these objectives can be pursued by very different means. The fiscal, economic, and political shocks of recent years—not least, the stresses of deficit reduction and government restructuring—have caused governments of most political stripes to place a greater emphasis on **fiscal sustainability**—the capacity of governments to maintain current levels of public services under foreseeable circumstances without undermining economic growth (and the capacity to finance future public services) through excessive levels of taxation or public borrowing.

Provincial governments adopted a variety of political and budgetary strategies to balance their budgets during the 1990s and to maintain some degree of fiscal balance after doing so, as indicated in Tables 13.8 and 13.9. Despite variations in political priorities, economic circumstances and fiscal policy choices, provincial fiscal and tax policies reflected several trends in common since the early 1990s.

Table 13.8. Different Paths to Balanced Budgets

	Surplus / Deficit[1] (% of revenue)			Spending Increase (+) / Decrease (-) Adjusted for Inflation/Population	
	1992	1995	1999	1992-95	1995-99
All provinces	- 18.1	- 5.5	3.3	- 3.1	- 3.5
NF	1.1	- 2.1	5.9	+ 7.6	+ 2.3
PEI	- 6.1	2.3	7.5	- 6.3	+ 5.3
NS	- 10.3	0.0	- 0.4	- 0.7	+ 5.0
NB	- 1.5	2.7	1.5	+ 3.7	+ 4.2
QC	- 16.9	- 10.4	0.2	+ 2.6	- 3.3
ON	- 28.9	- 12.0	3.2	- 4.3	- 7.7
MB	- 14.0	2.0	5.3	- 8.3	+ 1.7
SK	- 11.8	- 0.2	10.9	- 12.2	- 4.5
AB	- 16.3	7.1	8.2	- 14.0	- 2.3
BC	- 8.8	3.0	0.6	- 6.6	+ 6.0

1. National Accounts Basis—current revenues less current expenditures.
Source: Statistics Canada, *Provincial Economic Accounts*, Cat. # 13-213, (Ottawa: Statistics Canada, April 2002; author's calculations).

Table 13.9. Provincial-Territorial Fiscal Balance since 1999 (in $ billions)

	1999-00	2000-01	2001-02	2002-03	2003-04	2004-05
Public accounts basis	2.6	10.5	0.2	- 1.8	- 4.1	5.2
	1999	2000	2001	2002	2003	2004
National accounts basis	2.8	8.1	- 8.5	- 15.1	- 6.7	- 3.9

Source: Canada, Department of Finance, *Fiscal Reference Tables* (Ottawa: Department of Finance, October 2005) 34, 45.

1. All provincial governments moved towards a more consistent fiscal balance during the 1990s, although by very different methods, at different speeds, and with significantly different emphasis in the use of tax increases, spending reduction, and debt reduction. Depending on the accounting method used, as many as seven provinces had balanced their budgets by 1995-96.[28] Three of the laggards—Ontario, Quebec, and BC—had followed suit by 1999-2000, joined by Nova Scotia in 2000-01.

Table 13.10 summarizes the provinces' relative success in balancing their budgets since the mid-1990s and, more importantly, the ratio of cumulative surpluses or deficits to overall provincial revenues during this period. This approach allows observers to discern broader patterns in overall fiscal performance rather

Table 13.10. Managing within Fiscal Constraints

	Initial budget balance[1] after 1990	Years budget balanced[1] 1994-95—1998-99	Years budget balanced[1] 1999-00—2003-04	Average surplus/deficit:[1] 1995-96—1998-99 [% of revenue]	Average surplus/deficit:[1] 1999-00—2003-04 [% of revenue]
All provinces, territories	1999-2000	na	na	- 4.2%	0.8%
AB	1994-95	5	5	11.1%	14.4%
SK	1994-95	5	5[2]	2.3%	0.5%
MB	1995-96	4	5	1.5%	0.4%
NB	1995-96	3	3[2]	- 0.5%	0.3%
QC	1998-99	1	3[2]	- 5.7%	- 0.2%
ON	1999-2000	0	4	- 10.5%	- 0.7%
NS	2000-01	0	2	- 3.2%	- 1.9%
BC	1999-2000	0	2	- 2.8%	- 2.4%
PEI	1995-96	2	0	0.0%	- 4.1%
NF	1995-96	2	0	- 2.5%	- 14.2%

1. Public Accounts Basis; includes stabilization fund transfers.
2. Proceeds of stabilization fund used to balance budget.
Source: Canada, Department of Finance, *Fiscal Reference Tables* (Ottawa: Department of Finance, October 2004).

than focusing on year-to-year fluctuations, which may subject to considerable volatility as well as manipulative accounting techniques and other forms of fiscal illusion.[29]

2. There was a broad trend towards higher taxes during the early 1990s, before major reductions in federal transfers after 1995, along with more widespread dependence on non-tax revenues, particularly from provincially sponsored gambling activities.[30] Between 1990 and 1995, provincial income tax revenues increased from 53.7 per cent to 58.8 per cent of federal taxes collected—an average increase of 9.6 per cent.[31] Appendix 13.4 summarizes trends in provincial tax rates between 1990 and 2002.

3. There was a broad trend towards lower taxes during the second half of the 1990s, despite sharp reductions in federal transfers between 1995 and 1998, as Ottawa took decisive steps to put its own fiscal house in order. Between 1995 and 1999, provincial income taxes dropped by 10.1 per cent as a proportion of federal taxes collected—14.6 per cent outside Quebec. Although relative tax rate reductions were relatively modest in most provinces, ranging from 0.8 per cent in Alberta to 4.2 per cent in New Brunswick, Ontario cut its income tax rates by an average of 24 per cent.[32]

4. The intensity and nature of these tax reductions varied significantly by province and region. This trend appears to have dissipated in most provinces by 2002-03, with several provinces increasing user fees and consumption taxes to finance increased spending or limit budget shortfalls. Alberta and Saskatchewan were exceptions to this national trend.

5. Provinces most likely to reduce taxes in the late 1990s—particularly Ontario, but also BC and New Brunswick—tended to be those that had imposed the highest tax increases earlier in the decade. However, provincial decisions to reduce taxes often had little relationship to their overall budget balances.[33]

6. Most provinces that had balanced their budgets by 1996 took advantage of the subsequent economic recovery to restore the spending cuts occasioned by deficit reduction while reducing taxes to varying degrees. Table 13.8 compares the different paths taken to balanced budgets by provinces during the 1990s, along with spending patterns before and after the initial burst of deficit reduction (in most provinces) between 1992 and 1995.

The three large provinces that deferred serious deficit reduction strategies—Ontario, Quebec, and BC—took different approaches to balancing their budgets between 1996 and 1999. Ontario cut both taxes and spending, riding the economic boom of the late 1990s to an eventually balanced budget. Quebec made more modest spending reductions, while spending actually increased in BC.

7. Most provinces introduced various forms of "fiscal rules," including balanced budget legislation and "sustainability funds" as a way of imposing discipline on budgetary policies and structuring public expectations and public debate on provincial fiscal and tax policies.[34] Political commitment to these rules—and to

balanced budgets—declined sharply with the end of the 1990s boom and the renewed effects of the political business cycle.

8. Provinces moved towards a greater degree of autonomy and diversity in their tax policies, culminating in changes to the federal-provincial tax collection agreements between 1998 and 2001.[35]

Some provinces, notably Ontario (and, to a lesser extent, Manitoba), increased the progressivity of their tax systems, cutting tax rates for all income groups, but more so for lower and middle income earners.[36] The three Westernmost provinces—particularly Alberta—and New Brunswick moved towards "flatter," or more proportional, tax rates structures, particularly for middle and upper income earners. The other Atlantic provinces and Quebec made relatively modest changes to their tax structures. As noted earlier in this chapter, most provinces have reduced their reliance on income taxes in favour of a variety of consumption taxes and user fees for specific public services.

9. During the late 1990s, most provinces attempted to reduce pressures for internal fiscal discipline by mounting a sustained political campaign to extract commitments for a steady, predictable escalation of transfer payments from Ottawa, based largely on accusations that regular federal surpluses indicated the emergence of a chronic **fiscal imbalance** between the two levels of government.[37]

10. The economic slowdown of 2002-03 found most provinces in a "precarious" fiscal position, with rapidly increasing health care costs and slowing revenue growth (except for federal transfers). Several provinces cancelled or deferred planned tax reductions and increased user charges. However, a combination of increased economic growth, higher resource revenues, and increased federal transfers helped to strengthen the fiscal performance of most provinces in 2004-05.

In summary, the fiscal positions of most provinces are significantly better in 2005 than they were ten years earlier. However, as most provinces have spent the fiscal dividends resulting from having balanced their budgets and, in a few cases, from having paid down debt, neither provincial governments nor their citizens can take the fiscal or economic progress of the past decade for granted.

Recent fiscal developments: 2000 to the present

Economic growth contributed to significantly higher revenues in most provinces during the late 1990s, along with increased expectations of tax reductions as a "reward" for the sacrifices imposed in the name of deficit reduction. Competing pressures for increased spending on core services such as health care, education, and infrastructure (e.g., roads, bridges, sewers, and water systems) encouraged most provinces to attempt to transfer these fiscal pressures to the federal government by demanding increased transfer payments rather than raising their own taxes, particularly after the federal government began to report regular annual surpluses after 1999.

Table 13.11 compares the major components of provincial fiscal performance between the balancing of provincial budgets in 1999-2000 and 2003-04. Total revenues in three provinces grew faster than spending, although energy-producing provinces such as Saskatchewan, Nova Scotia, and Newfoundland were penalized for rapidly rising oil and gas prices by lower federal equalization payments.

Six provinces reported moderate spending growth, although tax cuts in Ontario resulted in a decline in its overall fiscal balance. Alberta's sizeable budget surpluses allowed it to finance rapid spending growth. Since 2001, BC has opted for a totally different approach to fiscal policy that combines sharp tax reductions and spending cuts with record budget deficits as it seeks to reduce the size and scope of its public sector. It subsequently reported a $ 2.6 billion surplus, with modest spending increases, for 2004-05—with consistent surpluses projected in future years.

Table 13.11. Where Did the Surpluses Go? 1999-2000, 2003-04

	Average annual growth in				
	Total spending	Total revenues	Own-source revenues	Transfers from other governments	Net change in fiscal performance
All provs/territories	4.4	3.3	2.2	9.5	-1.1
Moderate spending growth					
NS	3.0	4.7	7.7	0.3	1.7
MB	3.7	3.8	3.1	5.3	0.1
ON	3.8	1.4	-0.2	17.0	-2.4
QC	3.9	3.7	2.2	13.7	-0.2
NB	4.0	3.5	4.8	1.4	-0.5
SK	4.3	3.0	4.7	-3.6	-1.3
Above average spending growth					
NF	4.6	3.8	6.3	0.5	-0.9
PEI	5.0	2.8	3.2	2.3	-2.2
Spending outliers					
AB	6.4	7.2	6.1	19.6	0.8
BC	5.5	3.9	3.8	4.9	-1.6

Sources: Canada *Fiscal Reference Tables* (Ottawa: Department of Finance, October 2004); author's calculations.

The fiscal performance of provincial governments during the past decade points not only to the potential value but also to the limitations of formal and informal budget rules as a means of imposing fiscal discipline, managing public priorities, and shaping public expectations of the role and limits of governments.

Budget Rules: Good Intentions Gone Astray?

A major innovation of the 1990s was the introduction of fiscal rules by which most provincial governments committed themselves to a variety of formal disciplines on budgetary processes and government decision-makers. Although political commitment to these disciplines has declined somewhat in recent years, the politics of fiscal rules can still be used as a means of challenging politicians or interest groups to accept a greater degree of responsibility for making the trade-offs that are an inherent part of budgetary processes.

The capacity of governments to exercise effective policy choices is closely linked to their capacity to mobilize and reallocate financial resources to key priorities. Chronic deficits undermined the capacity of federal and provincial governments to meet their political commitments to Canadians without creating a "negative-sum game," which would leave most citizens and businesses economically worse off as a result, as ever larger shares of rising tax loads were used to pay interest charges on past borrowings, while levels of public services declined.[38] The increasing openness of the Canadian economy to international economic shocks—particularly sharp shifts in global commodity prices and fluctuations in capital markets—was reinforced by the rapid growth in Canada's domestic and international indebtedness to finance huge public deficits and the borrowings of Crown corporations.[39]

As in most other industrial countries, the fiscal crisis of the early and mid-1990s forced most Canadians governments to rewrite at least some of the rules of the budgetary game in order to regain control of their finances and to restore the margin of financial discretion necessary to balance their political, economic, and social objectives. Federal and provincial finance ministers of all political stripes discovered that budget rules could be used to restore their control over public finances, set priorities, and reallocate scarce resources. These rules, which may be policy based or enshrined in legislation, include such measures as:

- the creation of contingency funds or "fiscal cushions" to protect against revenue shortfalls from lower than expected levels of economic growth or higher than expected interest rates within a single budgetary cycle (fiscal year);
- the creation of fiscal stabilization or reserve funds to offset the effects of unforeseen fluctuations in economic activity or federal transfers from year to year;
- balanced budget laws, requiring governments to balance their budgets, with limited exceptions and varying consequences for non-compliance;
- provisions for the allocation of part or all of budgetary reserves or surpluses towards debt reduction or sinking funds; and
- legislation introduced in four provinces requiring a referendum before the imposition of new taxes, although Ontario retreated from this position in 2002.[40]

Appendix 13.5 summarizes the application of these practices by federal and provincial governments in recent years.

While stabilization funds can be used to indulge pre-election spending sprees—a tendency visible in governments of all political stripes—they can also provide a hedge against unsustainable levels of spending growth during years of relative prosperity.

By 2000, eight provinces had passed balanced budget legislation of varying degrees of stringency.[41] Progressive Conservative governments in Manitoba, Ontario, and Alberta added requirements requiring referendums on the creation of new taxes or tax increases, with different exceptions, although the Ontario Tories revoked this legislation following the retirement of Premier Mike Harris.[42] Harris's successor, Ernie Eves, ran up a deficit initially estimated at $5.6 billion in attempting to stave off electoral defeat in 2003.[43] A post-election report by Quebec's former auditor-general, released in April 2003, suggested that the defeated Parti Québécois government's ostensibly balanced budget concealed a projected deficit of $4.37 billion before corrective action initiated by its Liberal successors.[44] This retreat signals the inherent political limits of fiscal rules, which will only be observed as long as they retain strong public and political support.

One area in which the development of fiscal rules has not kept pace with public sector management practices is the application of standardized accounting rules intended to provide accurate, consistent financial information to citizens and financial markets. The absence of such rules and their timely application through public financial disclosure makes it difficult to compare provincial financial performances or to hold governments accountable for their actions within an electoral cycle.

One tool used by some provinces to increase the transparency of their fiscal accounts is the introduction of consolidated budgets—which bring together accounts for all provincially funded agencies including public enterprises and special provincial agencies—in order to reduce governments' capacity to "manipulate the fiscal message through the use of inter-fund transfers of revenues and expenditures."[45] However, the presence of multiple budget accounts in a single document can create confusion enough to reduce transparency and create "multiple bottom lines" that lend themselves to whatever political "spin" may be chosen by the government of the day.

On balance, the development and application of fiscal rules has been most consistent in the three prairie provinces, regardless of ideological or partisan affiliation, resulting in consistently balanced budgets and a larger share of tax revenues available to pay for government services or lower taxes without returning to deficit budgeting. Their introduction and application in Ontario and BC was delayed or diluted by fiscal populism—first of the left, later of the right. Their application east of the Ottawa River has been even less consistent and more discretionary, reflecting the different political cultures and priorities of each province and the governments of the day. The return of eight of Canada's ten provinces into budgetary deficits in 2002-03 and 2003-04 suggests that the effectiveness of budget rules in helping provinces to restore the sustainability of their public services is highly subject to political opportunism and shifts in the broader public mood.

Fiscal Imbalance: Political Injustice or Political Tactic

Traditional approaches to fiscal federalism emphasize the importance of organizing tax and spending powers to offset the effects of economic and fiscal disparities on the capacity of governments to provide comparable levels of public services while enhancing their accountability and responsiveness to the citizens who elect them. Some of these decisions are embedded in Canada's political and economic systems. However, others are very much within the control of individual governments depending on their political skills and their capacity to build public support for clear and coherent policy priorities.

The issue of fiscal autonomy in Canada has been linked traditionally to issues of **vertical fiscal imbalance** between federal and provincial governments, particularly since the advent of the modern welfare state between the mid-1940s and mid-1960s. Despite shared jurisdiction over most fields of taxation, smaller provinces, in particular, have traditionally lacked the revenue-raising capacity to finance their responsibilities for major areas of spending responsibility such as health, education, social services, and transportation without significant federal assistance

Despite recent increases in federal cash transfers, rising provincial health costs and budget pressures have triggered a renewed debate over the nature and extent of vertical fiscal imbalances in Canada. As Boothe has said, "The key issue in the debate over vertical fiscal imbalance is the relative capacity of each order of government to raise its own revenues to fund its own expenditures."[46] In addition to the usual federal-provincial squabbling over money and power and the usual tendency of politicians to deflect blame when their budgetary decisions fail to live up to the expectations of powerful interest groups, this debate addresses both the nature of the Canadian federation and the relationship between fiscal policies and the role of the state.

The highly politicized nature of this debate means that there are wide differences in views of what constitutes a fiscal imbalance between the two levels of government, whether such an imbalance exists at all, and its main causes if it does exist. Lazar, St. Hilaire, and Tremblay suggest that these divisions are rooted in fundamentally different normative or ideological views of the role of government and the appropriate relationship between federal and provincial governments.[47] These issues are directly related to the competing visions of fiscal federalism addressed earlier in this chapter.

The question of relative fiscal capacity is inherently subject to the political and economic assumptions used by each side in the debate to make its case.[48] The federal government contends that provinces, collectively, have access to all the revenue sources necessary to finance their operations, and provincial deficits of recent years are largely the by-product of decisions taken by their political leaders to reduce taxes and increase spending while seeking increased federal subsidies to make up the difference.[49] Table 13.11 indicates that this accusation is plausible for as many as five provinces (including the four largest ones), which have increased their spending significantly faster than the national average or which have cut taxes without taking offsetting action to limit spending growth. Ottawa also notes that it still faces significantly higher levels of public debt and interest charges than most provinces, despite significant efforts at debt reduction in recent years.

Provincial governments have countered with voluminous consultants' reports arguing that, barring policy changes, federal surpluses are likely to grow substantially in coming years while rapidly growing areas of public spending—health care and education—are likely to result in growing deficits in most provinces. As a result, they advocate either substantial transfers in taxing powers to provinces, combined with increased federal equalization payments, or a federal commitment to fund a fixed proportion of health care costs. [50] Federal commitments to increase transfers by an annual average of more than $4 billion, announced in late 2004, are a partial response to these challenges.

Independent economic studies suggest that both levels of government are subject to rising costs driven by external economic and demographic forces, many of which are beyond the immediate control of governments, although not necessarily immune from more effective management.[51]

Ultimately, the responses to these issues are inherently political, based on the short- and medium-term trade-offs faced by politicians and other senior policymakers. The experience of the past 30 years suggests that most medium- or long-term fiscal projections are inherently subject to regular revision as a result of underlying economic conditions and the political decisions made in annual budget cycles. Circumstances change. Growth rates ebb and flow. Budget surpluses trigger renewed public expectations for new spending or tax reductions for which politicians always prefer to take credit in the first person rather than through transfers to other governments.

Although claims of vertical fiscal imbalance provide provinces with a convenient political rallying point in dealing with fiscal pressures, the political and economic differences between provinces are great enough that no "one-size-fits-all" solution seems either feasible or likely in the foreseeable future. The individual circumstances and choices of individual provinces and their government play at least as great a role in shaping their fiscal and tax policies as do the actions of other levels of government or the wider economic forces of globalization.[52]

Canadians, and their governments, have the "capacity for choice"[53] if they are prepared to recognize and face up to the trade-offs between short and longer term objectives that are an inherent part of setting policy priorities. Canada's relatively decentralized system of federalism allows both citizens and their governments a wider variety of choices than in most other countries. The variety of fiscal and tax policy choices examined in this chapter suggests, if anything, that these choices will continue to reflect the political, economic, and cultural diversity of Canada's regions and provinces.

Glossary

balanced budget legislation: Laws which require governments to balance their budgets within a particular time frame, involving a variety of constraints on overall levels of taxation, spending, or borrowing.

benefit-related taxation: Taxes or fees directly related to the provision or use of particular public services by individual citizens or businesses.

budget deficits: The amount by which government spending is greater than revenues for a particular time period (usually one year). Cumulative budget deficits are a major part of the public **debt**.

budget surpluses: The amount by which government revenues are greater than spending for a particular time period (usually one year). Cumulative budget surpluses allow governments to repay debt, thus increasing the share of tax revenues that pay for current services rather than **debt service charges**.

contingency funds: Budget accounts set up to "cushion" spending against economic shocks or unanticipated changes in economic activity; may be allocated to debt reduction if governments meet fiscal targets.

debt (public): The total value of government borrowing by a particular jurisdiction. Gross public debt is the total value of public borrowing to finance government deficits and capital spending from budget revenues. Net public debt is the total value of borrowing less the current value of public assets (after depreciation).

debt service charges: The cost of interest payments on public **debt**.

effective tax rate: Total taxes paid as a percentage of personal or family income.

expenditure-driven budgeting: An approach to budgeting based on calculating the total cost of public services to be provided and then determining how taxes or public borrowing will be adjusted to pay for them.

federal spending power: The ability of the federal government to spend money and use its jurisdiction over taxation in areas of provincial jurisdiction and to affect provincial priorities by setting conditions on its transfers to other levels of government.

fiscal autonomy: The capacity of governments to finance their activities without reference to the decisions of other levels of governments and the degree to which they can exercise discretion in choosing how to do so. Provinces' fiscal autonomy is affected by their relative dependence on federal transfers and other policies.

fiscal capacity: The ability of governments to finance, maintain, or expand public services.

fiscal federalism: The structures and processes for sharing revenues and spending responsibilities between different levels of government.

fiscal illusion: The use of creative accounting or economic forecasting methods to disguise the true state of public finances.

fiscal imbalance: Differences in the capacities of governments to provide services within their areas of constitutional responsibility; may reflect differences among provinces—"horizontal fiscal imbalance"—or between different levels of government—**vertical fiscal imbalance.**

fiscal rules: Legislated requirements or policy tools used to manage the trade-offs of the budgetary process.

fiscal sustainability: The capacity of governments to maintain current levels of public services under foreseeable circumstances without undermining economic growth (and the capacity to finance future public services) through excessive levels of taxation or public borrowing.

horizontal fiscal imbalance: Differences between the capacities of provincial governments to provide services within their areas of constitutional responsibility; may be produced by structural factors, such as the capacity to raise sufficient revenues, or by policy choices of either or both levels of government.

marginal income tax rate: Tax rate imposed on each additional dollar of income or profit earned by an individual or business.

net debt: See **debt.**

own-source revenues: Tax and other revenues collected by governments under their own legislative authority.

payroll taxes: Taxes imposed on employment income (payroll), collected and remitted by employers, usually to finance social insurance or other social programs (e.g., Canada/Quebec Pension Plans, Workers' Compensation, health care payroll taxes); may be levied on employees, employers, or both.

political business-cycle: Theories suggesting that overall levels of fiscal stimulus or government spending vary in proportion to the proximity of an election or to public moods shaped by relative degrees of prosperity.

progressive tax rate structure: A tax structure in which tax rates increase with the amount earned (income tax) or consumed (consumption tax); tax rates may increase sharply ("high progressivity") or moderately ("lower progressivity") as levels of income increase.

proportional tax rate structure: A tax structure in which taxes are levied at a fixed rate on each dollar earned (income tax) or consumed (consumption tax) over a basic threshold amount.

revenue-driven budgeting: An approach to budgeting that sets provincial spending priorities and decisions on anticipated revenues, usually adjusting spending estimates to function within expected revenues.

vertical fiscal imbalance: Differences between the capacities of federal and provincial governments to provide services within their areas of constitutional responsibility; may be produced by structural factors, such as the capacity to raise sufficient revenues, or by policy choices of either or both levels of government.

Appendix 13.1. Provincial Personal Income Tax Rates, 2005

Provincial / Territorial tax rates (combined chart)

Federal Basic personal/spousal exemptions:[1] $8,148 / 6,919[2]	16.0%[2] on taxable income of $0–35,595 22.0% on taxable income of $35,595.01–71,190 26.0% on taxable income of $71,190.01–115,739 29.0% on taxable income over $115,739.01
Provinces / Territories	*Rate(s)*
Newfoundland and Labrador Basic personal/spousal exemptions:[1] $7,410 / 6,055 (no inflation indexing)	10.57% on taxable income of $0 to 29,590 16.16% on taxable income of $29,591 to 59,180 18.02% on taxable income over $59,180 9% surtax on provincial tax paid above $7,032
Prince Edward Island Basic personal/spousal exemptions:[1] $7,412 / 6,294 (no inflation indexing)	9.8% on taxable income of $0 to 30,754 13.8% on taxable income of $30,755 to 61,509 16.7% on taxable income over $61,509 10% surtax on provincial tax paid above $5,200
Nova Scotia Basic personal/spousal exemptions:[1] $7,231 / 6,140 (no inflation indexing)	8.79% on taxable income of $0 to 29,590 14.95% on taxable income of $29,591 to $59,180 16.67% on taxable income of $59,180.01 to $93,000 17.50% on taxable income over $93,000 10% surtax on provincial tax paid above $10,000
New Brunswick Basic personal/spousal exemptions:[1] $7,888 / 6,698	9.68% on taxable income of $0 to 32,730 14.82% on taxable income of $32,730.01 to 65,462 16.52% on taxable income of $65,462.01 to 106,427 17.84% on taxable income over $106,427
Quebec Basic personal/spousal exemptions:[1] $9,330 / 9,330	16% on taxable income of $0 to 28,030 20% on taxable income of $28,030.01 to 56,070 24% on taxable income over $56,070 Abatement (reduction) of 16.5% of federal income taxes payable.
Ontario Basic personal/spousal exemptions:[1] $8,196 / 6,960	6.05% on taxable income of $0 to 34,010 9.15% on taxable income of $34,010.01 to 68,020 11.16% on taxable income over $68,020 20% surtax on provincial tax paid over $3,909 36% surtax on provincial tax paid over $4,956 In addition to personal income tax rates: Ontario Health Premium charged on incomes over $20,000: 6% on incomes between $20,000 and 36,000 to maximum of $300 6% on incomes between $36,000 and 48,000 to maximum of $450 25% on incomes between $48,000 and 72,000 to maximum of $600 25% on incomes between $72,000 and 200,000 to maximum of $750 25% on incomes over $200,000 to maximum of $900.

Manitoba
Basic personal/spousal
exemptions:[1] $7,634 / 6,482

10.9% on taxable income of $0 to 30,544
14% on taxable income of $30,545 to 65,000
17.4% on taxable income over $65,000

Saskatchewan
Basic personal/spousal
exemptions:[1] $8,404 / 8,404

11% on taxable income of $0 to 36,770
13% on taxable income of $36,770.01 to 105,056
15% on taxable income over $105,056

Alberta
Basic personal/spousal
exemptions:[1] $14,523 / 14,523

10% of taxable income

British Columbia
Basic personal/spousal
exemptions:[1] $8,676 / 7,429

6.05% on taxable income of $0 to 33,061
9.15% on taxable income of $33,061.01 to 66,123
11.7% on taxable income of $66,123.01 to 75,917
13.7% on taxable income of $75,917.01 to $92,185
14.7% on taxable income over $92,185

Yukon
Basic personal/spousal
exemptions:[1] $8,148 / 6,919

7.04% on taxable income of $0 to 35,595
9.68% on taxable income of $35,595.01 to 71,190
11.44% on taxable income of $71,190.01 to 115,739
12.76% on taxable income over $115,739

Northwest Territories
Basic personal/spousal
exemptions:[1] $11,609 / 11,609

5.9% on taxable income of $0 to 33,811
8.6% on taxable income of $33,811.01 to 67,622
12.2% on taxable income of $67,622.01 to 109,939
14.05% on taxable income over $109,939

Nunavut
Basic personal/spousal
exemptions:[1] $10,674 / 10,674

4% on taxable income of $0 to 35,595
7% on taxable income of $35,595.01 to 71,190
9% on taxable income of $71,190.01 to 115,739
11.5% on taxable income over $115,739

1. Technically, non-refundable credits on these amounts.
2. 15% if Nov. 2005 measures confirmed by Parliament; above basic exemptions of $8,648 / 7,344.
Sources: ADP Payroll; Peachtree Accounting; rates subject to change in annual budget cycles.

Appendix 13.2. Interprovincial Comparison of Annual Personal Taxes, 2004

Combined costs of personal income taxes (net of child benefits), property taxes, sales and fuel taxes, and health premiums, and retail sales taxes.

	Two-income family of 4 earning $30,000		Two-income family of 4 earning $60,000		Two-income family of 4 earning $90,000	
	$	% of income	$	% of income	$	% of income
BC	$ 3,540	11.8	$6,349	10.6	$8,700	9.7
AB	$ 1,502	5.0	$5,527	9.2	$8,325	9.3
SK	$ 3,950	13.2	$6,998	11.7	$ 10,761	12.0
MB	$ 5,091	17.0	$9,345	15.6	$ 14,987	16.7
ON	$ 4,081	13.6	$7,281	12.1	$ 11,114	12.3
QC[1]	$ 4,594	15.3	$ 10,323	17.2	$ 17,374	19.3
NB	$ 3,522	11.7	$6,691	11.2	$ 11,422	12.7
NS	$ 3,990	13.3	$7,228	12.0	$ 11,130	12.4
PEI	$ 3,632	12.1	$6,992	11.7	$ 10,738	11.9
NF	$ 4,668	15.5	$8,768	14.6	$ 13,460	15.0

1. Includes 16.5% federal tax abatement. Source: British Columbia, *Budget and Fiscal Plan: 2004-05 to 2006-07* (Victoria: Ministry of Finance, April 2004) 142-43.

Appendix 13.3. Building/Escaping Debtor's Prison: Trends in Net Debt Per Capita, 1992–2001

	1992 $ / capita	% of prov. average	1997 $ / capita	% of prov. average	2001 $ / capita	% of prov. average	Per capita debt % change 1992–01	% change 1997–01
All provinces, territories	5060	100.0%	8087	100.0%	7800	100.0%	54.2%	-3.5%
NF	9726	192.2%	14000	173.1%	16271	208.6%	67.3%	16.2%
PEI	5350	105.7%	7474	92.4%	7363	94.4%	37.6%	-1.5%
NS	5919	117.0%	9243	114.3%	11719	150.2%	98.0%	26.8%
NB	6702	132.5%	7388	91.4%	8141	104.4%	21.5%	10.2%
QC	7327	144.8%	11648	144.0%	11900	152.6%	62.4%	2.2%
ON	4870	96.2%	9300	115.0%	8720	111.8%	79.1%	-6.2%
MB	6402	126.5%	7544	93.3%	8082	103.6%	26.2%	7.1%
SK	8622	170.4%	9576	118.4%	8983	115.2%	4.2%	-6.2%
AB	1583	31.3%	1426	17.6%	3279	net assets	-100.0%	-100.0%
BC	960	19.0%	1906	23.6%	3779	48.4%	293.6%	98.3%
Federal	15162	299.6%	19684	243.4%	17074	218.9%	12.6%	-13.3%

Source: Statistics Canada, *Public Sector Statistics*, Cat. # 68-213 (Ottawa: Statistics Canada, 2003) 30, 34-35; author's calculations.

Appendix 13.4. Average Effective Provincial Income Tax Rates
(As Percentage of Federal Personal Income Tax Payable)

	1990	1995	1999	2002	% change 1990-95	% change 1995-99	% change 1999-2002
NF	59.1%	67.0%	69.5%	72.5%	13.2%	3.7%	4.3%
PEI	55.5%	59.3%	59.5%	64.1%	6.8%	0.4%	7.8%
NS	57.3%	56.9%	56.2%	66.2%	-0.6%	-1.3%	17.7%
NB	57.2%	62.7%	60.0%	62.8%	9.5%	-4.2%	4.7%
QC[1]	88.6%	91.6%	94.4%	na	3.4%	3.1%	na
QC[2]	61.9%	64.4%	66.9%	na	4.2%	3.8%	na
ON	50.7%	58.5%	44.7%	46.0%	15.5%	-23.7%	2.9%
MB	61.7%	63.5%	62.7%	66.3%	2.8%	-1.2%	5.7%
SK	61.9%	68.5%	67.0%	61.8%	10.6%	-2.3%	-7.8%
AB	47.3%	47.2%	46.8%	39.0%	-0.2%	-0.8%	-16.7%
BC	49.0%	54.8%	53.4%	42.2%	11.9%	-2.6%	-21.0%
Territories	42.2%	45.0%	45.6%	39.9%	6.8%	1.3%	-12.5%
Canada (incl.Quebec)	53.7%	58.8%	52.9%	na	9.6%	-10.1%	na
Canada (ex. Quebec)	51.1%	57.0%	48.7%	46.8%	11.6%	-14.6%	-3.8%

1. Actual.
2. Adjusted for 16.5% Quebec abatement.
Sources: Revenue Canada, *Taxation Statistics: 1992* (Ottawa: Revenue Canada, 1994); Revenue Canada, *Income Statistics, 1997* (Ottawa: Revenue Canada 1999); Canada Customs and Revenue Agency (2001, 2002), *Income Statistics: 1999, 2000* (Ottawa: CCRA, 2001-02); Quebec, Ministère des Finances (2002), *Statistiques fiscales des particuliers: annéee d'imposition 1999* (Quebec: Ministère des Finances, 11 June 2002), Tableau 18; author's calculations.

Appendix 13.5. Managing the Budgetary Process

	Budgetary Conventions			
	Cautious Economic Forecasts	Budgetary Contingency Funds	Fiscal Stabilization Funds	Debt Reduction Policy or Requirement
Canada	X	X		X
NF				
PEI				
NS				X[1]
NB		X		
QC	X			
ON	X			
MB		X[2]	X[2]	
SK		X	X[3]	
AB	X	X	X[4]	X[4]
BC	X			
YT				

Notes:

1. Nova Scotia: Provincial law prohibits growth of foreign currency denominated debt until foreign currency debt exposure below 20 per cent of total public debt (see Kennedy and Robbins 22).

2. Manitoba: legal debt repayment schedule requiring minimum annual payment of $75 million into Debt Repayment Fund; all surpluses not required for legislated debt reduction are to be paid into the province's Fiscal Stabilization Fund until it reaches a target balance of 5 per cent of operating expenditure.

3. Saskatchewan: surpluses must go to debt retirement; province must submit four-year debt management plan annually.

4. Alberta: Between 1994 and 2002, legislated rules required the government to allocate 75 per cent of unused "economic cushions" (contingency funds) in budget forecasts and 75 per cent of surpluses to debt reduction every year. In 2002, Alberta joined other provinces in creating a stabilization fund to reduce the province's vulnerability to fluctuating energy revenues. It promised to allocate annual energy revenues over $3.5 billion (increased to $4 billion in 2004) to the stabilization fund and to an infrastructure fund intended to smooth fluctuations in infrastructure.

Source: Kennedy and Robbins; modified by author to reflect subsequent changes.

Legislated Fiscal Rules in Canada, 2001

	Budgetary Balance Controls	Debt Restrictions	Tax or Expenditure Controls	Referendum for New Taxes
Canada			X	
NF	—————————————none—————————————			
PEI	—————————————none—————————————			
NS	X		X	
NB	X			
QC	X			
ON	X			X[1]
MB	X	X		X
SK	X			
AB	X	X	X	X
BC	X			
YT		X		X

1. Rescinded, June 2002.

Source: Kennedy and Robbins 5; modified by author to reflect subsequent changes.

Notes

1. Alexander Hamilton, "Federalist #30," in Clinton Rossiter, ed., *The Federalist Papers* (New York: Mentor Books, 1961) 188.

2. Direct Taxes on Personal and Corporate* Income as Shares of Provincial Own-Source Revenues: 2001

	Personal	Corporate
NF	27.5%	3.6%
PEI	24.5%	4.9%
NS	32.8%	5.4%
NB	27.5%	4.6%
QC	38.0%	5.3%
ON	31.6%	10.3%
MB	26.6%	4.9%
SK	21.9%	4.4%
AB	19.5%	10.2%
BC	23.6%	4.5%

   * Includes government business enterprises.
   Source: Statistics Canada, *Provincial Economic Accounts, Annual Estimates*, Cat. 13-213 (Ottawa: Statistics Canada, April 2004) Table 8.

3. Average Family Incomes by Province / Percent of Canadian Average, 2002

	Income	% of Cdn. Average
NF	$55,400	75.7
PEI	$57,600	78.7
NS	$65,600	89.6
NB	$59,500	81.3
QC	$66,000	90.2
ON	$81,400	111.2
MB	$65,300	89.2
SK	$63,800	87.2
AB	$77,100	105.3
BC	$72,400	98.9

   Source: Statistics Canada, *Income in Canada: 2002*, Cat. # 75-202 (Ottawa: Statistics Canada, June 2004) 54–64.

4. In New Brunswick, Nova Scotia, and Newfoundland.

5. Harry Kitchen, "Provinces and Municipalities, Universities, Schools and Hospitals: Recent Trends and Funding Issues," in Harvey Lazar, ed., *Canada: The State of the Federation: 2000–2001: Towards a New Mission Statement for Fiscal Federalism* (Kingston: Institute for Intergovernmental Relations, 2000) 323.

6. Total government spending (all levels: FMS basis): $463.4 billion; total provincial and territorial government spending: $258.0 billion; provincial "general government" spending, excluding general purpose transfers to other levels of government: $207.0 billion. Source: Statistics Canada, *Public Sector Statistics: 2003–2004*, Cat. # 68–213 (Ottawa: Statistics Canada, 2004) Tables 2.0, 2.5, 2.6.

7. Statistics Canada, *Public Sector Statistics: 2003–2004*, Table 1:10, 39.

8. Kitchen.

9. Alberta, Canada's third fast-growing province, has chosen to pay down its provincial debt, both to insulate itself from fluctuations of oil and gas prices (which have

made up between 14 per cent of provincial revenues in 1998–99 and 41 per cent in 2000–01, averaging 21.9 per cent between 1993–94 and 2002–03) and to prepare for the eventual depletion of a non-renewable resource. Source: Alberta, "Historical Fiscal Summary," *Fiscal Plan 2003–04 to 2005–06* (Edmonton: Alberta Finance, 8 April 2003).

10. *Citizens Insurance vs. Parsons*, (1881) 7 AC 96; *Hodge vs. the Queen*, (1883) 9 AC 117; see also Garth Stevenson, *Ex Uno Plures: Federal Provincial Relations in Canada: 1867–1896* (Montreal and Kingston: McGill-Queen's University Press, 1993) 286–97.

11. Canada, Department of Justice, *The Constitution Act, 1867*; available at <http://laws.justice.gc.ca/en/const/c1867_e.html>.

12. Statistics Canada, *Public Sector Statistics*, Cat. 68–213 (Ottawa: Statistics Canada, November 2001).

13. Harvey Lazar, France St. Hilaire, and Jean-Francois Tremblay, "Vertical Fiscal Imbalance: Myth or Reality," in France St. Hilaire and Harvey Lazar, eds., *Money, Politics and Health Care: Reconstructing the Federal-Provincial Partnership* (Montreal: IRPP, 2004) 156; Statistics Canada, *Public Sector Finance*, Cat. 68-214 (Ottawa: Statistics Canada, 2004).

14. Keith Banting and Robin Boadway, "Defining the Sharing Community: The Federal Role in Health Care," St. Hilaire and Lazar, eds. 1–78; this analysis was anticipated by Alain Noel in his 1998 article "Les trois unions fiscales," *Policy Options* (November).

15. Noel 152–54.

16. Lazar, St. Hilaire, and Tremblay 153.

17. Noel.

18. Lazar, St. Hilaire, and Tremblay 176. Federal spending, including transfers, amounted to 41.6 per cent of total public sector spending in 2003–04 (FMS basis); however, excluding transfers, it was only 33.2 percent; see Statistics Canada, *Public Sector Finance: 2004*.

19. Alain Noel, *Power and Purpose in Intergovernmental Relations* (Montreal: IRPP, November 2001).

20. For more details, see Karin Treff and David B. Perry, *2001 Finances of the Nation* (Toronto: Canadian Tax Foundation, 2001), Chapter 8; and Canada, Senate Standing Committee on National Finance, "The Effectiveness of and Possible Improvements to the Present Equalization Policy," *Fourteenth Report* (Ottawa: The Senate, March 2002).

21. The cash component of these transfers, ranging from $627 per capita in New Brunswick to $537 in Ontario in 2001, is larger in "have less" provinces; Canada, "Major Federal Transfers to Provinces and Territories" (Ottawa: Department of Finance, February 2002).

22. Treff and Perry 8:2.

23. Statistics Canada, *Provincial Economic Accounts, 2003 Preliminary Estimates*, Cat. # 13-213 (Ottawa: Statistics Canada, April 2004) 394, 397; author's calculations.

24. Peter Hogg, *Constitutional Law of Canada*, 4th ed. (Toronto: Carswell, 1996) 134–6.

25. Bev Dahlby and Dagmar Dyck, "Alberta and the Provincialization of the Canadian Fiscal System," in B. Dahlby, ed., *Alberta's Fiscal Frontiers: Essays in Honour of A.D. O'Brien* (Edmonton: Institute for Public Economics, 2002) 19–44.

26. Canada, Department of Finance, "Tax Transfers" 2003; available at <http://www.fin.gc.ca/FEDPROV/taxe.html>.

27. For a more detailed analysis of federal and provincial sales taxes, see Karin Treff and David B. Perry, *Finances of the Nation: 2002* (Toronto: Canadian Tax Foundation, 2003) Chapter 5.

28. Saskatchewan balanced its budget in 1995–96, measured on a public accounts basis, even though running a slight budget deficit for calendar year 1995, when measured in Statistics Canada's system of national accounts.

29. Some observers have suggested that trends in net debt or debt to GDP ratios may be a better long-term assessment of fiscal performance. However, as most provinces have emphasized balancing budgets rather than long-term debt trends as a major basis for their accountability to voters, I have chosen this measurement as a way of comparing relative performance.

30. John Richards, "Now That the Coat Fits the Cloth...," *Commentary 143* (Toronto: C.D. Howe Institute, June 2000).

31. Revenue Canada, *Taxation Statistics: 1992* (Ottawa: Revenue Canada, 1994); Revenue Canada, *Income Statistics, 1997* (Ottawa: Revenue Canada, 1999); Canada Customs and Revenue Agency, *Income Statistics: 1999, 2000* (Ottawa: CCRA, 2001–02); Quebec, Ministère des Finances, *Statistiques fiscales des particuliers: année d'imposition 1999* (Quebec: Ministère des Finances, 11 June 2002) Tableau 18; author's calculations.

32. Revenue Canada, Canada Customs and Revenue Agency, Quebec, Ministère des Finances. Quebec, Newfoundland, and PEI actually raised income tax rates slightly in the late 1990s. Ontario's tax cuts followed sharp tax increases in the early 1990s. Although BC's NDP government reduced taxes slightly in the late 1990s, while increasing spending substantially, these patterns were sharply reversed by its Liberal successors, elected in 2001.

33. This point has been made repeatedly by federal officials faced with provincial demands for the restoration of the 1995–98 cuts to federal-provincial transfers; Canada, *The Fiscal Balance in Canada* (Ottawa: Department of Finance, August 2001).

34. For an excellent summary of budgetary rules and practices in comparative perspective, see Suzanne Kennedy and Janine Robbins, "The Role of Fiscal Rules in Determining Fiscal Performance," Working Paper 2001-16 (Ottawa: Department of Finance, 2001).

35. Geoffrey E. Hale, "The Tax on Income and the Growing Decentralization of Canada's Personal Income Tax System," in Harvey Lazar, ed., *Towards a Mission Statement for Fiscal Federalism: State of the Federation 2000–2001* (Montreal and Kingston: McGill-Queen's University Press, 2000).

36. Ontario's nominal reduction in tax rates between 1996 and 1999 averaged 30 per cent across all income groups, but changes in provincial surtaxes and other factors resulted in a net reduction of 24 per cent.

37. For a concise and balanced summary of the debate, see Lazar, St. Hilaire, and Tremblay 145–50.

38. Douglas Hartle, *The Federal Deficit*, Discussion Paper 93-30, Government and Competitiveness Series (Kingston: School of Policy Studies, Queen's University, 1993); Geoffrey Hale, *The Politics of Taxation in Canada* (Peterborough, ON: Broadview Press, 2001).

39. Provincial net debt grew 64.5 per cent faster than inflation and population between 1990 and 1995—compared with almost 25 per cent for the federal debt. As usual, these averages disguised considerable variations between provinces. See Statistics Canada, *Public Sector Statistics* Cat. # 68-213 (Ottawa, November 2001) Appendix II.; author's calculations.

40. For an excellent summary of budgetary rules and practices in comparative perspective, see Kennedy and Robbins.

41. Kennedy and Robbins 5.

42. Ontario, *Budget 2002–03* (Toronto: Ministry of Finance, 17 June 2002). Ontario's *Taxpayer Protection and Balanced Budget Act, 1999* required that "Before a tax rate under a specified statute can be increased, before a new tax can be imposed, and before the authority to tax (as described in section 3) can be given to another person or body, there must be a referendum authorizing it (sections 2 and 3). Certain exceptions are set out (sections 4 and 5). For example, no referendum is required if the action was clearly stated as part of the election platform of the party that forms the government. Nor is a referendum required for an increase or new tax if, in the opinion of the Minister of Finance, it is not designed to generate a net increase in provincial revenues and revenues raised for school tax purposes." *Explanatory Notes: Bill 7—Taxpayer Protection and Balanced Budget Act, 1999* (Toronto: Ontario Legislative Library, 1999). See also Manitoba, *The Balanced Budget, Debt Reduction and Taxpayer Accountability Act* (Winnipeg: Ministry of Finance 1995). Alberta's referendum legislation is restricted to the creation of a provincial sales tax but, unlike the other two provinces, places no restrictions on increases in existing taxes; Alberta, *Alberta Taxpayer Protection Act*, RSA 2000 (Edmonton: Queen's Printer for Alberta, 2000) Section 4, Chapter A-36.

43. Erik Peters, "Report on the Review of the 2003–04 Fiscal Outlook" (Toronto: Government of Ontario, 29 October 2003); available at <http://www.premier.gov.on.ca/english/erikpeters/PetersReport.pdf>. Subsequent estimates place Ontario's 2003–04 deficit closer to $1.9 billion; see Drew Hasselback, "Alarm raised on provincial deficits," *Financial Post*, 17 February 2004: FP1.

44. Guy Breton, "Rapport sur la situation financière prévisible du gouvernement du québec au 15 avril 2003" (Quebec: Bureau du premier ministre, 2003); Robert Dutrisac, "Un trou de 4,3 milliards," *Le Devoir*, 1 May 2003; TD Economics, "The 2003 Quebec Budget," (Toronto: TD Economics, 13 June 2003).

45. Paul Boothe (2002), "Government Spending in Alberta: The O'Brien Years and Beyond," Dahlby, ed., 5.

46. Boothe 5.

47. Lazar, St. Hilaire, and Tremblay 141–57.

48. For a detailed comparison and analysis of competing analytical frameworks, see Lazar, St. Hilaire, and Tremblay 157–71. Sources for the competing political and economic arguments are noted below.

49. Canada, *The Fiscal Balance in Canada: The Facts* (Ottawa: Department of Finance, semi-annual); see also Chris Matier, Lisa Wu, and Harriet Jackson, "Analyzing Vertical Fiscal Imbalance in a Framework of Fiscal Sustainability," Working Paper 2001-23 (Ottawa: Department of Finance, 2001); Kenneth Norrie, "On Fiscal Balance in the Federation," in Robert D. Brown, ed., *Canadian Conundrums: Views from the Clifford Clark Visiting Economists* (Toronto: C.D. Howe Institute, 2002) 32–33.

50. Quebec, Commission on Fiscal Imbalance, *Report* (2002); available at <www. desequilibrefiscal.gouv.qc.gc.ca/en/document/rapport_final.htm>; Conference Board of Canada, *Fiscal Prospects for the Federal and Provincial/Territorial Governments— Economic Performance and Trends* (Ottawa: Conference Board of Canada, July 2002) 1. This definition reflects the usage of the Western and Territorial Finance Ministers, *Towards Fiscal Balance: A Western Perspective* (Brandon: May 2000), and *Revitalizing Federal-Provincial/Territorial Fiscal Relations* (Moose Jaw: May 2001).

51. For example, see Robert Stowe England, *The Fiscal Challenge of an Aging Industrial World* (Washington, DC: Centre for Strategic and International Studies, 2001); OECD, "Fiscal Sustainability: The Contribution of Fiscal Rules," *OECD Economic Observer* 72 (December 2002): 123; "In The Long Run We Are All Broke," *The Economist* (22 November 2003): 76; William B.P. Robson, "Time and Money: The Fiscal Impact of Demographic Change in Canada," *Commentary 185* (Toronto: C.D. Howe Institute, July 2003); Peter S. Heller, *Who Will Pay? Coping with Aging Societies, Climate Change, and Other Long-Term Fiscal Challenges* (Washington, DC: International Monetary Fund, November 2003).

52. Hale, Chapter 12; John A. Helliwell, *Globalization and Well-Being* (Vancouver: University of British Columbia Press, 2003); Christian Lammert, *Modern Welfare States under Pressure: Determinants of Tax Policy in a Globalizing World*, Working Paper 2004-01 (Montreal: IRPP, 2004).

53. George Hoberg, ed., *Capacity for Choice* (Toronto: University of Toronto Press, 2002).

PART V

Provincial Public Policy

CHAPTER 14

The Realignment of Government in the Provinces[1]

KAREN BRIDGET MURRAY
(with the research assistance of Victoria Miernicki)[2]

Introduction

Among political scientists in Canada and elsewhere, the question of the changing role of "the state" has been a central research theme. Especially since the
mid-1990s, a large body of research has attempted to evaluate the extent and
causes of government retrenchment, a focus captured in phrases such as the "retreating," "shrinking," "hollowing out," or "dismantling" of the state. Others have
questioned theories of retrenchment, emphasizing what they argue to be the development of a "new kind of state."[3]

Canadian researchers, as one study suggests, have been particularly influential in enhancing our understanding of the role of federalism in shaping the
evolution of the state.[4] Most often, however, these studies focus on evaluating
intergovernmental relations rather than on how particular governmental configurations take shape within specific provinces. Indeed, it is striking how little is
known about recent governmental transformations at the provincial level.[5] What
we do know is largely based on case studies dealing with a single policy or administrative field. Much of the research is dated, and the lion's share is focused on
Ontario and, to a lesser extent, Alberta.[6] It is precisely because of this imbalance
in the literature that the time is ripe for considering the limits of our knowledge
with regard to provincial governmental change.

This chapter contributes to developing our understanding of provincial
government transformations by using a qualitative approach to identify major governmental themes and processes at play in the provinces since the early
1990s. It focuses on the English-language secondary literature and selected primary sources.[7] Of course, an emphasis on English publications invariably has its
limitations, most obviously since many French-language studies are left unex-
amined. Nevertheless, given how little we know from a comparative provincial
perspective, an examination of this kind will allow us to stand back and discern
possible patterns and trends that are not readily apparent in studies of particular
policy domains or provinces. At the same time, an exploratory study such as this
is also beneficial for highlighting areas for future research. While this study is
not a comprehensive overview of provincial government transformations, the

evidence underscores the need to consider how relations between provincial governments and "extra-governmental" domains are shaping, and indeed shaking, the very foundations of what we once thought government to be. In this regard, both the "retrenchment thesis" and the "new state" arguments are found wanting as they fail to adequately address domains beyond the state that are also integral to governing.

The first part of this chapter explores how provincial governments have changed governmental practices through 1) internal administrative transformations, 2) the selling off of government business enterprises, and 3) the trend towards public-private partnerships. The second section explores some of the major patterns of change in the areas of health, education, and welfare, policy domains that have historically been the driving force behind the growth of the state. In the third, I look at how provincial governments have sought to shift the responsibilities of municipal governments.

Markets, Governments, and Non-Profits

The idea that government should be run as a business became popularized with the publication of David Osborne and Ted Gaebler's *Reinventing Government*.[8] Osborne and Gaebler's central thesis was that governments had grown too big, sluggish, and rule-bound to work well. Their solution was to reorient government towards steering rather than rowing, with a focus on results-driven policies that harness market principles of competition, "customer" needs, and profits. We see provincial governments adopting this orientation toward governing through internal administrative reforms, as well as by seeking to mobilize for-profit and non-profit entities towards activities once undertaken by official institutions of power.

Running government as a business

It is difficult to estimate the extent to which the idea of "running government as a business" took hold, as very little research has been conducted on internal bureaucratic restructuring. Nevertheless, we do know that some provincial governments have experimented with market techniques. Except for Prince Edward Island and Newfoundland, provincial governments increasingly emphasized the bottom line by passing balanced budget legislation.[9] Departmental-level business plans and employer-employee contracts were used in Quebec, Nova Scotia, and Ontario as part of personnel management reforms.[10] In some instances, front-line managers were given more discretion in their activities as accountability came to be defined in terms of performance measurements rather than adherence to strict rules.[11] New technologies and organizational forms, such as "single-window services," often facilitated changes.[12] In other cases, special operating agencies operating with a degree of managerial flexibility were set up according to predetermined performance targets.[13] Such initiatives sometimes effectively pushed responsibilities once undertaken by governments to the private sector.

Crown corporations

The sale of Crown corporations would appear to be a straightforward measure of one area where provincial governments are reducing their activity in economic life. Apart from Alberta, however, provincial governments have not kept easily accessible records of these transactions. Provincial governments, moreover, do not always own 100 percent of the stakes in Crown corporations; hence, simply counting the number of Crown corporations sold does not give a full picture of the extent to which governments have reduced their economic interests. And even though a Crown corporation may be dismantled, it is not always the case that it will be sold to the private sector. Some are integrated into government departments or transformed into government interests or investments.[14]

Nevertheless it is clear that, since at least the late 1980s, provincial governments, with the exception of PEI, have moved out of some government business enterprises. Quebec sold its stakes in Donohue Inc., the Madelipeche fishing operation in Iles-de-la-Madeleine, as well as Quebecair Inc.[15] Alberta sold 14 Crown corporations (see Table 14.1), including some of the largest sold in Canada during the early half of the 1990s, as shown in Table 14.2. Those that Saskatchewan sold were also among the largest.

Table 14.1. Crown Corporations Sold by the Alberta Government since 1990

1990	The Alberta Government Telephones Commission
	Alberta Terminals Ltd.
1994	The Workers' Compensation Board
1995	Alberta Educational Communications Corporation
	Alberta Electric Energy Marketing Agency
	Alberta Resources Railway Corporation
1996	Alberta Liquor Control Board
	Alberta Racing Commission
	Alberta Special Waste Management Corporation
	Glenbow-Alberta Institute
1997	Alberta Intermodal Services Limited
	Alberta Motion Picture Development Corporation
2001	Alberta Oil Sands Technology and Research Authority
2002	Alberta Dairy Control Board

Source: E-mail correspondence with Richard Lowen, Ministry of Finance, Government of Alberta, 24 July 2003.

A number of provincial government enterprises were sold in Saskatchewan, Manitoba, and Nova Scotia (see Table 14.2). Alberta sold its liquor outlets in

1993 and 1994, and New Brunswick, Quebec, and Ontario are moving in the same direction;[16] British Columbia privatized the BC Ferries Corporation, and is undertaking a review of other Crowns corporations;[17] Newfoundland sold Newfoundland and Labrador Computer Services Limited, along with the assets of several others; and New Brunswick is considering divesting itself of NB Power.[18]

Table 14.2. Largest Privatizations of Provincial and Municipal Crown Corporations (1975–96)

Name of Corporation	% Ownership	Year of Sale
Alberta Government Telephones	100.0	1990
Manitoba Telephone Systems	100.0	1996
Cameco (Saskatchewan)[1]	61.5	1991
Nova Scotia Power Corporation	100.0	1992
Alberta Energy Company	100.0	1975
Syncrude Canada (Alberta)	16.7	1993
Edmonton Telephone	100.0	1995
Postash Corp. of Saskatchewan	100.0	1989
Suncor (Ontario)	25.0	1992
Vencap Equities Alberta	31.0	1995

1. The Saskatchewan Government continued to hold 10.3 per cent of Cameco's shares until year-end of 2001. See Levac and Wooldbridge 31; and Jasen Clemens, Joel Emes, and Nadeem Esmail, "Saskatchewan Prosperity: Taking the Next Step," *Public Policy Sources* 57 (Vancouver: The Fraser Institute, 2002): 31.

Source: Adapted from Mylène Levac and Philip Wooldridge, "The Fiscal Impact of Privatization in Canada," *Bank of Canada Review* (Summer 1997): 31.

Sales of Crown corporations have not, however, proceeded in ineluctable fashion. New Brunswick, after Premier Lord almost lost the election over high car insurance rates, opted to modify its private car insurance system, only after exploring the possibility of establishing a public system.[19] In other instances, privatization efforts proved problematic. Following the path of California, Ontario back-pedaled on privatizing hydroelectric power.[20] These high-profile failures steered BC away from privatizing British Columbia Hydro and Power Authority.[21]

Public-private partnerships

Provincial governments have appeared increasingly eager to engage in "partnerships" with various private for-profit and non-profit organizations. The emergence of the phrase "public-private partnerships" (P3s) is one indication of this trend. P3s encompass a wide range of procurement methods, such as contracting out services and joint ownership of property or production. Such partnerships are not new. For many years, municipal governments have contracted out in areas such as roads, snow ploughing, and garbage collection. While it seems clear that partnerships are taking on a greater centrality in governing processes, it is difficult to evaluate the extent to which governments have increased the use of P3s. In many cases, contracting out is initiated at the individual agency level, with little or no direction from political authorities.[22] Even the Alberta government, which implemented one of the most aggressive deficit-busting programs, did not instigate a centrally directed system for promoting P3s.[23] As well, because private firms are not always subject to the same standards of information disclosure, the knowledge that we do have of partnerships is invariably partial. Nevertheless, it is apparent that every province engages in some form of P3, and that P3s are used in a variety of settings, some of which are identified in Table 14.3.

Table 14.3. Selected Provincial Government Public-Private Partnerships

BC	JobWaveBC
	BC Justice Integrated System
	BC Online
	South Surrey Interchange
AB	Telus Learning Connection
	Twin Brooks Elementary School
	Alberta Wellnet
SK	Saskatchewan Multi-Party Training Plan
MB	Manitoba Government Online Services
ON	Toronto Better Transportation Partnership
	Telehealth Ontario
	Ontario Correctional Facility Modernization
	407 ETR
	Bruce Nuclear Power Plant
NB	Belledune Port Authority Refinancing
	Fredericton-Moncton Highway Project
NS	Atlantic Canada On-Line
	Nova Scotia TeleHealth Network
	Cobequid Pass

Source: Compiled from The Canadian Council for Public-Private Partnerships, *100 Projects: Selected Public-Private Partnerships Across Canada* (Toronto: The Canadian Council for Public-Private Partnerships, 2001).

While many P3s are geared toward major infrastructure projects, partnerships with the non-profit sector—charities, voluntary organizations, and the like—are becoming more integral to programs and services aimed at supporting the health and well-being of people and populations. Michael Hall and Keith Banting maintain that the "nonprofit sector appears to be emerging as a chosen instrument of collective action in a new century." The evidence bears this out as most provinces, including British Columbia, Manitoba, Ontario, Quebec, Manitoba, New Brunswick, Newfoundland, Saskatchewan, and PEI have set up formal processes to promote this sector in the social welfare fields.[24] The federal government has played an important role in this regard by spearheading several major initiatives to promote collaboration between the non-profit sector and governments, both federal and provincial, as well as with the for-profit sector. In 2004, for instance, the federal government launched a new "social economy" initiative to promote a larger role for the voluntary sector in addressing issues pertaining to social and economic inequalities. The implications of this are significant and worthy of far more critical academic attention.[25] Yet, while it is clear that the non-profit sector is becoming increasingly vital to the development and provision of social welfare services, our knowledge of it is far from complete. What is clear is that registered charities alone constitute a significant segment of the Canadian economy. In 1994, non-profit organizations received roughly $90.5 million in revenue, with 60 per cent coming from government grants, mostly from provincial governments.[26] Non-registered charities would not be included in these data, so these figures are inevitably partial.

Figure 14.1. Charities per 1,000 Population

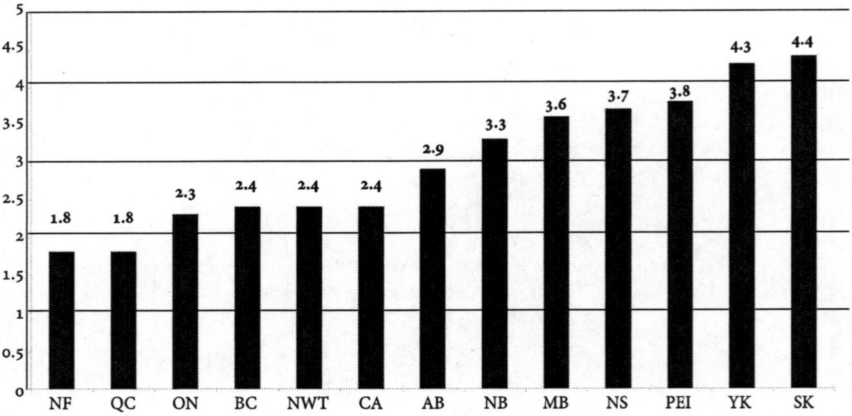

Source: Compiled from Michael Hall and Laura Macpherson, "A Provincial Portrait of Canada's Charities," Canadian Centre for Philanthropy Research Bulletin 4, 2 and 3, (Spring/Summer 1997): 3.

In terms of registered charities, it is clear that provincial variations are wide. As Figure 14.1 demonstrates, Saskatchewan, at 4.4 per cent, has the most charities per 1,000 people, whereas Quebec and Newfoundland, each at 1.8 per cent each, have the fewest. As well, as indicated in Figure 14.2, PEI charities obtain only 44 per cent of their funding from government grants, compared to Newfoundland's 74 per cent, 65 per cent for both BC and Ontario, and 67 per cent for Quebec.

Differences are also apparent in relation to the percentage of government funding directed towards health, education, and social services. As Figure 14.3 reveals, health charities in Saskatchewan (82 per cent), Manitoba (83 per cent) and New Brunswick (77 per cent) receive more government funds than charities in the areas of education or social services. At 74 per cent, Newfoundland social

Figure 14.2. Percentage of Revenues Obtained from Government Grants and Payments,[1] by Province

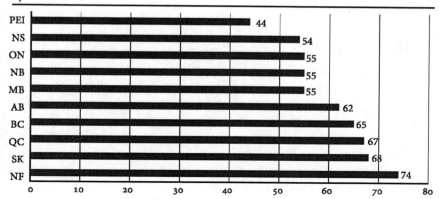

1. Grants and payments include disbursements from all governments including municipal, provincial, and federal.
Source: Adapted from Hall and Macpherson 8–9.

Figure 14.3. Percentage of Revenues Obtained from Government Grants and Payments by Type of Charity[1]

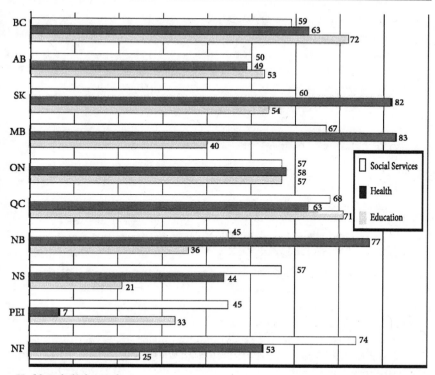

1. Health excludes hospitals.
Source: Adapted from Hall and Macpherson 8–9.

service charities receive more government funding than similar charities in other jurisdictions. At 45 per cent each, social service charities in New Brunswick and PEI receive the least amount of government funding than in other parts of the country. Education charities in the four Atlantic provinces, at between 21 and 36 per cent, receive the lowest percentages of government funding, with charities in Quebec (71 per cent) and BC (72 per cent) receiving the highest levels of funding in the education field. As these figures suggest, the number of charities, the extent to which charities rely on government funding, and the types of charities receiving provincial government funding constitute a divergent mix from province to province. These differences have largely been ignored in the welfare state literature in Canada. Now that non-profit organizations are being touted as important social services domains, much more research is needed to ascertain the historical emergences and implications of these variations.

Summary

The activities of provincial governments over the last roughly 15 years suggests that more attention needs to be paid, not only to the changing role of "the state" but also to the types of relationships and initiatives being undertaken between governments, markets, and the non-profit sector. In this regard, analytical approaches that are focused on retrenchment or new paradigms of the state will prove inadequate to the task. The changing terrain of provincial government beckons for novel analytical strategies and techniques that allow for a much broader conception of government and governance. As will be discussed in the section to follow, this conclusion is also relevant to changes that have taken place in the policy fields of health, education, and welfare.

Health, Education, and Welfare

Provincial government bureaucracies grew as a percent of government expenditures by 400 per cent between 1945 and 1971. This growth was largely due to the expansion of programs relating to health, education, and welfare, which fall under the constitutional jurisdiction of provincial governments.[27] In 1991, one of the flagship federal-provincial funding arrangements supporting the growth of these programs at the provincial level—the Canada Assistance Plan (CAP)—was significantly altered as the federal government put a cap on CAP for the three wealthiest provinces. This was the first time a limit was imposed for transfer payments since the plan was established in 1966. In 1996, CAP was dismantled, and the Canada Health and Social Transfer (CHST) program set up in its place. Unlike CAP, which established national standards for health, education, and welfare programs, CHST allowed for greater provincial flexibility and experimentation. Within this context, provincial governments undertook significant changes to the design and delivery of programs and services in these policy fields. While more recently the CHST has been split into the Canada Social Transfer and Canada Health Transfer, this has not marked a return to the funding commitments under the CAP. And as the evidence to follow suggests, more attention needs to be paid to the complex web of relationships between governments, markets, and the non-profit sector in the domains of health, education, and welfare.[28]

Health

In the area of health care, for instance, the Canadian Healthcare Association found that in the early 1980s public spending in this area accounted for 75 per cent and private spending 25 per cent of health expenditures. In 2001, the public/private-spending ratio was 70/30. The degree of private spending was not, however, uniform. In 2000, it was forecasted that private health sector expenditures would be highest in Alberta (32 per cent), Ontario (31.7 per cent) and New Brunswick (29.7 per cent), with the lowest expected to be in Newfoundland (19.1 per cent).[29]

Major institutional changes were also undertaken. As shown in Table 14.4, with the exception of Ontario, by 2002 every provincial government had implemented some form of regionalized health care. Sometimes regionalization entailed devolving responsibilities from provincial governments to regional bodies;[30] in other cases, responsibilities were shifted upwards from local boards to regional structures. More recently, provincial governments in BC, Alberta, Saskatchewan, and Quebec have reclaimed authority previously devolved to regional entities.[31] No doubt these changes will have an impact on health care programs and delivery, but our knowledge is limited on how structural changes have shaped the scope and character of responsibilities in the health care field.

Education

In the area of education, provincial governments rolled back funding to universities, particularly between 1992 and 1997. By the end of the decade, university revenues began increasing, but these increases came largely from private funding. In the face of government cuts, universities began soliciting funding from other sources, such as private research contracts, endowments, donations, and rising student fees. The shift towards private funding was so dramatic that, in 2003, the Canadian Association of University Teachers argued that "the Canadian university is becoming less a public institution and more a private one, less accountable to the public interest and more beholden to private interests."[32]

This pattern of tightening the provincial purse strings was repeated in the area of K-12 education. Figure 14.4 shows that provinces were spending less on public schools per student as a percent of gross domestic product in 2001 than they were in 1995.[33] Provincial governments have in some cases sought to promote a larger role for the private sector by, for instance, allowing Charter schools.

Table 14.4. Key Dates in Provincial Welfare Reform Initiatives

1992	New Brunswick commences welfare reform agenda.
1993	Alberta overhauls administrative culture of Family and Social Services Ministry.
1994	PEI commences restructuring and downsizing of the Department of Health and Social Services, including the reduction of benefits.
1995	Mike Harris elected as premier of Ontario; soon after welfare benefits are reduced by 21.6 per cent; eligibility is tightened, and fraud reduction scheme implemented.
	New Brunswick replaces the *Social Welfare Act* with the *Family Income Security Act*.
1996	Manitoba introduces the Employment and Income Assistance Program; dismantles Social Allowances Program.
	Newfoundland government releases a consultation paper: the *Strategic Social Plan*.
	Nova Scotia embarks on welfare reform.
	Saskatchewan government releases *Redesigning Social Assistance: Preparing for the New Century*.
	Quebec tightens eligibility requirements and reduces benefits for welfare recipients. Legislative assembly tables consultation paper, *The Road to Labour Market Entry, Training, and Employment*.
1997	Nova Scotia commences the Social Assistance Restructuring Initiative.
1998	Newfoundland implements a new social plan, *People, Partners and Prosperity*, which transfers responsibility over policy development to community organizations.
	Ontario introduces Ontario Works Program; also implements the *Social Assistance Reform Act* and the *Services Improvement Act*, which together transfer funding obligations, new cost-sharing agreements, and responsibilities for programs formerly run provincially to the municipalities.
2000	PEI increases welfare benefits.

Source: Compiled from Chris Schafer, Joel Emes, and Jason Clemens, "Surveying US and Canadian Welfare Reform," *The Fraser Institute Critical Issues Bulletin*, available at <http://oldfraser.lexi.net/publications/critical_issues/2001/welfare/index.html>.

Alberta has been a particularly strong advocate of this trend.[34] From a different angle, parents are increasingly turning to private tutoring to offset the perceived limitations of public education resulting from government reforms.[35]

Initiatives to devolve more authority to the local level appear, on the surface, to provide further evidence that provincial governments were trying to reduce their role in K-12 education. With the exception of BC and Saskatchewan, every province as well as the Yukon introduced a relatively new organizational form of school councils. These reforms were lauded as a means to enhance education policy and augment citizen and local involvement. Participation was not, however, without its limits. In 2002, for instance, when three "rogue" school districts failed to balance their budgets, the Ontario government stripped them of administrative and financial authority, even though school trustees maintained that it was impossible to meet provincial demands without undermining educational quality.[36] Provincial governments provided little instruction to school councils on how to expand local input. In some cases, councils were not given access to information on school performance, and few if any mechanisms were put in place to hold councils accountable for their decisions.[37] In other words, despite the rhetoric of increasing local participation, the mechanisms required for meeting this goal were weak, taking little away from the capacity of central provincial authorities to dictate education policy.

Figure 14.4. Total Public School Expenditures per Student as a Percentage of GDP per Capita

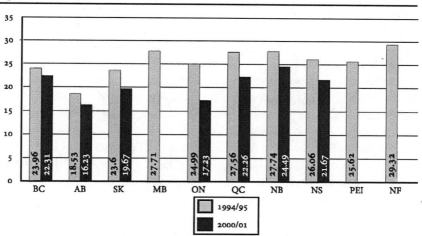

Italicized figures are estimates. Figures not available for 2000/01 for MB, PEI, and NF.
Source: Compiled from British Columbia Ministry of Education Statistics, Summary of School Statistics from the Provinces and Territories, Data Covering School Year 2000/2001 (Victoria, BC: Interprovincial Education Statistics Project, April 2002): 23.

In fact, in other ways, provincial governments were trying to augment their authority. Across the country provincial governments centralized policy development in the education field by imposing new initiatives for teacher training and standardized student tests, report cards, and curricula. In some cases, school boards were slashed or eliminated. For example, the Alberta government cut school boards from 181 to 64; in Quebec, 158 boards were trimmed down to 72; and in Ontario the reduction was from 172 to 108. These cuts further augmented the authority of provincial bureaucrats. Moreover, every province reinforced central government control over revenues, with Ontario, in 1998, becoming the last province to adopt a funding system drawn from the provincial tax base.[38]

Thus, in the education field, there have clearly been contradictory trends. In some cases it appears as though the provinces have attempted to reduce their roles and responsibilities, but in other instances, it is clear that central authorities have sought to rein in the power held by local authorities. Such contradictions do not fit neatly into the "retreating state" thesis, which again highlights the importance of exploring new interpretations of contextually specific differences both within policy domains and across different political settings.

Welfare

In the welfare field provincial governments were not only more eager to rely on the charitable sector in the provision of social services, but they also were shifting managerial supervision of public social services to regional or municipal bodies and focusing, instead, on setting program guidelines. Moreover, every province adopted a new social framework based on tightening up social assistance eligibility requirements, and reducing and eliminating benefits (see Table 14.4).[39] Of particular note, every province introduced some form of a work-for-assistance or "workfare" scheme linking income support to a combination of labour market participation and training through incentives or requirements. Mandatory workfare programs, used in at least six provinces, were prohibited under the CAP, but under the CHST (and later under the Canada Social Transfer) provincial governments were free to require work for social aid. Even though poverty activists argued that workfare violated the rights of the poor, the court upheld the Quebec Government's contention that the *Charter of Rights and Freedoms* does not impose an obligation on governments to provide for the poor.[40] The relationship between the individualization of responsibility for social and economic security and the growing expectations placed on the non-profit sector has yet to be fully explored. However, both appear to be an integral dimension to what many contend is a paradigm shift within government as the assumptions about the role, scope, and aims of governing have clearly altered in some fundamental ways.

Summary

In the areas of health, education, and welfare—three of the main pillars of provincial government growth after the Second World War—it is evident that provincial governments have introduced a wide variety of changes. Here, too, a major tendency has been to promote larger roles for the private domain in areas once considered core features of the bureaucratic state. These three policy fields often have a direct and immediate impact on the lives of individuals and populations, particularly those on the lower rungs of the social and economic ladder. This suggests that far more attention must be given to how changing governmental processes and practices are shaping the boundaries of citizenship, not just in terms of conferring rights and entitlements, but also in relation to the basic pre-suppositions and assumptions shaping discourses and practices of citizenship.

Municipal Government

In recent years, there has been a growing interest in the role of municipal governments in Canada's political system, in large part due to efforts by governments to promote a larger role for communities, cities, and local governmental entities in governmental processes. We are only just beginning, however, to fully grasp the implications of these changes.[41] This section highlights contradictory trends as provincial governments have decentralized some services while centralizing others.

Decentralization versus centralization

The contradictory tendencies of reducing the role of provincial government on the one hand and centralizing provincial government authority on the other were evident in the area of municipal government. Centralization tendencies were apparent as every province (except for BC, which had already created regional districts in the 1960s) embarked on some form of municipal amalgamation, sometimes in the face of widespread resistance. Some of the most dramatic changes occurred in Ontario, where Mike Harris's Progressive Conservative government, between 1996 and 2001, cut the number of municipalities by over 40 per cent, from 815 to 447.[42] Like most governmental transformations, the shifting of municipal structures was promoted as a way to reduce expenses and coordinate services.

At the same time, however, some provincial governments also began shifting some responsibilities downward to municipalities and communities. In Quebec, the provincial government downloaded responsibility for public transit and road maintenance to municipalities, and the Ontario government, while taking responsibility for elementary and secondary school funding, passed responsibility for social and other services to the municipal level. This was done despite the recommendations of the "Who Does What Panel," which argued against further downloading of social services.[43] These additional responsibilities, as Figure 14.5 shows, were not accompanied by an increase in provincial government transfers to the municipalities; with the exception of Manitoba, government grants constituted a smaller source of municipal government revenue between 1988 and 1998.

This pattern of municipal government transformation was not wholly consistent. In Nova Scotia, for instance, the provincial government steadily implemented a plan to release municipalities from responsibility for social service financing.[44] And changes played out differently depending on the municipality in question. According to Enid Slack, rural areas were "hard hit by the downloading of provincial highway maintenance costs, policing costs, and the elimination of the farm tax rebate."[45] In Nova Scotia, disentanglement resulted in municipalities with the weakest tax base facing increasing costs, while those with the strongest tax base saw expenses reduced.[46] Elsewhere, municipalities in large urban areas were hardest hit by the downloading of social housing and assistance. Urban centres felt even greater strains as a result of the aging population and relatively high immigration levels. Offering at least a modicum of services, urban centres increasingly were becoming destinations for those who are most socially and economically marginalized.[47] In the face of their inability to meet increased service demands, municipalities also began turning to non-profit organizations to pick up the slack.[48]

Figure 14.5. Distribution (in per cent) of Municipal Government Revenue[1] from Grants (Federal and Provincial Combined) by Province, 1988 and 1998

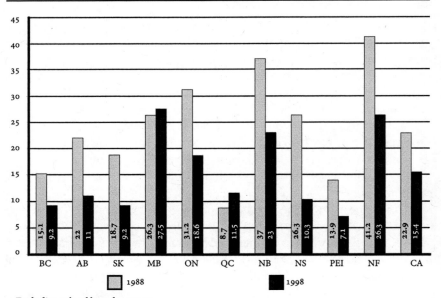

1. Excluding school board revenue.
Source: Adapted from Harry Kitchen, "Provincial-Municipal Fiscal Trends: An Interprovincial and Intertemporal Comparison." Paper presented at UBCM Convention, Waterfront Centre Hotel, Vancouver, British Columbia (September 27, 1999): 10–11.

Summary

Now that the cities' agenda is firmly on the political agenda, it is worth considering the implications of focusing on mechanisms of the state in driving governmental change in this area. The evidence suggests that municipalities, cities, and com-munities—generally "the local"—emerged as *de facto* vital elements of Canada's political system as a result of the widespread shifts toward market-based and non-profit program and service delivery and design. The "private" sphere inevitably focuses on relationships among individuals, through competition or cooperation—processes that are inherently local in nature, although obviously holding much broader implications in practice. Now that so many provincial government activities have been "shifted out," it seems clear that much more attention needs to be paid to how private dynamics and processes have altered the terrain of "the political" in Canada.

Conclusion

By design, this discussion has been rather broad in order to show the range of evidence that demonstrates discernible patterns of provincial governmental change. This literature scan suggests that analyses that focus centrally on "the state" cannot be anything but partial, as "extra-governmental" domains have clearly emerged as central domains in areas that were once considered central to political and governmental activity. Some people might argue that this suggests a constitutive reduction in government, but clearly the evidence is more complex than the retrenchment thesis. And even the "new kind of state" thesis is wanting, because it cannot adequately take into account the role of "private" activity in shaping human conduct. The current context, therefore, calls out for more than a new paradigm of the state. Analytical approaches that encompass a much broader terrain of human action as central to governmental processes would appear to be essential to understanding the contemporary political context, and the study of provincial governments is a field that offers many opportunities to explore these issues. And, indeed, if there is in fact a paradigm shift underway, then by definition new questions, tools, and analytical frames are essential. This point, of course, was made by Thomas Kuhn who argued in *The Structure of Scientific Revolutions* that our theories, methods, and approaches, and the assumptions to which they are tied, inevitably shape and are influenced by the paradigm within which we live.[49]

Notes

1. Gratitude is extended to Christopher Dunn, Peter Graefe, and Denis Saint Martin for reading and providing detailed comments on earlier drafts. Thanks also to Graham White for his helpful observations in the early phases of the research. Errors are, of course, my own.
2. Karen Murray is an Assistant Professor in the Department of Political Science at the University of New Brunswick. Victoria Miernicki is an MA student in Political Science at the University of New Brunswick.
3. Paul Pierson, *Dismantling the Welfare State? Reagan, Thatcher, and the Politics of Retrenchment* (Cambridge: Cambridge University Press, 1994); R.A.W. Rhodes, "The Hollowing Out of the State: The Changing Nature of the Public Service in Britain," *The Political Quarterly*, 65 (1994): 138–51; John Shields and B. Mitchell Evans, *Shrinking the State: Globalization and Public Administration Reform* (Halifax:

Fernwood Publishing, 1998); Susan Strange, *The Retreat of the State: The Diffusion of Power in the World Economy* (Cambridge: Cambridge University Press, 1996).

4. Ian Forbes and Dominic Abrams, "International Social Science Research: Craft Industry or Baby Behemoth?" *International Social Science Journal* 56,180 (June 2004): 237.

5. David R. Cameron and Jacqueline D. Krikorian, "The Study of Federalism 1960–1999: A Content Review of Several Leading Canadian Academic Journals," *Canadian Public Administration* 45,3 (2002); Richard Simeon, *Political Science and Federalism* (Kingston: Institute of Intergovernmental Relations, 2000).

6. Recent edited collections of case studies include: J. Bourgault, M. Demers, and C. Williams, eds., *Public Administration and Public Management: Experiences in Canada* (Québec: Les Publications du Québec, 1997); Evert Lindquist, *Government Restructuring and Career Public Service* (Toronto: IPAC, 2000); and Gene Swimmer, ed., *Public-Sector Labour Relations in an Era of Restraint and Restructuring* (Don Mills: Oxford University Press, 2001). Book-length case studies include: David Cameron and Graham White, *Cycling into Saigon* (Vancouver: University of British Columbia Press, 2000); Peter Clancy, James Bickerton, Rodney Haddow, and Ian Stewart, *The Savage Years: The Perils of Reinventing Government in Nova Scotia* (Halifax: Formac Publishing Company Limited, 2000); Robert I. McLaren, *The Saskatchewan Practice of Public Administration in Historical Perspective* (Lewiston: The Edwin Mellen Press, 1998); William J. Milne, *The McKenna Miracle: Myth or Reality?* (Toronto: University of Toronto, Faculty of Management, Centre for Public Management, 1996); Sylvie Morel, *The Insertion Model or the Workfare Model? The Transformation of Social Assistance within Quebec and Canada* (Ottawa: Status of Women Canada, 2002); Donald J. Savoie, *Pulling Against Gravity: Economic Development in New Brunswick During the McKenna Years* (Montreal: Institute for Research on Public Policy, 2001). *Canadian Public Administration, Optimium: The Journal of Public Management*; and *Canadian Government Executive* are the primary journal locations of provincial case studies of government reform.

7. Comparative research includes: Sandford Borins and S. Kocovski, *Public Management Innovation in the Provinces*, in J. Bourgault, M. Demers, and C. Williams, eds., *Public Administration and Public Management: Experiences in Canada* (Québec: Les Publications du Québec, 1997) 219–28; J. Church and P. Parker, "Regionalization of Health Services in Canada: A Critical Perspective," *International Journal of Health Services* 28,3 (1998): 467–86; Jeremiah Hurley, Jonathan Lomas, and Vandna Bhatia, "When Tinkering is Not Enough: Provincial Reform to Manage Health Care Resources," *Canadian Public Administration* 37,3 (Fall 1994): 490–514; Evert A. Lindquist, "Government Restructuring and the Evolution of Career Public Service in Canada's Provinces and Territories," in J. Bourgault, M. Demers, and C. Williams, eds., 230–41; Evert A. Lindquist and Karen B. Murray, "A Reconnaissance of Canadian Administrative Reform During the Early 1990s," *Canadian Public Administration* 37,3 (Fall 1994): 468–489; John Fryer, "Provincial Public Service Relations," in Gene Swimmer and Mark Thompson, eds., *Public Sector Collective Bargaining in Canada: Beginning of the End or the End of the Beginning?* (Kingston: IRC Press, 1995) 341–67; Richard Simeon and Robert E. Miller, "Regional Variations in Public Policy," in David Elkins and Richard Simeon, eds., *Small Worlds, Provinces and Parties in Canadian Political Life* (Toronto: Methuen, 1980); Gene Swimmer, "Provincial Policies Concerning Collective Bargaining," in Christopher Dunn, ed., *Provinces: Canadian Provincial Politics* (Peterborough: Broadview Press, 1996)

351–78; Terry H. Wagar and Shelley Arsenault, "Workforce Reduction in the Public Sector: Evidence from the Maritime Provinces," *Canadian Public Administration* 37,1 (Spring 1994): 177–84.

8. David Osborne and Ted Gaebler, *Reinventing Government: How the Entrepreneurial Spirit is Transforming the Public Sector* (New York: Plume, 1992).

9. TD Economics, "TD Report on Canadian Government Finances: Newfoundland 5-Year Fiscal Forecast," available at <http://www.td.com/ economics/finances/newfo1. html>.

10. Luc Juillet, ed., "Special Issue on Provincial Trends," *Public Service Commission Quarterly Updates* 1,4 (December 1999): 12–15.

11. See Sandford Borins, "The New Public Management is Here to Stay," *Canadian Public Administration* 38,1 (Spring 1995): 125; and Michael Power, *The Audit Society: Rituals of Verification* (Oxford: Oxford University Press, 1999).

12. Stephen Brent, Kenneth Kernaghan, and D. Brian Marson, *Innovations and Good Practices in Single-Window Service* (Ottawa: Canadian Centre for Management Development, 1999); F. Leslie Seidle, *Rethinking the Delivery of Public Services to Citizens* (Montreal: IRPP, 1995); Anil Verma and Zsuzsanna Lonti, *Changing Government Workplaces* (Ottawa: Canadian Policy Research Networks, May 2001). See also Evert A. Lindquist and Graham White, "Streams, Springs, and Stones: Ontario Public Service Reform in the 1980s and the 1990s," *Canadian Public Administration* 37,2 (Summer 1994): 267–301.

13. Paul Thomas and John Wilkins, "Special Operating Agencies: A Culture Change in the Manitoba Government," in Robert Ford and David Zussman, eds., *Alternative Service Delivery: Sharing Governance in Canada* (Toronto: IPAC, 1997) 99.

14. Interview with Jason Clemens, the Fraser Institute, August 8, 2003.

15. Gary Regenstreif, "Quebec Government Sees Even More Sales of Assets," *Toronto Star*, 24 March 1987: E6.

16. David Israelson, "Sober Second Thoughts: Premier Elect Mike Harris Wants to Know Why Government is in the Business of Selling Booze," *Toronto Star*, 24 June 1995: C1; Colin Perkel, "Ontario to Franchise Some LCBO Outlets," *Toronto Star*, 22 September 2001: A31.

17. Sylvia Fuller, *Protecting the Crowns: The Role and Value of Public Enterprises in BC* (Vancouver: Canadian Centre for Policy Alternatives, November 2002).

18. Correspondence with provincial government officials: Heather Jacobs, Department of Justice, Newfoundland; Lynn Ellsworth, Executive Council Office, PEI; Peggy Goss, Legislative Assembly Library, New Brunswick.

19. Tali Folkins, "Panel's Advice Could Come by Fall: Weir," *Saint John Telegraph-Journal*, 7 August 2003: A1/A6.

20. Caroline Mallan, "Eves: Hydro One Not For Sale," *Toronto Star*, 13 June 2002: A06.

21. Brent Jang, "No Privatization for B.C. Hydro, Province Says," *The Globe and Mail*, 26 November 2002: B7.

22. See, for example, Evan Atwood and Michael J. Trebilock, "Public Accountability in an Age of Contracting Out," *The Canadian Business Law Journal* 27,1 (July 1996); James C. McDavid, "Solid Waste Contracting Out, Competition and Bidding Practices Among Local Governments," *Canadian Public Administration* 44 (Spring 2001); James C. McDavid and Eric Clemens, "Contracting Out Local Government Services: The B.C. Experience," *Canadian Public Administration* 38,2 (Summer 1995): 177–93; and Philip de L. Panet and Michael J. Trebilock, "Contracting-out Social Services," *Canadian Public Administration* 41,1 (Spring 1998): 21–50.

23. Christopher Bruce, "Rethinking the Delivery of Government Services," in Christopher J. Bruce, Ronald D. Kneebone, and Kenneth J. McKenzie, eds., *A Government Reinvented: A Study of Alberta's Deficit Elimination Program* (Toronto: Oxford University Press, 1997) 421–55.

24. Quote from Michael Hall and Keith G. Banting, "The Nonprofit Sector in Canada: An Introduction," in Keith G. Banting, ed., *The Nonprofit Sector in Canada: Roles and Relationships* (Montreal and Kingston: McGill-Queen's University Press, 2000) 1–2. See also Kathy L. Brock, ed., *Improving Connections Between Governments and Nonprofit and Voluntary Organizations: Public Policy and the Third Sector* (Montreal and Kingston: McGill-Queen's University Press, 2002). Internet information on provincial voluntary sector initiatives include Alberta <http://www3.gov.ab.ca/ gs/services/cnfb/>; Manitoba <http://www.voluntarysector.mb.ca>; Ontario <http:// www.gov.on.ca/ mczcr/english/citdiv/voluntar/index.html>; Saskatchewan <http:// www.saskjustice.gov.sk.ca/pdfdocs/cons.pdf>;Quebec<http://www.mess.gouv.qc.ca/ anglais/index.htm>; and Newfoundland <http://www.cedresources.nf.net>. See also the government of PEI, "Province And UPEI Launch Year Two of The Save Program," News Release, 29 November 2002. The New Brunswick government established, in 1983, and continues to support, the Community Voluntary Action Program; see internal document of the Department of Family and Community Services, "Major Policy and Program Changes at HRD Over the Past 15 Years."

25. Karen B. Murray, "Do Not Disturb: 'Vulnerable Populations' in Federal Government Policy Discourses and Practices," *Canadian Journal of Urban Research* 13,1 (2004): 50–69.

26. Michael Hall and Keith G. Banting, "The Nonprofit Sector in Canada: An Introduction," in Michael Hall and Keith G. Banting, eds., *The Nonprofit Sector in Canada: Roles and Relationships* (Kingston: Queen's School of Policy Studies, 2000) 13. See also David Sharpe, *A Portrait of Canada's Charities* (Toronto: Canadian Centre for Philanthropy, 1994); and Susan D. Phillips, "Redefining Government Relationships with the Voluntary Sector: On Great Expectations *and* Sense and Sensibility," available at <http://www.vsr-trsb.net/publications/phillips-e.html>.

27. Rand Dyck, *Provincial Politics in Canada: Towards the Turn of the Century* (Scarborough: Prentice Hall, 1996) 19.

28. J. Pulkingham and G. Ternowetsky, "The Changing Context of Child and Family Policies," in J. Pulkingham and G. Ternowetsky, eds., *Child and Family Policies: Strategies, Struggles, and Options* (Halifax: Fernwood Publishing, 1997).

29. Canadian Healthcare Association, *Policy Brief: The Private-Public Mix in the Funding of Health Services in Canada: Challenges and Opportunities* (Ottawa: Canadian Healthcare Association, 2001) 26–28. On provincial government approaches to healthcare reform see *CHA Summary of Key Recommendations and Government Responses: Recent Provincial and Territorial Health Systems Reports*, Canadian Healthcare Association, 2002, available at <http://www.canadian-healthcare.org/ documents/Comprehensive_Grid.pdf>.

30. See J. Church and P. Barker, "Regionalization of Health Services in Canada: A Critical Perspective," *International Journal of Health Services* 28,3 (1998): 468. See also Jonathan Lomas, "Devolving Authority for Health Care in Canada's Provinces: 1. An Introduction to the Issues," *Canadian Medical Association Journal* 156 (1997): 373; Jonathan Lomas, Gerry Veenstra, and John Woods, "Devolving Authority for Health Care in Canada's Provinces: 2. Backgrounds, Resources, and Activities of Board Members," *Canadian Medical Association Journal* 156 (1997): 817–23. For

a discussion of provincial differences in health care, see G.W. Boychuk, "Public Health-Care Provision in the Canadian Provinces and American States," *Canadian Public Administration* 45,2 (Summer 2002): 217–38.

31. Denise Kouri, Kelly Chessi, and Steven Lewis, *Regionalization: Where Has All the Power Gone? A Survey of Canadian Decision Makers in Health Care Regionalization* (Saskatoon: Canadian Centre for Analysis of Regionalization and Health, 2002).

32. Canadian Association of University Teachers, *Education Review* 3,1 (1999) and 6,3 (2003).

33. On educational reforms see Stephen B. Lawton, "Trends in Canadian Educational Expenditures: Is the Worst Over?" *Journal of Education Finance* 24,2 (Fall 1998): 220–36; Thomas Flemming, "Provincial Initiatives to Restructure School Governance in the 1990s," *Canadian Journal of Educational Administration and Policy* 11 (1997); Helen Raham, *Education K-12 Policy for Canadian Global Leadership* (Kelowna: Society for the Advancement of Excellence in Education, 2000); and Council of Ministers of Education, "What is Happening in Education?" available at <http://www.cmec.ca/publications/rec98/prov.en.htm>. See also Paul Barker, "Education in Canada: Options for Change," in Martin W. Westmacott and Hugh P. Mellon, eds., *Public Administration and Policy: Governing in Challenging Times* (Scarborough: Prentice Hall Allyn and Bacon Canada, 1999) 180; Stuart Landon, "Education Costs and Institutional Structures," *Economics of Education Review* 18,3 (June 1999): 327–45; Suzanne Majhanovich, "Change in Public Education: Globalization in Action? The Case of Ontario, Canada," *Planning and Changing* 33,1–2 (January 2002): 53–76; Peter Woolstencroft, "Education Policies: Challenges and Controversies," in *Urban Policy Issues: Canadian Perspectives*, 2nd ed. (Don Mills: Oxford University Press, 2002) 280.

34. Canadian Centre for Policy Alternatives, "Provinces Pursue Deregulation of Tuition Fees: Further Limit Access to Higher Education Report" (March 2002), available at <http://policyalternatives.ca>; CUPE, *Dollars and Democracy* 13–24.

35. Scott Davies, Janice Aurini, and Linda Quirk, "New Markets for Private Education in Canada," *Education Canada* 42,3 (Fall 2002): 36–38.

36. Karla Scoon Reid, "Province Takes Over Toronto Schools," *Education Week* (11 September 2002), available at <http://edweek.org/ew/ewstory.cfm?slug"02takeover. h22>.

37. Raham 10–11.

38. Raham 9–11.

39. Chris Schafer, Joel Emes, and Jason Clemens, "Surveying US and Canadian Welfare Reform," *The Fraser Institute Critical Issues Bulletin*, available at <http:///oldfraser. lexi.net/publications/critical_issues/2001/welfare/index.html>.

40. *Gosselin v. Quebec* (Attorney General), 2002 SCC 84, File No: 27418.

41. See for instance, Christopher Dunn, "Urban Asymmetry: The New Reality in Intergovernmental Relations?" *Policy Options* (November 2004); Mary Louise McAllister, *Governing Ourselves? The Politics of Canadian Communities* (Vancouver: University of British Columbia Press, 2004); Murray n. 24.

42. See <http://www.yourlocalgovernment.com/ylg/muniont.html>.

43. Katherine A. Graham and Susan D. Phillips, "'Who Does What' in Ontario: The Process of Provincial-Municipal Disentanglement," *Canadian Public Administration* 41,2 (1998): 175–209; Enid Slack, "Have Fiscal Issues Put Urban Affairs Back on the Policy Agenda?" in Caroline Andrew, Katherine A. Graham, and Susan D. Phillips, eds., *Urban Affairs: Back on the Policy Agenda* (Montreal and Kingston: McGill-Queen's University Press, 2002) 315–16.

44. Slack 315.
45. Slack 316.
46. Igor Vojnovic, "The Fiscal Distribution of the Provincial-Municipal Service Exchange in Nova Scotia," *Canadian Public Administration* 42,4 (Winter 1999): 512–41.
47. Caroline Andrew, "The Shame of (Ignoring) the Cities," *Journal of Canadian Studies* 19 (2001): 100–10. See also A. Kazemipur and S.S. Halli, *The New Poverty in Canada* (Toronto: Thompson Publishing, 2000).
48. Michael J. Skelly, *Alternative Service Delivery in Canadian Municipalities* (Toronto: ICURR, February 1997); Glenna Carr, Jeff Bowden, and Judi Storrer, *New Directions in Municipal Services: Competitive Contracting and Alternative Service Delivery in North American Municipalities* (Toronto: ICURR, June 1997).
49. Thomas Kuhn, *The Structure of Scientific Revolutions* (Chicago, IL: University of Chicago Press, 1962).

CHAPTER 15

The Policy Implications of Provincial Demographics

DAVID K. FOOT

Introduction

Demographers study human populations, including their characteristics, needs, and behaviour. People are the cornerstone of all government. In a democracy, they vote for the members that constitute the government. They pay taxes that provide the means by which government can initiate and implement policies and deliver programs, and they are the beneficiaries of these government services. They constitute the workforce of government. In many jurisdictions, including Canada, population numbers are used to define electoral boundaries. In all of these aspects, therefore, demographic analysis provides useful insights into the workings of government.

Variations in demographic profiles are likely to result in different government outcomes. For example, a jurisdiction dominated by a young demographic profile is likely to appeal to children and their parents using policies and programs related to day care and education, while a jurisdiction with a dominant older demographic profile will find the need to pay more attention to security and health care issues. In a jurisdiction where the dominant demographic profile is of working age, employment and welfare are likely to dominate the agenda. If a jurisdiction has a relatively large Aboriginal profile, policies and programs oriented to Aboriginal peoples are likely to be higher on the agenda than otherwise.

Changes in populations over time, therefore, result in changing needs in the electorate. Policies and programs that are viewed favourably by an electorate in one election may be rejected in a subsequent one because they no longer meet the needs of a changed population within the electorate. The gradual ageing of the populations of Canada and many other developed nations since the 1960s is one example. Immigrant populations that alter the ethnic composition of electorates is another.

Even at a given point in time, governments in jurisdictions with different demographic profiles will face electorates with different needs. Under these conditions, concurrent governments responding to their electorates can be expected to have different legislative and fiscal priorities and a different mix of policies and programs. The greater are the differences in demographic profiles, the greater the likelihood of diversity in government outcomes.

Governments facing communities with different demographic profiles *within* their jurisdictions are especially "demographically challenged." Nations with different ethnic communities within their borders (such as the former Yugoslavia, Sri Lanka, and many African nations) come readily to mind. Urban and rural differences within a jurisdiction are another example. Federations of regional states may be particularly challenged because the regional jurisdictions usually have legislative and fiscal powers to support their jurisdictional needs. The greater are the regional demographic differences, the greater the potential for regional tensions within the federation.

The policies, programs, and priorities of Canadian provincial governments are inevitably influenced by the demographic compositions of the peoples within their jurisdictions. This demographic influence on government is the core of representative government. It applies to changes over time within any one province (or territory) and to comparisons among provinces (and territories) at any point in time. For example, it should come as no surprise that a demographically younger Alberta has different priorities from a demographically older Quebec. The challenge for the Canadian federation, as with any jurisdiction with demographically distinct components, is to find appropriate mechanisms to respect and adjudicate the diversity of demographic challenges within its borders.

For all of these reasons, the study of demographics provides a useful foundation for understanding governments—their electorates and workforces, policies and programs, successes and failures, and their priorities in intergovernmental discussions and negotiations. It is not only a descriptive tool that provides an understanding of the past, but it is also a proactive tool that can provide a vision of the future. While there are many influences on observed government behaviour, demographic developments determine the underlying trends within which governments must operate if they are to enjoy continued success. The longer the time period, the more relevant demographic trends become in influencing outcomes. Moreover, much like a jig-saw, demographics provides an overall picture or framework within which the pieces represented by the multitude of government issues can be integrated and interpreted—from revenues sources to individual program expenditures, from intergovernmental negotiations to workplace policies, and, perhaps, from electoral policies to taxpayer revolts.

This chapter provides an introduction to the use of demographic analysis in the context of Canada's provinces and territories. It starts with a review of the size and growth of the total population of each province and territory. The next section examines the associated age structure and introduces the concept of demographic dependency as a convenient summary measure of demographic influences on government. This concept and the associated data are then extended in the following section to incorporate relevant economic information. Armed with these measures, population projections are introduced to develop an overall vision for the future for each province and territory. Finally, the overall picture is broken down, and selected individual program expenditures are briefly reviewed to illustrate the role that demographics plays in influencing specific government policies and programs. With this information the student of government is equipped to better understand provincial and territorial governments in Canada, both in the past and into the future.

Population Size and Growth

Table 15.1 summarizes the size and growth of the provincial and territorial populations in Canada for the decennial census years between 1971 and 2001. Over this period the Canadian population grew from 22 to 31 million people for an average annual growth rate of 1.2 per cent. This growth rate was lower than world population growth but higher than that in many other developed countries. As with many countries in the developed world, the growth of the Canadian population gradually slowed over the period.

Ontario is the most populated province with 11.9 million people in 2001, which represented 38.2 per cent of the Canadian population. This share increased from 35.7 per cent 30 years earlier, reflecting the faster growth of the provincial population compared to the Canadian average, especially over the 1980s. The population of Ontario is larger than the populations of many other countries, such as Greece, Hungary, or Sweden.

The second most populous province is Quebec with 7.4 million people in 2001, which represents 23.8 per cent of the Canadian population. Quebec's share decreased from 27.9 per cent 30 years earlier, reflecting the comparatively slower growth of its population over the period. Nonetheless, the population of Quebec is still larger than the populations of Switzerland, Denmark, or Singapore.

Perhaps of some interest in discussions of political authority and power in Canada is the fact that in 1971 there were 128 Ontarians for every 100 people in Quebec. By 2001 this figure had risen to 160.

Together these two central provinces of Canada are home to over 19 million people, which is about equal to the population of Australia and larger than the populations of the Netherlands, Belgium, or the Czech Republic. By 2001 Ontario and Quebec together accounted for 62 per cent of the Canadian population, down slightly from 63.6 per cent 30 years earlier. This decreasing share indicates that the Canadian population has gradually dispersed from the centre to the periphery over this period.

The major beneficiaries of this population redistribution were the two most western provinces of British Columbia and Alberta, both of which grew much faster than the Canadian average over the period (see Table 15.1).[1] BC was the third most populous province in Canada with over 4 million people, and Alberta was the fourth most populous province with over 3 million people by 2001. Together they are approaching the population of Quebec, accounting for over 7 million people or 23 per cent of the Canadian population by 2001, up from 17.8 per cent 30 years earlier. Individually, the population of BC is still larger than Ireland or New Zealand, while that of Alberta exceeds Latvia or Kuwait.

Again it is interesting to note that for every 100 people in Quebec there was almost 97 people in the two western provinces in 2001, up from 64 30 years earlier. When compared to Ontario, the western increase—from 50 to 60 for every 100 people in Ontario over 1971-2001—was not as large.

The remaining two western provinces, Manitoba and Saskatchewan, each were home to over one million Canadian residents in 2001, but their combined share of the Canadian population had fallen to 7 per cent from 8.8 per cent 30 years earlier, thereby indicating that their population growth rates had not kept pace with the national average over the period. Nonetheless, individually they still were home to more people than the countries of Luxembourg or Malta.

The other declining shares in this population redistribution were the four Atlantic provinces of New Brunswick, Prince Edward Island, Nova Scotia, and Newfoundland and Labrador. Together they accounted for almost 2.4 million Canadian residents or 7.6 per cent of the Canadian population in 2001. While their combined population was up from 2.1 million people 30 years earlier, their combined share was down from 9.5 per cent in 1971, also a reflection of the comparatively slower growth of the population in this region over the period. Nonetheless, Atlantic Canada was home to more people than the recently created East European nations of Slovenia or Macedonia.

Table 15.1. Provincial Populations: Size and Growth, 1971-2001

	Size (millions)				Growth (% per year)		
	1971	1981	1991	2001	1971-81	1981-91	1991-2001
NF	0.531	0.575	0.580	0.534	0.8	0.1	-0.8
NS	0.797	0.855	0.915	0.943	0.7	0.7	0.3
PEI	0.113	0.124	0.130	0.139	0.9	0.5	0.6
NB	0.642	0.706	0.746	0.757	1.0	0.5	0.2
QC	6.137	6.548	7.065	7.411	0.6	0.8	0.5
ON	7.849	8.811	10.428	11.874	1.2	1.7	1.3
MB	0.999	1.036	1.110	1.150	0.4	0.7	0.4
SK	0.932	0.976	1.003	1.016	0.5	0.3	0.1
AB	1.666	2.294	2.593	3.064	3.3	1.2	1.7
BC	2.240	2.824	3.373	4.096	2.3	1.8	2.0
YT	0.019	0.024	0.029	0.030	2.3	1.9	0.3
NWT[1]	0.036	0.048	0.061	0.069	2.7	2.5	1.3
Canada	21.962	24.820	28.031	31.082	1.2	1.2	1.0

1. Including Nunavut.

Source: Statistics Canada, *Annual Demographic Statistics 2001*.

Finally, Canada's territories—Yukon, Nunavut, and the Northwest Territories—accounted for slightly less than 100,000 persons in 2001. While this was only 0.3 per cent of the Canadian population, the combined population of the territories almost doubled in 30 years, making this the fastest growing region in Canada over 1971-2001. There are countries with similar sized populations such as Tonga and Kiribati in Oceania or St. Vincent in the Caribbean.

Births and deaths

Provincial population sizes and growth are determined by births, deaths, and migration, both international and interprovincial.[2] Populations with higher birth rates experience more rapid population growth and increased size relative to those with lower birth rates. Conversely, populations with higher death rates experience less rapid growth and lower population size relative to those with lower death rates. Similarly, populations with more in-migrants than out-migrants experience population growth, while those with more out-migrants than in-migrants experience population decline.

Demographers frequently refer to the concept of demographic transition that links births and deaths to economic development and, therefore, to each other.[3] Early stages of economic development associated with low incomes per person are characterized by high birth *and* high death rates. As economic development advances and incomes rise, death rates fall first as many of the necessities for life can now be provided for. This is associated with a period of rapid population growth since the difference between high birth rates and lower death rates is enlarged.[4] Later, with continued economic development, birth rates fall as improved education permeates the population and people, especially women, have other opportunities besides raising children. In this era, population growth declines, usually to a level below that experienced in the early stages of economic development.

Based on international comparisons of per capita incomes, Canada has been considered a highly developed country for much of the twentieth century and certainly for the last half of the century. This means that by the end of the century both birth and death rates are low relative to earlier times and relative to many other countries.[5] This comparatively high level of economic development has been reflected in all provinces, although there have been slight differences between the provinces at different periods.[6]

In a broad sense, therefore, provincial economic development could be considered to be part of a provincial demographic policy. While economic development is, probably, the single most important determinant of the trends in births and deaths and therefore of population growth, there are other provincial policies that can also have a limited impact. For example, health care that prevents deaths, especially of the most vulnerable members of the population (infants and the elderly), contributes to population growth. Education, especially of women, provides better knowledge and opportunities for paid employment, which can influence the number of births and hence population growth.

Perhaps the most celebrated recent example of a provincial population policy occurred in Quebec where the government offered potential parents escalating non-taxable cash incentives to have children. The *Allowance for Newborn Children* (ANC) was introduced in the provincial budget of 12 May 1988 and took effect retroactively on 1 May 1988. All permanent residents of Quebec were eligible for this provincial program. Initially new parents were given a one-time $500 for the first and second child, and $3,000 for the third and each additional child, paid in eight quarterly installments of $375. By the time the program was terminated on 30 September 1997 the comparable amounts were $500, $1,000 (including a further $500 payment on the child's first birthday), and $8,000 respectively, the latter paid in 20 quarterly installments of $400. All obligations under the ANC were honoured, so payments continued until 2002. While the provincial fertility rate did not rebound significantly, Quebec no longer has the lowest fertility of the Canadian provinces. Consequently, the effects of this pro-natalist policy remain a topic of debate.[7] A substantial expansion of public subsidies for day care was announced at the same time as the cancellation of the ANC. Besides meeting social objectives by supporting family-friendly policies, this program lowers the effective cost of child-rearing and, therefore, also provides an incentive for more children. It remains to be seen if this program will meet its objectives.[8]

Migration

The differences in provincial population growth rates and the resulting implications for provincial population shares primarily reflect the diversity in migration patterns. While natural increase (the difference between births and deaths) still contributes more to the change in the national population than net migration (immigration minus emigration), provincial population changes also reflect movements of people *within* the country. When combined, migration (international plus interprovincial) is the major determinant of provincial population changes.

International migrants are attracted to regions where there are communities of similar cultures to provide their needs (food items, places of worship, etc.). In Canada these communities are the largest and most diversified in the metropolitan areas of Toronto in Ontario, Vancouver in BC, and Montreal in Quebec. Consequently, international migration favours population growth in these provinces. In recent years, the federal government has signed bilateral agreements with provinces regarding sharing responsibility for immigration.[9] The *Canada-Quebec Accord* is the most comprehensive of these agreements. Signed in 1991, it gives Quebec selection powers and control over its own settlement services. Canada retains responsibility for defining immigrant categories, setting levels and enforcement. Agreements with Manitoba (1996) and BC (1998) give those provinces a greater role in planning, funds, and responsibility for settlement services and an agreement to attract business immigrants. By 2003 most other provinces had signed Provincial Nominee agreements, which allow them to select a small number of immigrants to meet specific labour market needs.[10] Yukon Territory signed a Cooperation Agreement that included a nominee annex in 2001.

Interprovincial migration, on the other hand tends to follow job creation, which largely reflects the relative growth of the provincial economies. In this regard, Ontario and the two western provinces of BC and Alberta outperformed the rest of the country over 1971-2001, so these provinces gained residents from other provinces, thereby simultaneously contributing to their own population growth and reducing the population growth of the province of migrant origin. In this sense, provincial economic growth acts as a provincial demographic policy.[11]

The provincial populations, summarized in Table 15.1, reflect the net outcomes of these various population movements and are the basis for many of the provincial (and territorial) comparisons found in this book. Since the national population is the total of the provincial (and territorial) populations, national population growth is a weighted average of the provincial population growth rates, where the weights are the provincial population shares in the Canadian population. A province growing faster than the national average will increase its population share in the Canadian federation, while one growing slower will experience a decreased share. Since population size is the basis for defining electoral boundaries in Canada, provinces with increased population shares will ultimately have greater opportunity for influence in the Canadian federation.[12]

Age Structure

Besides population size, the age structure of the population also has an impact on government behaviour. Foot notes that Canada experienced a "boom, bust and echo" demographic profile over the post-war period.[13] After the conclusion of World War II, Canadian soldiers returning home and immigrants who found Canada to be an attractive country to settle far from the theatre of war started to raise families. By 1960, Canadian women were averaging almost four children each. This resulted in the post-war Baby Boom generation, which was especially large in Canada.

Then in the early 1960s the availability of the birth control pill and the re-entry of Canadian women into the work force in substantial numbers resulted in a dramatic fall in the average family size. By the end of the decade, fertility was down to under two children per woman and continued to decline into the 1970s. A birth dearth, called the Baby Bust generation, was the result.

In the late 1970s the early boomers (born in the late 1940s and early 1950s) reached their child-bearing ages in significant numbers and births started to rise again. Note that the increase in births came from the increased size of the parent "pool," not from a change in their behaviour. In fact, the fertility rate remained around 1.6 children per woman, well below the replacement level of 2.1 (two to replace the two parents plus 0.1 to account for children who do not reach child-bearing age or did not have children).

Foot defines the Baby Boom generation in Canada as those born between 1947 and 1966 inclusive. By 2001 almost 10 million boomers were aged 35 to 54 years. Following the boom was the Baby Bust generation born between 1967 and 1979. By 2001, the 5.5 million busters were aged 22 to 34 years. The "echo" of the boom appeared over the 1980s and continued into the early 1990s. Foot defines the Baby Boom Echo generation as born between 1980 and 1995. By 2001 the 6.6 million echo boomers were aged 6 to 21 years. [14]

In an update Foot notes that the number of births decreased noticeably over the late 1990s as the smaller bust generation entered their child-bearing ages. He defines this birth dearth as the millennium generation. He notes that the early members of the echo generation will reach their child-bearing ages late in the first decade of the new millennium at which time births can be expected to rise moderately again. [15]

The advantage of the boom, bust, and echo template is that it provides a useful lens through which to view population change over time. A birth year provides an irrevocable time marker to measure demographic change. Since the boomer generation is so numerically dominant in the Canadian population, its ageing results in the ageing of the Canadian population, which has major impacts on society and governments.

Not surprisingly, this demographic profile also pervades each of the provincial demographic profiles to a greater or lesser degree. Interprovincial migration has had a moderating effect on the profiles of some provinces, so some diversity in provincial age profiles has emerged over the years. Provincial demographic profiles also reflect the cumulative effects of slight differences in provincial birth (fertility) and death (mortality) rates and the continued impacts of international migration.

Finally, Foot notes that the demographic profiles for those over age 54 years in 2001 are also subject to considerable variation. [16] Low births during World War I were followed by the Roaring Twenties decade when births increased. The arrival of the Depression years of the 1930s reduced births. The delay in child-bearing and a growing economy during World War II resulted in an increase in the number of births in Canada, which then led into the postwar Baby Boom. These birth trends on the population were accentuated by immigrant intakes and moderately influenced by mortality and emigration trends. Since many of these births define the 55-plus population of 2001, these demographic events continue to be of importance for current government policies and programs.

Demographic dependency

A useful method of capturing these demographic variations is presented in Table 15.2. For analytical convenience, the population of any society (denoted P) can be separated into three mutually exclusive and exhaustive age groups—the pre-working age young (denoted Y), those of working age (denoted W), and the post-working age seniors (denoted S), that is,

$$P = Y + W + S.$$

By definition, the pre-working age young are too young to work and the post-working age seniors are too old to work. In this simplified world, both non-working age groups are "dependent" on those of working age to provide for their sustenance and survival.

The support of those unable to work is the foundation of the extended family in many societies, where both children and grandparents (and perhaps great-grandparents) live together and share family resources. In modern societies, the extended family has been modified by the movement of seniors into their own family units and increasingly requires that they depend on their own resources for sustenance and survival. In this modern world, societies have turned to governments to provide assistance with this task, through poverty assistance where appropriate, the provision of demogrants (such as Old Age Security) and public pensions, whether contributory or not. In many countries some assistance with health care costs (including drugs) is also provided, particularly for those in need. These programs are paid for by taxes generally levied on those of working age, usually on their incomes, expenditures, assets, and the products (and profits) of their labour. Consequently, a larger senior population makes greater demands on these revenues, whereas a larger working age population alleviates the per capita impacts of these needs.

While most expenses associated with children remain within the family, many modern societies have chosen to provide public education for the young, which is primarily paid for by taxes on the financial resources of the working population, such as the value of their property or their wealth. Policies to provide some tax relief to those parents who choose to send their children to private schools are, essentially, paid for from the same source. Consequently, a larger child population makes greater demands on these resources, and a larger working population alleviates the per capita impacts for the provision of education and any other government-funded programs for the young (such as child care).

These demographic demands on a society can be conveniently captured by the concept of a dependency ratio. The young dependency ratio is defined as the size of the young population divided by the size of the working age population, or Y/W. Since both numerator and denominator can be divided by the total population, this measure is equivalent to the ratio of the respective shares of the two population groups—Y/W = (Y/P)/(W/P).

444 DAVID K. FOOT

The senior dependency ratio is defined analogously as the size (or share) of the senior population divided by the size (or share) of the working age population—S/W = (S/P)/(W/P). An ageing population is likely to result in a higher senior dependency ratio for that population over time.

Together, the young and the senior dependency ratios (Y/W + S/W = (Y + S)/W) define the total dependency ratio.[17] High values of a total dependency ratio are a signal of high pressures on the society's resources as a result of the demographic profile, while low values of the ratio signal the opposite.

The definition of a "high" or "low" total dependency ratio inevitably involves some comparator. Comparisons over time in one jurisdiction provide one method of comparison. This is commonly used to assess the impacts of population ageing in a jurisdiction. Comparisons across populations at a point in time provide another method. This is particularly useful in assessing the comparative demographic pressures on the government budgets of different jurisdictions, such as provinces or countries, at any point in time. In both methods, a lower total dependency ratio is considered to be more favourable than a higher total dependency ratio.

Table 15.2 presents demographic information on the two dependent age groups for Canada and the provinces over 1971-2001. In this application, the pre-working age population is defined as the population aged under 15 years (since persons 15 and over could legally work in some provinces during this period), while the post-working age population is defined as the population aged 65 years and over (since this was the retirement age for both the Quebec and

Table 15.2. Provincial Populations: Under 15 and 65 and Over, 1971-2001

	Under 15 (%)				65 and Over (%)			
	1971	1981	1991	2001	1971	1981	1991	2001
NF	36.9	29.2	22.2	16.9	6.1	7.7	9.6	11.8
NS	30.3	23.3	20.3	17.8	9.1	10.9	12.5	13.4
PEI	31.5	24.7	22.5	19.2	11.0	12.1	13.1	13.3
NB	31.8	24.7	20.7	17.7	8.6	10.0	12.0	13.0
QC	29.3	21.5	19.8	17.6	6.8	8.8	11.1	13.0
ON	28.4	21.6	20.1	19.2	8.3	9.9	11.6	12.6
MB	28.8	23.1	21.9	20.7	9.6	11.8	13.3	13.5
SK	30.1	24.5	23.9	21.2	10.2	11.9	14.1	14.6
AB	31.2	23.9	23.6	20.5	7.2	7.2	9.0	10.2
BC	27.6	21.2	20.1	17.7	9.3	10.7	12.7	13.2
YT	34.1	25.9	24.3	20.4	2.9	3.3	3.9	5.7
NWT[1]	41.8	34.1	32.3	30.8	2.3	3.0	2.7	3.6
Canada	29.3	22.3	20.7	18.8	8.0	9.6	11.5	12.6

1. Including Nunavut.
Source: Statistics Canada, *Annual Demographic Statistics 2001*.

federal pension plans). The data are presented as population shares to enable easy comparisons over time and across provinces and territories.

For Canada, the share of the young dependent group in the population has decreased over time, from 29.3 per cent in 1971 to 18.8 per cent in 2001. In 1971 half of the boomer generation were still under age 15. Over the subsequent ten years they aged into the working age group. The last boomer born in 1966 reached age 15 in 1981, so much (two-thirds) of the reduction in the young share over the period occurred between 1971 and 1981. Since 1981 the decline has continued at a much slower pace. This trend signals a relative decline in the need to support the young in Canadian society.

At the same time, the share of the senior group has been increasing, from 8 per cent in 1971 to 12.6 per cent in 2001. The largest decadal change over the period occurred between 1981 and 1991 when the Roaring Twenties generation began to reach the senior ages. Someone born in 1920 turned 65 in 1985, and thereafter the senior population share rose rapidly. This trend signals a growing importance in the support need of the senior group in Canadian society. However, the first of the boomers born in 1947 do not turn 65 until 2012, so there is no impact of the boomer demographic on the senior population in these historical data.

These two conflicting trends have clear implications for government priorities, policies, and programs. The total dependency ratio measures the net impact of these on society. This will be examined after a review of the provincial differences.

Young dependency

A comparison over the provinces reveals noticeable provincial variations in these shares. In 1971 the highest young shares were in Canada's territories and in Newfoundland, reflecting in large part the higher fertility of the northern Aboriginal communities and delayed decline in fertility in Newfoundland.[18] Above average young shares were also recorded in all Maritime provinces and in Saskatchewan and Alberta, with the most populous provinces of Ontario, Quebec, and BC experiencing below average young population shares. The gap between the highest province (Newfoundland) and the lowest (BC) was 9.3 percentage points, or 33.7 per cent. Including the territories in the comparison raises the gap in 1971 to 14.2 percentage points, or a substantial 51.4 per cent.

By 2001 the interprovincial gap still persisted, although it had narrowed somewhat. However, there were noticeable changes of the provincial positions in the ranking. The Atlantic provinces were no longer above average (except for PEI), and Ontario had now become an above-average province because of its substantial echo generation. The highest provincial young dependency ratio was in Saskatchewan, which had a substantial echo generation reflecting, in part, the contribution of its higher population share of Aboriginal peoples to provincial fertility. Note, however, that the highest provincial share in 2001 was still substantially lower than the lowest ratio in 1971. The lowest young share was in

Quebec,[19] followed closely by New Brunswick, BC, and Nova Scotia. The inter-provincial gap was down to 3.6 percentage points, or 20.5 per cent. The territories (excluding the Yukon) still had the highest young share at 30.8 per cent, down 10 per cent from 30 years earlier. Meanwhile, the Canadian share had dropped 10.5 per cent so the territorial-provincial gap only narrowed slightly to 13.2 percentage points, which implied a widening of the relative gap to 75 per cent.

Senior dependency

The senior dependency share also exhibited substantial interprovincial variations over the period 1971-2001. In 1971 the highest senior share was in PEI, reflecting the substantial out-migration of working age people (especially boomers) over the previous 20 years. Saskatchewan was the only other province with a senior share above 10 per cent, while the territories were the lowest with less than 3 per cent. The gap between the highest share (PEI) and the lowest share province (Newfoundland) was 4.9 percentage points, or a substantial 80 per cent. Including the territories in this comparison increases the gap to 8.7 percentage points, or a 378 per cent difference. By 2001 all provinces and territories had experienced noticeable increases in the senior population shares, but at different rates. The largest increase occurred in Quebec where the senior share almost doubled over the 30 years from 6.8 to 13.0 per cent—an increase of 6.2 percentage points, or 91 per cent. The second largest change was in Newfoundland where the share increased 5.7 percentage points for an even higher 93 per cent increase over 1971. In both cases the out-migration of the working age population and the stability of the senior population drove these trends. All other provinces experienced changes below the average Canadian increase of 4.6 percentage points, or 58 per cent. The highest growth was in the Yukon population where the senior share almost doubled.

Between 1971 and 2001, the interprovincial gap in the senior share narrowed slightly from 4.9 to 4.4 percentage points. However, the gap between the highest share (Saskatchewan) and the lowest share province (Alberta) was still substantial (43 per cent). In fact, Alberta is a standout in these interprovincial comparisons with a senior population share 2.4 percentage points below the national average. Without Alberta, the interprovincial gap narrows to 2.8 percentage points. Nonetheless, the lowest senior share in Table 15.2 is still in the Northwest Territories at 3.6 per cent, which means that the provincial-territorial gap in the table actually increased over the period from 8.7 to 11.0 percentage points.

It is interesting to note that, because Alberta and Saskatchewan are at the opposite ends of these interprovincial comparisons of the senior population shares in 2001, they might be expected to take different policy positions with respect to national programs involving seniors, such as pensions and health care. The senior share gap between the remaining eight provinces is much narrower at 1.7

percentage points, or a 14.4 per cent difference, which provides a greater opportunity for consensus than might otherwise be indicated by the interprovincial gap comparisons.

Total dependency

Both the young and senior population shares enter the calculation of total dependency.[20] These calculations are presented in Table 15.3. They present a similar picture to Table 15.2, but with some additional interesting features.

Table 15.3. Young and Senior Dependency Ratios, Provinces, 1971-2001

	Young (Under 15)				Senior (65 and over)			
	1971	1981	1991	2001	1971	1981	1991	2001
NF	0.65	0.46	0.32	0.24	0.11	0.12	0.14	0.17
NS	0.50	0.35	0.30	0.26	0.15	0.17	0.19	0.19
PEI	0.55	0.39	0.35	0.29	0.19	0.19	0.20	0.20
NB	0.53	0.38	0.31	0.26	0.14	0.15	0.18	0.19
QC	0.46	0.31	0.29	0.25	0.11	0.13	0.16	0.19
ON	0.45	0.32	0.29	0.28	0.13	0.14	0.17	0.18
MB	0.47	0.35	0.34	0.32	0.16	0.18	0.21	0.21
SK	0.51	0.39	0.38	0.33	0.17	0.19	0.23	0.23
AB	0.51	0.35	0.35	0.29	0.12	0.10	0.13	0.15
BC	0.44	0.31	0.30	0.26	0.15	0.16	0.19	0.19
YT	0.54	0.36	0.34	0.28	0.05	0.05	0.05	0.08
NWT[1]	0.75	0.54	0.50	0.47	0.04	0.05	0.04	0.05
Canada	0.47	0.33	0.30	0.27	0.13	0.14	0.17	0.18

1. Including Nunavut.
Source: Statistics Canada, *Annual Demographic Statistics 2001*.

For Canada between 1971 and 2001 the young dependency ratio (Y/W) decreased from 0.47 to 0.27, a decrease of 43 per cent. Another way of expressing the same trend is to say that in 1971 there were 2.1 persons of working age for every young non-working age person. By 2001 this number had increased to 3.7, thereby indicating less per capita pressure on those of working age to support the young. Once again Newfoundland experienced the biggest drop of any jurisdiction, falling from a provincial high young dependency ratio of 0.65 in 1971 to a provincial low of 0.24 by 2001, a change of 0.41 or 63 per cent. The smallest drops were in Manitoba (0.15) and Ontario (0.17), followed by Saskatchewan and BC (0.18). By 2001 the lowest young dependency ratio provinces were Newfoundland and Quebec, followed by Nova Scotia, New Brunswick, and BC. Besides the Northwest Territories, the highest young dependency provinces were Saskatchewan and Manitoba.

Meanwhile the senior dependency ratio (S/W) was increasing in every province and territory. For Canada, this ratio increased from 0.13 to 0.18, an increase of 38 per cent. Another way of looking at the numbers is that in 1971 there were 7.7 people of working age for every senior. By 2001 this number had been reduced to 5.6, a decrease of 27 per cent over 30 years, thereby indicating more per capita pressure on those of working age to support the seniors. In this respect Quebec faced the biggest increase and PEI the smallest increase of the provinces. By 2001, the highest senior dependency ratio was in Saskatchewan (0.23), followed by Manitoba (0.21), and PEI (0.20). Besides the territories, the lowest senior dependency ratio was in Alberta (0.15). Once again the difference between Saskatchewan and Alberta (of 0.06 or 40 per cent) indicates a substantial provincial difference that might be expected to affect government priorities and positions on national programs for seniors.

With decreasing young dependency and increasing senior dependency representing conflicting trends, it is useful to combine them into a single measure of dependency. The total dependency ratio is defined as the addition of the young and senior dependency ratios (= Y/W + S/W). It shows the number of people in the non-working ages for every person of working age. These calculations are presented in Table 15.4 (left half).

Table 15.4. Total Dependency Ratios, Provinces, 1971-2001

	Unweighted[1]				Weighted[2]			
	1971	1981	1991	2001	1971	1981	1991	2001
NF	0.76	0.58	0.47	0.40	0.92	0.77	0.68	0.65
NS	0.65	0.52	0.49	0.45	0.88	0.77	0.77	0.74
PEI	0.74	0.58	0.55	0.48	1.03	0.87	0.86	0.78
NB	0.68	0.53	0.49	0.44	0.89	0.76	0.75	0.73
QC	0.57	0.43	0.45	0.44	0.73	0.62	0.69	0.72
ON	0.58	0.46	0.46	0.47	0.77	0.68	0.72	0.74
MB	0.62	0.54	0.54	0.52	0.86	0.81	0.85	0.83
SK	0.68	0.57	0.61	0.56	0.93	0.86	0.95	0.90
AB	0.62	0.45	0.48	0.44	0.80	0.61	0.68	0.66
BC	0.58	0.47	0.49	0.45	0.80	0.70	0.77	0.73
YT	0.59	0.41	0.39	0.35	0.65	0.48	0.47	0.47
NWT[3]	0.79	0.59	0.54	0.52	0.85	0.66	0.60	0.61
Canada	0.60	0.47	0.47	0.46	0.79	0.68	0.73	0.73

Notes: 1. Population Under 15 plus Population 65 and Over divided by Population 15 to 64.
2. Population Under 15 plus 2.5 × Population 65 and Over divided by Population 15 to 64.
3. Including Nunavut.
Source: Statistics Canada, *Annual Demographic Statistics 2001*.

For Canada, total dependency fell from 1971 to 1981 and again from 1991 to 2001. It remained unchanged between 1981 and 1991. This suggests that the decrease in young dependency more than offset the increase in senior dependency over this period. In 1971 there were 1.7 working age persons for every non-working age person in Canada. By 2001 this figure had risen to 2.2, thereby indicating a noticeable (30 per cent) improvement in the abilities of the average Canadian to meet the needs of those not in their working ages. Consequently, this simple calculation suggests that governments were facing favourable demographic trends in regard to their expenditure obligations, at least over the 1970s and 1990s.

However, as noted above, the provincial governments experienced these demographic trends to different degrees. According to the total dependency ratio measure, Newfoundland and PEI faced the most unfavourable demographic profiles in 1971, the former because of its relatively high young population and the latter because of its relatively high senior population. The large provinces of Quebec, Ontario, and BC were the most demographically favoured provinces in 1971. The territories faced even more unfavourable demographics than the provinces in 1971 because of their relatively young populations.

By 2001, demographic trends had altered the complexion of interprovincial comparisons. Between 1971 and 2001 Newfoundland moved from facing the most unfavourable to facing the most favourable demographic situation because the dramatic decline in its young dependency more than compensated for the large increase in the senior dependency. Second and third in the list of demographically favoured provinces were Quebec and Alberta, the former because of its relatively low young ratio and the latter because of its relatively low senior ratio. The province facing the most challenging demographic population profile by far was Saskatchewan because of its relatively high young *and* senior dependency ratios. The only other province with a total dependency ratio above 0.50 in 2001 was Manitoba. In general, the Maritime Provinces (except PEI) faced below average demographic pressures, as did BC. Ontario moved from a slightly favourable demographic situation in 1971 to a slightly unfavourable situation in 2001, primarily because of the relatively larger echo generation in Ontario than in many other provinces.

As for territories, the Yukon is facing the most favourable demographic situation in Canada because it has the largest share of the population of working age, whereas the Northwest Territories (including Nunavut) face the most demographically challenging situation of any jurisdiction in Canada because of their relatively young populations.

Provinces with a relatively high young dependency ratio and a relatively low senior dependency ratio (for example, Alberta) can be expected to have policies that emphasize youth needs, such as sports and recreation and education. Provinces with a relatively low young dependency ratio and a relatively high senior dependency ratio (for example, Nova Scotia) can be expected to have policies that place greater emphasis on senior needs, such as health care. Provinces with more average demographic age structures (for example, Ontario) can be expected to have policies that balance the needs of both dependent groups. The ability to pay for these policies is indicated by the total dependency ratio. Provinces with low total demographic dependency ratios (such as Alberta) are likely to have lower taxes and/or better funded programs, whereas provinces with higher total demographic dependency ratios (such as Saskatchewan) are likely to have higher taxes and/or more poorly funded programs. Alternatively, low total demographic dependency ratios will make it easier to achieve surpluses in government budgets, while high ratios will have the opposite impact.

Economic Dependency

In the calculation of total demographic dependency there is an assumption that a decrease in the population share of one non-working group can be offset by an equivalent increase in the population share of the other non-working group. If, for example, the young population share falls from 25 to 22 per cent at the same time that the senior share rises from 7 to 10 per cent, the working age share remains unchanged and so does the total dependency ratio. This suggests that the budgetary implications for society and, hence, governments were unchanged, even though the population had clearly become older.

However, the total demographic dependency for a population and the total demographic dependency for a government elected to provide public programs (and taxes) to satisfy the needs of that population will not be the same if the per capita costs of serving the two non-working groups are different. This would occur if, for example, seniors were more costly to service than the young on a per capita basis. In this case, population ageing that reduced the share of young and increased the share of seniors in the population would result in increased pressures on society and, probably, on the public sector or government. It would also occur if the young were primarily cared for in the private sector family, but responsibility for the seniors was primarily transferred from the private sector family to the society or public sector. In this case, population ageing may reduce the pressures on the private sector because there are fewer children to look after but increase the pressures on the public sector because there are more seniors to look after. Obviously, a combination of these two cases could lead to considerable upward pressures on the public sector dependency ratio as a result of population ageing.

In either case the automatic link between demographic dependency and the economic implications for the public sector are severed. A reduction in the share of young matched by an equal increase in the share of seniors that leaves the total demographic ratio unchanged would not have a neutral impact on government because the *public* per capita costs associated with programs for the young are lower than those associated with programs associated with the seniors.

By examining the age distribution of government spending on all programs, Foot calculated that the per capita cost of seniors in the public sector in Canada was approximately 2.5 times higher than the young.[21] While Foot's calculation was based on public expenditure data from the late 1970s, similar calculations for other countries show a range of between two and three times.[22] Consequently, 2.5 is a representative number for illustrative calculations, especially for the historical period 1971-2001.

These illustrative calculations, presented in Table 15.4 (right half), assign a weight of 2.5 to the senior population in the numerator, while the young population weight remains at 1.0. This implies that the young share in the population must decline by 2.5 percentage points for every one percentage point increase in the senior share for the weighted dependency ratio to remain unchanged.

For Canada, the calculations show the weighted total dependency ratio decreased noticeably between 1971 and 1981 as the last of the boomers entered their working ages and then increased between 1981 and 1991 as the Roaring Twenties generation entered their senior ages. It remained unchanged between 1991 and 2001 at a level lower than in 1971. This is a different time profile from the unweighted total dependency ratio (left half of the Table 15.4), thus suggesting that per capita cost differences may be important in assessing the impact of changing demographics on governments.

Using the same calculation at the provincial level also reveals interesting conclusions (see Table 15.4). In 1971 PEI ranked above Newfoundland because its high dependency came from a high share of seniors, whereas Newfoundland had a high dependency because of a high share of young in its population at that time. Once again the lowest provincial ratio was in Quebec, although the Yukon Territory had an even lower weighted ratio. All the Atlantic provinces and Manitoba and Saskatchewan had above average weighted ratios, whereas the two central provinces of Ontario and Quebec were below average. Alberta and BC were only slightly above average in 1971.

By 2001 the provincial landscape had changed noticeably. Saskatchewan followed by Manitoba remained at the top of the list with the highest provincial weighted dependency ratios, and Newfoundland remained at the bottom followed by Alberta. These results suggest that while weighting modifies the overall trend, the provincial rankings are much less affected because demographic change impacted all provinces similarly over the period. However, the provincial rankings are not totally unaffected. The older provinces of Nova Scotia and Quebec moved up a rank (to 4 and 8 respectively), while the younger provinces of Ontario and Alberta moved down a rank (to 5 and 9 respectively). In other words, Nova Scotia and Ontario exchanged ranks, as did Quebec and Alberta. All other provinces maintained their same relative position between 1971 and 2001.

However, the Northwest Territories (including Nunavut) demonstrate the potential impact of weighting. In the list of 12 jurisdictions presented in Table 15.4, the Northwest Territories in 2001 ranks second using the unweighted ratio and 11 using the weighted ratio. This is because the most important source of their dependency is their young population, and they have the smallest share of seniors (Table 15.2).

Since the weighted dependency ratios in Table 15.4 are illustrative indices only, gap measurements based on numerical calculations do not make sense. Nonetheless, the difference between Newfoundland and Alberta at the bottom and Saskatchewan at the top is substantial. This suggests that by 2001 demographic composition favoured the governments of Newfoundland and Alberta and severely challenged the governments of Saskatchewan and, to a lesser extent, Manitoba. All other provinces were between these extremes. By this measurement, the territories are even more favoured than the provinces since the main source of their dependency is their young populations, not the more costly seniors.

Finally, Foot calculated that the appropriate weighting factor for the provinces as a group based on data from the late 1970s was a much lower 1.1, since within the Canadian federation provinces have responsibilities for all age groups.[23] The federal government had residual responsibility for seniors and, therefore, had a higher weighting factor, while the municipal governments tended to deliver programs to the younger end of the age spectrum (especially education) and, therefore, had a lower weighting factor. Subsequent reallocations of program responsibilities between the three levels of government may have changed the relative weighting factors.

Consequently, the impacts on Canada's provinces from demographic variations probably lie somewhere between the left half of Table 15.4 (with a senior weight of 1.0) and the right half of Table 15.4 (with a senior weight of 2.5). Dependency fell between 1961 and 1971 and has not changed much since then, especially over 1991 to 2001. It is less in 2001 than it was in 1971 despite the ageing population. At the provincial level, the "winners" from demographic change have been Newfoundland and Alberta, while the "losers" have been Quebec and Ontario since 1981. However, the province most challenged by its age structure was Saskatchewan, while the least challenged province over the period was Alberta. Finally, the ranking of Canada's provinces remains almost unaffected by which dependency measure is used.[24]

The Future

Population projections explore the demographic future for Canada and the provinces. A population grows when births exceed deaths and/or in-migration exceeds out-migration. For the country, migration covers international migration, while for a province it includes both international and interprovincial migration. By making assumptions about fertility, mortality, and migration patterns for the future, the associated population implications can be derived. Each population projection reflects the combination of assumptions used to generate the numbers. Different assumptions lead to different projections. A "medium" projection, based on the *status quo* assumptions that reflect the continuation of past trends (for fertility, mortality, emigration, and interprovincial migration) or stated government policies (for immigration) is usually used for analysis.

It is important to note that population projections also reflect the truism that "every year we get a year older." For example, the basis for next year's projection of 40-year-olds is this year's number of 39-year-olds. Since the net addition to this base over a year is so much smaller than the base, the current size and age structure of the population provides the most important determinant of the future population, including its age structure and, hence, dependency. Therefore, for example, it is easy to project that the first boomer born in 1947 enters the senior population 65 years later in the year 2012, and the last boomer born in 1966 will not be there until 2031. Similar calculations are possible for all generations or age cohorts.

Since these generational calculations do not depend on the numbers of births, deaths, or immigrants, and since the net additions to the population are less than 1 per cent annually, the dependency implications of all alternative population projections are dominated by the existing population characteristics. Consequently, examining the dependency implications of a "medium" population projection provides a solid foundation for exploring the likely implications of future populations on government priorities, policies, and programs. Similar calculations are possible for every population projection.

Dependency projections

Statistics Canada regularly produces population projections for Canada, the provinces, and territories. The production of provincial projections together ensures consistency of assumptions. Not only do the provincial numbers have to be consistent with the national number, the interprovincial migrants must also sum to zero since, by definition, every in-migrant to one province (or territory) must be an out-migrant from another province (or territory). These consistency requirements were incorporated into the Statistics Canada population projections in 2001.[25]

The connection between the assumptions necessary to produce population projections and dependency works through age structure. For example, a higher fertility assumption will result in more births and a higher young dependency ratio, while a slower increase in life expectancy will generate more deaths than a faster increase and likely result in a lower senior dependency ratio. Since most migrants are of working age, higher immigration levels increase the working age population and, hence, lower the dependency ratios, while interprovincial migration largely transfers people of working age from one province to another, thus raising dependency in the sending province and lowering it in the receiving province. All of these impacts are captured together in any population and dependency projection.

The "medium" Statistics Canada population projection incorporates *status quo* assumptions that include slight declines in fertility, moderate increases in life expectancy, a somewhat high immigration level (of 250,000 persons a year), and emigration patterns reflecting the average of 1997-99. The interprovincial migration assumptions reflect the average pattern of selected previous years to average out the effects of cyclical economic activity in the provincial economies.[26]

Figure 15.1 summarizes the dependency ratio projections for Canada for the period 2001-2051. It shows a young ratio that decreases until around 2016 and then increases slightly until 2031 as the echo boomers go through their child-bearing years. By 2041 the young dependency ratio is back to where it was in 2016 and stays there until 2051. The senior dependency ratio continues to increase throughout the projection period, which reflects the impact of an ageing population, especially the ageing boomer generation. A noticeable jump in senior dependency occurs between 2011 and 2016 when the first boomers reach age 65. Thereafter, large increases are experienced every five years until 2031 when the last of the boomers enter the senior age group after which increases are much more moderate. By 2051 the senior dependency has more than doubled compared to the level at the beginning of the millennium.

Total dependency, which combines the young and senior dependency ratios, *declines* in Canada between 2001 and 2011 because falling young dependency as a result of lower births more than offsets moderately rising senior dependency. Thereafter, rising senior dependency dominates young dependency, primarily because of the ageing boomers. By 2051 the total dependency ratio is projected

Figure 15.1. Dependency Ratios, Canada, 2001-2051

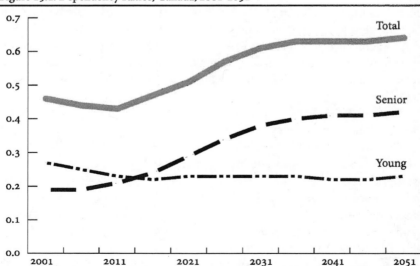

Source: Statistics Canada, *Population Projections for Canada, Provinces and Territories, 2000-2026.*

to be 48 per cent higher than the 2011 minimum. It is at about the same level that was experienced in 1921 and still *below* (by 10 per cent) the level of the total dependency ratio in 1961 at the peak of the Baby Boom.[27] In 2051 Canada will be approximately where it was in 1966 according to the total dependency measure.

The reasons are, of course, quite different. In the 1960s high total dependency came from high young dependency, whereas in the 2040s it comes from high senior dependency. The implications for specific government priorities, policies, and programs are, therefore, very different. Moreover, the implications for government budgets may also be different if the per capita costs of servicing seniors are higher than the young.

Weighted dependency calculations using a relative per capita weight of 2.5 for the seniors (as in Table 15.4), show a total dependency ratio increasing 72 per cent between 2001 and 2051 compared to a 40 per cent increase for the unweighted ratio. The increase for Canadian provinces (which have a lower weight) is, therefore, likely to be closer to the lower end of this range. However, compared to 1961,[28] the weighted total dependency ratio in 2051 is 40 per cent higher whereas the unweighted ratio is almost 10 per cent *lower*. Once again, the provinces are likely to be at the lower end of this range.

Table 15.5 summarizes the dependency implications of the provincial (and Canadian) populations for the period 2011 to 2026 associated with the Statistics Canada population projections. These provincial projections to 2026 (26 years) covers a similar period of time as Tables 15.1 to 15.4 (30 years) and includes the entry of the most populous boomer age group (born in 1960) into the senior age group.

Table 15.5. Dependency Ratios, Provinces, 2011-2026

	Young			Senior			Total[1]		
	2011	2021	2026	2011	2021	2026	2011	2021	2026
NF	0.19	0.19	0.19	0.21	0.35	0.43	0.40	0.54	0.62
NS	0.20	0.20	0.21	0.22	0.33	0.39	0.43	0.53	0.60
PEI	0.24	0.24	0.24	0.21	0.31	0.37	0.45	0.55	0.61
NB	0.20	0.20	0.20	0.22	0.34	0.41	0.42	0.54	0.61
QC	0.21	0.22	0.22	0.23	0.32	0.38	0.44	0.54	0.61
ON	0.23	0.23	0.24	0.20	0.27	0.31	0.43	0.50	0.55
MB	0.25	0.26	0.27	0.22	0.29	0.34	0.47	0.55	0.61
SK	0.26	0.27	0.27	0.23	0.31	0.36	0.49	0.57	0.63
AB	0.24	0.25	0.25	0.17	0.26	0.32	0.42	0.51	0.57
BC	0.22	0.22	0.23	0.21	0.28	0.33	0.43	0.51	0.56
YT	0.22	0.23	0.24	0.13	0.21	0.26	0.34	0.45	0.50
NWT[2]	0.34	0.34	0.33	0.08	0.14	0.17	0.42	0.48	0.50
Canada	0.23	0.23	0.23	0.21	0.29	0.34	0.43	0.51	0.57

Notes: 1. Young plus Senior.
2. Including Nunavut.
Source: Statistics Canada, *Population Projections for Canada, Provinces and Territories, 2000-2026.*

By 2026 the Canadian province with the most favourable total dependency ratio is Ontario, followed by BC and Alberta. Since these are the dominant migration-receiving provinces, this finding underscores the ultimate importance of migration in future dependency ratio calculations. Migrants are mainly of working age and therefore lead to lower total dependency. The Canadian province with the most unfavourable dependency ratio is still Saskatchewan, primarily because of its relatively high young ratio, followed by Newfoundland and New Brunswick, primarily because of their relatively high senior ratios. The total dependency ratios in the territories are well below the provinces by 2026 because of their continued relatively low senior ratios.

However, in 2026 the total dependency ratios for all provinces are *below* the comparable numbers in 1961[29] (by about 20 per cent). Interestingly, Ontario experienced the most favourable dependency in both years. Newfoundland had the least favourable dependency in 1961 and the second least favourable dependency in 2026. In general, the provinces with above average total dependency ratios in 1961 have above average total dependency ratios in 2026, with the exceptions of Alberta (which moved from above average to below average) and Quebec (which moved from below average to above average).

Public Policy Implications

The historical and projected future trends in dependency have important implications for public policies in Canadian governments. First and foremost, lower total dependency results in more flexibility in government budgets, both because the revenue base is higher and the expenditure needs are lower. A higher share of the population of working force age means a larger tax base, while a smaller share of the population in the young and senior groups means lower demands for many expenditure programs. Consequently, increases in total dependency constrain government in two ways—by reducing the tax base and by increasing the expenditure needs.

Second, and of almost equal importance, is the role of the human life cycle. Dependency calculations recognize three important stages in a person's life—the pre-working years, the working years, and the post-working years. While dependency calculations *per se* do not explicitly recognize the order in which these stages occur, there is a clear chronological order to the three stages from young to senior. This was clearly recognized by the labels used for the two components of the total dependency ratio.

The human life cycle

A person's needs change over a lifetime. This is often called the human life cycle or the life course. Of course, these needs seldom neatly follow the three-stage approach of the dependency calculation, but the concept provides a useful foundation for understanding a population's demands on governments and on society in general. For example, day care needs are the domain of the pre-school population, usually under six years of age. This need may be satisfied at home or in the marketplace in the private sector or it may be transferred to a public sector program, perhaps using government subsidies (such as currently occurs in Quebec). Almost no person in any other life stage will need day care in this form. In the senior years, a comparable need is home care, although not every person in their senior years will require home care, and some people, such as persons with disabilities, may need home care at earlier stages of their life. Once again, such care can be provided in the private sector, using relatives and friends or paid help, or it can be transferred, partially or fully, to the public sector.

A high young dependency is likely a signal for more day care, while a high senior dependency is likely a signal for more home care. A high total dependency is likely a signal for both, although it could be the signal of very high need for one or the other. These needs may be supplied by the private sector, the public sector, or some combination. Although a large pre-school population aged zero to five years does not automatically mean a large pre-working age population age zero to 15 years, there is likely to be a strong connection. Similarly, a large senior population does not automatically translate into a high demand for home care, but there is likely to be a strong connection. This is the connection between dependency ratios and government priorities, policies, and programs, whether realized or not.

While many public policies and programs are *de facto* related to the human life cycle, many are not, especially those that are considered public goods. "Peace, order and good government" would be examples of government outputs that are needed by all and consumed by all independently of age. National defence is another example where presumably the "need" is generated and consumed by all equally. National (and provincial) parks may be a somewhat less clear example of age independent consumption, especially if certain age groups who are more active make greater use of the facilities. National (and provincial) health care is even more life cycle dependent because, although available to all when needed, the elderly are much more likely to need it more frequently and more intensely that any other age group. National pensions are strongly related to the human life cycle because they cannot be received until a prescribed retirement date. Here there is a direct connection between the human life cycle, the public program, and dependency ratios.

The human life cycle concept is also useful in another context. Those who receive public pensions frequently argue that they have "earned" them. Here they are voicing the idea of lifetime equity—that over a lifetime a person uses public programs when young (such as education), pays taxes that exceed program use over their working ages, and then returns to being a net beneficiary of government programs in their senior years (through, for example, old age security and health care benefits). The idea being expressed is that, on average over an individual lifetime, the net benefits approximately sum to zero. Such an idea clearly links the human life cycle to government expenditures and revenues.

Dependency ratio calculations implicitly recognize the human life cycle impacts on government budgets by relating the numerator (the young and the seniors) to the expenditure obligations of society or a government, and the denominator (the working age population) to the revenue capacity of society or a government. Whether or not a deficit or surplus on the government account exists, however, depends on the effective benefit rates (per capita) and the effective tax rates (per capita).[30] A surplus may be indicative of a high share of the population of working age, a high tax rate, a low benefit rate, or a combination of all three elements. A deficit may be indicative of the opposite, namely a low share of the population of working age, a low tax rate, a high benefit rate, or some combination of the three elements. In short, dependency calculations provide the demographic input into government budget analysis, but the complete "story" requires more than demographic information alone.

However, increasing total dependency does imply increasing pressure on government budgets from demographic change *alone*. *If* this is considered to be unmanageable or undesirable, the impacts can be offset by appropriate adjustments in the benefit rate (down) or the tax rate (up). These are the only policy options available since policies to change the demographic structure, including immigration policy, have little impact. In this regard government policies are contingent on the demographics of the populations they serve.

Public expenditure programs

This section provides examples to show how demographic information can be used to inform the past and outline the future for selected expenditure programs common to all provinces. No attempt is made to be exhaustive over programs or provinces. The intent is to be illustrative, informative, and, in some cases, provocative. While emphasis is on those programs funded by provincial governments, the analysis is not limited to those programs because there is much joint funding and fluidity in responsibility over time.

The first boomer born in 1947 reached elementary school age (six) in 1953 and secondary school age (13) in 1960. Consequently, *school enrolments* expanded rapidly over the 1950s and1960s in all provinces. Growth then slowed noticeably in the 1970s and early 1980s as the bust generation of the late 1960s and 1970s reached their elementary and secondary ages. The first boomer reached post-secondary education age (19) in 1966. Post-secondary enrolments grew over the subsequent 25 years as the boomers moved through their college and university years.

In many provinces births started up in the mid to late 1970s as the boomers began to have their children, resulting in the echo generation. As indicated in the young dependency ratio calculations, the echo of the 1980s and early 1990s was larger in some provinces than others. This placed considerable demands on governments for the provision of *child care* and pre-school programs over this period. These needs and the associated demands gradually became less prominent over the late 1990s as the millennium bust generation entered these ages.

Meanwhile, the first echo boomers reached elementary school age in the mid-1980s and secondary school age in the early 1990s. As a result, after a decade and a half of no growth and no jobs for teachers over the 1970s and early 1980s, the elementary-secondary education system expanded again over the second half of the 1980s and 1990s in those provinces that had an echo and high young dependency (such as Ontario, Manitoba, and Saskatchewan). Demands for capital grants for new schools increased along with needs for expanded operating funds and new teachers. For those provinces that experienced a strong out-migration of people of working age (such as New Brunswick), the echo did not materialize, and they found it necessary to continue to consolidate their education system by closing and amalgamating elementary and secondary schools.

Declining young dependency in all provinces indicates that school enrolments will decline as the smaller millennium generation reaches school age. In Ontario, for example, where the echo is large, the peak of the echo generation was born in 1991. This group moved through the mid-point of their elementary education (age nine) in 2000. Suddenly school closings were introduced as new policies by many school boards. Similar outcomes have been experienced in other provinces.

In Ontario the peak of the echo generation moves through the mid-point of its high school years (age 15 or 16) in the mid-2000s, and thereafter school boards in the province will face both declining elementary and secondary enrolments. Of course, there will be some variation around the province as regional demographic differences and intraprovincial migration play a role in the experiences of individual school boards. While the decline will be most noticeable in provinces that experience the biggest decline in young dependency, the big-picture trend is clear for all provinces. In the future, children will form a smaller share of the population; therefore, adjustments to provincial (and local) government priorities, policies, and programs will be increasingly necessary. Provincial governments can choose between improving the quality of elementary-secondary education in the form of higher per capita transfers or using the funds elsewhere. And there are likely to be many alternative uses for these funds, even within the education portfolio.

Not surprisingly, the increasing births of the late 1970s in a number of provinces started to result in increasing *post-secondary enrolments* 20 years later, in the late 1990s. At the turn of the new millennium, many colleges and universities in Canada are facing increasing applications and enrolments. Consequently, post-secondary institutions in those provinces have been requesting more funding both for capital and operating expenses to meet these challenges. From a demographic viewpoint, this is the educational growth sector of the new millennium.

But how long will it last? Not very long in Quebec, where the echo is comparatively small. In Ontario the peak of the echo born in 1991 will reach age 19 in 2010 and will be halfway through their first degree by 2012. But these post-secondary institutions should also be doing their demographic strategic planning much earlier. Capital facilities last a long time, and so strategic planning should embrace a similar time horizon. If births in Ontario started to go down in 1992, first admissions will start down 19 years later, namely, in 2011. Consequently, if careful planning is not undertaken, excess capacity in both staff and built facilities may emerge in the post-secondary sector in Ontario and other provinces over the 2010s.

Foot has suggested one possible solution for this challenge.[31] Since the eastern provinces have a smaller youth share in the population but also contain many well-established post-secondary educational institutions, excess capacity is likely to emerge in these institutions in the 2000s. Consequently, these institutions might well be closing facilities at the same time that Ontario and the western provinces are establishing new facilities. This is not a problem from a faculty and staff perspective, since people are mobile and some employees no longer needed in eastern Canada will be able to find opportunities in Ontario and western Canada. However, this is not the case for the bricks-and-mortar facilities that are not mobile. From a national perspective, it might be desirable to share post-secondary students around the provinces. This sharing policy, which could be achieved formally through bilateral arrangements among the provinces, might preserve well-established institutions in eastern Canada while at the same time easing pressure on post-secondary facilities in Ontario and western Canada. Moreover, over-expansion in Ontario and western Canada in the 2000s might not be wise in light of the likely easing of post-secondary enrolment needs in the subsequent decade.

In summary, with demographic change driving declining elementary enrolments and expanding post-secondary enrolments over the first decade of the new millennium, resource reallocations within the education portfolio appear to be a sensible policy. Thereafter, education enrolment growth will decrease, and resource transfers outside of the traditional education sector are likely to be necessary. An ageing workforce is likely to make increasing demands on training resources, but the largest demand on government is likely to be elsewhere, namely in health care.

The first boomer born in 1947 reaches age 65 in 2012 and age 75 in 2022. While people use *health care* throughout their lives, use of physicians and drugs increases in a person's fifties, and use of hospital facilities increases in a person's sixties and especially their seventies. Those born in the Roaring Twenties are currently in their seventies. Funding cutbacks and expanding demands from this generation have resulted in hospital space becoming a contentious issue in all provinces. Meanwhile, expensive new drugs and expanding demands from both the boomers and their parents have resulted in escalating drug costs within the health portfolios.

Relief is on the horizon as the Roaring Twenties generation gradually passes away and is replaced by the slower growing 1930s Depression generation who will be in their seventies and eighties in the first two decades of the new millennium. Of course, longer life expectancy will mean more patients in their eighties and older, but the slowdown of growth in needs from the younger generation can be pleasant news for the challenged health care sector.

However, the growth in health care demands will still exceed population growth by a substantial amount. For example, the Final Report of the Provincial and Territorial Ministers of Health estimates that health expenditure growth due to population ageing will exceed health expenditure growth due to population growth after the mid-2000s.[32] By the early 2020s, the Report estimates annual health expenditure growth due to population growth of 0.5 per cent compared to 1.25 per cent due to population ageing. Combined, these two components result in annual health expenditure growth of 1.75 per cent (in constant dollars), which is 2.5 times the population growth but is probably below the real growth potential of the economy.

The ministers of health estimate that health expenditure growth in Ontario will be slightly above the national average, but it will still lag behind Alberta and BC. The growth in other provinces will be lower. Based on these estimates, the growth potential of the provincial economies is likely to be sufficient to generate the revenues needed to provide health care to an ageing population. The Achilles heel of the health care system is likely to be elsewhere, namely, in the health care workforce. An ageing and retiring workforce will result in an increasing challenge to recruit workers.

Parenthetically, it is interesting to note that since rural areas, however defined, have higher senior shares in their populations and seniors are the most intensive users of hospitals, customer-oriented public policy would ensure good hospital access in rural areas. Recent decisions on hospital closings in Ontario, Alberta, Saskatchewan, and other provinces do not appear to recognize these demographic imperatives to provide accessible health care to demographically older rural areas.

Other quantitatively less important provincial budget items are also affected by the changing demographics of the provinces. For example, since it is the males in their teens and twenties that are responsible for most *crime*, an ageing population tends to lead to a reduction in the overall crime rate. This has happened throughout North America over the 1990s as the massive boomer generation aged out of its crime-prone ages. The continuing (negative) impact of the ageing boomer generation more than offsets the (positive) contribution of their echo children to the crime rate, so crime rates can be expected to continue to decrease in the years ahead, especially in the 2010s and beyond. This should be welcome news for the justice portfolios of the provincial governments.

Once again there are differential impacts within the justice sector. One area of growth is fraud, since this is the preferred crime of older criminals. This crime category covers the gamut from blue collar through white collar to starched collar crime. Detecting and solving fraud requires different police training than is part of the traditional curriculum. Moreover, police on the fraud beat do not need the same physical attributes that police on the drug or homicide beats need. Well-experienced but ageing officers could be trained in forensic accounting and other relevant disciplines to be used in the fraud division for many more years of successful police work.

Another portfolio impacted by changing population is *transportation*. On average, public transportation is the preferred transportation mode of the young. It is cheap, and young workers in their twenties tend to locate in the downtown cores that are well served by public transportation. As the boomers grew up over the 1960s and 1970s, demands for public transportation grew rapidly. They also rode the intercity buses. Then in the 1980s the boomers reached their thirties, started their families, and moved out to the suburbs, thereby leading to suburban sprawl. Sprawling suburbs cannot be well serviced by public transportation, and they were ready to drive their automobiles anyway. Transit got into financial trouble, and the roads became crowded in many jurisdictions. By the mid-1990s the children of the boomers were teenagers and, as expected, riding public transportation. This moderate growth can be expected for another decade, when they too will start families and move to areas conducive to raising their children and pets.

Transportation surveys show that automobile use peaks in the early forties, when parents drive their children to their numerous activities. The peak of the baby boom, born in 1960, turned 40 in 2000 and entered their peak driving ages. Not surprisingly, traffic congestion is a problem in many urban areas in Canada as the boomers are driving their automobiles. Population growth and population ageing have both contributed to traffic congestion in the major urban centres. Population growth will continue to contribute to congestion, but since, on average, a person drives increasingly less after their mid-forties, population ageing will contribute to less traffic congestion in the years ahead. However, population ageing produces other traffic related challenges. Road signs (and maps) need to be bigger and easier to read. Traffic lights need to be longer to enable slower moving pedestrians to cross the road.

Culture and recreation are other government expenditure items influenced by population ageing. In essence, the young are interested in discos and sports, while the older members of the population are interested in live theatre and birding. Capital and operating project funding policies need to adapt to the changing needs of the population if a government wishes to serve the needs of its electorate.

Many other government policies and programs are also impacted by population change. Demographic and life cycle information can be used to explain and understand past trends and to project likely future trends and policy needs. They can be used to determine priorities that are future-oriented and connect policies and programs so that new needs in one area may be funded using resources from another area where needs are shrinking. But perhaps of even more importance, they are forward-looking and can contribute to proactive rather than reactive government.

Workforce implications

People are also employees. Demographic change has important workforce implications. Again, some historical analysis can contribute to understanding the trends. The first boomer born in 1947 reached age 16 in 1963. Consequently, from the mid-1960s to the late 1980s the labour force in Canada grew rapidly as the boomers entered their working ages. Youth unemployment became a major issue as ever more youth faced the challenge of finding their first job. Then over the 1990s workforce growth slowed noticeably as the smaller group born in the 1970s entered their working ages. The labour market became tighter, and the unemployment rate fell. By the late 1990s reports of labour market shortages were commonplace, as were accounts of bonuses for young workers. Canada had moved from youth unemployment to bonuses for youth in a decade.

Concern for future labour market shortages continued into the new millennium, despite the slowdown in hiring attributable to slower economic growth. At the national level, these concerns have some legitimacy since the lack of an echo generation in older provinces (such as Quebec and Atlantic Canada) offsets the impact of the echo generation in younger provinces (notably Ontario, Manitoba, Saskatchewan, and Alberta). The US has an even larger echo, so it is unlikely that young Canadians will find expanded employment opportunities south of the border. The echo generation means growing numbers of new workforce entrants for the first decade of the new millennium. Consequently, a labour market shortage is unlikely to emerge over this period.

The ageing of the existing workforce also produces policy challenges. There are now more workers aged 40 and over (40-64) than under 40 (15-39) in the workforce of Canada. This increasing share of older workers in the workforce will continue despite the workforce entry of the echo generation over the first decade and a half of the new millennium. Innovative retraining programs are likely to be in more demand as increased numbers of older workers find the skills, largely acquired in their younger years, no longer appropriate for a changing economy.

The first boomer born in 1947 reached age 55 in 2002. Over the first decade of the new millennium there will be a rapidly increasing number of workers in their fifties who have largely finished raising their children, are becoming grandparents, and are finding elder care an increasing part of their lives as they assume responsibility for their ageing parents. They are not yet able or ready to retire, but they could use more free time in their schedules. The time is now right in the new millennium to implement flexible workplace and phased retirement policies.[33]

An increasing number of workers are likely to embrace the offer of a reduced workload for a proportionate reduction in pay. For example, a policy that permitted a worker to work four days a week between age 50 and 54, three days between 55 and 59, two days between 60 and 64, and one day between 65 and 69 with an associated proportionate reduction in pay might be attractive to an increasing number of employees. Other flexible workplace policies, such as half-days for 50 per cent pay or nine months of the year for 75 per cent pay, might also be attractive.

These flexible workplace policies have the advantage of being adapted to individual employee needs while at the same time releasing monies that can be used to renew the workforce with new younger workers at no increase in the wage bill. Moreover, they facilitate two-way mentoring where the older employees transfer their experience to the younger employees and the younger employees transfer the latest technology skills to the older employees, thereby raising productivity in the organization.

Unfortunately, many existing public policies impede such progress. The most important are pension policies where it is frequently not possible to be both a contributor (on work days) and a beneficiary (on non-work days) at the same time. Pension plans need to be made flexible to accommodate more flexible workplace policies. Mandatory retirement is another policy in need of review. Even small changes could be considered for implementation. For example, working half-time for five years before and half-time for five years after the mandatory retirement age could still be considered consistent with a policy of mandatory retirement.

Similarly, many workplace taxes or contributions, such as employment insurance or workers compensation, have caps or fixed costs that encourage employers to work existing employees longer hours rather than introduce the flexible hours and workforce renewal indicated by these new policies. Governments need to examine the role of their various workplace policies with regard to flexible workplace arrangements if society is to proactively reap the benefits of an ageing workforce rather than be saddled with all the costs without any benefits. These are not easy tasks, but progress is required to suit the ageing workforce of the new millennium.

Conclusions

Demographic analysis provides a powerful tool to understand the past and foretell the future. Good government requires an understanding of the needs of the members of the society. People are consumers and workers, as well as taxpayers and voters. Proactive strategic planning based on demographic and life cycle analysis at the provincial level can anticipate their needs and assist in the formulation of appropriate provincial government policies. It can both identify areas of increasing resource needs and, perhaps more importantly, areas of decreasing resource needs. In this way resources can be gradually transferred from programs in diminishing need to those with growing needs. Demographic information is readily available but insufficiently used. The future roles of provincial governments will, in large part, be determined by the demographic trends outlined in this chapter. It is all about satisfying the needs of people—the people who elect the government to help them satisfy their own life cycle needs.

Notes

1. In increasing the number of seats in the House of Commons from 301 to 308 in 2003, Elections Canada allocated two additional ridings to Alberta and BC, and three to Ontario.
2. See J.R. Weeks, *Population: An Introduction to Concepts and Issues*, 8th ed. (Belmont: Wadsworth, 2002) for an introduction to demographic concepts and definitions and F. Trovato, *Population and Society: Essential Readings* (Toronto: Oxford University Press, 2002) for examples of demographic analyses. S.T. Wargon, *Demography in Canada in the Twentieth Century* (Vancouver: University of British Columbia Press, 2002) provides a review of demography in Canada in the twentieth century.
3. See, for example, R. Beaujot, (1991), *Population Change in Canada: The Challenges of Policy Adaptation* (Toronto: McClelland and Stewart, 1991) chapter 3.
4. Note that it is the *difference* between the birth and death rate that contributes to population growth.
5. However, many other developed countries, particularly in Europe, have even lower population growth rates, and some countries such as Germany, Russia, and Japan are now experiencing population decline.
6. For a review of historical demographic developments in Canada see D.K. Foot, *Canada's Population Outlook: Demographic Futures and Economic Challenges* (Toronto: Lorimer, for the Canadian Institute of Economic Policy, 1982); M. Haines and H. Steckel, eds., *A Population History of North America* (Cambridge: Cambridge University Press, 2000); and R. Beaujot and D. Kerr (2004), *Population Change in Canada*, 2nd ed. (Toronto: Oxford University Press, 2004).
7. Milligan argues that the program did have a statistically significant positive impact on the provincial fertility rate. See K. Milligan, "Subsidizing the Stork: New Evidence on Tax Incentives and Fertility," NBER Working Paper 8845 (2002), available at <http://www.nber.org/papers/w8845>.
8. These are examples of a different provincial culture influencing provincial demographic policy (see the chapter in this book by Nelson Wiseman).
9. See <http://www.cic.gc.ca/english/policy/fedprov.html> for details.
10. In chronological order these include New Brunswick, Newfoundland and Labrador (1999); PEI (2001); and Alberta, Nova Scotia, and Saskatchewan (2002).
11. See the chapter by Michael Howlett in this book for further evidence of the impacts of provincial economies on government policies.
12. See note 1.

13. D.K. Foot, with D. Stoffman, *Boom, Bust & Echo: How to Profit from the Coming Demographic Shift* (Toronto: Macfarlane, Walter and Ross, 1996).
14. Foot, *Boom, Bust & Echo.*
15. D.K. Foot, with D. Stoffman, *Boom, Bust & Echo 2000: Profiting from the Demographic Shift in the New Millennium* (Toronto: Macfarlane, Walter and Ross, 1998).
16. Foot, *Boom, Bust & Echo.*
17. The total dependency ratio can be expressed in many mathematically equivalent ways: in terms of population numbers (=$(Y+S)/W$); as the sum of the young and senior dependency ratios (= $(Y/W) + (S/W)$); or using population shares (= $((Y/P) + (S/P)) / (W/P)$).
18. This could be viewed as confirmation of the demographic transition hypothesis (see note 2) since these were also the regions of Canada that were further behind in economic development. Newfoundland includes Labrador throughout this chapter.
19. This could explain Quebec's policies to increase births noted above.
20. See note 13.
21. D.K. Foot, "The Demographic Future of Fiscal Federalism in Canada," *Canadian Public Policy* 10 (1984): 406–14.
22. See, for example, R.L. Clark and J.J. Spengler (1980), "Dependency Ratios: Their Use in Economic Analysis," in J.L. Simon and J. DaVanzo, eds., *Research in Population Economics: A Research Annual*, Vol. 2 (Greenwich, CT: Jai Press, 1980) 63–76; and D. Dixon and C. Thame, "The Relative Costs to Governments of the Young and Old," *Australian Quarterly* 56 (1984): 41–52.
23. Foot, "The Demographic Future of Fiscal Federalism in Canada."
24. Further adjustments to dependency ratios to account for differences in unemployment and labour force participation rates, and in the costs to the public purse from programs used by people of working age (such as employment insurance and welfare) are not considered here. See Foot, "The Demographic Future of Fiscal Federalism"; and D.K. Foot, "Public Expenditure, Population Aging and Economic Dependency in Canada, 1921–2021," *Population Research and Policy Review* 8 (1989): 97–117 for details.
25. Statistics Canada, Population Projections for Canada, Provinces and Territories, 2000–2026 (Ottawa: Ministry of Industry, 2001).
26. Statistics Canada.
27. Foot, *Canada's Population Outlook.*
28. Foot, *Canada's Population Outlook.*
29. See Foot, *Canada's Population Outlook* for comparable data.
30. For further details, see D.K. Foot, (1993), "Demography, Dependency and Deficits," in A.M. Kruger, D. Morley and A. Shachar, eds., *Public Services Under Stress: A Canadian-Israeli Policy Review* (Jerusalem: Magna Press, 1993) 140–53.
31. D.K. Foot, "Canadian Education: Demographic Change and Future Challenges," *Education Canada* 41 (2001): 24–27.
32. Provincial and Territorial Ministers of Health, Understanding Canada's Health Care Costs, Final Report, available at <http://www.health.gov.on.ca/english/public/pub/ministry_reports/ptcd/ptcd_mn.html> .
33. D.K. Foot and R. Venne, "The Time is Right: Voluntary Reduced Worktime and Workforce Demographics," *Canadian Studies in Population*, 25 (1998): 91–114.

CHAPTER 16

Women's Status Across the Canadian Provinces, 1999-2002

Exploring Differences and Possible Explanations[1]

BRENDA O'NEILL

To what extent does the status of Canadian women vary across the provinces? Much attention has been devoted to the economic restructuring brought on by the federal government's offloading of social program financial obligations onto the provinces, and some attention has been directed to evaluating how this offloading has specifically affected women in Canada.[2] The shift from targeted funding under the Canada Assistance Plan (CAP) and Established Program Financing (EPF) to block funding under the Canada Health and Social Transfer (CHST) in 1996 and the overall reduction in funding accompanying the shift have necessarily had negative consequences for provincially based programs. But less attention has been directed to the question of how variation in provincial policy response to the new economic climate has translated into differential effects for Canadian women. Given that the provinces assume constitutional responsibility for policy areas of particular importance to women's status, the focus would seem to be an important one to adopt. Moreover, provincial variation in policy capacity makes it highly likely that women's status varies provincially.

Policy response and fiscal capacity are not, however, developed in a vacuum. Economic restructuring brought on by the "need" to balance budgets occasions significant policy room. Particular government responses are shaped by numerous factors. Provincial government policy responses necessarily respond to the political agenda that is itself driven in part by the province's political culture and public opinion, by the type and degree of social activism targeted at bringing about specific policy reform, and by the nature of partisan competition within the provincial party system. Additionally, governments can and do independently drive policy responses that are themselves shaped by party platforms, party leaders, and elite and party competition. Canadian research has shown that policy response—particularly that which promotes women's status—can additionally be driven by the level of female representation in legislatures.[3] This relationship is, however, seriously constrained by "the institutional and ideological constraints and opportunities confronting women legislators."[4] Additionally the political opportunity structures feminist activists face can have consequences for their ability to shape policy.[5]

467

The goal of this chapter is twofold. The first is to evaluate and compare women's status in a select number of areas across the provinces in an effort to determine its variation. The questions of how provincial policy responses have varied given the reality of economic restructuring and, as such, how they have differently affected women across the country are important ones, for they extend the limited investigations to date of the relevance of federalism (and place) to women's status. More than this, identifying and assessing the "lived reality" of horizontal fiscal imbalance and policy variation more broadly constitutes an important starting point for understanding how women's political activism is "grounded in their experiences of particular places."[6] The second, and more difficult, goal is to identify those factors that help to explain any existing variation in provincial policy. As expressed by Richard Simeon, the objective is a "scholarly one of increasing the understanding of political reality."[7] This chapter necessarily provides only the first stage of a longer and more exhaustive evaluation of provincial policy variation and the multiple factors accounting for it across the provinces.

The concept of status is multifaceted and open to varying interpretations. It necessarily implies the application of a rank or position relative to others. The goal here is to position women in one province relative to women in others.[8] There are, indeed, an unlimited number of bases on which to evaluate and compare women across the provinces. One is simply to define key "women's issues" and to comparatively evaluate women's status on those issues across the provinces. The weakness in this approach is that is suggests that only a limited number of issues are relevant to gender, when, in reality, few policy areas do not have gendered effects. A more comprehensive approach is to assess women's status in each of three key areas: political, economic, and social. This risks the possibility of falsely compartmentalizing women's lives, but it does provide the potential for ensuring a comprehensive picture. The approach taken here is to evaluate and compare women's status across the provinces in four areas: economic independence, reproductive freedom, child care, and political representation.[9] The first provides an indicator of women's economic status, a clear determinant of women's capacity overall. Reproductive freedom and child care are included as both have been and are significant policy areas for women, given their direct connection to women's freedom and independence. Moreover, feminist activism has been directed towards these two policy areas, indicative of their overall importance for women.[10] The last, political representation, provides a rough indicator of women's formal political power, at least to the degree that it resides in the legislative and executive branches of government.

Comparing Women's Status

Research into comparative provincial policy invariably butts up against the reality of the difficulty of collecting data that allows for meaningful comparisons across the ten provinces. Research that comparatively evaluates public policy by gender exponentially increases the level of difficulty encountered by the researcher, given the difficulty often encountered when attempting to collect provincially based statistics separately for women and men.[11] Evidence of these difficulties is to be found in the propensity for research on gender and public policy in Canada to concentrate on the federal level of government or to be limited to a comparison of two to several, rather than all ten, provinces.

As such, the data collected in this chapter provide a comparative snapshot of women's status on a limited number of dimensions for the 1999 to 2002 period. The time period reflects the fact that these are the most recent figures available for several of the indicators (most notably, child care); although the data might at first glance seem dated, the reality is that this snapshot provides one of the first attempts to collect these statistics and, as such, provides an important benchmark for future research. The data also allow for a preliminary and exploratory account of the source of variation in women's status across the provinces. Accounting for this variation necessarily means that the data collected on all measures had to be restricted to a relatively short time period.[12]

Economic independence

Women's status in many respects is directly dependent on their economic independence. Several indicators provide a snapshot of women's economic status across the provinces: share of women holding a university degree, participating in the labour force, employed in managerial and professional occupations, and with low incomes or living below the Low Income Cut-Off Measure (LICO), as well as women's average income and the ratio of women's to men's average income (see Table 16.3). Higher levels of each correspond with higher economic status, the exception being the share with low incomes where the correspondence is reversed. Although the federal government is involved in many of these areas, provincial governments assume primary responsibility for economic conditions, labour, and post-secondary education, and, as such, variation in these indicators might be anticipated.

A comparative evaluation of several indicators of women's economic independence reveals a certain degree of provincial variation, a variation, moreover, that often corresponds to the economic climate of the province generally. That is, women tend to have a higher economic status in "have" as opposed to "have not" provinces. There are, however, some interesting and important exceptions to this result.

With a few exceptions, women in British Columbia, Alberta, and Ontario enjoy a higher economic status than other women in Canada. On all of the indicators included in Table 16.1, women in BC are above average: in the share of women holding a university degree, participating in the labour force, on average income, in the share living below the LICO, and in the ratio of their full-time/

full-year income to men's. Women in Ontario also fare better on several indicators when compared to women across the country. The one exception is in the ratio of women's to men's income, where women earn the same as the overall provincial average, 72 cents per male dollar. Women in Alberta also earn a high ranking on economic independence over the set of indicators included here. The same exception, however, holds in Alberta as it does in Ontario: the ratio of women's to men's income in Alberta, 68.9 cents per male dollar, ranks the province at significantly below the provincial average; indeed, it is the lowest score across all the provinces.

Table 16.1. Women's Economic Independence across the Provinces, 1997–1999

Province	University Degree (1999)	Partici-pation in the Labour Force (1999)	Employed in Managerial & Professional Occupations (1999)	Average Income (1997)	Below Low-Income Cut-Off (1998)	Ratio of Women's to Men's Income (FT/FY) (1998)
NF	8.4	42.5	32.9	$14,289	21.3	72.3
PEI	11.4	52.5	32.3	$16,920	—	73.5
NS	12.4	50.1	33.0	$16,105	21.8	72.7
NB	11.4	49.8	31.0	$16,138	17.2	69.5
QC	12.9	50.2	35.3	$18,275	24.1	71.9
ON	15.4	56.5	35.0	$21,731	15.3	72.3
MB	12.3	57.5	32.9	$18,635	22.6	73.9
SK	10.5	56.7	31.7	$18,080	18.7	75.4
AB	13.4	62.2	33.1	$19,202	16.7	68.9
BC	14.2	54.8	34.8	$21,044	15.9	74.9
Average	12.2	53.3	33.2	$18,041	19.3	72.5

Note: With the exception of average income, all measures are percentages. The low income cut-off point is calculated by Statistics Canada as that income level below which individuals spend at least 20 per cent of their income on food, shelter, and clothing.
Sources: Statistics Canada, *Women in Canada 2000: A Gender-Based Statistical Report* (Ottawa: Minister of Industry, 2000) and *Women in Canada* (Canadian Centre for Justice: Statistics Profile Series), Catalogue No. 85F0033MIE (Ottawa: Minister of Industry, 2001).

Women in the Atlantic provinces, by comparison, are economically much less well-off than women generally across the country. On the six indicators employed to assess economic status, women in the eastern provinces come in below average on at least four of the indicators, and in the case of Newfoundland, on all six. In each of the four provinces, women earn less than women in Canada on average, are less likely than average to be employed in managerial and professional occupations, and are less likely to be participating in the labour force. With the exception of Nova Scotia, women in the region earn fewer university degrees than the average for women across the provinces. New Brunswick stands out among the Atlantic provinces in that it is the only province in the region for which a lower than average share of women live below Statistics Canada's

LICO level. Alternatively, women in Nova Scotia and Prince Edward Island fare comparatively well, at least in the level of income that they earn relative to men. Yet the overall assessment of women's economic independence in the region is particularly weak when compared with women elsewhere in the country.

Results are mixed in the remaining provinces. In Quebec, women fare above the national average on half of the economic independence indicators: in the earning of university degrees, the share employed in managerial and professional occupations, and in average income. In Manitoba and Saskatchewan, women fare worse than the average in two of the six indicators. In both provinces, women make up less than the average share of women employed in managerial and professional occupations across the country. Additionally, women in Saskatchewan earn fewer university degrees than the average, while a greater than average share of women in Manitoba lives below the LICO point.

The results suggest that the degree of economic independence enjoyed by women in a province depends in some measure on the overall economic climate within the province. Without a doubt, however, women's economic independence does vary across the provinces and underlines the importance of place for their day-to-day economic reality.

Reproductive freedom: Abortion

A key policy issue in many respects for women is abortion. The Supreme Court of Canada ruled in the *Morgentaler* case in 1988 that the existing abortion legislation was unconstitutional on the grounds that it violated security of the person provisions in the *Charter of Rights and Freedoms* (section 7). The result meant that no criminal action could be taken against providers of abortion services. Although the Mulroney government attempted to re-criminalize abortion through *Bill C-43*, its narrow defeat in the Senate in 1999 has meant the absence of a federal criminal abortion law since the late 1980s.

The absence of criminal penalty attached to abortion services has not meant, however, that access has significantly improved. Rather, the provincial governments' responsibility for regulating health care has provided them with considerable power in this policy area. The combination of a legislative vacuum and abortion's quasi-medical status has provided significant government policy discretion, and the result is a "patchwork" of policy across the country (see Table 16.2). *The Canada Health Act* 1984 provides the federal government with a possible avenue for ensuring relatively consistent access and cost reimbursement across the country in its guarantees of portability, accessibility, and comprehensiveness of service. Threats to withhold federal funds from provincial governments, however, have been few in number and have not been carried out. Adding yet a third dimension to the complexity of the issue, while provincial policy can set a standard for service, local regional health authorities and hospital boards have also had a lengthy history of challenging access to abortion services.[13]

Table 16.2. Reproductive Freedom: Abortion and Teen Pregnancies, 2000–2002

Province	Abortion Access[1]		Abortion Funding		Number of Abortions Performed per Year	Abortion Rate (per 1,000 people)	Teen Pregnancy Rate[2] (per 1,000 people)
	Hospitals	Clinics	Hospitals	Clinics			
NF	2	1	Complete	Complete	859	1.65	28.5
PEI	0	0	Complete	Partial	0	0	30.4
NS	5	1	Complete	Partial	2105	2.26	31.5
NB	2	1	Complete	None	1039	1.39	33.4
QC	30/11/3[3]	5	Complete	Partial	31038	4.20	39.7
ON	76	6	Complete	Complete	38831	3.26	34.1
MB	2	1	Complete	None	3515	3.05	58.7
SK	3	0	Complete	Partial[4]	1752	1.75	48.2
AB	3	2	Complete	Complete	10894	3.56	44.5
BC	37	3	Complete	Complete	15820	3.88	35.5
						Average: 2.50	Average: 43.12

1. Abortion access and funding current to August 2002; abortion statistics for 2001.

2. For women aged between 15 and 19 years, for 2000.

3. Includes 30 hospitals, 11 health centres, and three women's health centres.

4. Reciprocal billing plan with clinics in Edmonton and Calgary; requires facility fee.

Sources: Childbirth by Choice Trust; Statistics Canada, "Teen Pregnancy," Catalogue No. 82-221-XIE, accessed November 25, 2005; and Statistics Canada, "Canadian Statistics: Therapeutic Abortions by Province and Territory of Report," Health Indicators (2002), available at <http://www.statcan.ca/english/Pgdb/People/Health/health40a.htm>, accessed 4 July 2002.

Two bases for assessing women's status on the issue of abortion across the provinces are service access and fees. In all provinces, access to abortion services occurs predominately in hospitals (64 per cent of all cases in 2002), with the remainder being performed in private clinics.[14] The fact that not every hospital within a province provides the service, and that clinics are not found in every province, however, leads to significant provincial variation in access. For example, more than half of all the country's abortion clinics are found in Ontario and Quebec alone.

Without question women in PEI have the most limited access to abortion services in Canada. Without a single hospital or clinic providing abortion services, women are forced to travel outside the province for access to service. Women in the remaining Atlantic provinces do not fare much better, however; access is limited to few hospitals and clinics in the region, resulting in lower abortion rates than in every province except Saskatchewan. The average abortion rate (per 1,000 people) across the provinces is 2.5; not one of the Atlantic provinces exceeds this rate.

Women in Saskatchewan are similarly restricted in their ability to access abortion services. The overall abortion rate in that province is 1.75 per 1,000 people. Although two hospitals and one clinic within a hospital provide abortion services (in Regina and Saskatoon), the province's opposition to the establishment of free-standing clinics results in significantly fewer abortions than in many other provinces. A reciprocal billing arrangement with clinics in Edmonton and Calgary adopted in 1996 has improved access, but costs (including facility fees, transportation, and accommodation) remain prohibitive for many women. Research conducted in 2003 found that when not covered by provincial health care, charges for abortion services ranged from $250 to $1425.[15]

Access to abortion services in Ontario and Manitoba is higher than the provincial average overall (3.3 and 3.1 respectively) but is restricted predominantly to women in urban areas. Thus, while the number of abortions performed is relatively high compared to the remaining provinces, women in the rural parts of the two provinces face increased difficulties in accessing abortion services. In Manitoba, women's access is restricted to the City of Winnipeg where two hospitals and one free-standing clinic offer the service. Access in Ontario is superior to many other provinces given the existence of 76 hospitals and six free-standing clinics that provide the service. Access is not regionally balanced, however, but rather is concentrated in the southern part of the province.

Women in BC, Alberta, and Quebec appear to have the best access to abortion services across the provinces. The abortion rate is 3.9 abortions per 1,000 people in BC, 3.6 per 1,000 people in Alberta and 4.2 per 1,00 people in Quebec, each well above the provincial average. The existence of 37 hospitals and three clinics that the 1992 government designated as providers of abortion services has meant that access is more regionally distributed across BC and that a relatively high number of women have access to the service. In Alberta, hospitals in the cities of Edmonton, Calgary, and Grande Prairie provide abortion services, although the majority take place in the two major urban centres. Clinics in Edmonton and Calgary increase the degree of access in that province, although the limit on the number of abortions performed at Calgary's Kensington Clinic increases waiting lists. Women in Quebec enjoy the greatest access to abortion services of all Canadian women; 29 per cent of all Canadian abortions take place in the province's 40 hospitals and clinics. Regional concentration of service is also evident in the province, however, with 75 per cent of the province's abortions performed in Montreal alone.[16]

Access to abortion services is, however, only one element of the policy. The second involves the degree of funding available to women to procure such services. Variation in funding occurs primarily through the decisions of provincial governments regarding the imposition of user fees charged directly to women. In many ways, decisions regarding funding are as, if not more, important that those regarding access, given that a surfeit of private clinics would mean little if women could not afford to pay to procure their services. Quite apart from user fees, however, the regional concentration of hospitals and clinics that provide abortion services imposes significant travel and accommodation costs on women, in addition to any user fees attached to the service. The costs associated with travel to urban centres (often as many as three such trips are required) are not covered by provincial health insurance plans and remain significant barriers to access for many women.

Provincial governments have control over the existence of private clinics in the province, as well as the level of funding provided for services provided within those clinics. It is also the case that abortion is excluded from many provincial reciprocal billing lists despite the fact that portability of service is a cornerstone of the *Canada Health Act* (1984). Portability is meant to ensure that Canadians have uninterrupted access to medical services when they move from one province to another. This is not, however, the case for abortion services in most provinces, and, for many, the required three-month waiting period can deny access to publicly funded services, given hospital waiting lists.

Abortion services provided in hospitals are fully funded in every province, although there are restrictions on this in some.[17] Significant variation exists, however, in the degree of funding provided for abortions performed in private clinics. Four provinces provide full funding for private clinic abortions: Newfoundland, Ontario, Alberta, and BC (see Table 16.2). In four provinces—PEI, Nova Scotia, Quebec, and Saskatchewan[18]—women must pay partial costs for abortion services provided in clinics. New Brunswick and Manitoba remain the only two provinces that do not cover any of the costs associated with abortions performed in private clinics.

Thus, any assessment of abortion policies across the provinces suggests one of three rankings. In the highest ranked group of provinces—BC, Alberta, and

Ontario—women have an above-average access to service relative to the average across the provinces, as well as complete funding for abortion services performed in private clinics. In the second group—Newfoundland, Quebec, and Manitoba—women have either above-average access to the procedure or complete clinic coverage, but not both. In the provinces with the lowest ranking—PEI, Nova Scotia, New Brunswick, and Saskatchewan—women have below average abortion service access and either partial or no funding provided for private clinic services.

Reproductive freedom: Teen pregnancy rate

A not-unrelated issue to abortion is the rate of teen pregnancy in each province. The provincial variation in the rate tells us something about the relative importance provincial governments assign to sex education and to making information and prophylactics readily available to teens. On this issue, three provinces stand out for the high rates of teen pregnancy recorded in 2000: Alberta, Saskatchewan, and Manitoba. In Alberta and Saskatchewan, the rate per 1,000 women aged between 15 and 19 was 44.5 and 48.2 respectively. In Manitoba, this rate jumps to 58.7. These figures reflect the relatively high Aboriginal population in these provinces: 5.3, 13.5, and 13.6 per cent respectively in 2001[19] and the more limited access to services enjoyed by young Aboriginal women.

Child care services

The importance of access to affordable child care for women's economic and personal freedom should not be underestimated. The provinces assume constitutional authority for child care policy as it is considered a social service, although the federal government has assumed a direct role in the policy field through its fiscal capacity, tax provisions, and provincial transfers. Provincial variation in the affordability, accessibility and quality of childcare services is nevertheless substantial.[20] While all provinces provide subsidies to service providers to allow low-income parents to afford care for their children, other policies regarding regulated and unregulated child care can vary widely. Not all provinces, for example, require service providers to be regulated in order to obtain government subsidies. Quebec, as another example, is unmatched among the provinces in that it currently provides a very successful $5/day child care program for children aged between 0 to 12 years that puts pressure on the supply of child care spaces. No other province currently comes close to providing this level of service.

Provincial child care services are necessarily shaped by federal funding, provincial fiscal capacity, and ideological factors. Under the provisions of the CAP, introduced in 1966, funding targeted for child care services was directed to the provinces for programs on a 50/50 cost-shared basis. The shift to block funding under the CHST in 1996 ended federal transfers targeted specifically to child care. The bulk of current federal involvement in the policy field is in the form of tax expenditures available to individual Canadians. According to Linda White, federalism constrains the development of successful child care policy more so than fiscal and ideological factors.[21] The latter are not, however, irrelevant in shaping to some degree the variation in child care policies found across the provinces.[22]

Developing indicators that reflect and capture the multiple elements of the policy sphere is particularly difficult, and with child care the task is particularly complex. Two indicators are included in this evaluation: share of children (0-12 years of age) in regulated child care spaces and per child expenditures on regulated child care. While these indicators capture only a limited number of the multiple dimensions of the policy arena, they nevertheless provide a direct and comparable indicator of the availability of and provincial resources devoted to providing child care spaces.

Table 16.3 provides two indicators by which to evaluate provincial child care policies and level of services in 2001.[23] Unlike other policies, variation here does not correspond closely with provincial fiscal capacity. Women in the "have" provinces do not by definition fare especially well on the child care front compared to women in the "have not" provinces. Four provinces come out above average[24] on the two indicators: PEI, Quebec, Manitoba, and BC. Without question, child care services in Quebec are superior to those available in the remaining provinces; the number of spaces and the total budget allocated to child care services there exceed by a wide margin those found elsewhere. Women in PEI also fare com-

Table 16.3. Child Care Services across the Provinces, 2001

Province	Regulated Child Care Space Availability[1], 2001	Total Allocation for Regulated Child Care per Child in the Province, 2001($)
NF	5.5	101
PEI	14.0	187
NS	8.1	91
NB	9.9	105
QC	21.1	980
ON	8.9	232
MB	12.4	338
SK	4.2	97
AB	9.1	110
BC	12.1	273
Average (Median)	10.5	251.4 (148.5)

1. Measure indicates the percentage of children in the province, aged 0 to 12 years, for whom a regulated child care space exists.
Source: Martha Friendly, Jane Beach, and Michelle Turiano (2002) *Early Childhood Education and Care in Canada 2001* (Toronto: Childhood Resource and Research Unit, University of Toronto, 2002).

paratively well on these two indicators: data reveal that regulated spaces were available for 14 per cent of children in the province and that the government allocated $187 per child in the province to regulated child care. The percentage of children for whom a child care space is available is also higher than average in Manitoba and BC, but compared to PEI, these provinces must allocate greater funding to bring this result about. One province, Ontario, directs more funding to child care per child than six of the other provinces ($232 per child in 2001) yet does relatively poorly in translating this funding into regulated child care spaces. On this second measure, the province ranks seventh in its availability of regulated child care spaces.

In the remaining five provinces, the scores on both of the child care indicators are lower than those in the remaining provinces. In each case, regulated child care spaces exist for fewer than 10 per cent of children in the province, and in the case of Saskatchewan for fewer than 5 per cent of children. In terms of child care spending, governments in the five provinces spent approximately $100 per child in the province on regulated child care, while the median spending on child care for all provinces was roughly $150 per child.

Political representation

As an indicator of women's status, the level of women's political representation in the legislature and executive provides an indicator of the level of formal power possessed by women within traditional political institutions. The indicator is limited, however, in that women in the legislature and executive are constrained in the degree to which they can advance women's issues by institutional rules and structure, their positions within caucus and cabinet, and by party discipline. Nevertheless, the level of women's political representation matters, for as "more women enter Canada's Parliament and legislatures, they alter the style, tone, content, and outcomes of political debate," and, importantly, "women can only make a gender-sensitive difference in political life if they are present to do the work."[25]

Table 16.4 provides a snapshot of women's levels of political representation in each provincial legislature, governing caucus, and cabinet in July 2002. The legislatures in several provinces reveal a higher than average share of women among legislators: in PEI, Quebec, Manitoba, Saskatchewan, and BC women made up more than 20 per cent of the legislative membership. It is not immediately clear why these provinces performed better than average across all provinces.[26] Alternatively, Nova Scotia stood apart for the small share of women in its legislative chamber: only 9.6 per cent of all legislators in that province were women.

The level of representation in the governing caucus provides a better indicator of women's potential for political power, since it provides the supply from which cabinet members are chosen. In four of the provinces women constituted more than one-quarter of the members of the governing caucus: Newfoundland,

Table 16.4. Women's Political Status across the Provinces (2002)

Province	Women in Legislature	Governing Party	Women in Governing Party Caucus	Women in Cabinet
NF	16.7	Liberal	25.9	27.7
PEI	22.2	Progressive Conservative	23.1	20.0
NS	9.6	Progressive Conservative	9.7	8.3
NB	18.2	Progressive Conservative	17.0	20.0
QC	23.2	Parti Québécois	26.1	20.0
ON	17.5	Progressive Conservative	15.8	24.0
MB	24.6	NDP	28.1	31.3
SK	22.4	NDP	24.1	13.3
AB	20.5	Progressive Conservative	20.3	20.8
BC	22.8	Liberal	20.8	28.6
Average	19.8		24.1	21.4

Note: All entries are percentages.
Source: Trimble and Arscott.

Quebec, Manitoba, and Saskatchewan. In only two of these provinces, however, was this increased share translated into greater representation for women in cabinet; in Newfoundland and Manitoba, 28 and 31 per cent of cabinet members were women. And although Ontario and BC did relatively poorly in terms of the share of women found in the legislature, women were nevertheless well-represented in cabinet. Only in these two provinces was women's share of cabinet higher than average: at 24 per cent and 29 per cent respectively. Women's cabinet representation in the remaining provinces appears relatively consistent, averaging approximately 20 per cent. Only in Saskatchewan, at 13 per cent, and Nova Scotia, at a particularly low 8 per cent, was women's representation significantly lower than average.[27] Thus, the degree to which women enjoy political representation in the key political institutions varies significantly across the provinces.

Explaining Provincial Variation in Women's Status

An important task for this chapter is also to assess the causes of any provincial variation in these four areas. In a classical essay, Richard Simeon identified several factors as possible explanations for variation in policy outcomes across space and over time: the environment, the distribution of power, prevailing ideas, institutional frameworks, and the process of decision-making.[28] More recently, Louis Imbeau and Guy Lachapelle identified the following factors as those which analysts have identified as "policy determinants" in the context of Canadian provincial politics: non-political factors including cultural, economic, and social factors; and political factors including institutions, federal transfers, workers' militancy and the election of left-wing governments, and electoral competition and electoral cycles.[29] Focusing on policy variation of particular importance for women, however, narrows the set of factors likely to provide explanatory mileage. Three sets of variables are examined here as possible determinants of provincial variation in women's economic independence, reproductive freedom, and child care services. First, a province's fiscal capacity is likely to directly determine its ability to manipulate policy outcomes. As such, three indicators are employed to assess fiscal capacity: per capita federal transfer payments, per capita social services expenditure, and per capita gross domestic product (GDP). The first has been linked to the provinces' ability to provide services, while the second provides a direct indicator of social service spending.[30] The third—per capita GDP—provides an indicator of overall economic capacity. A fourth measure—share of urban population—is included as greater urbanization can provide economies of scale and, as such, may be linked to provincial policy capacity.

Table 16.5 provides the correlation of each indicator of fiscal capacity to the various indicators of status.[31] Three indicators of fiscal capacity—per capita federal transfers, per capita GDP, and urbanization—are closely related to women's economic independence across the provinces. In general terms, women's economic independence is greater where federal transfers are lower and where per capita GDP and urbanization are greater.[32] This relationship holds for each of the indicators of women's economic capacity except for the ratio of male to female

Table 16.5. Relationship between Women's Status and Fiscal Capacity

Status Indicator	Per Capita Federal Transfers	Per Capita Social Services Expenditure	Per Capita GDP	Share of Urban Population
University Degrees	-.78**	-.33	.51	.71
Participation in Labour Force	-.75*	-.46	.77**	.53
Share of Managerial and Professional Occupations	-.54	.39	.26	.79
Average Income	-.88**	-.22	.61	.83**
Share Below LICO	.48	.42	-.52	-.28
Ratio of Female to Male Income	-.05	.34	-.36	.03
Abortion Rate	-.75*	.01	.55	.93**
Teen Pregnancy Rate	-.40	-.24	.36	.38
Child Care Spaces	-.12	.19	-.13	.24
Child Care Spending	-.26	.24	-.05	.43

Notes: Entries are Pearson correlation coefficients. An "urban" area is defined as one having a minimum of 1,000 people and a population density of at least 400 people per square kilometre. Urbanization data collected from the 2001 census. Remaining data based on 2000/2001 data figures.
* indicates $p < .05$; ** indicates $p < .01$.
Sources: Statistics Canada (2001 Census; 2000-2001 Public Sector Statistics; 2001 Provincial Economic Accounts) and Eric Beauchemin and Paul Judson, *The Canadian Federal and Provincial Governments: 2002 Overview* (Toronto: Dominion Bond Rating Service, 2003).

income. Variation in this ratio does not appear to depend on any of the provincial fiscal capacity indicators included here, indicative perhaps of the necessity of directed and purposeful action on the part of government to remedy the situation beyond general attention to economic position. Alternatively, per capita social services expenditures appear to matter little to women's economic capacity. And beyond economic capacity, fiscal capacity appears to provide little explanatory value towards women's reproductive freedom and child care services. The one exception is the negative relationship between per capita federal transfers and the abortion rate. Although the relationship is unlikely one of direct causality, it does suggest that increased federal transfers will not necessarily result in increased spending to improve women's access to abortion services. Additionally, provincial fiscal capacity is related neither to the availability of child care spaces nor to the overall spending allocated to child care. There exists, then, important mediating factors that shape provincial government decisions regarding access to abortion and the provision of child care services.

A second set of indicators were evaluated to assess their relevance for variation in women's status across the provinces. Research suggests that the presence of women in political institutions can bring about more "women-friendly" policy and legislation.[33] As such, the share of women in the legislature, governing caucus, and cabinet are evaluated for their potential explanatory value. A third set of cultural and social factors were also evaluated as possible factors in shaping provincial policy responses on the issues of abortion and child care. The first taps into the religious identity and strength of religious belief across the provinces. Provincial policies, particularly in the area of access to abortion services, may reflect public opinion on the issue, at least as shaped by religious beliefs. Religiosity can also serve as a proxy for traditionalism. And finally, public opinion on specific issues can have a direct effect on government response to an issue if the issue is on the agenda and the government perceives pressure to address it.[34] Thus, levels of support for increased access to abortion and on sympathy towards feminism are evaluated as possible influences on government policy towards women. Table 16.6 provides provincial scores on religiosity and provincial attitudes on abortion and feminism. The level of variation on these scores across the provinces provides for the possibility that they might influence governmental policies of particular concern to women.

Table 16.7 reveals the correlation scores for this second set of possible explanatory factors and the various indicators of women's status in the provinces. The first conclusion to draw from this admittedly preliminary analysis is the lack of correspondence between women's political representation and policy performance. In no case does the relationship exceed a correlation score of .47. The remaining relationships—between religiosity, public opinion, and policy—suggest a more fruitful line of inquiry. Frequency of religious attendance is strongly and negatively correlated with provincial abortion rates, suggesting that public pressure

Table 16.6. Religious Identity, Religious Attendance, and Support for Feminism and Abortion across the Provinces

Province	No Religious Affiliation	Religious Attendance (once per month or more)	Very or Quite Sympathetic towards Feminism	Very or Quite Easy to Get an Abortion
NF	11.0	44.0	54.7	12.3
PEI	13.0	53.7	61.0	7.3
NS	17.6	44.0	63.8	7.10
NB	14.1	46.3	66.7	8.10
QC	6.5	33.7	72.3	18.8
ON	23.7	36.1	60.5	16.1
MB	24.9	39.6	60.9	15.5
SK	21.8	42.1	51.5	8.9
AB	31.0	33.0	50.2	11.0
BC	44.5	20.8	61.0	17.8
Average	21.2	38.8	59.9	12.9

Note: All entries are percentages.
Sources: Religion data: National Survey on Giving, Volunteering, and Participating (2000); public opinion data from Canadian Election Study (2000).

(whether explicitly applied or perceived by government) might play some part in shaping access to abortion services. Similarly, we find that the greater the share of the population that agrees that an abortion should be "very or quite easy to get" the higher the provincial abortion rate. And it appears that governments' willingness to devote funds to increasing child care access may be dependent to a degree on the existence of sympathy for feminism generally across the population. As shown in Table 16.7, opinion sympathetic to feminism is strongly and positively correlated with the number of regulated child care spaces in the province (.75) and to the level of child care spending per child in the province (.66). Thus, on policies for which provincial governments have considerable flexibility, public opinion might provide the necessary impetus for developing "women-friendly" policies such as child care and abortion.

Discussion and Future Directions

This chapter has provided a simple and preliminary assessment and exploration of the causes of variation in provincial policy of particular importance to women. The results have shown that substantial variation is found on a range of policy issues and in women's status. "Place" matters for Canadian women in the degree of economic independence and reproductive freedom that they enjoy, the level of child care services available to them, and the level of political representation afforded to them. Such variation can assist in explaining provincial variation in the nature and focus of women's activism.

Table 16.7. Relationship between Women's Status and Levels of Political Representation, Religiosity, and Public Opinion

Status Indicator	Women in Legislature	Women in Governing Caucus	Women in Cabinet	No Religious Affiliation	Religious Attendance (Once per Month or More)	Very or Quite Easy for Women to Get an Abortion	Very or Quite Sympathetic to Feminism
University Degrees	.09	-.38	.09	—	—	—	—
Participation in Labour Force	.42	-.01	.04	—	—	—	—
Share of Managerial/Professional Occupations	.12	.03	.31	—	—	—	—
Average Income	.40	-.05	.29	—	—	—	—
Share Below LICO	-.01	.39	-.10	—	—	—	—
Ratio of Female to Male Income	.28	.28	.07	—	—	—	—
Abortion Rate	.20	.05	.28	.45	-.89**	.81**	.16
Teen Pregnancy Rate	.59	.48	.22	.29	-.23	.25	-.23
Child Care Spaces	.45	.29	.20	-.29	-.21	.51	.75*
Child Care Spending	.43	.41	.16	-.29	-.34	.69*	.66*

Notes: Entries are Pearson correlation coefficients. * indicates $p < .05$; ** indicates $p < .01$.

This investigation has also suggested that provincial variation in policy and status is shaped in part by a mix of factors and that this mix depends on the policy or status indicator in question. Provincial fiscal capacity seems to provide considerable mileage in explaining women's economic independence. The less a province relies on federal transfers and the higher its GDP, the better off are women economically. Similarly, women's economic independence increases with the level of urbanization in a province. Provincial fiscal capacity is not, however, easily manipulated, and, thus, provinces have a limited ability to significantly improve women's economic independence. This is not to suggest, however, that policy changes designed to improve women's economic status would be of little consequence.

Fiscal capacity appears to play little part in shaping how closely women's income approaches that of men in the provinces. The factors that determine women's status on this score have not been examined here (for instance, the share of women working in pink collar ghettos), but governmental action on the part of the provinces, in areas such as employment equity, might also be of benefit to women.

The level of political representation in key provincial institutions does not, at first glance, appear to vary with any of the indicators of women's status that were examined. The indicator employed here, at one point in time, is likely too blunt an instrument to adequately capture the importance of this factor for the development of women-friendly policies and the improvement of women's status.

Indicators designed to capture the social context within the provinces do, on the surface, provide some potential insight into variation in policies for which the provinces have considerable flexibility. The provinces have, for example, considerable flexibility in determining access to abortion. Notwithstanding the *Canada Health Act*, there exists significant variation in women's access to, and the costs associated with, abortion services across the provinces. This variation appears to be linked with public opinion on the issue and with the strength of religious attendance within a province.

Significant policy flexibility also exists in the provision of child care services given the lack of any national standards or a federally driven program in the area. But one potential explanation for provincial variation on this issue is the degree of support that exists within the province for feminism. The development of women-friendly policies may depend on the existence of a "women-friendly" public.

The next step is to add to this understanding by developing a more sophisticated set of indicators for assessing the various factors that might be brought to bear on policy-making at the provincial level and by collecting data over a longer time period. In particular, any evaluation of policy-making must include an evaluation of the nature of partisan politics. Moreover, a more rigorous evaluation would include an evaluation of the degree to which the existence of a "women-friendly" administrative branch can assist in the development of policy and legislation. And, finally, feminist organizing in these various policy areas, including the nature of the organizing and the strategies adopted, are a further area of investigation to be tackled.[35]

Notes

1. An earlier version of this paper was delivered at the 2003 Canadian Political Science Association Meetings, Dalhousie University, Halifax, Nova Scotia, May/June 2003. Revisions were undertaken with the research assistance of Kirstin Stokes-Smith.
2. Caroline Andrew and Sandra Rogers, eds., (1997) *Women and the Canadian State* (Montreal and Kingston: McGill-Queen's University Press, 1997); Maureen Baker and David Tippin, *Poverty, Social Assistance, and the Employability of Mothers: Restructuring Welfare States* (Toronto: University of Toronto Press, 1999); Janine Brodie, ed., *Women and Canadian Public Policy* (Toronto: Harcourt Brace, 1996); and Lorraine Davis, Julie Ann McMullin, William R. Avison, and Gale L. Cassidy, *Social Policy, Gender Inequality and Poverty* (Ottawa: Status of Women Canada, 2001).
3. Manon Tremblay, "Quand les femmes se distinguent: Féminisme et représentation politique au Québec," *Canadian Journal of Political Science* 25,1 (1992): 55–68; Linda Trimble, "Feminist Politics in the Alberta Legislature: 1972–1994," in Jane Arscott and Linda Trimble, eds., *In the Presence of Women: Representation in Canadian Governments* (Toronto: Harcourt Brace, 1997); and Linda Trimble and Jane Arscott, *Still Counting: Women and Politics Across Canada* (Peterborough: Broadview Press, 2003).
4. Trimble 130.
5. Louise A. Chappell, *Gendering Government: Feminist Engagement with the State in Australia and Canada* (Vancouver: University of British Columbia Press, 2002).
6. Pauline L. Rankin and Jill Vickers, "Locating Women's Politics," in Manon Tremblay and Caroline Andrew, eds., *Women and Political Representation in Canada* (Ottawa: University of Ottawa Press, 1998) 349.
7. Richard Simeon, "Studying Public Policy," *Canadian Journal of Political Science* 9,4 (December 1976): 554.
8. The goal is not to provide some subjective ranking of women's status within each of the provinces but rather to simply assess the degree to which status varies across the provinces on several indicators.
9. This list is not meant to be exhaustive but instead is a first attempt to capture women's status and reflects in part the difficulties in collecting provincially comparable data on women.
10. Susan Prentice, ed., *Changing Child Care: Five Decades of Child Care Advocacy and Policy in Canada* (Halifax: Fernwood, 2001).
11. Even the relatively simple task of calculating the proportion of women in each provincial legislature can be rendered somewhat difficult in the absence of information on the gender of legislators. In the absence of photographs, relying on given names runs the risk of increased measurement error since gender is not always evident.
12. One could not, for example, hope to explain variation in provincial child care spaces in 2001 by looking at variation in women's legislative representation in 2005. On the contrary, data for women's representation would need to be collected for roughly the same time period.

13. Hospital boards in Brandon, Dauphin, and Thompson, Manitoba, have, for example, experienced anti-abortion activist take-overs resulting in limited or a complete lack of abortion services in those cities. See Childbirth by Choice Trust, *Abortion in Canada Today: The Situation Province-by-Province* (2002), available at <http://www.caral.ca/facts/factsheets/Abortion in Canada Today: The Situation Province by Province.php>, accessed January 9, 2002; and Heather MacIvor, *Women and Politics in Canada* (Peterborough: Broadview Press, 1996).

14. Childbirth by Choice Trust.

15. Canadian Abortion Rights League, *Protecting Abortion Rights in Canada* (Ottawa: Canadian Abortion Rights League, 2003).

16. Childbirth by Choice Trust.

17. Abortions performed in hospitals outside the province are fully reimbursed in PEI but only if a five-doctor committee deems the abortion to be "medically necessary." Moreover, given that hospitals in Atlantic Canada will only admit PEI women for abortions in cases of medical emergencies, the result is that few of them have access to fully funded hospital abortion services (Childbirth by Choice Trust).

18. Women in Saskatchewan must travel to Edmonton or Calgary to access abortion services in private clinics. A reciprocal billing arrangement between the two provinces nevertheless requires that women pay a substantial facility fee (Childbirth by Choice Trust).

19. Statistics Canada, *Aboriginal Identity Population, Percentage Distribution, for Canada, Provinces and Territories—20% Sample Data* (Census 2001), <http://www12.statcan.ca/english/census01/products/highlight/Aboriginal/Page.cfm?Lang=E&Geo=PR&View=1a&Code=0&Table=2&StartRec=1&Sort=2&B1=Distribution01&B2=Total>, accessed 1 December 2005.

20. Prentice; Linda White, "The Child Care Agenda and the Social Union," in Herman Bakvis and Grace Skogstad, eds., *Canadian Federalism: Performance, Effectiveness and Legitimacy* (Don Mills: Oxford, 2002).

21. White 105, 107.

22. In 2005, the federal government signed Agreements-in-Principle with each province on early learning and child care designed to improve the quality of and access to such services.

23. For more recent data on child care services across the provinces see Martha Friendly and Jane Beach, *Early Childhood Education and Care in Canada 2004*, 6th ed. (Toronto: Childhood Resource and Research Unit, University of Toronto, 2005).

24. For the second indicator, total allocation for regulated child care per child in the province, the median rather than the average is the indicator of choice given the skewness introduced by Quebec's spending on child care services in the province.

25. Trimble and Arscott 155.

26. Although it is clear that women's representation in English Canada is connected to the electoral strength of the NDP, given its commitment to promoting women candidates, the weakness of the party in PEI and Alberta suggests that more than simply partisan strength is at play in bringing about these results.

27. Since the data were collected, women's share of cabinet seats in Saskatchewan has risen to 20 per cent, due to one additional seat being awarded to a woman. The limited number of cabinet seats (in this case, 15 seats) can lead to significant changes in the representation share resulting from small changes in the allocation of seats themselves.

28. Simeon.

29. Louis M. Imbeau and Guy Lachapelle, "Comparative Provincial Public Policy in Canada," in Christopher Dunn, ed., *Provinces: Canadian Provincial Politics* (Peterborough: Broadview Press, 1996).

30. Imbeau and Lachapelle.

31. The term "relationship" is used very loosely in this context. With only ten data points, the ability to assess relationships between variables is limited. The data should be read as providing evidence of the possibility of existing relationships rather than as evidence of their existence *per se*.

32. Correlations of .50 or greater are considered to be indicative of a substantive relationship between the two indicators.

33. Trimble and Arscott.

34. Of course, the public may feel strongly on an issue and governments may nevertheless refuse to address the issue directly.

35. Rankin and Vickers decry the lack of comparative research directed at women's feminist organizing and provide an important framework for undertaking such an investigation.

CHAPTER 17

Comparative State and Provincial Public Policy[1]

Debora L. VanNijnatten and Gerard W. Boychuk

Deepening continental economic integration has brought the issue of Canada's ability to maintain distinctive public policies relative to the US again to the forefront of Canadian political debates. While economic integration and globalization augur in favour of policy convergence, they are also, simultaneously, argued to favour decentralization, further heightening the importance of the Canadian provinces in public policy. Concerns about Canadian distinctiveness *vis-à-vis* the US *and* issues of growing provincial policy distinctiveness are, to some degree, two sides of the same coin.

American states also are becoming increasingly important policy actors in numerous policy fields, raising the possibility of significant subnational variation *within* both countries, a pattern that has significant implications for cross-national policy comparisons. First, Canada-US policy comparisons need to consider the issue of *national clustering*. Do states and provinces really form distinct national public policy clusters such that states generally look more like other states than they do like the various Canadian provinces and vice versa, thus forming a "continental policy divide"? How distinct is Canadian public policy viewed from this perspective? Secondly, regions of Canada are economically integrating not with some amorphous mass called the United States of America but, rather, with particular American regions and states. Is public policy, in those provinces and states where significant economic integration is taking place, converging? Do these cross-border patterns increasingly undermine national policy distinctiveness?

This chapter first reviews the existing literature on Canada-US policy differences as well as the effects of economic integration on both decentralization and policy distinctiveness. The next section outlines patterns of public policy using examples from two policy areas, social and environmental policy, to demonstrate important patterns of policy similarity that become evident only through a consideration of policy at the state and provincial level. The final section illustrates how certain pairs of cross-border states and provinces, across various policy fields, may look more similar to each other than to their national counterparts and considers whether, in specific policy areas, these cross-border similarities are increasing over time.

An examination of similarities and differences among American states and Canadian provinces in social and environmental policy reveals that, while there are important differences between the two countries, these are marked by differences among states and among provinces that challenge easy acceptance of images of a continental policy divide. Looking more closely at cross-border regions, in some specific cases policy differences between neighbouring states and provinces are less marked than differences between neighbouring states or between neighbouring provinces. However, an examination of cross-border patterns over time in income maintenance and overall patterns of redistribution does not suggest that cross-border similarities are growing over time or that policies in these areas are converging in the wake of accelerated cross-border economic integration.

Economic Integration, Decentralization and National Distinctiveness: A Review of the Literature

The dominant image in both the public and academic realms regarding the border between the US and Canada is one of a "continental divide"—a sharp cultural and political disjunction running along the 49th parallel. From this perspective, the border is a barrier where two distinct sets of values and political institutions are packed up against each other. As Lipset pithily argues:

> ... the two countries differ in their basic organizing principles. Canada has been and is a more class-aware, elitist, law-abiding, statist, collectivity-oriented, and particularistic (group-oriented) society than the United States. These fundamental distinctions stem in large part from the American Revolution and the diverse social and environmental ecologies flowing from the division of British North America. The social effects of this separation were then reinforced by variations in literature, religious traditions, political and legal institutions, and socioeconomic structures. [2]

This image continues to have considerable resonance. For example, a recent book comparing Canadian and American institutions and policy starkly embodies this image in its title: *Canada and the United States: Differences that Count*.[3] This image is similarly, though more modestly, captured in the title of another such study, *Small Differences That Matter*.[4]

In the shadow of this dominant perception, a radically different imagery has been developed, albeit sporadically and at the margins of academic discussions. Here, certain observers of Canadian and American social, economic, and political development argue that there are cross-border similarities among certain provinces and states that are more notable than national differences. Fifty years ago, Wrong, for example, noted that "[t]here are groups on opposite sides of the border resembling one another more closely in cultural outlook than they resemble compatriots on the same side of the border." He argued that "[i]n the prairie provinces ... the social atmosphere is more like that of the United States than in Ontario or the Maritimes."[5]

This outlook was later developed much more fully by Garreau in his best-seller, *The Nine Nations of North America,* in which he claimed that North America is really made up of nine distinct regions, many of which extend across the international border. With the exception of Quebec, which Garreau argues is a nation unto itself, all the other regions of Canada share their identities with parts of the northern US, and the commonalities within these regions are underpinned by political, economic, and social similarities. Political boundaries and differences in political institutions hold little substantive meaning in Garreau's interpretation: "Economically and philosophically, Calgary is far more akin to Fairbanks, Salt Lake City, or Denver than it is to Ottawa. [...] Vancouver shares far more with Seattle than it does with Halifax, Nova Scotia. And the poor but proud Maritimes are in the same boat as New England."[6]

The dominance of the continental divide imagery is reflected in the literature assessing the effects of North American economic integration on domestic policy autonomy. Driven by the concern, evident across Western industrialized countries, that economic integration constrains the latitude of governments to pursue policies reflecting national aspirations, analysts have focused their examinations on the traditional nation-state, which "stands at the intersection of international and domestic pressures."[7] The key question in these studies is determining whether national governments maintain the capacity to take a distinctive national approach to public policy in the face of global economic imperatives. Although the popular wisdom that increased economic integration reduces the scope for policy distinctiveness has achieved wide currency, there is now increasing scepticism among academic policy observers that deepening economic integration is generating such policy convergence across Western industrialized countries that policies in these countries come to look more like one another over time. Similar scepticism has emerged in Canadian debates regarding the convergent effects of continental economic integration on public policy at the national-level.[8] On both sides of this debate, however, the main focus remains overwhelmingly on national-level comparisons.

While national-level studies are important in terms of furthering our understanding of the relationship between economic integration and domestic policy autonomy, it is also critical that analysts assess the implications of the decentralizing tendencies associated with globalization. As a number of analysts have observed, one of the effects of globalization is to make the nation-state too small for the big problems of life and too big for the small problems of life. Certainly, national governments have reacted to the freer movement of factor inputs, goods, and services by transferring important powers to supranational institutions such as the World Trade Organization (WTO). Yet, as economic power shifts upward, subnational governments and regions within countries may find it advantageous in terms of their distinctive economic requirements to "leapfrog their national governments and tie themselves to overarching structures."[9] In the likely situation that some subnational governments are more economically integrated into international markets than others, these governments may demand more policy-making room to respond to integrating effects and trends. This line of reasoning implies that the policy independence of subnational units such as the Canadian provinces and American states will continue to grow as globalization and economic integration proceeds.

Thus, if there was something to Garreau's hypothesis in the late 1970s, these patterns might be expected to be *even* more evident in the contemporary context where economic integration at the subnational level is accelerating. Williams has argued that "[j]ust as the evolution of modern Canada has been marked by the development of a dense system of interregional relations, so too have Canada's regions developed in relation to specific, often geographically adjacent, local areas in the United States." He also notes that "... each of Canada's five geographic regions has developed its own intensive, deeply pervasive, north-south trading relationship with its closest American regional neighbor or neighbors."[10] More recently, Courchene and Telmer have argued that a significant economic shift has already taken place such that Ontario is now best thought of as a North American region rather than the Canadian heartland as it has more traditionally been cast. Closely paralleling Garreau, they argue:

> It is not just that nearly all Canada's provinces are more integrated (in terms of the exports) internationally than east-west, but also that Canada's regions, which in some cases would incorporate more than one province, are economically/industrially quite distinct from one another ... this means that it is time to view Canada as a series of north-south, cross-border economies with quite distinct industrial structures. British Columbia is oriented toward the Pacific Rim and the U.S. Northwest; the energy-based Alberta economy competes with oil and gas producing regions of the Texas Gulf; the breadbaskets of Saskatchewan and Manitoba keep a competitive watch on the U.S. midwest; the Great Lakes economies of Ontario and Quebec are integrated with each other and with their counterparts south of the border; and the fortunes of Atlantic Canada will increasingly be linked to the Atlantic Rim and the Boston/New York axis.[11]

If economic integration is expected to contribute to policy convergence more generally, then this should generate expectations for policy convergence at the cross-border subnational level.

In fact, there are several reasons to suspect that cross-border policy convergence resulting from economic integration would emerge earlier and more forcefully at the provincial rather than the federal level. Provinces already control some of the most important policy levers for adjusting to increasing economic integration and competitive pressures. Moreover, decentralization of the Canadian federation, driven in part by the politics of Quebec nationalism as well as the dynamics of economic integration and globalization described above, have reinforced provincial policy dominance. Secondly, provinces have distinct economic structures and trading patterns requiring unique policy adjustment. Provincial governments are arguably more sensitive than the federal government to the pressures generated by cross-border economic integration and competition. Thus, according to Courchene, provinces will increasingly tailor their public policies to the patterns prevailing in the American states with which they are integrating and/or competing.[12] Distinct provincial responses to cross-border patterns of economic integration and competition generates expectations not only of cross-border policy similarities but also of increasing cross-provincial policy diversity.

Central in this image of cross-border economic integration is the recognition mentioned at the beginning of the chapter: regions of Canada are economically integrating not with some amorphous mass called the United States of America but, rather, with particular American regions and states. Thus, it is crucial to recognize the significance of the American states in various fields of public policy and the degree to which this significance has been increasing over time.[13] The states have become increasingly important actors in terms of public policy provision. Gray points out that the "devolution revolution" initiated by Reagan and, in some respects, continued under Clinton has resulted in the transfer of more policy authority from the federal government to the states, thereby "intensifying" state responsibility in a variety of policy areas.[14] Moreover, the 1990s were good years for state coffers, and state governments had the resources to improve their policy capacity, take on new responsibilities, and, in some cases, innovate.

Thus, analyses must take into account the variation among provinces as well as among states in assessing patterns of national policy distinctiveness. Examining cross-border policy similarity and difference at the subnational level may well be a better test of the linkage between economic integration and policy convergence than national-level comparisons. Cross-provincial and cross-state policy variation creates the need to consider the issue of national clustering, and, in some crucial aspects of policy, the findings challenge existing images of national distinctiveness. Moreover, the possibility of cross-border policy convergence resulting from deepening economic integration obliges the analyst to undertake policy comparisons of cross-border pairs of American states and Canadian provinces.

Patterns of State and Provincial Public Policy: Examples from Two Policy Areas

Two crucial policy fields for examining national policy distinctiveness as well as the convergent effects of cross-border economic integration are social and environmental policy. Both policy areas, especially the former, are often considered to be hallmarks of Canadian policy distinctiveness. In terms of the convergent effects of economic integration, both ought to be particularly sensitive indicators of Canada-US policy convergence since they are seen to be key elements in determining competitive advantage. Social policy is tightly intertwined with labour market flexibility and encompasses several of the areas identified by Courchene and Telmer as being key to divergent responses to economic integration.[15] Environmental policy is an important determinant in shaping production processes, may impose significant additional costs on business, and, thus, may significantly alter the competitive environment. It is for these reasons that "[c]oncern about harmonization in each of these areas was central to the debate" over the FTA in 1988 and NAFTA in the early 1990s.[16]

National Clustering: A Discussion

Existing studies often use the border as an arbitrary line of demarcation for aggregating subnational units. Regardless of whether American states tend to more closely resemble other states than they resemble Canadian provinces and vice versa, subnational units on each side of the border are grouped together. The units making up these groups are aggregated and averaged; alternatively, analysis focuses on median states and provinces. In either case, the aim is to derive some overall national-level characterizations that are then compared and contrasted. However, as many students will be aware from their classes on statistics, the validity (or statistical significance) of the conclusion that there are significant differences between the two groups depends not only on the magnitude of difference *between* the two averages but also the magnitude of this difference relative to the range of variation *within* each of the groups being compared. If the variation within each group is relatively large and the differences between the two groups is relatively slight, one cannot confidently draw conclusions about the existence of differences between them. When the difference between the averages is relatively large and the variation within each group is relatively slight, conclusions about differences can be drawn with more confidence.

The same logic applies to comparisons of states and provinces. As we have argued in our earlier work,[17] there is the potential for policy variation among states and provinces (e.g., policy areas in which states and provinces are important actors), and such variation must be considered in drawing conclusions about differences between states and provinces as groups. Where variation within each of the two groups is relatively slight and the difference in the averages of the two groups is relatively large, *national clustering*—where subjurisdictions naturally fall into two clusters depending on whether they are American states or Canadian provinces—can be said to exist. Only once this pattern is demonstrated can one confidently make national-level generalizations and move to explaining such differences on the basis of national-level explanatory factors (e.g., *national* differences in political culture, political institutions, or patterns of political competition). The following section examines four policy areas identifying where national clustering exists and where it might be presumed to exist but does not. In all four areas, the dominant imagery of national clustering across the policy field is challenged.

Social assistance[18]

Social assistance—cash and in-kind (non-cash) benefits provided to those deemed to be without the means for an adequate level of subsistence—has been a point of constant comparison between the US and Canada. These comparisons have generally tended to point to Canada's generosity in stark relief with the meager levels of assistance provided in the US.[19] Not only is Canada's social safety net widely accepted to be more generous than that in the US, Canadians are also generally thought to be more favourable toward social welfare *per se* than their American counterparts. However, both states and provinces exercise important responsibilities in the provision of social assistance, and an examination of social assistance provision in the states and provinces reveals that rather than one country being consistently more generous than the other, an alternative characterization emphasizes the continuing lack of strong national clustering. Thus, there is need for considerable caution in overemphasizing national-level differences between social assistance provision in the two countries.

There are a range of aspects in which social assistance provision in the American states and Canadian provinces demonstrate a strong measure of national clustering. It is most apparent in terms of the reliance in the US on in-kind (such as food stamps) versus cash benefits.[20] These important in-kind benefits have no analogue in the Canadian provinces and clearly represent a nationally distinct approach to the provision of social assistance. National clustering is also strong in the case of assistance provided to single employables.[21] Certainly, benefits are considerably lower for this group of recipients across virtually all American states in comparison with the Canadian provinces.

In many respects, the type of national clustering which one might expect considering widespread generalizations about social assistance provision in the US and Canada does not emerge. Even excluding Medicaid expenditures, there is no national clustering between the American states and Canadian provinces in terms of per capita expenditures on social assistance programs. Expenditures are as high or higher in generous American states as is the case for generous Canadian provinces, and expenditures in the least generous Canadian provinces are comparable in low (though not the lowest) spending American states. Nor is there clear national clustering in the proportion of the population receiving benefits. The outcome of benefit comparisons depends largely on what benefits are counted and what categories of recipient are being compared. However, benefits both for single parent families and disabled persons—which constitute important segments of the recipient population in both countries—are not clearly more generous in the Canadian provinces than in the American states. Rather, such conclusions vary depending on the states and provinces being compared. National clustering in social assistance provision is, thus, not clear-cut.

Post-secondary education[22]

Post-secondary education is another area in which broad perceptions of national-level differences between Canada and the US exist. Again, comparisons are complicated by the role of the states and provinces in this policy field. In terms of direct central government involvement in higher education, the situation in both countries is similar, with central government involvement in the field limited to the direct provision of financial support both for research and financial aid for students. In both countries, the long-term trend appears to be one of a diminishing role for the central government. In the US, "[t]he most significant change during the 1980s in the relation of government to higher education was the resurgence of the states,"[23] and this trend does not appear to have been reversed.

There are some obvious distinctions between post-secondary education provision in Canada and the US. However, where significant differences do emerge, they are often not what one might expect. The clearest difference between the two countries is found in greater rates of participation and, by implication, higher levels of accessibility to university-level education in the US.

Many of the distinctions drawn between the two countries regarding higher education are not nearly as stark as the conventional wisdom suggests when viewed from the vantage point of American states and Canadian provinces. Although private institutions do exist in the US, they do not exist to any significant degree in some states, do not predominate in most states, and, in many cases, do not rival the public system of higher education. The situation is further confused by the fact that the mixed public/private systems in several states are as heavily reliant upon public funding as many Canadian provinces. While the public component of higher education provision is more significant both in terms of funding and enrolment in many states than in any Canadian provinces, public university enrolment in most Canadian provinces is comparable to public enrolment in low public enrolment states.[24]

Environmental policy in the American states and Canadian provinces[25]

Canadian provincial governments are constitutionally more powerful and more independent than are American state governments in most areas of environmental policy-making and standard-setting. Yet, despite the more developed framework for national environmental protection in the US, states are important actors in terms of how policy is provided *on the ground*, and there are considerable variations across states in almost all areas of environmental protection.[26] In a review of state environmental activities over the period 1986-98, the Environmental Council of the States (ECOS) declared the states to be "the primary environmental protection agencies across the nation."[27] Comparing states and provinces on different aspects of environmental policy reveals that, while there is a tendency toward different national policy styles, national clustering in pollution control and abatement expenditures is weak, and policy similarities between neighbouring Canadian provinces and American states are noteworthy.

States and provinces showed relatively similar levels of commitment to environmental issues in the early to mid 1990s, although provincial expenditures have declined relative to state expenditures over the past few years as a result of aggressive budget-cutting.[28] This more recent divergence is likely to lessen, however, as states initiate expected budget cuts in 2003. In addition, the provinces are likely to choose a policy approach calling for a mixture of public and private expenditure—that is, direct public expenditure with some regulatory requirements forcing private investment in pollution abatement and control—with the balance tilting toward public expenditure. The states, for their part, are more prone than provinces to employ a regulatory-driven system in which private investment constitutes the majority of expenditures on pollution abatement and control.[29]

In terms of actual policy outputs, comparisons in the areas of air quality and solid waste reduction, for example, reveal interesting patterns. With regard to air quality policy, there is national clustering in terms of national ambient air quality and emission standards as well as vehicle emission programs, with those in the American states tending to be more stringent than those in the Canadian provinces. Moreover, there exists a wider range of national-level air quality programs in the US applicable to industrial point sources in all states. However, a closer look also reveals a distinctly regional pattern across states, with the northeastern states and California pushing for and, in some cases, implementing more stringent standards than those mandated by the national government.[30] There also are significant variations across provinces; central Canadian provinces appear to resemble more their Great Lakes neighbours, while BC has been an outlier among the provinces as it more resembles California and the northeastern states.

Certainly, in the area of solid waste management, it would be difficult to argue that either the states or provinces are more stringent in their approach to waste reduction. There is some national clustering in terms of the policy instruments chosen to manage waste; for example, the provinces are more apt to employ deposits, environmental taxes/fees, and landfill bans to achieve their objectives than the states. In addition, almost all provinces have chosen to impose some type of restriction on product packaging, while some states have no restrictions whatsoever. Most provinces and most states, however, have some form of mandatory recycling program, and there is a distinct lack of national clustering among provinces and states in terms of actual recycling recovery rates. At the same time, there is also some evidence of regional, cross-border clustering; for example, Ontario, Quebec, Nova Scotia, and PEI possess policies similar to those in Vermont, Maine, New Jersey, and New York.

Health care in the American states and Canadian provinces[31]

In cross-national public policy comparisons between Canada and the US, "[h]ealth care traditionally has provided the most dramatic contrast ..."[32] Even in health care, the policy area generally thought to demonstrate the greatest differences between the two countries, an examination of policy at the state and provincial level raises some challenges to broad national characterizations.

Comparisons of health care policy in the two countries are complicated by the role of the states and provinces within each country. As Boase notes: "Any discussion of reform of the health care system in Canada is complicated by the shared federal-provincial nature of social policy ... the provinces have considerable freedom in the development of social policy, and the decentralized nature of Canadian federalism ensures that, within the broad federal standards, ten discrete provincial health care systems have evolved."[33] Similar complexity marks the American side of such comparisons: "Rarely heard in the debate over health care reform is a discussion of health care politics at the state level. This lack of analysis is surprising. Not only do state treasuries fund a large share of the nation's health care bills, but also state officials play a key policy role."[34] Furthermore, "[s]tate governments are increasingly taking responsibility for health and welfare programs."[35]

There are, to be sure, important differences in health care provision in Canada and the US; however, in many respects, these differences are less significant than is often thought to be the case. The most important national-level difference between the two systems of health care provision lie in the existence of large private insurance markets for hospital and physician care in the US. However, other oft-cited differences overstate the distinctions. Most notably, Canada does *not* have a universal system of health care outside of universal coverage for hospital and physician care (pharmaceuticals, for example), the American system has some elements of universality (in Medicare), and public health care expenditures per capita are actually greater, on average, in the US than in Canada.

At the same time, differences in health care provision among Canadian provinces and among American states are more significant than is generally thought to be the case. Though certainly less true for those aspects of the Canadian health care system falling under the rubric of federal health grants, provinces differ considerably in other aspects of their public provision of health care, especially pharmacare and long-term/home care. The differences among American states appear even more marked. Many of these differences soften the distinctions conventionally drawn between the two national health care systems.

The result of these two patterns is that in some limited—albeit important— aspects of health care provision, certain states are more similar to Canadian provinces than they are to some of their other national counterparts. In terms of their overall public expenditures, provisions for drug insurance coverage, and patterns of hospital control (private for-profit *versus* not-for-profit), provinces tend to differ among themselves considerably less than American states. However, as a result of the striking differences among American states on these indicators of health care provision, some states look more like Canadian provinces than like other states.

Summary

Those who engage in Canada-US comparative public policy study might well ask: can one say nothing on the topic, then, without conducting an exhaustive and arduous examination of specific policy provisions and activities in all 50 states and 10 provinces? Our answer is that while one can compare federal frameworks or national legislation and program provisions, one cannot generalize about the "generosity" or the "stringency" or the "accessibility" of programs that are created, delivered, and maintained by two levels of government without demonstrating national clustering. Weighing the significance of policy differences *within* each group relative to the differences *between* the two groups is, after all, an empirical question.

Cross-Border Regions

The existence or lack of national clustering among states and provinces as groups, however, does not really tell us much about the degree to which cross-border economic integration or cultural interpenetration leads to policy convergence between particular provinces and states. Rather, an examination of these dynamics requires examining specific matching pairs of states and provinces or regional groups of states and provinces.

An important issue here is identifying which pairs or subgroups of states and provinces warrant examination to determine if there is policy convergence between them. To some large degree, this depends on the suspected causes of convergence. If it is cultural interpenetration resulting simply from geographical proximity, considering neighbouring states and provinces may be most appropriate. If economic integration is the suspected cause of policy convergence, examination of provinces paired with those states with which they have the strongest economic ties (e.g., the highest levels of trade) may be best. If policy adjustment in reaction to direct competition is suspected, policy comparisons between provinces and their top competitor states might be considered.[36]

The examples outlined below are based on geographical contiguity and examine, in the first instance, whether cross-border neighbouring pairs of states and provinces look more similar to each other than they do to their domestic counterparts. Secondly, the section provides an example of a consideration of whether public policies in cross-border pairs of provinces and states are converging over time.

Comparing neighbouring provinces, states, and state-province pairs

Cross-border economic integration, cultural interpenetration, and the geographical similarity of policy problems raise the following question: are the differences one is likely to encounter in crossing the national border between geographically contiguous states and provinces greater than the differences one is likely to encounter in crossing between border states or between border provinces? In earlier work addressing this question,[37] we considered average differences between pairings of contiguous states, contiguous provinces, and contiguous state-province pairs across nine policy indicators in three policy areas (income maintenance, environmental protection, and post-secondary education).[38]

Table 17.1. Ranking of Similarity Among Contiguous Pairs

Ranking	Overall (Ordinal)	Overall (Numeric)	Income Maintenance	Environmental Protection	PSE Provision
1.	BC-WA	BC-WA	SK-MB	BC-WA	AB-SK
2.	SK-MB	ON-MI	MB-MN	ON-QC	SK-MB
3.	MB-MN	SK-MB	ID-MT	ON-MI	MB-ON
4.	ID-MT	MB-MN	BC-WA	QC-ME	BC-AB
5.	ON-MI	ON-QC	ON-NY	WA-ID	NH-ME
6.	WA-ID	WA-ID	QB-VT	MB-MN	SK-MT
7.	AB-SK	NB-ME	MB-ND	ON-MN	ID-MT
8.	ON-QC	AB-SK	ON-MI	NB-ME	AB-MT
9.	AB-MT/ SK-MT/ ON-NY	ID-MT	ON-MI	AB-MT	AB-MT
10.	MB-ON	AB-MT	ON-MI	AB-SK	AB-MT

In our results (Table 17.1), border states, as a group, tended to look less like the remaining American states than they resemble the Canadian provinces. Across our range of indicators, even neighbouring provinces were not more similar to each other than they were to neighbouring states. Even more interesting, border states were likely to be *less* similar to neighbouring border states than to neighbouring Canadian provinces. Thus, in the Canadian provinces and border states, crossing provincial and state boundaries may involve encountering greater policy differences than crossing the national border between Canada and the US.

In our results, three contiguous cross-border pairs[39] stood out in terms of their policy similarity: BC-Washington, Manitoba-Minnesota, and Ontario-Michigan. These three pairs of states and provinces are notable because the similarities between them are greater on average than similarities between neighbouring provinces.

BRITISH COLUMBIA AND WASHINGTON

The BC-Washington pairing topped our overall rankings in terms of similarity. No other pair of contiguous jurisdictions—whether contiguous states or contiguous provinces—looked more similar across our range of indicators. With regard to income maintenance, aggregate indicators suggested that BC and Washington are indeed very similar and are more similar to each other than virtually all other provincial and state pairings. In this area, the similarity between BC and Washington is striking in terms of benefit levels, recipiency rates, and unemployment insurance provision, with only total public expenditures constituting a slight exception.

While the absolute level of similarity is less marked in the case of environmental protection, BC and Washington are more similar in these regards than any other pairing of contiguous border states or provinces. However, there is more variability between indicators of environmental protection than was the case for income maintenance. For example, while there are very wide differences between BC and Washington in terms of public pollution abatement control expenditures, they are quite similar in terms of private pollution abatement control expenditures.

Even in post-secondary education—where BC and Washington rank tenth in terms of similarity—they are very similar, and their apparently unremarkable ranking is primarily a result of the fact that a number of provincial pairs are so alike. A pattern of variability across indicators similar to that found in environmental protection exists in terms of post-secondary education. BC and Washington are identical in terms of total public expenditure on post-secondary education, while they differ quite markedly in terms of average university tuition and enrolment.

MANITOBA AND MINNESOTA

According to both our rankings, Manitoba and Minnesota are only slightly less similar than the two most similar contiguous provinces (Saskatchewan and Manitoba) as well as being only slightly less similar than BC and Washington, the most similar cross-border pair. The income maintenance systems in Manitoba and Minnesota are more similar than income maintenance systems in any other contiguous states or provinces with the exception of Manitoba and Saskatchewan. The largest difference between them in these regards is in unemployment insurance.

As was the case with BC-Washington, the unremarkable ranking of Manitoba and Minnesota in post-secondary education provision obscures a significant level of similarity. Almost all of the differences here lie in the discrepancy between public institution tuition levels, with Minnesota being above the US average and Manitoba being below the Canadian average. However, this difference aside, they are quite similar in terms of post-secondary education expenditures and enrolment levels.

While the absolute levels of similarity between Manitoba and Minnesota in the area of environmental protection are less striking than in the two areas above, they are considerably more similar to each other than most pairs of contiguous provinces, Ontario and Quebec being the only exception. For example, both public and private pollution abatement control expenditures look quite similar in these two jurisdictions.

ONTARIO AND MICHIGAN

The Ontario/Michigan pair is also an interesting case. The income maintenance systems of these two jurisdictions are very similar, with the main outstanding difference being rooted in Michigan's lower level of per capita expenditure on social assistance. In contrast, they are quite similar in terms of benefit levels and recipiency rates while being virtually identical in terms of overall unemployment insurance generosity.[40]

In terms of environmental protection, Ontario and Michigan do differ in their level of public pollution abatement and control expenditures, although other indicators show similarity between the two jurisdictions.

Again, while the ranking of Ontario and Michigan in post-secondary education is quite low, the overall level of similarity between them is only marginally lower than that for environmental protection (where Ontario and Michigan ranked third in terms of similarity.) Again, the low ranking in post-secondary education is due to the marked similarity among contiguous province pairs. However, Ontario and Michigan are virtually identical in terms of full-time public enrolment. Differences are more marked for public post-secondary education expenditures, but much of the difference between the two jurisdictions lies in the considerably higher public institution tuition in Michigan. Even despite such differences, Ontario and Michigan appear more similar overall in post-secondary education than do certain contiguous provinces such as Ontario and Quebec.

Cross-border comparisons over time

While suggestive, static comparisons of similarities and differences in policies between cross-border neighbouring states and provinces at a given point in time do not adequately address the issue of policy convergence over time resulting from increasing economic integration between American states and Canadian provinces. Two studies which undertake such comparisons with regard to social policy and income redistribution focus on discrete social programs and, alternatively, the overall redistributive effect of taxation and social policies.[41]

In considering the former, Boychuk and Banting examine similarities and differences in income maintenance policy in selected cross-border regions over the period from 1980 to 2000. Their study examines both federal and provincial programs of income maintenance policy (including unemployment insurance, social assistance, and workers' compensation), comparing not only national systems but also specifically examining BC and Washington as well as Ontario and five Great Lakes states (Illinois, Michigan, New York, Ohio, Pennsylvania and Wisconsin).[42]

The study concludes that focusing on variation within Canada and the US as well as between them blurs the image of welfare state distinctiveness. Nevertheless, the findings were surprising. Most commentary has emphasized the scope for growing interprovincial diversity and cross-border convergence in programs managed by provincial governments, especially in the wake of greater decentralization in both Canada and the US. However, the propositions advanced by scholars like Courchene about growing diversity in provincial programming and a greater provincial focus on cross-border economies does not show up in the evidence on provincial programs. Interestingly, the strongest patterns of convergence are to be found in programs controlled by the federal government in Canada, unemployment insurance and family benefits. In contrast, provincial programs such as social assistance and workers' compensation show less consistent evidence of cross-border convergence.

Concluding Observations

We have argued here that two important patterns in North America—regional cross-border economic integration and decentralization—require that policy comparisons focus on the Canadian provinces and relevant American states rather than simply on national-level comparisons. Using selected subnational comparisons of social and environmental policy, we have shown that there are differences among provinces and among states that call into question the methodological appropriateness of generalizing about national policy attributes. This conclusion is supported by a closer look at neighbouring states and provinces where, in some cases, social and environmental policy differences are less marked than differences between neighbouring states or neighbouring provinces.

Whether cross-border examinations of policy at the provincial and state level reveal convergence or divergence, they constitute a more appropriate test of the impacts of increasing cross-border economic integration on policy distinctiveness than comparisons of national statistical aggregations or a more singular focus on federal-level policy. Such comparisons are suggestive of interesting patterns of similarity and difference that are likely to enrich our understanding both of the operation of federalism in Canada as well as the impacts of deepening economic integration on policy distinctiveness.

Notes

1. The authors would like to thank the Social Science and Humanities Research Council of Canada for its financial support of the research on which this chapter is based.
2. Seymour M. Lipset, *Continental Divide: The Values and Institutions of the United States and Canada* (New York: Routledge, 1990) 8.
3. David M. Thomas, *Canada and the United States: Differences that Count* (Peterborough: Broadview Press, 2000).
4. David Card and Richard Freeman, *Small Differences that Matter: Labor Markets and Income Maintenance in Canada and the United States* (Chicago, IL: University of Chicago Press, 1993).
5. Dennis H. Wrong, *American and Canadian Viewpoints* (Washington, DC: American Council on Education, 1955) 4, 25.
6. Joel Garreau, *The Nine Nations of North America* (Boston, MA: Houghton Mifflin, 1981) 6.
7. Keith Banting, "What's a Country For? The Social Contract in the Global Era," *SPS Policy Insights* (2001), available at <http://policy.queensu.ca/spspi/docs/kb0401.shtml>.
8. See Gerard Boychuk and Keith G. Banting, "Converging and Diverging Paradoxes: National and Sub-National Variation in Income Maintenance Programs in Canada and the United States," in Richard G. Harris, ed., *North American Linkages: Opportunities and Challenges for Canada* (Calgary: University of Calgary Press, 2003) 533-72; George Hoberg, Keith Banting, and Richard Simeon, "North American Integration and the Scope for Domestic Choice: Canada and Policy Sovereignty in a Globalized World," paper presented at the Annual Meeting of the Canadian Political Science Association, June 1999; William Watson, *Globalization and the Meaning of Canadian Life* (Toronto: University of Toronto Press, 1998).
9. Thomas J. Courchene and Colin R. Telmer, *From Heartland to North American Region State: The Social, Fiscal and Federal Evolution of Ontario* (Toronto: University of Toronto Centre for Public Management, 1998).
10. Glen Williams, "Regions within Region: Continentalism Ascendent," in Michael S. Whittington and Glen Williams, eds., *Canadian Politics in the 1990s* (Toronto: Nelson, 1995) 19-20.
11. Courchene and Telmer 289. There is a considerable literature on the effects of the Canada-US border on trade flows. See John McCallum, "National Borders Matter: Canada-US Regional Trade Patterns," *American Economic Review* 85,3 (June 1995): 615-623; John F. Helliwell, "Do National Boundaries Matter for Quebec's Trade?" *Canadian Journal of Economics* 29,3 (August 1996): 507-22; John F. Helliwell, *How Much Do National Borders Matter?* (Washington, DC: Brookings Institution Press, 1998); and Michael A. Anderson and Stephen L.S. Smit, "Do National Borders Really Matter? Canada-US Regional Trade Reconsidered," *Review of International Economics* 7,2 (May 1999). However, there are two important points in this regard.

While trade between Canadian provinces may be considerably higher than it would be in the absence of the border, the critical fact is the overall north-south orientation in which trade flows, particularly notable in cases such as Ontario. Secondly, the tendency of provinces to "overtrade" with each other is dropping (Courchene and Telmer 280).

12. Courchene and Telmer 289-91.

13. It is certainly the case that Canadian provinces are more powerful domestic political and economic actors than most American states. As Rocher points out, the Ontario budget is one-third the size of the Canadian federal government's budget, and total expenditures by provincial administrations are slightly more than Ottawa's; see François Rocher, "Dividing the Spoils: American and Canadian Federalism," in David M. Thomas, ed., *Canada and the United States: Differences that Count* (Peterborough: Broadview Press, 2000). Also, the American federal system has greater tendencies toward centralization, with the American Senate playing an important role in regional representation.

14. Virginia Gray, "The Socioeconomic and Political Context of States," in Virginia Gray, Russell L. Hanson, and Herbert Jacob, eds., *Politics in the American States: A Comparative Analysis*, 7th ed. (Washington, DC: CQ Press, 1999).

15. Courchene and Telmer 291.

16. George Hoberg, Keith Banting, and Richard Simeon, "The Scope for Domestic Choice: Policy Autonomy in a Globalizing World," in George Hoberg, ed., *Capacity for Choice: Canada in a New North America* (Toronto: University of Toronto Press, 1999) 2.

17. Debora VanNijnatten and Gerard Boychuk, "Comparative Public Policy and National Clustering: Environmental Protection, Post-Secondary Education, and Social Assistance in the American States and Canadian Provinces," paper presented to the Annual Meeting of the Canadian Political Science Association, Ottawa, May 1998.

18. The following discussion draws from Gerard Boychuk, "Resemblance and Relief: National Clustering and Social Assistance Provision in the United States and Canadian Provinces," *American Review of Canadian Studies* 29,2 (Summer 1999): 259-85.

19. See, for example, Keith Banting, "The Social Policy Divide: The Welfare State in Canada and the United States," in Keith Banting, George Hoberg, and Richard Simeon, eds., *Degrees of Freedom: Canada and the United States in a Changing World* (Montreal and Kingston: McGill-Queen's University Press, 1997); Rebecca M. Blank and Maria J. Hanratty, "Responding to Need: A Comparison of Social Safety Nets in Canada and the United States," in Card and Freeman 191-231; Gerard Boychuk, "Are Canadian and US Social Assistance Policies Converging?" *Canadian-American Public Policy* 30 (July 1997): 1-55; and John Myles, *When Markets Fail: Social Welfare in Canada and the United States* (New York: United Nations Research Institute for Social Development, 1995).

20. In all states, Medicaid is a crucial component of the social assistance benefit package. Similarly, although Food Stamps benefits vary widely in their significance relative to other cash benefits, in all states they provide an important part of the social assistance package. While average benefits vary from state to state as do recipiency rates, housing benefits are also significant.

21. Assistance for individuals without dependents has not been eligible for federal cost-sharing in the US and has been completely the prerogative of the states. In Canada,

such assistance was federally cost-shared and has been available in every province, although, historically, assistance has been denied to this category of recipients (or various subgroupings) in different provinces at various times.

22. The following discussion draws from Gerard Boychuk, "Differences of Degrees: Higher Education in Canadian Provinces and American States," *Canadian Public Administration* 43,4 (Fall 2000): 453-72.

23. Patrick M. Callan, "Government and Higher Education," in Arthur M. Levine, ed., *Higher Learning in America, 1980-2000* (Baltimore, MD: The Johns Hopkins University Press, 1993).

24. Comparisons of tuition are extremely complex. For an overview, see Boychuk, "Differences of Degrees."

25. The following discussion draws from VanNijnatten and Boychuk, "Comparative Public Policy and National Clustering"; Debora L. VanNijnatten, "Environmental Protection in Canadian Provinces and American States: Variations and Interactions at the Subnational Level," paper presented to the Annual Meeting of the Canadian Political Science Association, Quebec City, May 2001; Debora VanNijnatten, "The Bumpy Journey Ahead: Provincial Policy Differences and National Environmental Standards," in Debora L. VanNijnatten and Robert Boardman, eds., *Canadian Environmental Policy: Context and Cases* (Don Mills: Oxford University Press, 2002).

26. These variations stem from a number of factors. First, there are significant variations in the degree to which states have assumed implementation and enforcement of federal standards from the EPA and in the extent to which they have or can attain these national standards, a matter of capacity. See D. Hitchcock Jessop, *Guide to State Environmental Management*, 3rd ed. (Washington, DC: Bureau of National Affairs, 1994); Barry G. Rabe, "Power to the States: The Promise and Pitfalls of Decentralization," in Norman J. Vig and Michael E. Kraft., eds., *Environmental Policy in the 1990s: Reform or Reaction?*, 3rd ed. (Washington, DC: Congressional Quarterly Press, 1997); and Evan J. Ringquist, *Environmental Protection at the State Level: Policies and Progress in Controlling Pollution* (Armonk, NY: ME Sharpe, 1993). Second, some states have chosen to exceed existing federal standards for different air and water pollutants or to regulate in areas where the federal level has been inactive, such as toxic air emissions and non-point source water pollution. Third, in areas such as solid waste management, environmental assessment, parks and water use/ rights—the regulatory roles played by the Canadian provinces and American states are quite similar.

27. R.S. Brown, "The States Protect the Environment," *ECOStates* (Summer 1999), available at <http:www.sso.org/ecos/publications/statesarticle.htm>.

28. VanNijnatten and Boychuk, "Comparative Public Policy and National Clustering"; VanNijnatten, "The Bumpy Road Ahead."

29. VanNijnatten and Boychuk, "Comparative Public Policy and National Clustering."

30. VanNijnatten, "Environmental Protection in Canadian Provinces and American States."

31. The following discussion draws from Gerard Boychuk, "Public Health Care Provision in the American States and Canadian Provinces," *Canadian Public Administration* 45,2 (Summer 2002): 217-38.

32. Banting, "The Social Policy Divide" 285.

33. Joan Price Boase, "Health Care Reform or Health Care Rationing? A Comparative Study," *Canadian-American Public Policy* 26 (May 1996).

34. Michael S. Sparer, "The Unknown States," in James A. Morone and Gary S. Belkin, eds., *The Politics of Health Care Reform: Lessons from the Past, Prospects for the Future* (Durham and London: Duke University Press, 1994) 430.

35. Mark Rom, "Transforming State Health and Welfare Programs," in Gray, Hanson, and Jacob, eds., 349-92.

36. We are currently undertaking further work which adopts this latter approach. See Debora L. VanNijnatten and Gerard W. Boychuk, "Economic Integration and Cross-Border Policy Convergence: Social and Environmental Policy in Canadian Provinces and American States," *Journal of Borderland Studies* 19,1 (Spring 2004): 37-58; and Gerard W. Boychuk and Debora L. VanNijnatten, "Economic Integration and Cross-Border Policy Convergence," *Horizons* 7,1 (June 2004): 55-60.

37. See Gerard Boychuk and Debora VanNijnatten, "Continental Divide vs. Regional Divides: Evidence from a Review of Public Policy in the American States and Canadian Provinces," paper presented to the American Studies Association, Montreal, October 1999; and Gerard Boychuk and Debora VanNijnatten, "The Canadian 'West' as a Public Policy Space? Public Policies in Western Canadian Provinces from a National and Cross-National Perspective," *BC Studies* 133 (Spring 2002): 5-30.

Noting all the caveats that these generalizations do not hold for all specific indicators, that these comparisons would be different if we had chosen different indicators or measured them at different points in time, and that aggregate-level quantitative data may obscure important qualitative similarities and differences, the data presented here suggest the plausibility of the argument that cross-border differences may be less significant than differences among states and among provinces. These quantitative data suggest that further qualitative investigation is required.

38. *Income maintenance*: total expenditures by states and provinces on means-tested social assistance, benefits (social assistance income from all programs for a single parent with two children adjusted to the cost of living), social assistance beneficiaries (Aid to Families with Dependent Children, Supplemental Security Income, State General Assistance, and Food Stamps in the US; social assistance in Canada—as percentage of population), unemployment insurance beneficiaries as percentage of all unemployed persons.

Post-secondary education: total expenditures on post-secondary education by federal, state, provincial, and local governments for full-time enrolment, and the public tuition levels in four-year public institutions in the US and in selected Canadian universities.

Environmental protection: both public and private pollution and abatement (PAC) control expenditures.

39. The pairs were ranked both according to their overall numeric scores and according to their ordinal ranking across the three sets of indicators.

40. While these two jurisdictions are similar in terms of their unemployment insurance coverage index, this index masks differences between them in terms of beneficiaries as a proportion of the total unemployment ratios (with Ontario being somewhat lower) and replacement rates (with Ontario being somewhat higher).

41. See Boychuk and Banting, "Converging and Diverging Paradoxes"; and Gerard W. Boychuk, "Redistribution, Social Protection and North American Linkages: Social Policy Distinctiveness Under Increased Labour Mobility," in Richard G. Harris and Thomas Lemieux, eds., *Social and Labour Market Aspects of North American Linkages* (Calgary: University of Calgary Press, 2005).

42. Boychuk and Banting, "Converging and Diverging Paradoxes."

CHAPTER 18

Provincial Policies Concerning Collective Bargaining

GENE SWIMMER AND TIM BARTKIW

Unlike the US and most Western countries, the federal government in Canada has a limited role in private and public sector collective bargaining. Collective bargaining refers to the process by which unions and employers negotiate the wages, hours, and working conditions that apply in an employment relationship. According to the *British North America Act*, barring exceptional circumstances (like wartime), the federal jurisdiction for labour relations legislation is limited to a handful of interprovincial industries—transportation, finance, and communications—as well as federal government employees. Although that does not preclude the federal government from attempting to set an example through its legislation and policies for other levels of government, the bulk of responsibility for the collective bargaining resides with the provinces.

This chapter addresses the various and sometimes contradictory roles that a provincial government faces when dealing with collective bargaining, first in the private sector and then in the public sector. With respect to the private sector, the provincial government's role is to develop legislation covering the rules for business and union interaction, from the establishment of a union management relationship to the conduct of ongoing contract negotiations, and the procedures available to resolve impasses, including strikes. Since the provinces are not directly involved in private sector bargaining, one might expect that their role would be one of impartial umpire, setting and enforcing the ground rules and then letting the parties fight it out. At times provincial governments have extended their role to "protecting the public interest," which can mean many different things, including protection of the public from strikes and/or the suppression of union power and organization, purportedly to attract investor capital.

The second part of this chapter concerns provincial interactions with various groups of public employees. In most situations the province is at least an indirect party of interest as employer or funding agent as well as being "impartial umpire" and "protector of public interest." This complicates the question as to what the rules for collective bargaining should be in the public sector, particularly with respect to the right to strike. It also means that one of the parties to the collective bargaining process has the ultimate ability to change the rules in mid-stream by legislation. Finally, with public sector compensation being a major portion of provincial and local government budgets, provincial governments have been looking for sacrifices from their employees as a way of reigning in deficits.

Private Sector Dealings

Given provincial jurisdiction over most labour relations, it is hardly surprising that there are currently ten labour relations acts covering the private sector (except for the designated interprovincial industries covered by the *Canada Labour Code*). Although there are some differences among the acts, which will be discussed later, the core of all provincial legislation is extremely similar. This arises from the historical leadership role played by the federal government in developing the labour relations model. In 1944, during World War II, the federal government extended its jurisdiction into labour relations through the *War Measures Act*, on the basis that labour strife could hamper the war effort. The Mackenzie King government passed Privy Council Order 1003 (PC 1003) which extended many rights to organized labour in the hope of ensuring that unions would not conduct strikes in war-related industries.[1] The executive order transplanted the American legislative framework for labour relations and collective bargaining (known as the *Wagner Act*) to Canada, until the war ended. In 1948 the federal government passed collective bargaining legislation to succeed the wartime measures which served as the model for provincial bargaining laws in the postwar period.

An understanding of the basic aspects of the private sector model is necessary to comprehend the specific options currently facing provincial decision-makers. The model starts with the premise that employees have a right to join unions and participate in their lawful activities, and the remainder of the legislation operationalizes those rights. In particular, workers obtain the right to union representation through democratic means, rather than through a picket line. Before PC 1003, workers would have to go on strike to exert pressure on an intransigent employer who refused to recognize their union as bargaining agent. As a result of the new laws, if a majority of workers expressed their desire to be represented by a union (through casting ballots and/or signing union membership cards), then that union would be "certified" as the bargaining agent by the quasi-judicial board which oversees each act (usually referred to as the labour relations board). Certification is like an exclusive franchise: no other organization can represent the workers and individual workers lose the right to negotiate for themselves (even if they voted against the union). Certification rights can be revoked if a majority of employees vote to be represented by another union or by no union at all.

Once a union is certified, the employer is required to meet with it in an attempt to negotiate a collective agreement concerning wages, hours, and working conditions. There is no requirement that an agreement be reached, provided both parties "negotiate in good faith." If negotiations reach an impasse, the union may strike to put pressure on management, and the employer can lockout employees to pressure labour. The strike/lockout system presumes that the threat of strikes and/or lockouts is sufficiently costly to both sides that they will make concessions to avoid this outcome.

Assuming the bargaining relationship is established with the successful negotiation of a collective agreement, no strikes or lockouts are legal during the contract life. To help ensure that work stoppages do not occur, every collective agreement must include a grievance procedure to resolve differences of opinion about what the agreement means. A typical grievance procedure has three or four levels where the parties try to negotiate a solution to the dispute. The final step in the process must be arbitration, where a third party (usually a lawyer) hears both sides' arguments and then makes a binding determination of the issue in dispute for the life of the contract.

When the contract is up for renegotiation (usually 60 days before its expiration), this, or any other aspect of the contract can be brought forward for potential amendment. The parties must again "bargain in good faith." If the contract has expired, the parties generally do not have the legal right to strike or lockout. In most provinces, no work stoppages can occur until the process of third-party conciliation/mediation has been completed. These mediators or conciliators are labour relations experts appointed by provincial governments to aid the parties in reaching agreement without resorting to strikes or lockouts. Their only real power is their ability to leave, which then makes a legal strike or lockout imminent.

Finally, each provincial labour act contains a list of actions by one side or the other that are prohibited and that are enforced by the labour board, which has the power to grant various remedies, including orders for the payment of financial compensation and damages and the reinstatement of employees fired for illegal purposes. These "unfair labour practices" include discriminating against or intimidating anyone on the basis of union activity, encouraging or participating in an illegal strike or lockout, bargaining in bad faith, and interfering in the formation of a trade union. Most provincial labour acts have been regularly amended, reflecting changes in the industrial relations and political environments. Two main issues of contention concern the rules around establishing bargaining relations and management's use of substitute employees during a strike.

Over the years, employers have attempted to use strategies to keep unions from organizing their establishments. These range from tactics to delay certification votes while management mounts its own anti-union campaign to threatening to close the plant if the union is certified and illegally firing union sympathizers. This has particular relevance for unions as the growth area for jobs is the service sector, which has been historically difficult to unionize. If these workers cannot be organized, unions are destined to represent a smaller percentage of total employees and have correspondingly less political and economic clout.

Both unions and employers have lobbied for changes to the certification process over time, and there were shifts in these rules during the 1990s and the early 2000s in a few provinces. For example, unions have sought rules providing greater access to employees who work in shopping centres during an organizing campaign (shopping centres have historically been considered under common law to be "private" property) and more effective restrictions on employer tactics such as procedural delay and/or "unfair labour practices" designed to thwart union certification. As of 1995, only Ontario and BC legislation provided unions with the right to enter upon property owned by third parties that is subject to public access in order to conduct union organizing. By the time of writing, both of these provinces had repealed these protections, and now none of the provinces provide this right of access, which presumably has weakened the labour movement's ability to organize service sector workers such as those working in shopping centres. In another example, the Ontario PC government removed the longstanding power of the labour tribunal to certify unions in the face of employer unfair labour practices, but the new Liberal government re-instated this power in further legal reforms in 2005.

Equally important is the dispute resolution process for first collective agreements. Employers understand that even if they cannot prevent union certification through legal or illegal tactics, they can often prevent the union from becoming effectively entrenched through tough negotiating strategies in the early stages of the process. In particular, forcing a new bargaining unit of employees to go on strike over their first collective agreement, while the employer continues its operations during the strike, has often left workers so disillusioned that they subsequently decertify their union. Many unions argue that if the first collective agreement were subject to binding arbitration (where a neutral third party, usually a lawyer, determines all aspects of the agreement which remain in dispute), the labour relations relationship would begin on a more positive basis and would give the union until the end of the agreement (at least a year) to prove its utility. By 1995, four provinces (Alberta, New Brunswick, Nova Scotia, and PEI) had no provisions at all for first contract arbitration.[2]

The other controversial issue is whether employers should be able to use "replacement workers" during a strike. In most jurisdictions, the employer has the right to use alternative workers to maintain operations during a work stoppage. One obvious group of replacements is management personnel. In many situations these employees are not sufficient, so the employer hires replacement workers (also known as "scabs"). Unions often react strongly to the possibility of replacement workers by setting up picket lines to prevent these workers from entering the establishment. The employer may then demand assistance from the police to ensure that the replacement workers can enter the workplace. Historically, these have been explosive situations, which have sometimes resulted in violence. Therefore, unions argue that legislation should prohibit the hiring of

replacement workers during strikes. Employers respond that "anti-scab" legislation would allow unions to hold firms up for ransom in collective bargaining,
thus eroding their competitive position. Such an environment could force capital
to flee to other provinces or the US. In 1995, only Quebec, Ontario, and BC had
limited the rights of employers to hire replacement workers, but since changes
in 1995, Ontario law currently permits companies to use them.[3] Despite apoca-
lyptic predictions by employers, the impact of these provisions seems not to have
been dramatic, although empirical studies of the Quebec law found that the frequency and lengths of strikes increased.[4]

The allocation of competing rights and powers between unions and private
sector employers is seen by some as a difficult "balancing act" and by others as
an acutely political process in which the state, to a certain extent, actually *con-
structs* the particular distribution of political and economic power in society.[5]
Often, advances in union rights are made following the election of left-of-centre
governments, mainly the New Democratic Party (NDP). Changes are generally
incremental in nature and outlive the government in power, although there have
been several cases where the "reforms" of the previous government are quickly
repealed. For example, in 1991, Manitoba's Progressive Conservative government repealed a section of the *Labour Relations Act* which gave unions, but not
employers, the choice to substitute a form of arbitration for the strike right to
resolve collective bargaining impasses. This "final offer selection" option, where
the arbitrator must choose either the union or management position in total, had
been introduced by the previous NDP government in 1988.[6]

Recent history in Ontario and BC reveals dramatic shifts in the nature of the
labour relations framework, suggesting the importance of labour law as an instrument in the provincial public policy apparatus. In Ontario, governments made
repeated and significant shifts in the labour relations framework, as the pro-labour NDP reforms of 1992 were quickly revoked by the Progressive Conservative
government in 1995. Indeed, that government went far beyond simply "undoing"
the 1992 reforms by significantly rolling back certain union rights and removing
some of the long-standing framework that was designed to aid non-union employees to obtain access to collective bargaining.[7] One example of this was the
elimination of the speedy "card-check" system of union certification in favour of
a mandatory vote system similar to the American model. Under the "card-check"
system, unions merely had to submit membership cards signed by a stipulated
percentage of the employees in the group of employees the union was seeking to
certify.[8] Recent Liberal government reforms in BC also included a removal of
this "card-check" system. Some analysts argued that this system of union certification was a significant factor in historically enabling unions in Ontario, BC, and
other provinces with similar systems to organize and expand more quickly and
effectively than their counterparts in the US.[9] Recent events show that successive
governments in Ontario remain continually interested in revising these policies,

since the current Liberal government re-instated the "card-check" certification procedure for the construction industry in the province in 2005.

Occasionally, provincial governments, in their role of promoting economic development, have attempted to use collective bargaining legislation as a way to attract and maintain foreign capital. In 1979, the Nova Scotia government amended its legislation to require unions to get a majority of all employees working at multi-plant manufacturing firms, in order to be certified. The legislation became known as the "Michelin Bill," because it prevented a union from becoming the certified bargaining agent of one of the two Michelin tire plants in that province.[10] More recently, the Newfoundland government proposed legislation which would have given special collective bargaining (as well as tax) advantages to offshore capital which moved there. In particular, these off-shore firms would be guaranteed that no collective agreement could be less than five years in duration, with no strikes allowed during that period. All disputes would be decided by interest arbitration, with the most important criterion for the arbitrator's award being the financial health and viability of the firm. Not only was the union movement up in arms about the proposal, but the Board of Trade came out against these changes as providing these new firms with an unfair competitive advantage. In response to the widespread criticism, the government dropped the proposals.[11] Political struggles over the nature of labour laws, and events like the passage of the "Michelin Bill," lead some scholars, writing from a Marxist perspective, to emphasize the state's continual role in constraining union power as a significant function in its facilitation of modern capitalism.[12] This is fairly interesting in that in the Canadian example, unlike in the US and Britain, much of this particular struggle between the state and organized labour takes place at the subnational, provincial level of government.

Regardless of the legal environment, provinces always retain the ability to become involved in a bargaining dispute on an ad hoc basis. In their role of protecting the public, they can and sometimes do pass "back-to-work" legislation ending a specific work stoppage. Although disputes with the potential to damage the public interest can emanate from either the private or public sector, in practice provinces have rarely found it necessary to legislate an end to private sector work stoppages. Only eight of the 88 instances of provincial back-to-work orders between 1959 and 1993 involved private sector firms.[13]

Public Sector Interactions

Compared to the private sector, determining a province's appropriate role with respect to public sector collective bargaining is much more complex. Depending on the jurisdiction involved, the provincial government is the actual employer of public employees or has the indirect "power of the purse" through its transfer payments to the formal employer (i.e., hospitals, boards of education, social service agencies, etc.). In addition, many of these subsectors provide services that are viewed as essential to health and safety. As a result, the government must be more than an "impartial umpire"" when it comes to public sector labour legislation. It is a direct party of interest trying to increase efficiency and contain costs like any other employer, as well as being the "protector of the public interest." Over the past 30 years, most provincial governments have decided that various public sector jurisdictions should be covered by separate legislation, rather than simply extending the existing private sector laws (see Table 18.1). The major exception is municipalities, who have been considered as equivalent to private sector establishments in all provincial labour relations acts. There is substantial variation among provinces in how public sector collective bargaining regimes are structured, with some being more concerned than others about crafting specific rules for each area of the public sector.

Historically, the most contentious issue faced by provincial governments was whether to extend the right to strike to public sector negotiations. Generally speaking, provinces with fewer laws covering public sector bargaining are more willing to extend the strike-based model to the public sector. The related issue is what should be used as a substitute for the strike. There must be a basis for finality in resolving collective bargaining disputes, or there would never be an incentive for at least one of the parties to settle by making concessions. Realistically, there are only two substitutes for the strike right: interest arbitration and limited strike. Under interest arbitration, all unresolved issues at the time of impasse are sent to an independent third party who resolves the issues on the basis of merit. The limited strike alternative allows some, but not all, union members to go on strike to press for their demands.

It has been alleged that unlike the private sector where the parties hurt each other, a public sector strike penalizes innocent third parties, members of the public at large. The other side of the argument is that the public is not an innocent bystander, but rather a direct party of interest (like a corporate shareholder) who wants high quality public services at minimum cost. A more defendable argument against the right to strike in the public sector is that some public services are so essential that a strike could endanger public health and safety. The critical issue is where to draw the line between necessity and convenience. The overwhelming majority of Canadians would agree that firefighting and police services are absolutely essential. Others would add ambulance services, public utility workers during the winter, and perhaps hospital employees. Few would include education and provincial or municipal government services in the list. Using this logic, one might expect to see a relationship between the degree of essentiality and the use of substitutes for the strike right.

Table 18.2 presents the "failsafe" *dispute resolution process* used in various subsectors across Canada. The data are only partially consistent with expectations. Three provinces (Saskatchewan, Manitoba, and Nova Scotia) allow some (or all)

Table 18.1. Provincial Collective Bargaining Legislation

Juris-diction	Private Sector	Municipal	Police	Fire-fighters	Hospitals	Teachers	Civil Service	Govt. Enterprise
BC	Labour Relations Code	Labour Relations Code	Labour Relations Code/Fire and Police Services Collective Bargaining Act	Labour Relations Code/Fire and Police Services Collective Bargaining Act	Labour Relations Code/Health Authorities Act/Healthcare Services Collective Agreement Act	Labour Relations Code/Public Education Labour Relations Act	Labour Relations Code/Public Service Labour Relations Act	Labour Relations Code
AB	Labour Relations Code	Labour Relations Code, Municipal Government Act	Police Officers Collective Bargaining Act/Police Act	Labour Relations Code	Labour Relations Code	Labour Relations Code/School Act	Public Service Employee Relations Act/Civil Service Garnishee Act/Public Service Labour Relations Act/Labour Relations Code	Labour Relations Code
SK	Trade Union Act	Trade Union Act	Police Act	Fire Department Platoons Act	Trade Union Act/Health Labour Relations Reorganization Act	Education Act	Trade Union Act	Trade Union Act
MB	Labour Relations Act	Labour Relations Act	Labour Relations Act/The Provincial Police Act/City of Winnipeg Act	Labour Relations Act/The Firefighters and Paramedics Arbitration Act	Labour Relations Act/Essential Services Act	Public Schools Act	Civil Service Act/Essential Services Act	Labour Relations Act

Juris-diction	Private Sector	Municipal	Police	Fire-fighters	Hospitals	Teachers	Civil Service	Govt. Enterprise
ON	Labour Relations Act, 1995	Labour Relations Act, 1995, Public Sector Labour Relations Transition Act	Police Services Act/Public Service Act/ Public Sector Dispute Resolution Act	Fire Protection and Prevention Act, 1997, Public Sector Dispute Resolution Act	Labour Relations Act, 1995/ Hospital Labour Disputes Arbitration Act, Public Sector Disputes Resolution Act, Public Sector Labour Relations Transition Act, Ambulance Services Collective Bargaining Act	Labour Relations Act, 1995/ Education Quality and Accountability Office Act	Crown Employees Collective Bargaining Act	Labour Relations Act/ Crown Employees Collective Bargaining Act
QC	Labour Code	Labour Code	Labour Code/ Police Act	Labour Code	Labour Code/ Public Service Act	Labour Code	Labour Code/ Public Service Act	Labour Code/ Public Service Act
NB	Industrial Relations Act	Industrial Relations Act	Industrial Relations Act/ Police Act	Industrial Relations Act	Public Service Labour Relations Act	Public Service Labour Relations Act	Public Service Labour Relations Act/Civil Service Act	Public Service Labour Relations Act

Jurisdiction	Private Sector	Municipal	Police	Fire-fighters	Hospitals	Teachers	Civil Service	Govt. Enterprise
NS	Trade Union Act	Trade Union Act	Trade Union Act	Trade Union Act	Trade Union Act	Teachers Collective Bargaining Act	Civil Service Collective Bargaining Act/Highway Workers Collective Bargaining Act	Trade Union Act
PEI	Labour Act	Labour Act	Labour Act/Police Act	Labour Act	Labour Act	School Act	Civil Service Act	Civil Service Act
NF	Labour Relations Act/Labour Standards Act/Employer's Liability Act/Workplace Health and Safety Compensation Act	Labour Relations Act	Labour Relations Act/Royal Newfoundland Constabulary Act	Labour Relations Act/City of St. John's Fire Department Act	Public Service Collective Bargaining Act/Interns and Residents Collective Bargaining Act	Teachers Collective Bargaining Act	Public Service Collective Bargaining Act	Public Service Collective Bargaining Act/Labour Relations Act

Source: Allen Ponak and Mark Thompson, "Public Sector Collective Bargaining," in Morley Gunderson, et al., eds., Union-Management Relations in Canada, 5th ed. (Toronto: Pearson Addison-Wesley, 2005).

Table 18.2. Dispute Resolution Procedures in Provincial Public Sectors

Jurisdiction	Municipal	Police	Firefighters	Hospitals	Teachers	Civil Service	Government Enterprise
BC	Limited Strike[1,2]	Arbitration at request of either party	Arbitration at request of either party	Limited Strike[1,2]	Limited Strike[1,2]	Limited Strike[1,2]	Limited Strike[1,2]
AB	Strike[3]	Arbitration at request of either party	Arbitration at request of either party	Arbitration at request of either party	Strike[3]	Arbitration at request of either party	Arbitration[3,4]
SK	Strike	Strike	Strike or Arbitration at request of either party[5]	Strike	Arbitration	Strike	Strike
MB	Strike[6]	Winnipeg – arbitration at request of either party; others strike and/or arbitration at request of either party	Arbitration at request of either party	Limited Strike[6]	Arbitration at request of either party	Limited Strike or Arbitration at request of either party	Strike[6]
ON	Strike	Arbitration[7]	Mandatory Arbitration	Mandatory Arbitration	Strike[8]	Limited Strike[9]	Strike
QC	Limited Strike[10]	Arbitration at request of either party	Arbitration at request of either party	Limited Strike[11]	Limited Strike[12]	Limited Strike[12]	Limited Strike[12]
NB	Strike	Arbitration at request of either party	Arbitration at request of either party	Limited Strike[10]	Limited Strike[10]	Limited Strike[10]	Limited Strike[10]
NS	Strike	Strike	Strike	Strike[13]	Strike; Arbitration at request of either party for local/regional issues	Arbitration at request of either party	Strike

Juris-diction	Municipal	Police	Firefighters	Hospitals	Teachers	Civil Service	Government Enterprise
PEI	Strike	Arbitration by Minister's order	Arbitration by Minister's order	Arbitration by Minister's order	Arbitration	Arbitration	Arbitration
NF	Strike	Newfoundland Constabulary—arbitration at request of either party	ST. JOHN'S— Arbitration at request of either party	Limited Strike[14]	Strike	Limited Strike[15]	Strike[16]

Sources: Statutes of each province as available on the Internet, from each provincial government online consolidation, as of 18 March 2002.

Notes:

1. Legislation restricts employer use of replacement workers during strike.
2. General legislation restricts strikes relating to perishable property and/or public health and safety and threats to children's educational programs.
3. General legislation provides that the minister may order changes in strike behaviour or settle dispute in event of "emergencies" affecting public.
4. Limited strike if excluded from *Public Service Employees Relations Act*.
5. Arbitration provisions only available where union constitution prohibits strikes by members.
6. General legislation (*Labour Relations Act*) provides for arbitration at request of either party after expiration of 60 days into strike or lockout.
7. Arbitration at request of either party for municipal police forces, mandatory arbitration for OPP.
8. Specific legislation contains expansive definition of "strike," including "work-to-rule" campaigns.
9. Legislation requires essential services agreements between parties, affected workers barred from striking.
10. General legislation restricts striking by employees performing essential services.
11. Legislation restricts striking in essential services and prohibits strikes over local/regional issues. Specified levels of staff to be maintained in certain institutions during strikes.
12. Legislation restricts striking in essential services and prohibits strikes over local/regional issues.
13. Strikes prohibited in two large health services bargaining units, where arbitration is available at request of either party.
14. Legislation restricts strikes by employees performing essential services and also prohibits rotating strikes.
15. Legislation restricts striking by employees performing essential services, and government may invoke emergency provisions to prohibit strikes by certain bargaining units. Where emergency provisions invoked, or where entire unit deemed "essential," mandatory arbitration is required.
16. Unless designated essential, in which case note 15 applies.

of their police jurisdictions to strike. BC, Nova Scotia, and Newfoundland also permit firefighter strikes. Even when the law states that the dispute resolution process is the right to strike, an individual employer and union can substitute interest arbitration by mutual consent. This is not uncommon in police and firefighter bargaining. At the other extreme, three provinces (Alberta, Nova Scotia, and PEI) deny provincial employees access to the strike (despite the fact that all municipal government employees have the strike right). There appears to be some trend toward narrowing and restricting the scope of the strike right, transforming it into a "limited strike" mechanism. In the past 15 years several provinces have either imposed or expanded existing "essential services" restrictions on selected portions of the provincial public sector, and there appears to be some convergence towards the limited strike model.[14]

Obviously, essentiality is not the sole determinant of the process for resolving public sector collective bargaining impasses. Before trying to explain the present situation, ways of evaluating different dispute resolution alternatives should be addressed.[15] One common criterion is that a good dispute resolution process is rarely used. This apparent contradiction is based on the fact that if a dispute resolution process is sufficiently painful, rather than resort to the process, the parties will make concessions to arrive at a negotiated settlement. In particular, both labour and management know a strike can impose severe hardship on themselves. As a result, in approximately 90 to 95 per cent of negotiations the parties make concessions and reach agreement without resorting to a work stoppage.

By contrast, going in front of an arbitrator is not particularly unpleasant for the parties, so much of the deterrent effect of a strike does not apply. Both sides may find arbitration a more politically palatable way of resolving difficult issues and tend to rely on the process round after round rather than trying to resolve the issues themselves. In addition, if the parties expect the arbitrator's decision to be a compromise between the union and management positions, there is no incentive to compromise in advance of arbitration. In other words, the possibility of arbitration, rather than encouraging the parties to make concessions, can actually have a "chilling effect" on bargaining.

A related criterion is accountability. A good dispute resolution process makes the parties accountable for their actions. In a strike-based system, whether a dispute is resolved before or after a work stoppage, the parties sign on the dotted line of the new collective agreement and are responsible for the outcome. Under arbitration, leaders on both sides can escape accountability by refusing to modify their positions and letting the arbitrator impose the contract. Finally, Swan[16] argues that the dispute mechanism should fit the nature of the relationship. If a dispute arises between two parties which do not have an ongoing relationship, third-party resolution works well. For instance, if two drivers are involved in an automobile accident, using a judge to determine liability is a good procedure, because whatever the verdict, the parties go their separate ways. The work relationship is quite different, because the parties must deal with each other after the dispute is resolved. Here, an arbitration award can have long-term effects on the parties' relationship.

Based on these criteria most labour relations experts believe that the right to strike is superior to arbitration and should be denied only in extreme situations. Many would argue that even where essential services are involved, a limited strike right may be preferable to arbitration. Overall, arbitration is used in nine firefighter, eight police, three hospital, four teacher, four provincial civil service, and two government enterprise jurisdictions. PEI and Alberta rely most heavily on arbitration (all non-municipal employees are covered except for teachers in Alberta), while a few provinces seem to reserve its use primarily for police and firefighters.

An obvious question is why many provincial governments have opted for arbitration at certain times. Much of the reason transcends partisan politics. Arbitration has provided governments with a way to potentially de-politicize public sector collective bargaining.[17] From the perspective of an incumbent government, arbitration's weakness of limited accountability is also its major strength. In self-interested political terms, public sector collective bargaining has three potential outcomes, two of which are bad. Negotiations can involve a strike, which is a political minefield, regardless of the ultimate settlement. Secondly, even if a settlement is obtained without a work stoppage, it can cause political difficulty if it appears to be expensive and could lead to tax increases. The third outcome, an inexpensive settlement without a strike is ideal, for which the government would proudly assume responsibility. The beauty of arbitration is that it reduces the political cost of the other two outcomes. The possibility of a strike is virtually eliminated, and in the rare event of an illegal strike it would be very difficult for the union to obtain any public sympathy. Secondly, should an expensive salary increase be necessary which requires higher taxes or a larger deficit, the "wise" arbitrator can be blamed.

These arguments must be counterbalanced against the potential down side of interest arbitration: that an outsider (the arbitrator) determines what happens to public employee compensation and that, as a result, the government can lose control over a large portion of provincial expenditures. Not surprisingly, in the 1980s and 1990s as provincial deficits began to mount, many provincial governments lost enthusiasm for arbitration. For example, in 1981 the Progressive Conservative government of Alberta attempted to restrain arbitration awards by limiting the criteria that arbitrators could use to make decisions. The law requires third parties to consider the government's "ability to pay" and the current provincial fiscal situation as the major criteria when making an award. As a result, the arbitration system has lost much of its legitimacy with Alberta public sector unions, who have resorted to a number of illegal strikes. More recently, numerous governments have used legislative powers to suspend the arbitration process as a way of fighting the deficit. This situation will be discussed in the next section of this chapter.

What about the third option: a limited strike? The logic behind this dispute resolution process is that strikes should impose economic and political costs but not irreparable damage. A limited strike allows a union to withdraw all services, except those that are truly essential. In reality, it would never be in a union's interest to be even indirectly responsible for a loss of life or enormous damage to property. A number of provinces use this technique: BC for most of its public and parapublic sectors, Newfoundland and New Brunswick for provincial and hospital employees, Quebec for hospital employees, and Ontario for the provincial civil service and crown corporations (this legislation was passed in 1993). Manitoba adopted this model for its civil service and for certain other parapublic sectors. Adell, et al.[18] argue that in the 1990s, there was some convergence across the provinces towards the use of a limited strike model in which specific services were designated as being essential. The crucial aspect of limited strike legislation is how those workers who are designated as being essential (and must work during a strike) is determined. Although experience is limited, it has proven to be a difficult process to manage. Unions have often complained that too many of their members are forced to work, allowing the employer to provide much more than essential services and thereby weakening the impact of the strike.[19]

Governments face another trade-off when dealing with the appropriate bargaining structure. The structure of public sector bargaining refers to the way collective agreements are actually negotiated. At one extreme, negotiations can take place between an individual local union and employer (decentralization), while at the other end of the spectrum a single set of province-wide negotiations could determine wages, hours, and working conditions for an entire subsector (i.e., hospital employees). Where bargaining is highly decentralized, as is true in Ontario where police boards, school boards, and hospital boards are all defined as separate employers, the collective bargaining process is not particularly visible. Even the occasional work stoppage is just a local event, so there is less accountability for the provincial government. Unfortunately, the provincial treasury can lose direct control over a large portion of its budget particularly when decentralized budgeting is combined with arbitration. It has been argued that decentralized bargaining allows unions to divide and conquer employers, taking on the most vulnerable employers first, and using that victory to set precedents with other employers and arbitrators. If the employer has limited or no taxing power (as is usually true for the hospital sector), the province can ultimately be stuck paying for the higher settlements through transfer payments.

When bargaining is centralized, as is the case for Quebec where a few sets of negotiations determine all public sector wages, the government is directly involved in the bargaining process and can protect its budget. However, centralization also brings intense public scrutiny. If the government's refusal to accept

the union demands lead to a strike, there can a massive impact on the populace, which leads to further politicization of the process. At the same time, the
magnitude of a potential work stoppage makes it politically legitimate to impose "back-to-work" legislation. Quebec resorted to such legislation 22 times
between 1967 and 1993, which is 28 per cent of the total provincial legislation
ending strikes.[20] It is also worth mentioning that, aside from the Parti Québécois
(PQ) government of 1994 to 2003, no Quebec provincial government has survived more than two rounds of public sector bargaining since its inception in
1965. Hébert[21] has argued that Quebec's "hyper-centralization" has ultimately
destroyed the collective bargaining process by removing the possibility for local
decision-making and problem-solving.

Nonetheless, there appears to be a trend among governments to negotiate or
legislate more centralized structures. An example of this behaviour is the centralization of teacher bargaining in Ontario, initiated by the Progressive Conservative
government of Mike Harris. The province increased its control over the budgets
of local boards of education and used legislation to override locally negotiated
collective agreement provisions dealing with teacher workloads.[22] A difficult fiscal environment places a premium on direct control over the budget and tends
to reduce the political costs of "hard-nosed'" bargaining with public sector employees.

A final role which provincial governments must assume is that of regulator
of the provincial economy. This affects public sector labour relations in a profound way. As Table 18.3 indicates, public sector compensation represents a large
proportion of provincial expenditures, whether the expense is direct through
paying salaries or indirect through transfer payments to junior jurisdictions. For
example, 2001 wages and salaries for the sectors listed in Table 18.3 amounted to
almost $30 billion in Ontario and over $20 billion in Quebec. Even these values
are underestimates because employer contributions to fringe benefits, including
pensions, are not included. Typically, wages and salaries of employees in provincial government and health and social services account for 20 per cent of the
total provincial budget. In addition, provinces are either directly paying teacher
salaries and/or transferring money to school boards and local governments that
use much of the money to defray their labour costs.

The labour intensive nature of public services makes them an obvious target
of provincial restraint programs. When combined with the fact that governments
have the ability to change the rules at any time through legislation, it is not surprising that public sector employees were subjected to a series of "temporary
suspensions to collective bargaining" during the 1980s and 1990s. In 1982-83 six
provinces followed the lead of the federal government in imposing wage controls
on public sector employees in their jurisdiction in the name of fighting inflation and reducing government expenditures.[23] This was a harbinger of the much
more widespread and onerous control programs imposed in the early 1990s.

Table 18.3. Provincial and Local Government Wage and Salary Costs, 2003

Province	A. Total Wage and Salary Costs (thousands of current $)						B. Wage and Salary Costs as Percentage of applicable budgets[1]		
	Provincial General Government	Health and Social Services	Local General Government	Local School Boards	Provincial Govt Business Enterprises	Local Government Business Enterprises	Provincial General Government	Health and Social Services	Local General Government
BC	2,205,598	3,721,241	1,700,413	3,216,509	1,012,646	7,407	6.9	11.6	33.6
AB	1,752,739	2,704,702	1,733,933	2,752,666	75,391	244,534	7.5	11.6	36.8
SK	753,976	1,133,796	459,186	860,352	548,911	17,729	8.4	12.6	27.8
MB	724,818	1,292,750	448,502	1,006,779	402,050	71,522	7.9	14.1	29.1
ON	5,002,572	10,078,608	6,607,509	10,226,189	2,253,480	1,778,334	6.1	12.3	27.1
QC	4,490,112	8,688,800	3,008,021	5,380,404	1,943,152	411,194	6.6	12.9	29.2
NB	1,147,443	760,399	208,917	N/A	214,413	12,997	18.7	12.4	38.1
NS	488,467	1,052,213	255,967	660,898	63,040	14,093	7.0	15.1	33.2
PEI	141,672	158,949	16,676	112,732	7,654	N/A	12.3	13.8	26.1
NF	361,357	741,789	96,162	438,186	93,127	N/A	7.3	15.0	31.6

1. Note: 2003 figures for Provincial General Government and Health and Social Services are expressed as a percentage of total provincial government expenditure for fiscal year 2003 ending 31 March, whereas figures for Local Government Administration are expressed as a percentage of total local government expenditure for fiscal year 2003 ending 31 March. Total local government expenditure is calculated using data in Table 385-0001 and by subtracting total provincial expenditure from total combined provincial/local expenditure. Calculations of various percentages in Part (B) of this Table were not possible with readily available data.

Sources: Statistics Canada, CANSIM II. Data on wages and salary costs are from Table 183-0002. Data on total government expenditures are from Table 385-0001.

The Deficit and Provincial Collective Bargaining

A combination of high real interest rates, limitations on federal transfer payments and programs, and a severe recession in 1990 all contributed to large increases in provincial government deficits in the early 1990s (see Table 18.4). Between the 1990 and 1993 fiscal years, the level of provincial deficits increased dramatically, with every province in a deficit situation. By the 1993 fiscal year, provincial deficits ranged from $129 per capita in New Brunswick to $1,171 per capita in Alberta. Some provinces were facing the possibility of having their credit rating reduced. At that time, virtually all provincial governments became committed to restraining public sector compensation, regardless of political ideology. Making matters even more difficult was the fact that the rate of inflation was extremely low (between 0 to 2 per cent). During the early 1980s, real compensation could be substantially reduced by freezing terms of the collective agreement and letting inflation take its toll. By contrast, during the 1990s, provinces had to obtain actual reductions in wages and/or benefits to generate substantial restraint. This resulted in a great deal of conflict, since it is likely much harder to convince union members and their leaders to accept a wage roll-back as opposed to a "mere" wage freeze.

Table 18.4. Provincial Government Surplus/Deficits for Selected Fiscal Years ending 31 March

	1990		1993		2001		2003	
Province	Millions	Per Capita	Millions	Per Capita	Millions	Per Capita	Millions	Per Capita
BC	+783	+238	-1559	-437	+236	+58	-2922	-705
AB	-1981	-778	-3127	-1171	+7667	+2502	+2543	+806
SK	-495	-492	-130	-129	+1161	+1143	-478	-480
MB	-233	-211	-510	-456	+274	+238	+51	+44
ON	+1276	+124	-11939	-1117	+1145	+96	-4357	-356
QC	-1779	-254	-5821	-812	+1888	+255	-4072	-544
NB	-25	-34	-260	-347	+31	+41	-169	-225
NS	-655	-720	-754	-816	+182	+193	+69	+74
PEI	-24	-184	-81	-612	-38	-274	-71	-515
NF	+1	+2	-324	-558	-273	-511	-333	-641

Sources: Statistics Canada, CANSIM II, Tables 051-0001 and 385-0001.

Table 18.4 also illustrates that by the end of the decade, provincial government finances were much healthier. Eight provinces were in a surplus position, and deficit levels had been reduced in both of the remaining provinces. This suggested the possibility of easing and/or reversing the earlier restraint programs, an issue that will be addressed subsequently in this chapter, although by 2003 only three provinces remained in a surplus position.

An important issue is what constitutes the best way to restrain public sector compensation. Broadly speaking, three approaches have been used. One involves using legislation to impose restraint by suspending collective bargaining and/or overriding existing collective agreements. Alternatively, the government threatens to invoke legislation if the unions involved do not agree to negotiate concessions. The major cost of this strategy is that it inevitably outrages the labour movement who argue that governments have no right to tamper with collective bargaining which is the work equivalent to due process in the courts. Potentially, these protests can escalate into public sector strike actions. If legislative threats become common, the long-term viability of public sector bargaining can be put in jeopardy. On the positive side, laws bring quick results and have generally been viewed favourably by the public at large.

The second strategy is to obtain concessions through a combination of hard bargaining and reductions in transfer payments. This technique is identical to concession bargaining in the private sector. The province comes to the bargaining table with its own employees demanding that compensation must be reduced through concessions and/or layoffs and being prepared to take a strike over the issue, if necessary. At the same time, the province slashes its transfer payments to hospitals, schools, and local governments. Managers of these junior governmental agencies have no choice but to require concessions from their unions and/or lay workers off. Governments using this approach cannot be accused of restricting the collective bargaining process. On the down side, achieving restraint will take time particularly in a system with decentralized public sector bargaining, and the public may be subjected to strikes along the way. In addition, if some public sector jurisdictions use arbitration to resolve disputes, it is not clear that compensation can be reduced, regardless of management's resolve. This strategy becomes particularly problematic if unions and arbitrators find it difficult to accept rollbacks (as opposed to contract freezes).

The third strategy involves the provincial government attempting to develop a cooperative arrangement with the public sector unions where the unions voluntarily agree to increase productivity and/or restrain compensation in return for other policies. If attainable, this kind of "social contract" not only brings restraint but maintains the legitimacy of the collective bargaining process and public employee commitment. Four provinces, under left-of-centre governments, tried this approach at some point during the 1990s, with varying degrees of success.

Table 18.5 summarizes the strategies and results of the restraint programs during the decade of the 1990s for each province.

Table 18.5. Compensation Restraint Measures for Provincial Public Sector Employees

Province	Party in Office	Process	Restraint Outcomes	Relative Debt and Deficit[1]
NF	Liberal	Legislative and Adversarial Bargaining	1991: wage freeze; 1 year 1993: suspension of govt. pension contributions; wage freeze 1 year 1994: 1% reduction in govt. pension contributions and 1.5 leave days without pay per year, wage freeze; 2 years	Above average debt Above average deficit in 1991 improving to below average by 1994
NS	Progressive Conservative	Legislative	1991: contract extension with compensation freeze; 2 years	Average debt, above average deficit
PEI	Liberal (since 1993)	Legislative	1993: 5 leave days without pay; 1 year 1994: 3% salary cut for all employees earning over $25,000; 3 years	Above average debt and deficit
	Liberal	Legislative and Adversarial Bargaining	1992: negotiated 6% reduction for 4 months in return for 6 extra vacation days following year 1994: 7.5% legislated wage rollback	Average debt; below average deficit in 1991 worsening to above average by 1994, then improving to below average
NB	Liberal	Legislative and Adversarial Bargaining	1991: wage freeze; 1 year 1992: union choice of 2 year contract extension with 1%, 2% wage increases or regular collective bargaining 1994: agreements reached with all union groups, calling for no salary increase in 1994, followed by 7–8% raise over the next two years; 3 years	Above average debt, improving to average by 1994; Below average deficits
QC	Liberal	Legislative	1992: contract extension with compensation freeze until July 1993 1993: wage freeze plus measure to be negotiated to reduce annual payroll by 1%; 2 years	Average debt; average or above average deficits

Province	Party in Office	Process	Restraint Outcomes	Relative Debt and Deficit[1]
QC (cont.)	Parti Québécois (since 1994)	Cooperative and Adversarial Bargaining	1995: 1% reduction in payroll abandoned; salaries increase by .5% lump sum in 1996; followed by 2% raise over the next two years; 3 years 1997: government calls for contract re-opener to reduce salaries by 3%; after many threats from both sides, parties agree to voluntary pre-retirement plan to reduce employment, financed by the government (1/3) and pension plan surplus (2/3); salaries unchanged	Average debt increasing to above average by 1996; Above average deficits
ON	NDP	Cooperative first, then Legislative	1992: negotiated small salary increase (3% over 2 years) in return for guaranteed job security; 2 years 1993: 4% reduction in annual public sector compensation for employees earning above $30,000, partially paid for by about 6 days off without pay per year; 3 years	Below average debt; Below average deficits worsening to above average by 1993
	Progressive Conservative (since 1995)	Legislative and Adversarial Bargaining	1996: amended legislation to remove successor rights and "wind-up" pension provisions to ease privatization 1996: after 5 week strike, union agrees to removal of guaranteed job security, in return for some protection against privatization and greater bumping rights and severance payments; no wage increases retroactive to 1994; 4 years	Below average debt worsening to average; Above average deficits
MB	Progressive Conservative	Legislative and Adversarial Bargaining	1991: contract extension with wage freeze; 1 year 1993: 10 unpaid days; 2 years 1995, 1996: parties agree to two contracts, no wage increase and 10 unpaid days; 3 years	Average debt; Average or below average deficits

Province	Party in Office	Process	Restraint Outcomes	Relative Debt and Deficit[1]
SK	NDP (since 1992)	Adversarial Bargaining and Cooperative	1993: after six months of rotating strikes, union agreed to contract retroactive to 1991, with a 2.5% cost of living increase in the last year of contract; 4 years 1995: mutual gains bargaining used to reach agreement with annual salary increases of 1% for three years, job guarantee for one year, and establishment of departmental union management committees; 3 years	Average or above average debt; Deficits varying from above average to below average
AB	Progressive Conservative	Adversarial Bargaining	1993: parties agreed to 1.2% wage cut, 7 days leave without pay; 1 year 1994: parties agreed to 2.3% permanent wage cut in return for 3 days unpaid leave; temporary loss of 4 statutory holidays; 3 years	Below average debt; Deficits worsening to above average in 1993, then improving to below average by 1994
BC	NDP	Cooperative	1994: parties negotiated a "Partnership Agreement" to work jointly at improving work organization and public service delivery; in return union agreed to wage increase of 2.5% over four years 1998: parties agreed to two year wage freeze, followed by 2% in year 3; instituted joint committees to identify efficiencies and equally share the savings	Debts below average; deficits below average

1. Based on deficits and debt as a percentage of provincial GDP (presented in Tables 1.2 and 1.4), provinces were classified on an annual basis into below average, average, or above average. Below average was defined as more than 20% below the annual unweighted provincial average for deficit or debt, average was between 20% below and 20% above the mean, and above average was more than 20% above the mean.

Source: G. Swimmer, "Public Sector Labour Relations in an Era of Restraint and Restructuring: An Overview," in G. Swimmer, ed., *Public Sector Labour Relations in an Era of Restraint and Restructuring* (Toronto: Oxford, 2001) 20–24.

Although the timing varied, the Atlantic provinces used the legislative approach at some point. As the deficit situation worsened between 1990 and 1993, the extent of concessions demanded escalated from wage freezes to rollbacks and/or unpaid leave days. Despite this fact, it became clear that the legislative approach would not be all that unpopular with the public at large. For example, after a tentative deal with the Newfoundland Teachers Association to suspend the government's pension contributions fell apart, Premier Clyde Wells called a provincial election in May 1993, making public sector concessions the major issue. When the Liberals were returned as a majority government, the unions bowed to threats of legislation and "negotiated" contracts which allowed the government to reduce its pension contributions and required all public employees to take three days off without pay.[24] The story was similar in Nova Scotia and PEI. Although imposed rollbacks led to union demonstrations and some strikes, the measures remained in place until 1997, at which time the Liberal government was re-elected and negotiated a new agreement with the union containing limited wage increases.[25]

In contrast, the New Brunswick government used a mixture of the legislative and hard bargaining strategies. Following the one-year freeze in 1991 the government passed an innovative law in 1992 which gave public sector unions the choice between automatic wage increases of 1 and 2 per cent annually, with their existing contracts extended for two years, or having the right to full collective bargaining. Most unions chose the bargaining option, and subsequent negotiations lead to a province-wide strike by the Canadian Union of Public Employees in May 1992. It is possible that the New Brunswick experience dissuaded other *Atlantic* governments from relying on the bargaining process to obtain concessions. A similar example was the use of legislation to end a public service strike in Newfoundland in 2004, in which the PC government imposed the employer's pre-strike offers, including a two-year wage freeze, with severe penalties on unions and employees for failure to return to work under the legislation.

Quebec and Manitoba also relied on legislation. The PC government of Manitoba followed the previous pattern of more austere policies as deficits worsened (from a contract extension to unpaid leave days), yet had little trouble gaining re-election in 1995. In Quebec, a change in government yielded a change in approach. After the legislated three-year salary freeze, the Liberal government in 1993 legislated another two-year freeze, plus a 1 per cent reduction in public sector payrolls. Fortunately for the public sector unions, a provincial election intervened, and the PQ formed the new government. Given the joint commitment of the PQ government and the unions to sovereignty, public sector compensation restraint was put on hold, despite the high per capita deficit at the time. In May 1995, the PQ government formally abandoned the previously imposed 1 per cent payroll reduction, which would have generated $170 million in compensation savings.[26] Then, through a somewhat more cooperative approach, the PQ and the unions agreed to a 2.5 per cent wage increase over three years in 1995 and to cost reductions through other measures such as a pre-retirement program.

Saskatchewan and Alberta adopted the hard bargaining approach. The major difference between them was the severity of cuts demanded. Not surprisingly, the NDP government in Saskatchewan was content with a five-year virtual wage freeze from its employees and relied on other fiscal measures including a sales tax increase to reduce its deficit. By 1995, the government's approach became more cooperative, and the parties agreed to a three-year contract with modest wage increases and improved job guarantees. By contrast, in 1993 the newly elected Alberta premier, Ralph Klein, vowed to eliminate the deficit by 1997 through massive cuts to public expenditures. The cuts forced unions at the provincial and local level to accept substantial contract concessions (i.e., provincial salaries fell 2.3 per cent in return for four unpaid leave days, and employees lost four statutory holidays for 1994-97) and/or face major layoffs. Despite a union-led outcry about the cut to social services, Klein retained high popular support.

Ontario and BC were the other two provinces that presented a more cooperative approach to public sector unions on how to adjust compensation in light of the fiscal realities. Both provinces were led by NDP governments that relied at least partly on support from unions. Ontario's attempts failed, and the government reverted to legislation, while BC's more limited approach was sustained for a longer period of time.

The Ontario recession was much more severe than expected, leading to shrinking tax revenues and massive increases in welfare expenditure (not only were welfare rolls swelling, but the federal government had capped its transfer payments to Ontario for welfare). By 1993, the government was predicting a deficit of $17 billion for 1993-94 (up from $2.3 billion in 1991-92 and more than double its 1992 projected deficit for 1993-94), if corrective action was not taken. The three pronged approach to deficit reduction included higher taxes, an expenditure reduction plan to promote productivity and reduce public employment, and a "social contract" with public sector unions and employers. In early April 1993, the NDP government invited public sector unions and employers representing 900,000 public employees to meet in the hopes of negotiating a tripartite agreement to voluntarily reduce public sector compensation by $2 billion annually for three years. In return, unions would receive greater input into the organization and delivery of public services, as well as amendments to the provincial labour laws extending the right to strike and promotion of sectoral (centralized) bargaining. Following the government's attempt to demonstrate the severity of the situation by "opening the books," the negotiations were broken down into eight sectors, and the parties were charged with reaching voluntary agreements within two months. Given the scope of the exercise and the extremely short time line, it would have taken a miracle to succeed.

It was naive of the government to expect union leaders to sacrifice themselves in the eyes of the rank and file, despite the dire deficit situation. Negotiations reached an impasse in early June, and the government responded with legislation that required that public sector compensation be reduced by approximately 5 per cent for the mid-1993 to mid-1996 period. If the parties could not negotiate a way to generate the required reduction by 1 August 1993, then "failsafe" procedures were invoked which would include up to 12 leave days without pay per year to reach the target.[27] The NDP's interference with the collective bargaining process by overturning signed collective agreements was viewed by the labour movement as violating the party's basic philosophy. The public sector unions reacted to the entire exercise as a betrayal and were intent to exact revenge in the next provincial election. A number of public and private sector unions including the Canadian Union of Public Employees, the country's largest union, cut all ties with the Ontario NDP.

The failure of a social democratic government to obtain cooperation from public sector unions and its subsequent resort to unilateralism undoubtedly had a large demonstration effect, providing other provincial governments with ammunition in favour of legislated concessions. Indeed, this also set the stage for a dramatic shift in bargaining strategy upon the election of the Progressive Conservative government in 1995. In late 1995 and early 1996, the new government moved swiftly to legislate removal of union successor rights and wind-up pension provisions, and adopted a hard bargaining stance that led to a bitter five-week strike—and its first ever—by the Ontario Public Service Employees Union (OPSEU). While the new government achieved significant reductions in public service employment and wage expenditure, its demeanour helped transform OPSEU into a more vibrant political organization and increasingly politicized the Ontario public service overall.[28]

BC's attempts at cooperation were more successful because the initiatives were on a smaller scale, and its relatively strong economy during most of the decade allowed government negotiators more flexibility in negotiations. Their major achievement was the March 1993 "Social Accord" in health services, which was negotiated between the government and health sector unions. It called for an overall reduction of 4,800 health sector jobs as well as transferring thousands of jobs from hospitals to community service organizations. This conversion would occur through attrition and the implementation of a shorter work week with no loss in pay. In addition, salaries would increase by 3 per cent over the three-year agreement.[29] By 1998, with the provincial economy worsening, the NDP government and the unions cooperated and agreed to a three-year agreement including a two-year wage freeze in exchange for enhanced job security and pensions. Thompson[30] argues that this cooperation was somewhat spurred by a desire of both parties to avoid the Ontario experience—the election of a right-wing government following a split between the NDP and the unions. However, with the election of the Liberal government in June 2001, the province embraced a dramatic agenda of deep tax cuts, public sector retrenchment, and a highly confrontational style of public sector collective bargaining. This led to a lengthy and bitter Hospital Employees Union (HEU) strike in 2001 in which the provincial government used legislation to end the strike and narrowly avoided a threatened province-wide general strike involving numerous other sympathetic unions.[31] In 2002, the government again used legislation to prohibit strikes and impose its terms for three years on teachers in the province, and in 2004, it legislated a 15 per cent wage rollback on striking health support employees. These events illustrate that the BC public sector unions' strategic efforts aimed at avoiding the Ontario experience ultimately failed.

Prospects for the Future

What can be expected about provincial collective bargaining policies in the future? The answer for the private sector is likely a general continuation of the current scenario. Depending on the party forming the provincial government, there will be incremental changes to private sector labour law, favouring organized labour or employers. In most jurisdictions the contentious issues will likely continue to revolve around a union's ability to certify unorganized workers and obtain a first collective agreement, as well as the use of replacement workers during strikes. Predictions about how provinces will behave with respect to public sector employees are more difficult. In the short run, the pressure on public sector employees is not over. Although a number of governments have delivered balanced budgets, there is some concern, at the time of writing, over a possible economic slowdown or recession. In the event that governments are unwilling to raise taxes to pay for social services, provincial governments will again be looking at the largest controllable item in their budgets, public sector compensation.

Under these circumstances, several scenarios are possible. The most pessimistic is a continuation of "special legislation" to address the crisis of the day, be it the deficit or inflation. As the exception of legislation becomes the rule, the free collective bargaining system could wither away, with unions reduced to administering grievances and "consulting" as opposed to "negotiating" with their employers. Although this scenario is unlikely, one need only look at the experience of federal public service employee relations to understand that it could happen. Collective bargaining was effectively cancelled from 1991-97 by two successive governments, and the Liberals further resorted to back-to-work legislation in 1999.[32] Recent examples of this legislative approach being used to end nursing strikes in BC and Nova Scotia, and in teacher strikes in BC and Alberta, despite improvement on the deficit front, also support this pessimistic outlook.

At the other extreme is movement toward cooperation between provinces and public sector employers. Here the parties jointly come to terms with the fiscal realities. Unions would have to accept that compensation levels could be only maintained, let alone increased, by increases in their productivity and/or workload. Provincial governments would have to agree "not to change the rules in the middle of the game," offer unions a greater involvement in managerial decisions where they are direct employer, and use their "power of the purse" to ensure that junior-level employers (i.e., education, health, and local governments) behaved in a similar way. This positive scenario will not likely become the norm, but it is possible in isolated situations, as the BC experience throughout the 1990s demonstrates.

The most likely scenario for the future is a return to the "adversary" system of collective bargaining. Concession bargaining is a fact of life for the private sector during recessions, and there is no reason why the same cannot be true for the public sector. Certain provincial governments, like Saskatchewan and Alberta, have been able to bargain hard with their own employees and force junior-level agencies to behave the same way by cutting transfers. Relative to earlier time periods, there seems to have been a decline in the "political costs" facing governments that take adversarial and/or legislative approaches towards public sector unions.[33] If this political and ideological environment does not shift, there is reason to expect that provincial governments will be prepared to accept greater centralized control and accountability over public sector labour relations. Thus, the trend towards the limited strike as a dispute resolution mechanism will likely continue, and provincial governments will remain quite willing to override collective bargaining rights and impose legislated outcomes once they are again faced with similar fiscal pressures.[34]

To resist this state of affairs, public sector unions appear to have two options. The first is to continue to attempt to alter the political environment in which they function, either through direct electoral politics in the hopes of assisting left-of-centre governments to (re)capture provincial government power or through increased lobbying and public relations campaigns outside of election times. The other option available is to develop new and improved pressure tactics in hopes of maintaining and improving their bargaining power within the existing environment. It remains to be seen whether the conflict of the 1990s has sufficiently mobilized and/or politicized public sector unions towards meeting this challenge.

Notes

1. D. Carter, "Collective Bargaining Legislation," in M. Gunderson and A. Ponak, eds., *Union-Management Relations in Canada*, 3rd ed. (Don Mills: Addison-Wesley, 1995) 53–71.
2. Canada, Human Resources and Labour, *Industrial Relations Legislation in Canada 1995–96 Edition* (Hull: Minister of Supply and Services Canada, 1995).
3. The term "replacement worker" has been used throughout the text rather then the term "strikebreaker," although these terms are sometimes used interchangeably. This

phrase has been used intentionally, since the term "strikebreaker" is actually a legal term used in some jurisdictions (e.g., Ontario) to refer not to replacement workers but to individuals hired by an employer for the purpose of interfering in or disrupting the strike, possibly through intimidation or coercive means. While Ontario law does not prohibit the use of replacement workers, it does ban the use of these "professional strike breakers." See Ontario's *Labour Relations Act 1995, Schedule A*, S.O., 1995, C.1, S.78.

4. M. Gunderson, D. Hyatt, and A. Ponak, "Strikes and Dispute Resolution," in Gunderson and Ponak, eds., 400. The authors cite two studies that indicate a 24 per cent increase in the incidence of a strike and a seven-day increase in the length of an average strike. However, they state that the results must be viewed with caution because a number of other pro-labour legislative changes were introduced in Quebec at the same time as the replacement worker provision, which could also be responsible for the greater strike activity.

5. "Power-resource" theorists of political economy have emphasized how labour movement strength, which is arguably affected by public policy towards unions, plays a role in determining the extent to which social democracy develops within a political jurisdiction. See W. Korpi, *The Working Class in Welfare Capitalism* (London: Routledge Kegan Paul, 1978); and G. Esping Andersen, *Politics Against Markets: The Social Democratic Road to Power* (Princeton, NJ: Princeton University Press, 1985).

6. G. Swimmer, "Final Offer Selection: A Review of North American Experience," in W. Kaplan, J. Sack, and M. Gunderson, eds., *Labour Arbitration Yearbook, 1992* (Toronto: Butterworths-Lancaster House, 1992) 209–26.

7. K. Burkett, "The Politicization of the Ontario Labour Relations Framework in the 1990s," *Canadian Labour and Employment Law Journal* 6 (1998): 161.

8. "Card-check" certification is generally regarded as a faster system, making it easier for unions to win certifications than under mandatory votes in every case. Where certification votes are held, the process is delayed, which provides employers with more time to respond with their own anti-union campaign and to possibly frighten, intimidate, or otherwise coerce the employees into voting against unionization.

9. P. Weiler, "Promises to Keep: Securing Workers Rights to Self-Organization under the NLRA," *Harvard Law Review* 96: 1769–1827.

10. B. Langille, "The Michelin Amendment in Context," *Current and Future Perspectives in Canadian Industrial Relations—Proceedings of the 17th Annual Meeting of CIRA* (Ste. Foy: Université Laval, 1981): 141–85.

11. J. Pierce, "Worker's Rights for Sale: The Sad Saga of the Late and Little-Lamented Labour Relations Provisions of Newfoundland's White Paper on Economic Diversification," paper presented to the 32nd Annual Conference of CIRA, (mimeo).

12. For an introduction to Marxist theory concerning the interaction between the state and unions, see R. Hyman, *The Political Economy of Industrial Relations* (London: MacMillan Press, 1989).

13. L. Panitch and D. Swartz, *The Assault on Trade Union Freedoms: From Wage Controls to Social Contract* (Toronto: Garamond, 1993) 215–22.

14. B. Adell, M. Grant, and A. Ponak, *Strikes in Essential Services* (Kingston: IRC Press, 2001) 65.

15. G. Swimmer and M. Thompson, "Collective Bargaining in the Public Sector: An Introduction," in G. Swimmer and M. Thompson, eds., *Public Sector Collective Bargaining in Canada* (Kingston: Industrial Relations Centre, 1995) 1–19.

16. K. Swan, "Grating Expectations: The Limitations on the Development of Normative Criteria in Interest Arbitration," in M. Thompson and G. Swimmer, eds., *Conflict or Compromise* (Montreal: Institute for Research in Public Policy, 1984) 315–37.
17. Swimmer and Thompson, "Collective Bargaining in the Public Sector."
18. Adell, Grant, and Ponak.
19. L. Haivan, "Industrial Relations in Health Care: Regulation, Conflict, and Transition to the 'Wellness Model,'" in Swimmer and Thompson, eds., *Public Sector Collective Bargaining in Canada*, 236–27. See also G. Swimmer, "Collective Bargaining in the Federal Public Service of Canada: The Last Twenty Years," pages 368–405 in the same volume.
20. Panitch and Swartz 215–22.
21. G. Hébert, "Public Sector Bargaining in Quebec: The Rise and Fall of Centralization," in Swimmer and Thompson, eds., *Public Sector Collective Bargaining in Canada*, 201–35.
22. See J. Rose, "The Ghost of Interest Arbitration," *Canadian Labour and Employment Law Journal* 8 (2002): 253.
23. J. Fryer, "Provincial Public Service Labour Relations," in Swimmer and Thompson, eds., *Public Sector Collective Bargaining in Canada* 341–67.
24. Fryer 353.
25. T. Wagar, "Provincial Government Restructuring in Nova Scotia: The Freezing and Thawing of Labour Relations," in G. Swimmer, ed., *Public Sector Labour Relations in an Era of Restraint and Restructuring* (Toronto: Oxford, 2001) 36–65.
26. R. Séguin, "Quebec unions give support to sovereignty," *Globe and Mail*, 26 May 1995.
27. See Ontario's *Bill 48: The Social Contract Act*.
28. J. Rose, "From Softball to Hardball: The Transition in Labour Management Relations in the Ontario Public Service," in G. Swimmer, ed., *Public Sector Labour Relations* 66–95.
29. Haivan 268–69.
30. M. Thompson, "Labour Relations in the BC Public Service: Blowing in the Political Wind," in Swimmer, ed., *Public Sector Labour Relations* 155–77.
31. Doug Ward, "Campbell beats the HEU, but has he lost ground?" *Vancouver Sun*, 8 May 2004.
32. G. Swimmer and S. Bach, "Restructuring Federal Public Sector Human Resources," in Swimmer, ed., *Public Sector Labour Relations* 178–211.
33. G. Swimmer, "Public Sector Labour Relations in an Era of Restraint and Restructuring: An Overview," in Swimmer, ed., *Public Sector Labour Relations* 1–35.
34. G. Swimmer and T. Bartkiw, "The Future of Public Sector Collective Bargaining in Canada," *Journal of Labour Research*, Vol. XXIV, No. 4 (2003): 579–595.

Contributors

Carl Baar recently took early retirement from a teaching career at Brock University, during which time he established the M.A. program in judicial administration and taught courses on law and politics, judicial administration, and the judicial process. He then undertook part-time teaching at York University. He has written over 60 books, monographs, reports, and professional articles, from *Separate But Subservient: Court Budgeting in the American States* (1975) to *Final Appeal: Decision-Making in Canadian Courts of Appeal* (1998).

Tim Bartkiw recently received his PhD in public policy from the School of Public Policy and Adminstration of Carleton University. He is also a qualified member of the Ontario Bar and he currently teaches at Ryerson University in Toronto.

Donald E. Blake is a professor emeritus and former head of the Department of Political Science at the University of British Columbia. He is the author of *Two Political Worlds: Parties and Voting in British Columbia* (1985) and co-author of *Grassroots Politicians: Party Activists in British Columbia* (1991) and *Government, Parties, and Public Sector Employees: Canada, United States, Britain and France* (1997), as well as numerous articles and book chapters on related topics.

Gerard W. Boychuk is associate professor and associate chair (undergraduate studies) in the Department of Political Science at the University of Waterloo. His areas of interest include comparative public policy and public administration as well as US politics. He is co-investigator with Debora VanNijnatten (Wilfrid Laurier University) in a multi-year project comparing public policy in the American states and Canadian provinces in the fields of environmental protection (VanNijnatten) and social policy (Boychuk). The project was awarded a SSHRCC Research Grant (2002-06).

R.K. Carty is professor and former head of the Department of Political Science at the University of British Columbia. He is the co-author of *Politics is Local: National Politics at the Grassroots* (with Munroe Eagles, 2005) and *Rebuilding Canadian Party Politics* (with W. Cross and L. Young, 2000) and editor of *Politics, Policy, and Government in British Columbia* (1996) and *Canadian Political Party Systems: A Reader* (1992). He has written and edited several other books and published many articles on political recruitment, leadership, and electoral activities of parties in Canada, Europe, and Australia. He served as director of research for the British Columbia Citizens' Assembly on Electoral Reform and is currently working on a study of it. He holds the Brenda and David McLean Chair in Canadian Studies at the University of British Columbia.

Christopher Dunn is a professor of political science at Memorial University of Newfoundland.

Rand Dyck is a professor emeritus at Laurentian University, Sudbury, Ontario, and is the university's former vice-dean of Social Sciences and Humanities. He is the editor of *Studying Politics: An Introduction to Political Science* (2003) and several editions each of *Canadian Politics: Critical Approaches, Canadian Politics: Concise Edition*, and *Provincial Politics in Canada*.

David K. Foot, is a professor of economics at the University of Toronto and co-author (with Daniel Stoffman) of the bestselling books *Boom, Bust & Echo 2000: Profiting from the Demographic Shift in the New Millennium* (2000) and *Boom, Bust & Echo: How to Profit from the Coming Demographic Shift* (1998, 1996), as well as several other books, articles, and monographs.

Geoffrey E. Hale is an associate professor in the Department of Political Science at the University of Lethbridge. He teaches and has published in the fields of Canadian politics, public administration, public policy, political economy, and business-government relations. His first book, *The Politics of Taxation in Canada* (2001), was nominated for the 2001-02 Donner Prize. In April 2005, he was named Fulbright Visiting Chair in Canadian Studies at Duke University in Durham, NC.

Michael Howlett is a professor and Burnaby Mountain Chair at Simon Fraser University, specializing in public policy analysis, Canadian political economy, and Canadian resource and environmental policy. He is co-author of *Studying Public Policy* (1995, 2003), *In Search of Sustainability* (2001), *The Political Economy of Canada* (1992, 1999), and *Canadian Natural Resource and Environmental Policy* (1997, 2005). He edited *Canadian Forest Policy* (2001) and co-edited *Executive Styles in Canada* (2005), *Designing Government* (2005), *The Real Worlds of Canadian Politics* (2004), *The Provincial State In Canada* (1992, 2000), *Innovation Systems in a Global Context* (1998), *Policy Studies in Canada* (1996), and *The Puzzles of Power* (1994, 1998). His articles have been published in numerous professional journals in Canada, the US, Europe, Brazil, New Zealand, and Australia. He served as English Language Co-editor of the *Canadian Journal of Political Science* (2002-06).

Karen Bridget Murray is assistant professor in the Department of Political Science at York University, and teaches and publishes in Canadian and comparative politics and government, urban governance, and public policy.

Brenda O'Neill is associate professor in the Department of Political Science at the University of Calgary. She is principal investigator for a SSHRC-funded research project "Value Pluralism and Canadian Women," and co-editor of the books *Gender and Social Capital* (with Elisabeth Gidengil [forthcoming]) and *Citizen Politics: Research and Theory in Canadian Political Behaviour* (with Joanna Everitt 2002).

Alan Siaroff is an associate professor at the University of Lethbridge. His major area of specialization is Comparative Politics, particularly European politics, European integration, political development and democratization, comparative party systems and political parties, and comparative and international political economy. He is the author of *Comparing Political Regimes: A Thematic Introduction to Comparative Politics* (2005) and *Comparative European Party Systems: An Analysis of Parliamentary Elections since 1945* (2000).

David K. Stewart is professor and head of political science of the Department of Political Science at the University of Calgary. He is the co-author (with Keith Archer) of *Quasi-Democracy? Parties and Leadership Selection in Alberta* (2000) and several articles on parties and party systems.

Gene Swimmer is a labour economist whose major research interests are public-sector collective bargaining and incomes policies.

Gregory Tardi is senior legal counsel (team leader) in Legal Services at the House of Commons. He advises both the House of Commons as an institution and the individual Members of Parliament on a broad range of legal matters, including the corporate functioning of the House, the work of parliamentary committees, litigation on issues of political speech and defamation, and election and redistribution law. He has published *The Law of Democratic Governing, Vol. I: Principles* and *Vol. II: Jurisprudence* (2004), as well as *The Legal Framework of Government: A Canadian Guide* (1992).

Richard Tindal was a professor of government at St. Lawrence College, Kingston Campus, until June 1998. He has written several editions of *A Citizen's Guide to Government: Local Government in Canada* (with Susan Nobes Tindal), and *Structural Changes in Local Government: Government for Urban Regions* (1977). He has written a dozen training courses and manuals, as well as numerous articles on government and management. As president of Tindal Consulting Limited, a firm established in the early 1970s, he has conducted local government restructuring studies in several areas of Ontario, designed and delivered training seminars across Canada, and continues to undertake consulting and writing projects.

Susan Nobes Tindal is a lawyer and teacher. She has taught a course in law and municipal government for two decades. In addition to her private practice, she acts as legal counsel for a children's aid society in Eastern Ontario. She is a principal in Tindal Consulting Limited, a local government and management consulting firm.

Debora L. VanNijnatten is an associate professor in the Department of Political Science, Wilfrid Laurier University, and is the co-editor of *Canadian Environmental Policy* (2002). She was Fulbright Visiting Chair, Duke University, 2004-05. She researches Canadian and American environmental policy, including air quality and climate change policy, transboundary institutions, and state-province comparisons.

Graham White has written or edited 10 books, including *The Ontario Legislature: A Political Analysis, Inside the Pink Palace: The Government and Politics of Ontario, Northern Governments in Transition,* and several editions of *Politics: Canada* in addition to numerous articles in academic journals. His most recent book is *Cabinets and First Ministers* (2005). One of his books, *Cycling into Saigon: The Conservative Transition in Ontario* (with David Cameron) was shortlisted for the Donner Foundation's award for the best book in Canadian public policy in 2001. He is currently at work on a book about the regulatory and wildlife management boards established under the settled comprehensive land claims settlements in Nunavut and the NWT.

Nelson Wiseman is an associate professor of political science at the University of Toronto. He is the author of *Social Democracy in Manitoba: A History of the CCF-NDP* (1983), co-editor of *Government and Enterprise in Canada* (with K.J. Rea, 1985), and several articles on matters relating to Canadian and provincial politics.